BUSINESS AND GOVERNMENT IN AMERICA SINCE 1870

A Twelve-Volume Anthology of Scholarly Articles

Series Editor

ROBERT F. HIMMELBERG
Fordham University

A GARLAND SERIES

131319

Series Contents

VOLUME

9

GOVERNMENT-BUSINESS COOPERATION 1945–1964

CORPORATISM IN THE POST-WAR ERA

Edited with introductions by

ROBERT F. HIMMELBERG

GARLAND PUBLISHING, INC.
New York & London
1994

Library of Congress Cataloging-in-Publication Data

Government-business cooperation, 1945–1964 : corporatism in the
post-war era / edited with introductions by Robert F.
Himmelberg.
    p.   cm. — (Business and government in America since
1870 ; v. 9)
    A collection of articles that were originally published between
1958 to 1990.
    ISBN 0–8153–1411–6 (alk. paper)
    1. Industry and state—United States—History—20th century.
2. Trade regulation—United States—History—20th century.
3. United States—Commercial policy. 4. United States—Economic policy—1945–1960. 5. United States—Economic policy—
1961–1971. 6. Military-industrial complex—United States—
History—20th century. I. Himmelberg, Robert F. II. Series.
HD3616. U46G643 1994
338.973'009'045—dc20   93–46105
                                                      CIP

Printed on acid-free, 250-year-life paper
Manufactured in the United States of America

Contents

SERIES INTRODUCTION

This compilation of articles provides a very broad and representative selection of the scholarly literature found in learned journals on the subject of government-business relations in the age of industry, the period since 1870. The scope of this collection is wide, covering all the arenas of business-government interaction. Sectorially, the focus is on manufacturing and transportation, upon whose rapid expansion after the Civil War the modern industrial economy was founded.

For the volumes covering the years from 1870 to 1965 (Volumes I through IX) it has been possible, while exercising selectivity, to include a very high proportion of everything published within the past thirty years. This literature is found largely in historical journals. More selectivity had to be employed for Volumes X through XII, which cover the period since 1965. Historians have not yet trodden much on the ground of the very recent past but social scientists and legal scholars have offered abundant materials, so abundant as to require a relatively severe selectivity. By choosing articles that appear to have a long-term analytical value and by excluding those too narrow in scope, too preoccupied with methodological questions or otherwise unsuitable for a non-specialized audience, an extensive and accessible body of writing has, however, been assembled for the post-1965 period, mainly from economics and legal periodicals.

The volumes are designed to contain articles relating to a particular period and to one or more topics within a period. The literature of business-government relations has four logically distinct major topics: antitrust, regulation, promotion, and cooperation. These topics define distinctive aspects of the relationship. Yet, the distinctions sometimes in practice blur, the ostensible, publicly proclaimed purposes of policy sometimes differing from the actually intended purposes or the actual outcomes.

Antitrust policy emerges in Volume I, which covers the era 1870–1900 when big business appeared, and figures prominently throughout the series. Several volumes are devoted entirely to it. Uniquely American, at least until relatively recently, antitrust policy has a complex history and much of what scholars have discovered about its origin and evolution is recorded only in the articles gathered in this collection. The literature reproduced here makes clear that the intent and impact of antitrust policy has varied enormously during its one-hundred-year history, which dates from the Sherman Act of 1890. Tension between competing objectives has existed from the outset. Should the "trusts" be broken up on the grounds that super-corporations inevitably conflict with democratic government and entrepreneurial opportunity? Or should only "bad trusts", those guilty of crushing competitors through unfair methods, suffer dissolution? Is cartelistic behavior always an illegal restraint of trade, or should it sometimes be tolerated if it helps small business to survive? Put most broadly, should the aim of antitrust policy be simply promoting competition, or should other conflicting social and economic values be recognized?

Business regulation also arose during the early stages of industrialization, appearing at the federal level with the enactment of the Interstate Commerce Act in 1887. The term "regulation" is used here to denote government policies intended, not to promote or restore competition, but to require specific behavior from business. The classic justification for regulation was the argument that in some situations the public interest could be served only through governmental prescription, that in some instances a remedy simply could not be obtained through the workings of the marketplace. Theoretically there are two such instances. The first occurs in the case of "natural monopoly," market situations in which competition would be wasteful and competing firms do not and should not exist. Railroads and public utilities were early identified as industries of this sort and were the first targets of government regulation. Would-be regulators early discovered a second justification for applying the regulatory approach, the situation in which competition fails to provide rival firms with incentives to avoid methods that may injure public health or well being. The argument found early expression in regulation of the meat-packing industry and has over the course of the twentieth century created a remarkable body of federal regulatory practices. The history of regulation, however, has not unfolded, any more than the history of antitrust, according to the logic of theory. It has been determined by the interplay between many factors, including the ideas of reformers, the complaints of those who have felt injured, policy rivalries among businessmen themselves, and the capacity or incapacity of government to execute planned reform. A major focus of recent literature on regulation, and to an extent on antitrust also, is the thesis of capture, the notion that regulatory efforts have often fallen captive to the interests they were intended to oppose.

The third theme of relations between government and business, promotion and encouragement, also emerged during the initial stages of the industrial era. Railroad subsidies abounded during the age of building the transcontinentals, of course, and protective tariffs were almost as old as the Republic itself. In the early twentieth century government support of trade expansion abroad enlarged and gradually became a major thread of government policy. Resembling promotion but logically distinct in many respects is the fourth category of business-government interaction, the area of cooperative relationships. Few scholars, even those who believe ongoing conflict has chiefly characterized business-government relations, would deny that cooperation has occurred at certain points, as during American participation in the major wars of the twentieth century. But in recent years many writers who conceive of business-government relations as taking place within a "corporatist" framework have perceived the scope and continuity of cooperative tendencies as very broad.

These four categories describe the subjects or topics around which scholarly investigation of business-government relations has revolved. There is, however, another approach to analyzing the literature of this relationship, one in which we ask about a writer's interpretive perspective, the conceptualizations the writer brings to the subject. All historians and social scientists, including those who created the literature collected here, adopt an interpretive standpoint from which to view society and its workings. An interpretive standpoint is a way of understanding the structure of society and the way those structural elements relate and interact; in other words, it is a "model" of society. Several rival models have competed for acceptance among scholars in recent times. Readers will be better equipped for informed reading of the literature assembled in these volumes if they are knowledgeable about these interpretive standpoints and the aim here therefore is to define the most important of these and give them appropriate labels.

Until the 1950s the prevailing interpretation of business-government relations—indeed, of American history generally—was the progressive viewpoint. The term progressive refers in the first place to the reform ideology and activity of the early twentieth century, the period before World War I. The perspective of the progressive generation continued for many years to dominate historical writing, not only on the period itself but on the whole of American history. According to the progressive perspective, the rise of big business during the late nineteenth and early twentieth centuries created a radical shift in the balance of economic and political power in America in favor of concentrated wealth. The rise of the "trusts", the powerful firms that came to predominate in many industries in the years after 1880, and the creation of cartels and other arrangements for suppressing competition, threatened independent capitalists and consumers with raw economic exploitation. This concentration of economic power threatened to utterly suborn representative political institutions as well and reduce American democracy to a plutocracy. In the progressive view the predominating tone of business-government relations was therefore necessarily antagonistic and conflictual.

The progressive paradigm became deeply embedded in the American consciousness. Reformist politicians have often reverted to it in shaping their ideological and rhetorical appeals. Franklin D. Roosevelt's attack in the campaign of 1936 upon "economic royalists" and John Kennedy's denunciation in 1962 of Big Steel during the controversy over price guidelines as "utterly contemptuous of the public interest" are vivid examples. The progressive outlook is evidently a persistent element in the popular historical consciousness. The power of the progressive conception of American history is in fact readily confirmed by reference to the way twentieth-century history is periodized, in textbooks and popular histories, into epochs of reform (the Progressive, New Deal, Fair Deal and Great Society periods) and of reaction (the Twenties, the Eisenhower and Reagan eras).

But if the progressive interpretation of business government relations retains some force among some historians and in the consciousness of liberal opinion makers and the public, its hold on much of the academic mind has long since weakened. A reaction among historians and other academics against the progressive paradigm emerged soon after the end of the Second World War and gathered force during the 1950s. The reaction was especially sharp among historians writing business history. Writing at a time when a reinvigorated American economy appeared to have overcome the doldrums of the 1930s and to be demonstrating the superiority of capitalism over other systems, energetic business and economic historians completely revised the progressive interpretation of the founders of American big business. The revisionists interpreted the founders not as greedy robber barons but as heroes of the entrepreneurial spirit, the spirit of enterprise and productivity. This revisionist interpretation proved too one-dimensional and celebratory to be maintained without modification. Revisionism, however, did succeed in thoroughly discrediting the progressive point of view. This circumstance, together with the impact of interpretive concepts emanating from post-war social science, moved historians to replace the progressive paradigm with a new and more sophisticated framework for understanding American political economy, the pluralist framework.

Pluralism as the dominant interpretive mode replaced progressivism in the 1950s and 60s. Speaking broadly, the pluralist model understands public policy as the result of struggle between economic and social groups. A major by-product of industrialization is the sharpening of differences between groups playing distinctive economic roles and a heightened articulation of self-interested goals and purposes on the part of such groups. Thus, government-business relations, that is, the shape of government policies towards business, are the result of rivalries among the major interest groups, business, labor, consumers, and so on. But the nature of the struggle is complex because the major groups are themselves divided into more or less rivalrous sub-groups. Business itself is divided; both intra- and inter-industry rivalries exist, sometimes in acute forms. Government policy is not merely the result of nonbusiness groups seeking to shape that policy but also of some business interests seeking to impose their own wishes on others.

During the 1960s pluralist interpretation became more complex. One important source of this heightened complexity was what some commentators have called the "organizational" outlook. Again influenced by currents in American social science, this time sociology, practitioners employing the organizational perspective are struck by the ever-increasing importance of large bureaucratic organizations in American life since the onset of industrialization. Business has continuously evolved in terms of an ever larger role for the large corporation, but other spheres, including government and the professions, also are organized in terms of large hierarchical bureaucracies. Borrowing from Weberian sociological traditions, writers impressed by the organizational perspective have explored the thesis that large bureaucracies wherever situated have similar requirements and tend to develop in those who manage them similar values and expectations. Thus, this brand of pluralism stresses the extent to which group leaders, including the managers and technicians who run the large corporations, developed accommodative as well as merely self-seeking motives. Business leaders, many of them at least, came to share certain values, such as respect for stability in the overall economy, which leads them to seek harmonious and cooperative relationships between interest groups and between them and the government. Government is assigned the role, in this construct, of facilitating and stimulating cooperative modes of behavior and umpiring conflicts. In the literature on business and government, figures who have advocated this kind of polity are often dubbed "corporatists" or "corporate liberals." Broadly defined, corporatism is the practice of cooperation between government and the corporate world to resolve economic issues. The existence and the importance of corporatist relationships has been one of the major emphases of recent scholarship but there is much disagreement as to the intentions of its practitioners and its impact. Some scholars have interpreted corporatism in a more or less positive light, as an ideology and a practice entailing cooperation rather than conflict between government and business, as an alternative to an adversarial relationship, a way of obtaining desirable economic performance from business without resorting to governmental coercion.

But others, especially but not only those writing in the vein of the "New Left", have argued that members of the corporate elite have frequently pursued their own narrow interests under the cover of ostensibly cooperative endeavors. The New Leftists emerged in the 1960s, expounding a more radical criticism of business than the progressive-liberal historians had advanced. The New Leftists doubted or denied outright that the American system was pluralist at all in any meaningful sense. Control of public policy might appear as a contest between social groups, but in fact one group, or rather class, those who controlled big business, enjoyed such lopsided power that the contest was apparently not real. Behind the facade of political infighting over government policy toward business, the masters of the corporate world quietly steered events toward outcomes which cemented in place control of the economy by monopoly capital.

These four conceptualizations, the progressive, the pluralist, the corporatist, and the New Leftist, are essentially theories of the structure and process of American political economy. However, rarely are researchers slavishly devoted to a theoretical perspective. Thus, those who see, in the progressive vein, an ongoing conflictual relationship between the people and business sometimes argue against the reformers and in favor of the businessmen. Even more significant and widespread is the conclusion of many writers using the pluralist or corporatist modes of interpretation, that regulation has not fostered equity and economic progress but rather has hardened the economy's vital arteries. Pluralists initially assumed that policies arising from a political arena to which all organized interests have access will inevitably achieve benign results, that the policy outputs will construct a system of "countervailing power" among organized interest groups. The assumption of acceptable outcomes is still prevalent, but a skeptical version of the results of interest group rivalries became manifest in the late

1960s, holding that both in origin and ongoing impact, business regulation was too often subject to "capture." In this view, regulatory measures and agencies and other policies seeking to guide business behavior toward balanced and generally acceptable outcomes readily fall under the control of the very interests they were intended to regulate.

There has emerged in recent years still another approach to the origin and process of social-economic policy that has been applied to the business-government connection. In this interpretation of the connection, a few examples of which will be found in articles collected here, emphasis is placed on the relative autonomy of government administrators and regulators. Seen by the pluralists as merely the creatures of the organizational struggles that result in public policies, in this new view regulators are seen as possessing substantial room for independent action. Thus the state is not merely to be seen as a passive receptor and executor of outcomes that social forces determine but as having a partially autonomous role which the officers of the state presumably will use to extend their own interests rather than the interests articulated by social groups.

These categories, progressivism, pluralism, corporatism, Leftism and the "autonomous officialdom" viewpoint, represent the major schools of thought and interpretation that readers will discover in the literature reproduced in these volumes. Writers investigating specific historical incidents, trends or problems have, in most cases, written through the framework provided by one or another of these interpretive models. As an alert reader will discover, most writers do have certain assumptions about the structure and dynamics of social relationships, and these assumptions stem from one of the models that have been described.

Interpretation of the relationship between business and government in the age of industry has given rise to a literature that is large and complex. It presents a stimulating intellectual challenge and is certainly relevant for anyone seeking understanding of contemporary business-government relations and endeavoring to predict, or to shape, their future course.

Introduction

American businessmen emerged with spirits revived from the mobilization experience of the Second World War. The wartime economy's success in achieving rapid expansion, providing simultaneously for increased civilian consumption while supplying the insatiable needs of the armed forces, restored some luster to the American business system's reputation, so sadly dimmed during the years of depression, and renewed the public's faith in the capacity of American capitalism to provide growth and prosperity. Would the business community parlay this recovery of self-confidence and public esteem into political influence and enlarge its capacity to shape government policies?

Unquestionably, business success in influencing the government did recover after the war. Nor was this influence limited to or especially concentrated in the Republican Eisenhower years, as progressive-liberal writers might argue. Rather, it extended unbroken through the entire postwar epoch from Truman through Kennedy. The most interesting question the historians of political economy pose for the postwar era is whether businessmen, or at least a vital elite of them, consciously sought to build a corporatist order. Or were they merely opportunists seeking to blunt the force of government regulatory policy?

Many historians of postwar political economy make a clear and persuasive case for the corporatist interpretation. That is, they argue that a leadership cadre from the highest business circles, eschewing the sloganeering of business conservatives who still thought primitively in terms of stopping "big government" and preserving "free enterprise," endeavored, in a manner analogous to the corporatists of the 1920s and 30s, to build relationships with government that would leave a great deal of initiative in business hands but would also guarantee economic progress and social-political tranquility.

But the corporatist vision of these postwar business leaders clearly is more limited than the one their predecessors from the interwar period had sought to implement. Robert Collins characterizes the earlier generation as wanting to divert nearly all responsibility for economic welfare to business through welfare-

capitalist- and National Recovery Administration-like arrangements. The postwar corporatists, however, operating through the
Business Advisory Council of the Department of Commerce and its
offspring, the Council for Economic Defense (CED), accepted government social welfare programs, such as social security and the
existence of strong, independent labor unions simply as well-
established facts. The ideological leadership of these business
sophisticates gradually but surely reconstructed the thinking of a
large part of rank and file businessmen, many of whom had
emerged from the war hoping to recover all the ground lost during
the New Deal. The high command of business wasted no time in
futile efforts to turn back the clock but instead prepared strategies
for preventing further growth of government economic and welfare
policies and of labor militancy that might erode control over
investment and price decisions, the essential managerial prerogatives that still lay largely untouched in the hands of businessmen.

Perhaps the gravest challenge these postwar corporatists faced
was providing an alternative to the prescription postwar liberals
offered for the problems of lagging economic growth, recession and
unemployment. Known as Keynsianism, this prescription called
for heavy additional governmental social spending financed through
budget deficits. In the business view the new policy, if carried too
far, would inevitably promote government control of an ever-
widening share of national income and would end with bureaucratic domination of all economic decisions. The CED's success in
formulating and building a national consensus in favor of a conservative version of Keynsianism represented probably the single
most important and most visible victory for the new corporatists.
The sheer success of the postwar economy, coupled with increasing
promulgation of the ideology of productionism and the limited
renewal of welfare capitalist strategies, enabled business corporatists to prevent encroachment on managerial prerogatives from
the direction of labor unions. Labor leaders gradually abandoned
postwar plans to demand a role in running the corporations and
settled for the stream of higher wages and benefits generated by
postwar prosperity. (See the articles by Robert Collins and Kim
McQuaid.) The postwar program for promoting European economic recovery, the Marshall Plan, represents a third major
success for corporatist strategy, for the plan not only sought to
stimulate recovery of the European economy but also assurance of
government financed markets for American capital goods. (See the
articles by Michael Hogan.)

Robert Griffith's often cited article on Eisenhower and corporatism
makes it clear that during the 1950s corporatism took on an even
more expansive meaning, for the President extensively inter-

twined government policy planning with advisory groups from business. Progress on the solution of social and economic welfare problems, moreover, Eisenhower left as much as possible to private voluntary efforts.

In his 1956 book, *The Power Elite*, C. Wright Mills argued that an interlocking directorate of generals, businessmen and bureaucrats had formed and come to dominate American policy in the postwar era and was sustaining the Cold War to maintain government military spending. The authors represented in this volume do find plentiful evidence of advanced government-business cooperation in the postwar world but whether it advanced so far as to resemble the dominating "military-industrial complex" Mills and those who adopted and expanded his concept portrayed is problematical.

American Corporatism: The Committee for Economic Development, 1942-1964

By

Robert M. Collins*

T HE study of American political history is undergoing a significant reorientation. The process of change has been a long one.
From the early years of this century until the mid-1940s, the
Progressive interpretation dominated the study of American
history.[1] The Progressive historians argued that American political life
was characterized by a liberal-conservative dichotomy. Americans were
divided into warring camps: on one side stood liberal reformers,
pursuing the interests of the many and fighting battles on behalf of a
constituency which included capitalism's disinherited; on the other side
were the nation's conservatives, often clad in business suits and housed
in executive suites, struggling to further the selfish interests of the few.
The ongoing conflict between these groups—now waxing, now
waning—seemed to impart a rhythm to American history. This
deceptively simple focus yielded a body of scholarship rich in moral
fervor and relevant to the rhetoric of reform politics.

Since World War II, however, the Progressive school has come under
attack from several different directions. The consensus interpretation
which rose to prominence in the celebratory 1950s argued that
agreement, not conflict, has been the dynamic factor in American life.[2]
The New Left historians who appeared in the 1960s disagreed among
themselves on the question of conflict versus consensus but came
together in their denunciation of another aspect of the liberal-
conservative dichotomy; all agreed that liberal reformers were not the

*The author is Associate Professor of History at the University of Missouri,
Columbia.

[1]The historiographical categories in this introductory section are largely based on
John Higham et al., History (Englewood Cliffs, 1965). Progressive history is treated with
insight by Richard Hofstadter, The Progressive Historians (New York, 1968).

[2]Major statements of the consensus position include Richard Hofstadter, The
American Political Tradition (New York, 1948); Daniel Boorstin, The Genius of
American Politics (Chicago, 1953); and Louis Hartz, The Liberal Tradition in America
(New York, 1955). An important appraisal is John Higham, "The Cult of the 'American
Consensus': Homogenizing Our History," Commentary 27 (February 1959): 93-100.

151

heroes of American history.[3] When the smoke from these onslaughts cleared, it was apparent that the Progressive synthesis had been weakened—but largely in its own terms. The critics of the 1950s and 1960s had accepted the Progressive categories and reversed the Progressive conclusions. Conflict had become consensus, robber barons had become industrial statesmen, and good guys had become bad guys. The result was an inchoate attack which was persuasive but not suited to generating a new framework for historical analysis.

The question, then, for political historians has been where to go from there. One fruitful possibility lies in the recent emphasis by some historians on organization as a dominant factor in the shaping of modern American society. What Louis Galambos calls "the emerging organizational synthesis" has attracted the attention of historians in fields ranging from economic to social history.[4] The organizational approach focuses on different units of analysis than did its various interpretive predecessors. And while attention to institutions is not new, the approach is distinctive in that it deals with institutions *qua* organizations and emphasizes the organizational environment within which particular institutions function. The discovery of waves of organizational activity sweeping over American society in the last one hundred years thus provides a new conceptual window through which to view the process of state building in recent American history.

One result of this new interest in organization has been the attention given by political historians to the development of an American corporatism. Ellis Hawley has described this domestic corporatism as

> one whose basic units consist of officially recognized, noncompetitive, role-ordered occupational or functional groupings. . .one with coordinating machinery designed to integrate these units into an interdependent whole and one where the state properly functions as coordinator, assistant, and midwife rather than director or regulator.[5]

Although American corporatists have not been able to realize their vision in this ideal sense and to achieve a wholly corporative order, their ideas have commingled with the value systems of liberals and conservatives and with the nation's democratic traditions to influence the modern American political economy significantly. An emphasis on the corporatist impulse is in some ways reminiscent of earlier consensus history, but the new focus at least clarifies the nature of the agreement

[3]Irwin Unger, "The 'New Left' and American History," *American Historical Review* 72 (July 1967): 1237-63.

[4]Louis Galambos, "The Emerging Organizational Synthesis in Modern American History," *Business History Review* 44 (Autumn 1970): 279-90. See also John Higham, *Writing American History* (Bloomington, Ind., 1970), 160-64; and Jerry Israel, *Building the Organizational Society* (New York, 1972).

[5]Ellis Hawley, "The Discovery and Study of a 'Corporate Liberalism'," *Business History Review* 52 (Autumn 1978): 312 n.3.

and allows us to see more clearly the ways in which the consensus was forged and institutionalized.

Scholars have discovered important efforts by both business and government leaders to establish a corporatist order during the first three decades of this century.[6] Less attention, however, has been given to the resurgence of such activity following the collapse of the New Deal's National Recovery Administration (NRA) experiment in the mid-1930s.[7] The present essay examines the manifestation of the corporatist impulse in more recent times. It focuses on one important business organization, the Committee for Economic Development (CED), and on one area of public affairs, national macroeconomic policy. What follows is an attempt to examine the ways in which the CED sought to influence public policy during the period 1942-64 and to assess the broader implications of this process in terms of the general relationships between state and society in post-World War II America.

I

The Committee for Economic Development came into being in 1942, a creation of the Business Advisory Council of the Department of Commerce and of other unaffiliated businessmen who wanted the federal government to play a positive role in stabilizing the economy.[8] From the outset, the CED had a small, cohesive membership

[6]See, for example, James Weinstein, *The Corporate Ideal in the Liberal State, 1900-1918* (Boston, 1968); Charles Hirshfield, "National Progressivism and World War I," *Mid-America* 45 (July 1963): 139-56; Robert Himmelberg, "The War Industries Board and the Antitrust Question in November 1918," *Journal of American History* 52 (June 1965): 59-74; Murray Rothbard, "War Collectivism in World War I," in Ronald Radosh and Rothbard, eds., *A New History. of Leviathan: Essays on the Rise of the American Corporate State* (New York, 1972), 66-110; Ellis Hawley, "Herbert Hoover, the Commerce Secretariat, and the Vision of an 'Associative State', 1921-1928," *Journal of American History* 61 (June 1974): 116-40; idem, "Herbert Hoover and American Corporatism, 1929-1933," in Martin Fausold and George Mazuzan, eds., *The Hoover Presidency: A Reappraisal* (Albany, N.Y., 1974), 101-19; Robert Himmelberg, *The Origins of the National Recovery Administration* (New York, 1976); Richard Hume Werking, "Bureaucrats, Businessmen, and Foreign Trade: The Origins of the United States Chamber of Commerce," *Business History Review* 52 (Autumn 1978): 321-41; and Kim McQuaid, "Corporate Liberalism in the American Business Community, 1920-1940," *ibid.*, 342-68.

[7]Ellis Hawley, *The New Deal and the Problem of Monopoly* (Princeton, 1966); Kim McQuaid, "The Business Advisory Council of the Department of Commerce, 1933-1961," in Paul Uselding, ed., *Research in Economic History*, 5 vols., vol. 1 (Greenwich, Conn., 1976), 171-97. The theme is treated at greater length in Robert M. Collins, *The Business Response to Keynes, 1929-1964* (New York, 1981).

[8]Two general, sympathetic histories of the CED by an insider are Karl Schriftgiesser, *Business Comes of Age* (New York, 1960); and *Business and Public Policy* (Englewood Cliffs, 1967).

153

representative of medium-sized and, increasingly over time, very large business firms.[9]. The committee's aims were to help businessmen plan for the reconversion to peacetime conditions and to determine, by means of research and consultation between business leaders and scholars, how high employment might be achieved.

The ideology of the CED was rooted in the corporatist formulations which had become especially influential in the United States during World War I and the decade of the 1920s.[10] American corporatism had been less visible after the demise of the NRA in the mid-1930s, but the corporate ideal was kept alive during the second New Deal and after by the very men who came together during World War II to form the CED.[11] American corporatists sought a middle path between statist formulas for the organization of society and the traditional laissez-faire creed of conservatives. They stressed the importance of expertise and tried wherever possible to transform political decisions into technical ones. Corporatism cast private, functionally defined groups in the crucial role of partners with a cooperative, rather than oppressive, state apparatus; together they were to pursue an objectively recognizable general interest.[12]

[9]On the role of big business in the CED, see the Marion Folsom Memoir (Eisenhower Project), Columbia Oral History Collection; and William Benton to John K. Galbraith, 12 September 1944, William Benton MSS (privately held, New York City). At first, this issue worried the CED leadership, especially Benton and Paul Hoffman, but by 1965 the committee was openly characterizing itself as "a group made up predominantly of the executives of large companies." CED, *Report of Activities, 1965* (New York, 1966). The absence of small business representation undoubtedly increased the cohesion of the CED. Folsom observed, "The people in. . .large companies have got to keep up with the times. They've got to adjust themselves to social conditions whether they like it or not, and they go along. . .whereas the little fellow just keeps on kicking all the time. He doesn't see the picture as a whole." Folsom Memoir (Social Security Project), Columbia Oral History Collection.

[10]See note 6 above. The best historical overview is Hawley, "Discovery and Study of a Corporate Liberalism'."

[11]Robert Collins, "Positive Business Responses to the New Deal: The Roots of the Committee for Economic Development, 1933-1942," *Business History Review* 52 (Autumn 1978): 369-91.

[12]On the general nature of American corporatism, see Daniel Fusfeld, "Rise of the Corporate State in America," *Journal of Economic Issues* 6 (March 1972): 1-22; Arthur S. Miller, *The Modern Corporate State: Private Governments and the American Constitution* (Westport, Conn., 1976); Grant McConnell, *Private Power and American Democracy* (New York, 1966); Theodore Lowi, *The End of Liberalism* (New York, 1969); David Noble, *America by Design: Science, Technology, and the Rise of Corporate Capitalism* (New York, 1977); and Philippe Schmitter, "Still the Century of Corporatism," *Review of Politics* 36 (January 1974): 85-131. I have found particularly helpful two unpublished papers by Ellis Hawley: "Techno-Corporatist Formulas in the Liberal State, 1920-1960: A Neglected Aspect of America's Search for a New Order" (1974); and "The New Corporatism and the Liberal Democracies, 1918-1925: The Case of the United States" (1977).

Committee for Economic Development

Thus, the CED's first chairman, Paul Hoffman of Studebaker, held that it was "very important that we as a group think of ourselves not as 'right', 'left', 'conservative' or 'radical' but as 'responsible'."[13] The committee's faith in its own objectivity was so deeply rooted that in 1962 Herbert Stein, the group's research director, could indignantly rebuke those who viewed society "as sharply divided into a certain number of classes,—business, labor and possibly others." In contrast, he observed that the CED "believes that there is a general interest, and a truth independent of class interest."[14]

In the context of such an ideology, the CED sought to devise governmental economic policies which would, in the words of its Research Committee chairman, Ralph Flanders, allow "natural adjustments under the laws of supply and demand and under the incentives of the profit system, rather than efforts by direct regimentation."[15] Properly devised fiscal and monetary measures would be impersonal and would leave to the private sector the nation's basic decisions about resource allocation, production, prices, and wages. Ideally, such measures would necessitate little expansion of the government and would minimize further concentration of economic and political power in Washington.[16]

The means to this end were most clearly articulated in two policy statements issued by the committee in 1947 and 1948. The publication in November 1947 of the CED's program for "prosperity in a free economy" launched a frontal assault against the orthodoxy of the balanced budget. Balancing the budget on an annual basis, regardless of economic conditions, necessarily meant the adjustment of tax rates and spending programs "at times and in directions most harmful to high employment and stable prices."[17] The CED's alternative to annually balanced budgets was based on the concept of the high employment budget suggested by trustee Beardsley Ruml in 1944: "Set tax rates to balance the budget and provide a surplus for debt retirement at an agreed high level of employment and national income."[18] Tax rates would then be left alone barring "some major change in national policy

[13]CED, Minutes, Board of Trustees, 18 April 1947, Marion Folsom MSS, University of Rochester (cited hereafter as Folsom MSS).

[14]Stein to the CED Trustees, 10 January 1962, Folsom MSS. Interestingly, Stein went on to observe that the CED's pursuit of truth and the general interest furthered the class interest of businessmen; thus, objectivity and self-interest merged.

[15]Ralph Flanders, "The Research Activity of the CED" (cover letter, Flanders to Benton, 17 January 1943), Box 50, William Benton MSS, University of Chicago (cited hereafter as Benton MSS).

[16]Howard Myers, "If Anti-Depression Policies Become Necessary. . .?" (speech to the Conference of Business Economists, 25 June 1949), on Reel 33, CED Archives, Washington, D.C.

[17]CED, *Taxes and the Budget: A Program for Prosperity in a Free Economy* (New York, 1947), 20-21.

[18]*Ibid.*, 22.

155

or condition of national life."[19] In prosperous times, national income would rise and so also would the amount of taxes collected, even though tax *rates* would remain the same; the size of the budget surplus would increase and this in turn would help to dampen any inflationary tendencies generated by the economic surge. Conversely, in periods of recession national income and federal revenues would shrink and government expenditures such as unemployment compensation would rise; the budget surplus would decrease, and at some point an expansionary deficit would be incurred. Thus, an economic tool, the high employment budget, was made into a full-fledged policy prescription, which the CED called the "stabilizing budget."

The committee completed the basic framework for its response to the New Economics in 1948 with a call for a flexible monetary policy.[20] The CED recommended that in times of inflation the Federal Reserve System should pursue a contractionist monetary policy by tightening the reserve requirements of member banks, by increasing the rediscount rate, and by selling government securities on the open market. In periods of deflation, the opposite policies would be implemented. Thus, monetary policy, the efficacy of which many liberal Keynesians had come to doubt, would be wedded to the stabilizing budget policy. As Neil Jacoby, a longtime member of the CED's Research Advisory Board, subsequently commented, "Money controls operate impersonally and without any of the direct interference with the details of private business which is so irksome and inefficient in a free economy."[21] They were, in short, particularly appropriate for a private enterprise system.[22] By accepting that "Government holds the key to maintaining the variations of the whole social organism within safe limits" and· by liberating itself from the rigidity of the annually balanced budget, the CED gave the American business community a formidable program to promote.[23]

The CED's program represented an important alternative to the Keynesianism which had taken root in the United States in the wake of the Great Depression and the publication in 1936 of *The General Theory of Employment, Interest, and Money.* Developed by antibusiness liberals, this American Keynesianism posited that the United States had become a "mature economy" and that economic well-being therefore necessitated continuous, planned government investment to take up the slack which was inherent in American captalism. Led and inspired by Alvin Hansen of Harvard, publicized by

[19]*Ibid.*

[20]CED, *Monetary and Fiscal Policy for Greater Economic Stability* (New York, 1948).

[21]Neil Jacoby, *Can Prosperity Be Sustained?* (New York, 1956), 91.

[22]I. O. Scott, "Monetary and Debt Management Policies" (21 September 1956), on Reel 29, CED Archives.

[23]Flanders, "The Research Activity of the CED," Box 50, Benton MSS.

156

Stuart Chase, and supported by Henry A. Wallace, the stagnationist school of American political economists proposed secular deficit spending, heavily progressive taxation, and an extensive program of social-welfare expenditures, urban renewal, and regional development on the order of the TVA.[24] In contrast, the CED's program called for an active monetary and a passive fiscal policy, for automatic stabilization rather than discretionary management, and for reductions in taxation and increases in private spending rather than increases in expenditures and public spending. It opted for a modicum of unemployment over a modicum of inflation, and for economic stability and growth over a redistribution of income and a reallocation of resources.

II

At the very least, the development of a sophisticated "commercial Keynesianism" by even a relatively small segment of American business in the years immediately after World War II calls into question the common belief that the New Economics was somehow imposed on a reluctant business community by antibusiness liberals. CED chairman Donald David was probably correct in asserting in 1957 that "at every major economic watershed of these past 15 years you will find a reservoir of CED research and recommendations."[25] The committee's prescription of automatic stabilizing action through the federal budget coupled with a flexible monetary program constituted the heart of federal economic policy prior to the Kennedy-Johnson tax reduction of 1964.[26] Writing on the tenth anniversary of the 1947 publication of the CED's stabilizing budget policy, economist Walter Heller (later

[24]On the stagnationist approach, see Alvin Hansen, *Full Recovery or Stagnation* (New York, 1938); *idem*, "Economic Progress and Declining Population Growth," *American Economic Review* 29 (March 1939): 1-15; *idem*, "The Stagnation Thesis," in American Economic Association, *Readings in Fiscal Policy* (Homewood, Ill., 1955); and Richard Gilbert et al., *An Economic Program for American Democracy* (New York, 1938). Regarding Hansen's role, see "Alvin H. Hansen — The American Keynes," in William Breit and Roger Ransom, *The Academic Scribblers: American Economists in Collision* (New York, 1971), 85-110; and Richard Lee Strout, "Hansen of Harvard," *New Republic*, 29 December 1941, 888-90. An example of Chase's contribution is Stuart Chase, "If You Were President," *New Republic*, 15 July 1941, 888-90. Concerning Wallace's support, see Henry A. Wallace, *Sixty Million Jobs* (New York, 1945); John Morton Blum, "Portrait of the Diarist," in *The Price of Vision: The Diary of Henry A. Wallace, 1942-1946* (Boston, 1973), 32-33; and Norman Markowitz, *The Rise and Fall of the People's Century: Henry A. Wallace and American Liberalism, 1941-1948* (New York, 1973), 57-64, 141-43.

[25]"Remarks of Donald David before CED Trustees, Chicago, May 16, 1957," Box 102, Ralph Flanders MSS, Syracuse University (cited hereafter as Flanders MSS).

[26]A. E. Holmans, *United States Fiscal Policy, 1945-1959* (London, 1961), 296-99; Wilfred Lewis, Jr., *Federal Fiscal Policy in the Postwar Recessions* (Washington, 1962), 15-19; Robert Aaron Gordon, *Economic Instability and Growth: The American Record* (New York, 1974), 105-7, 133-36, 203-4.

157

Kennedy's chief economic adviser) observed that "a review of CED's tax policy for economic stability is a review of the dominant theme in postwar fiscal-policy thinking."[27] Throughout much of the postwar period, there existed striking parallels between CED and government policy.

Evaluating the precise impact of the CED's proposals on federal policy remains, however, a difficult task. Herbert Stein has argued that the "fiscal revolution" resulted largely from changes in the economic environment. Increasing concern with inflation and the gradual redefinition of the problem of macroeconomic management as instability rather than stagnation caused economists, and ultimately political leaders, to abandon the early, left-wing, stagnationist version of Keynes for a more conservative varient.[28]

But any such explanation remains incomplete without a consideration of the political component of the Keynesian revolution. Throughout the period, choices were made and options discarded. There appears to have been a very complex social and political process at work by which "radical" alternatives. were filtered out, or so emasculated and transformed as to render them *relatively* harmless to those who wielded power within society. Economics remained "partly a vehicle for the ruling ideology of each period as well as partly a method of scientific investigation."[29] The main reason for this was the power of businessmen and business institutions in American society. Expressed simply, business accommodated itself to the fiscal revolution and successfully turned aside the thrusts of those who sought to seriously limit its dominion.

However, the transmutation of Keynesian economics did not derive from business influence alone, for it was only the most important of several forces at work. The essential components included (1) a particular body of economic theory; (2) the scientific experts who continually refined that theory and enunciated its policy implications; (3) a business power structure which was itself characterized not by unanimity but rather by a spectrum of philosophical and political views and which naturally sought to control its political and economic environments; (4) a governmental sector which represented an even wider variety of interests and which attempted to reconcile these interests with its newly discovered responsibility for economic prosperity; and (5) a changing economic environment which was subject to conditions frequently beyond the control of either government planners or businessmen. No one of them was *solely* responsible for the process of transformation, nor can the process be explained merely by lumping the elements together. It was, rather, the

[27]Walter Heller, "CED's Stabilizing Budget Policy After Ten Years," *American Economic Review* 47 (September 1957): 634.

[28]Herbert Stein, *The Fiscal Revolution in America* (Chicago, 1969).

[29]Joan Robinson, *Economic Philosophy* (Chicago, 1962), 1.

Committee for Economic Development

interaction of these factors which led to the transformation of Keynesianism.

The corporatists of the CED were not alone in advocating what they did, but they played a significant role in gaining acceptance for their brand of commercial Keynesianism among the several constituencies involved. Addressing economists, government policy-makers, and their fellow businessmen, the CED contributed to the interaction described above in three distinct ways: (1) through its contributions to economic thought; (2) through the activities of its personnel; and (3) through its relationships, as an institution, with the various agencies active in formulating, selling, and implementing national economic policy.

The CED influenced national affairs by developing concepts which shaped the parameters of the debate over federal fiscal policy. Of special significance was the committee's sponsorship of the concept of "automatic stabilizers" and its emphasis on the "built-in flexibility" which such stabilizers would provide. While it is difficult to determine with precision the exact origins of the "automatic stabilizers" concept, the CED's 1946 study entitled *Jobs and Markets* and the pioneering work of staff economist Albert Hart seem to have played a crucial part in building "the basic framework for future considerations of built-in flexibility."[30]

The influence of the committee, moreover, extended beyond the mere development of ideas. More important, it worked to popularize such concepts among economists and laymen alike. From the very beginning, the CED had a shrewd appreciation of the value of public relations. "We got a lot of publicity," Marion Folsom later recalled laconically.[31] The committee aimed particularly at the "opinion-influencing group" in American society, especially those "equipped by education and desire to make a real study of our economy."[32] The organization's Information Committee included (in 1955) the head of the Book-of-the-Month Club, top executives from both Young and Rubicam and the J. Walter Thompson Agency, the editors of the *Atlanta Constitution* and *Look* magazine, the publisher of the *Washington Post*, the board chairman of the Curtis Publishing Company, and the presidents of Time-Life and the Columbia Broadcasting System. With such support, the CED was able to keep its recommendations in the public mind. For example, its 1958 pamphlet entitled *Defense against Inflation* was discussed within one month of its publication in 354 papers and magazines representing a total

[30]Norman Keiser, "The Development of the Concept of 'Automatic Stabilizers'," *Journal of Finance* 11 (December 1956): 436-37.

[31]Folsom Memoir (Eisenhower Project), Columbia Oral History Collection.

[32]CED executive director H. R. Johnson, quoted in CED, Minutes, Board of Trustees, 18 April 1947, Folsom MSS. See also CED, Joint Research Meeting, 25-26 September 1943, Box 127, Flanders MSS.

159

9

circulation of over thirty-one million.[33] Even so astute an economist as Paul McCracken of the University of Michigan (later a member of Eisenhower's Council of Economic Advisers) admitted that "the Committee for Economic Development, among others, has done a great deal to educate us on this point of built-in flexibility."[34] As a self-styled "merchant of ideas," the CED played a prominent role in the major postwar discussions regarding the government's role in the economy.[35]

In addition to its activities as an educational force, the committee affected public policy through the personal activities of its most fertile "idea man," Beardsley Ruml. An important element in the CED's style of Keynesianism was a shift in emphasis from the expenditure to the revenue side of the budget. The stabilizing budget would use automatic variations in revenue to cushion minor fluctuations and would rely on discretionary tax reduction rather than increased public spending to stimulate the economy in a depression. But before such a fiscal policy could be implemented, the rickety prewar tax structure of the United States had to be revamped.

The problem lay in the state of the personal income tax. First, it did not apply to enough people, for only four million persons or families were subject to the federal income tax in 1939.[36] Second, there was a lag in tax payment which delayed the impact of any change either in taxable income or in the tax rate assessed. Taxes on income earned in calendar year 1940, for example, were not paid until the following year, 1941, when payment would be undertaken in quarterly installments beginning in March.

Both of these difficulties were resolved, however, during World War II. The Revenue Act of 1942 brought nearly all working Americans into the income tax system; by 1944, 42.4 million persons or families were subject to the federal income tax.[37] But putting the tax on a pay-as-you-go basis proved to be a more difficult task. The problem of making tax payment current had been under discussion in the Treasury Department for some time, but no concrete proposals of scope and imagination were forthcoming. It was into this vacuum that Ruml swept in 1942 with a pay-as-you-go plan which was to make his name a household word and

[33]"Report on the Press Coverage of Defense against Inflation." on Reel 9, CED Archives. See also Nate White, "CED 'Idea Men' Scan Economic Horizons of U.S.," *Christian Science Monitor*, 10 October 1955, 10.

[34]Paul McCracken, "The Present Status of Monetary and Fiscal Policy," *Journal of Finance* 5 (March 1950): 42.

[35]This apt phrase was used by Robert Lenhart (vice president, CED, Administration) in an interview with the author, 8 May 1975.

[36]Gabriel Kolko, *Wealth and Power in America: An Analysis of Social Class and Income Distribution* (New York, 1962), 33.

[37]*Ibid.* On the Revenue Act of 1942, see Richard Polenberg, *War and Society: The United States, 1941-1945* (Philadelphia, 1972), 27-28; and Randolph Paul, *Taxation in the United States* (Boston, 1954), 294-326.

which was to allow taxation to play a more important role in economic stabilization.[38]

Ruml submitted his plan to the Treasury on March 30, 1942.[39] The proposal called for tax payments made in 1942, which were calculated on 1941 income, to be redefined as tentative payments on current 1942 income. In March 1943, income for the previous year would be known with certainty and the taxpayer could make up any sum owed the government (or vice versa) because of the difference between estimated and actual 1942 income. In the process, taxes for 1941 would be forgiven; they would simply be skipped. Tax payment would thus be made current and withholding procedures could be implemented with little trouble.

When the Treasury reacted coolly to his proposal, Ruml brought it to the attention of Congress in July 1942 by appearing "as an individual" before the Senate Finance Committee. The plan received much publicity, and a bitter controversy ensued over the issue of forgiveness. For some, the very idea that a year's taxes could be skipped without the Treasury losing money was incomprehensible. Liberals argued that to forgive a year's taxes across the board would result in unfair benefits for the rich.[40] Ruml continued to argue for equality of treatment (i.e., total forgiveness) regardless of income level, but he revised his plan to incorporate several windfall provisions to prevent the most blatant profiteering.

In the end, the appeal of the proposal and the extraordinary publicity that it received proved irresistible. Capitalizing on Ruml's abilities as an articulate and indefatigable promoter and utilizing such clever catch phrases as "setting the tax clock ahead" and "daylight saving for the taxpayer," the supporters of the scheme made pay-as-you-go a popular issue. By late 1942, 81 percent of those questioned in a Gallup poll had heard of the Ruml plan.[41] Additional notoriety was achieved when Ruml was made the subject of the $64 question on "Take It or Leave It," a popular radio quiz show.

[38]The account that follows is based upon Paul, *Taxation*, 326-49; "The History of the Pay-As-You-Go Income Tax" (unpublished memorandum, dated January 1957), Series II, Box 2, Beardsley Ruml MSS, University of Chicago (cited hereafter as Ruml MSS); "Chronology of Pay-As-You-Go Income Tax Plan 1942-1943" (revised September 1956), Series II, Box 1, *ibid.;* John Morton Blum, *From the Morgenthau Diaries: Years of War, 1941-1945* (Boston, 1967), 49-52, 58-64.

[39]Ruml to Morgenthau, 30 March 1942, Series II, Box 2, Ruml MSS.

[40]See, for example, the testimony of Randolph Paul, general counsel for the Treasury Department, in U.S., Congress, House, Committee on Ways and Means, *Individual Income Tax*, Hearings. . .on a proposal to place income tax of individuals on a pay-as-you-go basis, 78th Cong., 1st sess., 1943, 18-19. Representative Frank Carlson (R-Kans.) called the resulting legislative struggle "one of the hardest fights we had in Congress for years." Carlson to Ruml, 26 May 1943, Series II, Box 2, Ruml MSS.

[41]George Gallup, ed., *The Gallup Poll: Public Opinion, 1935-1971* (New York, 1972), 1: 366.

161

The Historian

On June 9, 1943, Roosevelt finally signed into law the Congressional compromise which put most wage and salary earners on a withholding basis beginning July 1 and which provided for the cancellation of 75 percent of one year's taxes (the lower of the 1942 or 1943 tax liabilities) or $50, whichever was higher. The unforgiven part of the tax would be paid in two installments, one due in 1944 and the second in 1945. What Representative Bertrand Gearhart (R-Calif.) derisively labeled "the plan that slogans built" was a reality.[42] Ruml's campaign had been a significant element in the process of change. His crusade also helped make practical the CED's policy of reliance on the built-in flexibility of the economy's automatic stabilizers.

Another way in which the committee influenced public economic policy was through the influx of CED members and alumni into federal service, a movement which established an important liaison between the CED and the government. In the first fifteen years of the organization's existence, thirty-eight CED trustees held public office.[43] Ralph Flanders and Ruml, respectively, served as presidents of the Boston and New York Federal Reserve Banks. William Benton and Flanders went to the Senate, and Paul Hoffman became administrator of the Marshall Plan. Marion Folsom relinquished the chairmanship of the CED to serve in the Eisenhower administration, first as Under Secretary of the Treasury and later as Secretary of Health, Education, and Welfare. Both of Eisenhower's secretaries of the Treasury, George Humphrey and Robert Anderson, were exposed—with varying degrees of agreement—to CED doctrine during their tenure as trustees. Indeed President Eisenhower and his brother Milton served for a time on the committee's board.[44] Nor were such contacts limited only to trustees. For example, Grover Ensley, who was recommended to Senator Flanders by research director Herbert Stein, became staff director of the Congressional Joint Economic Committee.[45] Theodore Yntema, who was the CED's first director of research, later served as chief economist in the government's Economic Stabilization Agency and ultimately returned to the committee as a trustee when he became a vice-president of the Ford Motor Company. Economist Neil Jacoby, a longtime

[42]Quoted in Paul, *Taxation*, 341.

[43]The figure is taken from Schriftgiesser, *Business Comes of Age*, 162.

[44]Of course, Eisenhower did not retain his membership in the CED during his presidency. Greater detail concerning the CED's old-boy network is provided in R. A. Hummel, "The Impact of CED on U.S. National Policy" (covering letter, Hummel to Flanders, 31 January 1958), Box 102, Flanders MSS. This document expresses a conspiracy theory which should be handled gingerly; the raw biographical data contained therein are useful, however. For a recent treatment, see Frank Fowlkes, "Washington Pressures: CED's Impact on Federal Policies Enhanced by Close Ties to Executive Branch," *National Journal*, 17 June 1972, 1015-24. The interchange described above has characterized both Republican and Democratic administrations.

[45]Interview, author with Herbert Stein, Charlottesville, Virginia, 20 June 1977.

162

12

member of the CED's Research Advisory Board, served on Eisenhower's Council of Economic Advisers.

An example of the impact of this sort of interchange is provided by the experience of CED alumnus Thomas McCabe, who had a role in implementing the flexible monetary policy proposed by the committee in 1948. McCabe, the president of Scott Paper, was one of the founding trustees of the CED and a member of its original Research Committee (under Ralph Flanders). Selected by President Truman in 1948 to succeed Marriner Eccles as chairman of the Board of Governors of the Federal Reserve System, McCabe became an important figure in the Fed's attempt to free itself from the domination of the Treasury Department. In 1948, the Fed was still committed, somewhat against its will, to the support of a favorable market for government securities. This relationship, which had hardened during the war because of the Treasury's undeniable need to borrow large amounts of money as cheaply as possible, meant that the actions of the Fed were determined more by the needs of the Treasury Department than by the Fed's own assessment of the needs of the economy.[46]

The policy views which McCabe brought to this battle had been provided to a significant degree by his CED experience. He explained to his CED associates in 1949,

> I can testify from personal experience to the impact that the effort left upon me as a participant. . . .I have been wrestling with the same type and range of problems as a public official. I can also testify, consequently, to the impact of the CED upon our public policies and upon the thinking of those who formulate policies. It goes without saying, of course, that the preliminary contact with the CED had been invaluable to me.[47]

The committee's repeated calls for the Federal Reserve to use to the maximum its statutory powers to maintain economic stability made a strong impression on McCabe.[48] Moreover, the CED's declarations generated support which helped McCabe succeed in the struggle to liberate monetary policy. He later recalled,

[46]The Fed-Treasury dispute is recounted in Stein, *Fiscal Revolution*, 241-80; Allan Sproul, "The 'Accord' — A Landmark in the First Fifty Years of the Federal Reserve System," *Federal Reserve Bank of New York Monthly Review*, November 1964, 227-36; James Knipe, *The Federal Reserve and the American Dollar: Problems and Policies, 1946-1964* (Chapel Hill, 1965), 50-62; Daniel Ahearn, *Federal Reserve Policy Reappraised, 1951-1959* (New York, 1963), 9-21; A. Jerome Clifford, *The Independence of the Federal Reserve System* (Philadelphia, 1965), 197-272; and Sidney Hyman, *Marriner Eccles: Private Entrepreneur and Public Servant* (Stanford, 1976), 341-51.

[47]CED, *The Committee for Economic Development: Its Past, Present and Future: An Address by Thomas B. McCabe . . . November 17, 1949* (New York, 1949), 3.

[48]McCabe, *The Role of CED Today* (New York, 1951), 2. This is the published text of an address to the CED trustees, 15 November 1950. See also McCabe's speech, Birmingham, Alabama, 12 December 1950, Box 11, Subject File 001.411, Records of the Federal Reserve System, Board of Governors, Washington, D. C.

13

...more and more public officials turn to CED for counsel and assistance, as it did when I was Chairman of the Board of Governors of the Federal Reserve System. I found CED gave me more aid in its statements on monetary and credit problems than any other group of business or financial people, especially in the very critical period prior to the Treasury-Federal Reserve accord, which was reached in 1951.[49]

While not all alumni of the CED were so inspired by their experience or so well positioned to affect events, the "old boy network" worked and, in the case of McCabe, exerted an important influence on public policy.

The committee's connection with the federal government involved in addition an organizational interaction that went beyond the exchange of personnel. Often such contact was informal. Leon Keyserling, chairman of the Council of Economic Advisers, reported to Truman that "we here in the Council have been in constant contact with various members of the Committee for Economic Development, have received from them much evidence of understanding and support for our work, and look upon them as the most forward looking of the major business organizations. . . .These gentlemen, most of whom you undoubtedly know, drop in to see me when they get a chance, and in general are helpful although they disagree with us on some points."[50]

The committee also enjoyed a close working relationship with the Federal Reserve System. From its inception during World War II, the CED found the Fed and its regional banks willing and active collaborators in various research activities.[51] Federal Reserve economist Ralph Young, a member of the CED's Research Advisory Board, served as an expert adviser and critic in the preparation of several CED policy statements; he actually represented the committee at a meeting of the Conference of National Organizations in 1948.[52] All the while, Young reported to his superiors regarding the views and activities of his CED

[49]McCabe, "We Dared Not Leave Economic Solutions to Chance," in Clarence Walton, ed., *Business and Social Progress: Views of Two Generations of Executives* (New York, 1970), 85. Regarding the importance of McCabe's role in bringing about the Accord, see the opinion of James J. O'Leary, chairman of the National Bureau of Economic Research, in the *New York Times*, 11 January 1978, D3.

[50]Keyserling to Truman, 15 February 1951, Subject File/Agencies/CEA, Box 143, President's Secretary's File, Truman MSS, Truman Library, Independence, Missouri (cited hereafter as Truman MSS).

[51]"Report of the Committee on Research and Statistics to the Presidents' Conference," 6 October 1943, Box 2256, Subject File 500.71, Records of the Federal Reserve System, RG 82, National Archives, Washington, D. C. (cited hereafter as FRS); "Minutes of Meeting of Subcommittee of the Presidents' Conference Committee on Research and Statistics. . .October 21, 1943," *ibid.*; memo, "Cooperation of Federal Reserve Bank Research Departments with Other Research Agencies," 26 February 1944, *ibid.*; Thomas McCabe to J. Cameron Thomson, 20 April 1950, Box 2186, Subject File 500.001, *ibid.*

[52]Paul Hoffman to Eccles, 12 August 1946, Box 2185; Young to Stein, 26 February 1948, Box 2186; Henry Johnston (executive director, CED) to Young, 15 March 1948, Box 2186; Young to Fed Personnel Committee, 3 April 1950, Box 2186; F. A. Nelson to Young,

14

colleagues.[53] Clearly, such connections served as liaisons for all involved; information and influence flowed both ways.

The CED often used its organizational relationships to direct government research into areas of mutual concern. In 1945, the committee gave $50,000 to another private group, the National Bureau of Economic Research, to finance a study of the flow of money payments through the principal sectors of the American economy. The CED arranged for representatives of the Federal Reserve System to serve on the project's technical advisory committee and induced the Fed to provide office space for this private study. Once it was underway, the Federal Reserve System agreed in 1946 to take over the entire effort.[54]

The CED utilized its ties in a similar fashion when it became concerned over the probable economic impact of the winding down of Korean War military spending. The committee prodded the Commerce Department into surveying the immediate economic prospects. Chairman Marion Folsom prevailed upon Commerce Secretary Charles Sawyer, and in 1952 the department launched a study designed "to inform the business community on factors affecting the level of civilian demand after the present defense program has reached its peak."[55] The CED advised Sawyer in the selection of outside experts to guide the project, and members of its own research staff "participated in an advisory capacity" and reviewed successive drafts of the study.[56] While the substance of the Commerce study was hardly reassuring, the CED had once again achieved an integration of private and public interests and organizations. In such instances the CED's corporatist ideology posited a mutuality of interests which played down the importance of determining who used whom; according to the corporatist outlook, private and public goals were the same. It was thus appropriate that during the Truman-Eisenhower interregnum, Eisenhower directed department and agency heads to maintain working relations with the CED. As Administrative Assistant for Economic Affairs Gabriel Hauge noted, ". . .this group has such connections with several government

---

5 April 1950, Box 2186; Young to E. A. Goldenweiser, 31 December 1952, Box 2188, all in Subject File 500.001, FRS.

[53]Young to Board of Governors, 17 October 1947, 5 January 1948, 13 January 1948; and Young to Eccles, 13 January 1948, 9 February 1948, all in Box 2186, Subject File 500.001, FRS.

[54]Woodlief Thomas to Board of Governors, 9 March 1945, Box 2256, Subject File 500.71, FRS; R. M. Evans to Flanders, 4 November 1946; Flanders to Evans, 6 November 1946; Ralph Young to Theodore Yntema, 20 December 1946, all in Box 2185, Subject File 500.001, FRS.

[55]U. S., Department of Commerce, *Markets after the Defense Expansion* (Washington, 1952), title page.

[56]*Ibid.*, iii-iv. On the CED's role, see Howard Myers to Folsom, 11 March 1952; Wesley Rennie to Folsom, 12 September 1952; and "CED, Summary Record of Meeting. . . September 18, 1952," all in Folsom MSS.

165

agencies and wants to keep them under the new administration; so does Ike.''[57]

In addition to such direct and indirect influence and interaction, the CED shaped events by providing conservative Keynesianism with a champion of impeccable credentials. As John Kenneth Galbraith has observed, ''In our tradition of economic debate, a proposition can often be more economically destroyed by association than by evidence. . . .The charge is that an idea is radical, unpractical, or long-haired is met by showing that a prominent businessman has favored it. Businessmen— successful ones at least—are by definition never radical, impractical, or long-haired.''[58] Once embraced by the CED, occasional deficit finance became less frightening. Respectability by association gave to the CED's Keynesianism a status and an influence never enjoyed by the earlier stagnationist formulation.

By such means, within a few years after its formation the committee had helped to alter the parameters of the public debate over economic affairs and to mold the content of public policy. By the mid-fifties the transformation of Keynesianism was well advanced. In the recessions of 1954 and 1957-58 the Eisenhower administration resisted the advice of both the laissez-faire advocates who held that the balanced budget was the *sine qua non* of political leadership and the spenders who viewed the expansion of public-sector investment as the salvation of American capitalism. In 1959, Secretary of the Treasury Robert Anderson, a CED alumnus, sought to explain the rationale underlying the administration's economic policy:

> We should, in my opinion, follow some variation of the stabilizing budget proposal, in which budget policy, year in and year out, would be geared to the attainment of a surplus under conditions of strong economic activity. . . .On this basis, the automatic decline in revenues and increase in expenditures during a recession—reflecting in part the operation of the so-called built-in stabilizers—would generate a moderate budget deficit. In prosperous periods, tax receipts would automatically rise and certain types of spending would contract, producing a budget surplus.[59]

His comments to the Congressional Joint Economic Committee could easily have been mistaken for a CED policy statement.

III

Even as Anderson spoke, however, the CED had begun to move away from its advocacy of fiscal automaticity towards a formulation which

---

[57]Gabriel Hauge to Robert Cutler, 15 January 1953, OF 114, Box 558, Eisenhower MSS, Eisenhower Library, Abilene, Kansas (hereafter DDEL).

[58]Quoted in Schriftgiesser, *Business and Public Policy*, 14-15.

[59]U. S., Congress, Joint Economic Committee, *January 1960 Economic Report of the President, Hearings. . .*, 86th Cong., 2nd sess., 1960, 455. See also Anderson's speech,

would allow greater discretionary action. This gradual shift had begun, in part, in response to the recession of 1953-54. It reflected also, however, the committee's belief that the return of the Republicans to power had lessened the danger of excessive government activism.[60] In March 1954, the CED issued a policy statement which indicated a new receptiveness to discretionary fiscal management. The automatic stabilizers were again appraised and suggestions for their strengthening put forth; built-in fiscal flexibility and monetary policy were judged sufficient for combating relatively minor economic fluctuations.[61] New, however, was the careful consideration given to deliberate measures to prevent or check a more serious recession.[62] In case of "either. . .an existing recession of some severity or. . .a recession that is forecast with a high degree of certainty," the committee recommended a temporary, general, income-tax rate reduction to stimulate demand.[63] This policy shift was reaffirmed during the recession of 1957-58, but in neither of the two Eisenhower recessions did the CED formally and firmly recommend the sort of tax reduction mentioned in its statements. In the end the committee decided that the patient was not quite sick enough to warrant the contemplated treatment.[64] But the CED had significantly lowered its threshold for discretionary tax reduction.

Such flexibility enabled the CED to continue to influence national economic policy when the Democrats returned to the White House in 1961. Its techniques were largely extensions of those which had worked so well during the period 1942-60. The Kennedy-Johnson tax cut of 1964 is often viewed as the culminating triumph of the fiscal revolution, and it was indeed an important departure from the reliance in the 1940s and 1950s on passive, automatic stabilization.[65] Yet, once again, important

---

Washington, D. C., 29 December 1959, in Box 3, DDE/Whitman File, Administrative Series, DDEL; and Anderson to Eisenhower, 12 December 1960, Box 2, *ibid.*

[60]Herbert Stein, "Budget Policy to Maintain Stability," 15 October 1953, Box 10, Arthur F. Burns MSS, DDEL; Stein, "Budget Policy to Maintain Stability," in CED, *Problems in Anti-Recession Policy*, CED Supplementary Paper (New York, 1954), 97; Robert Lenhart, "Case Study of 'Defense Against Recession'," (31 March 1953), on Reel 6, CED Archives.

[61]CED, *Defense against Recession: Policy for Greater Economic Stability* (New York, 1954), 10-26.

[62]*Ibid.*, 28-29, 31, 41, 48.

[63]*Ibid.*, 38, 34.

[64]Stein, *Fiscal Revolution*, 499 n45, 341.

[65]Some treatments mistakenly equate the postwar revolution in national economic policy with the Kennedy administration. See, for example, Robert Lekachman, *The Age of Keynes* (New York, 1966), 271; James Tobin, *The Intellectual Revolution in U.S. Economic Policy-making* (London, 1966), 1-4; and Arthur Okun, *The Political Economy of Prosperity* (Washington, 1970), 44-46. Correctives to this oversimplification are Holmans, *United States Fiscal Policy*, 303; and Walter Salant, "Some Intellectual Contributions of the Truman Council of Economic Advisers to Policy-Making," *History of Political Economy* 5 (Spring 1973): 36-49. The most sophisticated view of the entire

167

parts of the conceptual basis of the "new" New Economics had already been anticipated and popularized by the CED. The so-called high-employment budget, for example, was crucial to the Kennedy brand of Keynesian thought. The high-employment surplus, as it was termed by the Heller Council of Economic Advisers, provided a means of comparing alternative budget programs by canceling out the effects of economic fluctuations. Paternity of the concept can be traced to Beardsley Ruml's Littauer lecture at Hunter College in November 1943.[66] The idea first appeared in print the following summer and at Ruml's urging was early incorporated into CED policy, becoming the basis for the stabilizing budget formulation of 1947.[67]

As before, the educational efforts of the committee went far beyond the development of key ideas. In 1948. the CED had called for the creation of a national commission to undertake a comprehensive study of the government's monetary and budgetary operations. Eisenhower had proposed a similar undertaking in 1957, but had been rebuffed by Congress. The CED then acted to create a private group—the Commission on Money and Credit—to meet the need.[68] The bylaws of the new group were drawn up by CED secretary Robert Lenhart. Donald K. David, chairman of the CED and executive vice-president of the Ford Foundation, arranged for an initial Ford grant of $500,000 to finance the effort and selected the initial members. Frazar Wilde, chairman of the CED's Research and Policy Committee, was named to head the CMC and its membership of twenty-five included seven CED'ers. The committee provided office space in its New York headquarters, conference facilities, and some staff support. Formally established in October 1957, the CMC was a wholly private organization, legally separate from the CED, but the role of the committee in its formation had been crucial.

----

process — "an evolution with several critical points and gradual movement between them" — is in Stein, *Fiscal Revolution.*

[66]Ruml, "Free Enterprise and Post-War Planning," 12 November 1943, Series II, Box 3, Ruml MSS. See also Ruml to Arthur Schlesinger, Jr., 29 September 1959, Series I, Box 5, *ibid.*

[67]Ruml and H. Christian Sonne, *Fiscal and Monetary Policy,* National Planning Association Planning Pamphlet no. 35 (Washington, 1944), 8-9; CED, Joint Research Meeting, 25-26 September 1943, Discussion Notes, Box 127, Flanders MSS; CED, *Taxes and the Budget,* 22. At about this same time, Milton Friedman independently developed a version of the high employment budget. "A Monetary and Fiscal Framework for Economic Stability," *American Economic Review* 38 (June 1948): 248. See also Keith Carlson, "Estimates of the High-Employment Budget: 1947-1967," *Federal Reserve Bank of St. Louis Review,* June 1967, 6-13; and Robert Solomon, "A Note on the Full Employment Budget Surplus," *Review of Economics and Statistics* 46 (February 1964): 105-8

[68]This paragraph is based on Karl Schriftgiesser, *The Commission on Money and Credit: An Adventure in Policy-Making* (Englewood Cliffs, N.J., 1974), 3-43.

Committee for Economic Development

The recommendations of the CMC were consistent with the CED's increasing support for discretionary fiscal policy. The CMC's final report in 1961 recommended that Congress grant the president "limited conditional power to make temporary countercyclical adjustments in the first-bracket rate of the personal income tax."[69] The CMC report seems to have had a broad educational impact. The CED assumed responsibility for publishing and publicizing the CMC recommendations; over 35,000 hardcover and more than 110,000 paperbound copies of the CMC report were sold. In addition, a week after the report was published a sixteen-page supplement on its findings was distributed with the Sunday edition of the *New York Times*.[70] Through such activities, the CED helped to move discretionary tax reduction to the center of the public dialogue on national economic policy. In 1962, Kennedy's economic report specifically addressed the CMC's major recommendations and proposed a similar grant of power to allow the president to make necessary adjustments in tax rates.[71]

The committee also attempted to alter the course of events directly. As the president agonized in November and December 1962 over the question of whether to ask for a massive tax cut in the face of an already substantial deficit, the CED offered important support with the publication on December 14 of a call for "a prompt, substantial, permanent reduction."[72] Kennedy read the statement immediately and the White House legislative liaison office arranged to have copies distributed to all members of Congress.[73] Encouraged by this and other evidence of support within the business community, the administration drew up the details of its tax cut proposal during planning sessions at Palm Beach over the Christmas holiday.[74]

In the ensuing struggle for legislative approval, an organizational

[69]CMC, *Money and Credit, Their Influence on Jobs, Prices and Growth: The Report of the Commission on Money and Credit* (Englewood Cliffs, N.J., 1961), 137.

[70]Schriftgiesser, *Commission on Money and Credit*, 37, 43.

[71]U.S., President, *Economic Report of the President, 1962*, 18, 21-22.

[72]CED, *Reducing Tax Rates for Production and Growth* (New York, 1962), 7. Kennedy's path to the tax cut decision is discussed in Arthur Schlesinger, Jr., *A Thousand Days* (Boston, 1965), 620-31, 644-51, 1002-14; Theodore Sorensen, *Kennedy* (New York, 1965), 393-433; Seymour Harris, *Economics of the Kennedy Years and a Look Ahead* (New York, 1964); Walter Heller, *New Dimensions of Political Economy* (Cambridge, Mass., 1966), 1-82; Tobin, *Intellectual Revolution in U. S. Economic Policy-making*; Bernard Nossiter, *The Mythmakers: An Essay on Power and Wealth* (Boston, 1964), 1-42; Hobart Rowen, *The Free Enterprisers: Kennedy, Johnson and the Business Establishment* (New York, 1964); Jim Heath, *John F. Kennedy and the Business Community* (Chicago, 1969), 22-47, 114-22; and Stein, *Fiscal Revolution*, 372-453.

[73]Walter Heller to Herbert Stern, 22 December 1962, Box 22, Walter Heller MSS, Kennedy Library, Boston, Massachusetts (hereafter JFKL); Paul Sarbanes to Heller, 21 December 1962, *ibid*.

[74]On the mid-December turning point, see Heller, *New Dimensions*, 35; and Sorensen, *Kennedy*, 430.

169

The Historian

offspring of the CED played a significant role. In 1963 the Business Committee for Tax Reduction was formed at the suggestion of Secretary of the Treasury Douglas Dillon (who joined the CED as its vice-chairman after his government service) and was endorsed by Kennedy. The group served as the active lobbying agency for the CED constituency during the tax-cut battle; four of the six businessmen called upon by Dillon to mobilize support for reduction were trustees of the CED, as were twenty-three of the fifty executives invited to the formal organizational meeting in April 1963.[75] The Business Committee was, in Heller's words, "a potent outfit," with a membership of approximately three thousand and a budget which made it the third largest spender among registered lobbying groups in 1963.[76] It advocated a policy similar to that of the December 1962 CED statement. The voice was that of business corporatists rallying to the support of an administration which shared their appreciation of "commercial Keynesianism." The Revenue Act of 1964 was thus not an aberrant conversion experience for either government or business but was instead the culmination of a number of varied trends, long underway, in both the private and public spheres. The CED played a prominent role in facilitating these trends and in achieving the policy adopted in 1964.

IV

The development of Keynesian policies had taken two critical turns in the years after the statist, stagnationist formulation was first developed in the United States during the period 1938-45. The first of these changes involved a shift from an emphasis on fiscal activism and government spending to a new reliance on automatic stabilization. The second involved a new willingness to use discretionary management and to depend on tax reduction, rather than increased expenditures, to ensure economic stability and growth. At both junctures, the CED played an important role in changing the parameters of the public policy debate. These shifts resulted not simply from changes in the economic environment but also from the efforts of American businessmen to establish an effective economic role for the federal government—a role which would avoid statist regimentation or laissez-faire anarchy. The popular view of John F. Kennedy pulling a

[75]On the formation and membership of the Business Committee, see U.S. Congress, Senate, Committee on Finance. *Revenue Act of 1963*, Hearings on H.R. 8363, 88th Cong., 1st sess., 1963, pt. 3, 1263-78; and Frazar Wilde, "Some Comments on the History and Position of the Business Committee for Tax Reduction in 1963," 10 September 1963, Box 23, Heller MSS, jFKL. Kennedy's endorsement is in U.S., President, *Public Papers, Kennedy, 1963*, 351, 667.

[76]Heller to LBJ, 29 November 1963, Box 31, Theodore Sorensen MSS, JFKL; Stein, *Fiscal Revolution*, 551 n.38; Heath, *Kennedy and Business Community*. 171 n.46.

170

benighted business community, kicking and screaming, into the modern age of political economy is clearly mistaken.

As the CED's experience in the period 1942-64 illustrates, there was a revival in postwar America of the conscious corporatist impulse which had been so notable during 1900-1935. Both generations of corporatists shared a common, overarching vision; pursued a scientifically achieved social harmony to replace the all too chimerical, automatic one of laissez faire; and sought to use private agencies and expert knowledge for public purposes. Each generation derived inspiration from the experience and lessons of wartime mobilization but subsequently found itself compelled, by reasons of both principle and expediency, to give continued obeisance to the workings of the market mechanism and constitutional democracy. And each directed considerable attention to the problem of economic stability.[77]

The committee's program differed markedly, however, from that advanced by such earlier corporatists as Herbert Hoover in that it gave to the state a larger role in guaranteeing prosperity. As founder and vice-chairman William Benton explained to his CED colleagues,

> The historic attitude of business has been to use government if it could, and abuse it if it couldn't. Philosophically, business was committed to the doctrine that, "that government is best which governs least." The emerging CED attitude has been that "government has a *positive* and *permanent* role in achieving the common objectives of high employment and production and high and rising standards of living for people in all walks of life.". . . The greatest single achievement of CED. . .may turn out to be the clarification it has been developing on the role of government in the economy. . . .This is our present answer to the European brands of socialism. Long may it thrive.[78]

Yet the CED's departure in this regard was not as sudden as Benton's rhetoric made it appear. First-generation corporatists had posited the government's role as that of energizer and coordinator of private action, but the challenge of the Great Depression made it clear that a spectrum of opinion concerning the proper level of government activity had developed among domestic corporatists. Some, such as Henry Harriman of the Chamber of Commerce and Gerard Swope of General Electric, began to plump for government-sponsored cartelization of industry as both necessary and desirable, and the New Deal's NRA brought these suggestions to fruition. But not all who had been active in promoting the ideal of an associative state in the 1920s supported such developments; Hoover, for one, regarded them with distaste and

---

[77]See, for example, Evan Metcalf, "Secretary Hoover and the Emergence of Macroeconomic Management," *Business History Review* 49 (Spring 1975): 60-80; and Carolyn Grin, "The Unemployment Conference of 1921: An Experiment in National Cooperative Planning," *Mid-America* 55 (April 1973): 83-107.

[78]Benton, speech to CED trustees, 1949, Box 1518, OF 638-A, Truman MSS.

171

branded them fascistic. The businessmen of the CED in effect attempted to find some middle ground between these two wings of corporatist opinion. The problem, said Benton with an ad man's flair for the epigram, was to regulate the economic climate without rationing the raindrops.[79]

The corporatists of the CED also functioned in a more complex and demanding political world than did the corporate organizers of the 1920s; they operated in a much denser organizational environment than did their predecessors. In the wake of the Great Depression the state assumed new responsibilities and acted as the ultimate guarantor of prosperity. Thus, the post-1929 era saw the development and strengthening of secondary organizations in the public sector (such as the Council of Economic Advisers) designed to coordinate the activities of primary economic organizations.[80] Other complicating factors included the continued appeal of statist and conservative alternatives and the strengthening of potentially antagonistic countervailing interest groups and institutions, such as organized labor and Galbraith's technostructure. Yet the experience of the CED indicates that the post-Depression corporatists did very well.

In part, their success was due to the weaknesses of traditional reform liberalism and to the appeal of corporatist ideology for those outside the business community. As liberals came increasingly to see their political role as that of technocratic managers of the social order, they became amenable to corporatist solutions to their problems. Kennedy's assessment that "most of the problems, or at least many of them, that we now face are technical problems, are administrative problems. . .very sophisticated judgments which do not lend themselves to the great sort of 'passionate movements' which have stirred this country so often in the past," narrowed considerably the philosophical distance between the New Frontier and the new corporatism.[81]

The success of the CED also resulted from factors of technique and institutional location. The group's alliance with academe allowed it to generate sophisticated alternatives which seemed particularly applicable to the complex problems of a highly organized society. The CED's determination and ability to operate as a neither fully private nor fully official but rather somehow a "quasi-public" institution was also crucial. Nestled on the boundary between the private and public spheres

---

[79]Address to CED Trustees, 11 May 1949, Box 102, Flanders MSS.

[80]Alfred D. Chandler and Louis Galambos define primary organizations as large-scale, complex bureaucracies which essentially organized people in order to provide goods or services. Secondary organizations coordinated the activities of primary organizations. Their important essay, "The Development of Large-Scale Economic Organizations in Modern America," is reprinted in Edwin Perkins, ed., *Men and Organizations: The American Economy in the Twentieth Century* (New York, 1977), 188-201.

[81]U.S., President, *Public Papers, Kennedy, 1962*, 422.

172

and facing as it were in both directions at once, it was well placed to act as a combination training, recruiting, and legitimizing agency. Whereas the older variety of corporatists had worked most effectively on a localistic plane (often intraindustry) and in areas of clear, direct, and traditional self-interest (for example, the area of labor-management relations), the postwar corporatists enjoyed considerable success in the more rarified atmosphere of highly abstruse national economic policy as well.

173

Research

The Political Control of the Economy: Deficit Spending as a Political Belief, 1932-1952

DONALD T. CRITCHLOW

THE RELATIONSHIP BETWEEN electoral behavior and economic public policy presents a crucial problem for historians concerned with the meaning of democracy in a capitalist society. Yet this relationship is not readily discernible, even during periods of party realignment, when the intensification of electoral activity and the mobilization of new voters into the electoral process should lead, as Walter Dean Burnham observes, to "ideological polarization and issue distances between parties" and to "durable consequences which determine the outer boundaries of policy in general, though not necessarily of policies in detail."[1] The relationship between electoral activity and subsequent economic policy is only in a preliminary stage of investigation. Many scholars concerned with the nature of political parties in American history have pointed to possible ways in which electoral behavior influences economic policy.[2]

1. Walter Dean Burnham, *Critical Elections and the Mainsprings of American Politics* (New York: 1970), pp. 6–9.
2. The impact of electoral changes on subsequent policy outputs has been explored in Paul Allen Beck, "The Electoral Cycle and Patterns in American Politics," *British Journal of Political Science* (April, 1979); David W. Brady, "Critical Elections, Congressional Parties, and Clusters of Policy Changes," *Ibid.*

25

More specific empirical studies have pursued this relationship by examining congressional membership and congressional legislation during times of party realignment. Recently scholars have explored voting as it relates to economic policy in broader terms. In a recent article, "The Party Period and Public Policy: An Exploratory Hypothesis," Richard L. McCormick, Jr. described government's role in the period from the 1830s to the 1900s as little more than the accumulation of isolated, individual choices, usually of the distributive nature.[3] Edward Tufte, in turn, shows through regression analysis that the timing of elections has generally influenced the rate of employment, the growth of real disposable income, the short-term management of inflation and unemployment, and the flow of transfer payments. Tufte proves the existence of what others have sought to find, a politicized economy characterized by a close relationship between the business cycle and the electoral system.[4]

These studies make an important contribution to the new field of public policy history. Reflected in these studies, however, is a behavioral emphasis on the nature of voting and elections in American politics. Yet these studies suggest little concern for how public policy is formulated, particularly during periods of party realignment. This neglect of public policy formulation has left those with an interest in it with a one-dimensional view that ignores the role that government functionaries, academics, and

---

(January, 1978); Leon D. Epstein, "Electoral Decision and Policy Mandate," *Public Opinion Quarterly* (1964); Benjamin Ginsberg, "Critical Elections and the Substance of Policy Conflict: 1844–1968," *Midwest Journal of Political Science* (November, 1976); Michael R. King and Lester Seligman, "Critical Elections. Congressional Recruitment and Public Policy," *Elite Recruitment in Democratic Polities: Comparative Studies Across Nations*, Henry Eaulau and Moshe M. Czudnowski, eds. (New York: 1976); Warren E. Miller and Donald E. Stokes, "Constituency Influence in Congress," *American Political Science Review* (November, 1963); Barbara Deckard Sinclair, "The Policy Consequences of Party Realignment—Social Welfare Legislation in the House of Representatives, 1933–1954," *American Journal of Political Science* (February, 1978); Gabriel Almond and Sidney Verba, *The Civic Culture* (Princeton, N.J., 1963), p. 214; and John C. Wahlke, "Policy Demands and System Support: The Role of the Represented," *British Journal of Political Science* (July, 1971). On the nature of belief systems see Philip Converse, "The Nature of Belief Systems in Mass Politics," in *Ideology and Discontent*, David D. Apter, ed. (New York, 1964).

3. Richard L. McCormick, "The Party Period and Public Policy: An Exploratory Hypothesis," *Journal of American History* (September, 1979).

4. Edward Tufte, *The Political Control of the Economy* (Princeton, New Jersey: 1978).

intellectuals play in developing and implementing public policies and programs. If the field of public policy history is to contribute to our understanding of democratic politics in a capitalist society, it must understand the role that individual actors play in public policy formulation. This means that historians of public policy in the twentieth century must incorporate the findings of new political history and economic history with the insights of intellectual history, which perceives the importance of the individual and consciousness in shaping history.

This study proposes to show the complexity of policy formulation and its relation to electoral politics by examining the development of deficit spending as a political belief during the period from 1932 to 1952. The history of deficit spending as an accepted political belief reveals a non-linear relationship between election results and policy outcomes. For purposes of study, the development of deficit spending as a political belief can be divided into three phases. The first phase, from 1932 to 1937, was characterized by a profound ambivalence on the part of the Roosevelt administration to accept deficits as a regular part of government policy. In fact, following the election of 1936, which was marked by sharp class polarities, Roosevelt sought to balance the budget by cutting allocations for many of those relief agencies that had helped win him electoral support among the lower income groups.

The second phase, which occurred after the recession of 1937 and lasted until 1945, was distinguished by the institution of a planned deficit spending program. The initial advocates of planned deficits were a group of young Keynesian economists, New Economists, who were primarily concerned with the objective economic conditions of the time. Many regular Democratic politicians in the Roosevelt administration opposed the new economic program of spending. Furthermore, new economics became an instituted part of fiscal policy after Republican congressional victories in 1938. Thus a major policy shift, closely associated with the New Deal, occurred with a resurgence of Republicanism in Congress.

The third phase in this study shows that Republicans eventually came to accept much of the New Deal program, particularly social security, but were unwilling to endorse any further programmatic developments as advocated by the New Economists.

Nonetheless, Republican fiscal policy accepted deficits, in effect, through its support of incremental increases of transfer payments and defense expenditures.

During the presidential campaign of 1932, Roosevelt attacked Hoover's fiscal irresponsibility and promised to eliminate government waste and return the nation to a balanced budget. The story of Roosevelt's fiscal conservatism has been frequently told, but Roosevelt's promises to balance the budget should be seen as more than political rhetoric, even though once he was in office he would be forced into deficit spending practices in order to finance his relief measures. Immediately after the election of 1932, President-elect Roosevelt asked former Congressman J. Swager Sherley to examine ways in which government could be reorganized and expenses cut. Once in office Roosevelt temporarily dropped any immediate plans for reorganizing government, but his fiscal conservatism was evident in his appointment of Lewis Douglas, who was prevailed upon to resign his seat in Congress to become director of the Bureau of the Budget. Douglas was asked to attend all Cabinet meetings, and he had a standing appointment in Roosevelt's bedroom each morning between 9:00 and 9:30 to discuss the business of the day.[5] Furthermore, one of the first measures of the Roosevelt administration was to ask Congress on March 10, 1933, only six days after the inauguration, to pass an economy act which would reduce the compensation of federal employees and cut veteran's benefits.[6] Roosevelt's concern with increasing governmental deficits was expressed in terms of urgency:

With the utmost seriousness I point out to the Congress the profound effect of this fact upon our national economy. It has contributed to the recent collapse of our banking structure. It has accentuated the stagnation of the economic life of our people. It has added to the ranks of the unemployed. Our government's house is not in order and for many reasons no effective action has been taken to restore it to order.[7]

5. James E. Sargent, "FDR and Lewis W. Douglas: Budget Balancing and the Early New Deal," *Prologue* (Spring, 1974). For a summary of Lewis Douglas's own views see Douglas, "Address," *The Consensus* (January, 1935). Useful insights into Roosevelt's economic thinking can be found in Elliott Rosen, *Hoover, Roosevelt, and the New Deal* (New York, 1977) and Daniel Roland Fusfeld, *The Economic Thought of Franklin D. Roosevelt and the Origins of the News Deal* (New York, 1956).

6. Lewis Kimmel, *The Federal Budget and Fiscal Policy, 1789–1959* (Washington: 1959), p. 176.

7. *Public Papers and Addresses of Franklin D. Roosevelt* II (Washington, 1938), p. 175.

Roosevelt's early recovery program centered primarily on inflationary monetary schemes and industrial planning. It is interesting to note that many of those who proposed plans for industrial planning, men like Harold G. Moulton and Meyer Jacobstein, two Brookings economists who helped draft the initial legislation for the National Industrial Recovery Act, were fiscal conservatives.[8] Nevertheless, although Roosevelt was a fiscal conservative, his own political instincts allowed him to accept an expanded role for government in supporting relief appropriations and an extensive public works program. By fiscal year 1934, budget estimates placed the deficit at $7.3 billion. That same year Lewis Douglas resigned as budget director.

Relief appropriations paid direct political dividends to the Roosevelt administration. Considerable discretionary allocative authority was concentrated in the executive branch in spending these relief appropriations. Econometric studies now show a close interaction between political and spending forces. Gavin Wright, a University of Michigan economist, has shown that interstate inequalities in per capita federal spending can be explained in large part as a result of maximizing expected electoral returns. He estimated that between 58.7 and 79.6 percent of the variance in per capita spending in the period from 1933 to 1940 can be attributed to political concerns to deliver electoral votes in marginal states.[9] Furthermore, his analysis of work relief appropriations confirms Republican accusations made at the time that Work Projects Administration allocations were political in nature. It was well known at the time that WPA employment reached peaks in the fall of every election year. Clearly, a political component was built into

8. Moulton's role in the drafting of the NIRA was discussed in his memorandum, "History and Origins of the NIRA," (c. mid-1943), *Brookings Institution File* (The Brookings Institution); his fierce opposition to deficit spending is evident in his *A New Philosophy of Public Debt* (Washington, 1943). See also Theodore Rosenof, *Dogma, Depression and the New Deal* (New York, 1975), p. 56; Bernard Bellush, *The Failure of the NRA* (New York, 1975), especially pp. 1–30; Ellis Hawley, *The New Deal and the Problem of Monopoly* (Princeton, New Jersey, 1966), pp. 19–52; Ellis Hawley, "The New Deal and Business," in *The New Deal* I, John Braeman, ed. (Ohio, 1975); and Kim McQuaid, "Corporate Liberalism and the Business Community, 1920–1940," *Business History Review* (Autumn, 1978).

9. Gavin Wright, "The Political Economy of New Deal Spending: An Econometric Analysis," *The Review of Economics and Statistics* (February, 1974); 30–38. See also L. J. Arrington, "The New Deal in the West: A Preliminary Statistical Inquiry," *Pacific Historical Review* (August, 1969): 311–16; Arrington, "Western Agriculture and the New Deal," *Agricultural History* (October, 1970): 337–53. For conservative hostility to New Deal relief, see James T. Patterson, *Congressional Conservatism and the New Deal* (Lexington, 1967).

relief spending and this political factor must have reinforced Roosevelt's ambivalence toward deficit spending.

Nonetheless, Roosevelt was not solely motivated by politics, as evidenced by his fierce opposition to the veteran's bonus and in his desire to have a balanced budget by 1937. Roosevelt's veto of immediate payments of the veteran's bonus withstood a congressional override attempt in 1935, but his veto in 1936, an election year, could not withstand the pressure of an anxious Congress. Even a loyal Roosevelt Democrat and a fiscal conservative like Pat Harrison of Mississippi, whose state alone had $33.5 million at stake in bonus payments, fell to veterans' pressure. With telegrams coming at a rate of 250 by the hour in favor of the bonus bill, Congress rapidly overrode Roosevelt's veto.[10]

Bonus legislation, together with the Butler decision issued in early 1936, which ordered the return of $200 million of processing taxes by the Agricultural Adjustment Administration, created a threat of even greater deficits. Spenders within the administration, including Lauchlin Currie at the Federal Reserve, Leon Henderson and Aubrey Williams at the WPA, and a group of economists at the Treasury Department, urged the enactment of an undistributed profits tax as a means of releasing idle pools of capital and increasing government revenues.

At the same time Roosevelt continued to hope for a balanced budget by cutting government expenditures. Working with Daniel Bell, who replaced Douglas as director of the budget, Roosevelt retreated to Warm Springs, Georgia, in November 1935, where he systematically slashed budget requests. He halved the request of the Civilian Conservation Corps, cut road-building funds, speeded the discharge of employees from the now disbanded NRA, and took $150 million from Ickes' Public Works Administration. In January 1936, he renewed his efforts to cut funds from the Reconstruction Finance Corporation ($660 million), the Farm Credit Administration ($80 million), and the Federal Housing Administration ($750 million).[11]

Yet while Roosevelt undertook these budget cuts, and planned

10. *Congressional Record*, 74th Cong. 2nd Sess., (1936), 561, 7031; John Morton Blum, *From the Morgenthau Diaries, The Years of Crisis, 1928–1938* (New York, 1959): 247–58; and Martha Swain, *Pat Harrison, The New Deal Years*, (Jackson, Mississippi, 1978): 100–120.

11. Blum, *From the Morgenthau Diaries*, pp. 263–65.

more severe ones, a political polarization along class lines was in progress, culminating in the election of 1936.[12] The presidential election of 1936, which gave Roosevelt all but two states, revealed a clear-cut set of socioeconomic polarities. In the preceding presidential election of 1932, Democrats had outpolled Republicans among the upper income groups. Now, in 1936, the highest income groups swung sharply toward the Republican Party. Specifically, 71.7 percent of the voters who switched from the Democratic Party in 1932 to the Republican in 1936 came from the upper class. At the same time, Democrats gained the support of 77.5 percent of those 1932 voters who were poor or on relief.

TABLE 1: PERCENTAGE-POINT DIFFERENCE BETWEEN DEMOCRATIC AND REPUBLICAN VOTING BY INCOME CATEGORIES: THE NON-SOUTH, 1932–1948[*][13]

	1932	1936	1940	1944	1948
Income Category					
Above Average	+ 4.9	—29.1	—36.2	—21.3	—37.7
Average	— 4.8	+ 2.8	— 5.2	—11.4	— 2.1
Poor	+32.7	+42.8	+30.0	+14.4	+24.8
On Relief[**]	+59.4	+68.8	+50.0	+14.3	+29.0
N =	4058	1768	2578	2165	2528

[*] Dem % minus Repub %
[**] Very small N's for 1940–48

Nonetheless, Roosevelt's budget cuts following the election did not reflect his lower class support. Having initiated budget reductions in 1935, Roosevelt slashed appropriations of the very agencies that had helped bolster Democratic support among the lower classes—PWA, WPA, CCC, Farm Credit Administration, and the Federal Housing Authority.[14] Roosevelt felt he could afford to undertake these budget cuts because the economy appeared to be on its way toward revival. By early 1935, production was already 57 percent greater than the depression low of July 1932, and from the middle of 1935 through December, production rose another

12. The following analysis of electoral behavior in 1932 and 1936 was presented by Paul Kleppner and Stephen C. Baker, "The Impact of Depression on Mass Political Behavior: The United States in the 1870s, the 1890s, and the 1930s," (Unpublished paper, delivered at the 1979 Annual Meeting of the American Historical Association, December, 1979), pp. 28–33.
    13. This table is from Kleppner, *Ibid.*, p. 32.
    14. Blum, *From the Morgenthau Diaries*, pp. 263–83; Kimmel, *Federal Budget*, pp. 184–90.

13 percent. Wholesale prices advanced 33 percent and the cost of living had risen 18 percent from depression lows.[15]

Yet this economic recovery only heightened fears of runaway inflation. Many economists observed that recovery was based only on increased consumer spending rather than on increased capital investment, thereby reversing what appeared to be the traditional pattern of economic recovery in which increased consumer demand followed, instead of led, capital investment.[16] Business leaders found opportunity to attack Roosevelt's "extravagant waste of money, his reckless expansion of public credit, his policy of inflation ... his catering to class hatred ... ," but business spokesmen were not alone in their concerns of inflation.[17]

The editors of The Nation reported in 1936 that "talk of inflation is once more in the air." By the spring of 1937, even Marriner Eccles, one of the New Deal's most avid spenders, spoke in favor of returning to a balanced budget in order to combat inflation.[18] Consequently, federal reserve requirements were raised, and finally on April 7, 1937, Roosevelt, acting on the best advice offered

15. The recession of 1937–38 is analyzed in Kenneth D. Roose, The Economics of Recession and Revival; An Interpretation (New York, 1969) pp. 24–33.

16. Actually this recovery was not unique. Consumption led investment in the upturns following the recessions in 1924 and 1927. Furthermore, Kenneth Roose shows that, contrary to Keynesian arguments, the decline in net government contributions was not the primary cause of the recession. More important factors in this recession were the increase in marginal reserve requirements and monopolistic increases in prices while demand fell. Roose, The Economics of Recession, pp. 70–74, 102–18. Sumner Slichter, "The Downturn of 1937," Review of Economic Statisitcs (August 1938); M. D. Brockie, "Theories of the 1937–38 Crisis and Depression," The Economic Journal (June, 1950); and Douglas A. Hayes, Business Confidence and Business Activity, "Michigan Business Studies," 10 (Ann Arbor, 1951).

Concerns with inflation at the time were expressed by E. A. Goldenweiser, "How Can Credit Be Controlled," Academy of Political Science Proceedings (May, 1936); Arthur Marget, "Inflation: Inevitable or Avoidable," The Day and Hours Series of University of Minnesota (Minneapolis, 1937), and Sumner H. Slichter, "Must We Have Another Boom?" Atlantic Monthly (January, 1936) espec. 601–6.

17. S. Wells Utley, The American System Shall We Destroy It (Detroit, 1936), quoted in Roose, The Economics of Recession, p. 57; Robert L. Lund, The Truth About the New Deal (New York, 1936); and The Atlantic Monthly's series of editorials, especially "There is a Way Out," (September 1938), "The Danger of Mounting Deficits," (November, 1938); and "Sound Recovery Through A Balanced Budget," (December, 1935).

18. Maxwell S. Stewart, "Beware Inflation," The Nation (March 11, 1936): 306–8; Alvin Johnson, "Where Inflation Threatens," The Nation (September 5, 1936): 265; "Eccles Warns Fight Inflation Now," Business Week (March 20, 1937).

by both conservatives and liberals, ordered a further curtailment of government expenditures in an attempt to restore a balanced budget.

As the budget appeared to be nearing balance, with many predicting the year 1938 would be a particularly good year, suddenly economic disaster struck.[19] The rapid decline in income and production during the nine months from September 1937 to June 1938 was without precedent in American economic history. From August 1937 to June 1938, industrial production fell nearly 30 percent. Decline in non-durable goods was even more drastic, falling over 50 percent. By December 1937, over 1,800,00 workers had lost their jobs.

The recession unleashed a fierce political debate inside Roosevelt's administration which carried over to the press and the public. Secretary Henry Morgenthau continued to urge fiscal cuts. He even went so far as to encourage anti-trust action as a means of distracting Roosevelt from undertaking a spending program.[20] Morgenthau's arguments gained support from party regulars including John Garner, Cordell Hull, Jesse Jones, Pat Harrison, and James Farley, who told Roosevelt that the American people wanted to hear that the administration was going to reduce the cost of government.[21] Polls at the time revealed that 63 percent of the public stood against increased spending, but 37 percent stood in favor.[22]

Confronting the fiscal conservatives were a small group of economists, recent converts to Keynesianism. Since the publication of John Keynes' *General Theory of Employment, Interest and Money* in 1936, an increasing number of liberals, including Lauchlin Currie, Harry Dexter White, Isador Lubin, and Aubrey Williams had

19. National City Bank of New York, *Monthly Letter* (1937): 31, quoted in Roose, *Economics of Recession*, p. 78; Blum, *From the Morgenthau Diaries*, p. 393.
20. Blum, *From the Morgenthau Diaries*, p. 414.
21. *Ibid.*, pp. 392–3. Henry Morgenthau, "Federal Spending and the Federal Budget," *Academy of Political Science Proceedings* (1938): pp. 536–56; Harley L. Lutz, "Federal Depression Finances and Its Consequences," *Harvard Business Review* (Winter, 1938); Burt M. McConnell, "The Press Looks At Pump Priming," *Current History* (June, 1938): 32. *The New York Times* was particularly adamant against increased spending; see "The Panacea of Spending," (March 28, 1938): 14; "The President's Program," (April 15, 1938): 18; "The Right Prescription," (April 20, 1938): 22.
22. "The Fortune Survey," *Fortune* (March, 1939): 66, 135.

turned to Keynes to provide an economic rationale for deficit spending.[23] Keynes's theoretical construct showed that "pump priming" was not enough, and perhaps was even harmful, for economic recovery.[24] What was needed was a planned fiscal program determined by specific aggregate levels in the national economy to set government expenditures. Demand became the barometer and the target of economic policy. With the severity of recession, American Keynesians found their arguments for a liberalized spending program carrying more weight within the Roosevelt administration.

Thus in 1937 the Keynesians took the offensive. Lauchlin Currie articulated the Keynesian analysis of the recession by pointing to the previous cuts in government expenditures and the introduction of Social Security taxes as the primary cause of renewed inflation. At the same time, Marriner Eccles tried to interest the president in a massive federal housing program.[25] Finally, in the spring of 1938, Leon Henderson, Aubrey Williams, and Beardsley Ruml, acting through Harry Hopkins, presented Roosevelt with a detailed argument for an increased spending program. Shortly after receiving this program, Roosevelt, concerned at this point with the approaching fall election, called upon Congress for a "spend lend" program of $4.5 million dollars.[26] Roosevelt's program called for a public housing program, the building of a transcontinental highway, and increased appropriations of the agencies which had

23. There is a growing literature, mostly by economists, on this Keynesian revolution. See, John K. Galbraith, "Came the Revolution," New York Book Review (May, 1965): 1, 36. Lawrence R. Klein, The Keynesian Revolution (New York, 1966); Kimmel, The Federal Budget, pp. 195–228; Robert Lekachman, The Age of Keynes (New York, 1966) pp. 79–112; J. Ronnie Davis, New Economics and Old Economists (Ames, 1971); Herbert Stein, The Fiscal Revolution in America (Chicago, 1969); Alan Sweezy, "The Keynesians and Government Policy, 1933–1939," American Economic Review, (May, 1972): 116–121.

24. For an interesting discussion on the detriments of "pump-priming" see Alvin H. Hansen, "The Postwar Economy," in Postwar Economic Problems, Seymour Harris, ed. (New York, 1943) pp. 9–27.

25. Lauchlin Currie, "A Tentative Program to Meet the Business Recession," Emanuel Goldenweiser Papers (Library of Congress); Beardsley Ruml, "Warm Springs Memorandum," (April, 1938), and "Miami Memorandum," (April 6, 1938), Beardsley Ruml Papers, University of Chicago); Marriner Eccles, Beckoning Frontiers; Public and Personal Recollections, Sidney Hyman, ed. (New York, 1951), pp. 299–317; Paul W. Sweezy, "Why Balance the Budget," The Nation (January 15, 1938); Simeon Leland, "Some Recent English Books on Government Finance: A Review," Journal of Political Economy (April, 1938), 229–336; Alvin Hansen, Full Recovery and Stagnation (New York, 1938).

26. Public Papers of Franklin D. Roosevelt (1938), pp. 241–48.

been targeted for budget cuts the previous year. The Keynesian fiscal program now appeared to be in complete harmony with the social and economic objectives of the New Deal.

The first step in the Keynesian revolution had been taken by a small group of economists numbering only twenty to fifty men. In the next few years these Keynesians made further inroads in government. Shortly before America entered the war, a Division of Fiscal Analysis was established at the Budget Bureau to analyze the impact of budgetary operations, expenditure programs, tax programs, and debt management for the economy as a whole. During the war, Keynesians joined government to work for the National Resources Planning Board (NRPB), the National Housing Agency, Treasury, Agriculture, and the Securities and Exchange Commission. At the Division of Price Management, under Leon Henderson, a Macroeconomic Advisory Group would be formed to prepare programs for economic stabilization.[27]

From the outset of this revolution, it was clear that new economics could go in two directions—toward a restrained fiscal policy centered around automatic stabilizers and limited discretionary spending, or toward more government planning. Fiscal policy offered a means of avoiding the mistakes of do-nothingism without specific interference with the free decisions by many of what and how to produce.[28] On the other hand, Keynesianism presented an instrument for more direct programmatic planning through public works, public housing programs, urban renewal, and national resource development. Clearly, many Keynesians desired a more planned economy directed by the federal government. As early as 1936, the director of research at the Treasury Department, Emanual Goldenweiser, warned that "relatively little progress has been made toward developing an economic steering gear . . ." to keep the economy running smoothly. Until the development of conscious planning was encouraged, he declared, "we will continue to trust the more or less 'automatic' controls of our partial

27 Byrd L. Jones, "The Role of Keynesians in Wartime Policy and Postwar Planning, 1940–1946," *American Economic Review* (May, 1972): 125–33; Louis Fisher, *Presidential Spending Power* (Princeton, New Jersey, 1975), p. 45; Stein, *Fiscal Revolution*, pp. 169–97; A. E. Homans, *United States Fiscal Policy, 1945–1959* (New York, 1961); Donald Winch, *Economics and Policy: A Historical Study* (New York, 1969), pp. 274–80.

28. The use of fiscal policy in a market economy is discussed by Gerhard Colm, "Fiscal Policy and the Federal Budget," in *Income Stabilization for a Developing Democracy*, F. Millikan, ed. (New Haven, 1953), pp. 214–23.

capitalism."[29] During the recession of 1938, Keynes encouraged such planning efforts when he urged Roosevelt to nationalize the utility companies.[30] Similarly, William O. Douglas, chairman of the SEC, revised Adolph Berle's 1934 plan for government to form industrial banks to service capital requirements of small businesses through the purchase of preferred and common stocks.[31]

By World War II, the big issue, Leon Keyserling later recalled, was "how extensive the planning should be, and how large and imaginative the goals should be. . . ."[32] Perhaps the boldest and most elaborate planning proposal came from the National Resources Planning Board when it urged complete social security for all Americans from "cradle to grave" through the establishment of a national health insurance system, an extensive public works project to maintain full employment, and the extension of the Social Security system to include farm and domestic workers, the disabled and dependents.[33] Yet, at the same time that government planners drafted new proposals to extend the New Deal, electoral politics had shifted to the right.

Thus coinciding with the institution of new economics, Republicans began their political comeback in the congressional elections of 1938. That year Republicans doubled their strength in the House, increasing their membership from 89 seats to 164 seats. Furthermore, Republicans gained an additional 7 members in the Senate to increase their total to 23 members.[34] In 1942, Republicans further increased their representation to 208 members in the House, and 37 in the Senate. By 1946, the Republicans controlled

29. Emanuel Goldenweiser, "Memorandum to the Secretary of Treasury," November 5, 1936, *Goldenweiser Papers* (Library of Congress).

30. Quoted in Blum, *From the Morgenthau Diaries*, p. 403.

31. *Ibid.*, p. 415.

32. Leon Keyserling, "Comment," *American Economic Review* (May, 1972). For planning during the war, see Otis L. Graham, Jr., *Toward A Planned Society, From Roosevelt to Nixon* (New York, 1976), pp. 70–90.

33. *Congressional Record*, (1943), 690, 717, 979. Proposals for a full-employment economy were expressed in Lauchlin Currie, "Memorandum On Full Employment," March 18, 1940, President's Official Files 1820; and L. B. Currie to Franklin Roosevelt, "Expansion Possibilities," December 2, 1940, President's Personal File 1820; and G. Colm to Richard V. Gilbert, June 10, 1940, *Hopkins Papers*, (in Franklin Delano Roosevelt Library).

34. U. S. Bureau of Census, *Historical Statistics of the United States, Colonial Times to 1970* (Washington, 1975), p. 1083; Milton Plesur, "The Republican Congressional Comeback of 1938," *Review of Politics* (1962); and James L. Sundquist, *Politics and Policy; The Eisenhower, Johnson and Kennedy Years* (Washington, 1970), pp. 265–69.

the House and the Senate.[35] If there was a Keynesian revolution in 1938, this was to be the first instance of a revolution paralleled by thermidor.

The rise of Republicanism beginning in 1938 proved to have serious consequences for the new economic planners. Still the Republican gains might have been moderated if there had been an active independent left. By the late nineteen-thirties, however, the independent left was in full retreat.[36] In Wisconsin and Minnesota, for example, the Progressive Party and the Farmer-Labor Party had been decimated by the loss of twelve to four in their combined congressional delegation. In the West, the Commonwealth Federation was ousted from control of the state Democratic Party in Washington, and in California the EPIC movement was no longer a viable force in the state. The desultory performance of the CIO's Labor Nonpartisan League in the congressional elections of 1938 indicated that the left had lost its earlier momentum. By 1938, talk of forming a third party of the left had been silenced. As a consequence of this failure to build an independent left, economic planners within the government, although not radical themselves, lost what could have been an important source of political support.

The decline of the left in 1938 reflected a failure of leadership to rally popular support for its policies, not a mass desertion of the New Deal constituency for "conservative" Republican politics. Gallup polls taken in 1937 and 1938 reveal strong support for an activist federal government particularly among voters who had come of voting age in the 1920s and 1930s. Voters born after 1909 expressed overwhelming support for active government involvement in the areas of social security, fiscal policy, control of utilities and banks, and medical care for the indigent. Moreover, among this younger generation of voters, 55 percent described themselves as "liberal" (see Table II). These polls clearly indicate that the left had a potential social base for pushing the New Deal forward. Nevertheless, this failure to mobilize a constituency effec-

35. The Republican comeback is discussed in James L. Sundquist, *Dynamics of the Party System* (Washington, 1973), pp. 265–69.

36. For the decline of the independent left, see Donald R. McCoy, "The National Progressives of America, 1938," *The Mississippi Valley Historical Review*, (June, 1957); Hugh T. Lovin, "The Fall of Farmer-Labor Parties, 1936–38," *Pacific Northwest Quarterly*, (January, 1971); and Millard Gieske, *Minnesota Farmer Laborism: The Third Party Alternative*, (Minneapolis, 1979).

TABLE 2: PERCENTAGE SUPPORTING ACTIVIST POSITION
FOR FEDERAL GOVERNMENT BY AGE, NON–SOUTH[37]

1937–1938	Percentage of Support by Year of Birth	
	(after 1909)	(prior to 1909)
Compulsory Old Age Insurance	73.2	65.0
Copy TVA Elsewhere	70.3	61.2
Favor Increased Government Spending to End Business Slump	60.3	53.4
Government Control:		
Electric Power	72.0	62.5
Banks	53.0	46.0
Federal Medical Care for Indigent	83.3	78.6
Prefers to be Labeled "Liberal" as Opposed to "Conservative."	55.0	47.0
1945		
Favors Unemployment Insurance	58.4	46.8
Government Control:		
Electric Power	38.5	30.6
Mines	38.5	28.2
Railroads	35.0	25.2
Banks	32.5	23.7

tively in the election of 1938 proved to have dire consequences for the left.

Why popular support was not rallied in 1938 remains, for the most part, an unexplored question. There is no doubt, however, that voters moved away from support of active government policies in many domestic areas during the next few years. Gallup polls taken in 1945 revealed a dramatic shift in sentiment away from activist federal control of business. By 1945 those favoring federal control of utilities had fallen among the younger generation of voters from 72 percent in 1937–1938 to 38.5 percent in 1945, a decline of 34.4 percentage points. Similarly, those favoring federal control of banks had fallen from 53.8 percent in 1937–1938 to 32.5 percent in 1945, a decline of 21.3 percentage points.

37. AIPO 53; AIPO 60; AIPO 65; AIPO 66; AIPO 90; AIPO 95; AIPO 127; AIPO 355; American Institute of Public Opinion, Roper Center, University of Connecticut. The author would like to thank the Institute of Social Science Research at Northern Illinois University, DeKalb, Illinois, which provided access to this material. This specific information was collected by Stephen Baker, a doctoral student in political science at Northern Illinois University who is completing a dissertation on issue voting and generational effect from 1936 to 1976.

The benefactors of this shift away from an activist federal government would be the Republican Party, but it is interesting to note that the majority of younger voters favored unemployment insurance, which indicates continued support for government involvement in social economic areas.

Contrary to what some historians have assumed, Republicans in Congress never made absolute peace with the New Deal. Their hostility carried into the postwar period. As one Republican declared after the 1946 election, "The results of last November's election showed a strong protest against Federal bureaucracy and its dictatorial tactics. They indicate that our people are at last coming to realize the growing menace to our liberties under the New Deal regime." Anti-planning rhetoric rang through the halls of Congress throughout the war. Representative Harold Knutsen graphically expressed the sentiments of his fellow Republicans: "For years we Republicans have been warning that the short-haired women and the long-haired men of alien minds in the administrative branch of government were trying to corrupt the American way of life and install a hybrid oligarchy at Washington. . . ."[38] Republicans specifically targeted the NRPB as a "vicious body, and a menace to the American people." One Republican declared that investigations of the board revealed the "dangerous infiltration into our government of these enemies of our American way of life for the purpose of undermining and destroying this government of ours."[39] Led by Everett Dirksen of Illinois, Congress cut the entire appropriation for the NRPB in 1943, and then later complained when personnel from the disbanded board were transferred to other agencies.[40]

The ideal of a full-employment economy did not die an easy death, however. In 1945, Senator James Murray and Senator Robert Wagner introduced a Full Employment bill before Congress. Proposed initially by Lauchlin Currie, the bill was an attempt to legislate "new economics" into law by guaranteeing government's commitment to full employment through mandatory spending provisions in deflationary times, and the creation of a Council of Economic Advisors. The act expressed a certainty on the part of liberal economists that a postwar depression was im-

38. *Congressional Record*, 78th Congress, 1st Session, (1943), p. 717.
39. *Ibid.* p. 212.
40. *Ibid.*, A. pp. 708, 1146; Otis Graham, *Toward A Planned Society*, pp. 52–58.

minent.[41] In early 1946 Republicans forced Democrats to compromise the original bill. A modified Employment Act of 1946, which created a Council of Economic Advisors, would be passed. Many liberals understood the compromises to be only of symbolic importance, but for Republicans it marked another defeat for new economic planners.

Following the 1946 elections which gave Republicans control of Congress, they opened a vicious attack on the Democratic proposal for a national health insurance system. Liberals, who had dreamed of national health insurance since the Progressive era, had nearly succeeded in having a national insurance system included in the original Social Security Act of 1935 before the American Medical Association defeated their plans.[42] World War II revived their hopes when studies of military draftees showed significant inadequacies in the current health delivery system. Senators Robert Wagner and James Murray brought the issue into the national arena when they sponsored a new national health insurance bill in 1943. Although a *Fortune* magazine poll in 1942 showed that an impressive 74.3 percent of the American people favored national health insurance, the Wagner-Murray-Dingell bill quickly became stalled in Congress.[43] Truman tried to aid the passage of the bill when he sent a message to Congress which urged the establishment of a comprehensive medical system prepaid through Social Security taxes.

41. Concern about an approaching depression was evident in "Economic Projections: Prepared Within the Technical Staff of the Office of War Mobilization; Memorandum, September 8, 1945," *Official Files of Office of War Mobilization*, Record Group 250 (National Archives); Everett Hagen to John W. Snyder, "Implications of Present Trends in Output and Employment, November 22, 1945," Classified File of Deputy Director for Reconversion, Record Group 250 (National Archives). The subsequent failure of depression predictions are discussed in Everett E. Hagen, "The Reconversion Period: Reflections of A Forecaster," *Review of Economic Statistics* (May, 1947): 95–101; C. A. Blyth, *American Business Cycles* (New York, 1969): 88–102; Bert G. Hickman, *Growth and Stability of the Postwar Economy* (Washington, 1960): 27–70; and Angus Maddison, *Economic Growth in the West* (New York, 1964).

42. The early history of compulsory health insurance is discussed by Daniel S. Hirshfield, *The Lost Reform: The Campaign for Compulsory Health Insurance From 1932–1943*, (Cambridge, 1970); and Arthur J. Altmeyer, *The Formative Years of Social Security*, (Madison, 1968).

43. Compulsory national health insurance in the Truman period is described by Monte M. Poen, *Harry S. Truman Versus the Medical Lobby* (Columbia, 1979). The link made by Republicans between planning and national health insurance is evident in Robert Taft, "National Compulsory Health Insurance," *Congressional Digest* (July, 1949): 79–81; and George W. Bachman and Lewis Meriam, *The Issue of Compulsory Health* (Washington, 1948): 51–59, 69–70.

The A.M.A. immediately lashed out at the bill by spending over a million dollars to convince the American public of the ills of "socialized medicine." The bill would be attacked in Congress by Republicans who warned of increased government regulation and control. By 1948, national health insurance had been defeated.

Republicans were not prepared to turn the clock back to pre-depression days, however. They did not seek a counter-revolution, but only a halt in any further radical advances in social programming. The next decade, therefore, would be characterized by the politics of incrementalism, the gradual extension of existing programs. The politics of incrementalism in domestic programs was best symbolized in the passage of major amendments to the Social Security Act of 1935.[44] Following a report of the Social Security Advisory Council, Truman recommended in 1948 that Social Security benefits be increased and coverage extended to include the self-employed, widows and dependents of war veterans, and regular domestic and farm workers. After prolonged deliberations in Congress, amendments would be passed that increased benefit payments by 77 percent. Subsequently, expenditures for insurance benefits doubled between 1950 and 1951. Republicans initially had called Social Security a step toward totalitarianism; but in 1950 only fourteen House members voted against the amendments. A consensus had been reached, and in the process, government planning had been replaced by fiscal policy based on automatic stabilizers and some discretionary spending through transfer payments and defense expenditures.

New economic planners had offered an opportunity for the Democratic Party to become a "responsible" policymaking party. Instead, the defeat of new economic planning ensured that both American parties, the Democratic Party and the Republican Party, would remain what Theodore Lowi calls "constituent" parties, primarily concerned with winning and maintaining support from many different constituencies.[45] Moreover, both Democrats and Republicans discovered that discretionary spending through increases in transfer payments could be politically beneficial. Social

44. The politics of Social Security is thoroughly analyzed in Martha Derthick, *Policymaking for Social Security* (Washington, 1979), especially pp. 45–48, 214, 272–79.

45. Theodore Lowi, "Party, Policy, and the Constitution in America," in *The American Party Systems*, William Nisbet Chambers and Walter Dean Burnham, eds. (New York, 1975), pp. 203–38.

Security, unemployment, and veteran benefit programs become political devices to be used by incumbents, particularly during election years, to increase real per capita income among the voters.

The defeat of new economic planning also meant that automatic stabilizers would be relied upon to maintain a self-adjusting economy. In effect, stabilizers therefore come to play a similar role in America as had Smith's "invisible hand" in the previous century. It is not surprising that Keynesian policies found a congenial atmosphere for growth in America, a nation that took pride in its doctrinal belief in the free market system.[46] New economics provided a substitute for more direct economic controls. By 1952, discussion of a "planned capitalism" now appeared to be a contradiction in terms. Nonetheless, this reliance on fiscal policy, instead of conscious government planning, perpetuated economic maladjustment and obscured the need for genuine economic reform. Capitalism emerged in the postwar period only moderately reformed, incoherently regulated, and dependent on government spending. This economy was best described by Joseph Schumpeter as "capitalism in an oxygen tent."[47] Nevertheless, capitalism survived, neither having experienced a revolution, as liberals claimed it would, nor having taken the "road to serfdom," as some conservatives warned it might.

46. The failure to develop economic planning in America has been discussed by Andrew Shonfield, *Modern Capitalism: The Changing Balance of Public and Private Power* (New York, 1965), pp. 302–59. Also worth reading is Paul A. Baron, "National Economic Planning," in *A Survey of Contemporary Economics*, Bernard F. Haley, ed. (Homewood, Illinois, 1952), especially pp. 358–60. Otis Graham discusses this failure in *Toward A Planned Society*, pp. 1–90.

47. Joseph Schumpeter, "Capitalism in the Postwar World," in *Postwar Economic Problems*, Seymour Harris, ed. (New York, 1943).

Ferdinand Eberstadt, the National Security Resources Board, and the Search for Integrated Mobilization Planning, 1947–1948

ROBERT CUFF

The Crisis

A "war hysteria"[1] gripped Washington in the spring of 1948. A Communist coup in Czechoslovakia in February alarmed policymakers, and President Truman heightened public tension with a ringing denunciation of Soviet aggression before a joint session of Congress on March 17th. He asked Congress to pass universal military training legislation and to reinstitute the draft for five years. Other groups made their own recommendations, and airpower enthusiasts in Congress and in the administration demanded funding for a seventy-group force. According to *Business Week*, "officials [were] nerving themselves to take the initiative in the East-West struggle."[2] A rearmament program appeared imminent. On April 1st, Truman requested a $3 billion supplement from Congress to the fiscal year 1949 budget of $13.5 billion, including $775 million more for aircraft procurement. Allocations for the European Recovery Program—estimated at $13 billion over the next three years— were also about to pass into law. Washington rhetoric was tough and

The author wishes to thank Bertrand Fox, Terry Gough, Thomas McCraw, Richard Neustadt, and David Trask for assistance in the preparation of this article.

1. *Business Week*, March 20, 1948, 16.
2. *Ibid.*, March 6, 1948, 15.

expansive, and the defense appropriations were unprecedented in American peacetime history.[3]

The military services wanted still more. But some close observers wondered if the White House had thought through the implications of these sizeable increases. Had the administration considered the possibility of material shortages in military production? Could the government anticipate the relationship between military requirements and material supply? Did the administrative capacity exist to manage the mobilization of national economic resources?

James Forrestal worried about such questions, even as he lobbied for additional military appropriations. He sat at the helm of the national military establishment, the first secretary of defense appointed under the National Security Act of 1947. He was already under pressure from his military departments for increased defense spending and had a fight on his hands to keep under Truman's budget ceiling for fiscal year 1949. The spring crisis intensified military demands as well as Forrestal's political problems with the White House. The defense secretary also wondered if the administrative structure created under the National Security Act could respond effectively to the mounting pressure. That act produced a complicated set of new organizations. Key agencies had held their first meetings just six months before. Organization, like policy, remained unsettled. In February 1948, Forrestal called Ferdinand Eberstadt to Washington to evaluate the new security machinery—"the child of your brain,"[4] Forrestal described it.

Eberstadt was no stranger to Washington, or to Forrestal. The two men had known each other since undergraduate days at Princeton, and in the twenties they worked together at the Wall Street investment firm of Dillon, Reed. Forrestal became president of the firm, but then left for Washington in 1939, where, after a short stint as administrative assistant to President Roosevelt, he became undersecretary of the navy. Eberstadt in the meantime sold his partnership for several million dollars and set up his own investment firm. Something of a lone wolf on the street, Eberstadt branched out into mutual funds and underwrote a number of successful corporate reorganizations.

By 1940 military mobilization issues had heated up, and Forrestal began to call his old friend for advice and assistance. Eberstadt recruited business managers for the Navy Department and helped to break bottle-

---

3. For Truman's speech see *Public Papers of the Presidents of the United States. Harry S. Truman 1948*, vol. 4 (Washington: GPO, 1964), 182. For references to the spring crisis, see Walter Millis, ed., *The Forrestal Diaries* (New York: Viking Press, 1951), 397; David E. Lilienthal, *The Atomic Energy Years, 1945–50* (New York: Harper & Row, 1964), 313; Daniel Yergin, *Shattered Peace* (Boston: Houghton Mifflin, 1977), 343–65; and Robert A. Pollard, "The National Security State Reconsidered: Truman and Economic Containment, 1945–1950" (unpublished manuscript), 11–17.

4. Forrestal to Eberstadt, February 13, 1948, Papers of Ferdinand Eberstadt, Seeley Mudd Library, Princeton University (hereafter cited as Eberstadt Papers).

necks in machine tool production. More significantly, in December 1941 he took over chairmanship of the Army-Navy Munitions Board (ANMB) at the urging of Forrestal and Robert Patterson, Forrestal's counterpart in the War Department.

Forrestal and Patterson had made a brilliant choice. With characteristic tenacity and drive, Eberstadt made the ANMB a powerful advocate for military requirements in wartime Washington. He applied the same personal force in pushing through a managerial innovation that guaranteed delivery of critical materials to munitions producers. The Controlled Materials Plan, announced in November 1942, allocated steel, copper, and aluminum to military munitions programs and provided an effective method of administrative control over the entire industrial economy. In early 1943 Eberstadt fell from power, a victim of powerful tensions between New Deal partisans and the military services, but he remained close to Forrestal, and in the spring of 1945 he accepted the navy secretary's charge to draw up a plan for postwar security organization.[5]

The Plan

Eberstadt's report of October 1945 was a major contribution to the debate over America's postwar defense structure. He argued against army proposals for a centralized military structure, and his decentralized alternative became a rallying cry for navy opposition. This much is well known. Less appreciated, however, was his concern, fully shared by Forrestal, to ensure consideration of economic factors in the formulation of national security policy. Eberstadt regarded "linking strategic plans with their conversion into national resources" as among the "very desirable objectives" of an adequate postwar defense structure. But what kind of institutional arrangements could guarantee this outcome?[6]

Eberstadt looked to both the interwar period and the recent war experience for answers. The historical survey of the ANMB, which he had made before taking over the board in 1941, had made a deep impression on him. After World War I the government had placed responsibility for industrial mobilization planning in the Office of the Assistant Secretary of War, and that office, with the cooperation of other military agencies such as the ANMB, had gathered an impressive amount of information on American industry after a great many surveys

5. On Eberstadt's background and wartime activities, see Calvin L. Christman, "Ferdinand Eberstadt and Economic Mobilization for War, 1941–1943." (Ph.D. dissertation, Ohio State University, 1971). See also "Interviews with Ferdinand Eberstadt by Calvin L. Christman," Eberstadt Papers.

6. Eberstadt, "Memorandum for Secretary Forrestal," July 5, 1945, *ibid*. Eberstadt regarded his report as more than simply a rationalization for navy opposition to unification. See Eberstadt to Forrestal, November 15, 1945, *ibid*.

of mobilization requirements. It also produced a series of Industrial Mobilization Plans (IMPs), and in August 1939 President Roosevelt established the War Resources Board, made up of business executives and academics, to evaluate the fruits of army labors. The resources board quickly blessed the army plan and volunteered to implement it in case of war. But that was not to be. New Dealers abhorred the idea of mobilization management by big business representatives; labor spokesmen, unrepresented in the planning process and on the board, cried "foul"; and anti-New Dealers saw an "iron-heel dictatorship" in the making. So Roosevelt, apprehensive about isolationist sentiment and the 1940 presidential election, dismissed the board and buried its report.

It was a traumatic episode for industrial military planners, and for Eberstadt the lessons were clear: never again could industrial and economic mobilization planning become associated in the public mind with the military—it must remain under civilian control; and never again should the planning process be isolated in the services and disconnected from the rest of the executive branch. Any economic planning board would have to be seen clearly in civilian hands, and outside and above the national military establishment.[7]

Because of the World War II experience, Eberstadt took up the model provided by the Office of War Mobilization (OWM). The OWM (later called the Office of War Mobilization and Reconversion—OWMR) was established in 1943 under the direction of James F. Byrnes, who stepped down from the Supreme Court to take the chairmanship. OWM-OWMR was essentially a policy-coordinating body with a small staff, and Eberstadt had a similar agency in mind for the postwar defense structure. If the White House retained an organization like the OWM in peacetime, it "would enable the president in office at the time conflict threatened to avoid the political embarrassment of having to set up an organization clearly aimed at impending war." On this point Eberstadt combined the lessons of 1939 with the recent OWM-OWMR experiment. Eberstadt also wanted the permanent peacetime agency to involve the regular government departments in its planning activities—"it might then not be necessary in case of war to set up so many special agencies which conflict

7. On interwar planning see Albert A. Blum, "Birth and Death of the M-Day Plan," in Harold Stein, ed., *American Civil-Military Decisions: A Book of Case Studies* (Birmingham: Twentieth Century Fund, 1963), 61–94; Harry B. Yoshpe, "Bernard M. Baruch: Civilian Godfather of the Military M-Day Plan," *Military Affairs* 29 (Spring 1965), 1–15; Paul A. C. Koistinen, "The 'Industrial-Military Complex' in Historical Perspective: The Interwar Years," *Journal of American History* 56 (March 1970), 819–39; and Paul Y. Hammond, *Organizing for Defense* (Princeton: Princeton University Press, 1961), chaps. 2 and 3. On the War Resources Board episode see Jordan A. Schwartz, *The Speculator, Bernard M. Baruch in Washington, 1917-1965* (Chapel Hill: University of North Carolina Press, 1981), chap. 7. And on Eberstadt's interpretation of it, F. Eberstadt, *Report to Arthur M. Hill*, Washington, D.C., June 4, 1948.

with each other and with the regular departments."[8] Eberstadt had been at the center of those kinds of conflicts as head of the ANMB.

Eberstadt's final report embodied all these lessons. He called for creation of the National Security Resources Board "charged with the duty of formulating plans and programs—and keeping them up to date—and of maintaining a skeleton organization for the prompt and effective translation of military plans into industrial and civilian mobilization. It would be a logical outgrowth of the Office of War Mobilization and Reconversion." He recommended too that the NSRB chairman be appointed by the president "with full power of decision similar to the power now conferred upon the chairman of the Office of War Mobilization and Reconversion."[9]

It was an ambitious proposal, and Eberstadt treated it with real urgency: "The National Security Resources Board should be established promptly while the lessons of this war are still fresh in the public mind. If this is not done soon it will probably not be done at all."[10] The NSRB would function as the domestic analogue of the National Security Council, which Eberstadt's report also recommended. As he had explained earlier to Forrestal, the NSRB would serve as "the civilian counterpart of the proposed National Defense Council," later changed to NSC. "Just as the National Defense Council would consider, adopt, and implement measures in the military and related foreign policy fields, the National Defense Resources Board would carry over and implement these decisions in the civilian and industrial fields." Both innovations conformed to Eberstadt's general view that certain federal government procedures "ought to be adjusted to the faster pace here and in the world."[11]

A fierce political battle ensued over unification, but after two years of struggle, the National Security Act finally emerged in the summer of 1947, and it included both a National Security Council and a National Security Resources Board. According to Section 103 of the act, the NSRB, composed of a civilian chairman and such cabinet members as the president chose to designate, was established to advise the president on the coordination of military, industrial, and civilian mobilization in peacetime. Its specific duties included developing programs for the accumulation of strategic materials; for the unification of government activities in time of war; the balance of potential requirements for supplies

8. Eberstadt, "Memorandum for Secretary Forrestal," July 5, 1945, Eberstadt Papers. The standard study of the OWMR, completed in 1949, supported Eberstadt's approach. See Herman Miles Somers, *Presidential Agency OWMR, The Office of War Mobilization and Reconversion* (Cambridge: Harvard University Press, 1950), esp. 3, 214.

9. Senate Naval Affairs Committee, *Unification of the War and Navy Departments and Postwar Organization for National Security*, Report to Honorable James Forrestal, Secretary of the Navy, October 22, 1945, 79th Cong., 1st. sess. (hereafter cited as *Eberstadt Report*), 8, 9.

10. *Ibid.*, 8.

11. Eberstadt to Forrestal, January 15, 1945, Eberstadt Papers.

of manpower, critical materials, and productive facilities; the relocation of strategic industries; and the stabilization of the civilian economy in wartime. In addition, Congress made the NSRB chairman a statutory member of the National Security Council.[12]

When seen against the historical background of interwar mobilization planning and the dismissal of the 1939 Plan, as well as the chaotic administrative development that preceded American entry into World War II, the establishment of the NSRB was a considerable achievement. It lifted the economic mobilization planning function from a minor segment of the military bureaucracy, where it had rested in the twenties and thirties, to the highest levels of the executive branch. For the first time in its history, the United States government possessed a peacetime agency devoted to assessing the nation's economic capacity for war.

The gains were real, but the NSRB, as the charts reveal, also faced some major inter-organizational problems. Chief among them were its relationship to the national military establishment, to other civilian departments and agencies, and, above all, to the White House. Had the NSRB been able to resolve these relationships quickly in its favor, then its impact on subsequent events would have been far more substantial.

The board's initial failure to distance itself from the military was perhaps the agency's most surprising misstep. Forrestal and his aides were essentially responsible for this. They regarded the NSRB, like the NSC, as essentially an arm of the defense secretary. Documents from early planning sessions make this very clear. Pentagon officials wanted both agencies housed as close to the defense secretary as possible. They also drew the board's first budget from service appropriations. And Forrestal chose as the board's first chairman Greyhound Corporation president Arthur Hill, one of his wartime aides. These facts underscored the agency's virtual integration into the military establishment. Why Eberstadt, who participated in Pentagon strategy sessions after passage of the National Security Act, failed to object to these developments is unclear. The outcome may be understandable from Forrestal's point of view, but it certainly undermined Eberstadt's initial intention to have the civilian planning agency perceived as independent of military control.[13]

12. On the unification controversy see Hammond, *Organizing for Defense*, chap. 8. On the NSRB, see U.S. Senate, 80th Cong., 1st sess., *Congressional Record* 93, Part 7: 8291–92, July 7, 1947; Harry B. Yoshpe (U.S. National Security Resources Board), *A Case Study of Peacetime Mobilization Planning* (Executive Office of the President, April 30, 1953), *passim*. See also Edward H. Hobbs, *Behind the President, A Study of Executive Office Agencies* (Washington, D.C.: Public Affairs Press, 1954), chap. 7; and Ralph J. Watkins (Director, NSRB's Office Plans and Programs), "Economic Mobilization," *American Political Science Review* 43 (June 1949), 555–63.

13. Marx Leva to Eberstadt, August 11, 1947; and Leva, "Memorandum for the Secretary," August 2, 1947, both in Eberstadt Papers. See also *Business Week*, September 13, 1947, 8. Eberstadt had suggested a GM executive as board chairman in Eberstadt to Forrestal, August 6, 1947, Eberstadt Papers. On early NSRB history in general, see Yoshpe, *Peacetime Mobilization Planning*. Also, Interview of G. Lyle Belsley with author, July 16, 1982, Washington, D.C. Belsley was NSRB Secretary, 1947–49.

THE NATIONAL SECURITY RESOURCES BOARD

Its Position in the Executive Branch of the Government as Established by the National Security Act of 1947

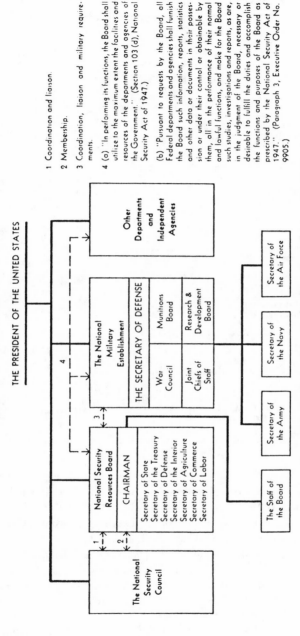

1 Coordination and liaison.

2 Membership.

3 Coordination, liaison and military requirements.

4 (a) "In performing its functions, the Board shall utilize to the maximum extent the facilities and resources of the departments and agencies of the Government." (Section 103 (d), National Security Act of 1947.)

(b) "Pursuant to requests by the Board, all Federal departments and agencies shall furnish the Board such information, reports, statistics and other data or documents in their possession or under their control or obtainable by them, all in the performance of their normal and lawful functions, and make for the Board such studies, investigations and reports, as are, in the judgment of the Board, necessary or desirable to fulfill the duties and accomplish the functions and purposes of the Board as prescribed by the National Security Act of 1947." (Paragraph 3, Executive Order No. 9905.)

Prepared by the National Security Resources Board, February 12, 1948

NATIONAL SECURITY RESOURCES BOARD BUDGET AND PERSONNEL STRENGTH, FISCAL YEARS 1948–53 [1]

Fiscal year	Budget	Personnel strength		
		Full time	Less than full time	Total
1948	$800,000 (appropriation transfer from the Departments of of the Army and Navy.			
First quarter		7	0	7
Second quarter		52	14	66
Third quarter		96	19	115
Fourth quarter		178	60	238
1949	$3 million.			
First quarter		254	87	341
Second quarter		295	151	446
Third quarter		294	124	418
Fourth quarter		293	118	411
1950	$3.5 million.			
First quarter		277	85	362
Second quarter		270	103	373
Third quarter		273	101	374
Fourth quarter		289	147	436
1951	$3.5 million.			
First quarter		359	181	540
Second quarter		358	185	543
Third quarter		170	40	210
Fourth quarter		105	24	129
1952	$1,627,000.			
First quarter		131	14	145
Second quarter		156	19	175
Third quarter		205	38	243
Fourth quarter		168	28	196
1953	$625,000 (through Apr. 30, 1953).			
First quarter		87	25	112
Second quarter		77	25	102

[1] Personnel data reflect the strength at the close of business on the last day of each quarter.

The board's early relations with industrial planners in the armed services, though cordial, were also uncertain. The National Security Act established the Munitions Board (MB) to coordinate logistics requirements for the services. Theoretically the MB would advocate military needs while the NSRB weighed all requirements—civilian and military—against material and industrial resources from a national perspective. "The National Security Resources Board is not an advocate," Eberstadt explained. "It is a judge."[14] The MB might do spadework for the board—as would the executive departments—but the board, the responsible civilian agency, would proclaim any final plans. Eberstadt put it this way: "The Resources Board should be like an automotive assem-

14. Eberstadt to Forrestal, October 2, 1947, Eberstadt Papers.

bly line, and should put together components of the plan, but should not itself undertake to manufacture the engine, fabricate the fenders, etc."[15]

In fact, the Munitions Board, able to draw upon experienced military personnel and wartime industrial connections, was first off the mark in postwar planning. The board engaged private consultants to draw up a mobilization plan even before final passage of the National Security Act, and the result, *The Industrial Mobilization Plan for 1947*, became a benchmark for subsequent work in the field. Even Eberstadt, who intended to have the NSRB, the civilian agency, publicize final plans, praised the 1947 effort. He was even more pleased when he learned the names of the plan's two major authors, Lincoln Gordon of the Harvard Business School and Bertrand Fox of Williams College, both of whom had worked with him on the Controlled Materials Plan during the war. As the minutes of an informal meeting in the Office of the Secretary of Defense record, "Mr. Eberstadt [upon hearing who had authored the plan] replied that he was not surprised and that he would like to lay claim to both of them as 'his boys'." In light of this plan, Eberstadt believed that "we are far more advanced with our planning than even those people who keep in touch with industrial mobilization would have believed possible."[16] The administrative challenge was to secure the central coordinating role for the NSRB.

The Department of Commerce, among civilian agencies in the executive branch, balked at the idea. During demobilization this department fell heir to a number of functions, programs, and personnel from various war agencies, and it refused to yield pride of place to the NSRB in industrial mobilization planning. Averell Harriman, the department's first postwar secretary, proved especially determined. "It would appear wholly consistent with the department's general responsibility," he wrote the president, "to have it work primarily in the field of mobilizing industrial production. Broadly this would mean the same area of responsibility as the War Production Board covered during the war."[17] Even

15. "Minutes of an Informal Discussion. . . " October 1947, Record Group 304, Records of the Office of Civil and Defense Mobilization, U.S. National Archives, Washington, D.C. (hereafter cited as RG 304). On early attempts to delineate NSRB-MB functions, see Marx Leva to Eberstadt, August 11, October 30, and November 21, 1947; and Eberstadt to Leva, November 22, 1947, all in Eberstadt Papers; and *Forrestal Diaries*, 329–30.

16. "Minutes of an Informal Discussion. . . " October 1947, RG 304. For information on the Plan, see U.S. Munitions Board, *Industrial Mobilization Plan for 1947*, Washington, D.C., 1947; and *Industrial Mobilization, Office of War Production, Annex Number 82 to 1947 Plan*, Washington: GPO, 1947. For a description and evaluation of the Mobilization Plan of 1947, see Roderick L. Vawter, "Industrial Mobilization: An Historical Perspective," Washington, D.C., Industrial College of the Armed Forces, 14–18. See also U.S. Munitions Board, *Military Procurement, A Guide for Joint Industry-Military Procurement Planning*, Washington, D.C.: National Military Establishment, June 1, 1948.

17. W. A. Harriman to Truman, n.d., attached to Truman to Harriman, August 4, 1947, in Record Group 51, Records of the Bureau of the Budget, Series 47.3, U.S. National Archives, Washington, D.C. (hereafter cited as RG 51). For persistent Depart-

Truman, who had his own reservations about the NSRB, felt compelled to intervene and hold off Harriman and the Department of Commerce until the NSRB sorted itself out. But the department continued to press its claims.

More significantly still, the NSRB-White House relationship remained ambiguous. The president proved wary of both the board and the National Security Council. During the unification battle the president had come out in favor of the army's centralized plan. He accepted the NSC-NSRB scheme in large part simply as one of the costs of gaining Forrestal's acquiescence in the ultimate compromise. Both boards were in this sense forced upon him. Moreover, Truman had no wish to share his autonomy and prerogatives in a process of collective decisionmaking through inter-departmental committees, and he realized very well that a British cabinet ideal pervaded the Eberstadt-Forrestal proposals. The idea had considerable vogue among government reformers in the immediate postwar years. Eberstadt and Forrestal hoped that in the new postwar defense structure a combination of NSC with appropriate elements of NSRB would constitute the basis of a war cabinet. Both agencies, in their view, were part of a broader, more ambitious agenda in national security organization, a reaction, in part, to the ad hoc ways of Franklin Roosevelt.

President Truman believed in tidy administration, but he resisted the idea of being hedged in by inter-agency committees. Officials at the Bureau of the Budget (BOB) reinforced his instincts. BOB staff came out of the war with a strong sense of "presidential mission and perspective."[18] They also shared a deeply held conviction that no coordinating authority in the executive branch ought to exist short of the president himself. They advised Truman to absent himself from NSC meetings, for example—which he generally did until the Korean conflict—and to treat both the NSC and the NSRB simply as extensions of the presidential staff. Truman later recalled:

> Secretary of Defense Forrestal for some time had been advocating our using the British cabinet system as a model in the operation of

ment of Commerce activity on this issue see Harriman to Hill, November 26, 1947, "Views of the Department of Commerce on the National Security Resources Board Operations," July 26, 1948; and Sawyer to Forrestal, September 23, 1948, all in RG 51, Bureau of the Budget records. See also Business Week, January 24, 1948, 14; and Charles Sawyer, Concerns of a Conservative Democrat (Carbondale: Southern Illinois University Press, 1968), 180–90. One employee of the Department of Commerce has claimed that "so far as administration goes, this Harriman period (October 1946–April 1948) represented in some ways the golden age of the Department of Commerce." See Columbia University oral history interview with Bernard L. Gladieux.

18. Allen Schick, "The Problem of Presidential Budgeting," in Hugh Heclo and Lester M. Salamon, eds., The Illusion of Presidential Government, (Boulder, Colo.: Westview Press, 1981), 89. For the intellectual and institutional tension between "presidential" and "cabinet secretariat" perspectives in a similar context, see Peri Arnold, "The First Hoover Commission and the Managerial Presidency," Journal of Politics 38 (February 1976), 46–70. Interview with David E. Bell, Cambridge, Mass.: October 5, 1984.

the government. There is much to this idea—in some ways a cabinet government is more efficient—but under the British system there is a group responsibility of the cabinet. Under our system the responsibility rests on one man—the president. To change it, we would have to change the constitution, and I think we have been doing very well under our constitution. We will do well to stay with it.[19]

So much for the British cabinet model.

Institutional tensions between the NSRB and the White House erupted early in debate over the status of the board chairman. On the one hand, Eberstadt had wanted the power of decision conferred on the chairman, subject only to the president. This followed the OWM-OWMR precedent. On the other hand, the enabling statute vested authority in the board. As a consequence Eberstadt advised Forrestal to go directly to the president and obtain for Arthur Hill, the NSRB chairman, a letter conferring "as his deputy the right to decide the problems within the scope of the board's authority." Without decisive delegated authority disaffected cabinet officers would have no incentive to cooperate and Hill would have to seek presidential support for each decision. A vacuum at the board's center, argued Eberstadt, "would be contrary to the basic purpose of the act, whose intent was to relieve the president of such burdens."[20]

White House aides defeated Hill's bid for power even before the board's first meeting in November 1947. Hill requested an executive order to empower him to direct other departments to undertake planning studies and provide information. Departmental spokesmen objected; so did the president. White House aides also insisted that authority flowed from the president to the board and thence to the chairman, not directly from the president to Hill. The outcome severely limited Hill's leverage with board members from the start, and the Department of Commerce resisted his informal initiatives in subsequent months.[21]

19. Harry S. Truman, *Memoirs: Years of Trial and Hope 1946–1952* (New York: Signet, 1965), 79. For an interesting recollection of the debate over cabinet committee or secretariat systems in inner circles, see Don K. Price, *America's Unwritten Constitution* (Baton Rouge: Louisiana State University Press, 1983), 180–87. See among recent documentation of Truman's wariness of NSC, Alfred D. Sander, "Truman and the National Security Council: 1945–1947," *Journal of American History* 59 (September 1972), 369–88; and Anna Kasten Nelson, "National Security I: Inventing a Process (1945–1960)," in *The Illusion of Presidential Government*, Heclo and Salamon, eds., 230–45. On Bureau of the Budget advice, see "Memorandum for the President . . . Suggestions Regarding the National Security Council and the National Security Resources Board," August 8, 1947, RG 51. See also Richard E. Neustadt, "Approaches to Staffing the Presidency: Notes on FDR and JFK," *American Political Science Review* 57 (December 1963), 860. For discussions of the influence of the cabinet model on Forrestal and Eberstadt, see John C. Ries, *The Management of Defense Organization and Control of the U.S. Armed Services* (Baltimore: Johns Hopkins Press, 1964), chaps. 5 and 6; and Paul Y. Hammond, "The National Security Council as a Device for Interdepartmental Coordination," *American Political Science Review* 54 (December 1960), 899–902.

20. Eberstadt to Forrestal, October 2, 1947, Eberstadt Papers.

21. Clark M. Clifford, "Memorandum," November 4, 1947; and undated memo from George M. Elsey, both in Papers of Clark Clifford, Truman Library, Independence, Missouri. See also *Forrestal Diaries*, 331–32.

Crisis Intervention

These then were among the existing deficiencies in the NSRB when the war scare hit Washington in March 1948. The crisis underscored the need for economic mobilization planning even as it highlighted the weakness of the NSRB's current position. But the crisis might also provide an opportunity to assert the NSRB's role. Eberstadt certainly took this view, and he devoted himself to the cause in Washington that spring. His official excuse for intervention was a request from Arthur Hill to investigate the NSRB's current status. More significantly, Eberstadt had been vitally concerned and involved with defense organization issues since at least 1941, and his close association with both the issue and the secretary of defense afforded him easy access to government officials whenever he wished. In April 1948 he took up residence at the Shoreham Hotel and made the rounds.

He undertook three major initiatives. He drafted a comprehensive set of proposals for mobilization authority and standby controls which the NSRB chairman sent to Truman on April 29, he made a formal investigation of the NSRB's role, and he organized and recruited staff for a Plans and Programs Division in the NSRB in anticipation of Truman's favorable response to his proposals, which would be funneled through the NSRB chairman.

Throughout these activities Eberstadt argued that if the United States were "to carry a broad band of defense and security burdens" on "a heavily occupied economy, there must be some agency in the government which [would] watch the impact of this burden upon the civilian economy and which [would] see that the security burden is fitted into the economy in such a way as to prevent undue strain. Unless some high-ranking civilian organization exercise[d] such functions," he believed, "the economy [would] be at the mercy of the vigorous efforts of the military and of other groups charged with the duty of consummating the security contracts." *Ad hoc* committees were inadequate to this function—"they haven't the knowledge, they haven't the staff, they haven't the prestige or the power."[22] The NSRB was the appropriate body and if it was to be "the top mobilization organization, it would be well to put it into business promptly."[23]

Eberstadt and Hill argued aggressively for this position in their report to Truman in late April. "The march of events compels us to turn from theory to practice," they asserted. "We have passed beyond the point where organizational charts and manuals or drafts of bills suffice. More substantial preparations are required to meet the needs of the moment and to prepare for what may come." Hill and Eberstadt wanted Truman

22. Eberstadt, "Memorandum for Mr. Millis," May 27, 1948, Eberstadt Papers.
23. "Memorandum," April 14, 1948, *ibid.*

to go before Congress, present the situation in these terms, request legislative authority for a variety of controls, and designate the NSRB the agency responsible for economic mobilization—"past experience and the preponderance of opinion of leading authorities in this field indicate the advisability" of such a course. They also wanted Congress to set aside the antitrust laws, clarify the conflict-of-interest issue to facilitate recruitment of business personnel, and re-enact World War II legislation authorizing the Reconstruction Finance Corporation to lend money for resource development tied to national security.[24]

Eberstadt lobbied hard to build support for his views among officials at the Bureau of the Budget, the Department of Commerce, and the Council of Advisors. He argued that "unless NSRB is given present responsibilities in the present context (and [is] properly staffed and equipped to discharge them), it will fail to fulfill the primary duty of preparation against an actual mobilization or war. Its product would most probably share the fate of the Industrial Mobilization Plan of 1939." Persuading the skeptics was a dispiriting task. One BOB official told him that some saw "military ghosts" under the desks at the NSRB; and James Webb, the BOB director, warned that mobilization planning "must not 'attenuate' the power of the president" or impinge upon "the prerequisites of the existing departments."[25] Eberstadt confided his anger in private memos:

> As a result of conditions down here I see the same type of thing developing as occurred in 1940. Just as Roosevelt concealed the War Resources Board report, Truman has concealed the report which the National Security Board made to him and their recommendations. They are dilly-dallying and fussing with expedients and failing to face the issues squarely. All this in spite of the fact that billions have been allocated for the European Recovery Program, billions for atomic energy, more billions for military. . . . It seems once more we are moving in the atmosphere of lipstick and soda preparations.[26]

24. "A Recommendation to the President by the National Security Resources Board on Steps and Measures Essential to the Fulfillment of the National Security Program (NSRB-R7)." Baruch and his aides also assisted with the report. See "Diary," April 18, 1948, Eberstadt Papers; and Baruch to Arthur Krock, August 25, 1949, Papers of Arthur Krock, Seeley Mudd Library, Princeton University. Government economists in the Bureau of the Budget and CEA also counseled the president to push for comprehensive controls to head off inflation. See Goodwin and Herren, "The Truman Administration," 54. Eberstadt also envisaged "hearings by the Armed Services Committee at which a formidable array of those experienced in war production and controls would support the President's recommendations." Eberstadt to Forrestal, April 16, 1948, Eberstadt Papers.

25. "Diary," May 5, 1948, and "Memorandum," April 14, 1948. According to Eberstadt in the latter diary note, "Webb continued rather confused and is somewhat affected by a constitutional reservation toward NSRB." Bureau of the Budget officials pushed the Department of Commerce as a substitute for the NSRB. See "Diary," May 12, 1948, all Eberstadt Papers.

26. "Memorandum," May 10, 1948. "The executive seems to be vacillating and having roused Congress and the people is now moving backwards," "Memo," May 15, 1948. Both *ibid.*

Defeat

Eberstadt's worst fears were confirmed on May 24, 1948. Truman turned down the NSRB initiative on almost every front. The president defined the current situation as "not one of mobilization for war" but "rather one of maintaining a firmer foundation of preparedness on which a more rapid mobilization could be based." Therefore, changes were unneccessary. Moreover, he opposed categorically the NSRB's quest for dominance in economic mobilization planning. "I do not intend to vest in the National Security Resources Board any responsibilities for coordination of the national security programs of the government which require the exercise of direct authority over any department or agency, or which imply a final power of decision resting with the board." The board should consider itself "a presidential advisory agency and conform its actions and recommendations to producing information and advice upon which presidential action may be taken."[27]

Eberstadt reacted philosophically to the White House rebuff. He did not give up on the NSRB, nor did he quit Washington. He continued to work with the board's Plans and Programs Division, and he also accepted the chairmanship of the Task Force on National Security Organization for the Hoover Commission and carried on his campaign to strengthen the NSRB from that position. That task force report, released in December 1948, called for more "cost consciousness" among the military and for "a greater sense of urgency in mobilization planning."[28]

Nor had Eberstadt's endeavors been in vain. The Plans and Programs Divison he inaugurated in 1948 was an important addition, and the NSRB did increase its staff and budget in subsequent months, despite its failure to obtain coordinating authority. The board's staff divisions provided a significant holding environment for pools of expertise and technical knowledge among personnel in both governmental and nongovernmental

27. Truman to Hill, May 24, 1948; Eberstadt to Hill, May 26, 1948, *ibid.* See also Webb, "Memorandum to the President," May 26, 1948, RG 51, Bureau of the Budget Records. Eventually, the Bureau of the Budget insisted that it receive MB reports on any industrial mobilization plans. Frank Pace, Jr., to Forrestal, June 24, 1948, and Forrestal to Webb, August 10, 1948, both *ibid.*

28. On the task force report, see *New York Times*, December 17, 1948. 1, 18. For Eberstadt's continuing missionary work, see "National Security Resources Board, Joint Meeting of Advisory Committee on Plans and Programs . . . 22 June 1948. . . " RG 304, Records of the Office of Civil Defense Mobilization. He wrote Forrestal on December 14: "This business of starting new agencies is a tough one (who knows better than you!) and I think Arthur has laid a firm foundation from which the board can move forward. . . . It has an exceptionally capable staff" (Eberstadt Papers). For another up-beat observation, see Robert H. Connery, "Unification of Armed Forces," *American Political Science Review* 52 (February 1949). The Plans and Programs Division, in the meantime, pursued its planning function. See "Preliminary Statement on Guiding Framework and Programs Framework for Mobilization Planning," NSRB Doc. 76 in RG 304, Records of the Office of Civil Defense Mobilization; and NSRB, *National Security Factors in Plant Location*, July 22, 1948.

institutions who were interested in mobilization issues. The board developed formal contracts with academic institutions, established voluntary advisory committees from various industries, and held informal consultations with such private organizations as the Committee on Economic Development, the Ford Foundation, and the National Bureau of Economic Research. Policy experts in the field pored over technical plans and draft legislation and did much to codify the knowledge they had gained from their years at the War Production Board and other World War II agencies. A great deal of work was done to refine methods of production and allocation controls, for example, and the legal staff of the NSRB laid the groundwork for the Defense Production Act of 1950, which provided the legal instrument not only for much of the Korean mobilization but also for industrial mobilization planning ever since. Moreover, in the early days of the Korean crisis, the board did become a coordinator for economic mobilization policies, and its chairman, W. Stuart Symington, did gain, finally, delegated presidential authority.[29]

And yet the NSRB's early failure to assert its coordinating authority over other departments in peacetime did prefigure its experience during the Korean War. In the wake of the Chinese intervention in the winter of 1950, Truman created a new Office of Defense Mobilization and vested authority in its chairman, General Electric president Charles Wilson. By 1951 the NSRB had become "a laughing-stock around town,"[30] according to a White House aide. It was reorganized out of existence in 1953.

Conclusion

Ferdinand Eberstadt's policy intervention in the spring of 1948 was only one in a series of recurring attempts by administrative innovators to create integrated forms of industrial and economic mobilization planning in the executive branch. Bernard Baruch had pressed for the same goal before World War I, and he supported Eberstadt's efforts in 1948. Eberstadt, like Baruch before him, possessed remarkably easy access to Washington officialdom, and that is an interesting and significant part of the

29. Yoshpe, *Peacetime Mobilization Planning*, 61–64. Harvard Business School faculty were active in this work, for example. See Bertrand Fox, Lincoln Gordon, Stanley F. Teele, "Memorandum on Relation of NSRB to Other Agencies in Economic Mobilization Planning," October 1, 1948. Available in RG 304, Records of the Office of the Civil Defense Mobilization, National Archives, Washington, D.C. For information on the NSRB's functions in the early days of the Korean build-up, see U.S. NSRB, *Report of the Chairman* (Washington: GPO, 1951), *passim*. See also U.S. NSRB, *The Objectives of United States Materials Resources Policy* (Washington: GPO, 1952).

30. Quoted in Crauford D. Goodwin, ed., *Energy Policy in Perspective* (Washington, D.C.: Brookings, 1981), 18. See also Richard E. Neustadt, "Presidency and Legislation: Planning the President's Program," *American Political Science Review* 49 (December 1955), 1018–19.

story. But equally significant is how the kind of coherent, centralized vision that Eberstadt cherished cracked apart on the competitive pluralism of the executive branch, and the determination of President Truman to protect his personal autonomy in the decisionmaking process.

The same fascination with integrated economic planning and coordinated policymaking has reappeared today in recent debates over industrial policy and in the contemporary interest in a Japanese model of national economic decisionmaking. And there is an analogue in defense as well. In 1978 the military services ran a series of exercises to test mobilization capacity, and they revealed problems. A critical evaluation by the Department of Defense (DOD), released to the public in 1980, cited shortcomings in existing mobilization plans and institutional arrangements and then called for "a master mobilization plan" and a cabinet-level Office of Defense Resources (ODR), which in the event of national emergency or attack "would provide policy advice to the president, adjudicate questions of priority and resource allocation, and coordinate a national response to mobilization—in short, . . . coordinate the civilian mobilization effort."[31]

The DOD's administrative ideal of centralized coordination resembles very closely the plans that administrative innovators like Ferdinand Eberstadt and James Forrestal pressed upon White House officials during military reorganization debates at the end of World War II, and those previous experiences can be instructive. This is not to argue for some necessary connection between the two eras, or to suggest that the outcome in the first case foreshadows outcomes today. The historical contexts are remarkably different. But the search for effective means of industrial and economic mobilization planning and coordination continues, and the fate of an earlier reform attempt suggests some of the underlying institutional factors that contemporary reformers need to consider, particularly the presidential quest for institutional autonomy.

31. Office of the Secretary of Defense, An Evaluation Report of Mobilization and Deployment Capability Based on Exercises Nifty Nugget-78 and REX-78 (June 30, 1980), 9. For recent interest in industrial mobilization policy in defense, see Lee D. Olvey, Henry A. Leonard, and Bruce E. Arlinghaus, eds., Industrial Capacity and Defense Planning, Sustained Conflict and Surge Capability in the 1980s (Lexington, Mass.: D. C. Heath, 1983); and Robert L. Pfaltzgraff, Jr. and Uri Ra'anan, eds., The U.S. Defense Mobilization Infrastructure: Problems and Priorities (Hamden, Conn.: Archon Books, 1983). For excellent recent guides to the controversial issues of defense economics, see J. Ronald Fox, Arming America, How the U.S. Buys Weapons (Boston: Division of Research, Harvard University Graduate School of Business Administration, 1974); and Jacques S. Gansler, The Defense Industry (Cambridge, Mass.: MIT Press, 1980). Seymour Melman connects the defense realm with the debate over declining industrial productivity in Profits Without Production (New York: Knopf, 1983).

By Robert D. Cuff

PROFESSOR OF HISTORY

YORK UNIVERSITY, TORONTO

An Organizational Perspective on the Military-Industrial Complex

❡ Is there a "military-industrial complex" in the United States? What is the relationship between business, government, and the military with its needs for vast quantities of goods and services? How has organization for war and defense changed since the demands of World War I first made such questions important? How much do we know about what actually happened between World War I and Vietnam to change the relationship between private and public organizations? Professor Cuff discusses the complexities involved in trying to answer such historical questions, and prescribes a professional historian's regimen for future work on this subject.

The study of business, government, and defense has generated an enormous body of work over the past two decades, much of it associated with social criticism of the "military-industrial complex." Historians, with some notable exceptions, have contributed very little to this literature, but recent interest in the evolution of large-scale organizations promises a fruitful source of interesting questions and appropriate strategies for future research. My purpose here is to propose a view of business, government, and defense studies that will integrate the "military-industrial complex" literature into an emerging perspective on American history, characterized a few years ago as the "organizational synthesis." [1]

The potential contributions of this integration, are threefold. First, the attention it directs to more precisely defined historical study can help to counter the heavy ideological content of so much

Business History Review, Vol. LII, No. 2 (Summer, 1978). Copyright © The President and Fellows of Harvard College.

[1] Louis Galambos, "The Emerging Organizational Synthesis in Modern American History," Business History Review, 44 (Autumn, 1970), 279–290. Paul Koistinen is the chief exception to this rule among historians. See Paul A. C. Koistinen, "The 'Industrial-Military Complex' in Historical Perspective: World War I," Business History Review XLIV (Winter, 1967), 378–403; "The 'Industrial-Military Complex' in Historical Perspective: The Inter-War Years," Journal of American History, LVI (March, 1970), 819–839; "Mobilizing the World War II Economy: Labor and the Industrial-Military Alliance," Pacific Historical Review, XLII (November, 1973), 443–478. See also Benjamin F. Cooling, ed., War Business and American Society: Historical Perspectives on the Military-Industrial Complex (Port Washington, N.Y., 1977).

of the current critical work. Second, the tension that this orientation demonstrates between contemporary description and institutional realities underscores the need to evaluate very carefully the relationship between ideology and organization in the history of business, government, and defense. And third, the questions it raises about continuities and discontinuities in the administrative and technological settings of particular wartime mobilizations argues for the crucial importance of a comparative historical perspective on the "military-industrial complex."

President Eisenhower introduced the phrase "military-industrial complex" into common parlance in his Farewell Address of 1961. The "conjunction of an immense military establishment and a large arms industry," he observed then, was "new in the American experience. The total influence — economic, political, even spiritual — is felt in every city, every State house, every office of the Federal government." [2] The consequences of a revolution in technology for relations among science, the universities, and the federal government also troubled Eisenhower. Indeed, the much broader question of how the American people could balance new international and technological demands with traditional democratic principles subsumed his specific illustrations. "Each proposal must be weighed in the light of a broader consideration," he urged: "the need to maintain balance in and among national programs — balance between the private and public economy, balance between cost and hoped-for advantage — balance between the clearly necessary and the comfortably desirable; balance between our essential requirements as a nation and the duties imposed by the nation upon the individual; balance between actions of the moment and the national welfare of the future." [3]

Eisenhower and his speech writers could not have guessed that the Farewell Address, an expression, in part, of a moderate Republican's apprehension about the statist and spending proclivities of crusading Democrats, would become a reference point in subsequent years for critics to the left of both groups. But it is true that the literature of the military-industrial complex, which self-consciously situates the Eisenhower speech at its origins, is linked almost without exception to a revisionist critique of American politics and society. It is, in a phrase, an intensely ideological body of work. Nor could Eisenhower have foreseen that his reference to a mili-

---

[2] From Carroll W. Pursell, Jr., ed., *The Military-Industrial Complex* (New York, 1972), 206.
[3] *Ibid.*

tary-industrial complex would become only one in a series of competing definitions of the phenomenon under investigation. It is rather surprising in light of the voluminous literature that commentators even now are by no means agreed upon what exactly they are studying: a warfare state; a weapons culture; Pentagon capitalism; a new industrial state; an industrial-military complex, and so on. Conceptual, evidential, and methodological differences are all characteristic, and these differences are both a cause and a consequence of competing definitions in the field. The literature itself has become an object of study as commentators attempt to construct typologies and isolate factors generally held to be most important in defining and explaining the subject. Indeed, it is now unclear whether a "military-industrial complex" should be regarded as "a fact" or as a product of ideology, in the sense of a definition of "reality" linked almost wholly with critics of American policies. In any case, students of the literature *qua* literature now ask questions about the origins of characteristic metaphors and their relationship to earlier, parallel debates in U.S. history — over similar questions of public and private power, civilian and military relationships, centralized and decentralized institutional relationships, morality and power. Such questions are central, of course, to Eisenhower's address, and to the current debate.[4]

Historical study offers no easy escape from ideology or partisanship to be sure, especially in the case of a controversial subject of contemporary political interest. And yet there is much to gain from reformulating questions about the military-industrial complex in terms of recent interest within American historiography in the causes and consequences of institutional growth, of the relationship between ideology and organization, and of the struggle for power among competing social groups in common institutional settings. The sources of these recent questions are evident in a variety of historical fields, but business history is especially important. Students of the modern business corporation have pioneered in the historical analysis of large-scale American organizations.

[4] Thomas A. Meeker provides a useful bibliography in *The Military-Industrial Complex: A Source Guide to the Issues of Defense Spending and Policy Control* (Los Angeles, 1973). On the issue of definitions, metaphors, and typologies, see Max L. Stackhouse, *The Ethics of Necropolis* (Boston, 1971), 25–42; Keith L. Nelson, "The 'Warfare State': History of a Concept," *Pacific Historical Review*, XL (May, 1971), 127–143; Charles C. Moskos, Jr., "The Concept of the Military-Industrial Complex; Radical Critique or Liberal Bogey?", *Social Problems*, XXI (Spring, 1974), 498–512. See also Steven Rosen, *Testing the Theory of the Military-Industrial Complex* (Lexington, Mass., 1973) and Sam C. Sarkesian, ed., *The Military-Industrial Complex: A Reassessment* (Los Angeles, 1972).

From this perspective, work among social scientists and publicists on the military-industrial complex converges with historical interest in such topics as the rise of the professions and the evolution of modern managerial capitalism. How the United States organized for war is another dimension of the rise of large-scale organizations. War organization is a species of administrative organization, and so it invites questions similar to those asked about how American higher education has been organized, or how American big business institutions might be distinguished from their French or Japanese counterparts.[5]

To approach the connection between business, government, and defense as an historical problem in the evolution of organizational forms also directs attention to the social science literature on public administration and organization. These literatures do not contain ready-made solutions to the ideological dimension of social scientific research, or to the methodological problems of research on organizations. Nevertheless, they are far more useful than contemporary social criticism in pointing to difficult yet necessary questions about what, specifically, the study of complex organizations implies.[6] They contribute more directly towards a conceptualization of business, government, and defense as a focus for systematic study, and they provide an opportunity to cast the subject in less ideological terms.

Samuel P. Hays reflected some time ago on a similar point in the context of political history when he called for closer scrutiny of the relationship between rhetoric and behavior in social change, noting that rhetorical devices can be misleading tools for historical research.[7] It would be misleading, for example, to take at face value the intellectual categories that historical actors employ to describe their situations and behavior, as in the "people"-versus-the-"interests" cry of progressive reformers. It is the same case with war organization. Without attention to the institutional environ-

---

⁵ Robert D. Cuff, "American Historians and the 'Organizational Factor,' " *Canadian Review of American Studies*, IV (Spring, 1973), 19–31. And see Harold F. Williamson, ed., *Evolution of International Management Structures* (Philadelphia, 1975), *passim* and James E. Hewes, Jr., *From Root to McNamara: Army Organization and Administration, 1900–1963* (Washington, 1975), esp. 411–412.

⁶ The social literature on complex organization is voluminous. Useful guides include Kurt Lang, "Military Sociology 1963–1969, A Trend Report and Bibliography," *Current Sociology*, XVI (1968), 1–66; James G. March, ed., *Handbook of Organizations* (Chicago, 1965); Renate Mayntz, "The Study of Organizations, A Trend Report and Bibliography," *Current Sociology*, XIII (1964), 93–156; D. S. Pugh *et al.*, *Writers on Organizations, An Introduction* (London, 1971); and David Silverman, *The Theory of Organizations: A Sociological Framework* (London, 1970).

⁷ Samuel P. Hays, "The Politics of Reform in Municipal Government in the Progressive Era," *Pacific Northwest Quarterly*, XL (October, 1964), 157–169.

ment of business, government, and defense during World War I, for example, a study of industrial mobilization in that period can become the study of Bernard Baruch's rise to production czar through the War Industries Board of 1918, a proposition that inhibits a comprehensive view of the period. Similarly, without a sense of the organizational structure of World War II, a study of industrial mobilization in those years may become the story of Donald M. Nelson's self-proclaimed fight against military attempts to take over the economy, when the issue is far more complicated and ambiguous. And on a broader canvas still, without some sense of the episodic in organizational growth, a description of business, government, and defense in the twentieth century may focus on how a decentralized social order gave way to an undemocratic centralism, when a very good case can be made for a constant dialectic between decentralization and centralization in the evolution of social organization.[8] From the perspective of organizational studies, then, one leaves open the question of what connection, if any, images of organization actually have with their institutional landscape. One might rather ask how actors have used characteristic images in their quest for administrative power and control.[9]

Take the case of the ideology of voluntarism during World War I. This is a persistent theme in the literature of national mobilization. The Wilson Administration, according to this canon, achieved planning without bureaucracy; regulation without coercion; cooperation without dictation. To be sure, state agencies had had to plan; administrators had had to coordinate; enlightened statesmen had had to lead. But their administration rested less upon manipulation and dictation than upon education, a general spirit of patriotism, and widespread consultation and cooperation with private groups. There is some truth to these claims, of course, but when one looks more closely at the activities of Bernard Baruch or Herbert Hoover, for example, we find such administrators using the images of voluntarism quite self-consciously as tools to defend their administrations against critics, to boost internal morale, and to in-

[8] The relevant literature here includes, Robert D. Cuff, *The War Industries Board: Business Government Relations During World War I* (Baltimore, 1973) *passim*; Bruce Catton, *The War Lords of Washington* (New York, 1948), *passim*; Calvin L. Christman, "Donald Nelson and the Army: Personality as a Factor in Civil-Military Relations During World War II," *Military Affairs*, XXXVII (October, 1973), 81–83; Eliot Janeway, *The Struggle For Survival, A Chronicle of Economic Mobilization in World War II* (New Haven, 1951); and G. William Domhoff and Hoyt B. Ballard, eds., *C. Wright Mills and The Power Elite* (Boston, 1968).

[9] See J. Kenneth Benson, "The Analysis of Bureaucratic-Professional Conflict: Functional Versus Dialectical Approaches," *Sociological Quarterly*, XIV (Summer, 1973), 376–394, esp. 387.

crease their jurisdiction both within the emergency bureaucracy and in society at large.[10]

The emotional civilian-military conflict of World War II is worth investigating from a similar perspective. How is it, for example, that Donald Nelson and Robert Patterson, two of the *dramatis personae* of the struggle between the War Production Board and the military services, could emerge from the same experience with such conflicting perspectives? It is not clear whether Nelson was consistent throughout the war in his attitude toward the Army, but by the time he sat down to write his memoirs, his antipathy was certainly clear. "The top men in the army's supply setup," he wrote, ". . . consistently opposed giving any consideration to even the most essential civilian needs." According to Nelson, "from 1942 onward the Army people, in order to gain control of our national economy, did their best to make an errand boy of WPB." It is a view that has passed into historiography, though not without challenge, through Bruce Catton's *War Lords of Washington.*[11]

Robert Patterson, Undersecretary of War, on the other hand, greeted Nelson's hostile memoir with a mixture of anger and despair, and so did Patterson's friends. The struggle between military and civilian forces for economic control "existed only in the minds of Nelson and some of his palace guards" in Patterson's view, "and it was a charge that was whispered around whenever the Army's requirements and our insistence that they should be filled became embarrassing to the War Production Board. I was on record repeatedly," Patterson claimed, "as being thoroughly in favor of control of the war economy being entrusted to a civilian agency like the War Production Board, the agency being headed by a civilian with power to make final decisions." [12] For Patterson, Nelson's personality and abilities as WPB head were the real issues. "The thing that irritated Nelson and caused him to make the charge of military control," he claimed, "was the Army's steady insistence that he take the measures necessary to get for the Army (or its contractors) the materials needed to produce the weapons for arming the soldiers. He had the necessary powers, and we pressed him to exercise

---

[10] Robert D. Cuff, "Bernard Baruch: Symbol and Myth in Industrial Mobilization," *Business History Review*, XLIII (Summer, 1969), 115–133, and "Herbert Hoover, The Ideology of Voluntarism and War Organization During the Great War," *Journal of American History*, LXIV (September 1977), 358–372.

[11] Donald M. Nelson, *Arsenal of Democracy* (New York, 1946), 358, 363. Eliot Janeway challenges Catton and Nelslon in *The Struggle For Survival, passim*. See also his "Where Was Mr. Nelson," *Saturday Review* (September 7, 1946), 11.

[12] Robert Patterson to Floyd B. Odlum, September 26, 1946, Box 21, Robert Patterson Papers, Library of Congress, Washington, D.C.

them."[13] Detailed study of the cases in dispute is required to arbitrate such antithetical views. But that in itself will not wholly explain the origins of the vast gulf in perception between Nelson and Patterson, or more importantly, what functions, machiavellian or otherwise, they may have served in the power games of wartime Washington.

Because it leaves open the relationship between rhetoric and behavior, ideology and reality, organizational study directs our attention to the nature of the administrative structure itself. How precisely do the politico-economic techniques of mobilization-control grow and change over time, irrespective of peoples' perceptions of them? How, for example, does one describe and account for the managerial instruments of business, government, and defense that enabled the United States to supply critical food supplies to the Allies during World War I; or allowed the country to process fifteen million men and women through the armed services during World War II, while simultaneously reaching unparalleled levels of industrial output; or encouraged the American government to conduct the enormous Vietnam escalation without the controls usually associated with war enterprise?

The issue here is not so much to define the shifting relationships between business and government, private and public institutions. It is more to understand why and how the administrative and managerial techniques of large-scale organizations have sometimes dissolved these distinctions altogether. The focus, once again, is less upon the tension between competing values and images and more upon how to describe and account for the kinds of administrative and managerial organizations that have emerged in the course of war mobilization. It is indicative of the growing sensitivity to these questions within the contemporary critical literature itself that Richard Barnet, in the most ambitious synthesis to date, places the idea of a "bureaucratic revolution" emerging from the World War II years at the center of his work.[14]

But how does one study bureaucratic growth? The vast dimensions of the organizations under consideration give one pause. As

[13] Patterson to George W. Healy, September 10, 1946, *ibid.*
[14] Richard J. Barnet, *Roots of War* (New York, 1972), esp. part 1. For additional references to the organizational factor in the critical literature, see John K. Galbraith, *The New Industrial State* (Boston, 1967), *passim*; Seymour Melman, *Pentagon Capitalism* (New York, 1970), *passim*; Morton H. Halperin, "The Limited Influence of the Military-Industrial Complex," in Warren F. Ilchman and Joe S. Bain, eds., *The Political Economy of the Military-Industrial Complex* (Berkeley, 1973), 1–20; and Graham T. Allison, "Organizational and Administrative Factors Affecting Shifts in Defense Expenditures," in Bernard Udis ed., *The Economic Consequences of Reduced Military Spending* (Lexington, Mass., 1973), 289–336.

Robert Dahl and Charles Lindblom observe in *Politics, Economics and Welfare*: "Large hierarchical organizations are so complex that simply to describe them is almost impossibly difficult."[15] When Secretary of War Henry Stimson recruited Robert Patterson to Washington in 1940, for example, Patterson inherited a position as Assistant Secretary that lacked staff, prestige, and jurisdiction. But by war's end, the administrative network, which he ostensibly supervised from his new office as Undersecretary of War, contained nearly two million civilian workers, the largest of all government organizations, and larger than the entire federal government at any time in its previous peacetime history. It is not obvious how one goes about understanding the internal structure of an organization of that size, to say nothing of the myriad ways it interacted with its economic environment both in the United States and around the world.[16]

Nor is it easy to comprehend the nature of the technological processes that have so intimately bound business, government, and defense mobilization. This is difficult enough in the case of World War I when, according to Murray L. Weidenbaum, four-fifths of the equipment that the armies first took to the field were derived from standard peacetime goods produced in ordinary civilian facilities.[17] Understanding our own period is even more difficult, given the accelerated pace of innovation and weapons specialization in the nuclear and missile age. Clarence Danhof points out an interesting measure of the complexity of the equipment and managerial capacity involved by noting the parts required in various weapons systems. The Lockheed C-141 Starlifter, he notes, for example, included a quarter of a million parts and required some 20,000 engineering drawings in manufacture, while the Army's Nike-Hercules system consisted of approximately 1,500,000 parts and required 80,000 Ordnance engineering drawings to depict on paper.[18] Clearly a focus on business, government, and defense as a study in large-scale organization offers no easy answers, given the enormous size of the organizations themselves and the complexity of their technological environment.

Two strategies hold particular promise as guides to the territory,

[15] Robert A. Dahl and Charles E. Lindblom, *Politics, Economics and Welfare: Planning and Politico-Economic Systems Resolved into Basic Social Processes* (New York, 1953), 373.

[16] R. Elberton Smith, *The Army and Economic Mobilization* (Washington, 1959), 105, 110–112.

[17] Murray L. Weidenbaum, *The Economics of Peacetime Defense* (New York, 1974), 134.

[18] Clarence H. Danhof, *Government Contracting and Technological Change* (Washington, 1968), 228, n. 11.

however. The first is to focus attention on the nature of the structures that have arisen to define strategy for business-government relations in defense mobilization, and to administer it. The analogy here is from business history, where Alfred Chandler's work has drawn attention to the importance of administrative structure in maintaining and advancing corporate strategies. And when one combines with this orientation a consideration of the power struggles that create and maintain administrative structures, then business, government, and defense becomes a study in the politics of administration.[19]

THE POLITICS OF ADMINISTRATION

A conception of organization-building as a study in the politics of administration has among its uses the advantage of countering assumptions about "bureaucratic imperatives" or "technological determinism," which frequently find their way into discussions of institutional development. In Richard Barnet's *Roots of War*, for example, there are references to "the technological imperative" and "tyranny of technique" that raise the dubious proposition that behavior and even consciousness itself are determined by impersonal bureaucratic or technical forces.[20] Whatever the sociological justification for such a view, it is ill-adapted to the historical study of the subtle interplay of ideas and actions of men struggling for power in and through organizations. It is one thing to attempt an understanding of the complexity of organization and technology exclusive of the perceptions that contemporaries might have of them, much as students of occupational and geographic mobility may usefully measure social movement without reference to its meaning for individuals and groups who are involved in the process. But it is quite another proposition to reduce ideologies, political struggle, and organizational growth to a function of bureaucratic drift or technological determination.

A key theme of recent work in business history, indeed, is of an on-going clash between technological "rationality" and ideological and political commitments in the organization of business-government relations. While students of business behavior document the powerful logic of such impersonal factors as market size and pro-

[19] Alfred D. Chandler, Jr., *Strategy and Structure: Chapters in the History of Industrial Enterprise* (Cambridge, Mass., 1962), *passim*. For a reading of Chandler's work that makes the idea of strategic choice the critical variable in a theory of organizations, see John Child, "Organizational Structure, Environment and Performance: The Role of Strategic Choice," *Sociology*, 6 (January, 1972), 1–22.

[20] Barnet, *Roots of War*, 16, 33.

duction velocity in shaping industrial organization – as, for example, in the emergence of oligopoly in some industries and fragmentation of others – they also note the devastating impact on public policy of political commitments to such "irrational" values as decentralized competition and antitrust. Thomas K. McCraw has summarized the point this way: "As the histories of railroad regulation suggest, a firm grasp of the 'railroad problem' and the distinctive features of the industry – its high ratio of fixed to variable costs, its powerful tendency toward huge integrated systems – are indispensable to the study of attempts at its public control. If, as seems likely, the inherent nature of an industry is the most important single context in which regulators must operate, then the range of policies open to them has been narrower than many observers have hitherto believed." [21] It is the political struggle over economic forces, in other words, rather than the economic forces themselves, that has determined the history of railroad regulation.

Ellis Hawley also illustrates the utility of avoiding generalizations about bureaucratic imperatives in favor of a close analysis of the clash between economic, political, and ideological interests in the development of public policy and bureaucratic organization in *The New Deal and the Problem of Monopoly*. He traces in rich detail the contradictory outcome of a regulatory policy designed to accommodate a mixture of competing commitments. His book is suggestive of the importance of focusing on the politics of administration as it affects organizational development. It also illustrates how useful connections can be drawn between the politics of administrative struggle on one level and a clash over general ideological systems on another, "particularly if one uses the ideological goals to identify policy directions rather than fixed positions." [22] Similarly, Martin Sherwin in *A World Destroyed: The Atomic Bomb and the Grand Alliance* illustrates the centrality of administrative politics in bureaucratic development; and, more importantly, as a crucial factor in the emergence of nuclear technology itself. The atomic bomb, with all its profound ramifications for administration and power in the postwar world, was less the inevitable result of scientific technique than a consequence of choices made by particular men in particular organizations for particular reasons at a particular time.[23]

Allied with a study of organization as the politics of administra-

[21] Thomas K. McCraw, "Regulation in American: A Review Article," *Business History Review*, XLIX (Summer, 1975), 181.
[22] Ellis W. Hawley, *The New Deal and the Problem of Monopoly* (Princeton, 1966), 36.
[23] Martin J. Sherwin, *A World Destroyed: The Atomic Bomb and the Grand Alliance* (New York, 1975), *passim*.

MILITARY-INDUSTRIAL COMPLEX   259

tion, a comparative approach to the problem also holds promise of considerable advance. Although a cross-cultural perspective might be the ultimate goal in this regard, a more limited comparison within American historical development is task enough. Tom Burns, a sociologist of industrial organization, suggested in a similar context: "The object is to use the contrast between two conditions of the same system separated by time as a basis for comparative study." [24] From the perspective of business, government, and defense, therefore, we might ask, how do the administrative structures binding and managing these institutions compare in World War I and World War II, or as between Korea and Vietnam? How, for example, was the connection drawn between the business of agriculture and defense during World War I compared to World War II? To be more specific in this case: why does an emergency food administration appear immediately during World War I, but not until comparatively late in World War II? Why, in both World War I and World War II, were there such gales of administrative destruction, with administrative reorganizations recurring across the administrative structure in bewildering confusion? [25]

Can one even speak of war mobilization as all of a piece? Or is it more accurate to define a series of stages, each with its own politico-economic strategies and subsequent administrative structures? Take the case of World War I, for example. The winter crisis of 1917–1918 had as great an impact on the administrative structures of the state and on the wartime political economy as entry into the war itself. A variety of crises converged in December and January of 1917–1918 in politics, administration, and supply. And the response they produced included yet another reorganization of military administration, creation of the Railroad Administration, the emergence of several Interallied war boards, the cry for a Munitions Ministry, and the ultimate introduction of the Overman Act, perhaps the central administrative document in Wilsonian war government. [26]

A similar number of interesting questions arise from this per-

[24] Tom Burns, "The Comparative Study of Organizations," in V. H. Vroom, ed., *Methods of Organizational Research* (Pittsburgh, 1967), 153. For a partial example of this kind of approach, though in the context of British history, see Clive Trebilcock, "War and the Failure of Industrial Mobilization: 1899 and 1914," in J. M. Winter, ed., *War and Economic Development* (Cambridge, Eng., 1975), 139–164.

[25] Luther Gulick made a pioneering attempt at charting and explaining the changing administrative structure of World War II in *Administrative Reflections from World War II* (Birmingham, Ala., 1948), but it was not followed up.

[26] Robert Cuff, *The War Industries Board*, 135–147; Daniel R. Beaver, *Newton D. Baker and the American War Effort, 1917–1919* (Lincoln, Neb., 1966), 94–109, 116–129; Austin K. Kerr, "Decision for Federal Control: Wilson, McAdoo, and the Railroads, 1917," *Journal of American History*, LIV (January, 1967), 550–560.

spective when we turn to the World War II years. To what extent did the wartime administrative structure flow from the administrative experiments of peace and the New Deal? On this point an interesting, if minor, debate occurred in the defense period over whether to base wartime mobilization on an expansion of preexisting units, or to establish emergency agencies. It is a tribute to the strength of existing government bureaus and their spokesmen in the wake of the New Deal expansion that the case for the professional public administrator was voiced with a vigor inconceivable twenty years before. As one of their number wrote in the summer of 1941, "With a farewell to normalcy and an appreciation of the greater opportunities that the crisis presents, public administrators today have an opportunity greatly to enhance and permanently to establish the prestige of their calling in the United States." [27]

It was in the context of this new administrative consciousness that Harold Smith, Director of the Budget Bureau, had earlier complained to his diary about the obtuseness in management matters he found in many of his colleagues. After a particularly discouraging encounter with economist Lauchlin Currie, Smith noted: "I have assumed that he knew something about administration which it is evident now that he does not. Currie is a person who, because of his technical background in economics, thinks in terms of subject matter, and when he has a problem thinks in terms of the individual rather than in terms of organization. There are too many people around here," Smith concluded, "who have that attitude of mind. The individuals come and go but the organization remains." [28]

In defining points of comparative reference for the study of business, government, and defense, the periods of major mobilization — World Wars I and II, Korea, and Vietnam — are particularly important. This is so because innovations in management structures for combining business, government, and defense proliferate most dramatically during periods of actual mobilization. Such advances are hardly confined to these periods to be sure. Each war mobilization begins at a higher organizational stage than the previous one as a result of the administrative and technical changes preceding it. Nevertheless, the development of new techniques and special-purpose organizations to embody them are of the essence during

[27] Herbert Emmerich (formerly deputy governor of the Farm Credit Administration, and Secretary of the Office of Production Management in 1941), "Administrative Normalcy Impedes Defense," *Public Administration Review* I (Summer, 1941), 325. See also Wayne Coy, "Federal Executive Reorganization Re-Examined: A Symposium I, *American Political Science Review* XL (December, 1946), 1124–1168.

[28] Diary of Harold D. Smith, 21 October 1939, Franklin D. Roosevelt Library, Hyde Park, New York.

wartime. More than that, each crisis reveals more clearly "the forms into which its governmental techniques can be converted" [29] for peace as well as for war.

WAR AND THE RATE OF ORGANIZATIONAL INNOVATION

Why are innovations in administrative techniques and organizations developed so rapidly during wartime? There is no definitive answer to this question, but Arthur Stinchcombe offers an interesting point of departure for speculating on the problem. In an enormously provocative article on the organizational capacity of populations, Stinchcombe posits five conditions conducive to the founding of organizations, which, it would appear, war mobilizations foster in a particularly intense and dramatic fashion:

> "People found organizations," he writes, "when (a) they find or learn about alternative better ways of doing things that are not easily done within existing social arrangements; (b) they believe that the future will be such that the organization will continue to be effective enough to pay for the trouble of building it and for the resources invested; (c) they or some social group with which they are strongly identified will receive some of the benefits of the better way of doing things; (d) they can lay hold of the resources of wealth, power and legitimacy needed to build the organization; and (e) they can defeat, or at least avoid being defeated by, the opponents, especially those whose interests are vested in the old regime." [30]

Many of Stinchcombe's general conditions are met during war mobilizations. Central to them is the way innovators in administrative and managerial controls can, through increased defense spending and the atmosphere of national crisis, lay hold of the resources of wealth, power, and legitimacy required to build organizations. William Leuchtenburg, for example, has illustrated in a widely noted article how World War I stimulated a variety of experiments in liberal collectivism and offered analogues for the crisis management of the depression years.[31] Business and government organizers have had consistently great success in ignoring the antitrust tradition in wartime on behalf of a wide diversity of experiments in coordination, cooperation, consolidation, and control. Perhaps no other theme of business, government, and defense is

[29] Dahl and Lindblom, *Politics, Economics and Welfare*, 126.
[30] A. L. Stinchcombe, "Social Structure and Organization," reprinted in part in Tom Burns, ed., *Industrial Man* (Baltimore, 1969), 157.
[31] William E. Leuchtenburg, "The New Deal and the Analogue of War," in John Braeman, Robert H. Bremner, and Everett Walters, eds., *Change and Continuity in Twentieth Century America* (Columbus, Ohio, 1964), 81–143.

262   BUSINESS HISTORY REVIEW

72

as well documented and avidly studied, from World War I through Korea. Major business corporations secured a legitimacy during both major wars that in each case had been under some strain in the immediate prewar years. It is equally clear as well that in every mobilization period major business corporations have been instrumental in shaping the nature of wartime controls, and staffing them as well.[32]

The war years also provide a process of education for social groups involved, as Stinchcombe suggests, as they devise the kind of social mechanisms not readily available from the administrative stocks on hand. As gaps in the knowledge of technical controls appear, groups rush in to fill them. Psychologists and engineers, social workers, and others spread the gospel of social efficiency during World War I; the new breed of public professional administrators personified by Harold Smith advocated developing knowledge of budgeting, accounting, and statistical techniques during the second great war; and defense intellectuals and economists have advocated varieties of problem-solving techniques on behalf of business, government, and defense in the Cold War and Vietnam years. Moreover, as the state has faced a situation of continuing war and war preparation, so it has invested in organizations like the Rand Corporation to provide continuing sources of administrative and organizational innovation. Likewise, the state after 1945 obviously believed that the future was such as to warrant investment in private academic and business institutions on behalf of research and development. This was done in part to cope with the instabilities inherent in the imperatives of advancing weapons technology.[33] In sum, from the perspective of management structures for business, government, and defense, it is the experimentation provided by mobilization itself that is most productive of leaps forward in the system's overall institutional evolution, and for the kinds of general reasons Stinchcombe suggests.

Even a cursory glance from a comparative perspective highlights some interesting aspects about the evolution of business, govern-

[32] For a very useful introduction to this theme, see Grant McConnell, *Private Power and American Democracy* (New York, 1966), ch. 8.
[33] Samuel Haber, *Efficiency and Uplift* (Chicago, 1964), ch. 7; David Novick, Melvin Anshen, and W. C. Truppner, *Wartime Production Controls* (New York, 1949); Charles J. Hitch and Roland N. McKean, *The Economics of Defense in the Nuclear Age* (Cambridge, Mass., 1960); Paul Dickson, *Think Tanks* (New York, 1971). Peck and Scherer write, concerning the instability of weapons technology: "In the postwar period, such a series of successive new weapons generations has appeared as to defy description. We can now pass through a weapon generation faster than we can complete a development cycle." Merton J. Peck and Frederic M. Scherer, *The Weapons Acquisition Process: An Economic Analysis* (Boston, 1962), 47.

ment, and defense as a managerial structure from World War I through Vietnam. It underscores, first of all, the large elements of discontinuity in the process as to both structure and values. By the end of 1941, for instance, not only had defense mobilizers exhausted most of the relevant social knowledge of the World War I experience, a point made both at the time and in the postwar years, but they had also proceeded much farther toward production and allocation controls in many respects than their predecessors had reached by the end of 1918. And to study the administrative and technical control mechanisms in business, government, and defense of World War I from the perspective of the Korea and Vietnam years is something akin to conducting an archeological excavation into a world we have lost.[34]

On the broadest level, one can cite the stupendous changes in defense expenditures and their acceleration; the transformation in the size and scope of the state; the enormous complexity of modern weapons technology; the great-power status of the United States; and more. But there are several arguments springing out of the nature of Wilsonian mobilization itself that might also be advanced on behalf of this proposition. First, the definition of war as emergency crisis rather than a permanent social condition carried a host of implications for war administration. In this case, legal self-destruct mechanisms were built into many wartime agencies. And those that did not wither at war's end ultimately disappeared into the administrative reorganizations of the New Deal period. As an administrative apparatus, in other words, very little of its parts reached forward to the World War II period. Second, bureaucratic controls were affected in their timing and their extent by the anti-statist bias characteristic of its central administrative personnel, almost all of whom were civilian volunteers serving government on a voluntary basis for the first time. Compared to the Wilsonian mobilization, the state since World War II has created a permanent career pattern in administrative management for business, government, and defense. Third, at the ideological center of the mobilization process during World War I was a vision of entrepreneurial or liberal capitalism that is not only very much at odds with the

[34] My comment on the comparative development of production and allocation controls is based on a reading of David Novick, et al., *Wartime Production Controls*, chs. 2-6. There is no equivalent study for the World War I period. In addition to the information that *Wartime Production Controls* provides on specific control procedures, the book also documents the intensified search for administrative "rationality" in the war and postwar years. Dahl and Lindblom's *Politics, Economics and Welfare* exemplifies this search as well. Both books provide a remarkable contrast in tone as well as substance to Harold J. Tobin and Percy W. Bidwell, *Mobilizing Civilian America* (New York, 1940), a book that codifies the Great War and interwar experience in economic planning for war.

managerial, bureaucratic heartland of the modern industrial economy today, but more important still, was at odds with its economic environment then, for the modern corporate form had already come into place by World War I. That is one reason why business-government relations during the first war were marked by hesitancy and ambiguity even among industries like meat-packing and explosives where, from a structural point of view, one might have expected a smoother transition by business and government to a war economy.[35]

From Ad Hoc Organization to Permanent Bureaucracy

A strong ideological component of the Wilsonian mobilization was the question of how to adjust private and public institutions. This concern, of course, has continuously pervaded business, government, and defense relations.[36] It found its spokesmen during both World War II and Korea; and it lies at the heart of criticism of the so-called military-industrial complex. But during World War II and after, this concern represented an ideological position and organizational image on the periphery of war organization. During World War I, in contrast, it stood at the ideological and administrative center. Even business members of the Wilson coterie, who more than Wilson concerned themselves with the technical means, were heavily imbued with the Wilsonian view. And that was to prove that private corporate leadership in conjunction with *ad hoc* agencies, gently coordinated by voluntary experts, could far outperform a bureaucratic state of any variety.

The prevailing view that springs from World War I is caught far more appropriately in Herbert Hoover's vision of an "associative state" than in the kinds of images typical of the literature of the "military-industrial complex." [37] And it is this vision that predominated in the administrative connections between business, government, and defense in the interwar years. From the perspective of the Cold War era, we might better regard the twenties and thirties as more a struggle for survival for wartime administrative techniques in an unsympathetic domestic environment than a tap root of the institutional complex of the fifties and sixties.

[35] These themes are developed in part in Robert Cuff, *The War Industries Board*, *passim*; and in "We Band of Brothers — Woodrow Wilson's War Managers," *Canadian Review of American Studies*, V (Fall, 1974), 135–148.
[36] Ellis Hawley, "Techno-Corporatist Formulas in the Liberal State 1920–1960: A Neglected Aspect of America's Search for a New Order," unpublished ms.
[37] Ellis Hawley, "Herbert Hoover, the Commerce Secretariat and the Vision of an 'Associative State' 1921–1928," *Journal of American History*, LXI (June, 1974), 116–140.

MILITARY-INDUSTRIAL COMPLEX   265

After the great emergency synthesis and unprecedented access to public funds occasioned by the war, the focus for innovators in business, government, and defense shifted back toward private, voluntary, professional activity, whence most of it had come in the first place. Such groups as the National Research Council, the National Advisory Committee for Aeronautics, and the Military Training Camps Association, which had been spawned by the war, continued their attempts to mediate between private and public institutions, but they now looked more to their own initiative in this quest than to the state.[38] It is this voluntarist context, far more than the images associated with the "military-industrial complex," that provides the best perspective on the kind of inter-war activity described in the pioneering articles by Albert Blum and Paul Koistinen. This is the kind of cultural-intellectual tradition, moreover, in which we might usefully situate President Eisenhower's famous address.[39]

Compared to the enormous attention that the administrative capacity and technical means of mobilization would receive at the height of World War II and after, one can regard the Wilsonian mobilization as providing a very ancient combination of administrative techniques indeed. The administrative capacity required for modern war was only dimly sensed before the First World War; and the advances of the war years, however important in the context of their own times, pale into significance when compared to the managerial tasks that routinely face business and government in providing for war and defense. It is equally true that the Wilsonians only dimly sensed that there was an inherent tendency in rationalization and the spread of administrative controls to obliterate altogether distinctions between private and public, business and government.

CONCLUSION

It is one of the great ironies in the study of business, government, and defense mobilization that what began in 1917 as an effort to rely upon private, and particularly business, institutions, for the

[38] A. Hunter Dupree, *Science in the Federal Government, A History of Policies and Activities to 1940* (New York, 1957), chs. 15–17; John G. Clifford, "Grenville Clark and the Origins of Selective Service," *Review of Politics*, XXXV (January, 1973), 17–40. A valuable article for establishing the politico-administrative context of these years is Barry D. Karl, "Presidential Planning and Social Science Research: Mr. Hoover's Experts," in Donald Fleming and Bernard Bailyn, eds., *Perspectives in American History* (Cambridge, Mass., 1969), II, 347–409.

[39] Albert A. Blum, "Birth and Death of the M Day Plan," in Harold Stein ed., *American Civil-Military Decisions: A Book of Case Studies* (Birmingham, Ala., 1963), 63–94; Paul A. C. Koistinen, "The 'Industrial-Military Complex' in Historical Perspective: The Interwar Years," *Journal of American History*, LVI (March, 1970), 819–839.

social, administrative, and technical bases of mobilization (and, thereby, to avoid a permanent state bureaucracy) has, over the intervening six decades, resulted in its opposite: a state management system for defense with a wide diversity of special-purpose organizations producing for a public market.[40]

It is the collapsing distinctions between private and public, business and government, civilian and military, and ultimately between the individual and the state, distinctions the Wilsonians were so eagerly determined to draw, that lies at the heart of so much of the critical debate over business, government, and defense policies today. And as critics such as Richard Barnet and others search for perspective on the structural relations that the military-industrial complex denotes, it is not surprising that, consciously or not, they should turn for inspiration as much to Weber as to Marx. For one of the central issues demanding historical understanding and analysis is the evolution of those administrative and technical systems of rational control that characterize large-scale organizations in both the state and the economy, systems that have been transformed in scope, complexity, and power since the days when Woodrow Wilson proclaimed a New Freedom and a generation marched off to a war to end all war.

[40] A controversial point to be sure. See Seymour Melman, ed., *The War Economy of the United States, Readings in Military Industry and Economy* (New York, 1971); William L. Baldwin, *The Structure of the Defense Market 1955–1964* (Durham, N.C., 1967); and Murray L. Weidenbaum, *The Modern Public Sector: New Ways of Doing the Government's Business* (New York, 1969) for relevant readings.

Hal Draper

neo-corporatists

and neo-reformers

THE REPLACEMENT of capitalism by a New Order is being discussed, even advocated or at least viewed with kindliness, by some very eminent and respectable thinkers in this country not usually associated with revolutionary ideologies. This trend, or school of thought, seems to have gained steadily in the last few years. Its meaning can best be understood in the context of a wider, a worldwide, trend in relation to which it constitutes only one strain or national form.

The wider, international, trend is the burgeoning of *bureaucratic-collectivist ideologies* in a broadspread infiltration of all bourgeois thought today. By "bureaucratic-collectivist" I mean in this connection the ideological reflection or anticipation of a new social order which is neither capitalist nor socialist, but which is based on the control of both economy and government by an elite bureaucracy—forming a new exploitive ruling class—which runs the fused economic-po-

87

litical structure not for the private-profit gains of any individual or groups, but for its own collective aggrandizement in power, prestige and revenue, by administrative planning-from-above. One premise of this conception is that the totalitarian statified economy developed under Stalinism in Russia, which is today consolidating its power over a good portion of the globe, is one well-developed form of bureaucratic-collectivism.

Whatever the label conferred on this system, however, it is less controversial that key elements characteristic of its structure have, in our own day, already had a massive impact on the capitalist world and its thought. The channels by which this society-wide pressure has been exerted are two related ones. First is provided by the contradictions and difficulties of capitalism itself, the solutions of which point to some type of collectivism and to some form of increased statification, whether under the Great Depression (with the New Deal as carrier) or under the Permanent War Economy of today. Second is the direct impact of the Russian advance-model on the system of the old world, in evoking emulation, triggering analogous patterns, enforcing imitation by the logic of rivalry.

1

The current—within the borders of this larger phenomenon—which this article proposes to investigate shares with all others a common desire to present itself as being "beyond capitalism or socialism." In a key document to be discussed, W. H. Ferry, of the Center for the Study of Democratic Institutions founded by the Fund for the Republic at Santa Barbara, says for example:

> I think there is something brand new emerging here as well as in Europe which is certainly not capitalism. If you wish, you can call it socialism. Several of my less friendly critics suggested that the new fascism was being proposed here. Naturally, I don't agree to that statement.

But what apparently distinguishes it from the other, more typical bureaucratic-collectivist currents is its hostility to statification or "statism," which it aspires to replace with a more pluralistic constellation of corporate powers. *Thus it finds itself developing a new corporatism*—which naturally leads right back to bureaucratic statism by a different theoretical route.

A. A. Berle Jr. strikes this keynote in his foreword to the recent book edited by Harvard's E. S. Mason, *The Corporation in Modern Society,* whose several chapters by leading authorities convey many of the leading conceptions of this neo-corporatism. Berle is discussing the "two systems" of modern industrialism, the one in Russia and the "modern corporation" in the U. S. He calls the corporations "these non-Statist collectivisms" and sees them as "suggesting an eventual non-Statist socialization" of profits. In another place Berle says the present system is really "Collectivism" or "non-Statist Socialism," and though (being unafraid of labels) he also calls it "People's Capitalism," he makes clear he believes the social order is traveling beyond capitalism or socialism.[1]

These neo-corporatist ideas have their roots, in the immediate sense,

88

not in a predilection for any of the older and more famous corporatisms which come to mind, but in a reaction to distinctively American conditions, in the soil of the one capitalism left in the world which seems to be a going concern.

One root is a wave of intensified soul-searching about the dominant institution of this capitalism, the corporation. "What Mr. Berle and most of the rest of us are afraid of is that this powerful corporate machine . . seems to be running without any discernible controls," writes Prof. Mason. Why does the system seem to them out of control?

It is certainly not controlled by the famous Invisible Hand of the Market, they agree. A new stage in the concentration of economic power has come into being. In *Power Without Property* Berle has laid great stress on the immense expansion of the fiduciary institutions (pension funds, mutual funds, etc.) and their economic consequences. These funds buy common stocks, i.e. formal shares in the ownership of the economy. They grow and their holdings proliferate. Then—

> A relatively small oligarchy of men operating in the same atmosphere, absorbing the same information, moving in the same circles and in a relatively small world knowing each other, dealing with each other, and having more in common than in difference, will hold the reins. These men by hypothesis will have no ownership relation of any sort. They will be, essentially, non-Statist civil servants—unless they abuse their power to make themselves something else.

This, he argues, is creating "a new socio-economic structure," with basic political effects. "Then, the picture will be something like this. A few hundred large pension trust and mutual fund managers (perhaps far fewer than this number) would control, let us say, the hundred largest American industrial concerns." Again: "In result, the greatest part of American economic enterprise, formerly individualist, has been regrouped and consolidated into a few hundred non-Statist, collective cooperative institutions."

> So, as noted, divorce between men and industrial things is becoming complete. A Communist revolution could not accomplish that more completely. Certainly it could not do so with the same finesse. When a Russian Communist government says to the workers that "the people" own the instruments of production but it will take care of them, it is assigning to its population a passive-receptive position closely comparable to the one we are studying. The difference lies in the fact that the criteria for reception are different, and that the political State exercises the power factor now gradually but steadily being aggregated under the American system in nonpolitical but equally impersonal fiduciary institutions.

This concentrated power of the fiduciary managers, a stage beyond the "America's Sixty Families" pattern, is only potential; in practice they eschew voting control. Thus the lack of any control over the corporate managements becomes institutionalized. But whether they exercise their power or not, the result is a small oligarchy of uncontrolled managers, continuously making decisions which have a vital impact on the society as a whole.

89

2

His next question is: What "legitimates" this uncontrolled corporative power? Not assignment of this power to the managements by the shareholders. Berle and Means took care of the fiction of shareholder control back in 1932; and even Adler and Kelso's *Capitalist Manifesto* only advocates that the shareholder *should* control, meaning that he does not now.

A second source of "legitimacy" could be the market, if one argues that it is the objective hand of the market which imposes decisions on the managers, not their whims. But our neo-corporatists do not believe this.

What then can legitimate the decisions of management? The solution of government control arises, of course, but to our subjects this means "state control," which means "statism," which means socialism, communism, totalitarianism, Sovietism and other unthinkable things. In general, they are in a flight from statism under the impress of the Russian horrible example. They grope for an alternative.

What then? Beardsley Ruml has suggested an appointed-trustee system: the Board of Directors co-opts a special member to act as "trustee" for a given interest-group (the company's customers, or suppliers, or employees, or the "community," etc.), protecting its interest against the board. I cite this mainly to illustrate what "groping" means.

The next grope is cited not only because it is Berle's but because it gives a proper sense of the hopelessness of the effort. This is the feudal analogy presented by Berle in *The 20th Century Capitalist Revolution* (1954), a much misunderstood book which does *not* present a Luce-type celebration of our economic system. In his strange chapter on "The Conscience of the King and the Corporation," Berle is trying to answer the question: How have absolute, uncontrolled powers been curbed in the past, not by upheavals from below but by organic dispensations from above?—for perhaps this will also apply to the absolute, uncontrolled power which is our present problem. He finds an answer in the medieval Curia Regis. Any man could throw himself before the king's feet and get justice dispensed on the spot by the king's conscience. The custom became institutionalized. Hence the beginning of equity courts and (one gathers, in this Berlean history) eventually other democratic counterpoises to the absolute power. "It is here suggested," Berle concludes, "that a somewhat similar phenomenon is slowly looming up in the corporate field through the mists that hide us from the history of the next generation."

The legitimation, therefore, is immanent in the historical process itself. The important thing, he is saying, is not whether the king's rule was legitimate but that this *was* the way the new system arose.

90

The approach stirs a reminiscence. It is our American school's analogue of the standard Stalinist "historical" justification of *its* absolute power: totalitarianism and terror are passing phenomena preparatory to a glorious morrow, mere flecks on the wave of the future. If it is dressed in feudal terms, this is partly because Berle has long been fascinated by the virtues of feudal society. (Compare his rather amazing paean of praise to medieval institutions, over 20 years ago in *New Directions in the New World.*) But this nostalgia for feudalism is not confined to Berle. In reaction to monolithic-statism, feudalism begins to appear "pluralistic," which in contemporary sociological jargon is high praise. Its integration of the individual in pre-capitalist community relationships looks good as against the alienation of man under capitalism. The feeling crops up especially in the neo-corporatists, as they view the "feudal" pattern of a society where overweening social power lumps up in a number of huge agglomerations, with a relatively small number of corporations lording it over their own "baronies," each one with vassals dangling after, like the auto dealers after the Big Three of Detroit.[2]

3

Berle's announcement in *The 20th Century Capitalist Revolution* that the big corporation not only has a soul but also a conscience was subjected to a good deal of understandable ribbing, even before those General Electric executives went to jail; but this discovery of the corporate conscience should be considered only one form of another grope, not yet examined. This is the proposal for the Statesmen-Managers. If the decisions made, without control, by the big corporation executives are so vital for society, these executives must be more than glorified shopkeepers.

Their decisive job cannot be simply to further the interests of the corporation, maximize profits, etc., with primary responsibility to the owners. They must train themselves to think in social terms, in terms of the impact of their decisions on the bigger world outside; in short, to be Statesmen rather than parochially profit-minded businessmen. This becomes also a solution, or part of a solution, to the problem of legitimacy. It may be soul-quaking to think that the fate of our whole society is in the hands of corporate overlords whose nearsighted eyes are fixed only on the shortest way to money-grubbing, but it is heartening to think that this fate is taken care of by Experts who, having proved their managerial skill in the rough-and-tumble of business, now blossom out as broadgauged Social Thinkers too. This is the meaning of the refrain in Philip Selznick's recent *Leadership in Administration*: "The executive becomes a statesman as he makes the transition from administrative management to institutional leadership." The theme can also be found in some of the contributions to the Mason book.

In this approach, then, the new irresponsibility of the uncontrolled Institutional Leaders is no longer a thing to view with alarm but rather a necessary precondition to freeing them from the petty, distorting influences of short-range, profit-maximizing considerations.

In this context we get demonstrations (which once would have sound-

91

ed like muckraking) of how our corporate barons are indeed making the vital decisions politically and socially, as well as economically: how the oil companies determine our foreign policy; how General Dynamics decides strategy in the struggle for the world, etc. The objection, of course, is not that this is done but that it is too often done by executives who are not also Statesmen.

But this line is inherently dangerous, as Mason points out:

> If equity rather than profits is the corporate objective, one of the traditional distinctions between the private and public sectors disappears. If equity is the primary desideratum, it may well be asked why duly constituted public authority is not as good' an instrument for dispensing equity as self-perpetuating corporate managements?

And Eugene V. Rostow warns that this trend invites the response that it is men elected to advance the general welfare who should make the decisions rather than uncontrolled oligarchs. But this implies *democratic control* of the decision-making apparatus, and democracy is the one way out which our neo-corporatists reject with unquestioning uncertainty.

4

Neo-corporatism presents itself, first of all, as another attempt to answer the problem of legitimacy. But this problem, after all, is only the current way in which its posers formulate to themselves the basic question of the underpinnings of the whole social system. Real solutions are bound to lie in radical, i.e., systemic, changes.

The outline of such a change appears under the name of "Constitutionalizing the Corporation" in the deliberations (already mentioned) of the Center for the Study of Democratic Institutions led by W. H. Ferry.[3] Ferry began with a number of complaints about the present system which could once have been part and parcel of a socialist propaganda pamphlet: against over-concentration of wealth, the "paradoxes and contradictions" of contemporary capitalism, alienation, the myth of the "self-regulating economy," the "creed of the affluent," economic individualism, "the messiness of the present economic arrangements," etc. This leads on to formulations favoring "a political economy based on the purposive use of law, politics, and government on behalf of the common good," "the primacy of politics" for "the rational control of our economic affairs," "bringing the economic order under political guidance," and so on.

These phrases seem to give the primacy to *political* power over the corporate power, subordinating the latter to the former, i.e. installing "statism,' in the terminology previously referred to. This general "socialistic" approach gave way to something else as the discussions at the Center advanced, with the participation of an impressive panel of eminent thinkers: Robert Hutchins, Berle, Scott Buchanan, Reinhold Niebuhr, I. I. Rabi, J. C. Murray, Walter Millis, and others. At a month-long meeting— a sort of enlarged plenum—of the Center held last summer, Ferry presented a programmatic paper for discussion by the group.

The concrete idea that emerged is the founding of a new political order

92

on a "commonwealth of corporations." Ferry proposed (after raising the question of a "fourth branch of government" for economic questions):

> A less dramatic form of constitutionalization might be the formation by statute of a commonwealth of corporations, an "association of free, self-governing nations." This would call for federal charters, or "constitutions," which would recognize the autonomy of the member-corporations but charge them collectively with specific powers and responsibilities . . . Along some such route might also come the legitimacy that Berle believes the modern corporation is seeking. Establishing a commonwealth or federation of corporations would necessitate, for example, a review of corporate charters.

He explains further:

> . . . we keep on thinking in the very limited terms of nationalization or non-nationalization, private ownership or national ownership. It is quite possible, for example, to give a good deal more authority and responsibility to corporations . . . I am looking for a legal order to enclose and to make coherent what is being done in this country by the corporations.

And he stresses several times that his vision means "a new and different type of state," "something new, a qualitatively different way of looking at the economy."

Father Murray, the Jesuit member of the panel of consultants, who took a prominent part in the discussions, thereupon spoke the following, not at all antagonistically:

> I know that you have expressly disclaimed that what you wish is socialism, and quite rightly, especially in the classic definition. It doesn't seem to me that that is what you wish. However, the tendency of your paper is to install intervention of a sort that is referred to technically as the corporative state. I don't mean the corporative state of the facist sort, which was frankly totalitarian . . . [Murray explains he means the corporative state as invented by "some German economists and political thinkers" as an alternative to both capitalism and socialism.] You seem to be aiming at something of the same sort. You seem to want an integration of the economic and political orders, a legalized incorporation of the economic processes and political processes, if you will, or a constitutionalization of it. The net effect would be radically new.

5

This observation by Father Murray, which was not a criticism, ties up with the views of another Jesuit social thinker who had recently published on the question. This is Father Harbrecht, whose brochure *Toward the Paraproprietal Society* (1960) had appeared with a laudatory introduction by none other than Berle.

Harbrecht's thesis is that our social system is turning into a system of property tenure which is neither socialism nor really capitalism. His analysis starts at the same place as Berle's discussion of the fiduciary institutions and the new stage of divorcement between property and power. In this new order "beyond property," inevitably "the economic power that

93

is growing in the institutions is being drawn, or shunted away, from the generality of the people." The result has "striking parallels" with feudal institutions, which also "began with a separation of control from the owner-ship of productive property." Today corporations correspond to the Great Domains of the baronial principalities. "A man's place in medieval society was determined by his place in the domain. Today men are bound to their corporations . . . the present-day corporate managers are like the vassals of the great domains. They have control, but not ownership of great wealth, yet their tenure in power is in fact limited by their continuing ability to perform a service."

Thus Father Harbrecht in his own book. It is easy to see why it de-lighted Berle. For Harbrecht, this process of "feudalization" of the corpo-rate-political structure is his own version of the Wave of the Future.

Now we learn from Father Murray (in the Center discussion) that Harbrecht made a criticism of Ferry's paper. He found that Ferry wants to go too far with "the *politization* of the economic process"—that is, the im-position of outside political (state) controls *over* the corporations (the baronial powers), whereas Harbrecht sees the increased power as going *to* the corporations.

Faced with the explicit posing of this question, Ferry denied that Harbrecht's criticism applied to his position: "I do not accept the criticism. *I will accept Father Harbrecht's own proposal for imposing larger re-sponsibilities on corporations.*" (Emphasis added.)

The distinction is very important for our purposes. What is being worked out here is not simply more of the familiar liberal-collectivist trend toward increased statification, a line running from Croly through the New Deal and on to Schlesinger and others today. This, as Berle likes to stress, is an attempt at a "non-statist" alternative: the assignment of political power not *over* the corporate bodies of the economy but *to* them.

6

The Center consultant who has developed a more clearly thought-out program of corporatism, perhaps thereby inspiring Ferry, is Scott Buchanan. Buchanan was a leader of the Wallace Progressive Party in 1948; I do not know what his politics became after that, but when he published his *Essay in Politics* in 1953, the preface explained that it was based on conversations in 1947 which led most of the participants to join the Wallace movement the following year. The 1953 book presents essen-tially the same views he has now.

In a 1959 discussion at the Center, Buchanan criticized Ferry along the same lines as Harbrecht: for wanting to give too much power to the government instead of giving more powers to the corporations. But the government, he argued, "is obviously incapable of dealing with the big economic, military, and other problems that arise . . . When you turn this all over to the government as is done in Sweden, you get a very dull, not necessarily stupid, kind of society." So—

94

> What I am thinking of, as some of you are guessing, is that you don't
> hand such a function over to the government—the national government.
> You hand over this function to a new kind of corporation which is
> chartered to determine its own function and legalize its own operation—
> a self-governing body. This might be some federal scheme. You would
> not have one national economic corporation. You would have 200 or 500
> corporations, or whatever they are, and some kind of congress of cor-
> porations that would deal with political-economic matters through legal
> means.

The corporation, said Buchanan, should "think about itself in terms of the
rule of law":

> This would mean that the corporation think of itself literally as a gov-
> ernment, as Berle has put it often enough, and try to constitutionalize
> itself in some way. This doesn't necessarily mean that we should impose
> a democratic dogma on it. It means that the corporation, if it isn't going
> to be democratic, should say it is not going to be and find a mode of
> operation that will discharge its responsibilities and be efficient in its
> own operation.

This is laudably clear: not democracy but efficiency. In another brochure
issued by the Center in 1958, Buchanan ties up a number of things in
one olio:

> The Marxist used to speak vividly, if not too accurately, about the con-
> centration of capital and the expropriation of the worker. If the dialectic
> is still working, he ought now to point out the next stage or moment when
> the labor union applies for corporate membership in the big corporation
> whose directors grant annual tenure and salaries, pensions, and the
> power of veto on the policy of the corporation instead of the right to
> strike. As a result, the corporation is a government by and with the con-
> sent of the workers as well as the stockholders. As Adolf Berle puts it in
> ".The 20th Century Capitalist Revolution," creeping socialism has be-
> come galloping capitalism, and, we might add, corporate communism,
> free-world variety.

It is not surprising to find him adding that Russia has gone ahead to
entrust its economy to "three separate but coordinated giant corporations"
and "The other socialist countries have invented other forms to meet their
needs. It is not to be supposed that we are lacking in inventive imagination."

The final chapter of his 1953 book even presents some modest details
of a New Order in which the corporations have taken on certain sovereign
powers making the corporate structure autonomous and coordinate with
the government. (Example: the N.A.M. becomes the "sponsor" of the
Federal Trade Commission.) There is a separate House "representing
managers, engineers and workmen." The same corporations which "moderate socialists mark for nationalization" are in this scheme to be given
wide self-governing "powers and privileges." The "chronic civil war between labor and the corporation" will be eliminated. The "three giant corporations" of the Soviet system (which are the Trade Unions, Soviet, and

95

Consumers Cooperatives!) "should be intelligible to us as a kind of preview of ourselves if we continue to increase our corporate development in the same way in the future as we have in the past . . ." The vision is global: "incorporated trading companies, making cartel treaties in the twentieth century, could become the United States of the World . . ."

7

Buchanan is the most unreserved of our neo-corporatists, but Berle is recognized as their leading theoretician. Berle, as far as I know, has not put it as bluntly as some others, and I am not certain how far he would go. He is, to be sure, entirely uninhibited in describing the present system as corporate collectivism. He militantly insists on labeling it collectivism as often as possible—"true collectivism," etc.—and since he also quite calmly describes the corporate system as "an automatic self-perpetuating oligarchy," we need not suppose he has any illusion that we are living under a *democratic* collectivism. Nor does he think there is an unbridgeable gulf between this system and the bureaucratic-collectivist system on the other side of the Iron Curtain:

> The private property system in production . . . has almost vanished in the vast area of American economy dominated by this system. Instead we have something which differs from the Russian or socialist system mainly in its philosophical content.

Nor, for this matter, is he even exercised about democratic controls over this spreading collectivism. One of the troubles with liberals, he writes, is that

> they thought of ownership by "the people" as something real, whereas a moment's thinking would make it clear that "the people" was an abstraction. Its reality meant some sort of bureaucratic management.

And if bureaucratic management is inevitable, it should be efficient bureaucratic management. The oligarchic methods of the corporation "work remarkably well" and "Conventional stereotypes of 'democratic procedure' are particularly useful in dealing with this problem."

"Public consensus" is counterposed to "public opinion." The important difference, of course, is that "public opinion" can finally be ascertained only by the conventional stereotypes of democratic procedure. But public consensus? This is the body of "unstated premises" lying behind the superficialities of public opinion. It does not emanate from the people, that abstraction; nor merely from the business community. Where then? Here is the answer: from "the conclusions of careful

96

university professors, the reasoned opinions of specialists, the statements of responsible journalists, and at times the solid pronouncements of respected politicians." These constitute "the real tribunal to which the American system is finally accountable," and it is their consensus which confers legitimacy upon the system.

So the bureaucratic nature of this corporate collectivism—which by Orwellian rules he sometimes calls "the reality of economic democracy in the United States"—does not give him pause. It would indeed take a riotous imagination to equip the new corporate order with the aforesaid "conventional stereotypes" of democracy. In his good society, "organizations in each industry and inter-industry"—like the Iron and Steel Institute, which is properly "not Statist"—can be encouraged to "synchronize or harmonize" their planning, with the assistance of "relief from some of the rigidities of the antitrust laws."

Like Buchanan, he sees that "in any long view the American and Soviet systems would seem to be converging rather than diverging . . ." For here too "power centralizes itself around a politico-economic instead of a governmental institution," the politico-economic institution on this side being the corporation. He is as enthusiastically in favor of cartels as Buchanan, with a similar vision of a corporate world government:

> In point of surprising fact, the large American corporations in certain fields have more nearly achieved a stable and working world government than has yet been achieved by any other institution. The outstanding illustration is the case of the oil industry.

For Berle, corporatism is the American surrogate for socialism. Socialism, he writes, was the instrument of the 20th century revolution in many countries, but "In the United States, the chief instrument has proved to be the modern giant corporation." If the corporations "do not assume community responsibilities, government must step in and American life will become increasingly statist." The corporation's powers are in fact "held in trust for the entire community."

> The choice of corporate managements [he writes in the chapter "Corporate Capitalism and 'The City of God,' " in The Twentieth Century Capitalist Revolution] is not whether so great a power shall cease to exist; they can merely determine whether trey will serve as the nuclei of its organization or pass it over to someone else, probably the modern state . . . It seems that, in diverse ways, we are nibbling at the edges of a vast, dangerous and fascinating piece of thinking.

Vast, dangerous and fascinating it is, and Berle is nibbling.

8

In discussions of corporatism, the word corporation is more often than not used in more than one sense. The broader and earlier sense is any body (of people) corporate, whose association for some purpose is recognized; the narrower sense is the business corporation. The "corporations" of Italian Fascist theory were, however, not business corporations nor

97

joint-stock companies, but associations of labor and capital assigned a given role in society. Corporatist ideologies have not necessarily begun with the business corporation; but as we have seen, our own neo-corporatists do begin this way. While beginning this way, however, do they go on to a broader conception of corporatism?

The bridge from the narrower to the broader sense is constituted by the question of who are the "members" of a corporation.

Once you entertain the idea of turning the corporation into a sovereign power, of turning autonomous political powers over to it in some fashion, you must bethink yourself that it will not do to confer this boon simply on the Board of Directors. The base must be widened to receive the weight. The corporation must be more inclusive, if it is to be turned into a political community or the base for one. We do not want to strengthen management at the expense of labor—no, we are all liberals and believe that labor must be treated equally. The solution is plainly to integrate labor *into* the corporation . . . on an equal basis, naturally . . . In a number of steps presented as expanding the "membership" of the corporation, the business corporation of today becomes the politically autonomous body of corporatist theory. Basic is the unity of all classes inside the confining forms of the corporate structure.

Buchanan has it all laid out: he wants "a highly structured corporation in which the union would be a part of the structure." Not only investors and managers but "creditors, workers and buyers" should all get "explicit status as members or citizens of these governments [corporations]." Hutchins opines it is labor itself, not the union as such, which should be included in the structure of the corporation, since the idea "does not necessarily involve the maintenance of a national union of any kind." We have seen that in Father Harbrecht's wave of the future, "men are bound to their corporations."

In the Mason tome, Prof. Abram Chayes of Harvard elaborates a "more spacious" conception of "membership" of the corporation: "Among the groups now conceived as outside the charmed circle of corporate membership, but which ought to be brought within it, the most important and readily identifiable is its work-force." Does this mean worker representation in its managing board? Apparently not, however. Still, something has to be done about the present sad state of affairs in which labor and management "are made to appear as hostile antagonists in a kind of legalized class-warfare." (The reference is to ordinary collective bargaining.) By bringing the labor force *into* the corporation, negotiations become merely an act of adjusting common relations. Chayes is arguing that class collaboration, as against class struggle, entails the corporatist principle as the method of tying up two now-warring constituencies into a single constituency.

For Frank Tannenbaum in *A Philosophy of Labor,* the unions must save the corporation by endowing it with "a moral role in the world, not merely an economic one." "In some way the corporation and its labor force must become one corporate group and cease to be a house divided and seemingly at war."[5]

98

In that one of his many, and not always consistent, books in which he comes closest to a kind of corporatism, Peter Drucker also naturally turns up with the notion that the trade union must be made an institutional part of the corporate structure. This is in his *The New Society* (1949), written under the impress of the British Labor government. A man who thinks in managerial terms from first to last, Drucker views the trade-union leader as just another type of manager, who, like the corporation executive, has a responsibility not to his organization's members but to the Organization as such. Integration of the union will also help to make the government of the corporation "legitimate," he argues.

Interesting is the context of Drucker's approach to corporatism in this book. Generally speaking Drucker is a militant conservative, and in his other books he is usually a fervent apologist for the corporation and its managers as a going concern. Here, however, Drucker has a remarkable section on "Democratic Socialism," plainly meaning mainly the ongoing British Labor regime, in which he *defends* it against American misunderstanding—in his own way. His own way is the corporatist way.

He announces that capitalism has failed at least outside our own charmed country, that the New Society will be (naturally) "beyond capitalism and socialism," and insofar as he concretizes this vision, it is in terms echoing what we have already considered. The modern industrial enterprise is already "collective," it is a "governmental institution"; it is, however, "independent of the State in its origin as well as in its function. It is an organ of Society rather than one of the state . . . There is not one prime mover in our society but at least two: State and enterprise." The investor (shareholder) deserves no special rights in the corporation; the thing to do is to put the de-facto situation on a legalized basis, so that the sovereign control of the corporation by its managers is institutionalized.

From here Drucker naturally goes over to the question of how to broaden the corporate structure in line with its broader role: we get an echo of Ruml's trustee-tribunes. We get the theory of the convergence of the capitalist corporation with the Russian system, a characteristic accompaniment.[6] And we also get the already mentioned integration of the trade unions into the "membership" of the broadened corporation, which is now ready to fulfill its bigger tasks.

9

Our neo-corporatist school consists of liberals, not conservatives or reactionaries.

The people of the Santa Barbara Center are in general conscious liberals, as evidenced by their output on other questions like war and nuclear disarmament, civil liberties and civil rights, etc. Berle is a certified liberal, being a leader of the New York Liberal Party. Buchanan was what I am accustomed to call a Stalinoid-liberal, and probably still is. Drucker the conservative proved the rule, as explained, in the book in which he approached corporatism. Tannenbaum is an ex-socialist; and so on.

The trend is cropping out of the bureaucratic-collectivist side of today's liberalism. It is not the only outcropping; the dominant one is still

99

what Berle would call "statist." But it is an especially interesting outcropping.

These are not the first liberals to discover corporatism. The famous German liberal capitalist Walter Rathenau embodied it in the new social order outlined in his book *In Days to Come,* written during the First World War. In 1947 John Fisher in *Harper's* (he was then one of its editors and is now editor-in-chief) offered a well-developed program of corporatism as platform for the revival of liberalism, very similar to Buchanan's finished product. In return for this dispensation, "In a few peculiarly vital industries, however, labor might have to forego its right to strike: and in return it would have to receive a special standing and special privileges comparable to those of the civil service." Rightists, he admitted, "might try to convert it into a corporative state."

Probably more significant are the views of the liberal whose economics is the bridge between liberalism and Laborism, J. M. Keynes. In *The End of Laissez Faire* (1926) Keynes advocated a status for corporations as "semi-autonomous bodies within the State":

> I propose a return, it may be said, towards medieval conceptions of separate autonomies. But, in England at any rate, corporations are a mode of government which has never ceased to be important . . .
> But more interesting than these is the trend of Joint Stock Institutions, when they have reached a certain age and size, to approximate to the status of public corporations rather than that of individualistic private enterprise. One of the most interesting and unnoticed developments of recent decades has been the tendency of big enterprise to socialise itself . . .
> . . . The battle of Socialism against unlimited private profit is being won in detail hour by hour . . . It is true that many big undertakings . . . still need to be semi-socialised . . . We must take full advantage of the natural tendencies of the day, and we must probably prefer semi-autonomous corporations to organs of the Central Government . . .

Note that views similar to those which our American school *counterposes* to socialism are here offered as socialistic. To confound the picture further, the reader has no doubt been aware that corporatism is most notorious as a fascist ideology. Well then, is corporatism liberal, socialist or fascist? Or are there three distinct kinds of corporatism? When a liberal adopts corporatism, is he falling for a fascist theory or is he rescuing this theory from the fascists? Where, in short, does this neo-corporatism fit in?

10

The difficulty arises because corporatism is thought of as being a fascist theory. It became so, of course; we shall see how. But historically it arises as a *socialist* idea, and as such it has a far from negligible past. Its liberal incarnation, which we have been observing, is only an extension of this phenomenon.

Its main appeal to socialist thought, as to Berle, was as a framework for the radical reform-from-above of capitalist society through what were thought of as "non-statist" or non-political channels. It looked to a trans-

100

formation of society not through a struggle for political power but through the assignment of social powers to autonomous economic bodies. (This in fact is the basic definition of corporatism in whatever form it presents itself.)

Some elements usually associated with corporatism go back very far in pre-Marxist socialist thought, particularly a beehive-view of society as an organic whole of which the human individual is only a cell (organicism) and a related "communitarian" outlook. But these are by no means peculiar to corporatism, being common in all forms of socialism-from-above. Fourier's phalanx, Cabet's Icaria and Robert Owen's model factory can also be taken as ancestors, but these utopian socialisms, of course, saw their autonomous economic bodies as infiltrators on the margin of society rather than commanders in the center.

The first prophet of a full-fledged corporatism was Saint-Simon—not a utopian and not really a socialist—who was fertile in schemes for the radical reform-from-above of society through autonomous economic and social bodies which would dispense with "politics" and rule by direct administration, under the benevolent control of financiers, businessmen, scientists and technicians. In Saint-Simon labor and capital were institutionally amalgamated not only in theory but in terminology: the very term "workers" meant primarily the capitalists who carried on productive work as distinct from the "idlers" of the old ruling class. (Derivative trends in bourgeois thought stem from Saint-Simon's disciple, Comte, and the schools of sociology basically inspired by him; *vide* Durkheim.)

The conception of a new order built along the lines of a corporate society was one element in Edward Bellamy's version of socialism. Bellamy's system, though mainly modeled after military organization, explained the great Change in terms of pushing the corporate development to its final conclusion, "the one great corporation in which all other corporations were absorbed."

Perhaps the classic statement of "socialist" corporatism was expounded by Charles P. Steinmetz, prominent socialist in his day as well as eminent scientist. In his *America and the New Epoch* (1916) "socialism" is a society where the giant corporations, like his employer General Electric, literally rule directly, having eschewed profit and embraced the goal of sheer efficiency.

But the most massive corporatist element in the development of socialist thought was injected by syndicalism. The basic conception of the reorganization of society through (presumably) non-political but autonomous economic bodies was here the distinctive content of the movement.

Here corporatism diverged in two quite different directions. Saint-Simon, Bellamy's *Looking Backward,* and Steinmetz were almost purely authoritarian, not to say totalitarian. But syndicalism, like socialism as a whole, was a movement with two souls.

One was a socialism-from-below which looked toward the organization of democratic control of governmental authority through workers' control; the other was a thoroughly anti-democratic, elitist and "admin-

101

istered" view of the new order which was associated with the anarchist element in anarcho-syndicalism.[7] The former strain later dissolved itself into the general socialist movement and early revolutionary Communist movement, where its positive outcome was represented in such tendencies as guild-socialism and acceptance of a workers-council basis for a new type of democratic state. (These can still be termed "corporative," if one absolutely insists, insofar as they look to the assignment of power in society to "occupationally" determined bodies, although these bodies were not "economic" but thoroughly political.)

The latter strain flowed into the later bureaucratic-collectivist ideologies of corporatism, the ones to which that term actually became attached. In the heartland of the syndicalist movement, pre-1914 France, this current in syndicalism was documented in the book which most bluntly concretized the syndicalist new order: Pataud and Pouget's *Comment Nous Ferons la Révolution* (1909). When syndicalism traveled north to England, its anarchist element tended to dissolve out, leaving guild-socialism as a deposit; but when it traveled south to Italy, it was anarcho-syndicalism and Georges Sorel's protofascist reading of syndicalism which expanded.

Now it was this latter wing or current of syndicalism which transformed itself organically into the "black socialist" wing of Italian Fascism, and which thereby created what we know as the corporatism of the fascist ideology. Its architects were Enrico Corradini, Edmondo Rossoni and other syndicalists-turned-fascist, plus D'Annunzio-type nationalists-turned-syndicalist like Alfredo Rocco and Dino Grandi. Corporatism was the *serious* ideology only of this "socialist" face of fascism. As is well known, though Mussolini later adopted it officially it remained an empty façade for purely social-demagogic purposes.[8]

In German fascism too, within the Nazi movement, it was the assigned manipulators of the "Labor Front" who played with it and it was the *serious* ideology only of the "black socialist" wing. Strasser developed it into a view of a new corporate order called "state feudalism," with a chamber of corporations, etc. Here it was not even officially adopted for demagogic purposes; the Hitler regime rejected it.

We see, then, that corporatism enters the fascist world not *as a* fascist ideology but as a socialistic idea, indeed as *the* program to transform fascism into socialism. In this role corporatism is a direct and organic outgrowth of that one of the

102

"two souls of socialism" which I have called socialism-from-above.⁹

Once having arisen in this way, fascist corporatism had a powerful reactive impact on the socialist movement itself. It attracted—sucked out toward itself, so to speak—precisely those socialist currents which felt their kinship to it. In the case of the Marquet group in the French Socialist Party and the Mosley group in the British Labor Party, wings of the socialist movement split off to become fascist themselves. But more significant were the currents which were attracted specifically by corporatism *without* going over to fascism.

A hand of ideological sympathy to the Strasser wing of Nazism was stretched out by the not-insignificant tendency in the Social-Democracy led by the German-Czech social-democrat Wenzel Jaksch. Bernard Shaw, the no. 2 architect of Fabianism, was enthusiastically pro-Mussolini before he became even more enthusiastically pro-Stalinist; in a sober lecture before the Fabian Society in 1933 he described the Italian corporate-state plan and added, addressing Il Duce in the name of Fabianism:

> I say "Hear, hear! More power to your elbow." That is precisely what the Fabian Society wants to have done . . . Although we are all in favor of the corporative state, nevertheless it will not really be a corporative state until the corporations own the land in which they are working . . .

In Belgium, the socialist party leader Henri de Man, who had made a great if now forgotten reputation as a "revisionist" offering a theoretical alternative to Marxism within the socialist movement, wrote *Corporatisme et Socialisme* in 1935 and later became virtually a Nazi collaborator. Lincoln Steffens—I list him here rather than as a liberal; the distinction becomes terminological—glowed with ardor for both Mussolini and the application of the corporative idea to the U. S. Without throwing him into the very same bag, I would also suggest a look at Leon Blum's introduction to the French edition of Burnham's *Managerial Revolution*.

Corporatism was also an element in the ideological jumble of the New Deal, but my impression is that it was more prominent in non-socialistic New Dealers like Hugh Johnson than in the radical wing, who tended to be overweeningly "statist."

11

This identification of corporatism as a *socialist* current—as one of the strains in the history of socialism-from-above—rather than as an idea necessarily connoting fascism, is the first key to understanding the burgeoning of new corporatist ideologies today. But now widen the focus on this picture:

"Socialism-from-above" did not arise from socialism. It was and is merely the form taken within the framework of socialism—the intrusion *into* socialism—of what is in fact all-pervasive in the entire history of man's aspirations for the good society and a better life. This is true everywhere, in all times, and in all ideological guises. It is the expectation of emancipation or reform from some powers-that-be who will hand down the new world to a grateful people, rather than the liberating struggle of the people

103

themselves, associated from below, to win and control the good society for themselves. It is the octroyal principle, which is still dominant as always, versus the revolutionary-democratic principle, which during most of man's history could be nothing but a phantasm and which could become a realistic aspiration *only* within the framework of socialism. What is distinctive about socialism is not its dominant "socialism-from-above" wing, for this is dominant everywhere, but the fact that it and it alone could generate the ever-arising and so-far-defeated movements for emancipation-from-below.

Reform-from-above, under the economic and political impulsions of a period when the dominant social system is decaying, characteristically takes the form of a bureaucratic-collectivist ideology. Corporatism is one of the bureaucratic-collectivist ideologies which arises. It arises quite inescapably both inside and outside the socialist movement. What we have examined in the case of the American school, in a country with a tiny socialist movement, is its rise in circles outside the socialist movement. But in most countries of the world, ideologists like Berle, Buchanan, Ferry, *et al.* would not be outside the broad socialist movement; they are social-democratic types. Their ideology would arise within the framework of socialism and take on a socialistic coloration and vocabulary, instead of taking care to couch itself in non-socialist or even anti-socialist terms. This American development is an anomaly in that it produces a corporatism stripped of any socialist dress.

But this means that if we look abroad, we should expect to see its analogues *with* a socialist dress. And we do plainly enough; in fact, the picture is gratifyingly simplified when we find that both sides recognize their affinity.

The British co-thinker of our American school is C. A. R. Crosland, the leading theoretician of the right (Gaitskell) wing of the British Labor Party. He, in turn, is the apostle of a new "revisionism" (his term) for which he claims most of the European social-democracies.

Prof. Mason appeals to Crosland's book *The Future of Socialism* for British evidence that "the form of ownership of large enterprise is irrelevant" and that the large corporation is fundamentally the same whether private in the U. S. (where it is called capitalism) or public as in Britain (where it is called an installment of socialism). If this is so, then the transplantation of Crosland revisionism to the private "corporate collectivism" of the U. S. produces a resultant ideology similar to the neo-corporatism we have been discussing.

Prof. Rostow states his understanding of Crosland-Gaitskellism in terms of the American problem as follows: "In England, socialists say that the managers have already socialized capitalism, so that it is no longer necessary to invoke the cumbersome formality of public ownership of the means of production." By the same token—this is Rostow's point—the managers may also be said to have already socialized capitalism in the U. S. Thus Crosland equals Berle plus a difference in latitude and longitude.

The chapter in Mason's book on the British corporation was, in

104

fact, assigned to Crosland himself, as collaborator with the American authors. Crosland winds up this essay by quoting the 1957 thesis of the Labor Party, *Industry and Society,* in which the anti-nationalization view was established: "The Labor Party recognizes that, under increasingly professional managements, large firms are as a whole serving the nation well." This is why nationalization is unnecessary, according to Crosland. It follows that the big corporations, under even more professional managements, are serving the U. S. at least as well if not better.

Industry and Society was the official theoretical exposition of this revisionism; and especially because it was a formal "resolution" and not simply an article, it is interesting to see, in "motto" form at the head of a chapter, not a quotation from Marx but one from Berle's 20*th Century Capitalist Revolution.* Quoted also is the Drucker of *The New Society.* This is symbolic of a fact. The line of analysis in *Industry and Society* is essentially Berlean.

If W. H. Ferry proposes a corporatist program for the U. S., he himself at any rate sees no great difference between this and the views of the Swedish social-democrat Gunnar Myrdal, or with the British and New Zealand welfare-states. Scott Buchanan says he wants to see his ideas worked out by a Fabian Society.

12

It is this relationship, mutually recognized, between American neo-corporatism and the new post-war trend of European social-democratic reformism which helps to explain both. I refer to the trend toward the repudiation of public or social ownership (*not* merely nationalization) as an important part of the socialist program. Crosland (*Encounter,* March 1960) chortles that "nearly all the European socialist parties" have gone this way.

But this is not traditional or historical social-democratic reformism in economic program, any more than Molletism in France has been traditional reformism in politics. The qualitative transformation that has taken place was pointed up when Crosland denounced "the extremist phraseology of the Party's formal aims" in its constitution regarding nationalization, and demanded that it be rewritten. This phraseology, now "extremist," was written in by Sidney Webb and Arthur Henderson.

Why is this neo-reformism engaged in a precipitous flight away from public ownership? First it should be seen as analogue to Berle's evolution from New Deal "statism" to his new enthusiasm for "non-Statist collectivism," which we have discussed. The line of thought goes like this:

Public ownership is no longer necessary for the gradual reform of capitalism into socialism because capitalism is socializing itself in other forms. The transference of power in the corporations to socially responsible managers means that the forms of private property are no longer incompatible with our ends. Socialization will now go forward with the inevitability of gradualism in these new corporate forms. Public ownership can now be stored away in the cellar of our program because the develop-

105

ment of the new corporate collectivism is adequately doing the job which the socialist movement once thought it was called on to perform. What is accepted as the road to "socialism" is the ongoing process of the bureaucratic-collectivization of the capitalist world. This neo-reformism of the European social-democrats and the neo-corporatism of our American liberal school are analogous forms of one type of bureaucratic-collectivist ideology.

FOOTNOTES

1. The role of the corporation in dissolving the property relations of capitalism was already explained in some detail by Marx in **Capital**, III, 516-22 (Kerr ed.); cf. 450-59; see also Marx-Engels, **Selected Correspondence** (N.Y. ed.), p. 105, and the passage which stands at the head of this article.

2. For an acadanese version of the comparison, see Richard Eells, **The Meaning of Modern Business** (N.Y., 1960), which invents the term "metrocorporate feudalism."

3. See W. H. Ferry, **The Economy Under Law** (1960), published by the Center; also his **The Corporation and the Economy** (1959). The Center also published Scott Buchanan, **The Corporation and the Republic** (1958) and Berle, **Economic Power and the Free Society** (1957). Ferry is also author of a pamphlet arguing for unilateral disarmament, published by the American Friends Service Committee, where a biographical note says he "has had long experience in newspaper work and as a consultant in labor relations. More recently he was partner in a public relations firm in New York City." His political involvements in the course of this career are hazy to me. Robert Hutchins, head of the Center and the Fund for the Republic, backs Ferry's views.

4. It should be remembered that the Catholic Church officially has its own program for a sort of corporatism (also called "industry council plan," etc.), a very elastic one; it has been interpreted into anything from Mussolini's fascist corporations to mere labor-management committees. Father Murray can therefore raise the question of corporatism more objectively than most.

5. In 1921 (**The Labor Movement, N.Y.**) Tannenbaum was for the revolutionary mission of the working class and socialism, and friendly to something he called the "dictatorship of the proletariat," but it is interesting to see how, even then, this revolutionism was based on as reactionary and anti-humanistic a version of the organicist theory of society as I have ever seen and was combined with insistence on the outlawry of strikes and the excommunication from society of strikers.

6. This theory of convergence and its popularity deserves an article by itself. One of the most amazing recent examples is **Industrialism and Industrial Man**, by Clark Kerr and three colleagues (Harvard, 1960), which paints the coming New Order as an authoritarian society ("a new slavery") extrapolated almost entirely from the convergence of a bureaucratized capitalism with a somewhat mellowed Stalinism. The authors insist this is the wave of the future to be accepted without vain "moral indignation."

7. I am aware that this passing remark flies in the face of the myth of anarchist "libertarianism" and "anti-authoritarianism." I hope to deal with this legend in the near future.

8. For the benefit of Berle, it should be emphasized that even if the corporative structure had ever been realized, it would not and could not have been "non-statist" in any meaningful sense. The state power would still have been omnipotent, however dressed up. The "non-statist" illusion about corporatism is analogous to the "non-political" illusion of its ancestor syndicalism, which was thoroughly political.

9. For a sketch of the meaning of "socialism-from-above" versus "socialism-from-below" in the history of socialist thought, see my "Two Souls of Socialism" in **Anvil**, Winter 1960.

HAL DRAPER, *former Editor of* The New International *and* Labor Action, *is on the Editorial Board of* New Politics.

106

Dwight D. Eisenhower
and the Corporate Commonwealth

ROBERT GRIFFITH

WE KNOW MORE ABOUT DWIGHT DAVID EISENHOWER than ever before. The papers of his presidency, now open to scholars, constitute a documentary record of extraordinary richness. Scarcely a month goes by, moreover, without the appearance of yet another new book or article on his life and times. But, although we know much more about him, we do not necessarily also understand what he was about or what the significance of his presidency was. Too much of the literature seems limited by the debates of the past: Was Eisenhower an active or passive president? Was he a skillfull politician or a bumbler? Was he dominant or subordinate in his relations with such powerful figures as John Foster Dulles? The answers to these questions have resulted in a useful but nevertheless limited sort of enlightenment.[1] It is possible to proceed somewhat beyond these limits, however, by focusing on what might be loosely called the political economy of the Eisenhower years: on Eisenhower's thinking about the relationship of government and the economy, on

I would like to thank the University of Massachusetts, the American Philosophical Society, and the John Simon Guggenheim Memorial Foundation for making possible the research and writing of this article. I am grateful for the valuable comments of Charles C. Alexander, Paul S. Boyer, Fred I. Greenstein, Ellis W. Hawley, Richard H. Immerman, Burton I. Kaufman, and Ronald Story. I owe a special debt to archivist David J. Haight and his coworkers at the Dwight D. Eisenhower Library. An earlier version of this essay was presented as a paper at the Ninety-Fifth Annual Meeting of the American Historical Association, held in Washington, D.C., December 27–30, 1980.

[1] A note on the historiography of the Eisenhower era. Most early interpretations of Eisenhower are dismissive. He had ended the Korean War and made the Republican party safe for internationalism and the New Deal, but he had provided little leadership in meeting the difficult new challenges of the mid-century, had reigned rather than ruled, was a somewhat naive and apolitical figure who, as Walter Lippmann put it, was never willing "to break the eggs that are needed for the omlette." Especially see Clinton Rossiter, *The American Presidency* (2d edn., New York, 1960). Historians seemed to agree. In a poll of seventy-five historians by Arthur M. Schlesinger in 1962, they rated Eisenhower twenty-second among American presidents, between Andrew Johnson and Chester A. Arthur; Schlesinger, "Our Presidents: A Rating by 75 Historians," *New York Times Magazine*, July 29, 1962, pp. 12, 40–41. Not until the late 1960s and early 1970s, against a backdrop of war and civil disorder, did historians and other intellectuals begin to revise this conventional portrait. See, for example, articles by Murray Kempton, Gary Wills, and Richard Rhodes, Arthur Larson's memoir, *The President Nobody Knew* (New York, 1968), and full-length studies by Herbert S. Parmet, Peter Lyon, and Charles C. Alexander. These works, despite important differences among them, portray Eisenhower as a far more complex, intelligent, and skillful chief executive. The opening in recent years of important new archival collections at the Eisenhower Library has resulted in an outpouring of books and articles extending and qualifying this reinterpretation. Especially see the work of Stephen E. Ambrose, Blanche Wiesen Cook, Robert A. Divine, Fred I. Greenstein, Richard H. Immerman, Burton I. Kaufman, Douglas Kinnard, Gary W. Reichard, and Elmo Richardson. The scholarship of these historians has been collectively labeled "Eisenhower revisionism," an unfortunately imprecise term that invites confusion with Cold War revisionism and obscures often profound differences among those so categorized.

the connections between this thought and the powerful constituencies that rallied to his support, and on the ways in which this thought shaped the politics and policies of his administration.

Eisenhower was not, of course, a profound or original thinker. He did, however, take ideas seriously, especially in the area of political economy; and, although he typically expressed these ideas in platitudes, he did create, beyond the banality of his language, a fairly coherent vision of how society ought to operate. For Eisenhower, this body of thought, which I have labeled "the corporate common-wealth," represented an attempt to resolve what he saw as the contradictions of modern capitalism and to create a harmonious corporate society without class conflict, unbridled acquisitiveness, and contentious party politics. This thought, this vision, this effort provides a unifying theme for his presidency and supplies us with at least one way in which to understand his significance.

Eisenhower was a product of the organizational revolution that had transformed American life in the twentieth century, a member of the new managerial class that led the nation's great public and private bureaucracies. Although he was not an intellectual, his thought nevertheless reflects the history, interests, and dilemmas of this new class. At West Point, he was at best an indifferent student, graduating well down in his class. His early years of military service seem to have been more crowded with coaching football and card playing than with any intellectual endeavor. His tour of duty in Panama under General Fox Connor, which he later described as "a sort of graduate school in military affairs and the humanities," was doubtless influential in his intellectual development, as was his subsequent attend-ance at the army's Command and General Staff School at Fort Leavenworth and the War College in Washington. So, too, was his political education, which began in the late 1920s and early 1930s, when he was attached to the office of the assistant secretary of war and charged with drafting plans for industrial mobilization in time of war, and which continued through nearly a decade of sometimes stormy service with General Douglas A. MacArthur. It was from the military itself, however, that Eisenhower absorbed the principal elements of his education: a respect for the efficiencies of organization, a contempt for politics and politicians, a distrust of popular democracy and of the masses whose "class fears and prejudices are easily aroused," and, finally, a strong commitment to duty and to the ideal of disinter-ested public service.[2]

These patterns of thought, widely shared among professional military men during the interwar years, were reinforced and deepened by the experience of command during the Second World War and by his service as army chief of staff immediately thereafter. He was especially alarmed by the strikes, inflation, and bitter partisan politics that characterized the postwar years. Nevertheless, as a

---

These historians nevertheless share a willingness to treat Eisenhower seriously and to see in the Eisenhower presidency an important subject for historical investigation. This essay becomes possible, at least in part, as a result of their efforts.

[2] Eisenhower, *At Ease: Stories I Tell to Friends* (Garden City, N.Y., 1967), 3–26, 185–87, 196–232, and "War Policies," *Infantry Journal*, 38 (1931): 489–93; and Peter Lyon, *Eisenhower: Portrait of the Hero* (Boston, 1974), 56–80. On military thought during the interwar years, especially see Morris Janowitz, *The Professional Soldier: A Social and Political Portrait* (New York, 1960), 233–56.

professional soldier, he refrained from political utterances. He did not register a party affiliation nor did he vote in presidential elections. He later confessed that, if he had voted, he would have voted Republican in 1932, 1936, and 1940 but Democratic in 1944, because of the war.[3] Not until 1948, when he left the army to assume the presidency of Columbia University, did he begin to express his views in letters and speeches. Although he still had neither the time nor the inclination for wide reading or systematic reflection, the pattern of thought that emerged during these years nevertheless suggests a fairly coherent social philosophy.

AT THE HEART OF EISENHOWER'S THINKING was a struggle to reconcile and resolve the most fundamental conflicts of modern society. Industrialization, mass production and distribution, and the growth of urban populations had, he believed, all combined to create a complex, interdependent social system—a system that possessed the potential for the production of great wealth and material abundance but that was also precariously vulnerable to destruction through the selfish antagonisms of class conflict. In the nineteenth century, as he traced America's recent past, the power of "concentrated wealth" had become "a menace to the self-respect, opportunities, and livelihood of great groups of ordinary citizens" and had "compelled drastic action for the preservation of the laborer's dignity—for the welfare of himself and his family." Although the legislative reforms of the Progressive and New Deal eras had, in his view, largely ameliorated such dangers, the threat of class conflict remained. The single most important source of "all our problems," he wrote a prominent business leader in early 1952, was the disunity born of "the great chasms separating economic groupings." Not only did capital, labor, agriculture, and other interests contend among themselves, but each also sought to bend public policy to its own selfish ends: "such divisions, even though economic in origin, inevitably become so clearly reflected in political organization and doctrine that they damage both our political and economic structures, thus enlarging and perpetuating initial effects." In his diary, he posed the question in terms of Lenin's analysis of the contradictions within capitalism and of the conflict between capital and labor, between antagonistic capitalistic states, and between

[3] Interview with Merriman Smith, November 23, 1954, Dwight D. Eisenhower Library, Abilene, Kans. [hereafter, DDEL], Dwight D. Eisenhower Papers as President of the United States (Ann Whitman File) [hereafter EPP], DDE Diaries series, box 3. The Ann Whitman File, a file maintained by Eisenhower's private secretary, contains some 265,000 documents that received the president's closest attention. It includes diary entries by and occasionally by Ann Whitman, correspondence between Eisenhower and members of his administration, close friends, and advisers, minutes of his meetings with the cabinet, legislative leaders, and national security advisers, notes and memoranda on other meetings in the Oval Office (some of which were recorded and later transcribed by Whitman), summaries of telephone conversations (which Whitman frequently monitored), and records of the president's pre–press conference briefings. Although most of the materials in this file cover the years 1953–61, there are scattered documents dated earlier and later. The Whitman file, of course, is augmented by the far larger collection of materials housed in other files, including Eisenhower's Pre-Presidential Papers [hereafter, EP], the White House Central Files, which total some six million pages, and the private papers of members of his administration, friends, and advisers. Eisenhower's correspondence during the war years, the occupation, and his tenure as army chief of staff appear in *The Papers of Dwight David Eisenhower* [hereafter, *Eisenhower Papers*], 9 vols. (Baltimore, 1970–). Numerous Eisenhower diary entries, drawn from both the Whitman file and other collections, have also recently been published; see Robert H. Ferrell, ed., *The Eisenhower Diaries* (New York, 1981).

capitalist and underdeveloped nations. Although he did not accept the inevitability of such conflicts, he did recognize that "the principal contradiction in the whole system comes about because of the inability of men to forego immediate gain for a long time good," and he worried that "we do not yet have a sufficient number of people who are ready to make the immediate sacrifice in favor of a long-term investment."[4]

Modern organization proved an especially difficult dilemma for Eisenhower. He extolled the new forms of corporate organization, the purpose of which, as he saw it, was "to produce orderliness, which means restriction upon irresponsible human action," but he feared that organization also posed grave dangers for traditional economic and political liberties. If organization was necessary for the orderly conduct of human affairs, it was nevertheless "difficult to define the exact line of demarcation between rules of conduct on the one hand, and unjustifiable seizure of power on the other." Even more threatening was the prospect that organized interests—"pressure groups," he usually called them—would impose their narrow ends upon the state or that the state itself would become little more than a battleground for class conflict. As he told a Columbia University audience in 1948, "danger arises from too great a concentration of power in the hands of any individual or group: The power of concentrated finance, the power of selfish pressure groups, the power of any class organized in opposition to the whole—any one of these, when allowed to dominate is fully capable of destroying individual freedom."[5]

For Eisenhower, as for other postwar conservatives, the dangers of such politicized conflict were all too readily apparent. Indeed, the Democratic party of the New and Fair Deals, built through appeals to selfish class interest, seemed to embody all of the most threatening tendencies of American democracy. In his inaugural address as president of Columbia in 1948, Eisenhower decried "demogogic appeals to class selfishness, greed, and hate" and warned against what he called "a regimented statism." Six months later, in a commencement address, he attacked "pressure groups" and politicians who appealed "to all that was selfish in humankind." Speaking to the American Bar Association in September 1949—an address to which he returned in later years as the touchstone of his political philosophy—he denounced Marxian concepts of class conflict and called for the defense of freedom from "the unbearable selfishness of vested interest" and from "the blindness of those who, protesting devotion to the public welfare, falsely declare that only government can bring us happiness, security and opportunity."[6]

Eisenhower nevertheless believed that the clash of classes was neither necessary

---

[4] Eisenhower to William E. Robinson, February 12, 1952, DDEL, Robinson Papers, box 2; Speech to the American Bar Association, September 5, 1949, DDEL, EPP, Speech series, box 3; and Eisenhower to George A. Sloan, March 1, 1952, in Robert L. Branyon and Lawrence H. Larson, eds., *The Eisenhower Administration: A Documentary History*, 2 vols. (New York, 1971), 1: 23–26. For Eisenhower's discussion of the contradictions of capitalism, see *Eisenhower Diaries* (July 2, 1953), 242–45.

[5] Eisenhower to Robinson, February 12, 1952; and Inaugural Address, Columbia University, October 12, 1948, DDEL, EPP, Speech series, box 1.

[6] Inaugural Address, October 12, 1948; Commencement Address, Columbia University, June 1, 1949, DDEL, EPP, Speech series, box 1; Speech to the American Bar Association, September 5, 1949; and Eisenhower to George Whitney, September 4, 1951, DDEL, EP, box 115.

nor inexorable. Indeed, the great lesson of the twentieth century was, for him at least, the interdependence of class interests, not their irreconcilability. "In our tightly knit economy, all professions and callings—no matter how widely separated they may be in purpose and technique—all have points of contact and areas of common interest," he declared in 1947. "Banker or housewife, farmer, carpenter, soldier—no one of us can live and act without effect on all the others." In early 1952 he suggested to businessman George Sloan "that agriculture, labor, management and capital frequently speak of themselves as if each were a separate and self-sufficient enterprise or community. Yet the simple fact is that each is helpless without the others; only as an effective member of an integrated team can any one of them prosper." Maximum production was possible "only when management, labor and capital work in harmony . . . ; no prosperity for one economic group is permanently possible except as all groups prosper."[7] Drawing heavily, though perhaps unconsciously, on the social thought of Herbert Hoover, Eisenhower repeatedly called for voluntary cooperation among America's diverse economic interests. Competition and self-interest, he insisted, must be "accompanied by a readiness to cooperate wholeheartedly for the performance of community and national functions." Indeed, the secret of American success in World War II, he declared on another occasion, was that "Americans welded into a cooperative unit the enterprise, initiative, spirit and will of many million free men and women." As William E. Robinson, a close friend, noted in 1948, Eisenhower believed not in "rugged individualism in the old-fashioned Republican sense of the word" but in "freedom and independence for the individual with its collateral responsibility for cooperation."[8] At Columbia, one of his proudest achievements was the creation of the American Assembly, in which he hoped the leaders of business, labor, government, and the professions would meet to study and plan cooperatively for the future. "We must find a way," he told the American Academy of Political Science in 1950, "to bring big business, labor, professions and government officials together with . . . experts and . . . study and work out these problems in the calmness of a nonpartisan . . . atmosphere."[9]

From his fears of class conflict and from his vision of a mutually cooperative, voluntarist society came Eisenhower's commitment to what he called "the middle way," a phrase that dominated almost all of his thinking after 1948. The "middle way" was not just a political platitude but rather signified his struggle to resolve the fundamental tensions of the modern state. The term defined not only a political position—between capital and labor, between entrepreneurial liberalism and socialism, between the Republican Right and the Democratic Left—but also a series of programmatic commitments and a style of leadership. Initially, the "middle way"

---

[7] Eisenhower, "Citizenship Responsibility in Relation to National Security," May 27, 1947, Harry S. Truman Library, Independence, Mo. [hereafter, HSTL], Paul G. Hoffman Papers, box 26; and Eisenhower to Sloan, March 1, 1952.

[8] Inaugural Address, October 12, 1948; Speech to the American Bar Association, September 5, 1949; Commencement Address, June 1, 1949; Robinson to Helen Rogers Reid, June 21, 1948, DDEL, Robinson Papers, box 9.

[9] Speech to the American Academy of Political Science, April 26, 1950, *Proceedings of the American Academy of Political Science*, 24 (1950): 144–47; and Eisenhower to Adolphus Andrews, Jr., September 29, 1950, DDEL, EP, box 15; and Eisenhower to Edward J. Bermingham, September 29, 1950, *ibid.*, box 4.

entailed arresting the momentum of New Deal liberalism and ensuring, as he wrote a prominent business supporter, that "our economy . . . remain, to the greatest possible extent, in private hands." In his diary, and in conversations and correspondence with friends, he worried about the dangerous "drift toward statism," a trend that, he declared, "must be halted in its tracks."[10] Yet he was also cautious enough and realistic enough to realize that this could not be done abruptly. He agreed with former president Hoover, who warned him in early 1953 that it would be impossible to accomplish a dramatic reversal and that the best that the new administration could hope to achieve would be a gradual "flattening of the curve of this particular trend." He believed, moreover, that at least some forms of state action were not only expedient but necessary. Government must, he argued, "prevent or correct abuses springing from the unregulated practice of a private economy" and must provide laws "necessary to an orderly and a measurably free life." The complexities of modern economic life "require the application to all of us of commonly agreed-upon rules and regulations in order that the accidents of mass production will not defeat or destroy the right of the individual to political and economic freedom."[11] More importantly, he believed that government should actively promote social harmony and encourage those mutually beneficial, voluntary, and cooperative activities that lay at the center of his vision of the good society; the essence of citizenship entailed "blend[ing], without coercion, the individual good and the common good." Above all, he told the American Bar Association, "we need more economic understanding and working arrangements that will bind labor and management . . . into a far tighter voluntary cooperative unit than we now have." The task of leadership, he wrote, was to bring "diversities together in a common purpose."[12]

The greatest obstacle to this corporatist commonwealth, in Eisenhower's view, was politics, a word he almost always used pejoratively to signify the selfish actions of special interests and classes. "Pressure groups," he warned a Columbia audience, "often pretend to a moral purpose that examination proves to be false. The vote-seeker rarely hesitates to appeal to all that is selfish in humankind." "When politicians begin to talk about *issues*," he wrote a friend, "they are often talking about those things on which they feel it expedient to make extravagant promises to various pressure groups." He distrusted popular opinion, which he believed was both uninformed and short-sighted, and he complained to friends that congressmen were oversensitive "to even transitory resentments in their several districts." The political game, he wrote his brother Edgar, was "a combination of gossip, innuendo, sly character assassination, and outright lies" in which "the demagogue tries to develop a saleable list of items to hold before the public." Disturbed by the bitter rhetoric of the 1948 election, with its fiery appeals to class interest, he

[10] *Eisenhower Diaries* (January 14, 1949), 153–54; Eisenhower to Everett E. Hazlett, Jr., February 24, 1950, and November 14, 1951, DDEL, EPP, Name series, box 17; William E. Robinson to Bruce Barton, December 13, 1949, DDEL, Robinson Papers, box 1; and Eisenhower to Sloan, March 1, 1952.

[11] *Eisenhower Diaries* (June 22, 1959), 364–65; Speech to the American Bar Association, September 5, 1949; Eisenhower to Robinson, February 12, 1952; and Eisenhower to Sloan, March 1, 1952.

[12] Inaugural Address October 12, 1948; Speech to the American Bar Association, September 5, 1949; Commencement Address, June 1, 1949; and Eisenhower to William Phillips, June 5, 1953, DDEL, EPP, Name series, box 25.

confided to his diary the wish that both Democrats and Republicans would embrace the middle of the road and "choose some issues outside the nation's economy on which to fight out elections."[13]

Eisenhower believed that the inevitable conflicts produced by the short-sighted and self-interested actions of classes and interest groups could be resolved only through the leadership of public-spirited and professionally skilled managers such as himself, who could exercise the disinterested judgment necessary to avoid calamities such as war or depression and achieve long-range goals such as peace and high productivity. The task of such leadership was to quell the passion of the masses, to encourage self-discipline on the part of business, labor, and agriculture, and to promote the pursuit of long-term, enlightened self-interest rather than immediate gain. "To induce people to do more," he wrote his close friend and former aide General Alfred M. Gruenther in May 1953, "leadership has the chore of informing people and attempting to inspire them to real sacrifice." Both at home and abroad people had to be prepared to endure hardship and discipline. The real question, as he wrote to a prominent Wall Street banker, was "whether national leaders here and abroad have the courage and strength to stand up and tell the truth and to keep repeating the truth regardless of vilification and abuse, until people at large will accept and act upon the clear facts."[14]

Eisenhower's commitment to social harmony, self-discipline, limited government, and a depoliticized, administrative state all dictated, in turn, an approach to leadership that stressed restraint, patience, moderation, and flexibility. "I am convinced," he wrote his friend Everett ("Swede") Hazlett in 1952, "that leadership in the political as well as in other spheres consists largely in making progress through compromise." He deplored "the table-pounding, name-calling methods that columnists so much love," not so much because he feared "a good fight" but because he thought that "such methods are normally futile." In a letter to a friend, he praised Lincoln as "the greatest compromiser and astute master of expediency that we have known" and confessed that he, too, was "a bit on the pragmatic side by inclination."[15] His belief in the mediatory role of government and his fear of popular politics was also reflected in his intense concern with public relations, which he saw not just as a means of political or personal aggrandizement but as a technique for defusing political conflict, limiting the role of the state, engineering support for administrative decisions, and forging consensus. He told the leaders of the Advertising Council in early 1953 that "the only way to avoid centralized domination" was "through an increased readiness to cooperate in the solution of group problems. As problems become more complex, we must find new ways to achieve cooperation—new mechanisms for discovering our problems and getting them

[13] Commencement Address, June 1, 1949; Eisenhower to Paul G. Hoffman, February 9, 1952, HSTL, Hoffman Papers, box 26; Eisenhower to Clarence Dillon, January 8, 1953, DDEL, EPP, Name series, box 7; Eisenhower to Edgar Eisenhower, January 27, 1954, DDEL, EPP, DDE Diaries series, box 3; and *Eisenhower Diaries* (July 7, 1949), 162. Also see Eisenhower to George A. Sloan, January 29, 1952, DDEL, EP, box 100; and Eisenhower to Bradford C. Chynoweth, July 20, 1954, DDEL, EPP, DDE Diaries series, box 3.

[14] Eisenhower to Gruenther, May 4, 1953, DDEL, EPP, DDE Diaries series, box 3; and Eisenhower to Dillon, January 8, 1953.

[15] Eisenhower to Hazlett, October 16, 1952, DDEL, EPP, Name series, box 17; Eisenhower to Phillips, June 5, 1953; and Eisenhower to Chynoweth, July 20, 1954.

over to the American people." The Advertising Council, whose conservative messages were carried annually in hundreds of thousands of so-called public service advertisements, was just such a mechanism, Eisenhower declared, "one of our great agencies for the preservation of freedom."[16]

Eisenhower's belief in an American commonwealth was paralleled by a Wilsonian faith in a world order through which, as he told a London Guildhall audience in 1945, "all nations can enjoy the fruitfulness of the earth." Like most other Wilsonians, he accompanied this idealistic vision with a fairly hard-headed grasp of America's postwar needs. Foreign policy, he wrote a friend in late 1951, should be based primarily on "the need for the United States to obtain certain raw materials to sustain its economy, and, when possible, to preserve profitable foreign markets for our surpluses." There is, he wrote John Foster Dulles in 1953, a "direct connection between a prosperous and happy America and the execution of an intelligent foreign policy." Like other prominent American leaders, he feared communism not only as a military menace but also as an economic threat that would close off to America "the great industrial complex of Western Europe" and the raw material–producing nations of Africa and Asia. "Where [then] would we get the materials needed for our existence," he asked a friend in 1951. Here too, he wrote in his diary in the summer of 1953, America confronted what Marxists called the "contradictions of capitalism," both the conflict among "capitalist states for the domination of the world's surface" and the conflict "between the advanced, industrialized nations of the world and the dependent masses of backward peoples." Here too, in Eisenhower's view, the conflict, though real, was necessary and inexorable *only* if nations could not abandon their immediate selfish interests for mutual cooperation As in domestic affairs he believed that politics was principally the expression of selfish interests and that the task of leadership was "to bring men and nations to the point where they will give to the long-term promise the same value that they give to immediate and individual gains." If we could resolve the issues of world trade and cooperation on the basis of the "long-term good of all," he concluded, "we could laugh at the other so-called 'contradictions' in

---

[16] Leo Burnett, "Cherry Blossom Time in Washington: An Informal Report on the 'Ninth White House Conference,' " March 23–24, 1953, DDEL, James M. Lambie, Jr., Records, box 1. For an extensive discussion of the Advertising Council, see Robert Griffith, "The Selling of America: The Advertising Council and American Politics, 1945–1960," paper presented at the Forty-Sixth Annual Meeting of the Organization of American Historians, held in Detroit, April 10–12, 1981.

As Supreme Commander during World War II and later as army chief of staff Eisenhower had repeatedly lectured his subordinates on the importance of good public relations. His job as president of Columbia was also, he believed, in large measure one of public relations. He was himself, by virtually every account, a master of the art, including the skillful and highly self-conscious management of his own image. When he began his campaign for the presidency, he drew about him not only prominent figures from banking and industry but also men and women from advertising, publishing, and public relations. He made more use of professional advertising and public relations in that campaign than any previous candidate in American history. "After watching Ike deal with the press, I don't think he needs a public-relations advisor," wrote Harry C. Butcher, who during World War II served as a public relations aide to Eisenhower; Butcher, *My Three Years with Eisenhower* (New York, 1946), 20. Also see Robinson to John S. D. Eisenhower, November 22, 1954, DDEL, EPP, Name series, box 29. Among Eisenhower's close political advisors were William E. Robinson (an advertising and sales executive at the New York *Herald Tribune*, who later headed his own public relations firm and still later served as president of Coca Cola), Sigurd S. Larmon (president of the large Young & Rubicam Advertising Agency, which handled, among other accounts, Citizens for Eisenhower during the primary campaign), and Paul G. Hoffman (who had risen

our system, and . . . be so secure against the Communist menace that it would gradually dry up and wither away."[17]

Like most prominent internationalists, Eisenhower generally supported the foreign and military policies of the Truman administration, yet here, too, his thinking was characterized by balance, moderation, and concern for long-term consequences. Thus, in endorsing the diplomacy of containment, he nevertheless remained more pacific than most of his military and civilian contemporaries. America must not seek "to preserve order in the sense of the Roman Peace, where one nation, due to its dominant position in the world, rules all others," he warned newspaper columnist Dorothy Thompson. To his father-in-law, he wrote, "We are traveling a long and rocky road toward a satisfactory world order but the big thing is that we never give up for an instant. No war can be anything else but a grave setback to such progress. The one thing that disturbs me is the readiness of people to discuss war as a means of advancing peace. To me this is a contradiction in terms." Eisenhower did not share the feeling of vulnerability that pervaded so much of the military during the early postwar era. "It is a grievous error to forget for one second the might and power of this great Republic," he cautioned Walter Bedell Smith in late 1947. He believed that both Soviet power and intent were limited and that in dealing with the Russians the United States ought to employ "patience, tolerance and a spirit of understanding." Following the Berlin blockade and Korea, he adopted a more hardline attitude toward the Russians, but he refused even then to be stampeded by those who believed that Armageddon was just around the corner.[18]

He believed in military preparedness, but only in moderation. As army chief of staff he had worked on behalf of military unification and universal military training and had attempted, without success, to restrain the abrupt contraction of defense budgets that followed the end of the war. He nevertheless believed that resources were limited and that armed forces were, as he put it, "nonproductive, sterile organizations whose purposes are, at the best, largely negative." By early 1952, following the rapid military expansion that accompanied the Korean War, he

through sales and advertising to head Studebaker, had been a founder of the Committee for Economic Development, had served as an administrator of the Marshall Plan under Truman, and was then President of the Ford Foundation). On the role of advertising and public relations in the 1952 campaign, especially see Stanley Kelley, Jr., *Professional Public Relations and Political Power* (Baltimore, 1956), chaps. 4–5; and Melvyn H. Bloom, *Public Relations and Presidential Campaigns: A Crisis in Democracy* (New York, 1973), chap. 3. These studies, if anything, understate the pervasiveness of professional advertising and public relations in the campaign, during the course of which Eisenhower employed—in one capacity or another—Young & Rubicam, Batten, Barton, Durstine and Osborn, the Kudner Agency, Ted Bates and Company, McCann Erickson, the Gallup Poll, and the Nielson rating service. His campaign, moreover, attracted the talents of many corporate advertising and public relations executives, including Charles F. Moore, Jr., of the Ford Motor Company and Abbott M. Washburn of General Mills.
[17] Eisenhower, "I Am Now a Londoner," Speech of June 12, 1945, DDEL, EPP, Speech series, box 3; Kevin McCann, ed., *Eisenhower's Creed* (New York, 1952), 12; Eisenhower to John Foster Dulles, November 16, 1953, DDEL, EPP, DDE Diaries series, box 3; Eisenhower to Edward J. Bermingham, February 28, 1951, DDEL, Robinson Papers, box 1; and *Eisenhower Diaries* (July 2, 1953), 242–45. Also see Eisenhower to M. W. Clement, January 9, 1952, DDEL, EP, box 24.
[18] Eisenhower to Thompson, June 25, 1946, in *Eisenhower Papers*, 7: 1149–50; Eisenhower to John Sheldon Doud, August 23, 1946, *ibid.*, 8: 1249–50; and Eisenhower to Smith, November 28, 1947, *ibid.*, 2084–85.

was worried over the expenditure of "unconscionable sums" for an indefinite duration. As in foreign and domestic affairs, concern for the enduring integrity of the system was the controlling issue. Every expenditure, he insisted, "must be weighed and gauged in the light of probable long-term *internal* effect."[19] Here again, however, selfish interests often threatened the collective good. The danger arose not just from the short-sighted partisanship of congressional budget-cutters but oftentimes from the service bureaucracies themselves. During World War II and again during the battles over unification and joint strategic planning, Eisenhower struggled to strike a balance among the competing claims of the services, and his letters and diaries are filled with angry denunciations of military self-interest. Here too, reconciliation of conflict and pursuit of the national interest rested with disinterested professional leadership and with the self-discipline and commitment to long-term goals of competing parties.[20]

For Eisenhower, then, the corporate commonwealth was not just a series of vague generalities, but a broad, internally consistent, social philosophy that brought together an interpretation of America's recent past, a vision of the good society both at home and abroad, and a style of leadership through which such an order might be obtained.

EISENHOWER'S VISION OF A CORPORATE COMMONWEALTH did not, of course, originate with him. Indeed, variations of this concept—with its emphasis on organization, cooperation, and social harmony—go back at least to the Progressive era and the National Civic Federation, to the businessmen such as Bernard M. Baruch and Gerard Swope who served on the War Industries Board during the First World War, to Herbert Hoover and his advocacy of the "associative state," to Edward Filene, Henry S. Dennison, and other apostles of welfare capitalism in the 1920s, and to the big businessmen who during the New Deal joined the Department of Commerce's Business Advisory Council (BAC) and helped shape the structure and operation of the National Recovery Adminstration. Common to all of these activities was an attempt to fashion a new corporative economy that would avoid both the destructive disorder of unregulated capitalism and the threat to business autonomy posed by socialism.[21]

---

[19] Eisenhower to Eric Larrabee, March 25, 1947, in *Eisenhower Papers*, 8: 1631; and *Eisenhower Diaries* (January 22, 1952), 209–13. Also see Eisenhower to M. W. Clement, December 4, 1951, DDEL, EP, box 24.

[20] *Eisenhower Diaries* (July 24, 1947), 142; *ibid.* (January 8, 1949), 152; *ibid.* (January 27, 1949), 154–55; and Eisenhower to Everett Hazlett, April 7, 1949, and February 24, 1950, DDEL, EPP, Name series, box 1. "There are few people outside the Armed Services and the higher echelons of the State Department that are giving their full attention to American interests as a whole and refusing to color their conclusions and convictions with the interests of party politics," he wrote Walter Bedell Smith in late 1947. "I should like to be numbered among this disinterested group." Eisenhower to Smith, September 18, 1947, in *Eisenhower Papers*, 9: 1933–34.

[21] Ellis W. Hawley has defined a "corporative system" as "one whose basic units consist of officially recognized, non-competitive, role-ordered occupational or functional groupings . . . , one with coordinating machinery designed to integrate these units into an interdependent whole and one where the state properly functions as coordinator, assistant, and midwife rather than director or regulator. In such a system there are deep interpenetrations between state and society, and enjoying a special status is an enlightened social elite, capable of perceiving social needs and imperatives and assisting social groups to meet them

In spite of their considerable power and prestige, "corporate liberals" remained a minority voice in national politics and even within the business community itself. By the mid-1930s, moreover, the depression and the sometime radicalism of the New Deal had disrupted their attempts to forge an alliance between business and government. After 1934 all but a handful of business leaders abandoned efforts at collaboration with the Roosevelt adminstration, while the president, in turn, now excoriated the "economic royalists." World War II, however, served to reinvigorate corporate liberalism. Mobilization brought thousands of executives into government, effectively dampened New Deal criticism, and created, at least temporarily, the kind of partnership between business and government that corporate liberals had long extolled. In addition, the wartime revival of corporate liberalism gave birth to important new organizations, such as the Committee for Economic Development (CED) and the Advertising Council.[22]

The relationship of corporate liberals to the Roosevelt and Truman adminstrations, however, remained uneasy. On the one hand, they welcomed cooperation between business and government and recognized that the state could serve as a powerful positive instrument for moderating economic conflict, regulating domestic markets, promoting international trade, and sustaining economic growth. On the other, they feared that the popularity of the New Deal and the power of its progressive constituencies might lead, piecemeal, to a semisocialist state whose fiscal and regulatory policies would ultimately destroy private enterprise. As William Benton, one of the founders of the Committee for Economic Development, wrote in 1944, the leaders of government ought to "rid the economy of injurious or unnecessary regulation, as well as adminstration that is hostile or harmful," and pursue "constructive fiscal, monetary and other policies that provide a climate in which a private enterprise system can flourish." Businessmen, for their part, he continued, must learn to cooperate with government in the exercise of

---

through enlightened concerts of interests." Hawley, "The Discovery and Study of a 'Corporate Liberalism,' " *Business History Review*, 52 (1978): 309–20. On the National Civic Federation, see James Weinstein, *The Corporate Ideal in the Liberal State* (Boston, 1968); for Hoover, see Hoover, *American Individualism* (New York, 1922); Joan Hoff Wilson, *Herbert Hoover: Forgotten Progressive* (Boston, 1975); and especially Ellis W. Hawley, "Herbert Hoover, the Commerce Secretariat, and the Vision of an 'Associative State,' " *Journal of American History*, 61 (1974–75): 116–40; on welfare capitalism, see Stuart D. Brandes, *American Welfare Capitalism, 1880–1940* (Chicago, 1976); and, on the Business Advisory Council, see Kim McQuaid, "Corporate Liberalism in the American Business Community, 1920–1940," *Business History Review*, 52 (1978): 342–67. Historians have used the term "corporate liberalism" to describe both the historical *process* through which liberal institutions have been adapted to the imperatives of large-scale organization and the *ideology* that has been used to promote and legitimate such a process. "Corporate liberals" have differed sharply among themselves on such important questions as the extent of state intervention, and historians have used the label to describe a fairly broad range of political behavior. Eisenhower's emphasis on voluntarism and cooperation most closely resembled the thought of Herbert Hoover. The history of corporate liberalism in America invites comparison and contrast with corporatist process and ideology outside the United States; see Matthew H. Elbow, *French Corporate Theory, 1789–1948* (New York, 1953); Ralph Bowen, *German Theories of the Corporative State* (New York, 1947); Samuel H. Beer, *British Politics in the Collectivist Age* (New York, 1965); Nigel Harris, *Competition and the Corporate Society* (London, 1972); Frederick B. Pike and Thomas Stritch, eds., *The New Corporatism: Social-Political Structures in the Iberian World* (South Bend, Ind., 1974); and especially Charles S. Maier, *Recasting Bourgeois Europe: Stabilization in France, Germany, and Italy in the Decade after World War I* (Princeton, 1975).

[22] Robert M. Collins, *The Business Response to Keynes, 1929–1964* (New York, 1981); and Griffith, "The Selling of America."

those powers that had become clearly necessary in a modern economy and display a "high degree of imagination, goodwill and inventiveness" in order to work out "improved rules of the game." If business failed to plan for the postwar, warned Paul G. Hoffman, another CED founder, "the Government will be forced to step in, and collectivism will come to postwar America—by default rather than design." "We must plan carefully and strike hard," one of Hoffman's business correspondents bluntly wrote. "Otherwise the new dealers will plan for all of us."[23] The strategic problem faced by corporate liberals in the postwar era was, thus, how to obtain the benefits of state intervention, while avoiding its dangers. Their immediate, tactical problem was how to win political power in an era still dominated by the passionate and well-remembered struggles of the 1930s. Not surprisingly, they quickly discovered in Eisenhower the solution to both dilemmas. As a widely admired war hero, he was pre-eminently electable. More importantly, as they were soon to discover, his political and economic views in many ways closely approximated their own.

No single generalization covers all the men and women who rallied about Eisenhower in the late 1940s, but the great majority of them were corporate liberals for whom the goals of cooperation and consensus were paramount, who saw in the New Deal a potentially dangerous threat to corporate enterprise, and who sought to refashion the federal state to their own needs. Some were progressive manufacturers such as Hoffman of Studebaker, Thomas J. Watson of I.B.M., Philip D. Reed of General Electric, and Harry A. Bullis of General Mills. Others, such as Clifford Roberts and John Hay Whitney, represented the financial community. Still others—William E. Robinson, Douglas M. Black, Eugene Meyer, and the Ogden Reid family—were in what might loosely be called "cultural production"—journalism, publishing, advertising, and public relations. Almost all were associated with the "internationalist" wing of the Republican party and frequently held membership in such groups as the Business Advisory Council, the Committee for Economic Development, the Advertising Council, and the Council on Foreign Relations.[24] Most of them would have agreed with William Robinson, who wrote Eisenhower in 1951 that the managerial revolution had created in America a new form of economic democracy in which management acted as "a referee between the three major elements in our economy—the customer, the worker and the capitalist"—or with Edward J. Bermingham, who insisted that "capitalism" was an inadequate description for the American economy, which was "an overall system of individual endeavor profitable to management, labor, and ownership, with vast numbers of labor among the stockholders and thus having ownership in their business." They shared Eisenhower's concern over "the insidious

---

[23] Benton, "The Economics of a Free Society," *Fortune*, October 1944, pp. 163–65; and Hoffman, as quoted in *The Republican*, April 1943, p. 1. Also see Hoffman, Speech to the Advertising Federation of America, June 30, 1943, HSTL, Hoffman Papers, box 104; and Lou Holland to Hoffman, March 20, 1943, HSTL, Lou Holland Papers, box 163.

[24] Herbert S. Parmet, *Eisenhower and the American Crusades* (New York, 1972), 33–34; Lyon, *Eisenhower: Portrait of the Hero*, 373–410; Ellis D. Slater, *The Ike I Knew* (New York, 1980), 3–27; and Clifford Roberts, *The Story of the Augusta National Golf Club* (Garden City, N.Y., 1976), 112–32.

inclination toward statism" and enthusiastically endorsed his call for "middle-of-the-road" government.[25]

These influential business and political leaders were convinced, out of both ideology and expedience, that the election of Eisenhower was a necessity. On the one hand, they greatly feared the implications of continued Democratic rule; on the other, they distrusted the views of Republican Senator Robert A. Taft of Ohio, especially on foreign policy. More importantly, they were certain he could not win. As Eisenhower later recalled in a letter to his brother Edgar,

> In 1948, '49, '50, '51 and early '52, many hundreds of people were urging me to go into politics. Scores of different reasons were advanced as to why I should do so, but in general they all boiled down to something as follows: "The country is going socialistic so rapidly that, unless Republicans can get in immediately and defeat this trend, our country is gone. Four more years of New Dealism and there will be no turning back. This is our last chance."[26]

No one put it more bluntly than Thomas E. Dewey, who in 1949 told Eisenhower that only he could "save this country from going to Hades in the handbasket of paternalism-socialism-dictatorship." The problem, declared the twice-defeated presidential aspirant, was that, although "all middle-class citizens of education have a common belief that tendencies toward centralization and paternalism must be halted and reversed, no one who voices these views can be elected." This meant, Dewey continued, that "we must look around for someone of great popularity and who has not frittered away his political assets by taking positive stands against national planning, etc., etc. Elect such a man to the Presidency, *after which* he must lead us back to safe channels and paths."[27]

The support of business men such as Robinson and Hoffman, publishers such as Helen Rogers Reid and Henry Luce, and politicians such as Dewey and Henry Cabot Lodge became absolutely critical to the Eisenhower campaign. These men and women not only convinced Eisenhower that he had a duty to run for the presidency but also reinforced his views on political economy, marshalled enormous financial and editorial support for his candidacy, and managed to force his nomination upon the reluctant regulars of the Republican party. Taft was more correct than not when he bitterly complained in the wake of the Republican convention that Eisenhower had been installed by "the power of the New York financial interests and a large number of businessmen subject to New York

[25] See, for example, Robinson to Eisenhower, March 4, 1949, September 6, 1949, and March 13, 1951, DDEL, Robinson Papers, box 1; Robinson to Reid, March 2, 1947, *ibid.*; Horace C. Flanigan to Robinson, February 18, 1948, *ibid.*; Clarence Budington Kelland to Robinson, September 1949, *ibid.*; Clifford Roberts, Memo, January 1950, *ibid.*; Edward J. Bermingham to Eisenhower, March 14, 1951, as cited in Lyon, *Eisenhower: Portrait of the Hero*, 397; Paul G. Hoffman to Eisenhower, December 5, 1951, HSTL, Hoffman Papers, box 26; and George Whitney to Eisenhower, January 16, 1952, DDEL, EP, box 115.

[26] Eisenhower to Edgar Eisenhower, May 2, 1956, DDEL, EPP, DDE Diaries series, box 9. Clarence Dillon wrote that Eisenhower was "the one best hope for the salvation of Western Civilization as we know it"; Dillon, as quoted in Robinson to Eisenhower, December 21, 1950, DDEL, Robinson Papers, box 11. Clifford Roberts urged Eisenhower to help arrest "the current trend of socialism and the serious threats to our liberty"; Roberts, Memo, January 1950. And, according to Paul Hoffman, only Eisenhower could "redeem the Republican Party"; Hoffman to Eisenhower, December 5, 1951. Also see *Eisenhower Diaries* (October 1949–February 1952), 165–205 *passim.*

[27] *Eisenhower Diaries* (July 7, 1949), 161–62 (italics in original MS). Clare Booth Luce told Eisenhower approximately the same thing; *Eisenhower Diaries* (September 27, 1949), 163.

influence" and by the nation's great newspaper, many of which "turned themselves into propaganda sheets."[28] The concept of a corporate commonwealth was, then, not just an exercise in political platitude but an ideology that rationalized a critically important development in American economic life and mobilized a powerful constituency behind the election of Eisenhower as president of the United States.

THE VISION OF A CORPORATE COMMONWEALTH, which was the touchstone of Eisenhower's political philosophy and which drew to his support so many progressive capitalists, also shaped the policies and politics of his administration. As president, Eisenhower sought to create a noncoercive, self-disciplined, and harmonious corporate society by limiting the New Deal state, forging cooperative relations between business and government, promoting social harmony and consensus at home, and maintaining a stable and Western-oriented international order abroad. These efforts represented a serious, in many ways even sophisticated, attempt to escape the dilemmas created by modern economic organization. They also revealed the sharp limitations of such an ideology, its class bias, and its profoundly antidemocratic character.

Eisenhower believed that the federal state posed a dangerous threat to economic liberties, and he was determined to arrest the growth of government and slowly but firmly to "bend the curve" away from public enterprise. He lifted wage-price controls, initiated new policies to prevent government competition with business, reduced the federal budget and lowered taxes on industry and capital. He signed legislation turning over oil-rich "submerged lands" to the states and strongly supported deregulation of natural gas. He withdrew federal opposition to private hydroelectric development in Idaho and California and sought to prevent further expansion of the Tennessee Valley Authority. In the critical new field of nuclear energy, he sponsored legislation that ended exclusive federal control of development.[29]

Eisenhower was not, however, a conservative ideologue, intent on returning the

---

[28] Taft, Memorandum on the 1952 Campaign, Library of Congress, Robert A. Taft Papers, box 1349. "It is hard for me to understand the attitudes of the businessmen, bankers and editors who seem to be determined to defeat any real Republican administration," wrote a bitter Taft shortly after his defeat; Taft to Hugh Butler, August 8, 1952, State Historical Society of Nebraska, Lincoln, Hugh A. Butler Papers, box 363. Taft was only partially correct, according to William Robinson, who later recalled that "Wall Street was about 3-to-1 in *his* corner." Taft was, however, "right about the newspapers. But what he didn't know was that some of us had been building up 'cells' of Eisenhower interest and enthusiasm among editors and publishers in every nook and corner of the country since about 1947. It is not strange that the Senator would not have known about this, since only a handful of people was even aware of it." Robinson to Eisenhower, DDEL, EPP, November 25, 1959, Name series, box 29.

[29] On wage-price controls, see Eisenhower, Press Conference, February 17, 1953, in *Public Papers of the Presidents of the United States: Dwight D. Eisenhower, 1953–1961* [hereafter, *Eisenhower Public Papers*], 8 vols. (Washington, 1960–61), 1: 45–47; Cabinet Meetings, February 6 and 12, 1953, DDEL, EPP, Cabinet series, box 1; and Eisenhower to Taft, January 9, 1953, DDEL, EPP, Name series, box 32. On public competition with business, see Cabinet Paper, "Government Competition with Business," January 15, 1955, DDEL, EPP, Cabinet series, box 4; and "Report on the Bureau of the Budget . . . , 1953–1961," January 19, 1961, DDEL, EPP, Administration series, box 37. On the federal budget, see especially *Congress and the Nation, 1945–1964: A Review of Government and Politics in the Postwar Years* (Washington, 1965), 361–74, 387–92. On taxes, see Annual Budget Message, January 21, 1954, in *Eisenhower Public Papers*, 2: 90–99; Council of Economic Advisors, "The Administration Program for Economic Expansion," May 17, 1954, DDEL, EPP,

nation's economic relations to those of 1900. He clearly recognized that the state must play an active role in sustaining high productivity and employment. As he wrote his brother Milton in early 1954, "Maintenance of prosperity is one field of governmental concern that interests me mightily and one on which I have talked incessantly to associates, advisers, and assistants ever since last January. In these days I am sure that government has to be the principal coordinator and, in many cases, the actual operator for the many things that the approach of depression would demand."[30] Like most conservatives, however, he feared inflation more than unemployment and was willing to accept slower growth and higher joblessness in return for wage and price stability. He preferred to act cautiously and often indirectly, avoiding a highly visible or intrusive federal presence. He believed strongly, moreover, in the necessity for self-discipline on the part of both business and labor. As he declared in 1957, the national interest must take precedence over the temporary advantages that might be secured by particular groups at the expense of all the people. "Should we persistently fail to discipline ourselves," he warned, there would be inexorable pressure for government to intervene and "freedom will step by step disappear."[31]

Cabinet series, box 3; and *Congress and the Nation, 1945–1964*, 415–17. On submerged lands, see "Notes on the President's Meeting with Congressional Leaders," January 26, 1953, DDEL, EPP, Legislative series, box 1; and Sherman Adams to Joseph Dodge, March 23, 1953, *ibid.*; and, for background, see Ernest R. Bartley, *The Tidelands Oil Controversy* (Austin, Texas, 1953); and *Congress and the Nation, 1945–1964*, 1401–04. On national gas legislation, see *Eisenhower Diaries* (February 11, 1956), 314–16; Eisenhower to H. R. Cullen, February 29, 1956, DDEL, EPP, DDE Diaries series, box 7; and Eisenhower to Sid Richardson, February 26, 1956, *ibid.*; and, for a fuller discussion of the natural gas issue, see Robert Engler, *The Politics of Oil: Private Power and Democratic Directions* (Chicago, 1961), 403–21; and Gerald D. Nash, *United States Oil Policy, 1890–1964: Business and Government in Twentieth-Century America* (Pittsburgh, 1968), 209–37. On public power, especially see Department of the Interior, "Power Policy," July 21, 1953, DDEL, EPP, Cabinet series, box 2; and Cabinet Meeting, July 31, 1953, *ibid.*; and, for the best brief summary of public power issues during the Eisenhower years, see *Congress and the Nation, 1945–1964*, 832–966, *passim.* On TVA, especially see J. M. Dodge, Proposed Statement with Regard to TVA, November 23, 1953, DDEL, EPP, Administration series, box 13; and also see *Congress and the Nation, 1945–1964*, 908–31; and Aaron Wildovsky, *Dixon-Yates: A Study in Power Politics* (New Haven, 1962). On atomic energy, see Walter Adams and Horace M. Gray, *Monopoly in America: The Government as Promoter* (New York, 1955), 163; *Congress and the Nation, 1945–1964*, 935–39; and Eisenhower, Message on Atomic Energy, February 17, 1954, in *Eisenhower Public Papers*, 2: 260–69. For a general account of resource policies during the Truman and Eisenhower years, see Elmo Richardson, *Dams, Parks, and Politics: Resource Development and Preservation in the Truman-Eisenhower Era* (Lexington, Ky., 973).

30 "Means available to the government include revision of tax laws to promote consumption, extension of credit and assuring of low interest rates; vigorous liberalization of all social security measures, extension of all kinds of reinsurance plans, as well as direct loans and grants; acceleration of construction programs involving everything from multiple purpose dams, irrigation projects, military equipment and public buildings on the one hand, to increased expenditures for soil conservation, upstream water storage and public housing on the other. There are, of course, other things the Government can and would do." Eisenhower to Milton Eisenhower, January 6, 1954, DDEL, EPP, Name series, box 12. Eisenhower's attentiveness to economic issues is revealed in frequent discussions with the Cabinet and, to a lesser extent, in meetings with Congressional leaders, in memoranda and private correspondence in the DDE Diaries series, and in extensive correspondence with economic advisers such as Arthur Burns and Gabriel Hauge, much of which is located in the Eisenhower Library, EPP, Administration series, boxes 9, 10, 19. Eisenhower quite typically acted indirectly and through subordinates in seeking to influence economic policy—for example, his efforts to put pressure on the Federal Reserve Board to relax credit restrictions in 1954 and 1956; *Eisenhower Diaries* (April 8, 1954), 277–78; Eisenhower, Telephone conversations, April 21, 1956, and May 17, 1956, DDEL, EPP, DDE Diaries series, box 8; Eisenhower to Harold Stassen, May 18, 1956, etc.; and Eisenhower to Lewis W. Douglas, September 30, 1956, DDEL, EPP, Administration series, box 13. On Eisenhower's fiscal policies, also see Herbert Stein, *The Fiscal Revolution in America* (Chicago, 1969), 281–371.

31 Eisenhower, Annual Message, January 10, 1957, in *Eisenhower Public Papers*, 5: 20. The danger, he

Eisenhower was also committed to at least maintaining the modest social welfare programs that had emerged from the New Deal. "Social gains," he told the Western Governors' Conference in 1952, were "not an issue any more" but a necessary "floor that covers the pit of disaster." He recognized what he called "the practical necessity of establishing some kind of security for individuals in a specialized and highly industralized age" and criticized business leaders who in the past had been "far too slow to understand the implications of the continuing social revolution" as well as "far too apt to take a completely indefinite, if not essentially a selfishly cruel, attitude toward the whole question." He also had a keen sense of the expedience of such programs. As he patiently explained to Edgar Eisenhower, the most conservative of the brothers, "Should any political party attempt to abolish Social Security, unemployment insurance, and eliminate labor laws and farm programs, you would not hear of that party again in our political history."[32] In 1954, at his urging, Congress expanded Social Security to as many as seven and a half million additional Americans, bringing fully five-sixths of the nation's paid work force under the law's provisions. He was less successful, however, in extending the minimun wage; despite his request that coverage be broadened to include "millions of low-paid workers now exempted," Congress declined to act. As late as 1960, minimum-wage protection applied only to a little over one-half of the nation's wage workers.[33]

Eisenhower's support for social welfare programs nevertheless remained sharply limited by his reluctance to enlarge the federal budget, raise taxes, or initiate new programs, the responsibility for which, in his view, lay clearly with the states. He strongly opposed national health care, proposing instead a plan whereby the government would reinsure private insurance companies against heavy losses in order to encourage them to expand their coverage.[34] He was reluctant to endorse federal aid to education, justifying his support for the National Defense Act of 1958 by stressing the "national security aspect" of the program and what he called "the dominating need for scientists."[35] During the last years of his presidency, fearful of inflation and facing large Democratic majorities in Congress, he waged a stubborn

---

declared, was "always present, particularly if the Government might become profligate or private groups might ignore all possible results on our economy of unwise struggles for immediate gains."

[32] Transcript, Western Governors' Conference, August 20, 1952, DDEL, EPP, Speech series, box 3; Eisenhower to Bradford C. Chynoweth, July 13, 1954, DDEL, EPP, DDE, Diaries series, box 4; Eisenhower to J. Earl Schaefer, September 30, 1954, *ibid.*; Eisenhower to Edgar Eisenhower, November 8, 1954, *ibid.*, box 5; Eisenhower to E. F. Hutton, October 7, 1953, *ibid.*, box 2; and Eisenhower to Milton Eisenhower, November 6, 1953, *ibid.*

[33] Eisenhower to Milton Eisenhower, November 6, 1953; and *Congress and the Nation, 1945–1964*, 641–44, 1249–53. Eisenhower opposed, but did not veto, the disability insurance program enacted in 1956 as well as increases in the federal share of public assistance monies in 1956 and 1958.

[34] Oveta Culp Hobby, Memorandum for the President, May 14, 1954, DDEL, EPP, Administration series, box 20. For the views of the insurance industry's chief lobbyist, see Eugene M. Thoré, Address of May 5, 1954, *ibid.* Even this modest proposal drew sharp opposition from the American Medical Association, which effectively blocked its passage. "How in the hell is the American Medical Association going to stop socialized medicine if they oppose such bills as this," declared an angry Eisenhower. "If they [the American people] don't get a bill like this, they will go for socialized medicine sooner or later and the Medical Association will have no one to blame but itself." James C. Hagerty Diary, July 14 and 19, 1954, DDEL, Hagerty Papers, box 1. A subsequent proposal, put forth by Hobby's successor, Marion Folsom, urged the relaxation of antitrust laws in order to enable insurance companies to pool their resources and thereby extend coverage, but this, too, made little headway; *Congress and the Nation, 1945–1964*, 1153; and James L. Sundquist, *Politics and Policy: The Eisenhower, Kennedy, and Johnson Years* (Washington, 1968), 292–93.

[35] On the NDEA, see Cabinet meeting, December 2, 1957, DDEL, EPP, Cabinet series, box 10; and Legislative Leadership meeting, December 4, 1957, DDEL, EPP, Legislative series, box 2. For the

and often effective battle against the further expansion of social welfare programs: "In my special seat I feel that it is not enough to know that an activity and its expenditure are merely *desirable*. We must be quite clear in the establishment of priorities so that these things can be done at a *rate* and in a sequence that will conform to the fiscal facts, as well as the clear requirements, of a nation that operates, primarily, on the *free enterprise system*." During the years of his presidency, federal transfer payments, the surest index to social welfare policy, remained unchanged as a percentage of the federal budget.[36]

EISENHOWER COMBINED HIS ATTEMPT to limit the role of the federal state with a strong and pervasive emphasis on cooperation between business and government. He drew about him a cabinet whose members he hoped would share his own faith in partnership and corporate self-government; he appointed representatives of business and industry to important regulatory boards and commissions; and he greatly expanded the government's already elaborate network of industrial advisory committees. The influence of existing groups such as the Business Advisory Council (BAC) and the National Petroleum Council was increased, while many new advisory committees were created. At the Department of Commerce, for example, Secretary Sinclair Weeks announced, following wide consultation with industry and trade association leaders, the creation of a new Business and Services Administration, which would preside over an extensive network of advisory committees designed to help allocate materials required by defense and atomic energy programs and make recommendations on applications for accelerated tax amortization, federal loan assistance, stockpiling, and other matters. Every department, Eisenhower assured the BAC in early 1953, was engaged in organizing similar bodies on a more or less formal or informal basis.[37] Similarly, the famous stag dinners to which he invited the leaders of America's great corporations were not just ritual celebrations of success but meetings at which Eisenhower hoped to

importance of scientific and engineering training in the minds of the president and his advisers, see Thomas S. Nichols, Memorandum for the President, April 26, 1955, DDEL, EPP, Administration series, box 30; Bryce C. Harlow, Memorandum for the Record (of discussion between Eisenhower and David Sarnoff), April 26, 1956, *ibid.*, box 19; and Memorandum for the President (on the Report of the President's Committee on Education beyond the High School), October 23, 1957, *ibid.*, box 16. For a recent study of the NDEA, see Barbara Barksdale Clowse, *Brainpower for the Cold War: The Sputnik Crisis and the National Defense Education Act of 1958* (Westport, Conn., 1981).

[36] Eisenhower to I. S. Ravdin, September 19, 1959, DDEL, EPP, DDE Diaries series, box 28. Also see Charles C. Alexander, *Holding the Line: The Eisenhower Era, 1952–1961* (Bloomington, Ind., 1975), 103.

[37] Eisenhower's appointments were more heavily Protestant (85 percent) than were Truman's, more likely to be political independents (20 percent), more likely to be recruited from the private sector (over 70 percent), and more likely to be drawn from elite educational institutions. Indeed, despite the educational backgrounds of Roosevelt and Kennedy, "the ivy influence was at its peak under Eisenhower." David T. Stanley *et al.*, *Men Who Govern: A Biographical Profile of Federal Political Executives* (Washington, 1967), 16–32, *passim*. On Eisenhower's appointments to regulatory boards and commissions, see Engler, *The Politics of Oil*, 323–25, 330–31, *passim*; David A. Frier, *Conflict of Interest in the Eisenhower Administration* (Ames, Iowa, 1969); and Bernard Schwartz, *The Professor and the Commission* (New York, 1959), 140–43, *passim*. For an excellent discussion of the evolution of the advisory system, see Grant McConnell, *Private Power and American Democracy* (New York, 1966), chap. 8. For Eisenhower's remarks to the BAC, see *Eisenhower Public Papers* (March 18, 1953), 1: 103. The use of industry advisory committees and unpaid consultants ("WOCs," meaning "without compensation") was extensively investigated by critical Democrats in Congress; see U.S. Congress, House of Representatives, 84th Cong., 2d sess., Committee on the Judiciary, Anti-Trust Subcommittee, *Interim Report . . . on WOCs and Government Advisory Groups* (Washington, 1956).

exchange views with men whose opinions he respected and whose support was indispensable to his broader purposes. He hoped, it seems clear, that such gatherings would also stimulate business leaders to think in broad, cooperative terms and not just according to their more immediate and parochial interests.[38]

Eisenhower's stress on cooperation and industrial self-government was nowhere better revealed than in his approach to fiscal and monetary policy. Although he believed that the state should play an important role in maintaining prosperity, he also believed in what he called "shared responsibility" between business and government. During the recession of 1954 he privately urged bankers to lower interest rates and make credit more easily available; in 1955 he attempted, unsuccessfully, to persuade auto industry leaders to restrain prices and production; during the recession years of 1954 and 1958 he enlisted the services of the Advertising Council, which launched massive advertising campaigns designed to promote "Confidence in a Growing America," and, though never explicitly stated, confidence in the administration as well; and in 1958–59 he quietly sought to organize corporate leaders behind his wage and price stabilization policies.[39]

The administration of antitrust policy under Eisenhower was characterized, similarly, by the widespread use of prefiling conferences, consent decrees, and premerger clearances, all of which emphasized cooperation and quiet negotiation. When business complaints of harassment reached the president, moreover, he admonished Attorney General Herbert Brownell, Jr., to reassure the business community as to "the true attitude of this Administration," which was that "continued prosperity and growth of the economy" could come "only through the cooperation of labor, management and government, and that such cooperation requires a readiness of all parties to observe the law (or to seek legislative changes in it) but the avoidance on the part of government of all kinds of petty annoyances brought about merely by personal bias."[40]

[38] Dillon Anderson to Eisenhower, January 29, 1954, DDEL, EPP, Administration series, box 8; George Whitney to Eisenhower, July 7, 1953, DDEL, EPP, Name series, box 34; and "Presidential Dinner," November 6, 1953, DDEL, Robinson Papers, box 2. To a fairly typical dinner, held on September 23, 1953, Eisenhower invited, among others, Frank Abrams of Standard Oil, C. F. Craig of A.T.&T., Harlow Curtice of General Motors, Benjamin F. Fairless of U.S. Steel, Henry Ford II of Ford Motor Company, John J. McCloy of the Chase Manhattan Bank, and Richard K. Mellon of Mellon and Sons; Stag Dinner, September 23, 1953, DDEL, EPP, DDE Diaries series, box 2.

[39] On bankers and credit, see George Whitney to Eisenhower, June 18, 1954, DDEL, EPP, Name series, box 43; Whitney to George Humphrey, July 27, 1954, DDEL, EPP, Administration series, box 22; and Cabinet Meeting, June 11, 1954, DDEL, EPP, Cabinet series, box 3. On the automobile industry, see George Humphrey to William Mc. Martin, April 24, 1956, DDEL, EPP, Administration series, box 23; and Eisenhower to Arthur Burns, March 20, 1958, *ibid.*, box 10. On the Advertising Council, see James R. Lambie, Jr., to Sherman Adams, December 9, 1953, DDEL, Lambie Records, box 3; Max Fox to Theodore S. Repplier, April 5, 1954, *ibid.*, box 12; Paul West to Sherman Adams, March 12, 1954, *ibid.* Also see Griffith, "The Selling of America," 31–45. Eisenhower also sought to enlist the Advertising Council in the fight against inflation, but with much more limited success. On Eisenhower's efforts to recruit business leaders in the campaign against inflation, see, for example, Eisenhower to Robert Anderson, November 3, 1958, DDEL, EPP, DDE Diaries series, box 32; Eisenhower to Richard K. Mellon, October 6, 1958, *ibid.*, box 22; and Eisenhower to Frank Stanton, February 23, 1959, DDEL, EPP, Administration series, box 39. Eisenhower told Mellon that "only by getting into politics up to our necks can we reverse these unfortunate trends" favored by Americans for Democratic Action and the Congress of Industrial Organizations. On the 1959–60 effort to enlist business support on behalf of wage and price stabilization, also see W. Allen Wallis to Richard M. Nixon, July 29, 1959, DDEL, W. Allen Wallis Records, box 3; Wallis to H. Bruce Palmer, January 20, 1960, *ibid.*, and Progress Report, The Council for Economic Growth and Security, Inc. (January 1960), *ibid.*

[40] Eisenhower to Brownell, June 12, 1957, DDEL, EPP, Administration series, box 8. For an extremely

The very success of such strategies, of course, depended on the ability and willingness of business leaders to exercise restraint and discipline. Eisenhower fully understood the enormous power of modern business and how decisions made by corporate boards could affect "the whole life of the United States." He understood also, as he told economic adviser Gabriel Hauge, how such a situation "could be very dangerous unless people act with the greatest wisdom and concert for the nation."[41] His speeches, his conversations, and his private correspondence are literally filled with appeals for corporate "statesmanship" and responsibility. Nothing so angered him, moreover, as what he considered corporate short-sightedness—the demand by some business groups for tax reduction regardless of the fiscal consequences, the pressure for tariff protection from inefficient producers, the refusal of steel and auto industry leaders to hold down prices, the unwillingness of the automakers to smooth out production and help stabilize the business cycle. When in mid-1955 steel companies announced an increase in steel prices of seven dollars per ton, he told Ann Whitman that he was "pretty disgusted with businessmen and didn't know when he would get over it." He was outraged by the heavy-handed lobbying and even bribery that accompanied the drive for deregulation of natural gas and that compelled him to veto a bill he otherwise favored. "I want to give business a honorable place," he angrily declared, "but they make crooks out of themselves." To the cabinet he worried aloud about "the contradiction that existed when the greatest exponents of a free economy failed to exercise the restraint necessary to a free economy."[42]

Yet even successful instances of corporate cooperation did not, as Eisenhower assumed they would, necessarily produce results that transcended corporate self-interest. In housing and urban affairs, for example, Eisenhower turned for assistance to a national advisory committee recruited for the most part from among realtors, builders, and bankers—groups notoriously hostile to public housing though not to other forms of federal intervention such as FHA and urban renewal. The Housing Act of 1954 and other administration programs, not surprisingly, reflected the political agenda of these powerful groups.[43] In the case of the federal

sympathetic, if unpersuasive, account of Eisenhower's antitrust policies, see Theodore P. Kovaleff, *Business and Government during the Eisenhower Administration: A Study of the Antitrust Division of the Justice Department* (Athens, Ohio, 1980). The administration's handling of the critical oil cartel case well illustrates its emphasis on negotiation and cooperative arrangements as well as the generally low priority it gave to antitrust enforcement; see Burton I. Kaufman, *The Oil Cartel Case: A Documentary Study of Antitrust Activity in the Cold War Era* (Westport, Conn., 1978), 50–101.

[41] Ann Whitman Diary, February 13, 1956, April 3, 1956, DDEL, EPP, Ann Whitman Diary series, box 8.

[42] Whitman Diary, June 1, 1955, DDEL, EPP, Ann Whitman Diary series, box 6; Whitman Diary, February 13, March 13, 1956, *ibid.*, box 8; *Eisenhower Diaries* (April 20, 1956), 326; Eisenhower, Telephone conversation with George Humphrey, January 31, 1956, DDEL, EPP, DDE Diary series, box 7; Jack Z. Anderson, Memorandum for the Record, June 19, 1958, *ibid.*, box 20; Cabinet meeting, June 5, 1953, DDEL, EPP, Cabinet series, box 2; Cabinet meeting, December 14, 1956, *ibid.*, box 6; and Memorandum of a Conversation between the President and T. S. Repplier, August 3, 1955, DDEL, Lambie Records, box 23.

[43] The Housing Act of 1949 had authorized construction of 135,000 public housing units per year, a rate never reached because of the intervention of the Korean War. Some 58,000 units were constructed in 1953, reflecting commitments entered into during the last years of the Truman administration. By contrast, construction fell off sharply during the Eisenhower years, averaging between 10,000 and 20,000 units per year. By the end of the decade, critics could rightly charge that far more poor people had been displaced through urban renewal than could be housed in newly constructed public housing. See Mark I. Gelfand, *A*

highway program, Eisenhower decided to name an advisory committee chaired by his close friend Lucius Clay, which he hoped would possess a national view of highway development and would therefore surmount the more parochial interests of truckers, auto clubs, state highway engineers, car manufacturers, oil companies, and others whose inability to reach agreement had deadlocked federal policy for more than a decade. The committee's report did receive broad support, and the bill that passed one year later embodied some, though by no means all, of its major recommendations. The Clay report and the Interstate Highway Act of 1956 also revealed, however, the sharp limitations of corporate stewardship; for, although the Clay committee took a broad, national view, that view was nevertheless narrowly circumscribed by those corporate and professional elites who saw highways solely as a means of moving more automobiles and trucks more cheaply and efficiently. The report, and subsequent Congressional testimony, was silent concerning the impact of such massive highway construction on the ecology of cities, on land use patterns and tax bases, on slum clearance and housing, on renewal and redevelopment, and on urban mass transportation. Thus, the program, though producing enormous growth in the auto, oil, construction, and other related industries, laid an enormous if immeasurable tax upòn the American people in the form of disintegrating cities, declining public transportation, air pollution, and wasteful energy consumption.[44]

In natural resource development, Eisenhower sought to replace what he called an "exclusive dependence on Federal bureaucracy" with "a partnership of state and local communities, private citizens, and the Federal Government, all working together." In practice, the "private citizens" involved were almost always large private utilities, owned and controlled by financial interests in New York, Boston, and other metropolitan districts; "local" rural electric cooperatives were actively discouraged, as were "partnerships" between cooperatives and federal power projects. Similarly, the Atomic Energy Act of 1954, which authorized the licensing of private corporations to produce and market nuclear electric power while explicitly prohibiting the Atomic Energy Commission from doing so, made it certain that the future development of this important new resource would be

---

Nation of Cities: The Federal Government and Urban America, 1933-1965 (New York, 1975), 157–97. Also see Noah P. Mason, "Report to the President on Housing," January 11, 1961, DDEL, EPP, Administration series, box 28. For Eisenhower's views on public housing, which were somewhat more liberal than those of Congressional conservatives, see Cabinet meeting, December 9, 1953, DDEL, EPP, Cabinet series, box 2; Cabinet meeting, December 10, 1954, *ibid.*, box 5; and Legislative Leadership meeting, December 17, 1953, *ibid.*, Legislative series, box 1.

[44] Both Eisenhower and the Clay Committee had recommended financing highway construction through revenue bonds, but this proposal was blocked in Congress. The final measure incorporated a Democratic-sponsored, "pay as you go" tax on highway users, to be administered through a Highway Trust Fund. Although this approach disappointed economic advisers such as Arthur Burns and John H. Bragdon, who had hoped to use highway construction as a countercyclical tool, it gained support from George Humphrey, Sinclair Weeks, and finally Eisenhower himself. It did, as Eisenhower desired, insulate highway finance from the federal budget. See Legislative Leadership meetings, June 21 and 28, July 6, and December 12, 1955, DDEL, EPP, Legislative series, box 1; and Legislative Leadership meeting, January 31, 1956, *ibid.*, box 2. For critical discussions of the federal highway program, especially see Mark H. Rose, *Interstate: Express Highway Politics, 1941–1956* (Lawrence, Kans., 1979), 95–100; and Gelfand, *A Nation of Cities*, 226–30.

controlled by large, private utilities.[45] Here, as in other areas, Eisenhower's policies thus decisively shaped the political agenda of future generations.

Eisenhower faced greater difficulties in those areas of public policy, such as agriculture and labor, where the power of corporate elites was contested by other powerful interests. He sought to shape agricultural policy with the cooperation of a national advisory commission representing the powerful triad of large commercial farmers, food processors, and land-grant economists who increasingly dominated national agricultural policy. He believed, as did most of the members of this commission, that the role of government in agriculture should be reduced and that price supports in particular should be lowered. Although the reduction of supports would, he believed, necessitate some "readjustment" in farming ("readjustment" was the then current administrative euphemism for recession), the long-term result would be production for demand and an end to costly surpluses. Eisenhower repeatedly defended the frequently unpopular efforts of Ezra Taft Benson to move in this direction, however much he differed from the tactless agriculture secretary on questions of pace, timing, and public relations. But Congressional leaders, less sanguine than Eisenhower about the social costs of "readjustment" and more sensitive to outcries from the farm belt, frustrated the president. He obtained some reduction of price supports in the farm bills of 1954 and 1958, but the government remained pledged, as it had since the 1930s, to an elaborate system of price supports and production controls. Indeed, even though farm income sharply declined and hundreds of thousands of small farmers were forced from the land, production continued to increase and surpluses to pile up in government warehouses. Eisenhower was convinced that, in agriculture as in other areas, the enemies of good policy were demagogic politicians and greedy partisans of self-interest, especially those farm-state leaders who insisted on the retention of high price supports or who declined to accept his version of the corporate commonwealth. By the end of the decade, however, he clearly realized the dimensions of his own failure, was more willing than before to seek compromise with Congressional leaders, and believed, as he put it, that the "application of . . . principles is not always easy and simple in a society as complex as ours."[46]

In the case of labor, Eisenhower's views and policies were divided. On the one

[45] *Congress and the Nation, 1945–1964*, 832–966. For opposition to the administration's power policies, see National Rural Electric Cooperative Association, "Washington Report," September 1953, HSTL, Wallace J. Campbell Papers, box 31; and James G. Patton, "Call for a National Electric Consumers' Conference," December 10–11, 1953, *ibid.*, box 40. For a critical analysis of the administration's atomic energy legislation, see Leland Olds to American Public Power Association *et al.*, August 9, 1954, Library of Congress, Clinton P. Anderson Papers, box 791; and National Rural Electric Cooperative Association, "The Atomic Energy Act of 1954," HSTL, Harry S. Truman Papers, Post-Presidential Name File, box 4.

[46] *Eisenhower Public Papers* (1953), 1: 28, 530, 574; Eisenhower, Memorandum for the Secretary of Agriculture, September 8, 1954, DDEL, EPP, Administration series, box 6; Legislative Leadership meeting, March 18, 1958, *ibid.*, Legislative series, box 2; and Eisenhower, *Mandate for Change: The White House Years, 1953–56* (Garden City, N.Y., 1963), 557–64. For Eisenhower's critical comments on the politics of agriculture, see *Eisenhower Diaries* (February 11, 1956), 317–18; L. Arthur Minnich, Staff Note, June 21, 1954, DDEL, EPP, DDE Diaries series, box 4; Eisenhower to Joel Carlson, April 5, 1956, *ibid.*, Name series, box 4; and Eisenhower to Benson, March 20, 1958, *ibid.*, Administration series, box 6. For a partisan critique of the Eisenhower program, see Wesley McCune, *Who's Behind Our Farm Policy?* (New York, 1956). For a defense of the Benson policies, see Edward L. Schapsmeier and Frank H. Schapsmeier, *Ezra Taft Benson and the Politics of Agriculture: The Eisenhower Years, 1953–1961* (Danville, Ill., 1975).

hand, he accepted the existence of labor unions as an unavoidable part of the nation's corporate order; on the other, he worried over what he saw as their divisive appeals to class selfishness and greed and over the possibility that the wage settlements they compelled might lead to a ruinous inflation. Nor could he bring himself to accord to labor leaders the same degree of legitimacy he bestowed upon the leaders of business and industry. In his diary he confessed to "disappointment" over his first secretary of labor, plumbers' union president Martin Durkin, who "could never free himself of the feeling that he was placed in the Cabinet to be a trade unionist." He was far more comfortable with Durkin's successor, James P. Mitchell, who had handled personnel and industrial relations for Macy's and Bloomingdale's and whose views and style more closely approximated his own. To his brother Milton he confided that, while his labor policies were designed to appeal to the mass of American workers, "most certainly" his administration was "not consciously seeking the favor of the so-called labor leader." In dealing with labor Eisenhower repeatedly returned to the themes of cooperation and mutuality that had characterized his thinking since at least the late 1940s. "The President," an aide recorded in early 1953, "made an eloquent presentation of the need for cooperation by free men . . . in order to make Democracy work. He emphasized the need for a cooperative climate rather than rigid specification by law." The foundations of the administration's labor philosophy, concluded Secretary Mitchell, were "cooperation, mutual understanding, self-respect and respect for other viewpoints, restraint and self-discipline."[47]

During the 1952 campaign Eisenhower had promised to seek changes in the Taft-Hartley law, only to be subsequently caught in a bitter struggle between the unions, who hoped to eliminate some of the law's antilabor features, and business leaders, who wanted even more restrictive legislation. He never permitted himself to become too closely identified with Taft-Hartley revision, however, and he quickly abandoned efforts to change the law once it became clear how difficult and politically costly this would be.[48] Four years later, following Senate revelations of corruption in labor unions, he again called for labor legislation. This time, however, he played an extremely active and skillful role in winning passage of the Landrum-Griffin Act, a measure that generally reflected the wishes of corporate lobbyists.[49]

[47] *Eisenhower Diaries* (January 19, 1954), 267; Eisenhower to Milton Eisenhower, January 6, 1954, DDEL, EPP, DDE Diaries series, box 3; Eisenhower, Conversation with Sinclair Weeks, November 7, 1953, DDEL, EPP, Administration series, box 42; Cabinet meeting, February 20, 1953, DDEL, EPP, Cabinet series, box 1; and Mitchell, "The Accomplishments of the Department of Labor, 1953–1961," DDEL, EPP, Administration series, box 29. Efforts to create a tripartite (labor, business, and the administration) advisory committee foundered on conflict between business and labor representatives; Legislative Leadership meeting, March 9, 1953, DDEL, EPP, DDE Diaries series, box 3.

[48] On administration attempts to resolve the conflict, see Bernard Shanley and Jerry Morgan, Memorandum for the President, September 20, 1953, DDEL, EPP, Administration series, box 41. On the opposition of business leaders, see Philip D. Reed to Eisenhower, December 23, 1953, *ibid.*; Lewis W. Douglas to Eisenhower, December 16, 1953, *ibid.*, box 13; Eisenhower to Clarence Francis, December 19, 1953, DDEL, EPP, DDE Diaries series, box 2; Memorandum of Conversation with Roy Roberts, December 11, 1953, *ibid.*; and Cabinet meeting, May 13, 1955, DDEL, EPP, Cabinet series, box 5.

[49] Summary Statement of the President's Proposals . . . [ca. November 8, 1957], DDEL, EPP, Cabinet series, box 10; and Cabinet meeting, November 8, 1957, *ibid.* The extraordinary role of the White House is detailed in the minutes of the president's meetings with Congressional leaders. See notes on meetings with legislative leaders, December 4, 1957–September 8, 1959, DDEL, EPP, Legislative series, box 3. Also see

Eisenhower sought, with some success, to limit the direct and formal role of the White House in labor conflict. He invoked Taft-Hartley far less frequently than had Truman, preferring to work indirectly and behind the scenes. When he did invoke the law, moreover, as he did during the long steel strike of 1959, he did so very reluctantly. The weight of White House intervention, more often than not, worked against high wage settlements that might, in the administration's eyes, prove inflationary. Thus in early 1960 White House leaders congratulated themselves for having achieved a steel settlement that was lower than those obtained in the can and aluminum industries and that, had the rank and file been allowed to vote, would have been rejected by an overwhelming margin. The administration also sought to encourage industry-wide bargaining and the negotiation of long-term contracts, thereby increasing industrial stability. The result, though Eisenhower could scarcely claim full credit, was a remarkable period of industrial tranquility during which, in comparison with the Truman years, there were far fewer strikes, far fewer workers involved, and far fewer workdays lost. Real wages improved somewhat during the decade, and most workers enjoyed a degree of security that stood in sharp contrast to their recollections of the 1930s. Yet these gains were modest, and large numbers of Americans, one-fifth or more of the population, remained in poverty.[50] Thus while labor and the laboring classes became partners in the corporate commonwealth, they remained very junior members at best.

THE SEARCH FOR STABILITY AND SOCIAL HARMONY underlying Eisenhower's vision of a corporate commonwealth also shaped his style of presidential leadership. This style was quite obviously a product of his experience as a military leader and of his conviction that modern government was so large and complex that no individual could master all of its intricacies. It was clearly reinforced by the practical necessity of working for the most part with a Congress organized by the opposing party. It was also shaped, however, by the conservative and consensual goals of his presidency and by his belief in the limited role of the political state, in the dangers of popular politics, in the importance of persuasion rather than coercion, and in the necessity for voluntary discipline, restraint, and cooperation among America's powerful economic groupings. Its purpose was to deflect attention not only from himself but also from the national government itself, to deflate and depoliticize

---

Alan K. McAdams, *Power and Politics in Labor Legislation* (New York, 1964), 71–74, 272–73: "The distinctive feature of the management side of the labor reform battle was the degree of participation by the White House," concludes this study of the bill's passage. "The direct coordination of the management groups by the Administration made possible working relationships which were smoother than had ever been achieved before among usually widely ranging groups."

[50] Cabinet meetings, April 3, December 15, 1953, DDEL, EPP, Cabinet series, box 2; Cabinet meeting, November 11, 1954, *ibid.*, box 4; and Allen Wallis, Memorandum for the President, August 7, 1954, DDEL, Wallis Records, box 1. On the steel strike, especially see the notes on Eisenhower's separate meetings with industry and labor leaders, Sepember 30, 1959, DDEL, EPP, DDE Diaries series, box 28; Summary of Steel Dispute, DDEL, Hagerty Papers, box 10; Eisenhower, Memorandum for the Record, November 9, 1959, DDEL, EPP, DDE Diaries series, box 11; Eisenhower, Telephone Conference Call with Richard M. Nixon, James P. Mitchell, Wilton B. Persons, January 2, 1960, *ibid.*, box 30; and Legislative Leadership meeting, January 12, 1960, DDEL, EPP, Legislative series, box 3. Also see *Congress and the Nation, 1945–1964*, 628–29, *passim*; and Harold G. Vatter, *The U.S. Economy in the 1950's: An Economic History* (New York, 1963), 221–48.

expectations raised by two decades of Democratic rule. Thus, he sought to govern by indirection, delegating authority to those he trusted and with whom he was in basic agreement, but insulating himself from the controversy and criticism their actions might provoke. He tried quite deliberately to appear above partisan politics, refused to be drawn into personal confrontations, and almost never displayed in public his legendary temper. To those around him, he repeatedly counseled moderation and restraint. The task of the political leader, he wrote in a long letter to Nelson Rockefeller, was "to devise plans along which humans [can] make constructive progress. This means that the plan or program itself tends to fall in the 'gray' category even though an earnest attempt is made to apply the black and white values of moral truths. . . . Perfection is not quickly reached; the plan is therefore 'gray' or 'middle-of-the-road.' "[51]

His experience as president also reinforced his distrust of popular democracy. People in the aggregate, he seemed to believe, were all too prone to self-seeking and all too vulnerable to the blandishments of demagogues. Congress was a warren of greedy special interests (an "occupational hazard," one aide quipped), while the press was little more than an endless source of "distortion and gross error."[52] Mistrustful of democracy, he opposed most efforts to modify the nation's constitutional arrangements. He believed that the Bricker Amendment would undermine the foundations of presidential authority in foreign affairs, and that attempts by Henry Cabot Lodge and others to change the electoral system by introducing proportional voting would make the American system "closer to a democracy, less of a republic." "We can't let just a popular majority sweep us in one direction," he told Vice President Nixon, "because then you can't recover." He defended the Supreme Court not because he always agreed with its decisions, but because he believed that "one of the great functions of the Supreme Court was to provide needed stability in a form of government where political expediency might at times carry parties and political leaders to extremes."[53]

Fear of popular politics and a commitment to voluntarism and corporate self-

[51] For discussion of Eisenhower's leadership by those who worked with him, especially see Emmet John Hughes, *The Ordeal of Power: A Political Memoir of the Eisenhower Years* (New York, 1963), 123–27; and Larson, *The President Nobody Knew*, 12–33. Also see Parmet, *Eisenhower and the American Crusades*, 175, 209–10. For the best and most recent appraisal of Eisenhower's leadership, see Fred I. Greenstein, "Eisenhower as an Activist President," *Political Science Quarterly*, 94 (1979–80): 575–99. For Eisenhower's own reflections on leadership, see especially Eisenhower to Emmet John Hughes, December 10, 1953, DDEL, EPP, DDE Diaries series, box 2; Eisenhower to Milton Eisenhower, October 9, 1953, *ibid.*; Eisenhower to Rockefeller, May 5, 1960, *ibid.*, box 32; Eisenhower to Henry Luce, August 8, 1960, *ibid.*, box 33; and Eisenhower to William Phillips, June 5, 1953, DDEL, EPP, Name series, box 25.

[52] On the public, see, for example, Eisenhower to Hughes, December 10, 1953; and Eisenhower to Lamar Fleming, Jr., December 5, 1958, DDEL, EPP, DDE Diaries series, box 23. For typical remarks on Congress, see Eisenhower to Everett Hazlett, July 22, 1957, DDEL, EPP, DDE Diaries series, box 10; and Eisenhower to Arthur Burns, March 11, 1959, DDEL, EPP, Administration series, box 10. The White House aide is quoted in the Whitman Diary, August 11, 1954, DDEL, EPP, Ann Whitman Diary series, box 2. On the press, see—again for fairly typical expressions—*Eisenhower Diaries* (January 19, 1954), 270–72; and Eisenhower to Edgar Eisenhower, January 27, 1954; Eisenhower to Everett Hazlett, April 27, 1954, DDEL, EPP, DDE Diaries series, box 4; and Eisenhower to Robinson, August 4, 1958, *ibid.*, box 21.

[53] On the Bricker Amendment, see Eisenhower to Edgar Eisenhower, December 12, 1954, DDEL, EPP, DDE Diaries series, box 3; Eisenhower to J. Earl Schaeffer, January 22, 1954, *ibid.*; and Eisenhower to John

government also shaped Eisenhower's preoccupation with public relations: if he hoped to avoid coercive state intervention and to encourage the resolution of conflict among powerful interests, his chief techniques had to be persuasive; and if the principle threat to this process arose from lack of discipline among the masses and the demagogic promises of politicians, then public relations must play an even more important role in encouraging restraint, defusing dangerous issues, dampening protest and legitimizing corporate rule. The administration faced problems "not unlike the advertising and sales activity of a great industrial organization," he noted in 1953; and, while it was necessary to have "a good product to sell," it was also necessary "to have an effective and persuasive way of informing the public of the excellence of that product."[54] He established a standing committee on public relations within the White House, followed closely the public relations efforts of the Republican national committee, and maintained a steady correspondence with friends and advisors from the world of corporate public relations. He directed the organization of special campaigns on agriculture, highways, public power, labor relations, and economic policy, and he enlisted the support of powerful private groups such as the Advertising Council in publicizing his policies.[55] He was exceptionally skillful in his press relations. He maintained a wide correspondence with many publishers and editors, invited them frequently to his stag dinners, and even employed them on occasion to conduct confidential surveys on his behalf. He was extremely sensitive to adverse comment in the press and frequently sought to counter such criticism, though almost always obliquely.[56]

J. McCloy, January 19, 1954, *ibid*. On electoral college reform, see the Whitman Diary, March 20, 1956, DDEL, EPP, Ann Whitman Diary series, box 8; and Pre-legislative Leadership meeting, March 20, 1956, DDEL, EPP, Legislative series, box 2. On the Supreme Court, see Eisenhower to E. F. Hutton, July 10, 1957, DDEL, EPP, DDE Diaries series, box 14. Those changes that Eisenhower did support were almost invariably those that would have strengthened the executive or further insulated political leaders from popular influence: for example, the item veto, the requirement of a two-thirds vote to reject presidential nominations, and four-year terms for Congress; Legislative Leadership meeting, September 9, 1959, DDEL, EPP, Legislative series, box 3.

[54] Eisenhower to George Humphrey, Arthur Summerfield, Henry Cabot Lodge, Sherman Adams, *et al.*, November 23, 1953, DDEL, EPP, Administration series, box 33.

[55] Cabinet meeting, July 3, 1953, DDEL, EPP, Cabinet series, box 2; Cabinet meeting, March 5, 1954, *ibid.*, box 3; Cabinet meeting, November 5, 1954, *ibid.*, box 4; and Cabinet meeting, July 8, 1955, *ibid.*, box 5. One of the president's sharpest and most frequently proffered criticisms was on the lack of public relations skill among his subordinates. See, for example, Eisenhower to Charles E. Wilson, November 2, 1953, DDEL, EPP, Administration series, box 44; and Eisenhower, Memorandum for the Files, March 12, 1955, DDEL, EPP, Ann Whitman Diary series, box 4. For Eisenhower's own concern with public relations, see, among others, Eisenhower to Sigurd S. Larmon, February 1, 1954, DDEL, EPP, DDE Diaries series, box 3; Eisenhower to William E. Robinson, August 4, 1954, *ibid.*, box 4; Eisenhower, Memorandums for Robert Montgomery, March 12 and August 18, 1954, DDEL, EPP, Administration series, box 29; and Eisenhower, Memorandum of Appointment [with Sig Larmon, of Young & Rubicam, Kenneth Dyke of Batten, Barton, Durstine and Osborne, and others], September 2, 1955, DDEL, EPP, Name series, box 20. For public relations in agriculture, see, for example, Belknap to Secretary of Agriculture, December 9, 1953, DDEL, Benson Papers, Public Relations, roll 27. On the role of public relations in economic policy, see Eisenhower to Raymond Saulnier, February 11, 1958, DDEL, EPP, Administration series, box 35. On public power, see Sherman Adams, Memorandum for Howard Pyle, June 1, 1955, DDEL, Pyle Records, box 37. On highways, see Whitman Diary, February 12, 1955, DDEL, EPP, Ann Whitman Diary series, box 4. On labor relations, see McAdams, *Power and Politics in Labor Legislation*, 74–75, 120, 178. And, on the Advertising Council, see Griffith, "The Selling of America," 28–47.

[56] On Eisenhower's use of newspaper editors in conducting confidential surveys, see Cabinet meeting,

Eisenhower did not, however, limit these efforts, which he frequently referred to as "selling the American people," to advertising his highly marketable personality or even to promoting the specific programs of the administration but directed them as well toward the broader, long-term goals of his presidency—winning popular acceptance of the discipline and self-restraint necessary to the corporate common-wealth and helping "our people understand that they must avoid extremes in reaching solutions to the social, economic and political problems that are constantly with us."[57] His approach to these broad aims was nowhere better illustrated than in the creation, near the end of his second term, of a commission to identify and publicize national goals for the 1960s. Chief among these goals, Eisenhower made clear in advance, was the "American aspiration . . . to develop a world in which all peoples will be living at peace under cooperative policies with maximum standards of living and opportunity for all." The most important purpose of the study, he noted privately, "was to outline for the American people problems involved in mobilizing public opinion in a democracy in order to make the hard decisions that would be needed to successfully compete in an indefinite cold war."[58]

Eisenhower's deep concern for public order and consensus influenced his response to Joseph R. McCarthy and the discordant Cold War politics of anticom-munism. While he repeatedly insisted on the importance of justice and fair play, he tended, almost without exception, to resolve conflicts between security and civil liberties in favor of the state. He supported legislation to strip citizenship from those convicted under the Smith Act of conspiring to advocate the violent overthrow of the government, to compel witnesses to testify in national security investigations, to legalize the use of wiretap information in internal security cases,

---

February 16, 1954, DDEL, EPP, Cabinet series, box 3; and Roy Roberts to Eisenhower, February 18, 1954, DDEL, EPP, Administrative series, box 21. For specific efforts to shape coverage and editorials, see, for example, Eisenhower, Telephone conversation with Arthur Hays Sulzberger, September 25, 1956, DDEL, EPP, DDE Diaries series, box 10; Eisenhower, Telephone conversation with William E. Robinson, February 6, 1957, *ibid.*, box 8; Gardner Cowles to Eisenhower, April 2, 1956, *ibid.*; Eisenhower to Cowles, April 3, 1956, *ibid.*; Eisenhower to Alfred M. Gruenther, January 15, 1958, *ibid.*, box 18; and Eisenhower to John S. Knight, October 6, 1954, DDEL, EPP, Name series, box 20. On efforts to clean up *Fortune*'s handling of an administration scandal, see C. D. Jackson to Sherman Adams, July 22, 1955, DDEL, C. D. Jackson Papers, box 12. On the seeming indifference of the press to Republican scandals generally, see Frier, *Conflict of Interest in the Eisenhower Administration*, 9–10, 51–52, 89. On the administration's successful effort to kill a *Denver Post* story on the production of nerve gas, see Special Staff Note, April 1, 1957, DDEL, EPP, DDE Diaries series, box 13. On Eisenhower's efforts to place a defeated Republican senator at CBS, where he might "insure key television appearances for more good Republican speakers," see Ed McCabe, Memoran-dum for Ann Whitman, December 18, 1958, *ibid.*, box 23. "As you know, Spyros Skouras is trying to publicize a few of our younger Republicans by keeping them on the newsreels whenever they attend some ceremony or other"; Eisenhower to Adams, October 29, 1957, *ibid.*, box 16.

[57] Eisenhower to Everett Hazlett, March 2, 1956, DDEL, EPP, DDE Diaries series, box 8.

[58] Memorandum Concerning the Commission on National Goals, February 7, 1960, in *Eisenhower Public Papers*, 8: 159–60; and Robert Merriam, Memorandum for the Record, March 19, 1959, DDEL, EPP, DDE Diaries series, box 25. For the commission's report, see The American Assembly, *Goals for Americans: The Report of the President's Commission on National Goals* (Englewood Cliffs, N.J., 1960), 1–31. Not surprisingly, the report reflected the president's own belief in a limited federal state ("Government participation in the economy should be limited to those instances where it is essential to the national interest and where private individuals or organizations cannot adequately meet the need"), in cooperation between business and labor, in a free market for agriculture, in economic growth and modernization, in an "open and peaceful world" characterized by free trade and mutual interdependence, and his conviction that the American people should be summoned to "extraordinary personal responsibility, sustained effort, and sacrifice."

and to broaden and redefine espionage and sabotage laws. One of his earliest actions as president was to institute a drastic new internal security program that broadened the criteria for federal employment to include not only loyalty and security but also "suitability," abolished the hearing and review procedures established by the Truman administration, and extended the power of summary dismissal, previously reserved to heads of sensitive departments such as state and defense, to all federal agencies and departments. He continued the Truman administration's prosecution of Communist leaders under the Smith Act and approved, in outline at least, the FBI's covert and extralegal COINTELPRO efforts "to promote disruption within the ranks of the Communist Party." He was well aware, moreover, of the FBI's euphemistically labeled "custodial detention" program and was prepared to order suspected subversives rounded up in time of national emergency.[59] Although he believed that little new evidence had been produced to implicate J. Robert Oppenheimer and that the case had been "constantly reviewed and reexamined over a number of years," Eisenhower nevertheless quickly ordered the famous physicist's security clearance lifted and later defended the AEC's finding that Oppenheimer was a security risk. And, although he considered commuting the sentences of Julius and Ethel Rosenberg, he finally decided, as he wrote his son, that "the exemplary feature of the punishment, the hope that it would deter others, is something that cannot be ignored."[60]

Although Eisenhower had himself on occasion employed the communist issue for political purposes, he nevertheless loathed McCarthy and was sharply critical of the highly publicized investigations in Congress. What he objected to most strenuously in the Congressional proceedings, however, was not so much their arbitrary violation of individual liberties but rather the disorderly and partisan atmosphere in which they were conducted. The job of routing subversives, he believed, was primarily administrative, not legislative—a task for orderly and bureaucratic resolution, not partisan debate. His strongest and most direct stand against the Congressional inquisitors came in the spring of 1954, when he invoked the doctrine of executive privilege in order to protect the privacy of advice offered within the executive branch. He bluntly told Congressional leaders, "Any man who testified as to the advice he gave me won't be working for me that night. . . . I will

---

[59] Athan Theoharis, *Spying on Americans: Political Surveillance from Hoover to the Huston Plan* (Philadelphia, 1978), 54, 55, 82–83, 107–10, 155–65, 209–18; and *Congress and the Nation, 1945–1964*, 1656–60. The president's program, boasted Walter Bedell Smith, would have the effect of outlawing the Communist party "without becoming involved in the constitutional complications of actual outlawry." Cabinet meeting, April 2, 1953, DDEL, EPP, Cabinet series, box 2. On rounding up political subversives, see Whitman Diary, June 25, 1954, DDEL, EPP, Ann Whitman Diary series, box 2.

[60] On Oppenheimer, see *Eisenhower Diaries* (December 2, 3, 1953), 259-60; and Hagerty Diary, May 29, June 1, 10, 1954, DDEL, Hagerty Papers, box 1. The strongest evidence against Oppenheimer, in Eisenhower's view, was the fact that he continued, through 1953, to visit socially with Haakon Chevalier, long after the 1943 "kitchen conversation" in which Chevalier had initiated a discussion about supplying technical information to the Soviet Union; Whitman Diary, June 25, 1954, DDEL, EPP, Ann Whitman Diary series, box 2. On the Rosenberg case, see Eisenhower to John S. D. Eisenhower, June 16, 1953, DDEL, EPP, DDE Diaries series, box 2; and Eisenhower to Clyde Miller, June 10, 1953, DDEL, EPP, Administration series, box 35. Eisenhower was impressed by trial judge Irving R. Kaufman and subsequently sought to elevate him to the U.S. Court of Appeals; Eisenhower, Telephone conversation with Herbert Brownell, February 22, 1955, January 27, 1957, DDEL, EPP, DDE Diaries series, boxes 5, 12.

not allow people around me to be subpoenaed and you might just as well know it now."[61]

He refused to be drawn into a direct confrontation with McCarthy, however, despite repeated entreaties from friends and advisors who feared that the senator's continued depredations would undermine the president's leadership. This reluctance arose in part from his realistic, if cynical, respect for McCarthy's support among Senate Republicans, in part from his personal dislike for the philippic mode. It also derived, however, from his sophisticated analysis of the relationships between McCarthy, the media, and the presidency. McCarthy, he wrote, owed "his entire prominence and influence . . . to the publicity media of the nation." The president, on the other hand, also possessed a "terrific headline value." He noted to his friend Hazlett that, "whenever the President takes part in a newspaper trial of some individual of whom he disapproves, one thing is automatically accomplished. This is an increase in the headline value of the individual attacked."[62] He chose instead to combat McCarthy through indirection: he urged Republican senators to attack him, ordered a reluctant Richard M. Nixon into combat in order to prevent McCarthy from monopolizing network television, encouraged Paul Hoffman and others to organize an anti-McCarthy movement, prevented McCarthy from addressing party gatherings, and suggested, with great circumspection, that publishers and media executives resist the senator's demands for time and space. He even suggested—only half jokingly—that since McCarthy had been built up by the press, the press should "develop a collusion to ignore him."[63] In the end, of course, the Senate did act, however reluctantly, in censuring the senator from Wisconsin. Eisenhower remained publicly aloof from the controversy, the press began to ignore McCarthy, and a measure of tranquility returned to American politics. By his own terms, if not by those of liberals or civil libertarians, the president had succeeded in bringing an era to an end.

The sharpest challenge to Eisenhower's quest for consensus, however, and the one that revealed most clearly the class and racial bias of his ideology, was the struggle by black Americans for civil rights and economic justice. Like most men of power, Eisenhower fully subscribed to the hierarchical values of corporate America. Though he believed in the principle of equality of opportunity, he also subscribed

---

[61] Eisenhower to Charles E. Wilson, May 17, 1954, in *Eisenhower Public Papers*, 2: 438–84. "I've gone to utmost lengths to be cooperative with Congress," Eisenhower told Republican majority leader William Knowland. "I have declined to get into this mess even when I have been needled by the press, but this is one thing I will fight with all my power—I will not have my men subpoenaed." Hagerty Diary, May 17, 1954, DDEL, Hagerty Papers, box 1.

[62] Eisenhower to Everett Hazlett, July 21, 1953, DDEL, EPP, DDE Diaries series, box 2; Eisenhower to William E. Robinson, March 23, 1954, *ibid.*, box 3; Eisenhower to John Reagan McCrary, Jr., December 4, 1954, *ibid.*, box 4; Eisenhower to Philip D. Reed, June 17, 1953, DDEL, EPP, Administration series, box 32; and Eisenhower to Paul H. Helms, March 9, 1954, DDEL, EPP, Name series, box 18.

[63] Hagerty Diary, May 20, 29, 30, 1954, DDEL, Hagerty Papers, box 1; Eisenhower, Telephone conversation with Nixon, March 8, 1954, DDEL, EPP, DDE Diaries series, box 3; and Paul G. Hoffman to Sherman Adams, November 26, 1954, HSTL, Hoffman Papers, box 84. Hoffman was one of the key supporters of the campaign to censure McCarthy in 1954; see Robert Griffith, *The Politics of Fear: Joseph R. McCarthy and the Senate* (Lexington, Ky., 1970), 228, 279–81. Hoffman also sought—together with former White House aide and Time-Life executive C. D. Jackson, columnist Roscoe Drummond, and others—to

to its less frequently stated corollary—that such opportunity inevitably created inequality of condition. He shared many of the conventional prejudices common among upper-middle class white Americans toward blacks and other minorities. He believed in equality before the law but not in "social equality." He did not think, he told Arthur Larson, that everyone had to mingle socially "or that a Negro should court my daughter."[64] These attitudes shaped his response to the emerging racial crisis of the 1950s and reinforced the fundamentally conservative elements of his political philosophy: his narrow construction of what was permissible and desirable for the national government to do, his fear of popular passion and his distrust of politics, his preference for cooperation over coercion, and his tendency to insulate the presidency from controversial issues. As president, he opposed the establishment of a Federal Fair Employment Practices Commission as well as any efforts that might project the national government any deeper into the school desegregation controversy opened up by the Brown decision in 1954. Not until 1956 did he call for civil rights legislation, and then only at the insistence of Attorney General Brownell. His support was limited, moreover, to the area of voting rights, where federal responsibility seemed clear, and to the creation of a bipartisan commission to study the problem. The proposed legislation, he assured Senate Majority Leader Lyndon B. Johnson, represented "the mildest civil rights bill possible"; even so, the measure was drastically weakened before enactment in 1957. Three years later, prodded by his own Civil Rights Commission, he again called for legislation, this time an extremely modest proposal that became the Civil Rights Act of 1960.[65]

In civil rights, as in other areas, he preferred to act administratively, without widespread publicity, and where federal jurisdiction was uncontested—for example, in the desegregation of navy yards and the integration of public facilities in the District of Columbia. He also sought, privately, to persuade prominent Southerners

mount a public and press relations campaign aimed at "replacing, in the public mind, the disuniting symbol of McCarthyism with the unifying image of the President as the effective instrument of anti-subversion"; Hoffman to Eisenhower, April 30, 1954, HSTL, Hoffman Papers, box 27. On Eisenhower's efforts to influence the press, see William S. Paley to Eisenhower, May 22, 1954, DDEL, EPP, Name series, box 25; Eisenhower to Gabriel Hauge, September 30, 1954, DDEL, EPP, DDE Diaries series, box 4; Whitman Diary, April 27, 1954, DDEL, EPP, Ann Whitman Diary series, box 2; William E. Robinson to Eisenhower, July 22, 1953, DDEL, EPP, Name series, box 29; and Eisenhower to Robinson, July 27, 1953, DDEL, EPP, DDE Diaries series, box 3. Many of the liberal businessmen who had supported Eisenhower in 1952 were extremely critical of McCarthy; for example, Harry A. Bullis, Philip D. Reed, and Paul H. Helms. It is especially interesting to note that among the most important contributors to McCarthy's downfall were three of the founders of the Committee for Economic Development—Democratic Senator William Benton, Republican Senator Ralph Flanders, and Hoffman.

[64] Larson, *The President Nobody Knew*, 124–33; and Lyon, *Eisenhower: Portrait of the Hero*, 556–57. "Maybe the President might get a chuckle out of this," observed his close friend Robinson, enclosing a racial joke; William E. Robinson to Ann Whitman, May 10, 1955, DDEL, EPP, Name series, box 27.

[65] On the 1957 law, especially see Legislative Leadership meetings, April 17, 1956, July 9–August 27, 1957, DDEL, EPP, Legislative series, box 2; Cabinet meeting, March 9, 1956, DDEL, EPP, Cabinet series, box 6; Cabinet meeting, March 23, 1956, *ibid.*, box 7; Cabinet meeting, August 2, 1957, *ibid.*, box 9; and Eisenhower, Telephone conversation with Lyndon B. Johnson, June 15, 1957, DDEL, EPP, DDE Diaries series, box 14. For Eisenhower's misgivings, see Gerald D. Morgan, Memorandum for the Record, March 24, 1956, *ibid.*, box 8. On the 1960 law, see Legislative Leadership meetings, February 2, April 26, 1960, DDEL, EPP, Legislative series, box 3. For a chronology of civil rights legislation, see *Congress and the Nation, 1945–1964*, 1621–30. For an excellent legislative history of the Eisenhower program, see Steven F. Lawson, *Black Ballots: Voting Rights in the South, 1944–1969* (New York, 1976), 140–249.

to embrace his own goals of moderation and gradual progress.[66] He feared the passions aroused by civil rights, both among blacks and Southern whites, and repeatedly preached patience, calmness, and forbearance. As he told Booker T. Washington's daughter, "I like to feel that where we have to change the hearts of men, we cannot do it by cold lawmaking, but must make these changes by appealing to reason, by prayer, and by constantly working at it through our own efforts."[67] He insisted, moreover, on insulating himself from the actions of the Supreme Court, the Civil Rights Commission, and even his own attorney general. Thus, in the school desegregation cases he carefully avoided identification with Attorney General Brownell, whose *amicus curiae* brief had drawn sharp criticism from Southern conservatives. He repeatedly refused to endorse the Brown decision or to identify himself publicly with the goal of desegregation. Privately, he thought the decision a mistake that would set back racial progress throughout the South. Desegregation, he believed, would require over thirty to forty years to complete.[68] When efforts at conciliation failed and he was compelled, however reluctantly, to dispatch federal troops to Little Rock, Arkansas, he carefully couched his actions in terms of defending civil order, not civil rights. As he explained to his friend Hazlett, "My biggest problem has been to make people see . . . that my main interest is not in the integration or segregation question. My opinion as to the wisdom or timeliness of the Supreme Court's decision has nothing to do with the case. . . . If the day comes when we can obey the orders of our Courts only when we personally approve of them, the end of the American system . . . will not be far off." In civil rights, as in other areas, a concern for order and stability predominated; and it was the president's firm intention, as he told South Carolina Governor James F. Byrnes, "to make haste slowly."[69]

EISENHOWER'S QUEST FOR A CORPORATE COMMONWEALTH at home was paralleled and inextricably bound to the struggle to create, at least among the so-called free nations, an interdependent and cooperative world order. Like other American leaders he believed that freedom, security, and prosperity were indivisible and that little domestic progress was possible in the absence of an international "atmosphere

---

[66] Larson, *The President Nobody Knew*, 124–33; Staff meeting, April 9, 1953, DDEL, EPP, DDE Diaries series, box 2; Eisenhower, Speech to the NAACP, March 10, 1954, in *Eisenhower Public Papers*, 2: 310; Eisenhower to James F. Byrnes, August 14, 1953, December 1, 1953, DDEL, EPP, DDE Diaries series, box 3; Eisenhower to Billy Graham, March 22, 1956, *ibid.*, box 8; Eisenhower to Ralph McGill, November 4, 1957, *ibid.*, box 17; Eisenhower to Billy Graham, March 30, 1956, DDEL, EPP, Name series, box 16; and Eisenhower to C. C. Warren, March 30, 1956, DDEL, White House Central Files, O.F. 141-B-1, box 730.

[67] E. Frederick Morrow, *Black Man in the White House: A Diary of the Administrative Years* (New York, 1963), 98.

[68] Eisenhower to James F. Byrnes, December 1, 1953, DDEL, EPP, DDE Diaries series, box 3; Maxwell M. Rabb, Memorandum for Governor Adams, November 12, 1957, DDEL, E. Frederick Morrow Records, box 10; Eisenhower, Telephone conversation with William P. Rogers, August 22, 1958, DDEL, EPP, Administration series, box 35; Larson, *The President Nobody Knew*, 124–26; and Hughes, *The Ordeal of Power*, 200-01. In 1956, Eisenhower demanded that the Republican platform committee excise any words to the effect that the Eisenhower administration supported the Court's decision; Eisenhower, Telephone conversation with Herbert Brownell, August 19, 1956, DDEL, EPP, Ann Whitman Diary series, box 8.

[69] Eisenhower to Everett Hazlett, November 8, 1957, DDEL, EPP, Name series, box 18; and Eisenhower to Byrnes, July 23, 1957, DDEL, EPP, DDE Diaries series, box 14.

in which America can be safe and prosperous." The challenge to such a system, he believed, was threefold: most obviously from the Soviet Union and other Communist nations but also from the Western nations, which might unthinkingly allow the world to fall victim to communism because each was "too preoccupied with its own local and selfish interests," and from within the United States itself, where greedy pressure groups might undermine long-run national and international interests. If, on the one hand, a disorderly and dangerous world could disrupt America's future progress and prosperity, so, on the other hand, greed and shortsightedness at home could undermine American goals abroad.[70] The purpose of foreign policy therefore lay in the mastery of these contradictions. This meant, to begin with, convincing Western nations that their (and America's) long-run interests demanded cooperation and mutual restraint. Too often, he believed, such cooperation was sacrificed to what he considered parochial interests and loyalties: the Arab-Israeli conflict in the Middle East, the Indian-Pakistani struggle over Kashmir, Korean antagonism toward Japan, and the unwillingness of European colonial powers to yield their prewar empires, to cite some of the examples he most frequently used in his private correspondence.

Sound foreign policy and broad, long-term national interests also meant that it was often necessary to restrain domestic interests. Expanded international trade, for example, which he considered absolutely vital to American and world prosperity, demanded a willingness to lower barriers to foreign imports, even at the expense of domestic producers; and nothing so irritated him as the clamor of businessmen for protection. "Daily I am impressed by the short-sightedness bordering upon tragic stupidity of many who fancy themselves to be the greatest believers in and supporters of capitalism . . . but who blindly support measures and conditions that cannot fail in the long run to destory any free economic system," he angrily wrote in his diary. Many businessmen, he complained, were "so concerned for their own particular immediate market and prosperity that they utterly fail to see that the United States cannot continue to live in a world where it must, for the disposal of its products, export vast portions of its industrial and agricultural products unless it also imports a sufficiently great amount of foreign products to allow countries to pay for the surpluses they receive from us."[71] Similarly, Americans had to be willing to bear the costs of collective security, if for no other reason than to avoid what he believed would be the far greater costs of military and economic isolation. To his friend Hazlett he wrote that "we must pursue a broad and intelligent program of loans, trade, technical assistance and, under current conditions, mutual guarantees of security. We must stop talking about 'give aways.' We must understand that our foreign expenditures are investments in America's future." He gave what he called a "simple example: No other nation is exhausting its irreplaceable resources so rapidly as is ours. Unless we are careful to build up and maintain a great group of international friends ready to trade with us, where do we hope to get all the

---

[70] Eisenhower to C. D. Jackson, April 30, 1957, DDEL, EPP, DDE Diaries series, box 13; Eisenhower to Frank Altschul, October 25, 1957, *ibid.*, box 16; and *Eisenhower Diaries* (February 9, July 2, 1953), 228–30, 242–45.
[71] *Eisenhower Diaries* (July 2, 24, 1953), 242–49.

materials that we will one day need as our rate of consumption continues and accelerates." He bluntly told a group of prominent businessmen at a White House dinner that "we cannot have prosperity without security and we must have friends with whom to trade."[72]

Eisenhower shared the conservative, anticommunist premises that animated both earlier and subsequent administrations, and he could act with ruthless efficiency when he believed that risks were limited and important national interests at stake. In Iran, where he had directed the overthrow of Muhammad Mossadegh and the return of young Shah Muhammad Reza Pahlevi, he believed that "we were in imminent danger of losing Iran, and sixty percent of the known oil reserves of the world," and he boasted privately that through his actions "that threat had been largely, if not totally, removed." In Guatemala, he ordered a highly secret CIA operation that overturned the moderately leftist government of Jacobo Arbenz Guzman and replaced it with the reactionary, but pro-American, dictatorship of Carlos Castillo Armas. In the Far East he was even willing to threaten nuclear war, especially against the Chinese, who had no capacity to retaliate in kind.[73] Yet for the most part his conduct of foreign affairs was distinguished by restraint, especially when the risks seemed high and the dangers of miscalculation great—he understood that the refusal to act was often the wisest course of action. As Robert Divine recently concluded, "Almost all of Eisenhower's foreign policy achievements were negative in nature. He ended the Korean war, he refused to intervene militarily in Indochina, he refrained from involving the United States in the Suez crisis, he avoided war with China over Quemoy and Matsu, he resisted the temptation to force a showdown over Berlin, he stopped exploding nuclear weapons in the atmosphere."[74]

Yet Eisenhower could never quite transcend the logic of his premises, as his response to revolutionary nationalism clearly revealed. Like many sophisticated conservatives, he opposed traditional European colonialism as costly, impractical, and ultimately self-defeating. From his experience in the Philippines, moreover, he knew firsthand of "the intensity and force of the spirit of nationalism that is gripping all peoples of the world today." He believed, as he wrote George Humphrey, that the "*protection of our own interests and our own system demands* . . . that we . . . understand that the spirit of nationalism, coupled with a deep hunger for some betterment in physical conditions and living standards, creates a critical situation in the under-developed areas of the world."[75] He had at

---

[72] Eisenhower to Everett Hazlett, August 3, 1956, DDEL, EPP, DDE Diaries series, box 8; and Harlow, Memorandum for the Record, January 30, 1958, *ibid.*, box 18. For a critical examination of economic diplomacy under Eisenhower, see Burton I. Kaufman, *Trade and Aid: Eisenhower's Foreign Economic Policy, 1953–1961* (Baltimore, 1982).

[73] Eisenhower to Edgar Eisenhower, November 8, 1954, DDEL, EPP, DDE Diaries series, box 5, On Iran, especially see Stephen E. Ambrose, *Ike's Spies: Eisenhower and the Espionage Establishment* (Garden City, N.Y., 1981), 189–214. On Guatemala, see Richard H. Immerman, *The CIA and Guatemala: The Foreign Policy of Intervention* (Austin, Texas, 1982); and Blanche Wiesen Cook, *The Declassified Eisenhower: A Divided Legacy of Peace and Political Warfare* (Garden City, N.Y., 1981), 217–92. On Asia, especially see Robert A. Divine, *Eisenhower and the Cold War* (New York, 1981), 28–70.

[74] Divine, *Eisenhower and the Cold War*, 154.

[75] Eisenhower to George Humphrey, March 1957, DDEL, EPP, Administration series, box 23; Eisenhow-

first believed that the free flow of goods and capital would in itself sustain economic development and that cooperation among nations and a friendly door to private investment would promote growth throughout the world. He later came to believe that enlightened self-interest required that the operation of the international market be supplemented by public capital. He expected, however, that new nations would follow the American model of capitalist growth.[76] Self-determination did not include the right to choose a radical road to development. Nor could he ever disentangle his response to social revolutions from his reaction to the foreign and military policies of the Soviet Union and China, as in the case of Indochina. If Eisenhower displayed restraint by refusing to intervene on behalf of the French in Indochina, it was a restraint produced more by France's refusal to grant its colonies full independence and permit the United States a decisive role in the military conduct of the war than by any particular reluctance on Eisenhower's part to employ force against social revolutions. The president wrote Hazlett in October 1954 that he had been unable to obtain "the conditions under which I felt the United States could properly intervene to protect its own interests." Eisenhower was determined, moreover, to draw the line in Southeast Asia—"we have got to keep the Pacific an American lake," he told his advisors.[77] Following the French collapse he committed the United States to the support of a client state south of the seventeenth parallel and to the undermining of the agreements reached at Geneva in 1954. These actions, as much as any, led to the expanded American involvement in Vietnam in the decade that followed.

Nor, finally, could Eisenhower escape the costly and destructive momentum of the warfare state. He believed that the Soviet challenge to the United States was indefinite, not immediate, and that it posed an economic and political threat as well as a military one. He was convinced that high levels of defense spending, such as those that had accompanied World War II and Korea, could not be indefinitely sustained without producing economic disorder and a resort to pervasive state intervention. As president he sought to reduce the level of America's defense effort, the so-called New Look, and was willing to permit by the end of the decade a relative increase in Soviet power. He embraced the concept of deterrent sufficiency rather than superiority—"why have more when we have as much destructive power as we do now," he asked Congressional leaders. Although he understood the problems posed by limited wars—"the enemy's political and military nibbling," he called it in a letter to Winston Churchill—he remained reluctant to "deploy and tie down our forces around the Soviet periphery in small wars."[78] His efforts to hold

---

er to Paul G. Hoffman, June 23, 1958, HSTL, Hoffman Papers, box 28; and Legislative Leadership meeting, July 2, 1957, DDEL, EPP, Legislative series, box 2.

[76] See, for example, Eisenhower's speeches to the Brazilian Congress, to a luncheon in São Paulo, Brazil, and to the Argentinian and Chilean congresses, during his 1960 trip to Latin America; *Eisenhower Public Papers*, 8: 216–20, 225–37, 256–61. "Investment capital is limited," he told the Chileans. "Competition for it is keen . . . and it will flow only to those areas where it is actively sought, welcomed, and treated fairly." *Ibid.*, 260.

[77] Eisenhower to Everett Hazlett, October 23, 1954, DDEL, EPP, Name series, box 18; and Conference in the President's Office, June 2, 1954, DDEL, EPP, Administration series, box 11.

[78] On defense policies, see Eisenhower to Charles E. Wilson, January 5, 1955, DDEL, EPP, Administration series, box 45; Eisenhower to Churchill, January 25, 1955, DDEL, EPP, DDE Diaries series, box 5; and

down military spending drew sharp criticism from within the armed services and Congress, however, and during his second administration the struggle to maintain what he believed was an appropriate balance between the nation's military and economic requirements consumed much of his energy.

The battle to hold down defense spending also forced Eisenhower to confront some of the dilemmas raised by his reliance on partnership and professionalism. He had deliberately chosen an industrialist to head the defense department—"We have earlier tried two investment bankers, a lawyer and a soldier," he observed—in the hope of imposing discipline and order on the services and strengthening cooperative relations with business. Many of his other defense appointments were also drawn from industry and finance, and the industrial advisory system begun during earlier administrations was expanded and strengthened. Similarly, Eisenhower hoped to recruit disinterested and expert military advisors, especially for the Joint Chiefs of Staff, who could rise above the petty loyalties of the services and, together with the civilian leadership, help promote broad national goals. He was, in all of this, disappointed. Wilson and the other businessmen who staffed defense failed to impose order, and, although Eisenhower succeeded in reorganizing the department in 1958, he increasingly came to believe that its problems were systemic. Service rivalry continued almost unabated, with each branch seeming to believe that it was "exclusively responsible for the defense of the United States." The Joint Chiefs of Staff failed to provide "distinterested, competent advice," and instead in many instances they became special pleaders for their services. Most importantly, Eisenhower came to believe that defense contractors themselves were exercising far too much influence over military budgets, and he expressed a keen interest in John J. McCloy's observation that "the inter-service game extends right down through the corporations, depending upon which branch their contracts flow from and it even goes into the academic institutions depending from where their research grants flow." In his farewell address Eisenhower noted the "conjunction of an immense military establishment and a large arms industry" and warned against "the acquisition of unwarranted influence . . . by the military industrial complex."[79]

THE EISENHOWER PRESIDENCY was thus shaped by the self-conscious quest for a corporate commonwealth in which the contradictions of modern capitalism would

---

Eisenhower to Frank Altschul, October 25, 1957. On the concept of sufficiency, see Eisenhower's remarks, Legislative Leadership meeting, March 1, 1955, DDEL, EPP, Legislative series, box 1; Legislative Leadership meetings, February 28, 1956, June 24, 1958, December 15, 1958, *ibid.*, box 2. On limited wars, see Eisenhower to Churchill, January 25, 1955; Andrew J. Goodpaster, Memorandum for the Record, May 23, 1956, DDEL, EPP, DDE Diaries series, box 8; and Cabinet meeting, May 23, 1958, DDEL, EPP, Cabinet series, box 11. Also see Douglas Kinnard, *President Eisenhower and Strategy Management* (Lexington, Ky., 1977).

[79] Eisenhower to Alfred M. Gruenther, November 26, 1952, DDEL, EPP, Administration series, box 16; Eisenhower to McCloy, May 10, 1958, DDEL, EPP, DDE Diaries series, box 20; Andrew J. Goodpaster, Memorandum for the Record, May 18, 1956, *ibid.*, box 8; Eisenhower to Everett Hazlett, August 20, 1956, *ibid.*; Legislative Leadership meeting, June 2, 1959, DDEL, EPP, Legislative series, box 3; Notes on Pre-Press Conference Briefing, June 3, 1959, DDEL, EPP, Ann Whitman Diary series, box 10; and *Eisenhower Public Papers*, 8: 1038.

be resolved through cooperation, self-restraint, discipline, and disinterested public service. The power of the state would be carefully limited, budgets prudently managed, cooperative arrangements forged between business and government, and conflicts defused through skillful governance and public relations. Enlightened diplomacy would similarly resolve potential conflicts among both developed and developing states and ensure a stable and harmonious world order. Only by understanding the centrality of this quest can we begin to grasp the inner coherence of the Eisenhower presidency and, more importantly, its relationship to the twentieth-century search for a new political economy. Indeed, the struggle to define the character of that new system has been the most important issue in modern American politics, from Populism and Progressivism through Hoover and the New Deal to the contemporary debate over "reindustrialization" and the proper relationship between government and economic life. In understanding Eisenhower we begin to understand our past, our present, and—at least in part—the alternatives before us. It is precisely because of this resonance, however, that we must be careful to avoid facile and misleading analogies and to label any conclusions provisional.

Eisenhower's quest for a new order was, on one level at least, an enormous success. The years of his presidency were among the most prosperous, peaceful, and politically tranquil in this century, and he left office one of the most popular chief executives in American history. But this was, as he himself would have been quick to note, a calculus of only short-term results. He had succeeded in slowing the growth of the federal state and, as in the case of the highway program, insulating its operations from popular politics. He had also succeeded in expanding cooperative arrangements between government and business and in accelerating the interpenetration of public and private sectors. In all of this, of course, his presidency served to rationalize the efforts of American business to refashion the New Deal state. But he did not succeed in securing that concert of private interests that would insure stable and orderly growth and on which his vision of a corporate commonwealth depended. Indeed, before his presidency had ended there was already widespread evidence of disorder and dysfunction: business leaders had repeatedly failed to exercise the restraint and self-discipline that such a system demanded, the problems of agriculture had proven politically irresolvable, and employers and labor unions were increasingly "tending to settle their differences without regard to the impact on the economy." Nor did he succeed in surmounting the tensions of class, race, and sex that surged like powerful undercurrents just beneath the surface of American culture. The tendency, encouraged during his presidency, to substitute private consumption for public politics laid a heavy—if then still invisible—tax on limited resources, increased political alienation, and undercut his own emphasis on sacrifice and discipline. Revolutions throughout the Third World created growing international tension and heightened the conflict between his tactical emphasis on the limits of American power and the globalism to which he and other American leaders continued to subscribe. Critics, including some former supporters, now began to accuse the president of lack of leadership, demanding not only a more activist foreign policy but also a level of military spending that he clearly feared would produce disastrous consequences. By 1958 he was wondering plaintively "whether immediate greed would ever surrender to the long-term good of the whole world." His attempt to fashion a corporate commonwealth foundered, finally, on the problem of succession and on the inability of the Republican party to generate a disinterested leadership capable of sustaining his vision. His deep ambivalence over Nixon turned on precisely this point—"it is terrible," he pointedly told Ann Whitman, "when people get politically ambitious."[80]

Within a decade the fragile consensus of the 1950s shattered on the hard realities of war and revolution, of class and racial conflict, of repression and indulgence. Such a failure was probably inevitable; for despite his pragmatism and lucid intelligence Eisenhower was at heart a visionary. Alarmed by the self-interested destructiveness of contemporary economic life, he had fashioned a deeply conservative image of a good society in which conflict would yield to cooperation, greed to discipline, coercion to self-government. Such a vision was no match for the vast and powerful forces of modern America.

[80] Cabinet meeting, December 14, 1956, DDEL, EPP, Cabinet series, box 6; Legislative Leadership meeting, May 13, 1958, DDEL, EPP, Legislative series, box 2; and Whitman Diary, June 11, 1959, DDEL, EPP, Ann Whitman Diary series, box 10.

American Marshall Planners
and the Search for a European Neocapitalism

MICHAEL J. HOGAN

IN THE LAST DECADE OR SO, NEW LEFT, NEW RIGHT, organizational, and institutional historians alike have begun to see the emergence of a corporative capitalism as one of the most important developments in recent American history. In the Progressive-era policies of the National Civic Federation, in Herbert Hoover's brand of associationalism, in the business-government commonwealth promoted by many New Dealers, and in the political economy of the Eisenhower years, they have traced the development of an integrated economic system and of new patterns of collaboration and interpenetration between private groups and government authorities. In this system, group conflict and natural market forces are tempered by institutional mechanisms of regulation and control and by a host of cooperating committees and other voluntary frameworks through which public and private leaders share responsibility for economic policy and management. In theory, at least, the resulting fusion of market forces and institutional controls, of private and public power, works to preserve the economic and political advantages of an older, more competitive capitalism, while avoiding the threat to private enterprise that supposedly inheres in an unregulated pursuit of self-interest or in an oppressive and paternalistic statism.[1]

The existing literature, however, says little about the international dimension of this evolving neocapitalism. It tells us little about how American leaders have applied their corporative strategies to the management of foreign policy and the organization of the international system or about the specific institutional mechanisms through which they have worked to integrate economies and blend public and private power in ways that would maximize the chances for social peace and

I would like to thank the Miami University Faculty Research Council, the Harry S. Truman Library, and the Woodrow Wilson International Center for Scholars for financial assistance in the completion of this work. I would also like to thank Kurt S. Schultz for research assistance, Pamela Messer for help with the typing, and Ellis W. Hawley, John Lewis Gaddis, Burton Kaufman, Melvyn Leffler, and the anonymous referees of the *American Historical Review* for stylistic, organizational, and substantive suggestions.

[1] James Weinstein, *The Corporate Ideal in the Liberal State* (Boston, 1968); Joan Hoff-Wilson, *Herbert Hoover: Forgotten Progressive* (Boston, 1975); Ellis W. Hawley, "Herbert Hoover, the Commerce Secretariat, and the Vision of an 'Associative State,'" *Journal of American History*, 61 (1974–75): 116–40, *The Great War and the Search for a Modern Order* (New York, 1979), and *The New Deal and the Problem of Monopoly: A Study in Economic Ambivalence* (Princeton, 1966); and Robert Griffith, "Dwight D. Eisenhower and the Corporate Common-

productive efficiency.[2] An examination of the Marshall Plan can tell us more than we now know about this facet of public policy. Through the Marshall Plan, American leaders sought to recast Europe in the image of American neocapitalism. They envisioned a Western European system in which class conflict would give way to corporative collaboration, economic self-sufficiency to economic interdependence, international rivalry to rapprochement and cooperation, and arbitrary national controls to the integrating powers of supranational authorities and natural market forces. One line of their policy aimed at liberalizing trade and making currencies convertible, another at forging national and transnational networks of private cooperation and public-private power sharing, and a third at building central institutions of coordination and control. Through these and related initiatives American Marshall planners hoped to create an integrated European market—one that could absorb German power, boost productivity, raise living standards, lower prices, and thus set the stage for security and recovery on the Continent and for a fully multilateral system of world trade.

THE IDEA OF EUROPEAN ECONOMIC INTEGRATION first appeared in American policy planning in the early months of 1947. By then it was clear that previous programs of piecemeal assistance had failed to bring economic and political stability to Europe. Economic conditions there actually worsened in the wake of the winter crisis of 1946–47, and this combined with political turmoil in France and Italy, failure of Allied leaders to agree on terms for Germany's unification, and fear that Soviet policy would gain from confusion and weakness in the West led American officials to consider a major foreign aid initiative. Their planning now envisioned a

---

wealth," *AHR*, 87 (1982): 87–122. Also see Hawley, "The Discovery and Study of Corporate Liberalism," *Business History Review*, 52 (1978): 309–20; Kim McQuaid, "Corporate Liberalism and the American Business Community," *ibid.*, 342–67; and Robert M. Collins, *The Business Response to Keynes, 1929–1964* (New York, 1981). As Griffith explained in the essay cited above, historians use the terms "corporatism," "corporate liberalism," and "neo-capitalism" interchangeably to describe "both the historical *process* through which liberal institutions have adapted to the imperatives of large-scale organization and the *ideology* that has been used to promote and legitimize such a process"; "Dwight D. Eisenhower and the Corporate Commonwealth," 97 n. 21. The historical advocates of neocapitalism differ on important questions, particularly on the proper balance between public and private power, and this balance has tended to shift over the course of the twentieth century. Nevertheless, neocapitalists differ from both laissez-faire and welfare state theorists in that they accept a positive role for the state in such areas as social welfare and economic regulation, while seeking to contain this role by organizing public-private power-sharing arrangements and voluntary frameworks of self-regulation, enlightened group action, and intergroup cooperation. For a general discussion of the continuities and changes in the neocapitalist approach to domestic and foreign economic policy over the course of this century, see my "Revival and Reform: America's Twentieth-Century Search for a New Economic Order Abroad," *Diplomatic History*, 8 (1984): 287–310.

[2] For efforts in this direction, see Hoff-Wilson, *Herbert Hoover*; Hawley, *Great War*; Griffith, "Dwight D. Eisenhower and the Corporate Commonwealth"; Michael J. Hogan, *Informal Entente: The Private Structure of Cooperation in Anglo-American Economic Diplomacy, 1918–1928* (Columbia, Mo., 1977), "Thomas W. Lamont and European Recovery: The Diplomacy of Privatism in a Corporatist Age," in Kenneth Paul Jones, ed., *U. S. Diplomats in Europe, 1919–1941* (Santa Barbara, Calif., 1981), 5–22, and "Revival and Reform"; and Melvyn P. Leffler, *The Elusive Quest: America's Pursuit of European Stability and French Security, 1919–1933* (Chapel Hill, 1979). Also see Thomas J. McCormick, "Drift or Mastery? A Corporatist Synthesis for American Diplomatic History," *Reviews in American History*, 10 (1982): 318–30. On the European side, see, especially, Charles S. Maier, "The Two Postwar Eras and the Conditions for Stability in Twentieth-Century Western Europe," *AHR*, 86 (1981): 327–52, and *Recasting Bourgeois Europe: Stabilization in France, Germany, and Italy in the Decade after World War I* (Princeton, 1975).

comprehensive recovery program for Europe as a whole, one based on the principles of collective action, joint programming, and resource sharing and one aimed at breaking bottlenecks to production, making currencies convertible, reducing trade barriers, and integrating economies.

Such an approach, it was assumed, could eliminate the territorial constraints, government restrictions, and bilateral trade and payments agreements that prevented the most efficient use of resources, hampered productivity, and slowed the pace of recovery in Europe. It could also fortify the Western democracies against communist attack, forge a collective framework for controlling German nationalism, and, in this way, reconcile the revival of Germany's productive power with the security and economic needs of its former victims. This was the thinking embodied in the public and private pronouncements of American policy makers on the eve of Secretary of State George C. Marshall's celebrated commencement address at Harvard University on June 5, 1947. Marshall himself was "deeply sympathetic" to the idea of European integration, and, although he thought that European leaders should take the initiative in devising a recovery program, the emphasis in his Harvard speech on a comprehensive scheme and on collective responsibility, mutual aid, and "joint" action in "Europe as a whole" was designed to point the Europeans in the right direction.[3]

The American position became even clearer in the summer and fall of 1947, when the Committee on European Economic Cooperation (CEEC) met in Paris to draw up a recovery program. American leaders urged the sixteen countries represented to draft proposals for mutual aid and resource sharing and to establish procedures for the collective screening of individual country requirements and the coordination of national investment decisions on an area-wide basis. They then worked with their European counterparts to devise a plan that acknowledged these principles and procedures, called for a "new era of European economic cooperation," and promised "concerted action" to maximize production, reduce tariffs, and stabilize currencies. American policy makers, according to a CEEC delegation that visited Washington in October, believed that such measures could "bring benefits to Europe through the creation of a larger domestic market and [the] concentration of productive effort." Indeed, the aid proposal that the Truman administration submitted to Congress in December and the Foreign Assistance Act that Congress passed the following spring urged Europeans to replace the old "self-defeating" pattern of "narrow nationalism" with new forms of economic cooperation and integration. This, they agreed, was the path to "lasting peace and prosperity" on the Continent.[4]

---

[3] For Marshall's sympathetic view of European union, see Marshall to Senator Arthur H. Vandenberg, June 4, 1947, Department of State *Bulletin*, June 22, 1947, p. 1213. Marshall's speech at Harvard is printed in U.S., Department of State, *Foreign Relations of the United States* [hereafter, *FRUS*], *1947*, 3 (Washington, D.C., 1972), 237–39. For a general discussion of American policy planning see Michael J. Hogan, "The Search for a 'Creative Peace': The United States, European Unity, and the Origins of the Marshall Plan," *Diplomatic History*, 6 (1982): 267–85.

[4] For the CEEC's report, see Committee on European Economic Cooperation, *General Report*, 1, and *Technical Reports*, 2 (London, 1947). For the remark by the CEEC delegation in Washington, see its telegram to the participating governments, October 31, 1947, in *FRUS*, *1947*, 3: 456–61. For the quotations from the administration's aid proposal and the Foreign Assistance Act, see Ernst H. Van Der Beugel, *From Marshall Aid to*

Thereafter, policy makers in the State Department and in the Economic Cooperation Administration (ECA), the American agency established to administer the European Recovery Program (ERP), employed a variety of strategies to integrate Europe and create the new era of "lasting peace and prosperity." One such strategy involved the ECA's decision to make Marshall Plan countries, through their Organization for European Economic Cooperation (OEEC), collectively responsible for reviewing national requirements and integrating these into consolidated annual recovery programs that would include plans for raising production, liberalizing trade, placing government finances on a sound basis, and making collective use of European resources. Any program for putting Europe on a self-supporting basis, as ECA Administrator Paul G. Hoffman told the OEEC in July 1948, could not be "traced on an old design" or "brought about by old ways of doing business," by "old concepts of how a nation's interests are best served," or by "old separatist lines" of economic activity. It would require "new patterns of intra-European trade and exchange," new efforts to adjust national economies to the needs of "Europe as a whole," and "new directions in the use of Europe's resources."[5]

These should include Germany's resources as well as those of the other participating countries. The need, according to this line of American strategy, was for a balanced recovery program that would incorporate western Germany into a "strong common structure of free Europeanism." A policy that "segregated" Germany might lead to the "rebirth of aggressive German nationalism," German economic domination of the Continent, or a dangerous Soviet-German rapprochement. But one that fitted Germany into the framework of a "general European union" could capture its resources for the West, aid European recovery, benefit the "strategic position" and reduce the "security preoccupations of the Western powers," and encourage the growth of democratic politics in the former Reich. If Germany could not, for political reasons, be made a member of the Brussels Pact and North Atlantic Treaty, its resources could at least form part of a larger Western European economic system.[6]

Another strategy centered on the so-called counterpart funds, the local currency equivalent of American grants set aside by participating countries for use under terms approved by the ECA. The agency employed these funds to restrain inflation where this would revive "internal production and foreign trade" and to underwrite

---

Atlantic Partnership: European Integration as a Concern of American Foreign Policy (New York, 1966), 106; and U.S. Congress, House of Representatives, Committee on International Relations, Historical Series, *Selective Executive Hearings, Foreign Economic Assistance Programs,* part 1: *Foreign Assistance Act of 1948* (Public Law 472), 80th Congress, 2d sess., 1948 (Washington, D.C., 1976), 254–72 [hereafter, House, *Foreign Assistance Act of 1948*]. For additional details on this part of the story, see my "Paths to Plenty: American Marshall Planners and the Idea of European Economic Integration, 1947–1948," *Pacific Historical Review,* 53 (1984): 337–66.

[5] Hoffman, as quoted in W. Averell Harriman to ECA, July 25, 1948, Washington, D.C., Agency for International Development Records, ECA Telegram File [hereafter, ECA File], Acc. 53A278, box 5.

[6] See the State Department paper of March 31, 1949, attached to Secretary of State Dean Acheson's memorandum to President Truman, March 31, 1949; the paper of March 23, 1949, prepared by Robert Murphy of the State Department's Office of German and Austrian Affairs; the State Department's undated annex and appendix to Murphy's paper; and the memoranda of February 7 and March 8, 1949, by George Kennan, director of the State Department's Policy Planning Staff, *FRUS, 1949,* 3 (Washington, D.C., 1974), 142–55, 118–37, 90–93, 96–102.

capital investment where this would enhance "national productivity" and contribute to recovery in "Europe as a whole."[7] Initially, it used counterpart funds to control inflationary pressures, for example, by enabling the British government to reduce short-term public debt and encouraging the Italian and French governments to balance budgets, limit bank credit, and maintain wage and price stability.[8] Once inflationary pressures seemed under control, however, policy makers in the ECA began discussing a "critical sectors" approach to counterpart financing by which they hoped to direct investment into those industries that had a natural advantage in labor costs or raw materials and could thus compete without government subsidies, protective tariffs, or restrictive arrangements. The result, or so it was expected, would be an integrated European economic system in which freer trade, greater specialization, and more efficient use of resources would work to raise productivity, lower prices, and close the Continent's trade deficit with the Western Hemisphere.[9]

The same goal guided the ECA's attack on exchange restrictions, quantitative import quotas, and bilateral trade agreements in Europe. These, too, discouraged the most efficient use of resources. They made participating countries dependent on the United States for goods generally available on the Continent, slowed the pace of European recovery, and hampered efforts to expand trade and increase production. Both the ECA and State Department thus lent support to the formation of a European customs union and encouraged negotiations for a Franco-Italian tariff union and a merger of this union with the Benelux group.[10] In addition, they supported the intra-European payments plans of 1948 and 1949, under which ECA dollars helped creditors finance a system of drawing rights that debtors used to balance their accounts without resorting to quantitative import quotas and other restrictions on trade.[11]

Before these strategies could work, however, British opposition to European

[7] Harriman, circular, August 31, 1948, Washington National Records Center, Suitland, Md., Department of State Records, Record Group 84, London Embassy Files [hereafter, RG 84], box 1035, folder 850, Marshall Plan. Also see Hoffman to Harriman, September 14, 1948, Washington, D.C., Department of the Treasury Records [hereafter, Treasury Records], Acc. 66A1039, box 4, Marshall Plan, Local Currency Counterpart folder; and Harry Bayard Price, *The Marshall Plan and Its Meaning* (Ithaca, New York, 1955), 104.

[8] Price examined policy in France and Britain; *Marshall Plan and Its Meaning*, 104–07. For American policy in Italy and Italian-American discussions over counterpart funds, see Harriman to Hoffman, October 14, 1948; William Foster to Hoffman, December 29, 1948, ECA File, box 5. Also see the ECA aide-memoires of September 30, 1948, resumes of conversations between the ECA mission chief and Italian Premier Alcide de Gasperi, October 1, 12, 1948, and the memorandum by Arthur Marget of the ECA to Harriman, December 21, 1948, in Washington National Records Center, Suitland, Md., Records of the Agency for International Development, Record Group 286 [hereafter, RG 286], Acc. 53A177, box 33, Italy folder.

[9] Harriman to Hoffman, October 11, 14, November 29, 1949; Harriman to Hoffman, December 20, 1949; Philip Bonsal to Hoffman, December 28, 1949, ECA File, box 8; Hoffman to Harriman, October 12, 1949; Foster to Hoffman, October 12, 1949; Hoffman to Harriman, November 11, 1949, *ibid.*, box 50; and Harriman to Hoffman, December 2, 1949, RG 286, Acc. 53A405, box 50, Finance-Investments folder.

[10] For American support of the European Customs Union Study Commission, see Marshall to the American Embassy, Brussels, March 10, 1948, National Archives, Washington, D.C., Department of State Records, Record Group 59 [hereafter, RG 59], file 640.002/2–448. On the Franco-Italian negotiations, see *ibid.*, file 651.6531/12–947, 1–1248, 1–1648, 1–2448, 1–2848; and Raymond Vernon, memorandum to Paul Nitze, January 14, 1948, *ibid.*, file 840.50 Recovery/1–1448. For the American position on French efforts to merge the Franco-Italian and Benelux groups, see Marshall to the American Legation, Luxembourg, January 29, 1948, *ibid.*, file 655.5631/1–2948.

[11] William Diebold, Jr., *Trade and Payments in Western Europe: A Study in Economic Cooperation, 1947–51* (New York, 1952), 34–46, 64–80.

union and French opposition to German integration had to be overcome. The French were reluctant to compromise their security or their Monnet Plan for industrial modernization in order to expedite Germany's revitalization. By 1948 their demands for reparations and proposals for ownership and management of the Ruhr industries, limitations and prohibitions on German production, and political decentralization in the western zones were colliding with American plans to revitalize German industry, reduce Allied occupation controls, and unify the western zones under a new German government.[12] The British, on the other hand, were refusing to submerge their sovereignty in a European economic union at the cost of their control over domestic policies, their ties to the Commonwealth, and their leadership of the sterling bloc. They conditioned their participation in a European customs union on special arrangements to protect the system of imperial preference. They played an indirect role in scuttling French proposals for merging the Benelux group with the proposed Franco-Italian tariff union. And to safeguard their position as leaders of the sterling area, they demanded special consideration for this area in the intra-European payments plans of 1948 and 1949.[13]

The political accommodation that resolved some of these differences in 1949 was offset by stubborn economic problems and ongoing Anglo-American disagreement over how to address them. The Allies agreed to loosen the restrictions on German industry, reduce the number of plants to be dismantled for reparation, establish an international authority to oversee the Ruhr, and replace military rule in the western zones with an Allied high commission of civilian officials.[14] These and other agreements brought French policy more into line with American thinking and set the stage for the formation of the Federal Republic and its subsequent accession to the OEEC and Council of Europe. At the same time, however, European exports to the dollar area began to decline, in part because of economic recession in the United States but also, as the Economic Commission for Europe reported, because of resistance to coordinated economic planning and the desire among European nations for self-sufficiency. Too many Marshall Plan countries were still pursuing policies that prevented gains in specialization, economies of scale, and labor productivity required to drive down prices, make their commodities more competitive, and balance their accounts with the dollar area.[15]

The need to redress the trade imbalance, as well as the different British and American strategies for doing so, grew apparent in mid-1949. By then the sterling area's dollar deficit had reached proportions that threatened to drain the Bank of

[12] John Gimbel, *The American Occupation of Germany: Politics and the Military, 1945–1949* (Stanford, 1968), 194–225; John C. Campbell, *The United States in World Affairs, 1948–1949* (New York, 1949), 70–79, 464–75; and Hogan, "Paths to Plenty." I have examined the German question in some detail. See my "European Union and German Integration: Marshall Planners and the Search for Recovery and Security in Western Europe," in Charles S. Maier, ed., *Germany and the Marshall Plan* (forthcoming, 1986).

[13] For these developments, see RG 59, file 640.002/11–647, 12–1847, 1–1648, 1–1948, 2–1148, 2–2448, 4–2448, and file 655.5631/11–1447, 2–448, 2–848; and Diebold, *Trade and Payments in Western Europe*, 34–46, 64–80.

[14] The Allied agreements came at the Washington Foreign Ministers Conference of late March and early April. On the discussions there and the agreements that resulted, see *FRUS, 1949*, 3: 156–86. Also see Hogan, "European Union and German Integration."

[15] United Nations, Economic Commission for Europe, *Economic Survey of Europe in 1948* (Geneva, 1949), esp. 211–28.

England of its gold and dollar reserves. To stabilize the situation, the Labour government relied on bilateral controls, restrictions on dollar-area imports, and international agreements to bolster the price of sterling-area exports.[16] Such measures were expected to stanch the dollar hemorrhage at the expense of the ECA's plans for an integrated European economic order and a fully multilateral system of world trade. And in response to them, American leaders called for a strategy that was more compatible with these plans and with the findings of the Economic Commission for Europe. They urged a maximum liberalization of trade and payments on the Continent and a substantial devaluation of the pound sterling and other European currencies. Such measures, they said, would improve the dollar position of Marshall Plan countries and create a "single-market Europe" in which "large low-cost production" could help "close the dollar deficit" and lessen the need for discrimination against American exports.[17]

Hoffman and other American leaders appealed for British cooperation during Anglo-American financial talks that opened in Washington on September 7. In reality, however, they had left the British with few alternatives to devaluation. The American executive director of the International Monetary Fund (IMF) had already overcome British opposition and won support for a resolution authorizing the IMF to study European exchange rates. He subsequently took charge of a special committee established to investigate the "dollar gap" and drafted a report that called for a downward revision in European exchange rates. The report was almost certain to have the support of the IMF's board of directors when it met in September, and the prospect of this, particularly of the pressure it would put on sterling, made it virtually impossible for the British to avoid devaluation. During the Anglo-American financial talks in Washington, they privately informed the Americans of their decision, and on September 18, six days after the talks had adjourned, they officially announced a 30 percent depreciation of pound sterling.[18]

British devaluation ended the sterling crisis, and, by prompting a general devaluation and realignment of other European currencies, it also fulfilled one of

---

[16] Ambassador Lewis Douglas, London, to Acheson, June 16, 22, 1949; Willard Thorp, assistant secretary of state for economic affairs, memorandum for the secretary of state, June 27, 1949; and Secretary of the Treasury John W. Snyder to Acheson, July 9, 10, 1949, *FRUS, 1949*, 4 (Washington, D.C., 1975), 784–86, 787–90, 793–96, 799–801, 801–02.

[17] Harriman to ECA, August 15, 1949, ECA File, box 8. Also see Acheson to Douglas, June 27, 30, 1949; Hoffman to Acting U.S. Special Representative Milton Katz, August 3, 1949; National Advisory Council on International Monetary and Financial Problems, undated paper, *FRUS, 1949*, 4: 796–97, 797–99, 412–15, 419–21.

[18] J. Burke Knapp, memorandum to Thorp, April 4, 1949, with attached memorandum by Frank Southard, under secretary of the treasury and U.S. executive director, IMF, to Snyder and Assistant Secretary of the Treasury William McC. Martin, Jr., March 31, 1949, RG 59, file 840.50 Recovery/4–449; Acheson to Douglas, April 7, 1949, *ibid.*, Recovery/4–2449; Acheson to certain diplomatic offices, April 12, 1949, *FRUS, 1949*, 4: 382–83; Thomas Finletter, ECA mission chief, London, to Harriman, April 13, 1949, Washington, D.C., W. Averell Harriman Papers [hereafter, Harriman Papers], United Kingdom folder; Southard, memoranda to Snyder and Martin, September 5, 8, 12, 1949, Harry S. Truman Library, Independence, Mo. [hereafter, HSTL], John W. Snyder Papers, box 20, Alphabetical File, International Monetary Fund folder. As these documents point out, Snyder agreed to delay action by the IMF's board until mid-September. It seems likely that he did so, however, only after British officials at the Washington financial talks had informed him of their decision to devalue. Also see Dean Acheson, *Present at the Creation: My Years in the State Department* (New York, 1969), 324–25. For the text of the announcement by Chancellor of the Exchequer Sir Stafford Cripps, see *New York Times*, September 19, 1949, p. 6.

the ECA's requirements for narrowing the dollar gap and integrating European economies. To fulfill its second requirement, a maximum liberalization of intra-European trade and payments, the ECA proposed in December 1949 the creation of a European payments union. The proposed union aimed to offset the bilateral credits and debits of participating countries, leaving each in net surplus or deficit to the group as a whole. Net balances would then be financed partly with ECA dollars, partly with new credits or gold payments by surplus and deficit countries respectively. The latter provision would introduce an automatic incentive for creditors to correct persistent surpluses by diverting a larger share of their exports to the dollar area and for creditors and debtors alike to adjust their exchange rates and internal fiscal and monetary policies in the interest of European equilibrium. At the same time, the provision for multilateral offsetting would enable countries in net surplus with the group to manage their bilateral deficits without resorting to quantitative import quotas or other restrictions on trade: a deficit with one country could be offset by a surplus with another. Through such provisions, the ECA hoped to reduce the dollar gap, eliminate the barriers to intra-European trade, coordinate national monetary policies, and integrate economies.[19]

For policy makers in London, however, merging the British and Continental economies meant shelving their socialist programs, importing Europe's unemployment, and subjecting their economy to greater competition and a potential loss of markets, revenues, and reserves. Such sacrifices, they warned the Americans, would make it difficult to shoulder their share of Europe's defense burden, protect their leadership of the sterling area, and maintain their commitments in other areas of the world that were vital to the security and interests of the Western alliance. For these reasons, they insisted, any payments agreement would have to exempt sterling from multilateral offsettings, leave their bilateral agreements intact, and protect their right to impose quantitative import restrictions on a unilateral and discriminatory basis.[20] The British, as the ECA complained, refused to limit "the exercise of national sovereignty, confining its absolute and arbitrary exercise to the legitimate field in which it would not conflict with the economic needs of Western Europe as a whole." They would not submit to the automatic checks on national policy that were inherent in the idea of partial gold settlements. Nor would they abandon the bilateral bargaining and artificial restrictions that prevented readjustment and the "creation of a single, wide, competitive market" in Western Europe.[21]

[19] Hoffman to Harriman, October 25, 1949; Foster to Harriman, November 26, 1949, ECA File, box 8; Hoffman to Harriman, December 3, 1949, *ibid.*, box 51; Harriman to Hoffman, December 3, 9, 1949; Harriman to Hoffman, December 12, 14, 1949, *ibid.*, box 8; and Richard Bissell to Nitze, December 15, 1949, RG 59, Records of the Policy Planning Staff [hereafter, RG 59, PPS Records], box 27, Europe folder, 1949.

[20] U.S. Delegation at the Tripartite Preparatory Meetings in London to Acheson, April 25, 26, 28, 1950; U.S. Delegation at the Tripartite Foreign Ministers Meeting in London to Under Secretary of State James Webb, May 9, 1950; Acheson to Webb, May 14, 1950, *FRUS, 1950*, 3 (Washington, 1972), 865–69, 881–83, 886–90, 1018–22, 1061–67. Also see U.S. Department of State, "Essential Elements of US-UK Relations," April 19, 1950, *ibid.*, 869–81. For a summary of the British terms, see Hoffman to Katz, March 11, 1950, ECA File, box 64; ECA, report for the State Department, April 14, 1950, *FRUS, 1950*, 3: 646–52; and ECA, memorandum for the secretary of state, May 5, 1950, Harriman Papers, European Payments Union folder.

[21] ECA, report for the State Department, April 14, 1950. Also see Hoffman to Harriman, March 31, 1950, ECA File, box 64; and Henry Tasca, memorandum to Katz, March 13, 1950, Harriman Papers, European Payments Union folder.

Under these circumstances some policy makers began discussing a Continental payments union that would exclude Britain. But this idea had "an air of unreality" to most of those in the ECA. The Scandinavians would certainly refuse to participate without the British, and, even if other Marshall Plan countries could reach agreement, they feared that Germany would dominate a strictly Continental group or that "competitive jockeying" over its position would divide the Western system into separate British and Continental blocs, drive a wedge between the United States and Britain, and "mean a setback to Europe and to Atlantic community cooperation."[22] Similar thoughts came from George Kennan's Policy Planning Staff, from a meeting of American ambassadors in Paris, and from position papers composed in the State Department in the months prior to the London Foreign Ministers Conference of May 1950.[23] Those involved generally agreed that some form of economic union was needed to put Europe on a self-supporting basis and to contain both German and Soviet power. But they agreed as well that the prospects for union did not seem bright so long as the British refused to make the necessary sacrifices. Germany would dominate a Continental union, and fears of this would make it difficult to win continued French support for Germany's revitalization and reintegration.

The remaining alternative seemed to involve some formula for reconciling British commitments at home and abroad with American plans for an integrated Europe balanced between British and German power. And because the problem was one of financial constraints on British diplomacy, the solution seemed to lie in what one State Department memorandum termed a "'share-the-wealth' plan," under which the British would adopt a more positive approach to the Continent and, in return, "we [would] assume unto ourselves at least the partial obligations of the sterling block [sic]." British and American leaders actually hammered out an arrangement like this during the London Foreign Ministers Conference. The British endorsed American economic policy objectives so long as they squared with British responsibilities to the sterling area. The Americans pledged to assist in these responsibilities by supporting pound sterling.[24] This understanding then defined the basis for Britain's participation in a European payments union. Specifically, the

[22] Harriman to Hoffman, April 3, 1950, ECA File, box 18. Also see Hoffman to Katz, March 11, 1950, *ibid.*, box 64; and Hoffman to Harriman, March 31, 1950.

[23] Policy Planning Staff, Minutes of the 81st Meeting, May 20, 1949, RG 59, PPS Records, box 32, Minutes of Meetings folder, 1949; Minutes of the 84th, 87th, 99th, 100th, 101st, 102nd Meetings, May 25, 27, June 8, 13 (two meetings), 14 (two meetings), 1949, *ibid.*, box 27, Europe folder, 1949; Summary Record of a Meeting of United States Ambassadors at Paris, October 21–22, 1949, *FRUS, 1949,* 4: 472–96; Minutes of the Seventh Meeting of the Policy Planning Staff, January 24, 1950, *FRUS, 1950,* 3: 617–22; Department of State, "Essential Elements of US-UK Relations"; and Memorandum Prepared in the Bureau of German Affairs, [February 11, 1950], *FRUS, 1950,* 4 (Washington, D.C., 1980), 597–602. Also see Perkins, memorandum to Acheson, January 24, 1950, *FRUS, 1950,* 3: 1610–14.

[24] Memorandum Prepared in the Bureau of German Affairs, [February 11, 1950]. Also see Minutes of the Seventh Meeting of the Policy Planning Staff, January 24, 1950; and Department of State, "Essential Elements of US-UK Relations." For a summary of the American position, see Department of State, "Essential Elements of US-UK Relations." Ambassador Philip C. Jessup outlined this position for British officials during the Tripartite Preparatory Meetings that preceded the Conference of Foreign Ministers. See U.S. Delegation at the Tripartite Preparatory Meetings to Acheson, April 25, 1950. For the informal Anglo-American agreement, see U.S. Delegation at the Tripartite Preparatory Meetings to Acheson, April 30, 1950; Agreed United States/United Kingdom Report, "Continued Consultation and Co-ordination of Policy," May 6, 1950, *FRUS, 1950,* 3: 890–92, 1072–74.

British agreed to a multilateral offsetting of sterling balances, while the Americans accepted special terms that safeguarded Britain's reserves and assured sterling's position as a leading reserve and trading currency. They permitted countries that had an overall surplus with the union to accept settlement in sterling, rather than in gold or dollars. They also accepted provisions that gave the British a wider credit margin with the union than had been planned, limited their gold payments to the union, covered part of these payments with ECA dollars, and allowed the British to reimpose quantitative import restrictions on a multilateral basis, if this became necessary to protect their reserves.[25]

Anglo-American understanding led in July 1950 to OEEC agreement on the principles of the European Payments Union (EPU).[26] The agreement included the provisions for multilateral offsetting and partial gold settlement that the ECA had hoped would set the stage for intra-European monetary integration and trade liberalization. Indeed, concurrent with the EPU accord, the participating countries pledged to remove quantitative restrictions on 60 percent of their private imports from each other. They also agreed with the ECA that liberalization and nondiscrimination should go hand in hand. According to a set of trade rules that the OEEC adopted when approving the EPU accord, all existing and future measures of trade liberalization were to be applied equally to imports from other members of the group, as were any restrictions that remained after January 1951.[27]

As we will see, Anglo-American leaders were unable to forge a similar compromise when it came to giving the EPU's Managing Board positive powers to coordinate national policies. Nevertheless, the EPU agreement and the new trade rules seemed to give real substance to the idea of Western Europe as a single, integrated market. Nor was this the only front on which progress was made. In May 1950, for example, the Western powers agreed to relax further their controls on Germany.[28] By the end of June, they had raised industrial production in Marshall Plan countries 24 percent above prewar levels. European exports and intra-European trade had climbed 20 percent and 17 percent respectively. Agricultural production had gone up, the dollar gap had declined, and inflation had come under control. American Marshall planners saw these successes as a validation of their corporative vision of an integrated European economic system similar to the

[25] For this part of the story, see Hoffman to Harriman, March 3, 11, 31, 1950, ECA File, box 64; Office of the Special Representative [hereafter, OSR], "Possible Reconciliation Between the EPU System and the Sterling System," April 6, 1950, Treasury Records, Acc. 66A186, box 81, folder EPU/21/300–Original Negotiations and Drafting of EPU Agreement, vol. 1; John Kenney, ECA mission chief, London, to Hoffman, April 13, 1950, ECA File, box 16; Foster to Harriman, two telegrams dated April 17, 1950, RG 286, Acc. 53A177, box 112, Inter-European folder; Hoffman to Harriman, Katz, and Tasca, May 4, 1950, ECA File, box 65; Harriman to Hoffman, May 5, 1950, RG 286, Acc. 53A177, box 18; ECA, memorandum for the secretary of state, May 5, 1950; Kenney to Hoffman, May 14, 1950, ECA File, box 16; and Harriman to Hoffman, May 15, 1950, *FRUS, 1950*, 3: 658–59.

[26] For an outline of the terms of the agreement, see Katz to Hoffman, Foster, and Bissell, June 18, 1950, ECA File, box 18; and Harriman to Hoffman, June 20, 1950, *ibid.*, box 20. Also see ECA, *Ninth Report to Congress* (Washington, D.C., 1950), 26–31; and Harriman to Hoffman, July 11, 1950, ECA File, box 20.

[27] Foster to Harriman, June 27, 1950; Bissell to Harriman, July 4, 1950, ECA File, box 66; Katz to Hoffman, June 6, 1950; OSR to Hoffman, June 7, 1950, *ibid.*, box 18; and OSR to Hoffman, June 11, 1950, *ibid.*, box 20. Also see Diebold, *Trade and Payments in Western Europe*, 172–75.

[28] See "Declaration for the Three Foreign Ministers on Germany," May 22, 1950, *FRUS, 1950*, 3: 1089–91, and 1089 n.1.

one that existed in the United States, where "a large domestic market with no internal trade barriers" had supposedly made possible a remarkable record of economic growth and social stability.[29] At the same time, moreover, they had supplemented their trade and payments initiatives with simultaneous efforts to build supranational institutions of coordination and control in Europe and new national and transnational networks of public-private cooperation and power sharing. And since these efforts were also part of their plan to boost productivity, integrate economies, and re-create the American brand of neocapitalism in Europe, it seems worthwhile to consider them now in some detail.

ONE OF THE HALLMARKS OF AMERICAN RECOVERY POLICY was the ECA's effort to forge both national and transnational links between private economic groups and between these groups and government authorities. Through such links it hoped to build a private alliance behind the Marshall Plan, equip Europeans with American production skills, and maximize the prospects on the Continent for transnational action and economic integration, productive abundance and social peace. This effort started in the United States, where the ECA itself became the hub in an elaborate system of public-private cooperation and power sharing. It is therefore important to begin with this system in America and then see how it stretched across the Atlantic.

In the United States, the goals pursued in recovery policy were inextricably tied to the administrative structure that was used. For policy makers in the Truman administration, the need to revitalize industry, maximize output, and liberalize trade, together with the need to appease Congress, required a bipartisan recovery administration that could recruit managerial talent from the private sector and guarantee a business-like efficiency in operational matters. Accordingly, draft legislation submitted to Congress in 1948 called for a new agency, the Economic Cooperation Administration, to handle the operational aspects of the recovery program subject to the State Department's control in areas relating to foreign policy.[30] For Senator Arthur Vandenberg and other members of Congress, however, an efficient and successful recovery program required greater limitations on the State Department's authority and a larger role for managers from the private sector. The primacy of private management followed logically from their stress on the ERP's economic objectives in Europe. They were no less interested in relieving suffering and combating communism, yet achieving these goals meant stabilizing currencies, fixing realistic exchange rates, reviving industry, liberalizing trade, and, through these and other reforms, fostering integration and boosting productivity. Steering this course, they agreed, required expert management by men with a practical knowledge of the complicated agricultural, industrial, financial, and labor problems involved. But it also required an administrative structure

---

[29] House, *Foreign Assistance Act of 1948*, 254; and ECA, *Ninth Report to Congress*, 3–7.

[30] The administrative recommendations in this legislation were the result of intense bureaucratic bargaining inside the Truman administration. See Hadley Arkes, *Bureaucracy, the Marshall Plan, and the National Interest* (Princeton, 1972), 59–83.

that would permit these men to apply their knowledge without political interference from the State Department. It required, in other words, a truly independent agency managed by private leaders who controlled operational decisions and shared with public officials the responsibility for making policy.[31]

Those involved in the congressional hearings could cite numerous precedents for this kind of public-private power sharing. Some noted the wartime control arrangements worked out by public and private leaders under the aegis of the War Production Board. Others pointed to the President's Committee on Foreign Aid, a special fact-finding group of university experts and representatives of labor, industry, and agriculture that President Truman had established to investigate the impact of a major aid program on the American economy. Still others cited the Commerce Department's success with its Business Advisory Council (BAC) and voluntary agreements with industry. Secretary of the Interior J. A. Krug made the same point about his department's collaboration with such groups as the National Petroleum Council. "Government-industry action" and "maximum" cooperation, he told the Senate Foreign Relations Committee, would satisfy both European and American requirements without "centralizing authority" in Washington.[32]

Witnesses suggested a variety of proposals for achieving this kind of public-private cooperation in managing the recovery program. From business and farm leaders came calls for a policy board composed of both government officials and representatives of private economic groups, especially organized industry, labor, and agriculture. From labor leaders came proposals under which public policy makers would be guided by the views of private advisory committees. And from a variety of other witnesses came schemes for a blend of direct and indirect representation, to be achieved by staffing the ECA with representatives from private groups, establishing private advisory committees, and preserving some role in the recovery program for those government agencies, particularly the Commerce and Agriculture departments, that were closely tied to private interests through a network of cooperating committees.[33]

One organization embracing the latter idea was the Brookings Institution. Its report, solicited by Senator Vandenberg, acknowledged the "special character of the task" involved in rebuilding Europe, a task entailing "economic and business" responsibilities that the State Department could not assume. Needed was a "new and separate agency," headed by a single administrator of cabinet rank who would have direct access to the president and "primary responsibility for the formulation of operating policies and programs." This agency should be exempt from various

[31] U.S. Congress, House of Representatives, Committee on Foreign Affairs, *Hearings, United States Foreign Policy For a Post-War Recovery Program*, 80th Congress, 1st and 2d sess., 1947–48 (Washington, D.C., 1948), 247, 257, 810–11 [hereafter, House, *Recovery Program Hearings*]; and U.S. Congress, Senate, Committee on Foreign Relations, *Hearings, European Recovery Program*, 80th Congress, 2d sess., 1948 (Washington, D.C., 1948), 751, 806, 808 [hereafter, Senate, *ERP Hearings*].

[32] Senate, *ERP Hearings*, 366, 279, 359–60, 365, 851, 1394; and House, *Recovery Program Hearings*, 569, 1445. Even Secretary of State Marshall had noted the successful work performed "by a number of government agencies in cooperation with business, agriculture, and labor groups"; Arkes, *Bureaucracy and the Marshall Plan*, 67.

[33] Senate, *ERP Hearings*, 728, 734–35, 807–08, 835, 851, 1039, 1116–17, 1127, 1293, 1346–47; and House, *Recovery Program Hearings*, 582, 590, 594, 810–11, 941–42, 1311–12, 1386–87, 1413, 1445–46.

federal regulations, particularly those limiting salaries, in order to attract managers from the private sector, and it should have a public advisory board and private advisory committees to maintain regular consultation between its administrator and representatives of "industry, labor, agriculture, and . . . other private citizens." Because the ERP was not "a purely business job," the new agency must not encroach on roles properly played by government departments. The Commerce and Agriculture departments were to retain their authority over export allocations, the State Department was to negotiate bilateral aid agreements with the participating countries in Europe, and the National Advisory Council was to determine specific financial policies. These were often "political" as opposed to "business" responsibilities, and, although it was assumed that the two could be harmonized through consultation and cooperation, each had its own institutional requirements.[34]

These ideas were incorporated into the Foreign Assistance Act of 1948.[35] Included as well were provisions insuring the bipartisan nature of the Public Advisory Board, allowing the ECA to establish its own missions abroad, and making both its mission chiefs and its special representative in Europe directly responsible to the administrator rather than to the secretary of state. Through such provisions, Vandenberg and others hoped to insure the ECA's autonomy and substitute for the State Department's "political" control a bipartisan public-private partnership in which essentially private leaders made operational decisions, exerted influence through a network of advisory committees, and collaborated with their public counterparts in the formulation of policy. The administrator, to be sure, would be a "public" official appointed by the president with the consent of Congress. But he was to be recruited from the private sector, function like a private executive, and run his agency like a "business enterprise."[36] Because the job required a man with "particularly persuasive economic credentials unrelated to diplomacy," it was the "overriding Congressional desire," Vandenberg told Marshall in vetoing the appointments of William Clayton and Dean Acheson to this position, "that the ERP Administrator come from the outside business world . . . and *not* via the State Department." In the end, Vandenberg himself selected the administrator, choosing Paul G. Hoffman, president of Studebaker Corporation and one of the industry representatives on the President's Committee on Foreign Aid.[37]

The result was an administrative structure that deliberately dissolved the distinction between public and private spheres, and did so as part of a strategy for achieving the goals of economic integration and greater productivity. Under the Foreign Assistance Act, for example, the ECA had the Public Advisory Board, to which Hoffman appointed representatives of organized business, labor, and

---

[34] For the conclusions of the Brookings report, see Senate, *ERP Hearings*, 855–60. On Vandenberg's solicitation of the report, see *ibid.*, 74.

[35] See House, *Foreign Assistance Act of 1948*.

[36] Vandenberg to Carl M. Saunders, January 2, 1948, Bentley Historical Library, University of Michigan, Ann Arbor, Arthur H. Vandenberg Papers [hereafter, Vandenberg Papers], box 3, Correspondence folder, January 1948. Also see Vandenberg, as quoted in Arkes, *Bureaucracy and the Marshall Plan*, 84.

[37] Vandenberg to Marshall, March 24, 1948, HSTL, Harry S. Truman Papers, President's Secretary's File, Subject File: George C. Marshall. Also see Arkes, *Bureaucracy and the Marshall Plan*, 100.

agriculture. It also had private advisory committees to assist the administrator with specific problems, including the Oil Price Committee, Advisory Committee on Fiscal and Monetary Problems, Advisory Committee on Overseas Development with a subsidiary investment panel, and Advisory Committee on Reparations. In addition, Hoffman cooperated with the Council on Foreign Relations, commissioning that group to report on United States goals in Western Europe and the means for achieving them. He also worked closely with the President's Advisory Committee on Financing Foreign Trade, and he had the "benefit of advice informally given by men such as Russell Leffingwell and Bernard Baruch."

The advisory committees were dominated by prominent figures from the world of business and finance. The Committee on Financing Foreign Trade was headed by Winthrop Aldrich, board chairman of the Chase National Bank. William L. Clayton led the ECA's investment panel on overseas development. The Committee on Fiscal and Monetary Problems included George Harrison of the New York Life Insurance Company, Edward Brown of the First National Bank of New York, Walter Steward of the Rockefeller Foundation, and Joseph Dodge of Detroit Bank. The Advisory Committee on Reparations was headed by George Humphrey of the Hanna Company and included such "top-flight" industrialists as Charles Wilson of General Motors, Gwilyn Price of Westinghouse, John McCaffrey of International Harvester, and Frederick Geier of the Cincinnati Milling Machine Company.[38]

Similar men, "Wall Street wolves" according to Hoffman's critics, dominated the top positions in the ECA during its first year of operation. A number of important slots were occupied by professionals and career public servants.[39] But more typical were men with corporate backgrounds similar to Hoffman's. W. Averell Harriman, the special representative in Europe, was a senior partner in the Wall Street firm of Brown Brothers, Harriman. Howard Bruce, the deputy administrator in Washing-

---

[38] Hoffman to Clarence Francis, October 1, 1948, HSTL, Paul G. Hoffman Papers [hereafter, Hoffman Papers], box 21, ECA Correspondence folder. Also see Richard Heindel to Vandenberg, August 24, 1948, Vandenberg Papers, box 3, Correspondence folder, August 1948; Hoffman to C. A. MacDonald, August 23, 1948, Hoffman Papers, box 1, Chronological File folder; Hoffman to American Embassy, Paris, October 15, 1948, ECA File, box 45; Council on Foreign Relations, "Studies on Aid to Europe," November 30, 1948, HSTL, William L. Clayton Papers, box 73, Council on Foreign Relations folder. For information on the Aldrich committee and the ECA's investment panel, see RG 286, Acc. 53A405, box 50, Finance-Investments (Aldrich committee) folder.

[39] Hoffman to Frank Gannett, July 15, 1948, Hoffman Papers, box 1, Chronological File folder. By "top positions" I mean the administrator and the special representative in Europe, their deputies and assistants, the general counsel and comptroller, the ECA's mission chiefs abroad, and the directors of its key divisions as identified in the text. The directors of such divisions as administration and administrative services, statistics and reports, China program, organization and management, personnel, and security have not been considered. Information on the directors of the divisions of operations, strategic materials, procurement operation, and program coordination has not been located. The information that follows in the text is based on the roster of personnel listed in the second edition of the ECA's pamphlet, "American Business and European Recovery" (Washington, D.C., 1948). Except where noted in the text, biographical information on the men listed on this roster comes from *Who's Who in America, Who Was Who in America, Current Biography: Who's News and Why, The National Cyclopaedia of American Biography,* and *Biographical Dictionary of American Labor Leaders.* Arthur Smithies, director of the Fiscal and Trade Policy Division in Washington, and Arthur Marget, who held a similar position at the ECA's headquarters in Paris, were professional economists with considerable government experience. Dennis Fitzgerald and Ben Thibodeaux, who headed the Food and Agriculture divisions in Washington and Paris, were agricultural economists. Milton Katz, a professor at the Harvard Law School, and Richard M. Bissell, Jr., an MIT economist, served respectively as general counsel in Paris and assistant deputy administrator in Washington.

ton, was director and board member of several large business firms. William Foster, Harriman's deputy in Paris, was president of a steel products company. Among the chief assistants to the administrator and deputy administrator in Washington were C. Tyler Wood, formerly a partner in the law firm of Gilbert, Elliot, and Company; Wayne C. Taylor, a Chicago banker before entering government service in the 1930s; James Cleary, a vice president in a leading advertising agency; Samuel Richards, an executive with the Studebaker Corporation; and Maurice Moore, a partner in the law firm of Cravath, Swaine, and Moore. Men with similar experience held the positions of comptroller, budget director, general counsel, and director of information.[40] Business representation was particularly strong in the ECA's industry divisions. The one in Washington was headed by Samuel Anderson, a partner in several large investment companies. In Paris, George W. Perkins of Merck and Company served in a similar capacity. And under Perkins were Clarence Randall, a vice president of Inland Steel Company; Cecil Burrill, an executive with Standard Oil of New Jersey; George Green, formerly a vice president of General Motors; Walter Cisler, a vice president of Detroit-Edison; and Godfrey Rockefeller, "a director of quite a number of corporations."[41]

Prominent business leaders also headed most of the ECA's overseas missions in 1948: in the United Kingdom, Thomas K. Finletter of Coudert Brothers; in Italy, James Zellerbach, board chairman of Crown Zellerbach Corporation; in France, David K. E. Bruce, a Baltimore businessman; and in Belgium, James G. Blaine, president of the Midland Trust Company of New York. In addition, the mission chiefs in Norway, Denmark, Turkey, Austria, Greece, and Sweden were, respectively, August Staley, an Illinois banker; Charles Marshall and Russell Door, both prominent New York attorneys; Westmore Wilcox, a partner in various New York investment firms; John Nuveen, a Chicago businessman; and John Haskell, a financial executive.[42]

Noteworthy, too, was the previous government service of most of these business leaders.[43] Many belonged to one or more of those prestigious private associations, especially the BAC and the Committee for Economic Development (CED), that routinely advised public officials and served as recruiting pools for government positions. Hoffman had helped found the CED, and both he and Harriman were

---

[40] These were Eric Kohler, an accounting executive; Norman Taber, an investment and financial consultant; Alexander Henderson, a partner in the law firm of Cravath, Swaine, and Moore; and Bryan Houston, a vice president of the Pepsi-Cola Company.

[41] Perkins actually succeeded Langbourne Williams, who served briefly as division head in 1948. Harriman probably recruited Williams from the Business Advisory Council. For information on members of the Industry Division in Paris, see Summary of Conference of Hoffman, Harriman, Members of ECA—Paris Staff, and Country Mission Representatives, Paris, July 22–23, 1948, RG 286, Acc. 53A405, box 1, Paris Conference folder, July 22–28.

[42] The remaining four mission chiefs listed in the ECA's pamphlet, "American Business and European Recovery," were Harriman, who officially headed the ECA mission in bizonal Germany; Joseph Carrigan, a former dean of the Agriculture School of the University of Vermont, who was chief of mission in Ireland; Alan Valentine, president of the University of Rochester and a director of various business firms, who headed the ECA mission in the Netherlands; and Roger Lapham, board chairman of the American Hawaiian Steamship Company and a member of the Business Advisory Council, who led the ECA mission in China.

[43] It should also be noted that virtually all top positions in the ECA were held by college graduates, ten of them by Harvard graduates and over half of them by graduates of such other prestigious schools as Yale, Princeton, Brown, MIT, Swarthmore, Johns Hopkins, and the University of Pennsylvania.

leading figures in the BAC. Both could agree that "top people from every industry" were needed to manage the recovery program efficiently and to solve the difficult economic and technical problems involved in stabilizing finances, liberalizing trade, and boosting productivity. Harriman recalled turning to the BAC when staffing his Paris office, and he thought it likely that Hoffman had used the CED for similar purposes.[44]

Along with business leaders, Hoffman tried to incorporate other economic groups into schemes of corporatist collaboration with the government. The major farm groups were represented on the ECA's Public Advisory Board, cooperated with its overseas missions, and worked closely with its food and agriculture divisions. Organized labor also played an important part, not only in countering communist attacks on the Marshall Plan but in persuading European workers to work harder, defer consumption for the sake of investment, accept temporary unemployment, and make the other sacrifices necessary to raise production and achieve "effective European collaboration and economic integration." In Europe, it was argued, "deep-seated union policies and worker habits" would have to give way to the "[p]roductivity stress" typical of America. European labor leaders had to recognize the need to adjust wage and price differentials between countries, reduce the barriers to labor migration, and replace the old system of national "self-sufficiency with more efficient production through specialized industries" operating in a European-wide market. And to expedite this process, union officials in the United States had to start sharing with "European labor and management" some of their ideas on the best way to organize industry and increase productivity.[45]

Nor were American trade unions reluctant to assume such a role. They endorsed the ERP in public statements that emphasized the importance of "increased production" and "economic integration" in Western Europe. They also urged labor's participation in a bureaucratic management of the recovery program and cooperated with public officials in shaping the international aspects of American labor policy.[46] The Department of Labor, for example, had already organized an Office of International Labor Affairs under Philip Kaiser and a Trade Union Advisory Committee that was collaborating with Kaiser, and with officials of the War and State departments, in shaping overseas labor policy. The State Department had also created the new post of labor attaché (choosing for these positions men close to American trade unions),[47] and its Division of International Labor and

---

[44] Summary of Conference, Paris, July 22–23, 1948; and interview with W. Averell Harriman, January 6, 1982.

[45] Val Lorwin, "Labor Participation in the Organization for European Economic Cooperation," April 30, 1948, RG 59, file 840.5043/5–1448; Under Secretary of State Robert A. Lovett to American Embassy, Paris, December 8, 1948, RG 59, file 840.50 Recovery/11–2448; and Nitze, "Labor's Role in the European Recovery Program," August 15, 1948, copy in RG 59, PPS Records, box 50, Paul Nitze (Speeches & Articles, 1945–1953) folder.

[46] See, for example, the AFL's declaration on foreign policy, as quoted in Howard Bruce to Harriman, November 24, 1948, ECA File, box 45; and AFL memorandum to President Truman, December 19, 1947, HSTL, Truman Papers, President's Official File, folder 426-L (March 1951–1953).

[47] Peter Weiler, "The United States, International Labor, and the Cold War: The Breakup of the World Federation of Trade Unions," *Diplomatic History*, 5 (1981): 1–22. Also see Kaiser to Erick Kocher, American Embassy, Brussels, November 6, 1947, HSTL, Philip Kaiser Papers, box 2, Labor Attachés and State Department Officials–General Correspondence folder.

Social Affairs was acting as liaison between the trade unions and the secretary's office. At the same time, Marshall and others in the State Department were considering qualified labor leaders for ambassadorial positions when they became available and were supporting representation for organized labor on the American delegations to various international conferences and on such UN agencies as the Economic and Social Council and the World Health Organization. In addition, they were collaborating with American trade union leaders to combat communism in the European labor movement, break up the communist-led World Federation of Trade Unions, and organize the European Recovery Program–Trade Union Advisory Committee to mobilize European workers behind the Marshall Plan and the noncommunist labor international that was formed in 1949.[48]

A substantial foundation existed, therefore, on which those seeking to integrate labor into Marshall Plan initiatives could build. Kaiser represented labor's views on the interdepartmental steering committee that studied the recovery program. Officials of both the American Federation of Labor (AFL) and the Congress of Industrial Organizations (CIO) served on the President's Committee on Foreign Aid.[49] Secretary Marshall asked the AFL for a list of possible labor appointees to the ECA, an agency expected to have "quite an immediate tie-in" with the labor, farm, and industry groups that supplied commodities, services, and personnel to the administrator. The list and union participation led to actual appointments. Arlon Lyon of the Railway Labor Executives' Association, George Meany of the AFL, and James Carey of the CIO were appointed to the ECA's Public Advisory Board. Bert Jewell of the AFL and Clinton Golden of the CIO became Hoffman's chief labor advisors in Washington. Boris Shishkin of the AFL headed the Labor and Manpower Division at Harriman's headquarters in Paris.[50] In addition, trade union officials were eventually appointed as mission chiefs in Norway and Sweden and as labor advisors to missions in other participating countries. Their task was to develop ties between American and European labor organizations and to help formulate policy on various "economic, social, technical and other problems affecting the European workers and their trade unions." "The trade unions of America," as Hoffman explained in 1949, had "a status of full partnership in the ECA not only from the standpoint of operations but from the standpoint of making policy."[51]

[48] Lovett to William Green, AFL, April 14, 26, June 17, 1948, RG 59, file 840.50 Recovery/6–1548; Cleon Swayzee, director of the Division of International Labor and Social Affairs, memorandum, March 9, 1949, HSTL, Dean G. Acheson Papers, box 64, Memoranda of Conversations folder; Swayzee, memorandum to Acheson, March 8, 1949; memorandum of conversation, March 14, 1949; Matthew Woll, AFL, to Acheson, March 14, 1949; Acheson to Woll, April 4, 1949, RG 59, file 800.5043/3–1449; and Weiler, "The United States, International Labor, and the Cold War."

[49] Kaiser to Kocher, November 6, 1947, and "Attitude of Labor towards the ERP," February 2, 1948, RG 59, file 800.5043/2–248.

[50] Memorandum of conversation between State Department and AFL officials, April 6, 1948, RG 59, file 840.50 Recovery/4–648; Lovett to Green, April 26, 1948, and memorandum to Harriman, April 26, 1948, *ibid.*, Recovery/4–2048; and *New York Times*, June 3, 1948, p. 14. Also see the ECA's pamphlet, "American Business and European Recovery"; and Hoffman to American Embassy, Paris, July 2, 1948, ECA File, box 44.

[51] There are two letters from Hoffman to the American Embassy, Paris, dated July 2, 1948; both are noteworthy. See ECA File, box 44. Also see Harriman to Hoffman, July 8, 1948, *ibid.*, box 5; Hoffman, "Weekly Report of the Administrator," November 8, 1948, Hoffman Papers, box 22, ECA, Miscellaneous folder, 1948–1949; Harriman to Hoffman, February 23, 1949; Hoffman to Harriman, March 2, 1949, RG 286, Acc. 53A405, box 1, OSR folder, 1949; Hoffman to Harriman, April 9, 1949, ECA File, box 47; and Hoffman to Harriman, February 8, 1949, ECA File, box 46.

Nor were the patterns of partnership limited to the ECA and private economic groups in the United States. During the same period, Hoffman and others were also trying to link their system of power sharing to a similar system in Europe. The results amounted to a transnational network of public-private cooperation, one that reflected the ECA's faith in the capacity of managerial approaches and corporatist collaboration to achieve efficiency, minimize disruptive social competition, and mobilize private interests behind the interrelated goals of economic integration and greater productivity. In many of the participating countries public and private leaders were already cooperating to formulate social welfare and economic policies. But the ECA now wanted organized private groups to be tied to the OEEC and represented on the ERP consultative committees being established by some European governments. In France, for example, the ECA supported a government decision to establish a labor advisory committee that would meet regularly with the ministries responsible for the recovery program. In Italy, it brought noncommunist trade unions together in a similar body.[52] It also persuaded European leaders to permit regular meetings between the OEEC's technical groups and the Trade Union Advisory Committee on matters relating to the labor aspects of the recovery program. And, together with the OEEC, it established liaisons with the International Federation of Agricultural Producers, a group that would eventually function as the OEEC's advisory body on agricultural policies in Europe.[53]

Business and banking groups made up another part of this transnational network. With support from the ECA and State Department, the Aldrich committee established three American investment groups to cooperate with similar, government-recognized groups in Belgium, Britain, and France. Their job was to identify potential development projects for American investors.[54] The ECA also played a part in organizing American corporate groups to collaborate with the British Dollar-Exports Board, established jointly by the Associated British Chambers of Commerce, the Federation of British Industries, and the British Trades Union Congress. Other participating countries soon created their own dollar boards, which, together with their American partners, sought ways to increase European exports to the Western Hemisphere.[55] A similar pattern took shape around the Anglo-American Council on Productivity. Proposed by Hoffman and British Chancellor of the Exchequer Sir Stafford Cripps in July 1948, the council brought together British and American trade union and management leaders to investigate capital plant and bottleneck problems in Britain and determine how

[52] Harriman to Hoffman, October 27, 1949, ECA File, box 8; and W. K. Knight, memorandum of conversation, October 1, 1948, RG 59, file 840.50 Recovery/10–148.
[53] Foster to Hoffman, March 26, 1949; Caffery to Hoffman from Clinton Golden and Bert Jewell, April 13, 1949; Harriman to Hoffman, May 21, 1949, ECA File, box 6; Harriman to Hoffman, May 29, June 25, July 6, 1949, *ibid.*, box 7; and Harriman to Hoffman, October 28, 1949, *ibid.*, box 8.
[54] Harland Cleveland, memorandum to Foster and Bissell, November 10, 1949, HSTL, John D. Sumner Papers, box 8, Economic Cooperation Administration, General ERP and Marshall Plan folder; and Winthrop Aldrich, "Report on the Establishment of the Committees of Banking Institutions in France and Belgium to Facilitate the Implementation of the Point IV Program," attached to Cleveland memorandum to Foster, November 22, 1949; Cleveland to Barry Bingham, December 7, 1949, RG 286, Acc. 53A405, box 50, Finance-Investments (Aldrich committee) folder.
[55] See RG 286, Acc. 53A405, box 1, British Dollar Exports Board folder; and Bingham to Hoffman, October 22, 1949, Treasury Records, Acc. 67A1804, box 4, France, Aid Program folder, vol. 2.

American labor and management could assist the British in increasing productivity. The British group was nominated by the Federation of British Industries and the British Trades Union Congress, acting through the National Production Advisory Council established during the war. The American group was chosen by Hoffman, the industry representatives in consultation with Philip Reed of General Electric, who served as chairman, and the labor members in consultation with the ECA's labor advisors and the leading American trade unions.[56]

The council held its first meeting in London at the end of 1948, where it established committees for the study of industry organization, capital investment trends, and production bottlenecks. The American members then toured several British plants, where they found the biggest barrier to increased production to be the frequently "complacent attitude" of British labor and management toward scientific production procedures, technical efficiencies, and restrictive business practices. This they hoped to change. And while the British ruled out action in regard to restrictive practices, the council did agree on a program of "industrial education" at all levels of British industry, the creation of agencies to spread American "know-how," and arrangements under which teams of British managers, technicians, and shop foremen could study production methods in the United States.[57] By the time the council disbanded in 1952, it had sponsored visits to the United States by sixty-six productivity teams, distributed over five hundred thousand copies of their reports, and published major studies on standardization and simplification in industry.[58]

Still another example of transnational action and power sharing in the service of productivity was that connected with the technical assistance program launched by the ECA at the end of 1948. The goal in this case was to stimulate greater efficiency and higher productivity in European industry. To achieve this, the ECA disseminated American technical and scientific information in Europe, conducted "in-plant and academic training" programs for European engineers and plant foremen, and held management seminars, or "clinics," for European executives. It also used engineers and technical consultants as roving ambassadors of American science and selected teams of European technicians, labor leaders, and managers to study industrial organization, production techniques, and labor-management relations in the United States. In organizing the program, ECA officials worked closely with European industrial, labor, and governmental leaders. And on the American side, they cooperated with the National Association of Manufacturers, Chamber of Commerce, National Management Council, and leading labor unions, farm

---

[56] Douglas to Marshall, July 30, 1948, RG 59, file 103.ECA/7–3048; Douglas to Marshall, July 31, 1948, ECA File, box 4; Hoffman to American Embassy, London, August 4, 1948, RG 84, box 1035, file 850, Marshall Plan; Harriman to Hoffman, August 5, 1948, ECA File, box 5; Finletter to Marshall, August 5, 1948, ECA File, box 4; Hoffman to Finletter, August 27, 1948, RG 84, box 1035, file 850, Marshall Plan; Finletter to Hoffman, September 3, 1948, ECA File, box 4; Hoffman to Finletter, September 10, 1948, RG 84, box 1035, file 850, Marshall Plan; and Hoffman to Harriman, September 20, 1948, ECA File, box 45. Also see Paul G. Hoffman, *Peace Can Be Won* (Garden City, N.Y., 1951), 101–02.

[57] Finletter to Hoffman, November 1, 1948, ECA File, box 4; and Anglo-American Council on Productivity, "Report of the First Session" (November 1948), Hoffman Papers, box 24, Economic Cooperation Administration, Pamphlets folder.

[58] Anglo-American Council on Productivity, "Final Report of the Council" (September 1952), Hoffman Papers, box 24, Economic Cooperation Administration, Publications folder.

groups, and trade associations. Between 1948 and 1951, the ECA spent nearly $20 million to finance 625 technical assistance projects, maintain approximately three hundred American productivity "experts" abroad, and sponsor several thousand European labor and management visitors to the United States.[59]

Pains were taken to impress these visitors with the close ties between government and labor in the United States, and with the gains in productivity, living standards, and labor peace to be derived from cooperative labor-management relations. One delegation of key Italian labor leaders spent several days touring the plant facilities and talking to the workers of the Crown Zellerbach Corporation, a large paper manufacturer that had recently been selected by the National Planning Association as an outstanding example of labor-management harmony in the United States.[60] A group of British steel founders heard American labor officials lecture on how "cooperation between management and labor" had resulted in greater productivity and "rising standards of living" for workers in the United States.[61] Still other groups toured farm and industry facilities, learned about the cooperative links between the American government and private economic groups, and received instruction in American labor-training techniques, American methods for arbitrating labor-management disputes, and what Hoffman called the American "miracle of mass production." "American know-how, wage earners' freedom, and property available to all" were the blessings that the ECA promised to "bring to pass in Europe," and these would come, the agency believed, once the Europeans began adopting American ideas for "worker and employer teamwork," for "more efficient production," and for eliminating "waste motions and turning out products in [the] manner that American management and labor have worked out."[62]

The ECA thought its technical assistance program and the comparable work of the Anglo-American Productivity Council were helping to produce a new European outlook—including a "new spirit of cooperation between labor and management"—by pointing to the impressive gains that American industry had made through intensive competition in a large, internal market, strict methods of product simplification, standardization, and cost accounting, and close collaboration with organized labor, which, "despite occasional differences with management over wages," generally agreed "that a high standard of living must be supported by a continuously increasing rate of output."[63] The ECA urged other participating countries to emulate the British and establish their own productivity councils. These, too, should be led by labor, management, and government representatives and should sponsor productivity teams, disseminate technical information, and serve "as the central coordinating and directing force in increasing productivity." By the end of 1951, Austria, Belgium, Denmark, France, the Netherlands, and West Germany had followed the British lead. They had established national

[59] ECA, *Eleventh Report to Congress* (Washington, D.C., 1950), 49–51. Also see Hoffman to ECA, November 12, 1947; Foster to Hoffman, November 26, 1948; Foster to Hoffman, December 3, 1948, ECA File, box 5.
[60] Hoffman to Harriman, April 1, 1949, ECA File, box 47.
[61] Hoffman to Harriman, March 15, 1949, *ibid.*, box 46. Also see Hoffman to Harriman, May 19, 1949, *ibid.*, box 48.
[62] Hoffman to Harriman, February 14, March 10, 1949, *ibid.*, box 46. Also see Hoffman to Harriman, January 7, February 12, 16, 17, 1949, *ibid.*
[63] ECA, *Tenth Report to Congress* (Washington, D.C., 1950), 48, and *Ninth Report to Congress*, 65.

"productivity centers" and, through the OEEC, had launched an intra-European technical assistance program under which participating countries began exchanging information and visits between leaders of labor, management, and government.[64]

The European productivity councils and the OEEC's technical assistance programs became additional parts of the public-private alliance through which the ECA worked to export American skill, win support for the Marshall Plan, and replace old patterns of national rivalry and class conflict with a new order of economic integration and corporatist collaboration. To be sure, not all forms of economic integration and public-private cooperation were acceptable. Hoffman and others objected to government-sanctioned arrangements under which private leaders would negotiate economic specialization along national lines. Such arrangements, they worried, might lead to new cartels and other restrictive agreements that would frustrate the rule of comparative advantage, prop up prices, and discourage rational investment, efficient use of resources, and maximum productivity. There was no reason to believe, they concluded, that such agreements could yield "results approximating those attainable by competitive forces" and the normal incentives of a free market. Indeed, some in the ECA talked about using the technical assistance program to acquaint European labor and management teams with the antitrust activities of the Department of Justice and the Federal Trade Commission.[65]

Yet if cartel-type agreements were out of the question, so was an approach that relied wholly on market incentives. The ECA was not seeking "to impose a Hazlitt libertarianism" on Europe or to follow what Hoffman dismissed as a "policy of government non-intervention." He and others also believed in "administrative coordination" through central institutions with the power to harmonize national policies across the ERP area.[66] This was the third line of American recovery policy, and, like the ECA's attempts to liberalize trade and payments and forge new systems of national and transnational collaboration, it aimed to integrate markets, maximize production, and put the Continent on a self-supporting basis.

THE ORGANIZATIONAL DIMENSION OF THE RECOVERY PROGRAM in Europe, like that in the United States, reflected the intrinsic link between administrative strategy and corporative objectives of American policy. The payments plans of 1948 and 1949 and the European Payments Union of 1950 were organizational mechanisms that the Americans hoped would weld the Continent into an economic unit. They had similar hopes for the EPU's Managing Board and for the Organization for European Economic Cooperation. But in both cases the results fell short of

[64] ECA, *Seventh Report to Congress* (Washington, D.C., 1949), 53. Also see ECA, *Ninth Report to Congress*, 53, *Tenth Report to Congress*, 66, *Twelfth Report to Congress* (Washington, D.C., 1951), 49; and Bonsal to Hoffman, December 29, 1949, ECA File, box 8.

[65] Hoffman to Harriman, January 3, 1950, ECA File, box 63. The ECA's views were in response to the government-sanctioned arrangements being proposed by the French. See Katz to Hoffman, January 6, 1950; Harriman to Hoffman, January 10, 1950, *ibid.*, box 17; Hoffman to Harriman, January 11, 1950, *ibid.*, box 63; Katz to Hoffman, February 18, 1950, *ibid.*, box 17; and Hoffman to Harriman, March 31, 1950, *ibid.*, box 64.

[66] Hoffman to Harriman, January 12, 1950, *ibid.*, box 63. The reference is to Henry Hazlitt, the conservative economist.

expectations, in large part because of Britain's antipathy to central institutions that might compromise its sovereignty, socialist programs at home, and commitments to the Commonwealth and the sterling area. The diplomacy of organization thus concealed a far more profound struggle over the nature of the European and world systems and the British role in both.

The ECA's plan for the European Payments Union had combined market incentives and administrative mechanisms to induce debtors and creditors to move toward equilibrium in overall intra-European payments. As we have seen, the former involved an obligation for creditors and debtors to cover a portion of their surpluses and deficits through new credits or gold payments to the EPU. The administrative mechanism was to consist of continuous consultation among member states, mutual review of their fiscal and monetary policies, and collective recommendations for maintaining equilibrium by adjusting exchange rates or changing national economic policies. Consultation would be institutionalized in the EPU's Managing Board, which was to launch investigations, take action by majority rather than unanimous vote, and have positive powers to coordinate national policies. The board, to be sure, would be less than a supranational authority. But neither would it be another of those "OEEC-type committees" in which national bargaining and government vetoes made decisive action impossible. For policy makers in the ECA, the board represented a compromise between these two organizational strategies, one that would circumvent the question of sovereignty while limiting the exercise of sovereign power through what amounted to national vetoes. On the board, moreover, would be an ECA representative, and backing it up would be the ECA's control over part of the funds that supported intra-European clearings. These arrangements, it was thought, could make the Managing Board an effective instrument of transnational action and a stepping stone toward a truly supranational organization.[67]

Yet the ECA's plan went further than others were willing to go. The agreement on the principles of a payments union that the OEEC reached in July 1950 established the Managing Board of seven members with the right to make decisions by majority vote. But the board's powers were vaguely defined and its decisions subject to review by the OEEC, which could recommend changes in national policy only by the unanimous vote of its members. Nor did the ECA have voting membership on the Managing Board. These limitations were partly the result of opposition in the Treasury Department and the National Advisory Council to a strong European agency that could challenge the jurisdiction of the International Monetary Fund in matters relating to exchange rates or the internal fiscal and monetary policies of its members. But they were also the result of opposition from some OEEC delegations, particularly the British delegation, to a truly independent board with considerable power to dictate national policies. Whatever the source, the results were the same. Although Hoffman and others still thought that the board might develop into a strong coordinating agency, the EPU had to rely largely on

---

[67] In addition to the sources cited in note 19, see Hoffman to Harriman, October 25, 1949; Foster to Harriman, November 26, 1949, ECA File, box 50; Harriman to Hoffman, December 3, 1949, *ibid.*, box 8; and Hoffman to Harriman, December 5, 1949, *ibid.*, box 51.

market incentives, not administrative controls, to adjust national policies in the interest of European equilibrium and integration.[68]

Nor was the ECA more successful in shaping the OEEC into an independent agency of economic action and integration. In the months following Marshall's speech at Harvard in June 1947, he and others urged European countries to create a continuing organization with considerable power to transcend sovereignties, set national production targets, allocate scarce resources, and coordinate national investment decisions. By March 1948, when the Committee on European Economic Cooperation met in Paris to form a continuing organization, they were calling for a "major instrument" of economic "cooperation and further integration," one with an "active secretariat" under the leadership of an "outstanding man," national representatives "of standing," and real executive responsibilities.[69] But the Europeans, particularly the British, were skeptical of an organizational strategy that subjected their trade, investment, and production policies to supranational control. The CEEC's preliminary report of September 1947 called for a joint organization with none of the powers that American leaders envisioned, and the OEEC's charter of April 1948 offered little more than an organizational medium for traditional forms of intergovernmental cooperation. It provided for a secretariat of international character, headed by a secretary general, but with merely routine duties. Administrative responsibility would reside in an executive committee and ultimate authority in a council of national representatives acting through mutual agreement. The new organization could "promote," "investigate," "consider," and "recommend," but it could not act independently of home governments.[70]

Despite these setbacks, American leaders were determined to make the OEEC the "focal point around which closer Western European economic cohesion can be built." They decided to keep bilateral negotiations to a minimum, deal collectively with Europeans through their permanent organization, and saddle the OEEC with as many responsibilities as possible, including devising coordinated annual recovery programs, liberalizing trade, and hammering out the intra-European payments agreements.[71] They also urged participating countries to appoint their "best brains" to the executive committee and the council, convene these bodies at the ministerial level as often as possible, and empower the secretariat to launch investigations and make recommendations. Most important, they wanted the OEEC to create a new

---

[68] In addition to the sources cited in note 26, see Irving S. Friedman, Treasury Department, memorandum to A. N. Overby, deputy managing director, IMF, November 2, 1949; Overby to Snyder (with enclosed memoranda by Friedman), December 29, 1949, Snyder Papers, box 20, Alphabetical File, International Monetary Fund folder; Hoffman to Harriman, January 10, 1950, ECA File, box 63; Southard, memorandum to Snyder, January 16, 1950, Snyder Papers, box 11, ECA and International Trade Organization folder, 1950; G. H. Willis, Treasury Department, to Tasca, January 11, 1950, Treasury Records, Acc. 66A1039, box 3, Marshall Plan Correspondence (Official) folder; Acheson to American Embassy, London, January 27, 1950, *FRUS, 1950*, 3: 623–24; "The Outcome of the EPU Negotiations," unsigned memorandum, June 16, 1950, Snyder Papers, box 11, ECA and International Trade Organization folder, 1950; and Hoffman to Katz, Tasca, and Lincoln Gordon, June 17, 1950; Bissell to Harriman, July 8, 1950, ECA File, box 66.

[69] Marshall to Douglas, February 29, 1948, *FRUS, 1948*, 3 (Washington, D.C., 1974), 384–86; Douglas to Marshall, March 3, 1948, RG 84, box 1035, file 850, Marshall Plan; Marshall to Caffery, March 9, 1948, RG 59, file 840.50 Recovery/3–948; and Marshall, circular telegram, March 10, 1948, *ibid.*, Recovery/3–1048.

[70] Caffery to Marshall, March 24, 1948, RG 59, file 840.50 Recovery/3–2448; and Caffery to American Embassy, London, March 29, 1948, RG 84, box 1035, file 850, Marshall Plan. Also see Hogan, "Paths to Plenty."

[71] Lovett to Caffery, April 8, 1948, *FRUS, 1948*, 3: 414–17. Also see the sources cited in note 69.

office of director general, appoint a European of political stature to this post, and authorize him to direct the organization's activities. Such reforms, they believed, would help circumvent the "tortuously slow" process of decision making by national delegations and enable the OEEC to develop a *European* point of view. A committee of "country representatives," as Harriman put it, could not provide "effective leadership" because each national delegation would be "inclined to consider first the interests of [its] own country." Real leadership required a director general of "international political position," who could speak for Europe as a whole, "initiate or advocate matters requiring top-level consideration," and deal "on a basis of equality with senior government representatives."[72]

In October 1948, the OEEC agreed to appoint a Committee of Nine to study organizational reforms and make recommendations early in the next year.[73] During ensuing discussions the Belgians and the French generally endorsed Harriman's demand for stronger leadership, and Belgian Prime Minister Paul Henri-Spaak drafted a proposal to enhance the functions of the secretariat and create a high-level ministerial committee with considerable executive authority. But when the Committee of Nine convened in February 1949, Britain submitted an alternative plan that called only for a consultative group of ministers to review the OEEC's work between sessions of the council and the executive committee. The British plan denied the group control over the secretariat and hence any independent status and clear executive responsibilities. It reaffirmed instead the role of the executive committee and the council as the "supreme" bodies of the organization and made clear that all policy decisions must pass through both groups for approval by their national delegations.[74]

The outcome was a compromise approved by the council on February 17. The group of ministers was to be consultative in nature and have no authority to make decisions on its own. But it could meet frequently at the request of its chair, review the work of the organization, discuss "high-level" business, and work closely with the secretariat in the preparation of agenda for sessions of the council and executive committee. The resolution also instructed the council to convene at the ministerial level as often as necessary, but no less than four times a year, and endorsed a recommendation from the secretary general to enlarge the staff and functions of the secretariat.[75] The Americans were hopeful that additional steps would follow. Richard Bissell, Hoffman's deputy in Washington, thought it especially important that the OEEC act quickly to appoint "highly competent people" to the enlarged staff of the secretariat. The creation of a "competent and disinterested staff of international civil servants," he argued, would help to make the OEEC a "nucleus for greater European unity in the economic field."[76] In

---

[72] Harriman to Marshall and Hoffman, July 31, 1948, ECA File, box 5. Also see Harriman to Marshall, July 17, 1948, RG 59, file 840.50 Recovery/7–1748; Theodore Geiger, memorandum to Bissell, July 17, 1948, RG 286, Acc. 53A405, box 60, AAP Policy Series folder; Lovett to Harriman, July 22, 1948, *FRUS, 1948*, 3: 471–72; and Hoffman to Harriman, September 10, 1948, ECA File, box 45.

[73] Harriman to Hoffman, October 16, 1948, ECA File, box 5.

[74] Ambassador Alan G. Kirk, Belgium, to the secretary of state, January 5, 1949, RG 59, file 840.50 Recovery/1–549; and Harriman to Hoffman, January 10, 1949; Foster to Hoffman, February 10, 1949; Harriman to Hoffman, February 15, 1949, ECA File, box 6.

[75] Harriman to Hoffman, February 17, 18, 1948, ECA File, box 6.

[76] Hoffman to Harriman from Bissell, February 18, 1949, *ibid.*, box 46.

addition, Harriman and others continued to press for the creation of a new post of director general and for the appointment to that position "of a leader with sufficient authority, stature and international prestige to influence member governments" toward the sort of economic integration that Congress and the American people expected. The man they had in mind for the job was Henri-Spaak, a leading advocate of European union and of the OEEC as a strong, supranational authority.[77]

But the organizational imperatives of British diplomacy dictated a different course—one hostile to both the new position and Spaak's appointment. As Harriman pointed out, "the reasons why we want Spaak were the very reasons why the British were opposing him, namely, the making of the OEEC [into] an effective organization freed from the present British curb-rein."[78] Foreign Secretary Ernest Bevin told Ambassador Lewis Douglas in London that his government could not "accept the appointment of Spaak or any other Continental to a position of control in the OEEC," that the OEEC's functions should remain strictly "economic and factual," and that it must not become a European political authority with the power to coordinate national policies across the ERP area. After all, he said, Britain was a world power, "not merely a European power," and "could not accept integration in western Europe on a scale which would impair its other responsibilities."[79]

At meetings in late 1949, the British directed their "best efforts at smothering the [American] proposal." Under their influence, the OEEC's consultative group tentatively agreed to appoint a new official to act as liaison between the OEEC and outside organizations, present its views to world opinion, and harmonize differences between the participating countries. But his specific duties and powers were not clearly defined. He would not have a fully independent status, control over the OEEC's secretariat, or anything but a "consultative" voice in meetings of the council and consultative group.[80] Nor could he hold another office, either in his own country or in another international organization. Such a stipulation seemed designed to disqualify Spaak, because it would have forced him to resign as a member of the Belgian Parliament and as president of the European Assembly. Secretary of State Dean Acheson pointed out that the compromise did not provide an "acceptable basis for Spaak or any other strong European personality to consider taking [the] position."[81]

British opposition hardened in January 1950, after Spaak had publicly criticized British policy toward European unification. Sir Oliver Franks, the British ambassador in Washington, told Acheson that his government could never consent to Spaak's appointment as director general. Acheson would not urge Spaak to

[77] George Perkins, memorandum to Acheson, September 9, 1949; Acheson to Douglas, October 14, 1949; Douglas to Acheson, October 18, 26, 1949, *FRUS, 1949*, 4: 421–23, 429–30, 430–31, 435–37. Also see Harriman to Hoffman, September 27, 1949, RG 59, file 103.ECA/9–3049.
[78] Harriman to Acheson, October 12, 1948, Harriman Papers, OEEC folder.
[79] Douglas to Acheson, October 18, 26, 1949, *FRUS, 1949*, 4: 430–31, 435–37. Also see Ambassador Warren R. Austin to Acheson, from Ambassador Philip Jessup, September 30, 1949, RG 59, file 840.50 Recovery/9–3049.
[80] Douglas to Acheson, December 1, 1949, *ibid.*, Recovery/12–149. Also see Katz to Hoffman, December 21, 1949, *FRUS, 1949*, 4: 464–67.
[81] Acheson to American Embassy, Paris, December 23, 1949, *FRUS, 1949*, 4: 468. Also see Katz to Hoffman, December 22, 1949, ECA File, box 8.

withdraw his candidacy, as Franks had requested. Nor would he and other American officials abandon their demand for the new position. But given the British opposition, they stopped urging Spaak's appointment and made the Europeans primarily responsible for selecting a candidate and defining his responsibilities.[82]

This softening of the American position made it possible for European leaders to implement the agreement of late 1949 and to do so as part of a major reorganization of the OEEC in February and April 1950. The consultative group of ministers was abolished, the council and the executive committee were to meet more frequently at the ministerial level, and top officials of the council were to spend more time directing the work of the organization. Most important, the council created the new post of "political conciliator"—as opposed to director general—and elected Dirk Stikker of the Netherlands to this position and to the chairmanship of the council. Stikker was an advocate of European integration, and Harriman considered his appointment a "constructive" step "in strengthening OEEC at the political level." Hoffman heralded it as the "single most hopeful move since the inception of OEEC."[83] Despite this hyperbole, Stikker's authority was obviously ill defined, and real power still remained in the hands of individual governments. The reorganization strengthened the OEEC as a vehicle for conventional intergovernmental collaboration. But it stopped short of creating the kind of independent, corporate authority that the ECA considered essential to European integration.

Nor did things change when the Western powers met at the London Foreign Ministers Conference in May 1950. American policy planning for the conference envisioned a more active role for the United States in European economic affairs, to be achieved either by associating the United States with the OEEC or by enlarging the functions of the North Atlantic Treaty Organization (NATO). This was seen as necessary because Britain and France were no longer capable of acting as great powers without American aid and leadership. Only ongoing American involvement, through stronger institutions of coordination and control, would give the Europeans the assurances of support, security, and direction they needed to move forward with plans for harmonizing national policies, unifying economies, and integrating Germany.[84]

The difficulty came in reconciling British and French differences over which organizational framework to use. The French wanted to centralize authority, including authority over national policies, in the hands of a strong collective agency. French Premier Georges Bidault had first expressed this desire in a vague proposal for an "Atlantic High Council."[85] By the time the foreign ministers met, Bidault's

[82] Acheson to Harriman, January 24, 1950, *FRUS, 1950,* 3: 616–17; and *New York Times,* January 15, 1950, pp. 1, 19.
[83] Harriman to Hoffman, February 2, 1950, ECA File, box 17; Harriman to Hoffman, February 4, 1950, *ibid.,* box 20; Harriman to Hoffman, March 25, 1950, *ibid.,* box 17; Katz to Hoffman, April 4, 1950, *ibid.,* box 18; Harriman to Hoffman, February 4, 1950, *ibid.,* box 20; and Hoffman to Harriman, February 3, 1950, *ibid.,* box 63.
[84] Memorandum Prepared in the Bureau of German Affairs, [February 11, 1950]; Memorandum of Conversation by the Officer in Charge of United Kingdom and Ireland Affairs (Wayne G. Jackson), March 7, 1950, *FRUS, 1950,* 3: 638–42; and Joseph Jones to George Elsey (and enclosed memorandum by Jones, dated March 2, 1950), March 3, 1950, HSTL, George M. Elsey Papers, box 62, Foreign Policy Planning folder.
[85] Ambassador David K. E. Bruce, Paris, to Acheson, April 20, 15, 1950, *FRUS, 1950,* 3: 57–58, 54–55.

proposal had given way to more concrete French initiatives. One of these was the Schuman Plan for a European coal and steel community that would blend German and French interests under the guiding hand of a common authority. Acheson later recalled how the prospect of such a community without Britain hung like a pall over the deliberations. According to the records, however, the foreign ministers barely touched on the plan during their meetings.[86] Controversy turned instead on the French search for an organizational framework that would bring the British into a Continental group and facilitate cooperation between this group and the United States in economic and political matters of common concern. This could be achieved, the French suggested, by making the United States an associate member of the OEEC. The latter would remain a "European organization for purely European affairs," but its transatlantic link would deepen the American commitment in Europe, and this, together with Britain's active involvement there, would pave the road for Germany's further revitalization and reintegration.[87]

Yet the British steadfastly refused to be incorporated into a purely European "zone" that made no allowances for their longstanding commitments around the world and ignored their claim to a special relationship with the United States. They preferred a North Atlantic rather than a European framework—one that would embrace the United States, the United Kingdom, and "'some European entity'" and that could be brought about by developing NATO as an "umbrella" organization with separate arms for military and nonmilitary affairs. Such an arrangement, they insisted, would recognize Britain's three-cornered commitment to Europe, Commonwealth, and United States. It would also permit Anglo-American cooperation in areas outside of Europe and yet allow the Germans to collaborate in nonmilitary affairs of the North Atlantic community. Together with Anglo-American military guarantees under the North Atlantic Pact, it would actually absorb and contain German power, insure French security, and thus open the door for European union and German reintegration.[88]

The French, however, viewed things in a different light. They saw in such a proposal an alarming degree of British aloofness that would virtually guarantee German predominance in an integrated European economy. Nor were they inclined to use NATO as an organizing framework, a course, they insisted, that would lead to Germany's rearmament and preclude participation by European neutrals. The result, according to French Foreign Minister Robert Schuman, would be "new iron curtains on our side of [the] present Iron Curtain." With this Acheson seemed to agree.[89] And the outcome was a compromise that pointed in all

---

[86] U.S. Delegation at the Tripartite Foreign Ministers Meeting to Webb, May 12, 1950, *ibid.*, 1044–51; and Acheson, *Present at the Creation*, 393.

[87] U.S. Delegation at the Tripartite Foreign Ministers Meeting to Webb, May 16, 1950, *FRUS, 1950*, 3: 1069–71. Also see U.S. Delegation at the Tripartite Preparatory Meetings to Acheson, May 6, 1950; Acheson to Webb, May 9, 1950; U.S. Delegation at the Tripartite Foreign Ministers Meeting to Webb, May 11, 1950; Acheson to Webb, May 14, 1950, *ibid.*, 911–13, 1013–18, 1040–43, 1061–67.

[88] U.S. Delegation at the Tripartite Preparatory Meetings to Acheson, April 25, 1950, *ibid.*, 860–63. Also see U.S. Delegation at the Tripartite Preparatory Meetings to Acheson, April 26, May 6, 1950; Acheson to certain diplomatic offices, April 27, 1950; U.S. Delegation at the Tripartite Foreign Ministers Meeting to Webb, May 9, 1950; Acheson to Webb, May 14, 1950, *ibid.*, 881–83, 911–13, 71–72, 1018–22, 1061–67.

[89] Acheson to Webb, May 9, 1950, *ibid.*, 1013–18; and U.S. Delegation at the Tripartite Foreign Ministers

directions. Acheson pledged continuing interest in European economic problems; Bevin and Schuman called for a "working relationship" between the United States and the OEEC. This relationship would be "informal" and would detract neither from the OEEC's role as an agency "devoted primarily to European economic problems" nor from NATO's general responsibility for economic and political issues affecting the North Atlantic area. American leaders tried to put a good face on the compromise. The American delegation in London considered it the best possible, and Harriman thought it another step forward. The Europeans had at least agreed on the importance of continued economic collaboration and on the need to give this collaboration "organizational expression." In June, moreover, they brought the United States into the OEEC as an associate member.[90]

Although this development further strengthened the OEEC as an agency of intergovernmental cooperation, it still fell short of what American leaders wanted— central institutions that could transcend European sovereignties and coordinate national policies. This policy did not belie their faith in the integrating powers of the market. Rather, it reflected their conviction that economic integration was only possible between countries with roughly congruent monetary and fiscal policies and that achieving this congruence required supranational organizations of regulation and control. Through such organizations they had sought to build a unified system poised between British and German power and capable of producing abundance. Their efforts, however, kept foundering on the imperatives of British diplomacy, and the kind of Anglo-American compromise that had led to British participation in the European Payments Union could not be used to resolve the disputes over the OEEC and the Managing Board in a way that reconciled British commitments with American hopes for an integrated Europe.

NONETHELESS, AMERICAN MARSHALL PLANNERS had scored substantial gains since the inception of the recovery program nearly four years earlier. They had helped revive European production, stabilize currencies, liberalize trade and payments, and restore a measure of social peace and prosperity to Europe. They had done so by urging European leaders to cast off old habits of bilateralism and restrictionism, old concerns with self-sufficiency and autonomy, old traditions of class conflict and national rivalry, and old ways of doing business. All of these were seen as barriers to maximum productivity, higher living standards, lower prices, and equilibrium between the dollar and nondollar worlds. And they were to give way now to a new European economic community founded on the principles of American neo-capitalism.

These principles were not a prescription for laissez-faire capitalism. While there was room in the American plan for such free-market strategies as full convertibility

---

Meeting to Webb, May 11, 1950, *ibid.*, 1040–43. Also see U.S. Delegation at the Tripartite Preparatory Meetings to Acheson, April 29, 1950, *ibid.*, 896–98; and Acheson to Webb, May 9, 1950, *ibid.*, 1013–18.

[90] For the final communique issued by the ministers, see Department of State *Bulletin*, May 29, 1950, p. 827. Also see U.S. Delegation at the Tripartite Foreign Ministers Meeting to Webb, May 16, 1950; Harriman to Acheson, June 15, 1950, *FRUS, 1950*, 3: 1069–71, 662–63; Harriman to Acheson, June 2, 1950, Harriman Papers, OEEC folder; and Katz to Hoffman, June 30, 1950, ECA File, box 18.

and multilateralism and for such free-market principles as competition and comparative advantage, there was also room for government aid and action, public-private cooperation, and central institutions of coordination and control. Through their trade and payments initiatives, their technical assistance programs and productivity teams, and their support for a stronger OEEC, American leaders tried to forge an organic economic order in Europe. The new order would be balanced between a paternalistic statism and the old capitalism, would be tied together by market forces and institutional coordinators, and would be founded on economic interdependence and supranationalism, American mass-production techniques, and American labor-management programs for a productive abundance in which all could share. A similar order had supposedly cleared a path to social harmony and affluence in the United States. And once in operation, or so the Americans believed, it would also lead to a new era of peace and plenty on the Continent.

The new era, to be sure, had not come by the end of 1950. The British had refused to join the movement for economic integration. In addition, the declining volume of American aid, the shift from economic to military priorities after the outbreak of the Korean War, and the shortages and inflationary pressures that accompanied the rearmament effort, all combined to reduce the leverage that American officials could use to integrate Europe. They also discouraged further steps to liberalize trade and payments on the Continent and revived old disputes over how best to harmonize national policies and divide resources. By that time, however, American Marshall planners had helped generate a vision of redemption on the Continent, one that saw a unified Western Europe arising from the rubble and the ruin of war, like Lazarus from the grave, with new life and productive vitality, and that led to the Schuman Plan of 1950, the European Coal and Steel Community of 1951, and ultimately the Common Market.

IN THE SHADOW OF THE LEFT:
THE POSTREVISIONIST HISTORY OF
AMERICAN ECONOMIC DIPLOMACY

Michael J. Hogan

William H. Becker and Samuel F. Wells, Jr., eds. *Economics and World Power: An Assessment of American Diplomacy Since 1789.* New York: Columbia University Press, 1984. xvi + 474 pp. Index. $35.00 (cloth); $10.00 (paper).

The publication of this collection of eight essays, each surveying between one and four decades of American history, symbolizes the resurgent interest in economic diplomacy among scholars of American foreign relations. The editors intended the essays to test, and ultimately to modify, the conclusions that have emerged from the work of New Left revisionists who did so much to stimulate our interest in economic diplomacy. The intention to test is evident in the list of questions they posed to their contributors, including: Were economic claims more or less important than strategic or political considerations in shaping American foreign policy? How often and to what degree did public officials respond to pressure from private economic interests? Were economic concerns central to the conceptualization and execution of American policy, or mere parts of a "larger constellation of considerations" (p. xv)? The intention to modify revisionism is apparent in the absence of the most notable members of this school from the list of contributors. The restrictions imposed by the questions and the choice of contributors virtually guaranteed that this volume would fall into that body of new literature called "postrevisionism," a school of thought that seeks to domesticate the Left by conceding the importance of economic considerations while rendering them harmless as one set among a great "constellation" of other factors that invariably are more important. Lacking an independent analytical model that matches or exceeds the explanatory powers of the neo-Marxist framework, the fruits of postrevisionism are, at worst, a repackaged version of traditional history; at best, a blend of arguments borrowed from the old orthodoxy and the New Left. For the most part, the essays in this volume fall into the second category.

The questions posed by the editors give this collection a thematic coherence unusual in multiauthored works, making it possible to review the volume as a whole and to focus on certain themes that run throughout the history of American foreign relations. By far the most celebrated of these is the American commitment to the principle of the Open Door: the principle, in Jefferson's words, that "the ocean, which is the common property of all, [should be] open to the industry of all" (p. 2). Together with such corollary principles as commercial reciprocity, freedom of the seas, and most-favored-nation treatment, an open door for trade and investment supposedly would contribute to greater economic efficiency and growth. This prescription for material gain through a thriving commerce dovetailed with the broad sense of mission that suffuses the history of American diplomacy. Three decades after Jefferson proclaimed the ocean to be the "common property of all," John Quincy Adams celebrated commerce as a "powerful means of civilization" (p. 61) which, if left unchecked, would spread American ideas and institutions across the globe. The essays by Melvyn Leffler, Robert Hathaway, Samuel Wells, and Robert Pollard point out how little this thinking changed in the following century. All stress the continuing American conviction, strengthened now by the increasing interdependence of the international economy, that open and reciprocal trade offered a reliable foundation for economic growth at home and peace, prosperity, and democracy abroad.

Another corollary to the open door principle was the persistent American faith in the power of individual initiative and private enterprise. Taken together, the essays in this volume show American policymakers continually linking the two principles in order to promote an open world system in which, as James Field neatly expresses it, "diplomacy would wither away" (p. 8). Field demonstrates how the founders of the Republic sought to eliminate the arbitrary government restrictions inherent in mercantilist colonial systems and replace them with a new liberal order based on private enterprise and the open door. Kinley Brauer repeats this theme in an excellent essay covering the period 1821 to 1860, citing pronouncements by American policymakers that both echo the words of the founding generation and foreshadow the rhetoric of such later-day Wilsonians as Herbert Hoover and Cordell Hull. For Hoover and Hull, as the essays by Leffler and Hathaway point out, unfettered private trade and investment brought peace and prosperity, while government restrictions hampered growth, fostered destructive economic rivalries, and led to both economic regimentation at home and war abroad. It was this line of thinking that linked Hoover's struggle against foreign raw-material cartels, and Hull's campaign against the British system of imperial preference, to Jefferson's earlier battles against the mercantilist policies of the European powers.

Universalizing the open door principle thus became synonymous in American eyes with universalizing the system of private enterprise. This conclusion hardly denies the trend toward state power in the twentieth century. But it does remind us of how history operates as a drag on this trend, forcing successive generations of policymakers to reconcile such old traditions as privatism, antistatism, and fear of monopoly with the modern need for artificial forms of government regulation and control. We see this most clearly in Leffler's excellent essay on the Republican Ascendancy of the 1920s. Building on his earlier book, which did so much to revise our thinking of the postwar decade, Leffler argues that Republican policy makers relied upon private officials to execute public policy because they shared the traditional conviction that government intervention was inefficient and a threat to peace, prosperity, and private enterprise. In their view, private leaders were more disinterested than public officials, possessed greater expertise and more experience in economic matters, and were thus more likely to organize the world economy along lines that guaranteed the public goals of economic growth and political harmony. Yet this view did not lead to the laissez-faire strategies of the past, but to new frameworks of collaboration in which public and private leaders worked together in an ultimately unsuccessful effort to achieve an ordered and efficient management of the domestic and world economies.[1]

The authors are careful to note the connection between the changing structure of the American economy and the interest in overseas expansion. The result is something close to a periodization of American economic diplomacy. In the first period, from the founding of the Republic to the 1850s, territorial acquisition and commercial expansion combined to serve the interest of an economy dominated by farmers, planters, shippers, and merchants who were hungry for new land, new ports, and new markets. Sectional struggles brought the era of territorial expansion to a halt on the eve of the Civil War, and in the three decades following that conflict the search for overseas markets took a back seat to the American preoccupation with assimilating older acquisitions and managing the social, economic, and political transformations that accompanied industrialization. Yet this second period, as David Pletcher points out, was a transitional era in which the mounting pressure of farm surpluses and the rise of modern industry set the stage for the economic internationalism of the next century. The essays by William Becker and Melvyn Leffler cover the third period, that between 1900 and the mid-1930s. Drawing upon his prize-winning study of business-government relations, Becker notes the efforts by large and small industrial firms, and their partners in the Commerce and State Departments, to build an American system of economic expansion similar to the one envisioned earlier by William Seward and James G. Blaine. As he and Leffler make clear, however, the new internationalism was stalled by old isolationist attitudes and congressional indifference, by a tendency to separate domestic and international economic imperatives, by traditional restraints on positive government action, and by incessant wrangling between private economic interests.

The breakthrough came in the aftermath of the world-wide depression and war of the 1930s and 1940s, when the new economic internationalism was institutionalized in the Reciprocal Trade Agreements Act, the Bretton Woods agreement, the General Agreement on Trade and Tariffs, and the principles of multilateralism which these and other initiatives promoted. It was founded on a broad consensus that domestic growth and overseas expansion were inextricably linked, and resulted in what Pollard and Wells call "The Era of American Economic Hegemony" (p. 333). But as David Calleo points out in a brilliant concluding essay, this fourth period would give way in the 1960s to a fifth. This is the era of America's decline, a byproduct, in Calleo's view, of the American-led recovery of prewar trade rivals, of declining rates of American productivity, and of the inflationary policies used by successive administrations to reconcile the needs of domestic welfare with the military demands of world leadership.

In linking these periods to systemic changes in the American economy, most of the authors draw conclusions contrary to those of the New Left. As the editors note in their epilogue, the transformation from an agrarian to an urban, industrial economy actually "*lessened* the impact of economic considerations on U.S. foreign policy, at least until recently" (p. 460, emphasis in original). The industrial economy of the twentieth century became less dependent on overseas trade and investment, more insulated from the vicissitudes of the international market. This meant that domestic economic concerns and domestic politics would play a greater role than overseas economic interests in molding American diplomacy. It also meant that policymakers would ignore the interests of private economic groups when these interests did not coincide with larger strategic and security imperatives. In short, or so the editors argue, it meant that American leaders would differentiate between the categories of national interest and rank them in a way that generally assigned economic imperatives lowest priority.

This argument has at least two important flaws. For one, it cannot explain the much-vaunted triumph of multilateralism during the fourth period of American diplomacy. In large part this is because the authors fail to appreciate how the political transformations that influenced American foreign policy were themselves a result of systemic changes in the domestic economy. Field and Brauer, to be sure, carefully delineate how foreign policy in the period before the Civil War reflected the expansionist requirements of a political economy dominated by a shifting coalition of sectional and functional groups. But the essays on the first half of the twentieth century are less successful in this line of analysis. Their discussions of congressional politics and bureaucratic rivalries, and of the important struggles between defenders of the home market and the advocates of multilateralism, convey a sense of the political stalemate that stalled the new internationalism through the 1920s. But they do not describe how underlying changes in the industrial structure finally broke this stalemate and assured a victory for the multilateralists. Here they might have been aided by Thomas Ferguson's suggestive argument that the rise of modern, science-based, capital-intensive firms had led by the late 1930s to a major political realignment, out of which emerged a dominant political coalition composed of progressive managers from the new firms and their allies in the trade unions, professions, and banking community. It was this coalition, according to Ferguson, that created the political basis for the New Deal at home and multilateralism abroad.[2]

In addition, this arbitrary effort to show how American leaders ranked the categories of national interest contributes to conceptual confusion and contradicts much of the evidence presented. This is especially the case in the essays by Pletcher, Becker, and Hathaway, the three contributors most hostile to New Left revisionism. Hathaway, to give one example, admits that Franklin Roosevelt was as ardent in defending and expanding the nation's capitalist system as any of his predecessors. But in an otherwise solid chapter, he undermines the validity of this assertion by confusing the short-term interests of specific capitalists, which often took a back seat to larger considerations, with the long-term interests of the capitalist system as a whole. This confusion is evident in his argument that the strategic, political, and ideological dangers raised by Nazi Germany, not the threat of its autarchic trading policies, finally led to an aggressive American diplomacy that at times sacrificed economic gains to larger security objectives. This line of reasoning contradicts two of the author's previous contentions – that public and private leaders agreed on ends, if not always on means, and that both equated autarchic trading policies with autocratic and aggressive regimes whose expansion in any form endangered the free enterprise system at home and abroad. It also leads Hathaway to the erroneous conclusion that in sacrificing short-term economic gains for immediate strategic and political objectives American leaders were following, or establishing, a permanent priority of interests that made such objectives more important than economic goals to the long-term survival of liberal capitalism. Leffler is surely more on target in talking about the unitary nature of American foreign policy objectives in the 1920s, as is Calleo in noting that economic diplomacy in the 1960s and 1970s must be understood to include political and military, as well as economic, dimensions.

The attempt to rank the categories of national interest constitutes a major flaw running through several otherwise excellent chapters in this volume. It succeeds only by assuming an absolute ordering of interests that did not exist in the minds of American policymakers, for whom economic, strategic, and political interests were parts of an interdependent whole that was not altered fundamentally by the priorities of the moment. The attempt to rank interests is a byproduct of the questions, noted earlier, which the editors framed for their contributors. Through these questions, the editors had hoped to produce a volume that went beyond the stale debate between traditional historians and their revisionist critics. But they succeeded instead in forcing most of their contributors into an ultimately hopeless attempt to reconcile the approaches of both schools. This is the fate of postrevisionism. It lives in the shadow of the New Left, and so long as it defines itself by reference to this school it will fail to break new ground in the way we conceptualize the history of American foreign policy.

Michael J. Hogan, Department of History, Miami University, Ohio, is the author of "American Marhsall Planners and the Search for a European Neo-Capitalism," The American Historical Review *90 (February 1985).*

1. These frameworks of collaboration survived the depression of the 1930s and continued to evolve in the decades that followed. See my article, "Revival and Reform: America's Twentieth-Century Search for a New Economic Order Abroad," *Diplomatic History* 8 (Fall 1984): 287–310.

2. Ferguson, "From Normalcy to New Deal: Industrial Structure, Party Competition, and American Public Policy in the Great Depression," *International Organization* 38 (Winter 1984): 41–94. Becker notes the rise of the large, capital-intensive firm, but without discussing its political implications.

Revival and Reform: America's Twentieth-Century Search for a New Economic Order Abroad

MICHAEL J. HOGAN*

Until recently the standard works on American diplomacy tended to juxtapose the two postwar eras. They saw in the isolationism and economic nationalism of the first postwar period policies that were overcome in the second, and they pointed to these policies as causes for the collapse of economic stability and world peace after 1929. This interpretation paralleled that in the original accounts of the Republican ascendancy at home. These accounts portrayed the 1920s as a reactionary decade squeezed between two dynamic reform periods, and together with the old standards on American diplomacy, they inspired textbook assertions about the New Deal and the Cold War as watersheds in the history of American domestic and foreign policy. Recent works, to be sure, have rehabilitated the Republican leadership of the first postwar decade. Those on domestic history have tied Republican policy to both the progressive period and the New Deal. Those on foreign policy have discovered links with Wilsonian internationalism. But few in the last category have connected their discoveries with developments in the 1930s and 1940s and have thus subsumed all three decades within the same analytical framework.[1]

*Stuart L. Bernath Memorial Lecture given at Los Angeles, 6 April 1984. The author wishes to thank the Miami University Faculty Research Conference, the Woodrow Wilson International Center for Scholars, and the Harry S Truman Library Institute for financial assistance. He would also like to thank his colleagues in the History Department, Miami University, for helpful comments; Kurt S. Schultz for research assistance; Pamela Messer for help with the typing; and Professors Lawrence E. Gelfand, Ellis W. Hawley, and Melvyn P. Leffler for stylistic, organizational, and substantive suggestions.

[1] In 1973, Gaddis Smith discussed "the Great Cycle Theory" of American diplomacy. According to this theory, Wilsonian internationalism was followed by America's "abdication of leadership in the 1920s and 1930s." This set the stage for totalitarianism, aggression, and war, which was then followed by American intervention and a reassertion of America's world leadership. See Smith's "The United States in World Affairs Since 1945," in William H. Cartwright and Richard L. Watson, Jr., eds., *The Reinterpretation of American History and Culture* (Washington, DC, 1973), pp. 543-54. For convenient summaries of the literature on American foreign

287

For this diplomatic historians would do well to adapt the corporative model that historians of the domestic scene have used to understand modern efforts to create an integrated American political economy—one founded on self-governing functional groups, tied together by institutional coordinators and market mechanisms, led by cooperating public and private elites, and nourished by limited but positive government power.[2] This essay employs such a framework to analyze America's twentieth-century search for a stable international economy. It focuses on American strategies for rebuilding Europe after both world wars and on some of the connecting developments in the 1930s. It argues that American leaders tried to project their vision of a corporative political economy on the European and world systems, to build, in other words, an economically ordered and organically integrated community of states. It also notes, as Charles S. Maier has done in connection with European politics and diplomacy, the critical links between American domestic and foreign policies during the thirty-year period and the important threads of continuity that run through both. And in doing so, it tries to show how American economic diplomacy in the first postwar era was in many ways an analogue of that in the second.[3]

relations, see the historiographical essays in Gerald K. Haines and J. Samuel Walker, eds., *American Foreign Relations: A Historiographical Review* (Westport, CT, 1981); John Braeman, "American Foreign Policy in the Age of Normalcy: Three Historiographical Traditions," *Amerikastudien/American Studies* 26 (2 November 1981): 125–58; Braeman, "Power and Diplomacy: The 1920's Reappraised," *Review of Politics* 44 (July 1982): 342–69; and Braeman, "The New Left and American Foreign Policy during the Age of Normalcy: A Re-Examination," *Business History Review* 57 (Spring 1983): 73–104. For the literature on the domestic side of the 1920s, see the works cited in subsequent footnotes and Burl Noggle, "Configurations of the Twenties," in Cartwright and Watson, *Reinterpretation of American History*, pp. 465–90.

   [2]For a discussion of this framework, see Ellis W. Hawley, "The Discovery and Study of a 'Corporative Liberalism,' " *Business History Review* 52 (Autumn 1978): 309–30. Thomas J. McCormick has discussed the prospect for a "Corporatist Synthesis for American Diplomatic History" in his "Drift or Mastery?" *Reviews in American History* 10 (December 1982): 318–30.

   [3]Charles S. Maier, "The Two Postwar Eras and the Conditions for Stability in Twentieth-Century Western Europe," *American Historical Review* 86 (April 1981): 327–52. Maier's portrayal of both postwar periods as "complementary and parallel alike" has been criticized by Charles P. Kindleberger. Kindleberger stresses the differences between the two eras and, in doing so, repeats the attacks on American isolationism and economic nationalism in the 1920s that had been popular in the older works on American diplomacy. American policymakers of 1945, he argues, "learned from the mistakes of 1919." They "did not try to withdraw from the European settlement . . . and corrected the mistakes of war debts, reparations, wrong exchange rates, and niggardly postwar assistance." See Kindleberger's critique of Maier's article in ibid., pp. 358–62. Kindleberger's argument also runs through some of the recent literature on European diplomacy in the first postwar era. This impressive literature is surveyed in a masterful essay by Jon Jacobson, "Is There a New International History of the 1920s?" *American Historical Review* 88 (June 1983): 617–45. Although the differences between this argument and my own will become clear in the text, it should be noted here that most Cold War policymakers had not been associated with the reconstruction efforts of the first postwar era and were thus unaware of the similarities between their approaches and those of their predecessors. In denouncing the "mistakes" of the interwar period, moreover, they were often referring to those of the 1930s rather than to those of the 1920s. As Braeman has pointed out, historians have also been guilty of confusing the two decades. See his "Power and Diplomacy," p. 369.

American policymakers started both postwar periods with similar suppositions. They believed that prewar patterns of economic autarky had discouraged growth, set the stage for German hegemony on the Continent, and led to both world conflicts. They also assumed that the path to peace and plenty lay in dissolving these prewar patterns and building an interdependent community of European nations. In their view, this would unleash productive energies in Europe, raise living standards there, and put the continental countries on a self-sustaining basis. It would also help to solve the German problem, which American leaders saw as a problem of reconciling conflicting economic and security imperatives. The problem, in other words, was how to harness Germany's resources to the cause of European recovery without restoring its prewar hegemony or reinvigorating the economic nationalism and autarky that had twice led to world war. And the answer, so far as American policymakers were concerned, lay in bringing a revitalized Germany within a European economic framework that was large enough to contain its power. European integration and German reintegration thus emerge as two of the major themes of both postwar eras, and bringing them about would be one of the central assignments of American diplomacy.[4]

American strategies of integration evolved during the thirty-year period, with policymakers in the second postwar era building on initiatives pioneered by their counterparts in the 1920s. In the decade following the First World War, the State, Commerce, and Treasury departments tried to promote stabilization through policies that stressed the importance of European initiative and self-help. They were willing to assist by funding war debts on a capacity-to-pay basis and by encouraging the flow of private capital to Europe. But the Europeans were to do their part by reducing reparations, funding war debts, balancing budgets, and making currencies convertible. Such initiatives, of course, would refashion Europe in the image of American liberal capitalism. In American eyes, however, they would also eliminate the economic causes of conflict and allow unfettered enterprise and normal market mechanisms to expand trade, integrate markets, and stimulate an economic growth in which all nations could share.[5]

In line with this thinking, Republican policymakers used their financial leverage, particularly their control over private loans and debt reductions, to pressure the Europeans into funding their war debts, reducing their reparation demands, and reforming their finances. Together with their collaborators in

----

[4]For these themes in the first postwar period, see my *Informal Entente: The Private Structure of Cooperation in Anglo-American Economic Diplomacy, 1918–1928* (Columbia, MO, 1977), pp. 1–77. For the second postwar period, see my article, "The Search for a 'Creative Peace': The United States, European Unity, and the Origins of the Marshall Plan," *Diplomatic History* 6 (Summer 1982): 267–85; and my "Paths to Plenty: American Marshall Planners and the Idea of European Economic Integration, 1947–1948," *Pacific Historical Review* 53 (August 1984). I have also dealt with these themes in "European Union and German Integration: Marshall Planners and the Search for Recovery and Security in Europe," in Charles S. Maier, ed., *Germany and the Marshall Plan*, forthcoming (1985).

[5]Hogan, *Informal Entente*, pp. 13–77.

the private and central banks on both sides of the Atlantic, they also engineered the Dawes Plan, arranged successful schemes of European monetary stabilization, managed European bond sales, and negotiated stabilization loans. All of these actions enabled the European countries to handle their balance of payments and achieve a fragile stabilization in the years after 1924. Republican leaders used the same leverage to supplant French plans for economic and political predominance on the Continent with an Anglo-American program that looked to Germany's revitalization and reintegration. The turning point here came with the Anglo-American debt-funding agreement in 1923. Out of this emerged a creditor entente, with both countries calling now for the prompt settlement and reduction of war debts and reparations. The results isolated the French and led directly to the Dawes Plan which, together with the Locarno agreements and the simultaneous and subsequent schemes of monetary stabilization, seemed to point toward the defeat of prewar autarchies, to Germany's reintegration into an interdependent European system, and thus to a new day of peace and plenty on the Continent.[6]

The new day failed to come, but this failure, and the tendency of later historians to denounce the mistakes of the 1920s, should not conceal the substantial coherence of American recovery policy after both world wars. Marshall planners, to be sure, were more interested than their Republican predecessors in reducing the restrictions on intra-European trade. But they also repeated the familiar demands for European self-help and redoubled efforts to reform European finances, balance budgets, and make currencies transferable. They argued again that such measures would loosen the constraints on European enterprise, permit free-market forces to forge an integrated European economy, and, in these ways, stimulate the gains in specialization, resource utilization, and economies of scale that were needed to boost productivity, put the Continent on a self-sustaining basis, and set the stage for full convertibility and multilateralism. Following this line of policy, moreover, they used their financial and political leverage to reduce quantitative import quotas and multilateralize intra-European trade, to underwrite the intra-European currency clearing schemes of 1948 and 1949, to

---

[6]The various parts of this story can be followed in ibid., pp. 17–104; Herbert Feis, *The Diplomacy of the Dollar: First Era, 1919–1932* (Baltimore, 1950); Lester V. Chandler, *Benjamin Strong, Central Banker* (Washington, DC, 1958); Stephen V. O. Clarke, *Central Bank Cooperation, 1924–1931* (New York, 1967); Joan Hoff Wilson, *American Business and Foreign Policy, 1920–1933* (Lexington, KY, 1971); Jon Jacobson, *Locarno Diplomacy: Germany and the West, 1925–1929* (Princeton, NJ, 1972); Charles S. Maier, *Recasting Bourgeois Europe: Stabilization in France, Germany, and Italy in the Decade After World War I* (Princeton, NJ, 1975); Stephen A. Schuker, *The End of French Predominance in Europe: The Financial Crisis of 1924 and the Adoption of the Dawes Plan* (Chapel Hill, NC, 1976); and Melvyn P. Leffler, *The Elusive Quest: America's Pursuit of European Stability and French Security, 1919–1933* (Chapel Hill, NC, 1979).

support the European Payments Union of 1950, and to back the European
Coal and Steel Community of 1952.[7]

As in the 1920s, Marshall planners also saw European integration as a
way to reconcile ostensibly incompatible economic and security imperatives.
It could provide a framework, that is, for absorbing and controlling Germany's
power and thus for reconciling her revival and reintegration with the security
concerns of the liberated countries. The French continued to pose the greatest
barrier to progress in this direction. Their demands for German disaggregation,
for industrial reparations and controls, and for limits on German sovereignty
recalled French policy in the 1920s; and if conceded, or so the Americans
believed, they would prevent the revival of Germany's productive power as
an aid to European recovery and security. As in the first postwar period,
American policymakers resorted to economic leverage and collaboration with
the British in order to overcome French obstructionism. They traded Marshall
Plan grants for concessions on reparations and joined the British in defeating
French proposals for international ownership of the Ruhr and permanent limits
on German production. These initiatives, together with supranational controls
over key resources, the division of Germany, and new security guarantees,
removed many of the political and financial impediments that had stalled the
process of economic recovery and integration after 1929. And out of them,
too, came a series of tortuously negotiated compromises that finally led to
the termination of military government, the formation of the Federal Republic,
and the integration of West Germany into a host of new European political
and economic institutions.[8]

In both recovery periods, then, the wartime alliance of western powers
gave way to an Anglo-American condominium that subordinated French hopes
for economic and political predominance to the reintegration of a revitalized
Germany. In the 1920s, British and American leaders resolved many of their
initial postwar differences and formed what Ernest Bevin later described as
a "financial partnership" in Europe. Public and private leaders in both countries
organized a united front on war debts and reparations and collaborated in the
great monetary and currency stabilization schemes of mid-decade. As Frank
Costigliola has shown, the Anglo-American partnership was fragile, was based
on American terms, and was superimposed on an underlying struggle for
national advantage and financial supremacy. For the British, in fact, success
in this struggle actually required a high degree of cooperation with their

---

[7]See the sources dealing with the second postwar period in footnote 4. See also, William
Diebold, Jr., *Trade and Payments in Western Europe: A Study in Economic Cooperation, 1947–
1951* (New York, 1952); and Diebold, *The Schuman Plan: A Study in Economic Cooperation*
(New York, 1959).

[8]I have discussed these developments in some detail in my "European Union and German
Integration." For general works on German policy, see John Gimbel, *The American Occupation
of Germany: Politics and the Military, 1945–1949* (Stanford, CA, 1968); John Backer, *Priming
the German Economy: American Occupation Policies, 1945–1948* (Durham, NC, 1971); and
Edward N. Peterson, *The American Occupation of Germany: Retreat to Victory* (Detroit, 1978).

American rivals. Once they had abandoned early hopes for a general cancellation of war debts and had negotiated a funding agreement with Washington, they were compelled to apply the American position to their European debtors, rely on American financial support to stabilize sterling, and join the United States in revising the reparation settlement and defending the gold standard. All of this was necessary if they were going to manage their own balance of payments, protect their leadership of the sterling area, and recapture London's historic position as the center of international finance.[9]

Much of this story repeated itself in the second postwar period. In this case, an Anglo-American partnership on behalf of Germany's revival and Britain's imperial commitments evolved out of initially different British and American strategies for rebuilding the European and world systems. The British again found themselves in a paradoxical position. They depended on American financial support to rebuild their economy, stabilize sterling, and protect their leadership of the sterling area, but the terms of this support were often incompatible with British ambitions. For the Americans, trade liberalization and currency convertibility were the surest routes to economic stability and growth. Together with new supranational institutions of coordination and control, they would also pave the road to an integrated Europe in which British power balanced that of a revitalized Germany. For the British, however, liberalizing trade, making currencies convertible, and integrating the British and European economies would increase the drain on their reserves, lead to devaluation of pound sterling, wreck their social-welfare programs at home, and undermine their leadership of an independent sterling area.[10]

These differences, already apparent in the Bretton Woods and Anglo-American loan negotiations and in the sterling debacle of 1947, came to a head during the second sterling crisis of 1949 when British threats to shelter sterling within a high-cost, soft-currency trading area promised to scuttle American hopes for an integrated Europe and a fully multilateral system of world trade. American pressure finally led to British devaluation,[11] and in

---

[9]Frank Costigliola, "Anglo-American Financial Rivalry in the 1920s," *Journal of Economic History* 37 (December 1977): 911–34; Hogan, *Informal Entente*, pp. 38–77; and Dan P. Silverman, *Reconstructing Europe After the Great War* (Cambridge, MA, 1982). For the quotation from Bevin, see the memorandum of conversation by the first secretary of embassy in the United Kingdom, 24 June 1947, U.S., Department of State, *Foreign Relations of the United States, 1947* 3 (Washington, DC, 1972): 268–76 (hereafter cited as *FRUS*, followed by appropriate year).

[10]For documentation, see the sources cited in footnote 12.

[11]For the wartime negotiations and the sterling crisis of 1947, see Richard N. Gardner, *Sterling-Dollar Diplomacy: The Origins and Prospects of Our International Economic Order*, rev. ed. (New York, 1969); Alfred E. Eckes, Jr., *A Search for Solvency: Bretton Woods and the International Monetary System, 1941–1947* (Austin, 1975); and Armand Van Dormael, *Bretton Woods: Birth of a Monetary System* (London, 1978). On the sterling crisis of 1949 and British devaluation, see the documentation in *FRUS, 1949,* (Washington, 1975), 4:781–852; and Dean Acheson, *Present at the Creation: My Years in the State Department* (New York, 1969), pp. 324–25.

subsequent negotiations the two countries defined the basis for a new accommodation. Under this, American leaders settled for British economic cooperation with the Continent in ways that stopped short of full structural integration. They then sought to facilitate this by absorbing some of the costs to the British treasury, underwriting sterling as an international reserve currency, and bolstering Britain's position outside of Europe. The result, as Charles Bohlen had predicted, was an Anglo-American "partnership" in which American aid made it easier for the British to collaborate in plans for reviving Germany and liberalizing trade and payments among the Marshall Plan countries.[12] As in the 1920s, however, this partnership shifted the greatest share of the responsibility for integrating and controlling German power to France, with the outcome in this case being the Schuman Plan and the European Coal and Steel Community of 1950 and 1952.

The Anglo-American partnership made up one link in an evolving transatlantic system. In the 1920s, the financial sinews of this system had consisted of German reparation transfers, allied debt payments, American bank loans, and the network of private and central bank cooperation. Marshall Plan grants reinforced this system during the second postwar period, as did a host of institutional linkages that had not existed earlier. These included the ties between American and European recovery authorities, between the American and European trade union movements, and between the American and European business, labor, and government leaders who worked cooperatively through such agencies as the Anglo-American Council on Productivity and the technical assistance program to boost European productivity and close the dollar gap. Out of these linkages, and those emanating from the North Atlantic Treaty and the military assistance program, emerged a transatlantic community that had remained essentially inchoate in the 1920s.[13]

During both postwar periods, then, American recovery planners had given Germany's revival priority over French predominance. They had forged an uneasy partnership with the British, had made this partnership one link in a transatlantic framework, and had sought within this framework to promote both European integration and German reintegration. The latter two were seen as the best ways to reconcile German recovery with European security and to put the Continent on a self-supporting basis. Together they made up central elements in an ongoing American effort to revive and reform the Old World and to do so by applying the American idea of federalism and creating a

---

[12]The Anglo-American accommodation grew out of negotiations dealing with the proposed European payments union and the British position in Europe. The British and American positions and the resulting understanding can be followed in *FRUS, 1950* (Washington, 1977), 3:617–22, 865–92, 1061–67, 1072–74; and *FRUS, 1950* (Washington, 1980), 4:592–602.

[13]On the transatlantic system of the 1920s, see Denise Artaud, *La Reconstruction de l'Europe, 1919–1929* (Paris, 1973). On the military assistance program and the North Atlantic Treaty, see Lawrence S. Kaplan, *A Community of Interests: NATO and the Military Assistance Program, 1948–1951* (Washington, DC, 1980); and Robert E. Osgood, *NATO: The Entangling Alliance* (Chicago, 1962). The other transatlantic linkages of the second postwar period are discussed later in the text.

unified European system—one, in the words of American Marshall planners, that was large enough "to justify modern methods of cheap production" and one "into which Germany can be 'integrated,' by which Germany can be 'contained,' and in which Germany can play a peaceful, constructive but not dominating role."[14]

To point out these parallels is not to deny important differences in American recovery policy after both world wars. Marshall planners were willing to match economic with military commitments. They used NATO and the military assistance program to safeguard European recovery and security and to integrate European defense systems. They also went beyond earlier notions of an interdependent European economic community of essentially independent states, envisioning now a structural integration that entailed some limitations on the exercise of sovereign power. They worked to build supranational institutions that could guide the process of integration. And they abandoned the earlier reliance on private credits in favor of a major government aid program that enabled the Europeans to rehabilitate their economies and manage their balance of payments without crippling deflation or excessive reparations. These innovations, most of which involved a greater reliance on government power and on new mechanisms of economic regulation and control, undoubtedly reflected the heightened fear of Soviet power and the impact of Keynesian thinking and New Deal experiences on American policy. Yet in the economic arena at least, these same innovations also built upon the rudimentary strategies and structures of an earlier day. They added increments, as it were, to the corporative order that Republican policymakers had started to build in the 1920s.

Seen from one perspective, both postwar periods witnessed a resurgence of conservatism in the United States. The McCarthyism of the latter period paralleled the Red Scare of the former, and American policymakers in both eras worked to isolate the Soviet Union internationally. Industrial peace gave way to union busting after 1918 and to a wave of disruptive strikes after 1945. Wartime planning agencies collapsed, and progressive coalitions yielded ground to conservative alliances. Left-wing defeats did not mean right-wing victories, however, but rather a search for a middle way that would finally triumph after World War II.

It is no longer fashionable to interpret the 1920s as a reactionary period in which Republican policymakers reverted to the laissez-faire prescriptions of a bygone day. Elements of a business progressivism survived and were personified in the policies of Secretary of Commerce Herbert Hoover, whose brand of associationalism envisioned an organic political economy in which public and private elites cooperated in the job of economic and social management. Hoover's associationalism built on the policies of Theodore Roosevelt and Woodrow Wilson, on the writings of men like Herbert Croly and

---

[14]John Foster Dulles, "Europe Must Federate or Perish: America Must Offer Inspiration and Guidance," *Vital Speeches of the Day* 13 (1 February 1947): 234–36; memorandum prepared in the Bureau of German Affairs [11 February 1950], *FRUS, 1950*, 4:597–602.

Walter Lippmann, and on the patterns of public-private cooperation and power-sharing that had surrounded the War Industries Board and other agencies of economic mobilization. It linked these prewar and wartime developments with the New Deal policies of the 1930s. It also had the support of important elements in the private sector, particularly of those progressive business leaders who had earlier formed the National Civic Federation, and of those labor leaders whose business unionism looked to a labor-management partnership based on increased productivity and bread-and-butter gains for workers. Those in the first group represented the great international investment banks and the new science-based, capital-intensive firms that were coming to dominate the American economy. They were tied to allies in the major private foundations and the new industrial relations research centers, and they were committed to policies of labor conciliation, scientific management, and overseas expansion.[15]

Hoover's associationalism, as Ellis Hawley has shown, accepted the economic collectivism and interdependence that came out of industrialization, the rise of organized and bureaucratized concentrations of private economic power, the concomitant decline of market forces, and the consequent need to supplement these forces with institutional ordering and coordinating devices. It tried to reconcile this need and the imperatives of modern science and technology with the older, nineteenth-century traditions of privatism, individualism, and voluntarism. It tried to do so by locating the apparatus of economic government in the private sector, specifically in the growing network of trade associations, professional societies, farm cooperatives, and labor unions. Enlightened functional elites, rather than public authorities, were to act as agents of an economic rationalization by working cooperatively within and between their groups to eliminate waste, allocate resources efficiently, tame the business cycle, and optimize output. In performing these tasks, moreover, they were to be guided by the dictates of modern science. They

---

[15]See especially, Ronald Radosh, "The Corporate Ideology of American Labor Leaders from Gompers to Hillman," *Studies on the Left* 6 (1966): 66–88; James Weinstein, *The Corporate Ideal in the Liberal State* (Boston, 1968); Murray N. Rothbard, "War Collectivism in World War I," in Ronald Radosh and Murray N. Rothbard, eds., *A New History of Leviathan* (New York, 1972); Robert D. Cuff, *The War Industries Board: Business-Government Relations During World War I* (Baltimore, 1973); Ellis W. Hawley, "Herbert Hoover, the Commerce Secretariat, and the Vision of an Associative State," *Journal of American History* 61 (June 1974): 116–40; Joan Hoff Wilson, *Herbert Hoover: Forgotten Progressive* (Boston, 1975); Robert H. Zieger, "Labor, Progressivism, and Herbert Hoover," *Wisconsin Magazine of History* 58 (Spring 1975): 196–208; Robert D. Cuff, "Herbert Hoover, the Ideology of Voluntarism, and the War Organization during the Great War," *Journal of American History* 64 (September 1977): 358–72; and David Burner, *Herbert Hoover: A Public Life* (New York, 1978). See also the essays by Ellis W. Hawley, Joan Hoff Wilson, and Robert H. Zieger, in Ellis W. Hawley, ed., *Herbert Hoover as Secretary of Commerce: Studies in New Era Thought and Practice* (Iowa City, 1981). My description of the business leaders involved in this progressive alliance, specifically my attempt to locate them in the industrial structure, is wholly derived from Thomas Ferguson's provocative essay, "From Normalcy to New Deal: Industrial Structure, Party Competition, and American Public Policy in the Great Depression," *International Organization* 38 (Winter 1984): 41–94.

were to rely on the new tools of scientific management and industrial sociology, and they were to look for assistance to those disinterested engineers and professional managers who supposedly possessed the knowledge and experience required to solve complex economic and social problems without the waste and inefficiency that inhered in an older, competitive individualism or in an oppressive and bureaucratic statism.[16]

The emphasis, to be sure, was on private, self-regulation by the groups, but government also had a positive role to play in the new associative order. It could provide useful information and services, defend legitimate group interests, promote associational activities, and champion the cause of countercyclical stabilization. It could collaborate with private elites in an organized system of power-sharing, working through this system to mediate disputes, eliminate destabilizing competition, encourage scientific management, and foster enlightened group action and self-regulation. And through these and other initiatives, it could work with its private partners to achieve the gains in productivity and living standards that would help to avoid both the redistributive conflicts and the pressure for greater government control that would supposedly result from economic stagnation and retrenchment. In Hoover's system, then, market forces and parliamentary forums would be reinforced with institutional coordinators, private governments, and new modes of public-private power-sharing. Political solutions would give way to technocratic formulations, and redistributive battles would be replaced by a corporative collaboration based on what Maier has called the "politics of productivity."[17]

In operation, to be sure, Hoover's associationalism failed to bring the promised era of permanent stability and abundance. It failed to correct structural flaws in the industrial, agricultural, and financial sectors, to appease the supporters of McNary-Haugenism, to satisfy the exponents of public-power development, to discipline the spokesmen for antitrust or private monopoly, and to elicit support from conservative business leaders who refused to forge partnerships with labor or engage in enlightened self-regulation. As these shortcomings and controversies point out, Hoover and the champions of associationalism competed throughout the decade with the defenders of an older, competitive capitalism and the advocates of a more active and expansive government.[18] Yet these same disputes and shortcomings should not obscure

---

[16]Hawley, "Herbert Hoover, the Commerce Secretariat." See also Hawley, *The Great War and the Search for a Modern Order: A History of the American People and Their Institutions, 1917–1933* (New York, 1979). My interpretation also draws on two unpublished papers by Professor Hawley: "Neo-Institutional History and the Understanding of Herbert Hoover," and "Techno-Corporatist Formulas in the Liberal State, 1920–1960: A Neglected Aspect of America's Search for a New Order."

[17]In addition to the sources cited in the previous note, see Charles S. Maier, "The Politics of Productivity: Foundations of American International Economic Policy after World War II," *International Organization* 31 (Autumn 1977): 607-33.

[18]In addition to the works cited in footnote 16, see Wilson, *Hoover: Forgotten Progressive;* the essays by Hawley, Wilson, and Zieger in Hawley, *Hoover as Secretary of Commerce;* Hawley, "Herbert Hoover and American Corporatism, 1929–1933," in Martin L. Fausold and George T. Mazuzan, eds., *The Hoover Presidency: A Reappraisal* (Albany, 1974); and Hawley's essay in Ellis W. Hawley, J. Joseph Huthmacher, and Warren I. Susman, *Herbert Hoover and the Crisis of American Capitalism* (Cambridge, MA, 1973).

Hoover's belief in positive government, his commitment to economic planning, coordination, and self-regulation, or his efforts to organize enlightened concerts of group action. Nor should they conceal the important transitional role that he and other Republican leaders played in a larger historical process that led from earlier progressive visions and wartime experiments to the organizational and economic adaptations of the 1930s and 1940s.

Hoover and other postwar policymakers played a similar role in the international economy where their blend of private and public power, market incentives, and new forms of regulation actually anticipated the managerial approaches and mixed economic policies of a later day. Some aspects of their policy reflected a lingering commitment to the older, nineteenth-century traditions of antistatism and antimonopoly. They waged a sustained campaign against European proposals to supplant the market with public planning or private cartels. They rejected European calls for government financing of economic recovery, British suggestions for preferential commercial and shipping arrangements, French proposals for intergovernmental control over key raw materials, and British, French, and German efforts to establish government-sanctioned resource monopolies. In their view, these and similar initiatives pointed toward a restrictionism and statism that would prevent the most efficient use of resources, hamper productivity, and lead to war. They relied instead on private finance to underwrite recovery on the Continent, and through monetary stabilization and currency convertibility they sought to release the constraints on individual initiative and create a climate in which private enterprise and the price mechanism could foster growth and integrate economies.[19]

Yet these aspects of policy did not mean that Republican leaders relied solely on an unregulated privatism to rebuild Europe and reorganize the world economy. In these areas, as on the home front, government had a positive if limited role to play and one it could best perform in collaboration with nonpolitical elites whose professionalism and expertise supposedly made them more reliable managers and less likely than their public counterparts to transform economic issues into dangerous political controversies. In these areas, moreover, Republican policymakers also promoted a business collectivism and self-regulation, devised transnational coordinators to supplement market forces, and then offered these strategies and their faith in technical expertise as the best way to resolve disputes, prevent excessive government intervention, and encourage a rational and productive integration.

On the American side, for example, Hoover divided the Bureau of Foreign and Domestic Commerce into commodity divisions. He staffed these divisions with experts drawn from the leading export industries and trade associations, tied them to the private sector through a network of cooperating committees, and worked through the resulting system to disseminate information, study trade and investment trends, and promote overseas resource

---

[19]Joseph Brandes, *Herbert Hoover and Economic Diplomacy: Department of Commerce Policy, 1921–1928* (Pittsburgh, 1962), pp. 63–147; Brandes, "Product Diplomacy: Herbert Hoover's Anti-Monopoly Campaign at Home and Abroad," in Hawley, *Hoover as Secretary of Commerce*, pp. 185–214; and Hogan, *Informal Entente*.

development.[20] He also envisioned the World War Foreign Debt Commission as an agency for adjusting claims on a nonpolitical and scientific basis. And he urged a technical management of tariff rates by a commission of experts who were to stand above political considerations and congressional logrolling. In addition, Hoover helped to establish a loan-control mechanism through which public and private leaders were to share the responsibility for directing capital exports into reproductive channels. Together with Secretary of State Charles Evans Hughes, moreover, he urged business and banking leaders to collaborate in promoting foreign trade, worked through a banking consortium to develop the China Market, and organized oil developers, raw material importers, and cable and radio builders to fight foreign cartels and open the door to American expansion.[21]

At the same time, Hoover and other Republican leaders tried to impose their associative system on the international economy. In dealing with European reconstruction, they asserted the primacy of economics over politics and sought to resolve outstanding issues by applying their technocorporative formulations. They encouraged banking leaders in Europe and the United States to join forces in devising constructive schemes of monetary stabilization and viewed the reparations imbroglio as a technical problem amenable to scientific solution by nonpolitical business experts. In promoting resource development, expanding communications facilities, and financing modernization, they abandoned initial plans for competitive action and a wasteful duplication of existing systems, worked with private American and European leaders to build collective structures of economic management and regulation, and then redefined the Open Door principle to accommodate the new forms of "cooperative competition" that resulted. Through the network of private and central bank cooperation, through the oil, financial, and radio consortiums, and through the loan-control procedure, the Agent General for Reparations, and the Bank for International Settlements, they also organized new frameworks of transnational action and public-private cooperation, new mechanisms of economic coordination and stabilization, and new instruments for an ordered development of the European and world economies.[22]

Even in the 1920s, then, key government and business leaders had applied their technocorporative formulations to the international economy. Their approach was flawed and failed to bring an enduring stability. They

[20]Brandes, *Hoover and Economic Diplomacy*, pp. 5–21; Hawley, "Herbert Hoover, the Commerce Secretariat," pp. 123–24.

[21]Hogan, *Informal Entente*, pp. 78–208; Melvyn P. Leffler, "Herbert Hoover, the 'New Era,' and American Foreign Policy," in Hawley, *Hoover as Secretary of Commerce*, pp. 148–79; and Hawley, *The Great War and the Search for a Modern Order*, especially chapter 6.

[22]Frank Costigliola, "The Other Side of Isolationism: The Establishment of the First World Bank, 1929–1930," *Journal of American History* 59 (December 1972): 602–20; Hogan, *Informal Entente;* Leffler, "American Policy Making and European Stability, 1921–1933," *Pacific Historical Review* 46 (May 1977): 207–28; Leffler, *The Elusive Quest;* Hogan, "Thomas W. Lamont and European Recovery: The Diplomacy of Privatism in a Corporatist Age," in Kenneth Paul Jones, ed., *U.S. Diplomats in Europe, 1919–1941* (Santa Barbara, CA, 1981), pp. 5–22; and Leffler, "Hoover, the 'New Era,' and American Foreign Policy."

attacked foreign cartels even while supporting American participation in oil, radio, and financial consortiums that amounted to multinational monopolies. They celebrated an impartial expertise, but often ignored "expert" advice when it contradicted preconceived notions or political expediencies. They applied the capacity-to-pay principle to debt settlements, yet the creditor position of the United States demanded a more generous policy. This was especially so in light of the American tariff which, Hoover's arguments notwithstanding, was seldom adjusted "scientifically" and never low enough for the continental countries to manage their balance of payments without serious deflationary consequences. Private American bank loans helped the Europeans to make ends meet until 1929, but even before then it had become clear that the loan-control mechanism was not working to guarantee reproductive investment on the Continent. In the end, Hoover remained an ambivalent internationalist whose primary concern with the home market, and whose commitment to the principle of privatism, ruled out more effective government action to regulate capital exports, reduce war debts, or fund European recovery.[23]

Yet, if Republican policymakers failed to achieve an enduring prosperity, they nonetheless made an important contribution to America's twentieth-century search for a new economic order. Internationally, as we will see, their technocorporative formulations were similar to those that would guide American leaders of a later era. And domestically, they added to an associative system that foreclosed both an older individualism and a statist syndicalism. New Dealers, to be sure, would bring additional components into the associative system and devise new forms of government action at home and abroad. To a large extent, however, both they and their counterparts in the Truman administration would live in a world shaped by historical forces, and not only by the powerful American commitment to privatism and the tradition of antimonopoly, but also by the frameworks of group action, public-private cooperation, and technical management coming out of the progressive period and the New Era of the 1920s. Indeed, these frameworks and others like them would often be used, as they had been in the 1920s, to contain government and reconcile its new role with the older tradition of laissez-faire.

In the 1930s, certain elements in the business community remained locked to a conservative variant of the New Era strategies. These included labor-intensive firms and the smaller- and medium-sized companies that were preoccupied with the home market and generally represented by the National Association of Manufacturers and the U.S. Chamber of Commerce. They supported the National Recovery Administration (NRA) so long as it emphasized private planning, industrial cartelization, and business self-regulation under the passive supervision of a cooperating government. But they broke with their collaborators in the public sector when New Deal policy pointed toward international expansion and a more active role for the state in such areas as economic regulation, social welfare, and budgetary policy. Nor would

---

[23]For an excellent brief critique of New Era foreign policy, see Leffler, "Hoover, the 'New Era,' and American Foreign Policy." See also, Hogan, *Informal Entente*, pp. 209–27.

they accept the Wagner Act and the New Deal's decision to recognize labor as a legitimate partner in the American political economy. After the NRA, this group retreated to private systems of economic planning and control, resisted government coercion, and rejected representation for organized labor and consumer groups.[24]

As Robert Collins, Kim McQuaid, and Thomas Ferguson have shown, however, economic depression and New Deal activism forced those progressive business leaders who headed the great investment houses and capital-intensive firms to redefine New Era formulations in a way that left more room for organized labor, conceded a larger role for the state, and included a conservative version of Keynesian economic theory. These were the men, such men as Lincoln Filene, Ralph Flanders, Henry Dennison, Beardsley Ruml, Paul Hoffman, and Averell Harriman, who organized the Business Advisory Council, staffed the NRA's Industrial Advisory Board, and founded the American Policy Commission. Their organic view of society, their faith in expertise, their flexible attitude toward labor, and their support for welfare capitalism, economic planning, and overseas expansion linked these men backward to the technocorporatism of the National Civil Federation and the associationalism of Hoover, and forward to what Robert Griffith has called the "corporate commonwealth" of the Eisenhower years.[25]

This group exerted only occasional influence during the early and middle years of the New Deal, when public programs for stimulating recovery oscillated between protecting the home market, breaking monopolies, promoting little NRAs, and expanding public-sector spending. In the NRA and other forums, its leaders waged a ferocious battle with private and public officials who were less conciliatory toward labor, supported strictly statist or free-market solutions to economic recovery, or favored a vigilant defense of the domestic market rather than reciprocal trade and overseas expansion. With the war mobilization, however, they began to occupy a dominant place in both business councils and government bureaucracies. They worked closely with their government and labor partners in such wartime agencies as the War Production Board and the War Labor Board, agencies that reconstituted the business-government détente achieved earlier under the War Industries Board. Through the Committee for Economic Development, moreover, they fashioned a postwar stabilization strategy that harnessed a conservative version of Keynesian theory to their vision of a collectivist democracy. According to

---

    [24]See Ellis W. Hawley, *The New Deal and the Problem of Monopoly* (Princeton, 1966); and Ferguson, "From Normalcy to New Deal."

    [25]Kim McQuaid, "Corporate Liberalism in the American Business Community, 1920–1940," and Robert M. Collins, "Positive Business Responses to the New Deal: The Roots of the Committee for Economic Development," in *Business History Review* 12 (Autumn 1978): 342–68 and 369–91, respectively; Robert M. Collins, *The Business Response to Keynes, 1929–1964* (New York, 1981); Kim McQuaid, *Big Business and Presidential Power: From FDR to Reagan* (New York, 1982); Ferguson, "From Normalcy to New Deal"; Robert Griffith, "Dwight D. Eisenhower and the Corporate Commonwealth," *American Historical Review* 87 (February 1982): 87–122.

this strategy, an active and flexible monetary policy and the largely automatic fiscal stabilizers in a full-employment budget would regulate the business cycle, limit government expenditures, and promote growth in the private rather than the public sector.[26]

By the end of the Truman administration, large elements of the business community, including the Chamber of Commerce, had accepted some variant of this "conservative Keynesianism" and had used it to define anew the basis for a public-private partnership. Defeated under the new arrangement were those antitrusters who opposed the modern trend toward concentration and collectivism. Defeated as well were those left-wing liberals whose gloomy predictions of economic stagnation had led them to demand more centralized planning, greater government direction of the economy, income redistribution, and permanent programs of public works. The new liberalism looked instead to a collectivist commonwealth in which government power would be enlarged, delimited, and shared. Following this vision, government planners would bring into the public sector much of the welfare capitalism pioneered by their corporate counterparts in an earlier day. They would organize and give representation to previously unrecognized labor, consumer, and professional groups, bringing them into the cooperative community and working with them to shape social and economic policy. They also would use the new tools of macroeconomic management and new ordering and stabilizing institutions to influence aggregate economic performance in the private sector. But they would leave in the hands of private business managers the fundamental decisions regarding production, allocation, prices, and wages, and through new frameworks of group action and power-sharing, they would collaborate with their private partners to boost productivity at home, promote expansion abroad, and thereby achieve an economic growth that would contain state power and prevent redistributive conflicts.[27]

Business reached a similar accommodation with organized labor. The National Labor-Management Conference of 1945 signified management's willingness to join government in recognizing the new status of independent trade unions. All sides looked to a three-cornered partnership as the basis for industrial stability and abundance. The central question involved the terms of this partnership, with Walter Reuther and other labor progressives urging worker codetermination in areas traditionally reserved for management. During the war years they had called for national economic planning through industrial councils in which government, labor, and business would jointly organize war industries and direct the process of postwar reconversion. After the war they demanded a voice for workers in industrial decisions relating to prices, profits, technological change, and plant location.[28]

---

[26]Collins, "Positive Business Responses to the New Deal"; McQuaid, "Corporate Liberalism in the Business Community"; Collins, *Business Response to Keynes,* especially chapters 4, 5, and 6; Hawley, "Techno-Corporatist Formulas in the Liberal State, 1920–1960."

[27]Collins, *Business Response to Keynes,* chapters 5 and 6.

[28]David Brody, *Workers in Industrial America: Essays on the Twentieth Century Struggle,* paperback edition (New York, 1981), chap. 5.

These demands went further than corporate leaders were willing to go. They rejected the idea of industrial councils, relegated labor leaders to the role of subordinate partners in the wartime mobilization agencies, and later refused to bend under trade union pressure for labor participation in pricing and profit policy. Yet neither did they revert to the big-stick policy of 1919. They accepted trade unions, tolerated strikes, and agreed to collective bargaining on issues of immediate interest to workers. With the acquiescence of government and the support of most trade union leaders, they also succeeded in defeating Reuther's demands and limiting the scope of labor-management conflict to basic bread-and-butter issues.[29] The result was a labor-management partnership similar to the one that Samuel Gompers and others had envisioned in the 1920s, one, in other words, that tied economic gains for workers to the rock of productivity and one that exchanged labor recognition of traditional managerial prerogatives for management recognition of independent trade unions.

These accommodations between government and business, business and labor, established the conditions for postwar stabilization at home. They built upon strategies and structures dating back to the first postwar period and beyond, and to a great extent, they were similar to the arrangements worked out for stabilizing the international economy in the 1930s and 1940s. In the 1930s, for example, the State Department's search for trade liberalization and the Treasury Department's quest for monetary stabilization recalled the liberal internationalism of an earlier era. They looked to a world system in which lower tariffs and fixed exchanges would enable such free-market maxims as competition and comparative advantage to stimulate growth and integrate economies. At the London Conference of 1933, however, this strategy suffered a major defeat at the hands of those New Dealers who defended the NRA and sought recovery at home through policies that combined economic isolationism with a crude neomercantilism.[30] The controversy that followed the London Conference was similar to the one that surrounded the NRA's approach to domestic economic management, just as the resulting compound of free-market and statist strategies would follow the lines of accommodation reached on the home front during and after the Second World War.

The famous battle between Secretary of State Cordell Hull and foreign trade adviser George M. Peek revealed one dimension of this controversy. Peek favored an autarchic commercial policy in which government would control, direct, and finance American commerce and seek national self-sufficiency through bilateral trade and barter agreements, surplus dumping, and policies of preference. For Hull, on the other hand, neither economic self-sufficiency nor state trading and bilateralism were desirable. They would

---

[29]Ibid.; Paul A. C. Koistinen, "Mobilizing the World War II Economy: Labor and the Industrial-Military Alliance," *Pacific Historical Review* 42 (November 1973): 443–78.

[30]Lloyd C. Gardner, *Economic Aspects of New Deal Diplomacy* (Boston, 1971), pp. 26–30; Dick Steward, *Trade and Hemisphere: The Good Neighbor Policy and Reciprocal Trade* (Columbia, MO, 1975), pp. 15–18; James R. Moore, "Sources of New Deal Economic Policy: The International Dimension," *Journal of American History* 41 (December 1974): 728–44.

further fragment the world economy, perpetuate the depression, lead to international conflict, and imperil private enterprise and political freedom in the United States. Hull called instead for reciprocal trade and nondiscrimination, stressing in his plea that such policies would allow unfettered market mechanisms and private enterprise to stimulate growth and integrate markets without the economic and political pitfalls inherent in state trading.[31]

By 1936, the State Department had defeated Peek and the economic nationalists. The Supreme Court had overturned the NRA; Hull was negotiating reciprocal trade agreements under the authority conferred by Congress in 1934; Secretary of the Treasury Henry Morgenthau, Jr., was arranging the Tripartite Currency Agreement; and together the State and Treasury departments were charting a course that would lead, from the Lend-Lease Agreement through the Bretton Woods Agreement, to a postwar world economy based on full convertibility and multilateralism. In the process, however, they lost ground to Henry A. Wallace and other public and private leaders whose middle way between Hull's laissez-faire and Peek's neomercantilism also shaped the American approach to international stabilization. This strategy, the strategy of the middle way, combined free-market incentives and private enterprise with modern forms of technical management, government aid, and public-private cooperation. By following it, American policymakers helped to organize private bondholders into the Bondholders Protective Association and cooperated with the group to negotiate debt-funding agreements with foreign governments. They also established the Export-Import Bank, linked it through advisory committees to the business and banking communities, and used it to underwrite private trade and development. In addition, they supported such international stabilizers as the World Bank and the International Monetary Fund, and through these agencies, the Inter-American Development Commission, the Point Four Program, and other institutions, they sought to banish restrictive policies and state trading, integrate the world economy along multilateral lines, and supplement market forces with new institutional regulators, new public-private partnerships, and new forms of government assistance and technical management.[32] This approach went beyond Hull's antistatism, but it also stopped short of the autocratic state trading that he and others saw as a fundamental threat to peace, prosperity, and private enterprise.

---

[31]Gardner, *Economic Aspects of New Deal Diplomacy,* especially chapter 2; Steward, *Trade and Hemisphere,* chapters 1 and 2; Frederick C. Adams, *Economic Diplomacy: The Export-Import Bank and American Foreign Policy, 1934–1939* (Columbia, MO, 1976), chap. 3.

[32]In addition to the works cited in the previous note, see Benjamin M. Rowland, "Preparing the American Ascendancy: The Transfer of Economic Power from Britain to the United States, 1933–1944," in Rowland, ed., *Balance of Power or Hegemony: The Interwar Monetary System* (New York, 1976), pp. 195–224; Thomas G. Paterson, "Foreign Aid Under Wraps: The Point Four Program," *Wisconsin Magazine of History* 56 (1972/73): 119–26; and James M. McHale, "National Planning and Reciprocal Trade: The New Deal Origins of Government Guarantees for Private Exporters," *Prologue* 6 (Fall 1974): 189–99.

American Marshall planners applied the same approach to the problem of European recovery after the Second World War. They again blended government action and institutional coordinators with private enterprise and free-market strategies and then tried to harmonize these two lines of policy by carefully delineating the government's role, stressing the importance of technical expertise, and building new systems of group action and public-private cooperation. Their formulations expressed the type of "conservative Keynesianism" that had triumphed in the United States. It left little room for the welfare programs and socialist experiments, the government controls, and the policies of preference by which the Europeans might avoid deflation, maintain employment, and preserve what remained of an independent world position. These were to give way now to a liberal capitalism, but one in which American aid, institutional ordering mechanisms, and new units of corporative collaboration would temper domestic and international adjustments, integrate economies, and create a productive abundance for all.

Although the Marshall Plan assigned government a significant role in the stabilization process, this role was carefully delimited. It was perceived as both a national security imperative and as an aid to private enterprise, and it was to be performed in collaboration with private elites. Some public and private leaders, to be sure, worried that a major government aid program might actually promote what Senator Walter George of Georgia called "a wholly new system of trade and commerce through state operation."[33] It would, in the eyes of conservative economist Henry Hazlitt, supplant market mechanisms and private initiative, support unproductive socialist experiments in Europe, delay monetary and fiscal adjustments there, and lead to shortages, inflation, and government controls in the United States.[34] But most thought government had a legitimate part to play in reinforcing private initiative at home and abroad. It could use its aid to alleviate the economic duress that had led European statesmen to experiment with socialist enterprise and state trading. It could also promote those trade, monetary, and fiscal reforms that would help to integrate the European economies and create the conditions in which private enterprise might thrive. In performing these functions, moreover, it could actually prevent the political and economic regimentation of American life that would invariably result from the diminution of American commerce, the collapse of liberal democracies in Europe, and the emergence there of a hostile coalition of totalitarian states dominated by the Soviet Union, committed to state trading, and controlling major markets and sources of supply.[35]

---

[33]U.S., Congress, Senate, Committee on Foreign Relations, *Hearings on European Recovery Program*, 80th Cong., 2d sess., 1948, p. 173.

[34]See Hazlitt's statement and testimony in ibid., pp. 684–705.

[35]Ibid., pp. 2, 31–32, 227–28, 233–34, 249, 354–56, 852, 1118; U.S., Congress, House, Committee on Foreign Affairs, *Hearings on United States Foreign Policy for a Post-War Recovery Program*, 80th Cong., 1st & 2d sess., 1947–48, pp. 73, 76, 182–83, 224–25, 334–35, 465, 578. See also, Senator Arthur H. Vandenberg, letter to Malcolm W. Bingay, 29 December 1947, Arthur H. Vandenberg Papers, box 3, folder: Correspondence, Nov.–Dec. 1947, University of

According to these arguments, government could shape aggregate economic performance. It could also act in areas too risky for businessmen and bankers, and in doing both, it could help to support private trade and investment. Congress incorporated this line of thinking into the Foreign Assistance Act of 1948. It was not simply that the act contained sops to particular private interests or provisions under which private surpluses could be dumped in Western Europe. More significant were those features designed to promote the very system of private enterprise. Included here were provisions guaranteeing currency conversion for certain American investments in Europe; provisions requiring the "maximum" possible use of private channels in furnishing technical assistance or in the procurement, processing, storing, transfer, transportation, and allocation of commodities and services; and provisions making American aid contingent on progress by the participating countries in stabilizing currencies, fixing realistic exchange rates, and liberalizing trade. All of these, according to American leaders, were essential to reestablishing a free world trading system.[36]

Significant too were the administrative arrangements for managing the American recovery program. Policymakers ruled out a government aid corporation, partly for reasons of bureaucratic politics, but partly because it would entail the sort of state trading which the United States had traditionally opposed and which politicized economic issues and violated the private character of the American economy. A massive government procurement operation, as Secretary of State George C. Marshall explained, would "constitute a threat to private enterprise in this country and to sovereign governments in Europe."[37] Instead, both Congress and the Truman administration agreed to establish an independent agency and to staff it with managerial talent from the private sector. Such an agency, it was argued, would guarantee a nonpolitical and businesslike administration of the recovery program. It would also win support from both political parties and from those organized functional groups that provided services and supplies for the program. And it would mobilize the private expertise that was required to solve Europe's difficult industrial, financial, and commercial problems, boost productivity there, and integrate the continental economies. In solving these problems, moreover, it would help to put the Marshall Plan countries on a self-supporting basis and to achieve those other goals, such as multilateralism, Communist

Michigan, Ann Arbor, MI (hereafter cited as Vandenberg Papers); and Secretary of State George C. Marshall, address to the Pittsburgh Chamber of Commerce, 5 January 1948, Lou E. Holland Papers, box 84, folder: Personal Correspondence, Marshall Plan, Harry S Truman Library, Independence, MO.

[36]The Foreign Assistance Act of 1948 is printed in U.S., Congress, House, Committee on International Relations, Historical Series, *Selected Executive Hearings, Foreign Economic Programs*, 80th Cong., 2d sess., 1948, pt.1:254–72. See also, Harold Lee Hitchens, "Congress and the Adoption of the Marshall Plan" (Ph.D. diss., University of Chicago, 1949), pp. 181–94; and Hadley Arkes, *Bureaucracy, the Marshall Plan, and the National Interest* (Princeton, NJ, 1972), pp. 166–71.

[37]The administrative arrangements are discussed in Arkes, *Bureaucracy, the Marshall Plan, and the National Interest*, pp. 59–128. The quotation is on p. 67.

containment, and German revival and reintegration, that also motivated American policy.[38]

Following this administrative strategy, the Foreign Assistance Act established an independent recovery agency, the Economic Cooperation Administration (ECA), under a single administrator who was to function as the "business head of a business operation."[39] The administrator, Paul G. Hoffman of the Studebaker Corporation, was to have his own special representative in Europe and economic missions in each of the Marshall Plan countries. These provisions aimed at ensuring ECA's autonomy and a nonpolitical administration of operational matters. But others, assigned specific responsibilities to such "political" agencies as the Commerce, State, and Treasury departments, urged these agencies and ECA to harmonize their differences through continuous consultation and collaboration, and thus created a framework for public-private power-sharing. Adding to this framework were ECA's links to the private sector through a Public Advisory Board, numerous advisory committees, and agency representation for various functional and technical elites. Business and banking leaders dominated the advisory committees, held the top management positions in ECA, and headed most of its overseas missions. Farm spokesmen sat on the Public Advisory Board and worked closely with ECA's Food and Agriculture Divisions. Trade union representatives also served on the advisory board, staffed ECA's Labor and Manpower Divisions, and functioned as labor advisors to its missions in the participating countries. Technical experts drawn from various government agencies and academic institutions were included as well.[40]

Hoffman, in other words, made ECA into a model of the technocorporatism championed by those large industrial and financial enterprises represented in the Committee for Economic Development and the American Policy Commission, both of which he had helped to found.[41] Like the Republicans in the 1920s, moreover, he and others tried to impose this model on the European system. On the one hand, they envisioned a liberal European capitalism founded on free-market mechanisms and American notions of sound fiscal management. They told the Europeans to reduce social expenditures, balance budgets, stabilize currencies, and fix realistic exchange rates. They also launched a campaign against monopoly in Germany, attacked bilateral trade agreements and government import controls, objected when the French

---

[38]For a fuller discussion of these arguments, see Michael J. Hogan, "American Marshall Planners and the Search for a European Neo-Capitalism," *American Historical Review*, forthcoming (1985).

[39]The quotation is from Senator Vandenberg as cited in Arkes, *Bureaucracy, the Marshall Plan, and the National Interest*, p. 84. See also, Vandenberg, letter to Carl M. Saunders, 2 January 1948, box 3, folder: Correspondence, January 1948, Vandenberg Papers. For the administrative provisions in the Foreign Assistance Act see the first source cited in footnote 36.

[40]Ibid.; Arkes, *Bureaucracy, The Marshall Plan, and the National Interest*, p. 100; Hogan, "Marshall Planners and the Search for a European Neo-Capitalism."

[41]For Hoffman's role in the founding of these organizations, see Collins, "Positive Business Responses to the New Deal."

tried to replace these controls with private cartels, and resisted British plans to organize a soft-currency trading bloc. As had been true of their Republican predecessors, Marshall planners saw in these European practices and proposals the sort of autarky and statism that generated conflict, hampered productivity, and prevented a rational integration of the European and world economies.[42]

On the other hand, Marshall planners tempered their conservative prescriptions with political realism and the modern tools of economic management. They settled for European trade and payments agreements that fell short of full convertibility and multilateralism, offset deflationary impacts with American grants, and urged the participating countries to cushion internal adjustments with compensatory fiscal policies.[43] They also tried to mix informal market mechanisms with formal institutions of coordination and control. They called for a European federal reserve bank and a federal trade commission. They made the Organization for European Economic Cooperation (OEEC) into a corporate body with a competent professional staff and limited authority to coordinate national recovery programs. And they won support for the European Payments Union through which a supervisory board of experts was to use both administrative controls and market incentives to adjust national monetary and fiscal policies in the interest of European stabilization and integration. In these and other ways, Marshall planners sought to reconcile their faith in market forces with the institutional imperatives of an integrated economic order, employing as the agents of reconciliation the same technical experts and politically neutral authorities that Hoover had celebrated in the 1920s.[44]

In addition, Marshall planners tried to transform political problems into technical ones that were solvable, they said, when old European ways of business and old habits of class conflict gave way to American strategies of scientific management and corporative collaboration. As a first step in this direction, they joined their labor allies in a concerted attack against the traditional pattern of cooperation between Communists and non-Communists in the European trade-union movement. They disrupted the Communist-led World

---

[42]On U.S. support for balanced budgets and opposition to British plans, see the last two sources cited in footnote 11. On U.S. opposition to bilateralism and import controls, see Diebold, *Trade and Payments*, pp. 153–85. On U.S. objections to French cartel proposals see *FRUS, 1949,* 4:443–45, 454–55. On the antimonopoly campaign in Germany and its eventual collapse, see Graham D. Taylor, "The Rise and Fall of Antitrust in Occupied Germany, 1945–48," *Prologue* 11 (Spring 1979): 23–39.

[43]Milton Katz of ECA, repto circular telegram 87 to Paul Hoffman, 15 April 1950, box 20, and Katz, repto 2359 to Hoffman, 1 May 1950, box18, ECA Telegram File, records of the Agency for International Development, Washington, DC (hereafter cited as ECA Telegram File).

[44]Theodore Geiger, Richard Bissell, and Harold Van B. Cleveland of ECA, "The Economic Integration of Western Europe,"15 October 1949, W. Averell Harriman Papers, folder: Policy-General, in his personal possession, Washington, DC; Hoffman, torep 3420 to U.S. Special Representative in Europe W. Averell Harriman, 18 February 1949, box 46, ECA Telegram File; Hoffman, torep 8769 to Harriman, 25 October 1949, and William Foster of ECA, torep 9606 to Harriman, 26 November 1949, box 50, ibid; Diebold, *Trade and Payments*, pp. 87–110; and Lincoln Gordon, "The Organization for European Economic Cooperation," *International Organization* 10 (February 1956): 1–11.

Federation of Trade Unions, organized a European Recovery Program-Trade Union Advisory Committee (TUAC), and used it as the nucleus for a non-Communist labor international devoted to the ideology of productivity that had defined the basis for a labor-management accommodation in the United States.[45]

Thereafter, American trade unionists and their ECA supporters urged TUAC to follow the American example, establish partnerships with the participating governments and the OEEC, and work through these partnerships to boost productivity and integrate economies. At a meeting in July 1948, TUAC responded with resolutions calling for the appointment of a labor "advisory" committee to assist OEEC and for new ties to ECA's overseas missions, to the labor representatives on its Public Advisory Board, and to the recovery authorities in the participating countries.[46] Similar recommendations came from another TUAC meeting later in 1948, one that American government and labor leaders had helped to organize in order to reiterate the "important part" that European trade unions and other "non-government groups" must play in the recovery program.[47] They made the same point to OEEC and the participating governments, and by the end of the year their efforts were showing signs of success. OEEC had recognized TUAC as the international representative of organized labor and the two bodies were laying plans to appoint labor advisors to OEEC's technical committees. TUAC had also decided to establish links with the International Trade Secretaries, a move that would open possibilities for transnational cooperation in those aspects of the recovery program that "extended beyond national boundaries."[48] In such countries as Italy and France, moreover, ECA had exerted pressure that was leading to the appointment of labor advisory committees whose members would collaborate with government officials in a variety of recovery projects.[49]

The ties between the American and European labor movements, between ECA and the European trade unions, and between these unions and the participating governments were important steps toward transnational integration

[45]Peter Weiler, "The United States, International Labor, and the Cold War The Breakup of the World Federation of Trade Unions," *Diplomatic History* 5 (Winter 1981): 1–22.

[46]Ambassador Lewis Douglas, London, tels. to SecSt., 26 April and 14 June 1948, Department of State Records, RG 84, London Embassy Files, box 1035, file: 850 Marshall Plan, Washington National Records Center, Suitland, Maryland; Samuel Berger, first secretary, American embassy, London, dispatch 1775 to SecSt., 13 August 1948, National Archives, Department of State Records, RG 59, file: 840.50Recovery/8-1348; memorandum of conversation between Clinton Golden of ECA and various State Department officials, 20 August 1948, RG 59, file: 840.5043/8-2048.

[47]Undersecretary of State Robert Lovett, tel. to the American embassy, Paris, 4 October 1948, RG 59, file: 840.50Recovery/9-2848; and Harriman, repto 1068 to SecSt., 7 October 1948, box 5, ECA Telegram File.

[48]Ambassador Jefferson Caffery, Paris, tel. to SecSt., 23 September 1948, RG 84, box 1035, file: 850 Marshall Plan; Caffery, tel. to SecSt., 24 November 1948, RG 59, file: 840.50Recovery/11-2448; Foster, repto 1762 to Hoffman, 2 December 1948, box 5, ECA Telegram File; Foster, reptos 2100 and 2131 to Hoffman, 29 and 31 December 1948, box 6, ibid.

[49]Lovett, tel. to Caffery, 9 April 1948, RG 59, file: 840.50Recovery/4-548; W. K. Knight, memorandum of conversation, 1 October 1948, ibid. /10-148.

on the labor front and toward a system of corporative collaboration between government and labor. They were followed, moreover, by additional organizational initiatives through which ECA tried to bring labor and management together in new integrating institutions, pool their expertise and that of technical elites, and, in this way, dissolve old frictions in common programs for productive abundance. One such institution was the Anglo-American Council on Productivity which British and American leaders established in late 1948 and through which cooperating groups of trade union, management, and technical representatives studied American management and labor procedures with a view to increasing the efficiency of British industry.[50] Another was the technical assistance program by which ECA brought similar European groups to the United States where they were to learn how American methods of mass production and labor-management teamwork had supposedly enhanced output, raised living standards, and created an industrial democracy.[51] Still other integrating institutions took the form of so-called "productivity centers" established, with ECA support, in several of the participating countries and used by collaborating labor, management, and professional groups to disseminate technical information, harmonize differences, and launch concerted drives to maximize productivity.[52]

Through these initiatives and those calling for compensatory fiscal policies and supranational coordinators, Marshall planners went beyond the prescriptions of their Republican predecessors in the 1920s. In doing so, however, they continued to pursue the same goal of an economically ordered and productive European and world community in which new integrating frameworks and new forms of technical leadership, enlightened group action, and public-private cooperation would prevent a dangerous and destructive statism, resolve Franco-German rivalries, harmonize class differences, and usher in an era of permanent peace and prosperity. Their policies tended to formalize, reinforce, and extend strategies and structures that had been informal and embryonic in the first postwar period. Old concepts of economic interdependence now gave way to modern notions of structural integration. Loose networks of cooperation between government and business became more definite and were enlarged to include representatives of organized agriculture and labor. Private finance and rudimentary ordering mechanisms were supplemented with more positive government action and central institutions of coordination and control.

These innovations undoubtedly grew out of what American leaders perceived as the shortcomings of past policy and the greater danger of Communist subversion and Soviet aggression. Yet they also involved evolutionary

---

[50]Paul G. Hoffman, *Peace Can Be Won* (Garden City, NY, 1951), pp. 101–2; reports of the council, Paul G. Hoffman Papers, box 24, folders: Economic Cooperation Administration, Pamphlets and Publications, Truman Library.

[51]ECA, *Sixth Report to Congress*, pp. 50–52; ECA, *Seventh Report to Congress*, pp. 51–53.

[52]ECA, *Tenth Report to Congress*, p. 49.

adaptations of the same technocorporative formulations that had guided America's search for a stable international economy since the First World War. Through these formulations progressive American business and political leaders, together with their allies in labor, agriculture, and the professions, had sought to adjust nineteenth-century verities to twentieth-century realities, and to do so in order to reconcile group interests, contain state power, and forge a stable and productive political economy at home and abroad. To a great extent, moreover, these same formulations continue to be sounded in the contemporary debates over economic policy, although now with a note of irony that had been missing in an earlier day. In the new age of economic instability, social division, and productivity crisis, one is indeed often struck by how American leaders seek to relearn from their international rivals the same strategies of scientific management, corporative collaboration, and public-private power-sharing that Marshall planners had exported in the 1940s.

The Political Economy of Crude Oil Cartelization in the United States, 1933–1972

GARY D. LIBECAP

This article examines a government-sponsored cartel that fixed domestic crude oil prices in interstate markets from 1933 through 1972. Although the cartel raised and stabilized nominal oil prices beyond earlier private efforts, it also resulted in politically driven constraints on price, output levels, and cartel rent distribution. Political factors molded quota assignments, diverted production from low- to high-cost producers, and raised production costs. Political pressures prevented Texas from acting as a residual or swing producer. Instead, the interstate oil cartel members maintained nominal prices and spread the political costs of output adjustments.

Cartels are interesting because of their potential impact on output and prices and the problems they often face in negotiating and policing output quotas. For these reasons private cartelization efforts have been the subject on considerable research.[1] The instability of private cartels, due to disagreements of industry output and price levels or to cheating on quotas and new entry, suggests that government assistance is necessary for success. The involvement of government, however, brings its own set of problems. Politics will mold the industry price and output levels and the nature of the production quotas assigned to members. Although monopoly rents may be earned through government-sponsored cartels, politically driven constraints will determine both the size of the rents and their distribution. These political factors

The Journal of Economic History, Vol. XLIX, No. 4 (Dec. 1989). © The Economic History Association. All rights reserved. ISSN 0022-0507.

The author is Professor of Economics and Director of the Karl Eller Center, College of Business and Public Administration, University of Arizona, Tucson, AZ 85721.

The author wishes to thank Lee Alston, Alberta Charney, Price Fishback, Jim Griffin, Robert Higgs, Betsy Hoffman, Mark Isaac, Ron Johnson, Ken Kroner, Ron Oaxaca, Ed Ray, Barbara Sands, Tom Weiss, this JOURNAL's referees, and participants in the 1985 Cliometrics Conference, the 1985 All-California Economic History Conference, and workshops at the University of Kansas, the University of Southern California, and Washington University. Statistical support was provided by Cliff Mangano.

[1] The cartel literature is both varied and large. A sample includes George W. Stocking and Myron W. Watkins, *Cartels in Action* (New York, 1946); Bjarke Fog, "How are Cartel Prices Determined?" *Journal of Industrial Economics*, 3 (Nov. 1956), pp. 16–23; Paul W. MacAvoy, *The Economic Effects of Regulation: The Trunk-Line Railroad Cartels and the Interstate Commerce Commission Before 1900* (Cambridge, MA, 1965); Gabriel Kolko, *Railroads and Regulation, 1877–1916* (New York, 1965); George A. Hay and Daniel Kelly, "An Empirical Survey of Price Fixing Conspiracies," *Journal of Law and Economics*, 17 (Apr. 1974), pp. 13–39; and Thomas Ulen, "Railroad Cartels Before 1887: The Effectiveness of Private Enforcement and Collusion," *Research in Economic History*, 8 (1983), pp. 125–44. There is also a large game-theoretic literature. See Jean Tirole, *The Theory of Industrial Organization* (Cambridge, MA, 1988), for a survey.

197

complicate the examination of cartel behavior, and the literature on the special problems associated with government-sponsored cartels is a much smaller one.[2] Even where research has been directed to the study of a particular cartel no clear picture has emerged.

The Organization of Petroleum Exporting Countries (OPEC) is a case in point. Since it quadrupled crude oil prices in 1974 there has been increased interest in the cartel, but a consensus on the appropriate modeling and interpretation of output coordination within OPEC has not emerged.[3] However, insights into the behavior of OPEC, as well as other government-sponsored cartels within the United States, may be learned from an important historical case also involving oil.

The cartelization of oil production by political bodies is not new. For 40 years, from 1933 through 1972, crude oil production in the United States was controlled by government-enforced prorationing of output among the states to fix prices. During that period crude oil prices were increased and stabilized beyond what had been historically possible through private means. Although the interstate cartel has received considerable attention, disagreement remains regarding the nature of oil production controls. Moreover, the constraints imposed by political conditions have not been explored for their implications for selecting prices, determining and coordinating monthly output levels among the states, and assigning individual well quotas.

There is general consensus that Texas played a pivotal role in the cartel, but the extent to which it acted as a swing or residual producer to offset the production of other states is one of the areas subject to dispute. One view, represented by Erich Zimmermann, and Melvin de Chazeau and Alfred Kahn, is that the Railroad Commission adjusted Texan output to insure that U.S. production equaled estimated aggregate demand at targeted prices.[4] Morris Adelman, and Wallace Lovejoy and Paul Homan, however, had a more moderate view of the role of

---

[2] Examples include Paul Joskow, "Inflation and Environmental Concern: Structural Change in the Process of Public Utility Regulation," *Journal of Law and Economics*, 17 (Oct. 1974), pp. 291–328; William Hallagan, "Contracting Problems and the Adoption of Regulatory Cartels," *Economic Inquiry*, 23 (Jan. 1985), pp. 37–56; Lawrence Shepard, "Cartelization of the California-Arizona Orange Industry, 1934–1981," *Journal of Law and Economics*, 29 (Apr. 1986), pp. 83–121; Jonathan Cave and Stephen W. Salant, "Cartels that Vote: Agricultural Marketing Boards and Induced Voting Behavior," in Elizabeth Bailey, ed., *Public Regulation: New Perspectives in Institutions and Policies* (Cambridge, MA, 1987); and Steven N. Wiggins and Gary D. Libecap, "Firm Heterogeneities and Cartelization Efforts in Domestic Crude Oil," *Journal of Law, Economics and Organization*, 3 (Spring 1987), pp. 1–25.

[3] For an overview of research and disagreements about OPEC, see Dermot Gately, "A Ten-Year Retrospective: OPEC and the World Oil Market," *Journal of Economic Literature*, 22 (Sept. 1984), pp. 1100–14; and James M. Griffin, "OPEC Behavior: A Test of Alternative Hypotheses," *American Economic Review*, 75 (Dec. 1985), pp. 954–63.

[4] See Melvin G. de Chazeau and Alfred E. Kahn, *Integration and Competition in the Petroleum Industry* (New Haven, 1959), pp. 123–25; and Erich W. Zimmermann, *Conservation in the Production of Petroleum* (New Haven, 1957), pp. 59, 213–24.

Texas, suggesting that interstate regulatory efforts may have been only loosely coordinated, with Texas primarily restraining its low-cost fields.[5] Other areas of concern regarding the cartel are the extent to which well quota assignments promoted profit maximization by minimizing production costs, and whether the cartel adjusted output to stabilize nominal or real crude oil prices.

I. INTERSTATE MARKET-DEMAND PRORATIONING

By 1920 there was a national market in the United States for crude oil, with most producing regions connected by pipelines and railroads to domestic markets. The midcontinent states of Kansas, Oklahoma, and Texas were the leading producers, accounting for 54 percent of total U.S. crude oil production. The other leading oil state was California, but it was isolated from the national market until after World War II, due to a lack of connecting pipelines.[6]

Prior to extensive government regulation in 1933, crude oil production decisions were made by firms that held leases from surface landowners. Since petroleum was migratory within reservoirs and property rights to it were assigned only upon extraction under the rule of capture, firms typically faced common pool conditions. On common pool reservoirs, firms had incentives to drill their leases and to produce as rapidly as possible to maximize their share of oil field rents. As a result, since the first discovery of oil in 1859, U.S. crude oil output and prices followed cycles with prices falling as new fields were discovered and drained and then rising as supplies again became tight.[7]

Sustained interstate efforts to create an oil cartel within the national market through government intervention began in 1926, following the unprecedented clustering of major new oil discoveries that drove prices to their lowest levels in the twentieth century. For example, the nominal Oklahoma price for 36-degree gravity oil, the industry standard, fell from $2.29 per barrel in 1926 to $0.10 per barrel in 1933.[8] Because of the magnitude of the oil discoveries, these falling prices seemed to go

[5] See Morris Adelman, *The World Petroleum Market* (Baltimore, 1972), p. 148; and Wallace F. Lovejoy and Paul T. Homan, *Economic Aspects of Oil Conservation Regulation* (Baltimore, 1967), pp. 226–27.

[6] U.S. crude oil production by state is in American Petroleum Institute, *Petroleum Facts and Figures* (Washington, DC, 1971), pp. 68–69. California had large oil reserves, but until the postwar period it served a separate West Coast market.

[7] For discussion of common pool conditions in crude oil production, their impact on prices, and efforts to secure government controls, see Gary D. Libecap and Steven N. Wiggins, "Contractual Responses to the Common Pool: Prorationing of Crude Oil Production," *American Economic Review*, 74 (Mar. 1984), pp. 87–98; and Gary D. Libecap, "The Political Allocation of Mineral Rights: A Re-Evaluation of Teapot Dome," this JOURNAL, 44 (June 1984), pp. 381–91.

[8] This decline in nominal crude oil prices far exceeds the decline in the consumer price index over the same period. See U.S. Department of Commerce, Bureau of the Census, *Historical Statistics of the United States, Colonial Times to 1970* (Washington, DC, 1975), p. 211.

TABLE 1
AVERAGE TOTAL PRODUCTION COSTS ACROSS THE STATES

State	Production Cost
Illinois	$1.35
Kansas	1.05
Louisiana	0.90
Oklahoma	1.02
Texas	
West	0.62
North	1.26
Central	1.08
East	0.56
State Average	0.69

Source: U.S. House of Representatives, Cole Committee Hearings, *Petroleum Investigation: Hearings Before a Subcommittee of the Committee on Interstate and Foreign Commerce on H.R. 441*, 73rd Congress, 2nd session, part 1 (Washington, DC, 1934), pp. 790–805.

beyond past oil production cycles, raising the urgency for an interstate agreement to control output. Nevertheless, conflict over state quotas delayed agreement on an interstate oil compact until 1935. The conflict centered on differences in oil production costs across the states and how much output reduction each state should bear.[9]

Texas was the location of most of the new oil discoveries, especially the giant East Texas field, discovered in October 1930, and the state had by far the largest reserves of low-cost oil.[10] In 1934 Texas had 45 percent of proved U.S. oil reserves and by 1940 had 56 percent. Kansas and Oklahoma, two other leading producing states at that time, had 3 percent and 6 percent of U.S. reserves.[11]

Oil production in Kansas and Oklahoma generally was from older reservoirs and more costly to extract than was much of Texas's production, as shown in Table 1, which lists average production costs for the leading producing states. Stripper well data shown in Table 2 underscore Texas's competitive advantage in the early 1930s. Stripper wells are high-cost wells on old fields or older parts of fields that

[9] Oil production costs are largely a function of geology and time. Newly developed reservoirs provide oil at very low marginal extraction costs, since underground pressures are sufficient to expel the oil to the surface once the reservoir is punctured by a well. Over time those pressures are dissipated, particularly if the field is exploited rapidly, as is likely under common pool conditions. Eventually, installation of pumping wells and the injection of natural gas, water, or other substances into the reservoir become necessary to extract the oil, but these actions raise marginal extraction costs.

[10] The Oklahoma City and East Texas fields were the largest during the 1926 to 1935 period, but East Texas dwarfed all others, being 10 to 12 *times* as large in area as Oklahoma City. See *Oil Weekly*, Apr. 24, 1931; and *Oil Weekly*, Feb. 11, 1935.

[11] Crude oil reserves data are from the *Oil and Gas Journal*, Jan. 18, 1937; and the American Petroleum Institute, *Reserves of Crude Oil, Natural Gas Liquids, and Natural Gas in the United States and Canada as of December 31, 1979* (Washington, DC, 1980), pp. 25–66. Proved reserves are defined by the American Petroleum Institute as crude oil that is recoverable with existing technology.

TABLE 2
NUMBER OF STRIPPER WELLS AND PERCENTAGE OF TOTAL STATE WELLS

State	1941	1950	1960
Illinois	16,065	24,245	28,930
	72%	88%	89%
Kansas	15,000	14,811	35,400
	65%	48%	87%
Louisiana	3,217	4,505	9,182
	49%	38%	37%
Oklahoma	47,378	42,810	68,836
	87%	75%	89%
Texas	31,126	46,197	84,690
	31%	36%	44%

Note: Stripper wells are defined by the National Stripper Well Association as wells producing 10 barrels of oil per day or less.
Source: Interstate Oil Compact Commission, National Stripper Well Survey (Oklahoma City, 1955, 1960); and American Petroleum Institute, Petroleum Facts and Figures (Washington, DC, 1971), pp. 40, 41.

produce 10 barrels or less of oil per day.[12] Stripper wells commonly were owned by small firms, and their large proportion of total wells in Kansas and Oklahoma, 65 percent and 87 percent in 1941, formed an influential political lobby in determining the stands of those two states in interstate prorationing negotiations. In Texas stripper wells were 31 percent of total wells and were located in the high-cost regions of north and central Texas (see Table 1).

High-cost wells in all states were vulnerable to the price effects of the new, low-cost production from the huge East Texas field, and, in interstate efforts for output control, Kansas and Oklahoma argued that Texas should disproportionately constrain its production. The argument was phrased in terms of conservation. It was asserted that the production from older fields would be lost if high-cost wells were shut in due to falling prices. While technical problems could be encountered in reopening wells that had been closed for significant time periods, the underlying political concern was the devastation to local economies and the careers of politicians if thousands of small, high-cost oil firms, refineries, and well service and supply companies were to fail.

Following the October 1930 discovery of the East Texas oil field, Oklahoma Governor William Murray organized the Oil States Advisory Committee to set total production quotas for Kansas, New Mexico, Oklahoma, and Texas. The quotas, however, were quickly violated by production from the East Texas and Oklahoma City fields, and they were struck down by the federal court.[13] In March 1933, as East Texas output approached one million barrels per day, despite a production quota from the Texas Railroad Commission of 400,000 barrels, the

[12] Stripper wells are defined in Lovejoy and Homan, Economic Aspects, p. 185.
[13] Constantin v. Smith, 57 F.2nd 227 (Feb. 1932).

governors of the oil-producing states met with U.S. Interior Secretary Harold Ickes to discuss a new quota structure to control production and raise prices. At the same time, Kansas Senator George McGill introduced legislation in Congress for federal enforcement of the proposed quotas. These efforts were shortly incorporated into the National Recovery Administration (NRA) Oil Code, which was established in September 1933.[14]

The NRA Oil Code placed interstate crude oil prorationing under the authority of the federal government and thereby beyond the local political pressures faced by the state regulatory agencies. This made the cartel much more effective. Ickes was named petroleum administrator, and quotas were assigned to each of the states to reduce total output. A target price of $1.11 was selected, and a Federal Tender Board was set up to issue affidavits certifying that any oil shipped interstate was within prescribed quotas. Under the NRA two critical services were provided to state regulatory agencies to assist interstate prorationing of oil production. One was the continuation of the monthly demand estimates for oil production provided by the Bureau of Mines in the Interior Department. The bureau had begun estimating demand for the Federal Oil Conservation Board from 1929 to 1932.[15] The second service was federal enforcement of state production quotas. From September 1933 through January 1935, Section 9(c) of the NRA Oil Code declared illegal any interstate shipment of hot oil, that produced in excess of state authorizations.

This arrangement for interstate coordination through the federal government, however, was struck down in January 1935, when the Supreme Court declared Section 9(c) of the NRA code unconstitutional.[16] The importance of federal enforcement was not lost on the oil-producing states. Texas Senator Tom Connally sponsored the Connally Hot Oil Act, which prohibited interstate shipment of any oil that exceeded the production

---

[14] Early efforts for interstate market-demand prorationing are outlined in *Oil Weekly*, Jan. 23, 1931; Apr. 10, 1933; Blakely M. Murphy, *Conservation of Oil and Gas: A Legal History, 1948* (Chicago, 1949), pp. 545–47; and *Oil and Gas Journal*, Mar. 23 and 30, 1933.

[15] The Bureau of Mines issued a *Monthly Petroleum Statement* for each state, which summarized current output, oil stocks (surface inventories), and forecasts of next month's demand. These estimates were for total U.S. demand, which was then divided among the states as a form of quota. This information was supplied to each of the state agencies in enough time to set next month's authorized output level. The output data were gathered by the bureau from crude oil producers, the Interstate Oil Compact Commission, the American Petroleum Institute, operators of pipelines and other means of transport, and refineries. The bureau based its forecasts of demand for crude oil on estimates of the demand for gasoline, fuel oil, kerosene and other petroleum products. Its procedures are discussed in the Cole Committee Hearings, *Petroleum Investigation: Hearings before a Subcommittee of the Committee on Interstate and Foreign Commerce on H.R. 441*, 73rd Congress, 2nd session, part 2 (Washington, DC, 1934), p. 1298; and Gary D. Libecap, "The Political Economy of the Establishment of the Interstate Oil Cartel, 1933–1940," in Robert Higgs, ed., *Emergence of the Modern Political Economy* (Greenwich, CT, 1985), pp. 53–81.

[16] *Panama Refining v. Ryan*, 293 U.S. 388 (Jan. 1935).

totals set by state regulatory agencies. The act passed in February 1935, within one month of the Supreme Court ruling.[17] It authorized the President to establish boards to issue certificates of clearance for the interstate shipment of oil. Oil shipped in violation of state authorizations could be seized by the government, and the individuals involved could be fined $2,000 and/or jailed for six months.

Interstate prorationing of crude oil production under NRA output restrictions worked extremely well, given the previous history of chaos in the industry. Total production was reduced, and crude oil prices quickly rebounded to over $1.00 per barrel. The allocation of total crude oil reductions, however, shows why Texas resisted the efforts of neighboring states to impose output controls in interstate production negotiations and feared any return to federal administration of the cartel. Under federal control through the NRA, the East Texas field bore virtually all of the production cuts to raise prices. By May 1934 East Texas was producing 509,000 barrels per day, less than half of its March 1933 output, and the rest of Texas was held to previous production levels. During the same period Oklahoma and Kansas actually increased output by 70,000 and 20,000 barrels per day, respectively. While total oil revenues in all three states rose with higher prices, Texas had no incentive to vest quota allocations to the federal government or an interstate body if it were to bear most of the constraints.[18]

Following the Supreme Court's decision, Oklahoma Governor E. W. Marland and Kansas Governor Alf Landon renewed their efforts to negotiate an interstate oil compact. To pressure Texas, Oklahoma Senator Elmer Thomas sponsored legislation for federal regulation of oil production, and related bills were considered by Congress through 1941, after the Interstate Compact was signed. Nevertheless, Texas Governor James Allred opposed federal intervention beyond enforcement of restrictions on hot oil shipments. Allred called for a compact among the states that would serve as a loose advisory body for regulatory agencies in coordinating output decisions. The compact was to have no independent authority to set output levels or quotas. Under the Texas plan regulatory authority would rest with state agencies, which would set monthly production totals and allocate them statewide.

An Interstate Oil Compact was finally accepted along the lines desired by Texas in February 1935. By 1935 each of the regulatory agencies in Kansas, Louisiana, Oklahoma, and Texas had authority to control output to fix oil prices through market-demand prorationing. The Illinois Commission did not have explicit authority for market-demand prorationing, but it could regulate output to minimize technological waste.

---

[17] "Connally Hot Oil Act," *U.S. Statutes At Large*, 49 (Feb. 1935), p. 30.
[18] Discussion of the impact of the NRA on Texas is provided in Wiggins and Libecap, "Firm Heterogeneities," pp. 18–19.

California, another major oil-producing state, did not formally join the compact in 1935 but did send observers to compact meetings.

Under the compact the governors of member states and representatives of their regulatory agencies met quarterly to discuss prices, oil production plans, and other regulatory issues. States where production was deemed excessive by compact members were criticized. For example, in the July 1939 meeting the Illinois Oil and Gas Division was condemned for "needless" output, which was threatening crude oil prices.[19]

With the signing of the Interstate Oil Compact in 1935, the essential elements for the interstate oil cartel were in place, and they remained through 1972. The elements included state prorationing rules to set monthly production totals and to allocate them among regulated wells; Bureau of Mines market-demand estimates for determining state production levels; the Connally Hot Oil Act for federal enforcement of state production rules in interstate commerce; and the Interstate Oil Compact to coordinate state production policies.

II. THE RECORD OF CARTEL SUCCESS AND THE STABILIZATION OF
NOMINAL PRICES

A major concern of the state regulatory agencies was maintaining the viability of high-cost wells. This required output controls on low-cost producers so that total domestic crude oil production could be reduced to equal estimated demand at a targeted price able to sustain high-cost producers. Average production cost figures in Table 1 show that in 1933 and 1941 average costs for old fields ranged from $0.92 to $1.35 per barrel. These costs are consistent with a target price of approximately $1.00 per barrel, set under the NRA and later by the Railroad Commission and the other state agencies under the Interstate Oil Compact.

Figure 1 plots estimated monthly U.S. demand for domestic crude oil production and domestic crude oil output from 1933 through 1972 as estimated by the Bureau of Mines.[20] The figure reveals a remarkable

---

[19] Article V of the compact stated that the purpose of the agreement was not to fix or stabilize prices. There were two barriers to explicit discussion of price fixing within the compact. One was a fear of violating federal antitrust laws; the other was Texas's concern that formal compact rules to equate interstate output to market-demand estimates would lead to regulation of its production by the Interstate Oil Compact Commission rather than by the Railroad Commission. For discussion of the pressure placed on compact members to conform to output rules, see *Oil and Gas Journal*, July 27, 1939.

[20] U.S. demand and production data are from the U.S. Department of the Interior, Bureau of Mines, *Minerals Yearbook* (Washington, DC, 1934–1973). As noted in fn. 15, the bureau provided total and state demand estimates each month to the state regulatory agencies. These demand forecasts for crude oil were based on estimates of demand for major oil products. See *Minerals Yearbook*, 1937, p. 978. Domestic crude oil demand figures are provided from 1943 through 1972. From 1933 through 1942 the demand estimates are for domestic crude oil and imports. Crude oil imports were small during that period, 2 percent of U.S. crude oil production in 1937, as reported

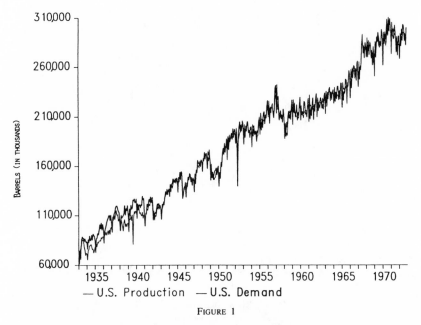

DEMAND AND SUPPLY FOR DOMESTIC CRUDE OIL, 1933–1972

Source: U.S. Bureau of Mines, *Minerals Yearbook* (Washington, DC, 1934–1973).

tracking of the two series over the 40-year period, indicating that the interstate cartel succeeded in matching domestic production with demand.

The impact of the cartel on nominal crude oil prices is shown in Figure 2. Figure 2 plots the nominal posted price for 36-degree gravity oil for the 60-year period of 1913 through 1972 to allow for comparison of price behavior in the period before and after interstate production coordination, which began under the NRA in September 1933.[21] Under the NRA, crude oil prices rose from their low of $0.10 per barrel in May 1933 to $1.00 per barrel by October 1933, and they remained relatively stable at $1.17 until 1946. In April 1946 the Office of Price Administration removed World War II price controls, allowing for an adjustment of 120 percent to $2.57 between 1946 and 1948. Beyond that, nominal crude oil

---

by the American Petroleum Institute, *Petroleum Facts and Figures*, p. 286. Imports of crude oil and refined products do not become a significant part of the U.S. market until later. In 1955 imports of crude oil were 11 percent of U.S. crude oil production. The bureau also published demand estimates for all oils, which include crude oil, refined products, and natural gas.

[21] Posted nominal crude oil prices are from American Petroleum Institute, *Petroleum Facts and Figures*, p. 449; and *Oil and Gas Journal*. Where there are discrepancies the *Oil and Gas Journal* price is used. Spot prices generally are not available, but movements in posted prices reflect the general path of spot prices.

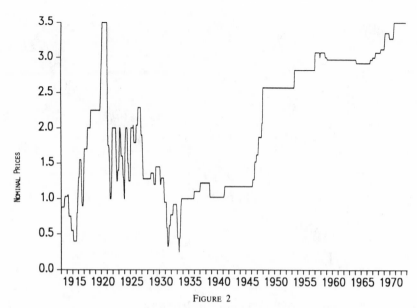

FIGURE 2

NOMINAL CRUDE OIL PRICES, 1913–1972
(dollars per barrel)

Source: American Petroleum Institute, *Petroleum Facts and Figures* (Washington, DC, 1971), p. 449.

prices followed a stable path until the end of 1972, when they peaked at $3.50 as OPEC output reductions began to affect crude oil prices.

On the other hand, Figure 2 shows that from 1913 through 1933, prior to interstate controls, nominal crude oil prices were extremely volatile, following swings in oil discoveries and unregulated common pool production. Between 1913 and 1933 there were 67 price changes with a mean price change of $0.0007 and a coefficient of variation of 24,828. From 1934 through 1972, however, nominal prices were not only higher, but considerably more stable. Over that period there were 24 price changes with a mean change of $0.005 and a coefficient of variation of 723.

It is noteworthy that this price stability occurred at a time of new oil field discoveries that contributed to increases in proved U.S. reserves. In 1934, when data are first available, U.S. reserves were 908 million barrels, by 1948 they had risen by 121 percent to 2 billion barrels, and they peaked at 3.3 billion barrels in 1970.[22] Moreover, through interstate

---

[22] Reserve estimates are from American Petroleum Institute, *Reserves of Crude Oil*, p. 25. It is possible that discoveries prior to 1933 represented larger percentage increases in total U.S. reserves than in the later period, contributing to the greater volatility of prices between 1913 and 1933 as shown in Figure 2. Nevertheless, an examination of reserve data, which are available after

production constraints after 1933, surface inventories declined. From 1921 to 1933 they averaged 353.5 million barrels, while from 1934 to 1968 average U.S. stocks were 259.2 million barrels.[23]

Although nominal prices were relatively stable under the cartel, real crude oil prices were not. Real prices rose from $0.66 per barrel in May 1933, prior to adoption of interstate output controls, to $2.89 in August 1938. By March 1946 they had fallen to $2.15 but increased to $3.66 in March 1948. Real crude oil prices declined slowly to $3.21 per barrel by July 1952, then rose, peaking at $3.71 in January 1957, and subsequently declined for the next 16 years, reaching $2.77 by December 1972.[24]

The goal of the state regulatory agencies seems to have been to stabilize nominal prices. As discussed below, most criticism of the Texas Railroad Commission from producers occurred when nominal prices fell. On the other hand, criticism of interstate oil production controls from Congress and the Justice Department, beginning in the 1950s, occurred when nominal prices rose. This focus on nominal prices by the regulatory agencies in the prorationing states is consistent with the observation made by Paul Joskow regarding the behavior of post-World War II utility regulatory agencies. He argued that the political process faced by those agencies led them to minimize conflict and criticism from consumer groups and politicians by maintaining stable nominal prices, regardless of the rate of return earned by the utilities.[25]

The observed decline in real crude oil prices indicates the limits of the interstate oil cartel. The Interstate Oil Compact and, indeed, state regulation of crude oil production were subject to continued scrutiny from Congress and federal agencies, and broader federal constituencies brought political pressure to limit crude oil price increases. By law Congress periodically reviewed the Interstate Oil Compact, and a chief concern after World War II was whether the compact violated antitrust laws. The major federal enforcement mechanism for interstate market-demand prorationing was the Connally Hot Oil Act, but federal restrictions on the interstate shipment of oil produced in excess of state authorizations could be lifted if the states were deemed to be using

---

1934, reveals large shifts in reserves from new discoveries which, if uncontrolled, could have caused prices to fall sharply. For example, between 1938 and 1939 reserves rose by over 36 percent. The successful efforts by the Interstate Oil Compact to address that problem associated, in part, with new Illinois production are described in the text. Similarly, U.S. reserves rose by nearly 32 percent between 1969 and 1970 with the discovery of the Alaska North Slope fields with no significant impact on prices.

[23] Stocks or inventories are from de Chazeau and Kahn, *Integration and Competition*, pp. 137–66; and American Petroleum Institute, *Petroleum Facts and Figures*, p. 109.

[24] Nominal crude oil prices for 36-degree gravity oil are deflated by the Consumer Price Index for all items, found in U.S. Department of Commerce, *Historical Statistics*, p. 210.

[25] See Joskow, "Inflation and Environmental Concern," pp. 291–328.

TABLE 3
DESCRIPTIVE STATISTICS AND VARIATION IN CRUDE OIL PRODUCTION AND
DEMAND
(Thousands of Barrels)

	Jan. 1933– Apr. 1941	Sept. 1933– Jan. 1935	June 1946– June 1958	July 1958– Dec. 1972
Texas Production				
Mean	37,242	31,631	78,999	89,054
Standard Deviation	5,177	2,035	10,864	10,762
Coefficient of Variation	0.139	0.064	0.138	0.121
Non-Texas Production				
Mean	57,249	43,859	105,936	160,896
Standard Deviation	10,566	2,334	14,918	20,783
Coefficient of Variation	0.185	0.053	0.141	0.129
Demand for Domestic Production				
Mean	103,165	85,758	184,886	250,031
Standard Deviation	15,249	3,660	24,884	30,948
Coefficient of Variation	0.148	0.043	0.135	0.124

Sources: Calculations described in text.

regulations to unduly raise nominal prices. Both the Justice and Interior departments monitored the Interstate Oil Compact and periodically charged it with price fixing. Moreover, beginning in 1937 through at least 1965 there were efforts to replace state regulation of crude oil production with federal regulation through agencies such as the Federal Power Commission.[26] This monitoring role by Congress and potential competition from federal agencies formed external constraints on how high nominal crude oil prices could be raised in order to maintain real prices.

III. PRODUCTION COORDINATION WITHIN THE CARTEL

One straightforward way of examining the production behavior of Texas and the other oil-producing states within the Interstate Oil Compact is to analyze the variation in monthly output for the various parties relative to the variation in demand for domestic production. If Texas acted primarily as a residual producer and absorbed most of the fluctuations in total U.S. demand so as to maintain nominal prices while the other states (fringe producers) maintained their output, the coefficient of variation for monthly Texas production would be larger than for the other states and approach or exceed the coefficient of variation for U.S. demand. Table 3 presents descriptive statistics, including the mean, standard deviation, and coefficient of variation for Texas and the other states, and total demand for domestic production for four relevant time periods.[27]

[26] See the following issues of *Oil and Gas Journal*: Mar. 20, 1941; Jan. 22, 1947; Dec. 28, 1950; Aug. 25, 1951; Sept. 20, 1954; Apr. 14, 1957; June 6, 1960; Feb. 25, 1963; and Jan. 11, 1971.
[27] It is not the aim of this article to explicitly model cartel behavior among the states. Griffin, "OPEC Behavior," tests various production hypotheses for OPEC and finds coordination among

The political environment and production potentials across the states were not stable over the 40-year period, and the four subperiods help to standardize for those changes. The first period, January 1933 to April 1941, was the period of organization of market-demand prorationing. In April 1941 federal war production rules were implemented, shifting political control from the state regulatory agencies. The second period was from September 1933 to January 1935, when Texas was more tightly constrained by the NRA Oil Code than the other states. The third period was the immediate postwar period from June 1946, after the removal of World War II price controls, through June 1958. This appears to have been a time when interstate market-demand prorationing functioned routinely. The fourth period ran from July 1958 to December 1972 and includes a crisis within the cartel over Louisiana production and the later rise of OPEC influence.

The results point to considerable coordination among the states in monthly production decisions to maintain crude oil prices. There is no evidence that Texas adjusted its output more than the other states in response to monthly fluctuations in U.S. demand. The coefficient of variation for Texas production is larger than that for the other states only during the NRA period when Texas output was under strict federal control. In the remaining time periods the coefficient of variation for the other states exceeds that for Texas and for U.S. demand. This suggests that all of the prorationing states within the framework of the Interstate Oil Compact adjusted their monthly authorized output to offset fluctuations in demand and that Texas did not assume the role of a swing producer on a monthly basis.

Another way to address the issue of interstate cartel production coordination is through time series analysis using a procedure outlined by Robert Engle and C. W. J. Granger. Residual production by Texas to maintain nominal crude oil prices would involve a long-term relationship between Texas output and U.S. market demand, whereby the two time series are cointegrated. Cointegration implies that a linear combination of Texas output and U.S. demand is a stationary time series. Further, residual production suggests that if U.S. demand unexpectedly increased during the period, Texas would raise production the next

---

OPEC members in output patterns. He does not find evidence that Saudi Arabia acts as a residual producer. While he does not examine the reasons for market-sharing behavior, the consistency of the results reported here with his suggest that political conditions may make residual production too politically costly, when governments are the cartelizing parties. Political and production conditions among the states are not stable over the 40-year period examined here. Comparisons of the coefficients of variation across the states avoid making any assumptions regarding the nature and stability of the underlying relationships. Estimations using Griffin's approach were investigated, and they also reveal market-sharing behavior among the states. For the purposes of this article, examination of the coefficient of variations is the preferable approach for determining the extent of coordination among the states.

TABLE 4
TEST FOR COINTEGRATION BETWEEN PRODUCTION AND DEMAND
(Ordinary Least Squares Estimation)

Output	Alpha Coefficient	R^2	Durbin-Watson	F-Value (1,479)
Texas	0.379 (207)	0.88	0.16	3,560
Other Cartel States	0.616 (319)	0.96	0.18	13,000

Note: The t-statistics are in parentheses.
Source: These are the results of the estimation of $Y_t = aMD_t + e_t$ as described in the text, using monthly data from 1933 through 1972 and following the procedure outlined by Robert F. Engel and C. W. J. Granger, "Cointegration and Error Correction: Representation, Estimation and Testing," *Econometrica*, 55 (Mar. 1987), pp. 251–76.

period as an "error correction" to bring total crude oil supply into line with demand at the target price. Testing for this behavior is a two-stage process, involving first a test for cointegration between the two time series as outlined in the equation:

$$Y_t = aMD_t + e_t$$

where Y_t is Texas output in month t; MD_t is U.S. market demand for crude oil; and e_t is the residual beyond the normal relationship between market demand and Texas production, arising from unexpected fluctuations in demand.[28] A finding of cointegration between Texas output and demand would be consistent with residual production behavior. If output and demand are cointegrated, then a second test for an "error correction" is warranted. On the other hand, a finding that the two time series are not cointegrated would lead to a rejection of the residual production hypothesis, since there is no stationary long-term relationship between them. The same test can be performed for the other cartel states as a group.

The results of ordinary least squares estimation of the equation for Texas and the other producing states, using monthly data from 1933 through 1972, are reported in Table 4. Engle and Granger state that the null hypothesis of no cointegration can be rejected if the Durbin-Watson statistic's value is greater than 0.386. Inspection of the Durbin-Watson values when Texas and other states' production are the dependent variables, however, indicates that the null hypothesis cannot be rejected. Accordingly, there is no evidence that output and demand are cointegrated or, hence, that Texas behaved as a residual producer.

Although the statistical analyses presented in Tables 3 and 4 provide

---

[28] For a discussion of the test for cointegration and error correction, see Robert F. Engle and C. W. J. Granger, "Cointegration and Error Correction: Representation, Estimation and Testing," *Econometrica*, 55 (Mar. 1987), pp. 251–76. See also G. S. Maddala, *Introduction to Econometrics* (New York, 1988), pp. 212–21, for a discussion of estimation techniques. A stationary time series implies that the relationship between the variables does not change significantly over time.

TABLE 5
RATIO OF SHARE OF U.S. PRODUCTION TO SHARE OF U.S. RESERVES

Year	California	Illinois	Kansas	Louisiana	Oklahoma	Texas
1934	0.67	1.72	1.56	1.18	2.01	0.93
1936	0.77	1.81	1.11	2.16	2.04	0.85
1938	1.01	1.26	1.19	1.70	2.46	0.75
1940	0.95	4.00	1.38	1.66	1.88	0.64
1946	1.15	2.59	2.13	1.02	1.84	0.78
1948	1.05	1.92	1.86	1.09	1.44	0.84
1950	1.14	1.42	1.90	1.19	1.52	0.78
1952	1.16	1.20	1.54	1.10	1.51	0.84
1954	1.19	1.32	1.57	1.00	1.22	0.83
1956	1.01	1.40	1.49	0.89	1.26	0.87
1958	1.04	1.71	1.67	0.89	1.34	0.82
1960	1.06	1.78	1.64	0.93	1.34	0.77
1962	1.00	2.11	1.59	1.00	1.40	0.75
1964	0.85	2.10	1.56	1.09	1.48	0.76
1966	0.82	1.88	1.56	1.19	1.58	0.78
1968	0.84	1.75	1.52	1.23	1.52	0.76
1970	1.09	2.24	1.83	1.61	1.84	1.07
1972	1.08	2.21	1.79	1.70	1.69	1.15
Average for 1934–1972	0.99	1.88	1.64	1.17	1.61	0.82

Source: American Petroleum Institute, *Petroleum Facts and Figures* (Washington, DC, 1971), pp. 68–69; *Oil and Gas Journal*; and American Petroleum Institute, *Reserves of Crude Oil, Natural Gas Liquids, and Natural Gas in the United States and Canada as of December 31, 1979* (Washington, DC, 1980), pp. 25–66.

no support for residual production by Texas, this does not rule out Texas having played a central role in other ways. Texas maintained the viability of high-cost producers by restraining its large, low-cost fields. This is illustrated by the data in Table 5, which lists the ratio of the share of U.S. production to the share of U.S. reserves from 1934 to 1972 for major prorationing states. Among them Texas had the largest reserves of low-cost oil, which could have displaced high-cost production in the other states. The data in the table indicate that the Railroad Commission so restrained low-cost output that Texas's market share was less than its reserve position would have warranted. Only for Texas is the ratio of the two shares routinely less than one. For the other prorationing states, production shares exceed their reserve shares.

All told, the evidence suggests an implicit agreement among the states. Texas would limit the output of its low-cost wells and channel much of its monthly production quota within the interstate cartel to its high-cost producers. These restraints on Texas's low-cost fields would maintain high-cost production in Kansas, Oklahoma, and elsewhere. In return, all of the prorationing states would share monthly production adjustments to maintain crude oil prices so that the responsibility was not left solely to the Railroad Commission.

IV. POLITICAL FACTORS AND THE ASSIGNMENT OF PRODUCTION QUOTAS

Under the Interstate Oil Compact each state agency set monthly production levels and allocated the state total among regulated wells. In Texas the Railroad Commission held hearings approximately the third week of each month to determine the next month's state production total. For its decision making, the commission assembled data on crude oil prices, supplies, and demand for the current and upcoming month. The *Monthly Petroleum Statement* of the Bureau of Mines provided the Railroad Commission and the other state agencies with market-demand estimates. These estimates included both total demand for domestic production and demand for each state's output within that total. In that way the Bureau of Mines helped to prorate output for the states. The Railroad Commission also collected data on planned purchases of Texas output based on firms' testimony at the agency's monthly allowable hearings. In setting monthly output levels, the regulatory agencies of the compact states met approximately at the same time and shared information on production plans.

The production and quota allocation decisions of the Texas Railroad Commissioners were molded by political considerations in ways that raised production costs. While the commissioners received only modest state salaries and there is no evidence that they received payments from the oil industry, the prestige and influence of their office was enormous. By restraining low-cost oil production, the commissioners raised and stabilized oil prices and increased industry rents. Through their quota assignments and other regulatory decisions, the commissioners determined the allocation of those rents. As shown below, the Railroad Commissioners aimed to protect the interests of the small independent oil producers who were found throughout Texas. While the most productive regions were East Texas in the 1930s and the Permian Basin of west Texas in the 1960s, only 40 of Texas's 254 counties never produced oil. It is difficult to overemphasize the importance of the oil industry in Texas. In 1935 the value of Texas agricultural production was approximately $74 million, but the value of mineral production, largely oil and natural gas, was over seven times greater, $528 million.[29]

In their production decisions, a major goal of the Railroad Commissioners was re-election. The three Railroad Commissioners were elected in statewide voting for staggered six-year terms. Since the commission was not a direct residual profit claimant, its regulatory policies could be based upon re-election considerations, rather than on

---

[29] The value of minerals production is from the U.S. Department of Commerce, Bureau of the Census, *Statistical Abstract of the United States 1939* (Washington, DC, 1940), p. 734. Value of agricultural products is from U.S. Department of Commerce, Bureau of the Census, *Census of Agriculture 1935, Statistics for State and Counties*, vol. 2, part 3, 2nd series (Washington, DC, 1936), pp. 742–43.

profit-maximization rules. The evidence suggests that the commission was extraordinarily successful in achieving its re-election goals. One commissioner, Ernest Thompson, served for 33 years (1932 to 1965), and in all periods the agency was characterized by stable membership. For example, during the 1950s there were no changes in the commission's makeup.

The political influence of numerous small producers and the election concerns of the Railroad Commissioners affected the allocation of crude oil production quotas. The initial demands made in 1931 for controls on low-cost East Texas oil came largely from the small, independent producers in north, central, and west Texas.[30] In July 1931 output per well ranged from 520 barrels per day in the East Texas field to 70 barrels in west Texas, 30 in the Panhandle, 22 in central Texas and the Gulf Coast, and 4 barrels in north Texas. In the legislature, representatives from the high-cost regions sought to control East Texas production as much as did producers in Oklahoma and Kansas. Prior to enacting regulatory legislation, however, the Texas Legislature exempted from any controls high-cost producers, who accounted for about 40 percent of Texas output.[31] As a legacy of this law the Railroad Commission's production constraints focused on low-cost producers for the next 40 years.

However, among low-cost producers there were both large and small firms, and their differential political influence affected how the regulations were imposed on low-cost firms. Small independent firms were numerous and closely tied to the local economy, giving them important political clout. Small independents were responsible for the discovery of the East Texas field in Rusk and Gregg counties, where no previous oil production had existed. Because of their risk-taking in exploration, independent producers were seen as critical for the continued development of the Texas oil industry. They also held leases from small landowners, refined their petroleum in nearby refineries, and relied upon local oil well service and equipment firms. Because they drilled more wells than did the larger firms, their demand for oil field equipment and service was a major contribution to the economy of east Texas communities. By 1935 there were over 1,000 small independent producers of the East Texas field, three times the number of firms in all of Oklahoma and more than the rest of Texas, and they had drilled over 12,000 wells. The 29 larger, integrated firms on the East Texas field had drilled approximately 10,000 wells.[32]

---

[30] See testimony regarding the need to restrain East Texas in the *Texas Senate Journal* (July 1931), pp. 418–52; and *Texas House Journal* (July 1931), pp. 428–59.

[31] See *Oil Weekly*, July 17, 1931; and 42nd Texas Legislature, *Acts*, 1931, regular session, chap. 50, art. 6049.

[32] *Oil Weekly*, Feb. 27, 1933; and David F. Prindle, *Petroleum Politics and the Texas Railroad Commission* (Austin, 1981), p. 50.

The coalition of small low-cost firms, landowners, refiners, and equipment suppliers was politically more potent than were the major low-cost firms. These larger firms typically had headquarters out of state, had fewer wells per acre, relied upon internal well service support (rather than contracting with local businesses), and had operations across fields and states.[33] While they had more resources, larger firms were viewed as having fewer ties to Texas, and they were unable to muster the political power of the low-cost independents. In 1931 East Texas independents opposed prorationing legislation because they feared it would be used to squeeze them in favor of the majors. The Railroad Commission responded by adopting regulations which favored small, low-cost producers relative to the larger major firms to mitigate their political opposition.

Within this political environment the regulatory system in Texas worked as follows: once the monthly state production quota was set by the Railroad Commission, it was prorated among all regulated wells. Since high-cost wells were exempt from regulation, their output had to be subtracted from the state total before individual well allocations could be made. For example, in November 1963, the commission set an authorized state production of 2,828,000 barrels, consistent with esti-mated demand for Texas production. Of the total, 1,248,000 barrels (44 percent) would come from exempt wells; hence, only 1,580,000 barrels were available for prorationing among the state's low-cost wells. The production capacity of the low-cost wells was estimated at that time to be 3,700,000 barrels; unregulated they could have displaced all high-cost stripper well production.[34]

After the production from exempt wells was subtracted from the total state quota, the remaining proratable production was divided by the capacity output of the regulated wells in Texas to give a "market-demand factor" (proratable production divided by capacity produc-tion). As such, the market-demand factor was the fraction of capacity production that would be allowed from all regulated wells in the upcoming month. Until late 1962 the market-demand factor was con-verted to a number of authorized producing days for the next month.[35] After 1962 it was expressed as the authorized percentage of capacity production. To arrive at each well's monthly quota, the state market-demand factor was multiplied by the top allowable or capacity produc-

---

[33] Hostility in Texas toward major oil producers has been noted in a variety of studies. See Prindle, *Petroleum Politics*; and Joseph A. Pratt, "The Petroleum Industry in Transition: Antitrust and the Decline of Monopoly Control in Oil," this JOURNAL, 60 (Dec. 1980), pp. 815–37.

[34] Lovejoy and Homan, *Economic Aspects*, p. 114.

[35] The number of producing days was a full-time equivalent number. In practice, firms produced for a fraction of each day during the month, calculated from the number of producing days authorized by the Texas Railroad Commission. Capacity production is defined in various ways (see Lovejoy and Homan, *Economic Aspects*, pp. 97–102). In general, it is maximum production for a specified period from existing wells.

tion for the individual well. In this manner, the monthly state production quota was prorated among the regulated wells in Texas.

For successful re-election the Railroad Commissioners adopted policies that balanced the political costs from regulating low-cost wells with the gains from sustaining high-cost wells through higher prices. From 1932 to 1964 the commission granted preferential production quotas to small firms, even though the practice raised production costs by encouraging the drilling of additional wells. The monthly quotas for regulated wells were based upon acreage and depth, but the commission placed more weight on depth to give advantages to small producers. For example, a well 1,000 feet deep servicing 10 acres had a top allowed production of 18 barrels per day. For every 500 feet of increased depth, nine more barrels were added through 7,000 feet. Beyond that depth, allocations increased, reaching 38 barrels per 500 feet for a well 10,000 feet deep. For acreage, however, only one barrel of additional allowable production was added for each additional surface acre drained by the well.[36]

Those administrative rules clearly promoted dense, deep drilling in Texas by firms to increase their monthly quota. Because the rules discounted acreage, they disadvantaged larger firms. To further promote drilling, the commission routinely granted exemptions to small firms to the 10-acre spacing rule to allow for denser drilling. The commission's biases were supported in 1946 by the Texas Court of Civil Appeals.[37] The court ruled that small landowners had the right to drill at least one well on their land with a sufficient monthly quota to cover drilling and operating costs. Organizations of small independent firms such as the Texas Independent Producers and Royalty Owners Association lobbied the Railroad Commission to maintain their favorable allocations.[38]

The internal political constraints on the Railroad Commission help to explain why the agency could not systematically regulate Texas production each month to be the residual within the Interstate Oil Compact. If output significantly expanded in the other states and Texas routinely cut back to maintain prices, at some point the restrictions upon low-cost Texas producers would be so great that they would resist and challenge the agency's political mandate. Further, given political pressures, the commission had limited degrees of freedom to fine-tune Texas output in response to production in the other states. Hence, the commission had incentive to seek coordinated output policies among the states to avoid having Texas bear the full costs of controlling crude oil output. The

[36] See Libecap and Wiggins, "Contractual Responses," for discussion of the initial prorationing allocation scheme in Texas. For discussion of acreage and depth, see Lovejoy and Homan, *Economic Aspects*, p. 144.

[37] *Railroad Commission v. Humble Oil and Refining Co.*, 193 S.W.2nd 824 (Mar. 1946).

[38] *Oil and Gas Journal*, May 8, 1961.

other members of the Interstate Oil Compact also had incentives to cooperate with Texas, since the Railroad Commission restrained the large reserves of low-cost Texas production. The clear beneficiaries were high-cost wells in the prorationing states (see Table 1).

V. COORDINATION WITHIN THE INTERSTATE OIL COMPACT:
TWO CRISIS PERIODS

The first crisis period between 1938 and 1941 involved rapid increases in output by Illinois, which threatened the structure of crude oil prices (see Figure 2). From September 1933 to September 1938 prices rose and stabilized, reaching $1.22 per barrel by February 1937, up from $0.10 per barrel in May 1933. Strains on interstate coordination, however, appeared as Illinois allowed new, essentially unconstrained production on the market in late 1937. Illinois temporarily left the Interstate Compact, and its production began displacing that of Kansas and Oklahoma in midwestern markets. By January 1938 Illinois's share of prorationed output was 1 percent, up from 0.4 percent in May 1937, and by June 1940 its share was 15 percent. At the same time, Kansas and Oklahoma shares declined from 6 and 21 percent in May 1937, to 5 and 13 percent, respectively, in June 1940.[39]

In response, Kansas called for a minimum market share for each state and tighter federal control of production; absent such controls, it threatened to leave the compact.[40] Moreover, increases in Illinois production contributed to a 16 percent fall in nominal crude oil prices from $1.22 to $1.02 per barrel in October 1938. As the states threatened to retaliate against Illinois by raising their own output, the interstate oil cartel seemed close to unraveling.

After an emergency meeting of the Interstate Oil Compact in August 1939, Arkansas, Kansas, Louisiana, Michigan, New Mexico, Oklahoma, and Texas agreed to temporarily cut production for up to one month. The cuts were led by Texas, which was concerned that the failure of interstate prorationing would lead to federal intervention and regulation of the industry. The results of the coordinated cutbacks were dramatic. Production in Kansas, Louisiana, Oklahoma, and Texas fell by 42 percent, 34 percent, 47 percent, and 41 percent, respectively, between July and August 1939. California, remote to the problem, increased its output slightly (by 1 percent), and Illinois output rose by 13 percent over the same period. Nevertheless, total output for the six states fell by 29 percent, from 98,070,000 barrels in July to 69,893,000 barrels of crude oil in August. Market shares correspondingly fell for Kansas, Louisiana, Oklahoma, and Texas. The states began to increase

---

[39] These shares are state output as a percentage of total prorationed output from California, Illinois, Kansas, Louisiana, Oklahoma, and Texas.

[40] *Oil and Gas Journal*, Aug. 4, Sept. 9, and Oct. 6, 1938.

production in September, but the evidence of state cooperation reduced the downward pressure on crude oil prices and, importantly, weakened prospects for new federal regulation.[41] Additionally, the flush period for Illinois fields quickly passed, reducing the state's production. By 1941 increased oil demand for World War II and greater controls on Illinois output brought an increase in crude oil prices.[42]

A second crisis period faced interstate prorationing in the late 1950s. Beginning in October 1958 nominal crude oil prices began to decline for only the second time since 1933. Nominal prices fell from $3.07 per barrel in 1957 to $2.97 by March 1959 and to $2.92 per barrel by February 1963. Prices did not recover until September 1966, when they rose to $2.97 and then continued to rise to $3.50 per barrel by December 1972. The threat to prices came in part from major increases in Louisiana production.[43] In January 1958 Louisiana produced 26,276,000 barrels of crude oil, giving it a 12 percent share of U.S. production. By January 1963, however, Louisiana production had risen by 62 percent to 42,512,000 barrels, giving the state a 19 percent share of U.S. production.

In 1958 the compact states of Kansas, Louisiana, Oklahoma, and Texas lowered production by an average of 1,034,000 barrels per day for the first half of the year.[44] Average daily U.S. output dropped from 7.4 million barrels on January 12, 1957, to 6.2 million barrels on April 12, 1958. The Railroad Commission continued to reduce allowed production in Texas. Allowable monthly production, which was approximately 48 percent of capacity output in October 1956, was lowered to 30 percent by September 1959 and 27 percent by June 1962. In addition to the actions taken in Texas, the Kansas Corporation Commission closed 40 fields in June 1960 to reduce crude oil supplies. The Kansas Corporation Commission was found later to be in violation of antitrust laws by the U.S. Supreme Court.[45] Louisiana's production was criticized by Texas, Oklahoma, and Kansas. In Interstate Compact meetings those three states urged fixed market shares for each member state.[46] The recommendations were not enacted because they could be

---

[41] Ibid., Aug. 24, 31, 1939; Oct. 6, 1939.

[42] Murphy, *Conservation of Oil and Gas*, pp. 92–120, outlines conditions in Illinois. Fear of federal intervention helped to persuade Illinois firms to support stricter state prorationing legislation.

[43] Imports also were a concern to the state regulatory agencies. In 1955 imports rose to 11 percent of U.S. domestic production. The state agencies, led by the Texas Railroad Commission, lobbied Congress for import controls. For discussion of U.S. oil import policies, see *Oil and Gas Journal*, Mar. 17, 1958; and Yoram Barzel and Christopher D. Hall, *The Political Economy of the Oil Import Quota* (Stanford, 1977).

[44] *Oil and Gas Journal*, July 28, 1958.

[45] Ibid., June 6, 1960; Feb. 25, 1963.

[46] Ibid., Dec. 14, 1959; June 20, 1960; Dec. 20, 1960.

enforced only by the federal government, an action opposed by the Railroad Commission.

The continued reduction of Texas output by the Railroad Commission brought criticism from the regulated oil firms in Texas, and they mounted a political offensive to have the Texas Legislature re-evaluate the Railroad Commission's regulatory mandate. In February 1961 the Texas Legislature considered a bill to fix minimum well production allowables, removing quota discretion from the Railroad Commission. In December 1962 Texas firms called on the legislature to force increases in state production and "not permit Texas to continue much longer its disproportionate share of the burden of curtailment to market demand. . . ."[47] More seriously, in April 1963 the legislature considered creating a new agency to assume oil and gas regulation from the Railroad Commission.[48] As adept politicians, the Railroad Commissioners soon began to slowly raise Texas output. This political maneuvering illustrates the limits on how far the Railroad Commission could go in reducing Texas's low-cost production to maintain U.S. nominal crude oil prices.

VI. CONCLUDING REMARKS

This article has examined the behavior of the domestic interstate oil cartel that controlled crude oil production to fix prices for 40 years, from 1933 through 1972. The cartel was administered by state regulatory agencies with the assistance of the U.S. Bureau of Mines, the Interstate Oil Compact, and the Connally Hot Oil Act. The cartel brought rents to the oil industry, but political factors determined both the size of those rents and their distribution.

The arguments of this article are summarized as follows. First, U.S. crude oil output was controlled to raise and stabilize nominal rather than real prices. Stable nominal oil prices appear to have been the concern of the industry and Congress, and the agencies had better influence over the path of nominal oil prices. The stabilization of real prices would have required more output intervention in the face of changes in prices elsewhere in the economy. Such adjustments would have exposed the regulatory agencies, particularly the Railroad Commission, to increased political risks. There would have been opposition from the low-cost firms that bore the output reductions and from Congress, which would have opposed any sustained nominal price increase as real oil prices began their long fall in 1957.

Second, the political influence of high-cost producers in all of the states and small, low-cost producers in Texas led to quota allocations that promoted high-cost production. High-cost producers in Kansas,

[47] Ibid., Dec. 17, 1962.
[48] Ibid., Apr. 22, 1961.

Oklahoma, and Texas were protected through restrictions on low-cost Texas firms. Among the latter, small firms were encouraged to drill excessive, deep wells. Although these cartel policies were responsive to political forces, they were inconsistent with monopoly rent maximization.

Third, there is no evidence that Texas acted as a residual or swing producer within the cartel. The internal political environment prevented the Railroad Commission from unilaterally adjusting Texas output in response to fluctuations in U.S. demand in order to maintain nominal prices. Rather, the regulatory agencies in the prorationing states coordinated their monthly production authorizations to adjust domestic output to fix prices. This coordination spread the political costs of fixing prices and allowed the Railroad Commission to constrain Texas's low-cost fields and channel production to high-cost firms.

Although the interstate oil cartel was long lasting, its behavior reveals that government-sponsored cartels may be very different from private ones. While government cartels can better police output limits, quota compliance, and restrictions on entry, they involve political trade-offs that lower monopoly rents through higher production costs or nonoptimal production patterns. Because explicit monetary side payments are either illegal or politically difficult to negotiate, a consensus on regulatory policies involves other forms of compensation, such as preferential production quotas, even if they lead to lower overall profits. In principle, at least, the parties within private cartels could negotiate monetary side payments to compensate those firms whose output was being differentially constrained in order to raise cartel profits. In this way, quotas and production patterns could be more optimally designed within private cartels. But history shows that private cartels suffer from cheating by members or from entry by nonmembers if prices are raised above competitive levels. Hence, to be more successful, cartels require government intervention, but their policies will be molded by political conditions and may not closely follow those predicted by economic theory. This may explain why Saudi Arabia, like Texas before it, apparently has not followed a strict residual producer policy. It also may explain why OPEC appears to target nominal crude oil prices in setting its production decisions.

AMERICAN BUSINESS AND AMERICAN LIBERALS

SLOGANS OR RESPONSIBILITY?

NORTON LONG

Ever since the thirties the liberal left in the United States has thought it knew where it was going. This confidence has been all the easier to maintain since it has been based on a set of unexamined and unstated premises. These premises were supposed to be implicit in the congery of expediential, frequently conflicting measures known collectively as the New Deal and Fair Deal.

The lively consciousness of humanitarian good intentions seemed sufficient to justify a rather nebulous faith, the more so as the faith was accompanied by sundry indubitably good works. After all the hungry had been fed, the aged secured, a T.V.A. had been built, the Ishmaels and the Insulls had been driven from the temple, labour had been organised and the party of Herbert Hoover banished to the outer darkness of seemingly permanent opposition. Such good works might be adorned by a theory but their self-evident merit seemed such as to permit them to stand by themselves, needing no justification beyond the certain immediate approbation of any man of honesty and good will. F.D.R.'s description of himself as a quarterback calling his plays on hunches characterised more than just his own lack of concern with theoretical consistency. There was a certain puckish, rollicking undergraduate good humour about the young men like Tommy the Cork who played at politics with the same technical zest that they had learned in law school. The probably apocryphal but widely publicised story of the elderly school superintendent of Gary, Indiana, in which he revealed to a delighted, half-credulous press how he had been taken to dinner by a band of young braintrusters and told while he quaked that " Roosevelt is only the Kerensky of this revolution," is indicative of a mood.

In some ways this light-heartedness of what Mauritz Halgren dubbed the Gay Reformer had a peculiar charm when contrasted

* The author is Professor of Political Science in Michigan State University; and at present Visiting Professor of Government at the Graduate School of Public Administration, Harvard University. Formerly served in the Office of Price Administration, National Housing Administration, and in other Government agencies.

with the fulsome seriousness of Wilson, Bryan, and the Chautauqua circuit. In comparison to the principled economic orthodoxy of Hoover it could even pose as an attitude both pragmatic and experimental—the very *avant garde* of a new political positivism.

This is not quite fair, however, for the humanitarian activists dreaming up assorted programmes to meet the multiplying articulate and inarticulate group demands born or nurtured by the depression were really concerned with the semantics of political feasibility, not the problems of a political philosophy. Their task was similar to that of colleagues in the advertising business concerned with the invention of slogans for merchandising. In this sense the tradition of Wilson, whom Irving Babbitt once described as a stubborn phrase-maker, was continued.

Fortunately for the peace of mind of those who felt they must sell policy, a nice concern with means was dulled by an overwhelming conviction of righteous intentions. The economics of Keynes, prized as a *post facto* rationale of public spending, was given an air of rustic virtue as pump priming, a slogan so efficacious in its tyranny of the mind that conservative Republican businessmen now talk knowingly and readily of priming the housing pump.

It is probably inevitable that those in the thick of it should emerge from the interest group battle of American politics with a contradictory assortment of special nostrums and advertising tags designed to mould an election day majority. The success of these nostrums and their brand names creates a vested interest in the continued manufacture and sale of popular political patent medicines. As in the drug trade, one is not too curious as to the objective consequences of the remedies, if not fatal, providing the customers come back for more.

And, indeed, the widespread medical use of the placebo indicates that political pseudo-action in soothing public neuroses may be therapeutic. Surely the three-ring circus of the N.R.A. gave the public a welcome relief from the high-principled inactivity of the Hoover Administration: The cases are too dissimilar for satisfactory comparison but it is just possible that the continuance of an American Bruening might have had nasty results. There is therefore a sense in which all the learned criticism of the economics of the recovery programme is both uncharitable and beside the point.

Fighting a depression, like fighting a war, has the great advantage of providing a white whale whose harpooning seems desirable beyond debate. The Churchillian reply to the question of war aims, that if we stopped fighting we would discover the reason we were fighting fast enough, seems both succinct and sufficient. No need for theory here. Perhaps the cold peace indicates this may have been a luxury, however momentarily satisfying.

In a sense the war rescued the New Dealers from having to think about the successes and failures of their policies. The continued overhang of large-scale unemployment and an industrial plant still operating way below capacity were evidence that all attempts to reflate the economy had proved inadequate. But these very evidences of the doubtful results of peacetime policy proved blessings in the war. The sour sense of frustration was transformed by the surging fact of wartime full employment.

The war thus rescued the liberal left from the pain of taking thought and the humanitarian activists happily switched to armaments. F.D.R. heralded the shift in slogans by calling for the exit of Dr. New Deal and the entrance of Dr. Win-the-War. This transformation came politically in the nick of time. The sagging fortunes of the Democratic Party were bolstered up by popular confidence in the leadership of its chief. An opposition confidently expecting a return to power was cheated of its expected victory and driven to an even more embittered guerilla warfare. A generation of Republican Congressmen grew up whose whole political experience consisted of the envenomed irresponsibility of seemingly hopeless and perpetual minority.

But while the war retained the Democratic Party in power, it largely restored the damaged prestige of the American businessman. It further transformed Big Business with all the techniques of scientific management and public relations. In the days of Coolidge the apothegm " The Business of America is Business," might meet the irreverent laughter of Mencken, but by and large it would be accepted as a Presidential wise saying worthy of respectful editorial comment in the press. The American intellectual, a-political since Tippecanoe and anti-business since Grant, had accepted European exile save for the hardy band that joined Mencken in mocking the booboisie. The American businessman was the work-giver who put two chickens in every pot and hopefully, some day, a Ford in every garage. The Wall Street crash of '29 crumbled the idols and as so often the angry tribe turned on its gods and, unable to beat them in person, beat their political shamen. The humiliation of this dethronement rankles yet and the restoration is no more solid than that of the Bourbons—a catch name in the New Deal arsenal.

At the outset of F.D.R.'s first term there seemed no compelling reason why the historic division of the classes between the parties

168

should be seriously or permanently disturbed. Businessmen were running like scared rabbits and were pathetically grateful for any lead from Washington. Paid advertisements sprouted in the subway carrying the slogan "As Right As Roosevelt." Many had preferred Hoover but not a few were in the Roosevelt camp. The N.I.R.A. had all the orthodoxy of the Chamber of Commerce. This experiment in organised scarcity was criticised by some but initially hailed by most. One grumbling Harvard economist did remark that the nation had been saved by the bootleggers once and he now put his hopes in the black market.

The minor provision enacted in section 7a in support of union organisation only slowly came to the forefront. It is still somewhat of a mystery why Roosevelt, who certainly conceived his mission as that of patching up American capitalism in accord with the enlightened views of an Episcopalian gentleman, should have become the subject of harsh and even scurrilous abuse as an enemy to his class. American politics has always used the rhetoric of invective. Washington himself complained of being used with language becoming to the description of a common pickpocket. Yet, in the past we have recovered from electoral bouts of mudslinging with little permanent damage. The partisan strife of the thirties has resulted in a high degree of polarisation of our political life. In particular it has generated self-perpetuating forces tending to increasingly identify all elements of business with the dominant spokesmen of big business in the Republican Party.

The intellectuals called back by the New Deal into political life after decades of scornful withdrawal became attached to the party of movement and ideas. This allegiance has seemed so self-evidently right that all those attaching themselves to the Republican Party have appeared as mere mercenaries. When the Republicans at election time have yielded to the temptation of proving that they too had an intelligentsia the organisations have had all the counterfeit air of a communist front.

It is difficult for intellectuals to carry on even a political struggle in a purely pragmatic and piecemeal way. The old war cries of the populists and the progressives, the New Freedom and the New Nationalism, were subtly altered by the new wave of ideas of the thirties. Charles Beard had been dismissed from Columbia for laying economic hands on the immaculate conception of the constitution in the twenties. The vulgarisation of a class struggle and the materialist interpretation of history was widespread and almost in the air to serve as a rationale for liberal and conservative alike.

169

When an economist of the Landon brains trust was quoted as advocating the sterilisation of the unemployed and the substitution of the title to a new car for a marriage licence it was easy to see in this the full diabolism of the Marxian capitalist rather than the sorry outcome of an outworn economics.

The curious thing about right and left in the politics of the thirties was the extent to which some vulgarised version of a Marxist theory of history controlled the background of the pictures in peoples' heads. The liberal intellectual with his humanitarian drive, his depression to be defeated, his specifics to be sold, legislated, and administered, had neither time nor will to put his intellectual house in order.

The conflict in American politics was played against a backdrop of an increasingly sinister European crisis. The popular theory of economic stagnation and the mature economy fitted in nicely with the Marxist rationale and the brutal facts of imperialism seemed so much confirmatory evidence.

The most powerful stream of creative new ideas in the thirties stemmed from Marx and Freud. Both lent themselves to easy popularisation, lent themselves in Walter Lippman's sense to teaching people new ways of looking at reality. A whole school of historians found Marx reread as Madison a useful scheme to give meaning to the American epic. Businessmen and New Deal liberals alike were taught without seriously thinking about it to look upon the New Deal as an expression of the class struggle. In the eyes of the businessmen the New Deal intellectuals were communist dupes if not the real thing. As bitterness rose in the thirties to the crescendo of the Spanish civil war it seemed to either side to divide the sheep from the goats. The Right was business, pro-Franco *ergo* pro-fascist, opposed to economic progress and grinding the underdog. The Left was pro-loyalist, preferring communist to fascist, believing in government control of the economy in support of the underdog.

The communists had taught the businessman how to look at his opponent in terms of their own version of history. Equally they taught the liberal intellectual how to view the "malefactors of great wealth." The price of having no ideas of one's own is to be controlled by those of others, even when the others are despised and rejected. Marxist thinking moved into a vacuum as naturally as an elemental force. It required no plot and succeeded intellectually far beyond the poor power of fronts and transmission belts to propagate it. Political artists like any others need fodder for their imagination

170

and the human quest for meanings will clutch at a powerful system capable of ordering an otherwise senselessness. No conscious acceptance was necessary for minds to take on a view of history that in the current world situation had compelling plausibility. It is possible to reject communism and yet be deeply affected by communist ways of thought. In no case is this more apparent than in the conspiracy-obsessed anti-communists, who resemble their antagonists in method and even in the ultimately dictatorial logic of their position.

The very vagueness of the New Deal-Fair Deal programme made it possible to treat it not as a pragmatic congery of political specifics but as a convenient cloak to hide sinister ambitions. It was politically convenient, too, to tar one's opponents with the blackest hues in the current symbolism of public distaste. This tactic, that went back at least to the Landon campaign and was carried on by dissident Democrats like Martin Dies, was mightily helped by the emergence of the Soviet Union as a real threat and the sudden collapse of the illusions of atomic supremacy. The deflation of this fond hope lent itself to the conspiratorial explanation. A public that had been led by slogans was ill-prepared to face the abrupt reality of the cold war. Lacking a vigorous foreign policy capable of curing public neuroses with the propaganda of the deed, the embittered men of the Right had a rich psychological field to exploit. We had won the war and lost the peace. A turn of events so startling could only be explained by conspiracy from within.

In the comparative calm of the moment it is hard to realise that only a few short months ago McCarthy was riding high. The massive complacency of the Eisenhower Administration with its adoption of the built-in economic stabilisers of the New Deal seems to have ushered in a Brave New World in which the President's personality provides the political soothing syrup for infantile alarms. The ex-communists and their fellows, who were making copy for the newspapers and entertainment for the right-minded, have been banished to the inside pages.

Even the displaced liberals are doing well in the colleges, in the magazines, in their law offices in Washington, even in the offices of big business. A short few years ago there was real fear for constitutional liberties, today the real fear is boredom. Arthur Schlesinger Jr. suggests in a recent issue of the *New York Times Magazine* that the liberal needs to recover his irreverent sceptical outlook and save our individual souls from being put in the production line of the advertising experts of Madison Avenue. The

171

dilemma of having the benefits of mass production and avoiding the evils of mass culture is a real one. On the economic and spiritual level it is the analogue of the dilemma presented by E. H. Carr in his *New Society* of reconciling individualistic, rational Lockean democracy with the unpleasant realities of contemporary mass democracy.

Certainly Schlesinger is right that a major weakness of American liberalism has been its too great preoccupation with things economic. There is a spiritual poverty as frightening as any economic poverty and quite compatible with our economic success. The early New Deal was not without concern in this regard and had Congress not shown a bitter opposition to federal aid to the theatre and the arts, a promising development might have taken place.

It would be folly to suppose in the present luxury of the Eisenhower Administration, when Messrs. Burns, Hauge, Larson, and Mitchell all but assure us " We are all Modeste Republicans, we are all New Dealers," that the black forces of McCarthyism are permanently exorcised.

The American liberal has a breathing space to think out where he wants to go and how he expects to get there. If he is wise he will realise the danger of having no more than a pragmatic set of expedientials developed on the spur of the moment to meet a crisis. The philosophies of history may be metaphysical and false but some view of history is essential if one is to do more than ride the wave of events. And some meaningful political philosophy is a prime necessity to provide a view of the New Society that can challenge our imaginations and, in doing so, give us more than material meaning to the world.

We are still faced with basic unsolved economic problems. The planless theory of *laissez faire* is still given formal lip service in certain quarters but is largely abandoned without being replaced. A national policy of full employment has been accepted without any thought of what is now to replace the older controls of inflation. The welfare state boggled at by Senator Taft is half accepted, half rejected in a curiously evolving stage.

The disenchantment with controls in the war and the post-war period, and the disgust with totalitarian excesses have shaken the liberal faith in his earlier half-conscious panacea—the government. The rules and roles of the game are in flux, and creative thought is badly needed to restore a sense of confidence and purpose. Nowhere is this more necessary than in the reintegration of the

172

American businessman into the scheme of things. His extra-ordinary isolation from political responsibility, at least until recently, has meant that his contact has been through paid political hacks and servile sycophants flattering his prejudices. This isolation has led to a politics of romantic reaction based on a dream world of *laissez faire*.

The isolation of the liberal intellectual from the business elite has left the field wide open to the McCarthyite and the huckster. The contempt for the booboisie symbolised by Mencken, carried forward into the heat of battle of the New Deal, has left a scarred hostility that is difficult to bridge. Yet unless the liberal intellectual intends, as the businessman fears, to place him with the spinning wheel and the bronze axe in the museum of history, an understanding between those responsible for creative thinking about our society and those responsible for posts of power, not only as economic commissars but as political powers at all levels of government, is a high priority endeavour. A major question for the liberal intellectual is what is the place of business in the New Society. The reports from Milovan Djilas about one alternative are not reassuring.

Unfortunately, the liberal is bound to certain positions, for the tested war cries of the political arena are so many brand names with good will. Short-run political expediency counsels their retention. Allies have been made in the course of many a political fight and one cannot be too critical of allies. A truly radical look at labour and agriculture is difficult when you are a political associate of the leaders. Even as a practising publicist the market of your wares dictates the product.

The re-entry of the intellectual into American politics has been a clear gain but while giving one kind of responsibility to his role it has sharply limited his capacity and perspective. He needs to be something more than a mouthpiece for the Democratic Party and the trade union leadership. However, the alternative to a servile dependence on business paymasters is a welcome one. How frustrating and degrading that can be has been well shown by Floyd Hunter in his study of community power structure.

In addition to the romantic reactionaries of the *National Review*, the communist hunters, and the Madison Avenue psychologists, the business community have acquired other intellectual resources of better promise. *Fortune* magazine, *Business Week*, and the *Harvard Business Review* have constituted themselves as a kind of missionary liberals of the Right and the Committee for Economic Development has made of itself a businessman's Fabian Society.

173

As promoters of intellectual fashion among those whom David Riesman calls the other-directed glad-handers their efforts have met with some success. They at least approach the hand that feeds them without making it fearful of being bitten. But their impact is confined, and while they are in a good way responsible intellectually for the conservative enlightenment of the Eisenhower Administration, they scarcely reach the provinces. Here are the stagnant waters from which a new fever of McCarthyism can rise.

Such a fever is likely to rise in the absence of a healthy sense of meaningful national direction. The Soviet Union, despite satellite and internal troubles, may still give us ugly moments. But, more than this, the boredom of a complacent Eisenhower epoch can generate its own demands for some things of the spirit, however perverse. The search for meanings will go on and the vacuum of the spirit will defy even the technics of Madison Avenue.

There is, then, a creative opportunity for liberal political thought to give a new definition of a national common good from which meaningful roles in an ethical society take their definition. Such thought will surely have to face up to the problems of economics, not only because they are unsolved as economics, but because for most of us they affect our significant social roles.

They need defining in ways that elevate human life not as mere bargaining postures. The aesthetic element in a society on the threshold of unprecedented leisure becomes a matter of first concern if we are to avoid mass exploitation in some version of Aldous Huxley's feelies. But blending a humanist view of economics and the arts we must relearn politics as a thing to be enjoyed in the Periclean sense, and structure our institutions with such an end in view.

For the first time, the material conditions for a widely shared democratic life are within our grasp. In some healthy pluralism of our institutions we may remedy the sodden and dictatorial tendencies of the threat of mass democracy. The liberal of today is conservative, in Huntingdon's sense, in seeking to preserve free institutions. The businessman, bemused by the name-calling of twenty years, deludes himself that romantic reactionaries, ex-communists and their fellows are true friends of our institutions. As Edward Shils has abundantly shown in " The Torment of Secrecy," nothing could be further from the case. It is an odd development of American politics that those who had most fundamentals in common should have so consorted intellectually, if not physically, with their enemies.

174

Our politics has been bedevilled by the twin slogans, " No Enemies on the Left," " No Enemies on the Right." This folly liberals and businessmen can ill afford. Neither can do anything but lose in the success of the extremes. The first step in cementing an alliance on fundamentals of what has been called the vital centre is a straight answer to the question: " What is the place of the businessman in the New Society? "

With the passage of the Full Employment Act of 1946 public policy in the United States has formally abandoned the regulation of the economy by uncontrolled market forces. The " economic whip " of unemployment has been laid aside and the search for substitute motivations begun. While many businessmen grumble and think wistfully of the wonders that a dose of unemployment would do for labour discipline, few have any idea that it is politically feasible to return to the days of the industrial reserve army. Few have a break-even point that would stand any substantial falling away of mass consumption. Politically it is recognised on all hands that a serious downturn would be met by drastic federal fiscal action. Governmental reflexes are conditioned to publicly expected roles and the conditioned spending response is almost too automatic for comfort.

The position of labour in the new economy is ill-defined and uneasy. No longer under the " economic whip," how is it to be held to responsible action? For generations it has been taught by management that it was a commodity and that all commodities were worth what they could get. As E. H. Carr has pointed out in his *New Society*, it seems hard to tell labour, haunted by fears of unemployment, that coming at last to the feast it must show a statesman-like moderation and restraint so alien to the business evangel.

The temptation to get what one can while the pickings are good is strong indeed. It comes with ill grace from the business world to cry shame at labour's exuberant pursuit of the profit motive. But morally justified or not, the problem of cost control remains, and labour discipline, though a harsh term, is a stubborn necessity of any functioning economy. The problem of labour leadership and its subordination to social needs is every bit as real as that of the social control of business. The liberal alliance with labour makes it relatively more difficulty to face up to this aspect of the new economic order.

Both business management and labour leadership have been brought up to play a game in which you got what you could and

175

had the comforting assurance that in doing so you were promoting the best interests of society. Few any longer believe this to be the case but while lip service is paid to a doctrine of social responsibility, no structured set of roles and institutions give it greater meaning than an expediential concern with public opinion. This borders in some cases on the sheerest Madison Avenue hypocrisy.

The massive forces of organised big business, big labour, and big agriculture that should have ground our free economy to a monopolistic halt, have, in Kenneth Galbraith's terms, created countervailing power which, with the active intervention of big government, has somehow avoided the dire consequences predicted in classic theory. We have, it seems, a system of administered prices and wages with those disadvantaged sectors of the economy if politically vocal receiving aid from the state.

This system seems inelegant, perhaps theoretically inefficient, but at least it works. Comparisons are odious but thus far no superior models ready for imitation seem at hand. The job of improvement will require originality and imagination in reshaping existing institutions in accordance with a sensitive awareness of the possibilities and limitations of American culture, political and economic.

Two immediate problems confront us. First the accelerating inflation of our full employment economy is failing to respond to the classic controls. The regressive and unequal impact of hiking interest rates has become apparent. The resort of the President to " jaw bone " price and wage control [1] is likely to prove no more successful than in the past. As a piece of moral ritual it may have totemic tribal value but it is doubtful that it can succeed as a politically efficacious Presidential washing of the hands. The reintroduction of cumbersome war-time controls can scarcely be used except as a last resort. A threatening buyers' strike might force down prices but at the cost of painful unemployment and the necessity of heavy deficit financing to check a downturn.

Clearly we are far from having discovered ways and means to structure the behaviour of big business and big labour, so as to insure that their demands are consistent with generally accepted social objectives. Some kind of new rules are needed for gearing wages, prices, and profits to productivity and reasonable concern for consumer interests. Thus far these latter concerns have received but lip service and their sanction is the adverse political effect of patently outrageous behaviour on public opinion. None the less, an

---

[1] *i.e.*, the attempt to control prices by executive exhortation without legal sanctions to enforce compliance.

176

emerging economic constitutional consensus in new standards of dividing the social product is not a forlorn hope. The unwritten constitution of an evolving economic order is taking shape and a new concept of fair shares consistent with economic responsibility may secure practical acceptance by labour and capital alike as the preferable alternative to continuous state intervention and control. Providing a framework of ideas to embody the desirable new rules of the game is a major job of responsible political economy.

The more basic problem confronting us is the unanswered question of whether we can maintain full employment without undue dependence on an arms programme. Clearly Marx has been proved wrong. Capitalism or our version of it can plan. But, can it plan only for war—be it hot or cold? Or can a sufficient volume of demand be generated by other socially desired ends to press our resources into full utilisation? Theoretically there seems no reason why it cannot. It is true that national patriotism and fear of the enemy provide a broadly inclusive common denominator which in our past symbolism has seemed the readiest basis for the manu-facture of consent. But much water has run under the bridge. While Hoover and Humphrey remain stubborn disciples of Henry Hazlitt's economics in one lesson, even Humphrey showed an expediential concern with the political effects of the recession his orthodoxy occasioned. The Taftian horror of the welfare state has receded and now seems almost as old-fashioned as Hoover. The basic political problem of the welfare state is its equation with socialism. And socialism unfortunately is branded with the stamp of class war and the objective of liquidating the bourgeoisie.

It is no wonder that an active, alert, and extremely able class of managers want no part of a political programme that proclaims them to be walking anachronisms if not worse. The role of manager in the New Society is a problem on both sides of the iron curtain. The recruitment, training, and properly motivating of the holders of key positions in the economy are a political problem of the first magnitude. It cannot be brushed aside. It is up to the liberal intellectual concerned with the fashioning of a free society to address himself to providing a proper and challenging place for the businessman in the New Society. There is reason to believe that many are interested and anxious to participate in the major task of social construction that provides the only hopeful alternatives to the great tyrannies menacing the individual and freedom itself.

177

Uneasy Partners: Government-Business Relations in Twentieth-Century American History

ALBRO MARTIN

"There are no simple congruences in human life: the cult of happiness assumes them." The late Reinhold Niebuhr doubtless intended this stern admonition to apply to the spiritual life of his congregation, but it well fits the experience that Americans have had in trying to accommodate vast economic power within a society that is supposed to be governed by a democratic political process. Except for the great constitutional issues, now largely resolved in favor of a unitary central government, there has been no more important issue in American politics than that of the proper role of government in the subordination of economic power, which, less than two generations after the industrial revolution took hold, threatened to eclipse that political power that had been the emblem and the shield of the Republic.

Americans did not begin to write what might

© 1979 by Albro Martin
  The author is Lecturer in Business History, Harvard University, and Editor of *Business History Review*. He acknowledges with thanks the thoughtful comments of W. Elliot Brownlee, Jr., Thomas K. McCraw, Richard S. Tedlow, and Paul J. Unselding.

pass as serious histories of government-business relations until well into the twentieth century. The primary sources of such works have been the universities, the foundations, and the government itself, and the "intellectual community" that these institutions represent is very largely a twentieth-century phenomenon. There was, moreover, relatively little direct government intervention in private economic decisionmaking before this century that could form the basis of histories of its origins and implementation, and almost none that had been in effect long enough to give meaning to studies of the effects of such intervention.

It would be a mistake, however, to suppose that the history of government-business relations is only the story of the sharing of economic decisions, or even of the subordination of economic to political power, after 1900. It is intellectual history, too. The history of ideas of what should constitute the proper relationship between government and business is an integral part of the subject, and no historiography of the field, however brief or tentative, can locate a seam between ideas and actions in this particular historical web. Americans may not have been writing anything of lasting value on this touchy subject before 1900, but they were certainly agonizing over it, and the histories that come later reflect a mind-set on the proper nature of government-business relations that was well established by 1900. So this essay, while it is no more than a prolegomenon to the subject, touches first on the vital influence of the nineteenth century on history that was written in the twentieth. The fact is that the history of what Americans have believed, since our beginnings, about the proper relationship between the people as a nation and the people as individuals going about their business is one of the three or four great pillars of the edifice we call history.

From the Idea of Commonwealth to the Age of Indignation—1825-1900

The incongruence between government and business began with the death of the only thing approaching a simple congruence that we have ever known: the idea of the commonwealth, the main feature of which was a broad agreement on the synergistic nature of national economic policy, as contrasted with the concept of public versus private interests that later captured the mind of pluralistic America. The decline of the commonwealth was breathtaking, so much so that a century later historians can still reach no real agreement on what happened. When James Monroe left the White House in 1825, after the most tranquil eight years that any American president has ever enjoyed, the second Bank of the United States was flourishing under the confident leadership of Nicholas Biddle and behind the shield of one of John Marshall's most famous Supreme Court decisions. With rising doubts, but in the realization that he had played a key role in the institution of a strong protective tariff policy barely nine years before, John C. Calhoun still kept his own counsel. Henry Clay, the eternal optimist, reflected cheerfully upon the fact that James Madison, strict constructionist though he was, had not left office without coming out in favor of federal aid for internal improvements. To a realist like Clay, Madison's condition that such aid would require a constitutional amendment seemed likely to get lost in the great shuffle that was taking place across the Appalachians, and in 1825 events seemed to be bearing him out.

And then, suddenly, the federal commonwealth idea was dead. What had seemed to be

such a close congruence between the public interest and the private interests who were soonest to be benefited came to be seen, in less than ten years, as nothing more than the contemptible jockeying of selfish private interests to get a handle on the sovereign power that would elevate their material welfare over that of the people. After the Jacksonian revolution, not even the exigencies of the Civil War would revive more than a limited constructive economic role for the federal government. By the end of the nineteenth century big business was under fire as violating the most basic element of economic faith. Until the Great Depression of the 1930s seemed to sweep away such simplistic ideas once and for all, that faith was laissez faire, and Adam Smith was supposed to have been its prophet.[1]

Next to the ideas of Karl Marx, Adam Smith's economic thought has probably been recycled more than any other practical philosophy. It became necessary long ago to abandon Smith's rejection of government intervention in the economic process in favor of the shaky logic behind the idea that intervention is necessary if self-regulation of the economy through the market process is to work in the modern world. If we have winced at the passage in Smith's *Wealth of Nations* about the "invisible hand" of enlightened self-interest being the only valid governor of the economic engine, we have been reassured by his warning that businessmen will inevitably conspire to constitute a very visible hand that will frustrate an otherwise benign and elegantly deistic self-regulating economic system.

---

[1] If the marshaling of capital for such internal improvements as canals and railroads through the agency of state governments is taken as an aspect of the commonwealth idea, then the idea survived at least to the Civil War. If minor civil divisions—counties and municipalities—are included in such a definition, the idea persisted in railroad development until the end of the century. What is significant, however, is that these policies, which grew up for the most part after 1825, were never accepted as entirely legitimate, and they were abandoned at the earliest possible moment. They led to repudiation of state obligations, to devastating contempt for both the integrity and competence of state legislators, and especially in the case of locally conceived railroad projects, to the building of many worthless lines that railroad men would never have undertaken on their own. In the mid-1950s, when historians began to "discover" the role of legislation to the idea of the federal commonwealth that the states had to play after 1825, Robert A. Lively published a review article, "The American System," for *Business History Review* 29 (Mar. 1955): 81-96, which is still an excellent, concise statement of the issues.

234

Henry Demarest Lloyd, 1847-1903, American reformer. Courtesy Library of Congress.

James Bryce (above right) in November 1912 during the time he was British ambassador to the United States. Courtesy Library of Congress.

Yearning for a simple congruence between Smith's apparently contradictory ideas, and between his pre-industrial world and our own, historians of government-business relations have swept this paradox under the rug. Their effort to recycle Adam Smith for use against large concentrations of economic power which businessmen acquired through their own efforts at concerted action (and not by successfully conspiring to subvert the sovereign into granting them economic privileges that have behind them the power of law) has led to unending confusion. Smith, in fact, had no conception of the modern industrial world, in which a few businessmen can conspire to make and maintain their own arrangements; a world in which the power of the sovereign is no longer something to be sought with flattery and specious arguments, but, in fact, something to be ignored because it is no longer needed.

This, then, has been the central infuriating fact about modern business: its economic *independence* of the political power. The revolution in the source of the businessman's power, however, has not meant a thing to rank-and-file Americans or to their political leaders. "Monopoly!" long ago became the rallying cry, and the possession of great wealth by individuals or—even worse—giant corporations run by salaried professionals, became prima facie evidence of successful exploitation of some kind of monopoly that originated not in the subversion of the state (although evidence to the contrary, where it existed, was always welcome) but in the monopolist's own . . . what? His greed? His devilish shrewdness? His great good luck? It has made no difference. The critical fact is that in the view of most Americans such power to affect the lives of citizens can come legitimately only from the state. Businessmen are not citizens of any nation, to paraphrase Adam Smith, and the history of government-business relations is the history of Americans' efforts to deal with the consequences of that phenomenon.

By 1900 Americans had a remarkable literature of indignation, and through it ran a secondary theme of regret at the loss of the older commonwealth. If that literature begins anywhere, it is with the essays collected and published as *Chapters of Erie* by Charles Francis Adams, Jr., and his brother Henry in 1866. Out of this tradition twenty-odd years later came a work which marked the apogee of the era of indignation and demonstrated, in the process, that big business and big businessmen are not effectively protected by the law of libel. That work was Henry Demarest Lloyd's *Wealth Against Commonwealth*, in which he savaged John D. Rockefeller and his associates in the Standard Oil Company. Lloyd has been to the antitrust movement what Harriet Beecher Stowe was to the antislavery crusade. The work takes leave of both facts and logic at innumerable points, but it has entered into American folklore, and not all the tears of modern business historians have washed away a word of it. In between there is a vast and mostly ephemeral literature that lays at the door of the "trusts" most of the very real hardships that a still largely agricultural America and an embattled society of small businessmen endured. To the most acute contemporary observer of America, James Bryce, there was no doubt about it. Bryce found here a fierce distrust and hatred of any kind of authority, especially when it was very large and was exerted from a distance. It was the corporation, Bryce noted in his celebrated *The American Commonwealth*, and especially the railroad corporation, that had become the hated symbol of this external authority.[2]

But academics and intellectuals meanwhile missed the point. Their indignation still centered on state-granted privilege. William Graham Sumner, with his talent for offending nearly everybody except his students, supported social Darwinism impartially against sturdy beggars and tariff-protected corporations. Frank W. Taussig reviewed the economic development of America in his *Tariff History of the United States*, demonstrating to the satisfaction of the thousands who bought edition after edition that the protective tariff had been an instrument not of growth of the commonwealth but of enrichment of a few privileged industrialists. The doctrine of laissez faire found strong advocates in a small but growing number of academics who discovered that dullness was no obstacle to publication of their work as textbooks. As late as the second decade of the

Progressive era, moreover, such diverse exponents of the era of indignation as Gustavus Myers and Charles A. Beard were still ploughing this field. Myers's *History of the Great American Fortunes* was a sustained sneer at the integrity, courage, and creativity of American business leaders, and ended up boring its few readers. It withered in the hot sun of national prosperity, but Beard's *An Economic Interpretation of the Constitution* created a sensation among academics and intellectuals, if not among ordinary Americans, who preferred their Founding Fathers legends straight.[3]

The Era of Optimism—1900-1930

William Allen White himself might have chiseled the two stone horses that stand outside the rather dowdy Federal Trade Commission building in Washington. Each beast, its massive WPA-aesthetic muscles rippling, pulls against the efforts of its groom to restrain its raw, equine power and, presumably, to direct it towards productive and philosophically appropriate ends. White, in his folksy way, had explained in 1910 what he and most Americans saw as the solution of the paradox of economic power transcending political power. "All of these fish will go on one string," he said, "the restriction of capital."[4] What marks the transition from mere indignation, with its destructive, revolutionary overtones, to the progressivism of the first third of the new century is the belief that a simple congruence between public and private power was not only devoutly to be wished but was, indeed, possible of attainment. That, it seems, is about all the agreement one can get on what the progressive movement was. It was a seductive philosophy for the times, which explains why the muckrakers struck it rich for the magazine publishers who employed them. The indignation was surely there, for the majority of prospering, on-the-make middle-class Americans could see themselves in Ida Minerva Tarbell's independent oil producers (not quite all of whom resented Standard Oil's offer they

---

[2] Charles F., Jr., and Henry Adams, *Chapters of Erie* (1866); Henry Demarest Lloyd, *Wealth Against Commonwealth* (1894); James Bryce, *The American Commonwealth*, 2 vols. (1888), 2: 404-406, 511, 705.

[3] Sumner's greatest effectiveness was on the lecture platform, but his philosophy is powerfully stated in *What Social Classes Owe to Each Other* (1883); Frank W. Taussig, *The Tariff History of the United States* (1888), reached its eighth edition in 1932; Gustavus Myers, *History of the Great American Fortunes*, 3 vols. (1910); Charles A. Beard, *An Economic Interpretation of the Constitution* (1913).

[4] William Allen White, *The Old Order Changeth: A View of American Democracy* (1910), p. 67.

236

Priming the old pump.

couldn't refuse) or, if not in Upton Sinclair's unbelievably unlucky immigrant packinghouse worker, at least among the innocents who bought and ate the unclean sausage he ground out. Ray Stannard Baker discovered that this new class of middle Americans was far more interested in wallowing in tales of the excesses of railroad magnates than of what resurgent white supremacists were doing to black people. It was a new era, and one in which Americans felt that their generation had been chosen to do something about the unrestrained power of the trusts that were multiplying around them.[5]

It was, in fact, a generation that thought it could do just about anything. Bitter medicine though it was, the long depression of the 1890s had razed much of the rickety Victorian social and economic structure and ushered in a long period of prosperity that even included the American farmer among its beneficiaries. Output of industrial goods rose dramatically, which was not surprising in view of the mushrooming growth of industries based upon remarkable new technologies. Farm output rose sharply, too, which surprised Americans as they watched the many young men and women who were deserting the farms for the cities and, perhaps more significant, for the colleges and universities that struggled to find room for them.

As Richard Hofstadter has so ably demonstrated, it was this prosperity and the surging growth in faith in the efficacy of education, especially higher education, that opened the field of college teaching to the lower middle class, and thus initiated a revolution in American leadership that has not yet run its course nearly a century later. The names of the intellectual leaders of the progressive movement, to be sure, remained for the most part eastern names. But alongside the scholarly tradition represented by Herbert Croly, Walter Lippmann, and Theodore Roosevelt, there grew up an oral tradition in the lecture halls of the rawboned campuses of the Midwest, the plains states, and the Far West that kept the progressive spirit supercharged with the indignation of the bad old days. Two progressive movements, in fact, existed side by side: eastern and western, or enlightened and "archaic," or liberal and reac-

[5] Ida M. Tarbell, *The Standard Oil Company* (1904); Ray Stannard Baker, "Railroads on Trial," *McClure's Magazine* 26 (Mar. 1906): 539.

tionary—the reader is free to choose his own label, so long as he frees himself from the old tradition of trying to make Herbert Croly, George Perkins, and Theodore Roosevelt stand under the same umbrella with Walter Weyl, Robert M. LaFollette, Albert B. Cummins, and Louis D. Brandeis.[6]

Americans, in short, as they attained greater leisure and more education also developed a faith in the efficacy of statecraft to solve basic economic problems. But had they more practical reasons to pour the molten anger of the nineteenth century into progressivism's legislative, judicial, and administrative molds? Indeed they did. If the period from 1900 to 1917 was one of great prosperity, full employment, and rising money wages, it was also one of inflation, which seemed all the more sinister after thirty years of declining prices. Why an immediate upturn in prices should go hand in hand with the advent of such a new age of prosperity was more than that naive era could understand; indeed, it is not a settled question today. The fact is that prosperity and rising prices were merely two sides of the same coin, for the rising price level reflected an astonishing rate of investment in nearly every creative aspect of American life.

The most thoughtful, if not the most readable, progressive interpretation of American government-business relations in the past and what it meant for the future was Herbert Croly's *The Promise of American Life*. Croly adopted the Hamiltonian stand that what is best for the commonwealth in the long run, that is, a free and unfettered business community that would continue to apply in the twentieth century the enterprising spirit that had worked such miracles (nearly everybody agreed) in the nineteenth, was good for everybody in the short run. It was the chief business of government, therefore, to create an atmosphere of permissive trust for business, while stiff-arming antimodernist efforts by unprogressive businessmen to trade on the public fear of strength, success, and power to demand special favors. Less ready to trust big business, but equally con-

[6] Richard Hofstadter, *The Progressive Historians* (1968), pp. 35-36, 41. "The [older generation of] historical writers," Hofstadter observed, "had commonly looked with incomprehension or stunned resentment at the trends of the times." Charles Forcey, *Crossroads of Liberalism: Croly, Weyl, Lippmann and the Progressive Era, 1900-1925* (1961), discusses the eastern brand of progressivism, which itself was far from monolithic.

vinced that America should take a positive, constructive attitude towards the operation and future shaping of its economic society, was the youthful Walter Lippmann, whose *Drift and Mastery* revealed that moderate detachment for which his punditry in national and international affairs was later famous.[7]

There was little of moderate detachment in the growing literature about the trusts, and even the mildest pieces seemed to call for action. John Moody, the financial editor who had begun to serve the business world so efficiently, made a good thing out of his *The Truth About the Trusts*, which succeeded in showing that the trusts were far more widespread, more successful, and more inclined to be a permanent trend, than many had supposed. Indeed, the book came on the heels of the greatest merger wave in American history and this time it was not only the railroads, who had been at this sort of thing for years, that were consolidating, but also industrial companies, nearly all of whom had only recently been good, grey, family-owned-and-operated firms.

In the gathering storm, hardly anyone noticed a small, paperbacked volume that the University of Wisconsin published in 1906 as volume 1, number 3, in its *Economics and Political Science Series*. Written by a Wisconsin professor of political economy, Balthasar H. Meyer, *A History of the Northern Securities Case* was a remarkable document for its time. Meyer had been echoing for some years what an older, sadder, and wiser Charles Francis Adams, Jr., had said at the time the Interstate Commerce Act of 1887 was before Congress—that all efforts to prohibit businessmen from doing those things that order and stability demanded would merely result in closer and more formal consolidation of interests. Now, in 1906, Meyer criticized the Supreme Court decision of 1904 forbidding James J. Hill, Edward H. Harriman, and J. P. Morgan from combining three western railroads into a single corporation. Meyer showed that there was no economic basis for the decision. He might have gone on and said that the decision merely proved once again that the Supreme Court was a political, not a judicial, institution, and that the Sherman Antitrust Act of 1890 would never have any meaning save what the Court said it meant the last time it ruled. A grateful James J. Hill bought several

dozen copies, but the book had no measurable effect. Meyer himself reversed his philosophy once he was appointed to the Interstate Commerce Commission, where he served for more than twenty years.[8]

More influential were men like Charles R. Van Hise, president of the University of Wisconsin and a leading economist during the waxing of institutionalism, and William Zenobia Ripley, holder of the prestigious Ropes chair in political economy at Harvard and unquestioned leader of that ill-defined but growing body of people who billed themselves as experts on the "railroad problem." Van Hise was an early wrestler with the question of how the rise of big business and the consolidation movement could be fitted rationally into the history of the development of the American economy. He never got much beyond lame generalizations about the economies of large-scale production, and for every thoughtful person who read his book *Concentration and Control* there were thousands who read the influential articles of Louis D. Brandeis in *Harper's* and *Collier's*.

Brandeis, who was seldom in doubt about anything, thought he knew precisely what was wrong with American business. He was convinced that small was better than big *even* if it was less efficient, and he was willing to use every weapon in the political arsenal to force a return to the atomistic competition that he believed had preceded the modern industrial era. Brandeis and other reformers received considerable help from Ripley, who ground out two massive volumes on railroad finance and regulation in 1913 and 1915. Packed with information about the origins and nature of the railroad problem, Ripley's books would lead any reasonable novice to conclude that railroad men were no longer competent to manage the properties in their charge. The coarseness of this Harvard economist's analysis of the new and ever-changing problems of finance that revolutionary enterprises like the railroads brought about is all the more remarkable in that he was probably the best informed "disinterested" party in America. Old notions die hard. Even after the financial innovations of World War I, for example, Ripley's quixotic polemic in favor of par-value stock (on which many of the jejune charges of stock watering are based) was

---

[7] Herbert D. Croly, *The Promise of American Life* (1909); Walter Lippmann, *Drift and Mastery* (1914).

[8] John Moody, *The Truth About the Trusts* (1904); B. H. Meyer, *History of the Northern Securities Case* (1906).

still being echoed by Columbia University's James C. Bonbright.[9]

It was a time for learning, for experimenting with far-reaching economic legislation, and for eventual disappointment with the realization that the calendar could not be turned back and that lawyers and college professors were no more the philosopher-kings that the progressive brand of optimism demanded than were the insurgent politicians.

World War I marked the beginning of a great advance in consumer spending power. Turning inward to the task of building upon the superb economic foundations they had perfected during the previous two decades, Americans transferred their optimism from government to business itself as the most important agent of a better nation and a happier life for the masses. Business as a profession (none other than Louis D. Brandeis, in fact, had called it that) beckoned, and the idea of formal education for business grew rapidly. There was something for everybody: from the ivied halls of Harvard, whose Graduate School of Business Administration was gathering momentum and prestige after a decade of experimentation, to the local business college with its promise of a place on the bottom rung of the ladder. The need was very real, as the integration of American industrial corporations and a burgeoning technology brought a quantum leap in business opportunities for the well educated. Inevitably, a constructively optimistic note was sounded in the history of government-business relations.

Significantly, it was not the professional historian who contributed the most to this literature. It was, rather, the rising band of "social scientists" that tackled the problems that had made up the "response to industrialism" of the previous two generations. Economics moved to front rank among the social sciences, and there emerged a stream of studies of economic problems that included more or less knowledgeable treatments of their history. The nation had reached that degree of economic superannuation which seemed to mark some vital industries, such as coal, railroads, housing, and agriculture as weak if not actually debilitated, and others as suffering from excessive economic

and political power on the part of their leaders. Financial institutions (especially in their role of suppliers of industrial financing and consumer credit), foreign investment banking operations and, most notably, the great new industry of the era, electric power, were subjected to a gaze that would intensify in the next decade. Meanwhile, a growing interest in the laws as they had affected such rising movements as labor unions and efforts to outlaw child labor, presaged the arrival of what Sumner Slichter would dub the "laboristic society."[10]

One team of professional historians, however, made a beginning at the task of integrating business into the broader history of the United States. Charles A. and Mary Beard's two-volume *The Rise of American Civilization* was the most important book on American history to appear in the decade of the 1920s, and its influence was profound. It marked a refreshing break with the stale political history that seemed to have passed the point of diminishing returns, and it offered something for everybody. Out of their genuine interest in social history came a mild brand of economic determinism that reached its climax in the Beards' concept of the "second American revolution," which is how they saw the centralizing effects of the Civil War on American national economic policy. From this one could derive support for the belief that big business had captured the American political system, or, equally, for the insistence that "the business of America is business." Southerners, viewing the virtual failure of sixty years of struggle to regain their antebellum pride and influence, found in the Beards' interpretation support for the century-old theory of conspiracy of northern economic interests against the South. And through it all, in the virile, enthusiastic, and sometimes breathless prose of its authors, the book told thousands of general readers for the first time the story of an America they could understand and be proud of in a new context.[11]

In the long view of history, however, the Beards' book is not the most significant in the evolution of the professional historian's ap-

[9] C. R. Van Hise, *Concentration and Control* (rev. ed., 1914); Brandeis's articles were collected in two volumes, *Other People's Money* (1914), and *Business: A Profession* (1914); William Z. Ripley, *Railroads: Rates and Regulation* (1913), and *Railroads: Finance and Regulation* (1915); J. C. Bonbright, *Railroad Capitalization* (1920).

[10] Some examples of problem-industry studies are H. S. Raushenbush and H. W. Laidler, *Power Control* (1929); W. H. Hamilton and H. R. Wright, *The Case of Bituminous Coal* (1925); W. M. W. Splawn, *Consolidation of Railroads* (1925); and G. W. Stocking, *The Oil Industry and the Competitive System* (1925).

[11] Charles A. and Mary R. Beard, *The Rise of American Civilization*, 4 vols. (1927-42), went through numerous printings and was still being sold as a textbook in the late 1940s.

Mary Ritter Beard, 1876-1958, who with her husband wrote the two-volume **Rise of American Civilization** (1927) and two sequels **America in Midpassage** (1939) and **The American Spirit** (1943). Courtesy Library of Congress.

proach to the subject of government-business relations. At almost the same time that the Beards were bringing out their masterpiece, an unknown history instructor at Cornell University, who at the age of 37 had turned his back on a successful newspaper editing career for a chance to study, research, write, and teach American history, published the first professional effort to understand the role of American business in the transformation of American life. In his *The Emergence of Modern America*, Allan Nevins combined a lust to know, a powerful ability to integrate, and a superb talent to write about the diverse subjects that are the true content of social history, in a book that is still a pleasure and a profit to read. It was the technique of "total history" that Nevins advanced so dramatically, and not a narrow interest in business. Only very slowly, during the depression and the war years, would the golden opportunity that lay in the subject of American business and its relations to the greater American society become apparent.[12]

[12] Allan Nevins, *The Emergence of Modern America* (1927). In that year the new campus of the Harvard Graduate School of Business Administration was opened and N. S. B. Gras

The Era of Confident Reformism: Since 1930

If Americans of the Progressive era drew their optimism from a confidence in their ability to improve upon the world their predecessors had made, Americans of the era since the onset of the Great Depression have been driven by the conviction that they *had* to find "the better way." The literature of government-business relations literally explodes after 1933. It is not a literature with which professional historians had much to do for some years, however. By 1935, in fact, a large proportion of all Americans holding a Ph.D. in history were unemployed. The rest were either keeping their noses to the academic grindstone—praying that somehow the college president would find the money to pay their shrunken salaries—or they were pursuing other occupations. Grants and leave for research, light teaching schedules for senior scholars, even tenure itself, were all in the future.

One of the most influential books in this period was Adolf A. Berle, Jr., and Gardiner C. Means, *The Modern Corporation and Private Property*, which analyzed the decline of the influence of stockholders (the nominal owners of corporate property), and the rise of professional managers as policymakers. The implications for public policy at a time when the stewardship of business leaders was being seriously questioned were profound, notwithstanding the fact that the changes Berle and Means described had been under way for a generation. I. Leo Sharfman meanwhile helped bring the long history of institutionalist economics to an end with his big study of the Interstate Commerce Commission. Crammed with information on the activities of this first important branch of administrative law, the work demonstrates, at least in hindsight, how little of government-business relations can be learned from studying the bare legal and administrative processes that encapsulate its real history. A landmark of business biography was Henrietta Larson's *Jay Cooke*, an early example of what a thorough grounding in historical

became the first professor of business history in the United States, occupying a chair established at the school by the descendants of Isidor Straus. Gras insisted upon the company history approach to the subject, which Nevins himself practiced on occasion, but it was Nevins's integration of economic and business history into a broader synthesis, most notably in his grandest work, *The Ordeal of the Union*, 8 vols. (1947-71), that is the most successful employment of this branch of history to date.

method and the subject matter of business, combined with a deep desire to understand the impact of the businessman upon American government, can accomplish. Finally, on the eve of Pearl Harbor, Merle Fainsod and Lincoln Gordon published the first full-scale synthesis of the subject in their *Government and the American Economy*.[13]

It was to be expected that the more we learned about the issues, about the narrowness of the limits in which both businessmen and statesmen had to maneuver, and about the fortuitousness—as opposed to the determinism—of human life, the fresher the history of government-business relations would become. The old legends have been a long time dying, however. At the depth of the depression John D. Hicks published an indulgent history of the populist movement that revealed the deeply felt need of historians writing about the American West for a native reform tradition. In 1934, the seed that Gustavus Myers had sowed twenty-five years earlier sprouted vigorously and lucratively for Matthew Josephson in his *The Robber Barons*. Instructors of American economic history who still reluctantly assign it do so in the increasingly desperate hope that someone who writes as well as Josephson did will synthesize the new history that has left it light years behind, or at least tackle the book's many sins of omission and commission.[14]

The newer tradition of blaming big business for the intervention of the United States in World War I found a further hearing in C. C. Tansill's much-discussed *America Goes to War*. Yet for almost a decade after the Second World War there continued to appear a series of books that clearly belonged to an earlier time. Among them was Fred A. Shannon's desperate effort

to breathe life back into the indignant pose that was already out of date when he was a young man. But Shannon's *The Farmer's Last Frontier*, an early volume in the uneven series *The Economic History of the United States*, will continue to be valuable for what it tells us about agriculture in the years when the last virgin land was being settled, until someone discovers that American agriculture is important enough to have its own definitive history. Another disappointment in this series was George Soule's *Prosperity Decade*, although there are passages that show Soule in command of the zeitgeist if not the definitive weaknesses of the 1920s economy. Like most studies, political and otherwise, of the New Deal era, Broadus Mitchell's *Depression Decade*, in the series, is useful mainly as an encyclopedia to the alphabetical fistfuls that Franklin D. Roosevelt flung at a problem that only the stimulus of war could solve. The role of business in the debacle of the 1920s still eludes us, while the economic policy of the New Deal, despite or perhaps because of the efforts of droves of scholars, continues to reveal an incoherence that may be as real as it is apparent.[15]

The Era of Revision, Reaction, and Disillusionment—Since 1945

Like the decade of the 1920s, the 1950s have little appeal for historians who seem to prefer those times when our leaders are energetically defending the nation against dangers internal and external, real or imagined. If we ignore bloody Korea, the 1950s decade was a time of peace, of rebuilding a Western world that had been drained by more than twenty years of depression and war, and of vouchsafing to the productive classes great freedom of action. As in the 1920s, times were good, productivity per manhour (than which there is no more basic evidence of material progress) rose steeply, American youth turned eagerly to business as a career (in 1949, according to the Harvard *Crimson*, $10,000 a year in salary from a large corporation was the dream of most Harvard undergraduates) and a placid, fatherly man occupied the White House for eight years. And, like the 1920s, the 1950s were a boom time

[13] Adolf A. Berle, Jr., and Gardiner C. Means, *The Modern Corporation and Private Property* (1932); I. L. Sharfman, *The Interstate Commerce Commission*, 4 vols. (1932-37); Henrietta Larson, *Jay Cooke, Private Banker* (1936); Merle Fainsod and Lincoln Gordon, *Government and the American Economy* (1941).

[14] Matthew Josephson, *The Robber Barons* (1934). Thomas C. Cochran and William Miller, *The Age of Enterprise* (1942), was no match for Josephson's literary style, and the authors also lacked the rich material that has been published since World War II. The topic now beckons invitingly, as the mythical character of the traditional interpretation seems finally to have been recognized. There is a large literature on the subject, of which one example, Hal Bridges, "The Robber Baron Concept in American History," *Business History Review* 33 (Spring 1958), has now been included in a college textbook, Nicholas Cords and Patrick Gerster, eds., *Myth and the American Experience* (2d ed., 1978).

[15] C. C. Tansill, *America Goes to War* (1938); Fred A. Shannon, *The Farmer's Last Frontier* (1945); George Soule, *Prosperity Decade* (1947); Broadus Mitchell, *Depression Decade* (1947). Harold U. Faulkner, *The Decline of Laissez Faire* (1951), another volume in this series, added little of fact or interpretation to the work of the previous generation.

If indignation passed out of historical writing in the post-war years, it remained a vital part of political cartooning. Courtesy Truman Library.

for those other fruits of peace and consensus, the arts, literature, and the world of the intellect. Colleges and universities finally resumed the rapid growth rate that had peaked on the eve of the depression. The sophistication and breadth of historians also grew, and the decade produced book after book reflecting that fact. And if the intellectual gears clashed raucously in the 1960s and seemed to reverse themselves wildly in the 1970s, at least the machine did not break down altogether.

Historians in the postwar period set out zestfully to revise the hackneyed old interpretations of the eras of optimism and reformism. The best books in the *Economic History of the United States* series made their appearance: George R. Taylor's *The Transportation Revolution*, on antebellum growth, and the late Edward C. Kirkland's *Industry Comes of Age*, covering the period from 1865 to 1897, left the traditional stance of indignation far behind. Even more striking was the impact of several monographs that shone the cool light of the professional historian on the question of the actual relationship between the state and business before the Civil War. Oscar and Mary Handlin's study of Massachusetts and Louis Hartz's for

Pennsylvania found the state and the business-man to have been highly productive partners; and Hartz concluded in a later book that "the master assumption of American political thought [is] the reality of atomistic social free-dom." Carter Goodrich greatly advanced our appreciation of the role of state aid in the first generation of the transportation revolution. Meanwhile, finding the Standard Oil archives open to him at last, Allan Nevins pushed aside the monumental two-volume biography of John D. Rockefeller that he had completed just before the war and wrote a second version to which all just and wise men and women re-paired from Henry Demarest Lloyd as rapidly as possible. If Nevins had not been revision enough, along came Ralph and Muriel Hidy's magisterial first volume in a cooperative his-tory of Standard Oil.

These lessons were not lost on others, who turned to that hardy perennial, the "railroad problem," for example, and found it ripe for revision, too. Lee Benson, Harry Scheiber, and George Miller showed that the old simplistic notions about the public versus the private in-terest were useless in understanding whence came the rage for government regulation of economic decisionmaking, and I have been honored to follow the signs which they (and Frederick Merk before them) posted.[16]

Bray Hammond, with a love and a deep familiarity for his subject that are rare in American scholarship, produced the best work

we have on the antebellum banking problem. His *Banks and Politics in America From the Revolution to the Civil War*, like the naive inter-pretation that it demolished, Arthur M. Schlesinger's *Age of Jackson*, received the Pulitzer Prize, an honor that was to come to books on economic and business history with greater frequency than before the war. Ham-mond, in his explanation of the early demise of central banking in America, relied upon the ignorance of Andrew Jackson and his followers of the true nature of banks and their role in society; but J. Willard Hurst has contributed powerful studies of the evolution of American law that reveal a pragmatic insistence upon the "release of creative energy" as the chief shaper of government-business relations. Stanley Kutler has shown this pragmatic force to be more powerful than the combination of Chief Justice Marshall's Dartmouth College decision and the legal talents of Daniel Webster. But Morton Horwitz's prize-winning effort to slam the tiller back in the direction of public versus private interests found no lack of admirers.[17]

The reaction was not long in coming. The work of the revisionists pointed unmistakably towards the conclusion, however distant, that Progressive intervention in economic deci-sionmaking had been an intellectual failure and a social mistake. The opportunity thus presented to the representatives of both the far left and right was not missed. Gabriel Kolko breathlessly announced in two books that throughout the eras of indignation and opti-mism the capitalists had coolly manipulated their political power to capture the entire regu-latory process and not merely to defang it but with it to attain a degree of economic power that had always eluded their own efforts. Kolko's use of the evidence is typical of the "usable history" school, but it would have been nothing new to the Charles A. Beard of *An Economic Interpretation of the Constitution*. Paul MacAvoy applied the techniques of the "new" economic history to the question of the economic effects of the Interstate Commerce Act of 1887 in its initial years. The result

[16] George R. Taylor, *The Transportation Revolution* (1951); Edward C. Kirkland, *Industry Comes of Age* (1961); Oscar and Mary F. Handlin, *Commonwealth: Massachusetts 1774-1861* (1947); Louis Hartz, *Economic Policy and Democratic Thought* (1948), and Hartz, *The Liberal Tradition in America: An Inter-pretation of American Political Thought Since the Revolution* (1955), p. 62; Carter Goodrich, *Government Promotion of Canals and Railroads* (1960); Allan Nevins, *John D. Rockefeller, The Heroic Age of American Enterprise*, 2 vols. (1940), and *Study in Power: John D. Rockefeller, Industrialist and Philan-thropist*, 2 vols. (1953); Ralph and Muriel Hidy, *Pioneering in Big Business, 1882-1911* (1955), but see also Harold F. Wil-liamson and Arnold R. Daum, *The American Petroleum Indus-try, 1859-1899* (1959), for the industry-wide picture; Lee Benson, *Merchants, Farmers, and Railroads: Railroad Regula-tion and New York Politics, 1850-1887* (1955); Harry Scheiber, "The Road to Munn: Eminent Domain and the Concept of Public Interest in the State Courts," *Perspectives in American History* 5 (1971):327-402; George H. Miller, *Railroads and the Granger Laws* (1971); Albro Martin, "The Troubled Subject of Railroad Regulation in the Gilded Age—A Reappraisal," *Journal of American History* 61 (Sept. 1974):339-371. Near the end of a long career in which he chronicled the western spirit of reform, the late Frederick Merk helped light the re-visionist fire with his "Eastern Antecedents of the Grangers," *Agricultural History* 23 (1949):1-8.

[17] Bray Hammond, *Banks and Politics in America From the Revolution to the Civil War* (1957); Arthur M. Schlesinger, Jr. *The Age of Jackson* (1945); J. Willard Hurst, *Law and the Con-ditions of Freedom in the Nineteenth-Century United State* (1956); Stanley I. Kutler, *Privilege and Creative Destruction* (1971), a study of the Charles River Bridge case; Morton Horwitz, *The Transformation of American Law, 1780-1860* (1977).

eemed to support Kolko's thesis and was widely acclaimed, but in the cold light of dawn it has failed to pass muster as history, as all such applications of deductive reasoning must fail. George Hilton, a laissez-faire economist of the "Chicago school" and a distinguished transportation specialist, saw in the Kolko thesis not proof that there is no salvation for industrial man outside the socialist church, but rather support for his belief that railroad men used their political power to cartelize their industry and frustrate the invisible hand of Adam Smith. This alienation of the right as well as the left from statist America is one of the most striking features of our times. Its chief exponents have been George Stigler, perhaps the strongest adherent to neo-Smithianism, and Milton Friedman, who looks even more hopefully to monetarist theory than to laissez-faire market mechanics for salvation.[18]

If the evidence that modern business has developed an independence of the state and its ministrations has infuriated many observers, the evidence of its independence of the flag has confounded the theorists of economic imperialism. At almost the very moment some historians were recycling the simplistic Leninist view of imperialism as the tool of a capitalist system, not only American corporations but more and more European and Japanese firms as well were creating the phenomenon of multinationalism. Since then Mira Wilkins has cataloged the extent of the movement and Raymond Vernon has demonstrated how little it has depended upon political hegemony. None of this, according to Robert L. Beisner, would have been any surprise to many eminently hardheaded Victorians, among them Andrew Carnegie.[19]

[18] Gabriel Kolko, *Railroads and Regulation, 1877-1916* (1965), and *Triumph of Conservatism: A Reinterpretation of American History, 1900-1916* (1963); Paul W. MacAvoy, *The Economic Effects of Regulation: The Trunk-Line Railroad Cartels and the Interstate Commerce Commission Before 1900* (1965); George W. Hilton, "The Consistency of the Interstate Commerce Act," *Journal of Law and Economics* 9 (Oct. 1966):87-113, which suggests that a need to see consistency in the political acts of mere mortals over long periods of time is one thing that distinguishes economists from historians; for a discussion of the inanity of the "capture theory" of government regulation, see James Q. Wilson, "The Dead Hand of Regulation," *The Public Interest* 25 (Fall 1971):46-49; Milton Friedman and Anna J. Schwartz, *A Monetary History of the United States, 1867-1960* (1963), is a magisterial study of the financial policies of the federal government and their effect on the American economy, in monetarist terms.

[19] William Appleman Williams, *The Tragedy of American Diplomacy* (1962); Walter LaFeber, *The New Empire* (1963);

It was Richard Hofstadter, however, who generated the greatest chorus of reaction, with his celebrated study *The Age of Reform*. In a glass that had been lately scoured, he saw the populist revolt as a provincial, materialistic, ignorant, and temporary aberration of Great Plains farmers whose defection from the mainstream of American philosophy lasted no longer than the blizzards, droughts, and low Liverpool prices for wheat that had produced it. He was almost as hard on the progressives, whom he saw primarily as small-town businessmen and professionals who were profoundly alienated by the vast and concentrated economic power that burst upon their comfortable world at the turn of the century. The incongruences in the relations between government and business during the administrations of Theodore Roosevelt, Taft, and Wilson, in Hofstadter's view, were reflected in the fatuous yearning of these provincial merchants, lawyers, bankers, and clergymen to recreate the world of the little man which, if it had ever really existed, was no more.[20]

The reaction has been massive, but the best-focused reaction was not to what Hofstadter said about the progressives, who finally have begun to bore historians of both the right and the left, but to his treatment of the populists. Two works published more than a decade apart stand out. Norman Pollack reacted by offering populism as a genuine American socialist movement that was aborted by the kinds of enemies that such movements have faced everywhere. He did not appear to realize that government ownership of basic industries, notably the railroads, was a frequently hurled threat during the age of reform that most people took no more seriously than a bad little boy's repeated threats to run away from home. More recently, Lawrence Goodwyn pumped up a good dissertation on the Southern Farmers' Alliance to a bulky polemic that insists that the alliance, especially in its most vital or Texas form, offered in its cooperative movement a true democratic alternative to the emerging industrial society. It may well be true, as Goodwyn insists, that the populist

Robert L. Beisner, *Twelve Against Empire: The Anti-Imperialists* (1968); Mira Wilkins, *American Business Abroad From the Colonial Era to 1914* (1970), and *The Maturing of Multinational Enterprise: American Business Abroad From 1914 to 1970* (1974); Raymond Vernon, *Storm Over the Multinationals: The Real Issues* (1977).

[20] Richard Hofstadter, *The Age of Reform* (1955).

star was bigger and brighter in Texas than elsewhere, but the case against the viability of the cooperative movement is very strong, and Goodwyn's tendency to deal with opposing views via the argumentum ad hominem is a serious weakness. Pollack and Goodwyn's efforts at history as what-might-have-been have been popular in our wistful times. More enduring, however, may be views of history like Lewis L. Gould's, which sees it as "the logic of the actual"; this, in Leonard Krieger's words, is the essence of the historical method. Americans of nearly all callings accepted the new industrial state, Gould says, and wanted positive measures, like a protective tariff and sound money, to make it work; and therein lay the failure of populism and the Democracy, and Republican victory.[21]

The history of government-business relations was a shambles by the late 1960s, the forces of massive intervention having fought the free-market forces to a draw. It was a juncture at which a sensible pragmatism that seeks to judge Americans' past ideas of the proper relationship between government and business in terms of their actual fruits might find a toehold. Indeed, historians should blush at the fact that after 150 years of government intervention in economic decisionmaking, and after a decade during which "regulation" has metastasized into every cell of the body politic, we have made scarcely any progress in assessing how well the forces we have unleashed have served us.

Several studies, however, signaled the arrival of an era of disillusionment that has been confirmed in the "deregulation" movement. Ernest Williams has shown that Interstate Commerce Commission policies prevented a rational integration of rail and truck transportation, a tragedy the proportions of which become greater with each rise in oil prices. John R. Meyer has reached similar conclusions. Stanley Caine demonstrated that if Wisconsin progressives wanted a railroad commission in 1905 that would slash railroad rates, then their commission was a failure, and their progressive "reform," a myth. Now that Elliot Brownlee has demonstrated how dearly the wage

earners of Wisconsin paid for the destructive effects of the state's corporation income tax, the once-sacred "Wisconsin idea" of scientific legislation is on the historical ropes. In the same pragmatic vein, I reported that federal railroad regulation in this period had amounted to de facto price fixing in this single industry at a time of rapid inflation, that the carriers' ability to raise fresh capital from retained earnings was therefore destroyed, and the spirit of enterprise so ravaged in the process that the railroads entered the era of decline which is their most familiar historical feature. Ellis Hawley has forced all but the most enthusiastic social engineers to face the conclusion that a thoroughgoing antimonopoly program is as politically unacceptable in America as a policy of benign neglect. And more recently, Robert Bork has waded into the Byzantine mess we call antitrust policy with a well-sharpened meat ax that may further encourage reform of a regulatory dissipation that, for the first time in its ninety-year history, promises to become truly debilitating.[22]

Strongly supporting the new era of disillusionment, if not actually a part of it, have been two studies of American business institutions that possess the vitality that the old school of institutional economics aimed at but so rarely achieved. Adolf A. Berle, Jr., capped his earlier work on the rise of the professional manager with *Power Without Property*, which demonstrated that only the form, and not the substance, of the earlier age of entrepreneurship had changed. Retained corporate profits, Berle noted, were now the chief source of risk capital in the modern business enterprise, and they are as critical to economic growth now as distributed profits and sheaves of stock certificates were before professional management took hold. If Berle is the most influential voice for the public policy implications of the age of

---

[21] Norman Pollack, *The Populist Response to Industrial America* (1962); Lawrence Goodwyn, *Democratic Promise: The Populist Moment in America* (1976); Lewis L. Gould, "The Republican Search for a National Majority," H. Wayne Morgan, ed., *The Gilded Age* (rev. ed., 1970), pp. 171-187.

[22] Ernest W. Williams, Jr., *The Regulation of Rail-Motor Rate Competition* (1958); John R. Meyer and Alexander L. Morton, "A Better Way to Run the Railroads," *Harvard Business Review* 52 (July-Aug. 1974); Stanley P. Caine, *The Myth of a Progressive Reform: Railroad Regulation in Wisconsin, 1903-1910* (1970); W. Elliot Brownlee, Jr., *Progressivism and Economic Growth: The Wisconsin Income Tax, 1911-1929* (1974); Albro Martin, *Enterprise Denied: Origins of the Decline of American Railroads, 1897-1917* (1917); Ellis W. Hawley, *The New Deal and the Problem of Monopoly* (1966); Robert H. Bork, *The Antitrust Paradox: A Policy at War With Itself* (1978). A more conventional study is Hans B. Thorelli, *Federal Antitrust Policy* (1954).

managerial capitalism, as Alfred D. Chandler, Jr., has called it, Chandler himself is the foremost historian of the technological and economic forces that created modern big business organization. It well may be that Chandler's Pulitzer Prize-winning study *The Visible Hand* will do as much to guide our understanding of the economy into the twenty-first century as John Maynard Keynes did to drag it into the twentieth.[23]

Where does this leave us on the subject of the history of government-business relations? In a sense, it leaves us about where we were in 1900. But this should not depress us. When we consider how the eras of optimism and confident reformism smothered the subject in an aura of professionalism and castrated it with a puzzling insistence that power to make business decisions could safely be separated from the responsibility for those decisions, it is a giant step forward just to be back in 1900. Americans appear to be about to realize that great economic power is not only fundamental to the good life but is as much a part of the American political process as the election of government officials. As with the enterprises that gave rise to the problem in the first place, the real economic performance of regulation, if we are to have it, must be the only criterion of its success. This point is made with great effectiveness by Thomas K. McCraw in an influential article on regulation, in which he notes, "If, as seems likely, the inherent nature of an industry is the most important single context in which regulators must operate, then the range of policies open to them has been narrower than many observers have hitherto believed."[24]

The work of understanding what government-business relations ought realistically to achieve has barely begun, but it is a work to which historians must make a fundamental contribution. Economists and political scientists will continue to lead in forming policy, but they have usually operated in the historical dark, and the assumptions they have made about how we got where we are have served them poorly. Reinhold Niebuhr went on to say that contentment lies only in the ability to rise above the incongruences in the human experience. Perhaps the best way to do this is to accept the fact that the social goals attainable by the intervention of government in the economic life of the people are remarkably limited in number and often incongruent. "I have no practical criterion except what the crowd wants," Mr. Justice Holmes wrote Sir Frederick Pollock as the government was declaring war on the railroads in 1910. "Personally, I bet that the crowd, if it knew more, wouldn't want what it does."[25] □

[23] Adolf A. Berle, Jr., *Power Without Property* (1959); Alfred D. Chandler, Jr., *The Visible Hand: The Managerial Revolution in American Business* (1977).

[24] Thomas K. McCraw, "Regulation in America: A Review Article," *Business History Review* 49 (Summer 1975):159-183.
[25] Mark DeWolfe Howe, ed., *The Holmes-Pollock Letters: The Correspondence of Mr. Justice Holmes and Sir Frederick Pollock, 1874-1932* (1961), p. 163.

President Eisenhower, Economic Policy, and the 1960 Presidential Election

ANN MARI MAY

This article examines economic policy in the Eisenhower years and the president's role in the 1960 election. I measure the impact of changes in fiscal policy on real GNP and show that policy in 1959 was unusually contractionary and cannot be dismissed as merely evidence of Eisenhower's fiscal conservatism.

Adlai Stevenson once described the "liberal hour" as that time before presidential elections when "even the most obsolete Republican becomes momentarily reconciled to the machine age."[1] For the most fiscally conservative president of the postwar period the liberal hour never arrived. In the 1956 and 1960 presidential elections President Dwight D. Eisenhower refused to engage in expansionary policies to enhance his or his party's chances for re-election.

Eisenhower's refusal to stimulate the economy before either presidential election raises serious questions about the validity of the political business cycle hypothesis.[2] According to this hypothesis, presidents will engage in contractionary policies in the early years of their terms to reduce inflation, then use expansionary policies before the presidential election to reduce unemployment and reap the electoral rewards of an expanding economy.

The economic policies of the Eisenhower administration provide a particularly intriguing case in the study of political business cycles because Eisenhower's policies were inconsistent with the general political business cycle pattern. Whereas real disposable income per capita increased in eight of eleven presidential and congressional election years during the administrations of Harry Truman, John Kennedy, Lyndon Johnson, Richard Nixon, and Gerald Ford, it declined in every election year during the Eisenhower administration.[3] As Stephen Weatherford points out, Eisenhower provides the deviant case

The Journal of Economic History, Vol. L, No. 2 (June 1990). © The Economic History Association. All rights reserved. ISSN 0022-0507.

The author is Assistant Professor of Economics, University of Nebraska, Lincoln, NE 68588. She would like to thank Martha Olney for helpful comments on an earlier draft.

[1] Adlai E. Stevenson, *Major Campaign Speeches of Adlai E. Stevenson* (New York, 1953), pp. 31–32.

[2] For example, see William D. Nordhaus, "The Political Business Cycle," *Review of Economic Studies*, 42 (Apr. 1975), pp. 169–90; and Edward R. Tufte, *Political Control of the Economy* (Princeton, 1978).

[3] Tufte, *Political Control*, p. 15.

because "conditions were ripe for a political business cycle in 1954, 1958, and 1960, yet he explicitly abjured the temptation."[4]

While Eisenhower had little need to stimulate the economy in 1956 with a solid lead in the polls over the Democratic front runner Adlai Stevenson, Vice President Richard Nixon could certainly have benefited from at least a momentary lapse in Eisenhower's fiscal frugality in 1960. Not only was the unemployment rate higher in 1960 than 1956, but the economy appeared to be sliding into another recession.[5] Moreover, voter surveys from August 1959 through August 1960 showed Kennedy and Nixon virtually tied in the polls.[6]

There are, of course, various interpretations of Eisenhower's economic policy actions before the 1960 presidential election. Economists have generally dismissed them as evidence of his unflinching fiscal conservatism.[7] Yet historians have consistently remarked upon the seeming ambivalence of Eisenhower toward Nixon's bid for the presidency in 1960.[8]

This article examines fiscal policy during the Eisenhower administration and explores President Eisenhower's role in the 1960 election. Impact measures are developed that provide a more complete picture of policy changes and allow us to assess their effect on economic activity and to understand the complex array of factors influencing Eisenhower's policies before the 1960 election.

OVERVIEW OF FISCAL POLICY IN THE EISENHOWER YEARS

Reflecting upon the 1960 presidential campaign Nixon later wrote: "In a losing campaign, only the candidate is responsible for the tactics that led to defeat."[9] Henry Cabot Lodge apparently agreed. Upon viewing the first Nixon-Kennedy debate Lodge erupted: "That son-of-a-bitch just lost us the election!"[10] At other times, however, Nixon expressed the belief that the outcome of the election was the result of something beyond his control—the state of the economy.[11]

The downturn which began officially in the second quarter of 1960 was

---

[4] Stephen Weatherford, "The Interplay of Ideology and Advice in Economic Policy-Making: The Case of Political Business Cycles," *Journal of Politics*, 49 (Nov. 1987), p. 932.

[5] The average annual unemployment rate in 1956 was 4.0 percent compared to an average annual rate of 5.4 percent in 1960. See the *Economic Report of the President*, 1988 (Washington, DC, 1988), p. 292.

[6] George H. Gallup, *The Gallup Poll Public Opinion: 1935–71* (New York, 1972), pp. 1622, 1642, 1682.

[7] For example, see Herbert Stein, *The Fiscal Revolution in America* (Chicago, 1969).

[8] See Stephen E. Ambrose, *Eisenhower: The President* (New York, 1984); and Stephen E. Ambrose, *Nixon: The Education of a Politician 1913–62* (New York, 1987).

[9] Richard M. Nixon, *Six Crises* (New York, 1962), p. 294.

[10] Fawn M. Brodie, *Richard Nixon: The Shaping of His Character* (Cambridge, MA, 1983), p. 427.

[11] Nixon, *Six Crises*, p. 310.

certainly not a complete surprise to administration officials. In February 1960 Arthur Burns, chairman of the Council of Economic Advisors during the first Eisenhower administration, advised the vice president that the economy was heading for another contraction and suggested that "steps be taken immediately" to increase federal expenditures and loosen credit.[12] Burns's advice was relayed to Eisenhower and discussed at the next Cabinet meeting.

Eisenhower did not take the advice. According to Nixon, the administration was unwilling to act to stimulate the economy until the downturn became more severe.[13] In subsequent quarters, however, unemployment increased from an already high 5.2 percent in the second quarter to 6.2 percent in the fourth quarter of 1960, and real GNP declined in the second, third, and fourth quarters.[14] The Eisenhower administration chose to deal with the economic downturn by ignoring it. Throughout 1960, until his final budget message in January 1961, Eisenhower warned of the hazards of inflation and promised not to "undermine our strength as a nation through deficits."[15]

Although Eisenhower was often accused of having a balanced budget fetish, he was, after all, a postwar Republican who, at least in principle, was willing to accept budget deficits during recessions.[16] While the actual federal budget was in surplus when economic activity was expanding, it moved to a deficit during the three recessions of 1953–1954, 1957–1958, and 1960, and there was no attempt to raise taxes to offset the reduction in revenue associated with the downturn.[17] In addition, although fiscal policy became more contractionary during the 1953–1954 recession, the full-employment budget showed a rather large deficit in early 1953. Likewise, while the full-employment budget was in surplus during the entire 1957–1958 recession, its size declined from $7.2 billion in the third quarter of 1957 to $2.4 billion by the fourth quarter of 1958.

Most interesting, however, is the full-employment budget for 1960. The full-employment budget surplus rose to $15.1 billion in the fourth quarter of 1960, its highest level of the entire Eisenhower term. Moreover, as the economy slid into recession, fiscal policy became tighter. The full-employment budget went from a surplus of $4.6 billion in 1958 to a surplus of $14.7 billion in 1960.

[12] Ibid., pp. 309–10.

[13] Ibid., p. 310.

[14] Quarterly data from Fairmodel macroeconometric model, July 1985.

[15] *Public Papers of the Presidents of the United States, Dwight D. Eisenhower,* 1960–61 (Washington, DC, 1961), p. 935.

[16] Stein, *The Fiscal Revolution,* pp. 281–84.

[17] All quarterly figures on the actual federal budget and the full-employment budget are reported in Keith Carlson, "Estimates of the High-Employment Budget: 1947–1967," Federal Reserve Bank of St. Louis, *Review,* 49 (June 1967), pp. 10–11.

May

IMPACT MEASURES OF FISCAL POLICY

While the full-employment budget provides a better measure of the thrust of fiscal policy than the actual federal budget, impact measures provide additional insight into the direction, magnitude, and composition of the changes in fiscal policy.[18] These measures are generated using a macroeconometric model to estimate the impact of changes in fiscal policy in a given quarter on real GNP four quarters in the future.[19]

The aggregate fiscal policy impact measure is generated by comparing simulated real GNP *with* the actual changes in fiscal policy that occurred in a particular quarter against simulated real GNP *without* them. The influence of fiscal policy in time t on real GNP Y, in period $t + j$ is thus:

$$F_y^j(t) = Y_{t+j} - Y^*_{t+j} \qquad j \geq 0$$

Ten fiscal policy variables are held constant in the Y^* simulation. They are real federal government purchases of goods, personal income tax rate, profit tax rate, indirect business tax rate, employee social security tax rate, employer social security tax rate, civilian jobs, military jobs, transfer payments to households, and grants-in-aid to state and local governments.[20]

The results presented in Table 1 indicate that fiscal policy was highly contractionary in Eisenhower's first term. Although fiscal policy in 1953 was expansionary, increasing estimated real GNP by $8.8 billion in 1954, this largely reflected the influence of the Truman administration.[21] The aggregate impact measures for 1954 reveal that fiscal policy was exceedingly contractionary, reducing estimated real GNP by $25.2 billion in 1955. This represents the largest yearly decline of the Eisenhower tenure. Moreover, fiscal policy was contractionary in every quarter of 1954—the only year in which this is true.

While contractionary policy in the early half of Eisenhower's first term is consistent with the political business cycle hypothesis, the impact measures do not indicate that fiscal policy became expansionary before the presidential election of 1956. While fiscal policy was more expansionary in 1955 and 1956 than it was in 1954, it still reduced estimated real GNP by $5.1 billion in 1956 and $490 million in 1957.

[18] The method used to estimate the impact measures is presented in Alan S. Blinder and Stephen M. Goldfeld, "New Measures of Fiscal and Monetary Policy, 1958–1973," *American Economic Review*, 66 (Dec. 1976), pp. 780–96.

[19] The four-quarter time horizon is used here because it represents a realistic impact lag and because the dynamic properties of the macroeconometric model produce highly correlated two-, four-, and six-quarter impact measures.

[20] See Ray C. Fair, *Specification, Estimation, and Analysis of Macroeconometric Models* (Cambridge, MA, 1984).

[21] When Eisenhower took office in 1953, government agencies were instructed to review their budgets and make cuts where possible. See the *Public Papers of the Presidents of the United States, Dwight D. Eisenhower*, 1953 (Washington, DC, 1960), pp. 53–54.

TABLE 1
AGGREGATE FISCAL POLICY IMPACT MEASURES ON REAL GNP
(billions of dollars)

		Quarters			Yearly Total
Year	First	Second	Third	Fourth	
1953	$ 3.885	$ 2.811	$-0.767	$ 2.852	$ 8.781
1954	-11.328	-8.199	-3.482	-2.177	-25.187
1955	-1.934	-3.459	2.566	-2.233	-5.059
1956	-0.400	1.360	-3.111	1.661	-0.490
1957	6.987	1.995	-1.051	2.146	10.078
1958	5.168	6.083	1.800	2.472	15.524
1959	-6.674	-1.105	-1.989	0.380	-9.388
1960	-4.927	2.162	2.375	2.524	2.134

Notes: The impact measure shows the effect of changes in fiscal policy on real GNP four quarters later. For example, fiscal policy in the first quarter of 1953 was expansionary, causing estimated real GNP in the first quarter of 1954 to be $3.88 billion higher than it would have been otherwise.
Sources: The impact measures were generated using the Fairmodel macroeconometric model, version 2.0, July 1985.

In contrast, the aggregate impact measures indicate that fiscal policy was quite expansionary in 1957 and 1958, increasing estimated real GNP by $10.1 and $15.5 billion in succeeding years. However, more interesting is the result which shows that fiscal policy in 1959 was highly contractionary, causing estimated real GNP to decline by $9.4 billion in the presidential election year of 1960. Furthermore, although fiscal policy was moderately expansionary in 1960, most of the expansionary policies occurred late in the year and would not have had an impact on the economy until after the election.

The disaggregated impact measures provide more detailed information concerning fiscal policy changes. These measures are generated in a similar fashion to the aggregate ones and allow us to isolate the impact of a single policy variable on real GNP.

The disaggregated measures in Table 2 reveal that real federal purchases of goods were indeed highly contractionary in 1954, causing estimated real GNP to decline by $28.3 billion. In addition, changes in military jobs exerted a contractionary influence early in Eisenhower's first term, reducing estimated real GNP $1.5 billion and $2.2 billion in 1954 and 1955. The reduction in federal purchases of goods and in military jobs reflects the decreased spending following the Korean conflict as well as the Eisenhower administration's attempt to reduce nondefense expenditures. In contrast, changes in transfer payments to households, personal income taxes, and indirect business taxes somewhat offset the contractionary influence of federal government purchases of goods.

In 1954 transfer payments to households increased estimated real GNP by a rather large $3.3 billion. Although this may appear to indicate

TABLE 2

DISAGGREGATED FISCAL POLICY IMPACT MEASURES ON REAL GNP

(yearly totals in billions of dollars)

Fiscal Policy	1953	1954	1955	1956	1957	1958	1959	1960
Federal Government Purchases of Goods	$ 8.390	$−28.304	$−2.819	$ 0.013	$ 3.701	$ 8.381	$−6.606	$ 0.428
Personal Income Tax Rate	0.164	0.994	−0.156	−0.385	0.065	0.306	−0.328	−0.369
Profit Tax Rate	0.097	0.118	−0.059	0.074	0.028	−0.036	0.009	0.190
Indirect Business Tax Rate	0.220	0.959	−0.232	−0.518	0.681	0.064	−0.119	−0.091
Employee Social Security Tax Rate	−0.032	−0.283	−0.070	−0.114	−0.265	0.019	−0.290	−0.489
Employer Social Security Tax Rate	0.057	−0.119	−0.042	−0.024	−0.048	0.062	−0.219	−0.213
Civilian Jobs	−0.961	−0.311	0.053	0.118	−0.353	0.153	0.297	−0.020
Military Jobs	−0.174	−1.524	−2.179	−0.811	−0.618	−0.742	−0.669	0.001
Transfer Payments to Households	1.120	3.332	0.398	1.626	4.163	3.724	1.139	2.639
Grants-in-aid to State and Local Governments	0.000	0.004	−0.002	−0.001	0.000	0.011	−0.009	0.003

Sources: See Table 1.

that discretionary fiscal policy was expansionary, it reflects instead the influence of nondiscretionary changes resulting from the recession of 1953–1954.[22]

Changes in the personal income tax rate do, however, reflect discretionary fiscal policy, and the 1954 changes exerted the largest expansionary influence of any of the Eisenhower years—increasing estimated real GNP by $994 million in 1955. This expansion does not, however, reflect countercyclical policy on the part of the Eisenhower administration. The reduction in personal income taxes was previously enacted by Congress and rather reluctantly signed into law by Eisenhower.[23]

Although the reduction in personal income taxes was offset somewhat by an increase in social security taxes in 1954, a reduction in excise taxes enacted by Congress and signed into law in March 1954 also exerted an expansionary impact on the economy. Changes in the excise tax rate during 1954 expanded estimated real GNP by $959 million in 1955—exerting the largest expansionary impact for that variable in any of the years reported. Although the reduction in excise taxes was instigated by Republicans in Congress as an antirecession action, the administration did not oppose the bill, given the state of the economy.

[22] Whereas other fiscal policy variables used here largely reflect discretionary changes in policy, transfer payments to households reflect both discretionary and nondiscretionary changes due to automatic stabilizers.

[23] See the *Economic Report of the President*, 1955 (Washington, DC, 1955), p. 19.

This result confirms Herbert Stein's observation that the "excise tax cut was the largest stimulating fiscal action of 1954 which would not have been taken if there had been no recession."[24]

The disaggregated measures provide further evidence that the contractionary policies before the 1956 presidential election were no accident. The largest expansionary influence of 1955 and 1956 came from transfer payments to households, which largely reflects nondiscretionary policy changes. All other changes in 1955, except that in civilian employment, exerted a contractionary influence on real GNP in the presidential election year of 1956.

Fiscal policy of 1957 and 1958 appears to have been quite expansionary, causing estimated real GNP to increase $10.1 and $15.5 billion. Although a significant proportion of the expansion was the result of increases in transfer payments to households and reflects the effect of automatic stabilizers, federal spending on goods was also expansionary.[25] Federal expenditures were buoyed up by an increase in the purchase of farm commodities for farm price supports, acceleration in defense contract spending, and an increase in highway expenditures.[26]

While fiscal policy was expansionary in 1957 and 1958, it became unquestionably contractionary in 1959. The disaggregated measures indicate that federal purchases of goods in 1959 were such that estimated real GNP would decline by $6.6 billion in 1960—the largest decline due to purchases for any year except the highly contractionary one of 1954. The decline in federal purchases of goods in part reflected a substantial reduction in defense-related expenditures.[27] In addition, an increase in social security taxes in both 1959 and 1960 also depressed estimated real GNP.

In 1960 changes in federal government purchases of goods were more expansionary than in 1959, increasing estimated real GNP by a modest $428 million. Most of the expansionary policies, however, came in the third quarter of 1960. Furthermore, the disaggregated figures show that increases in transfer payments to households provided most of the expansionary influence. Transfer payments to households in 1960 increased estimated real GNP by $2.6 billion, up from $1.1 billion the previous year due to the slowdown in economic activity in 1960.

The fiscal policy impact measures, along with the full-employment budget figures, provide interesting grist for our analysis of economic policy in the 1950s. Both the full-employment budget and the impact measures indicate that the policies of the Eisenhower administration do

---

[24] Stein, *The Fiscal Revolution*, p. 305.

[25] A proportion of the increase in transfer payments to households was due to the legislative extension of unemployment compensation payments.

[26] See Wilfred Lewis, *Federal Fiscal Policy in the Postwar Recessions* (Washington, DC, 1962), pp. 208–13.

[27] Ibid., pp. 237–39.

not correspond to the political business cycle pattern of contraction in the early years of the presidential term and expansion before the presidential election. Moreover, the fiscal policy impact measures show more clearly the highly contractionary character of policy in 1954 and 1959. While the contractionary policies of 1954 reflect the transition from a wartime to a peacetime economy, the economic policies before the 1960 election are less easily explained.

THEMES OF CONTINUITY AND DISCONTINUITY

Economists have traditionally dismissed the policies preceding the 1960 presidential election as evidence of Eisenhower's ongoing fiscal conservatism. While Eisenhower's undeniable commitment to Republican principles and his relentless budget surplus rhetoric made him appear to be "the rock of fiscal probity," the policies before the 1960 election cannot be dismissed as evidence of his conservatism.[28]

Throughout his tenure the president presented an unusually consistent theme reaffirming traditional Republican values and goals, chief among which was a belief in a minimal role for government in the economic sphere. For Eisenhower, this minimal role was inspired by the belief in the efficiency of the private sector in allocating resources and promoting economic growth.[29] Minimal taxation was desirable so as not to stifle individual initiative or put undue pressure on financial markets.[30] Moreover, the one goal which resonates throughout Eisenhower's papers is that of achieving economic growth without inflation. Maintaining a budget surplus was the primary mechanism through which low inflation was to be achieved.

Eisenhower's willingness to endure budget deficits became apparent during the 1953–1954 recession and again during the 1957–1958 recession. While it is no doubt true that a budget surplus had monumental significance to Eisenhower, as Stein points out, "the desirability of balancing the budget was not given by some eternal principle, but depended on economic conditions which would vary."[31]

In addition, the growing surpluses of the actual and full-employment budgets occurred in years when inflation became more problematic. In 1955, 1956, and 1957 the rate of inflation was above 3 percent, up from 1.6 percent in 1953 and 1954, and the full-employment budget surplus increased from $3.9 billion in 1955 to $6.4 billion in 1958.[32] Thus, Eisenhower's fiscal policy from 1953 through 1958 reflected consistent but flexible fiscal conservatism. The size of the budget surplus increased

---

[28] Jonathan Hughes, *American Economic Growth* (Glenview, 1987), p. 513.
[29] *Economic Report of the President*, 1956 (Washington, DC, 1956), pp. 72–79.
[30] *Public Papers of the Presidents*, 1960–61, p. 40.
[31] Stein, *The Fiscal Revolution*, p. 283.
[32] See the *Economic Report of the President*, 1988, p. 253.

with inflation but not during periods of recession. Fiscal policy after 1958, however, was quite different.

Both the actual and the full-employment budget figures indicate that fiscal policy became quite contractionary in 1959 and 1960. The actual federal budget went from a deficit of $10.3 billion in 1958 to a surplus of $3.4 billion in 1960 while the full-employment budget went from a surplus of $4.6 billion in 1958 to a surplus of $14.7 billion in 1960.[33] The impact measures demonstrate that fiscal policy became exceedingly contractionary in 1959, depressing estimated real GNP by $9.4 billion in 1960.

This severely contractionary fiscal policy is not consistent with the flexible fiscal conservatism of the early Eisenhower years. Whereas increases in the budget surplus were associated with increases in inflation from 1955 through 1958, as it moderated in 1958, 1959, and 1960, the surplus continued to expand significantly. Furthermore, while increases in the unemployment rate brought about more moderate fiscal policy in the first six years of the Eisenhower administration, increases in unemployment in 1959 and 1960 were met with a more contractionary policy.

It might, of course, be argued that Eisenhower was unaware of the extent to which fiscal policy was contractionary in the period before the 1960 election. After all, the full-employment budget was a new concept in the late 1950s. Nevertheless, estimates of the full-employment budget were publicly available in 1960. According to Stein, staff members of the Council of Economic Advisors presented estimates of the full-employment budget in 1960 and argued that the enlarged surplus was contributing to the sluggishness of the economy.[34]

Because fiscal policy is ultimately the result of the interaction of congressional as well as presidential action, it might be argued that fiscal policy reflected congressional rather than presidential influences. However, the contractionary fiscal policy in 1960 reflected the administration's conservative impulse more than the will of Congress. As Wilfred Lewis points out: "Congress showed far less enthusiasm for expenditure restraint in the 1960 election year than it had the year before, and appropriations were subsequently increased in virtually every category except foreign aid."[35]

Nor can it be argued that monetary policy was to provide additional stimulus to offset contractionary fiscal policy. In the period before the 1960 election, monetary policy was also exceedingly contractionary.[36] Furthermore, there appears to have been more agreement than dis-

[33] Carlson, "Estimates of the High-Employment Budget," pp. 10–11.

[34] Stein, *The Fiscal Revolution*, p. 364.

[35] Lewis, *Federal Fiscal Policy*, p. 240.

[36] See Milton Friedman and Anna J. Schwartz, *A Monetary History of the United States, 1867–1960* (Princeton, 1963), pp. 617–20.

agreement between the administration and the Federal Reserve on the thrust of monetary policy during this period. According to George Bach, "monetary authorities at the Federal Reserve by and large shared the White House view."[37]

While economists have traditionally focused on Eisenhower's ideology as an explanation for the economic policies surrounding the 1960 presidential election, historians and others have often focused on the ambivalence of Eisenhower toward Nixon's presidential campaign. Stephen Ambrose, perhaps the most thorough of Eisenhower's biographers, attributes his attitude, at least in part, to his complex and often antagonistic relationship with the vice president.[38]

Fueling the speculation about his limited endorsement of Nixon in 1960 were various public comments by Eisenhower. On the eve of the 1960 presidential election, in perhaps his most famous press conference, Eisenhower was asked repeatedly what decisions Nixon had participated in as vice president. The president finally remarked: "If you give me a week, I might think of one. I don't remember."[39] Two weeks earlier, when asked about Nixon's view on nuclear testing, Eisenhower remarked, "I can't recall what he has ever said specifically about nuclear underground testing."[40]

In reality, Eisenhower did very little to enhance the presidential prospects of Nixon and a great deal to jeopardize them. Under the guise of trying to further his vice president's career, Eisenhower suggested that Nixon take a Cabinet post to develop his administrative skills rather than remain on the ticket in 1956.[41] In 1959 Eisenhower suggested changing the structure of the administration to include two "Assistant Presidents"—one in foreign affairs and one in domestic affairs.[42] If, as Alben Barkley was fond of saying, the vice presidency wasn't worth a "bucket of warm spit," it would certainly be worth even less with this innovation.

Although Eisenhower did not dump Nixon in 1956 and did not pursue the "Assistant President" idea in 1959, he also did not help Nixon raise campaign funds or endorse his candidacy until after the Republican Convention had nominated Nixon.[43] Eisenhower remained a distant relative throughout most of the 1960 campaign. According to Nixon, it was Eisenhower who decided when it would be time to "move into action."[44] According to Eisenhower, however, it was Nixon who

[37] George L. Bach, *Making Monetary and Fiscal Policy* (Washington, DC, 1971), p. 102.
[38] Ambrose, *Nixon*, p. 509.
[39] *Public Papers of the Presidents*, 1960–61, pp. 657–58.
[40] Ibid., p. 626.
[41] For the official and unofficial story of this event, see Dwight D. Eisenhower, *Waging Peace* (Garden City, 1965), pp. 6–9; and Ambrose, *Eisenhower*, pp. 292–93.
[42] Ambrose, *Nixon*, p. 511.
[43] Ambrose, *Eisenhower*, p. 512. Also see *Public Papers of the Presidents*, 1960–61, p. 144.
[44] Nixon, *Six Crises*, p. 349.

"suggested he stay out of the active campaign until the last few days."[45] This, of course, was not the first time they had disagreed on who was making decisions.

CONCLUDING REMARKS

The Eisenhower presidency provides a compelling counterexample to the political business cycle hypothesis that presidents will manipulate the economy to enhance their re-election prospects. While Eisenhower engaged in highly contractionary policies upon entering office, he did not engage in significantly expansionary policies before the 1956 and 1960 presidential elections.

Economists have generally been satisfied with attributing these economic policies to Eisenhower's fiscal conservatism. For many, "Eisenhower epitomized the chief executive who sets an economic policy course early in the administration and holds tightly" to its central tenets.[46] The evidence presented here, however, indicates that the highly contractionary fiscal policy before the 1960 presidential election is not consistent with the flexible fiscal conservatism exhibited throughout much of the Eisenhower presidency.

Instead, the evidence on fiscal policy is consistent with those interpretations that view fiscal policy before the 1960 election as an anomaly—possibly influenced by Eisenhower's relationship with Nixon. As Ambrose has observed: "Time and again, Eisenhower could have done things that Nixon urged on him that could have swayed votes, but he always refused."[47] It is clear that for Eisenhower as for other presidents, ideology alone provides an insufficient explanation for policy actions which must be understood in the context of other political, economic, social, and, perhaps, personal factors.

[45] Ambrose, *Nixon*, p. 558.
[46] Weatherford, "The Interplay of Ideology," p. 944.
[47] Ambrose, *Nixon*, p. 513.

THE BUSINESS ELITE AND FOREIGN POLICY

DAVID S. MCLELLAN AND CHARLES E. WOODHOUSE

University of California, Riverside

INTRODUCTION

THE PURPOSE OF THIS STUDY is to examine the foreign policy perspective of the American business elite. By "perspective" we mean the set of premises in terms of which business leaders define America's situation with reference to the rest of the world and evaluate the courses of action to be taken in response. The sequence of foreign aid programs which has dominated the postwar landscape has challenged the business elite's conception of the way in which America's economic resources should be employed. By examining the way in which the business elite has reacted to these programs we can gain an insight into the process by which this elite exercises power over the making of foreign policy.

Part of this power process consists of carrying on the debate over specific foreign policy proposals within a framework of premises which have traditionally guided the thinking of American businessmen about the use of economic resources. So long as the participants feel obliged to argue in terms of these premises, this will limit the criteria by which policy alternatives are appraised. Therefore it is important at this point to specify these traditional premises and to indicate the basis for their persistence.

Given the history of businessmen as a status group in American society there is nothing exceptional about their incentive to influence the formulation of government policy. Economic development in the United States began under a constitution tailored to the needs of emergent mercantile and industrial interests. Governmental services and governmental economic controls have often been developed at the initiative of private interests and administered in close conjunction with private organizations. At the same time businessmen have learned to expect that government will take responsibility for securing people against economic deprivation and for regulating business in the interest of public welfare.

It is precisely within this context of pluralism that the sources of the businessmen's foreign policy perspective may be sought. The accommodation of business interests to the demands of social welfare has been fraught with controversy; in the process, businessmen have become sharply aware of the contrast between their interests and those of other groups and have had to defend business interests in ideological terms. As a consequence, the implications of alternative social and economic policies have come to be categorized in terms of mutually exclusive dichotomies: (1) the evils of government control have been contrasted with the virtues of private enterprise; and (2) the impersonal, self-regulating operation of the market system has been contrasted with the arbitrary application of social controls designed to serve purposes extraneous to the pursuit of economic self-interest. For a long time these dichotomies have constituted a stable part of the business elite's perspective on American domestic affairs. But with the onset of the cold war, and our consequent concern over the expansion of communism into countries beyond our borders, another set of categorical alternatives has entered the perspective of the business elite: (3) the contrast between our desire to avoid involvement in the domestic affairs of other countries, and the assumption that the American way of life is so inherently superior that every country, regardless of its cultural heritage, can benefit by emulating us.

In view of the well-established precedent for thinking in these terms, it could be anticipated that the business elite would appraise foreign policy on the basis of these categorical alternatives. However, in the course of debate over specific programs of foreign aid, a split has emerged which reflects a difference in perspective between two segments of the business elite. One group whom we shall call the "fundamentalists" appraises foreign economic policy in terms of a rigorous adherence to these traditional categories. The other group whom we shall call the "progressives" always manages to accept innovations in foreign economic policy without abandoning its belief in these traditional precepts. Members of both of these groups have high prestige and at different times they have enjoyed access to the centers of foreign policy decision-making.

To indicate the importance of this difference in perspective we shall analyze the positions each group has taken in testimony before Congressional committees and in recommendations submitted to the government pertaining to the enactment of the following major programs of postwar international economic policy:

1. The Bretton Woods Agreements Act and the British Loan Agreements
2. The European Recovery Program
3. Point Four
4. The Mutual Security Program
5. The International Finance Corporation
6. The Development Loan Fund

THE BRETTON WOODS AGREEMENTS AND THE BRITISH LOAN

The Bretton Woods Agreements Act and the Anglo-American Loan attempted to replace the defunct and defective mechanisms which traditionally regulated the international economy — the gold standard, free convertibility, and private investment — with new institutions. In the controversy which centered around these proposals we first see the emergence of an ideological division within the business elite — a division due to be exacerbated and sustained by subsequent efforts of the United States to take the lead in postwar international co-operation.

Among those who favored Bretton Woods and the Anglo-American Loan were groups having a direct stake in expanding United States trade and investment opportunities, and groups such as the National Planning Association and the Committee for Economic Development (CED). The latter organizations are representative of businessmen, generally big businessmen, who accept the increased role of government in the economy, possess an international outlook, are active in their local communities and professional organizations, are frequently consulted by the Administration or by Congress, and often serve as high government administrators. These groups exemplify the "progressive" perspective. Without their support it is doubtful whether the favorable testimony of other civic, religious, and trade-union associations would have secured adoption of Bretton Woods or the Anglo-American Loan.

Opposition to these new departures in American policy was spearheaded by a small but articulate group of congressmen, supported by the National Association of Manufacturers (NAM) and by publicists such as David Lawrence, Henry Hazlitt, and Henry Taylor, who distrusted and rejected the argument that the United States had to take an active role in international economic planning and foreign assistance. This group exemplifies the "fundamentalist" perspective.

"Progressives" and "fundamentalists" disagreed on practically every aspect of the Bretton Woods and British Loan Agreements. The bankers and traders, still smarting from their interwar experience with economic nationalism and monetary warfare, were acutely aware that failure to ratify these agreements would leave us isolated and vulnerable to "the worst depression that we have ever known, even worse than 1932 and 1933." [1]

In contrast to the bankers and businessmen who were virtually unanimous in their testimony that Europe, and especially England, were indispensable trading partners, Congressional "fundamentalists" adamantly refused to admit that the rest of the world might be important to American economic stability and prosperity. Instead they raised the spectre of "regimentation by an international bureaucracy" and the infringement of national sovereignty, to which the bankers and business spokesmen replied: "What have we had in the last 25 years? We have had the worst form of regimentation imaginable." [2]

Nevertheless it seemed immoral to the "fundamentalists" that American dollars should be employed "to keep Socialism going abroad" at the risk of undermining our own economy.[3] By contrast, the leading bankers — Burgess, Hemingway, McChesney Martin and others — deprecated the ideological issue and even argued that the loan "might be able to help the conservatives" by relieving Britain of the pressure of austerity.[4]

Thus America's postwar role in international economic affairs became the focus of two sharply contrasting perspectives, each destined to leave its imprint on subsequent American policy. For the "fundamentalists" life is a struggle and the competitive environment, in which the fit alone survive, is the only proper condition of existence. Reared in the American tradition of laissez-faire, this

---

[1] *Bretton Woods Agreements Act*, Hearings Before the House Committee on Banking and Currency, 79th Cong. 1st Sess., pp. 644–45. The following influential figures testified in behalf of the Bretton Woods Monetary Agreements, although sometimes with reservations about the Fund, and the British Loan: Randolph W. Burgess, National City Bank of New York; W. L. Hemingway, American Bankers Association; Charles Dewey, Chase National Bank; William McC. Martin, chairman, Export-Import Bank; Leon Fraser, president, First National Bank of New York; Leonard Ayres, vice-president, Cleveland Trust Co.; and Carl M. Wynne, president, Chicago Exports Managers Club. The only influential voice raised against both projects was that of Jesse Jones, former RFC administrator.

[2] *Ibid.*, p. 647.

[3] *Anglo-American Financial Agreement*, Hearings before the House Committee on Banking and Currency, 79th Cong. 2d Sess. (May and June, 1945), p. 395. As Representative Howard Buffett (Neb.-R.) summed it up: "The making of this loan, at this time, would remove the last sizeable barrier to the hog trough philosophy."

[4] *Bretton Woods*, p. 389.

group felt outraged by economic planning of the sort envisaged by the Bretton Woods Agreements, and "worthless" loans to a Socialist government. The "fundamentalist" appears to have little or no confidence in his capacity to take unorthodox risks or to assume responsibility for others. He views the world with such extreme suspicion and distrust that Under Secretary of State Acheson, testifying in favor of the Bretton Woods Agreements, was driven to remonstrate: "Who are we to sit around and suspect the motives of countries with whom we agree we must co-operate. These are the nations of the world. The people are just as honorable as we are. We do not have any premium on honesty." [5] But the "fundamentalist" holds that we must be on guard against nations which have not proven their worth by hard work, free enterprise, and economic independence.

By contrast, the "progressives" frankly accept America's obligation to assume economic leadership for its own best interest. Theirs is a perspective broadly tolerant of foreign differences, including European socialism. Appreciating that nothing should, or perhaps could, be done to interfere in the domestic economies of foreign countries, the "progressives" placed their faith in the impersonal operations of the Monetary Fund and the International Bank to bring about the desired redressment of the European economies.

THE MARSHALL PLAN

The Marshall Plan confronted the American people, and the business elite in particular, with a far more radical and costly departure in foreign policy. It demonstrated the State Department's conscious intention to employ an economic strategy, and it involved the control and expenditure by the federal government of a fearful sum of money. Although the persons involved were not all the same as had participated in the arguments over Bretton Woods and the British Loan, the response of the business elite exhibits the same ideological division, even more sharply than before.

One group of congressional witnesses consisting of Bernard Baruch, Paul Hoffman, Philip Reed (chairman of General Electric), John McCloy (president of the International Bank and later of the Chase National Bank) and R. W. Gifford (chairman, Borg-Warner International Corporation and representative of the Detroit Board of Commerce), enthusiastically endorsed both the principle and the sum involved in the Marshall Plan. They were strongly seconded by Senators Connally, Vandenberg, and Alexander Smith. Among those opposed to the Plan as recommended to Congress were former President Herbert Hoover, businessmen Curtis Calder (NAM) and Arnold J. Wilson (Illinois NAM), columnists Henry Hazlitt and Henry Taylor, Senator Burke Hickenlooper (Iowa–R.) and Representative John Davis Lodge (Conn.–R.).

To begin with, the two groups differed as to the seriousness of Europe's need. Those favoring the Plan accepted the State Department's contention that the need was great and urgent; those opposed deprecated the crisis and argued that only the prevalence of planning and socialism was preventing the natural economic forces from bringing about Europe's swift recovery. As the argument

[5] *Ibid.*, p. 63.

developed, it became clear that those in favor of the Plan shared the perspective we have identified as that of the "progressives" while those opposed shared the perspective of the "fundamentalists."

The "progressives" reasoned that if America could tutor Europe in the techniques of American productivity the European problem might be permanently solved. "Work, production, thrift — they made America. They can now save the world." [6] The European problem "is essentially a production problem" and ERP must be so viewed if it is to avoid being contaminated by politics.[7] Baruch, Hoffman, Gifford, Reed, and Lewis Douglas spoke with almost religious fervor of the redemptive quality of production; theirs was a Messianic zeal to make the Plan the instrument of Europe's conversion. This outlook, shared by senators, union leaders, and spokesmen for civic and professional organizations of a liberal persuasion, seems to express a traditional American compulsion to return to Europe and set it straight. So complete was their faith in the panacea of production that the "progressives" even argued that it was the answer to "false doctrines" such as communism and socialism.[8] The only political goal that the "progressives" were willing to endorse was European federation, a United States of Europe, justifiable in terms of American success with production for a mass market. Otherwise all that this group asked was that Europe prove itself worthy of each annual appropriation by its good works and economic progress.[9]

The "fundamentalists" — spokesmen for the NAM, publicists like Hazlitt and root-and-branch conservatives like former President Hoover — viewed the Marshall Plan as a New Deal or "planners' " concept. In principle, the Europeans should be made to work their way out of the crisis and to this end it would be more appropriate if the Plan took the form of outright relief and of hard-headed business loans rather than that of a specious aid program involving government interference in the economic system.[10] In the form in which it was proposed, the plan would only undermine the American economy through taxes and inflation and postpone the inevitable day of reckoning for the profligate European planners and politicians. While disclaiming any intention of interfering in the domestic affairs of the recipient countries, the "fundamentalists" argued that the Plan should be used to force the European governments to accept American conditions on several important economic and political points. The Plan must be: (1) handled as much as possible as outright charity or as loans between private interests; (2) a source of gain to the United States in the form of strategic materials, air bases, and rehabilitation of the German and Japanese economies; (3) predicated upon a stronger anti-Communist and anti-Soviet attitude on the part of American and European governments alike; and (4) conditional upon the willingness of

---

[6] *European Recovery Program,* Hearings before the Senate Committee on Foreign Relations, 80th Cong. 2d Sess., p. 556 (hereinafter cited as ERP).

[7] *Ibid.,* p. 848.

[8] *Ibid.,* p. 912.

[9] *Ibid.,* p. 556.

[10] *Ibid.,* pp. 692, 707–9.

Europeans to cease all socialistic programs and to afford American businessmen advantageous treatment in relation to the nationals of any other country.[11]

In light of these contrasting sets of attitudes it is possible to compare the perspectives of "progressives" and "fundamentalists" in terms of the premises implicit in each. Basically both groups were agreed that European economic recovery would depend ultimately upon the autonomous operation of the market system. But they disagreed on the extent to which this could or should be facilitated by the intervention of the American government. To the "fundamentalists" this intervention threatened to aid European governments already committed to Socialistic controls and to undermine our own security by diverting American resources from normal market channels.

On the one hand, "fundamentalists" denied the interdependence of America and Europe. They argued that the United States ought to limit its aid to those forms which would least involve us in responsibility for European recovery: "Charity with our surpluses we can afford and private loans are no drain upon the public economy."[12] At the same time "fundamentalists" disparaged the Marshall Plan as a dubious "substitute" for direct political action in the cold war: "What we ought to have done long ago . . . was to have taken a much firmer stand against Russia, and that is far more important than our lending money under the Marshall Plan."[13]

To the "progressives," the intervention of the American government appeared indispensable to Europe's economic recovery. They rejected the notion that Europe should be forced to "go it alone"; economic recovery would require political co-operation. It was on this note that Senator Alexander Smith replied to criticism of the Plan:

I do not think, Mr. Hazlitt, you can solve this matter by just dealing through private enterprise if you are looking always for the measure of cooperation between these countries that we have been insisting should be part of this whole process. Dealing with private industries will not handle the question of customs barriers, it will not handle the question of currency stabilization, it will not handle the question of a virtual economic federation of these countries to work together for their common ends, pooling their raw materials, pooling our western Germany resources, and all that we are trying to think through. Private industry won't meet that.[14]

Far from implying a threat to free enterprise, intervention by the American government was seen by the "progressives" as the way to remove the obstacles which had hindered the full development of Europe's productive resources. As

---

[11] In the end certain of these conditions found expression in the congressional enactment or in the bilateral agreements negotiated with recipient nations. For example, the European Recovery Act required that Marshall Plan funds be used to purchase surplus agricultural commodities in the United States, that about 25 per cent of total wheat shipments should be in the form of flour and that 50 per cent of all assistance should be carried in American ships. The original bilateral drafts required that recipient nations should undertake to consult the International Monetary Fund about rates of exchange *when in the judgment of The United States* this was necessary. Somewhat more tactful expedients were used to put an end to the dismantling of German factories and to restrict East-West trade to so-called nonstrategic materials.

[12] *Foreign Policy For a Post-War Recovery Program,* Hearings before the House Committee on Foreign Affairs, 80th Cong. 1st and 2d Sess., Part 1.

[13] *Ibid.,* p. 633.

[14] ERP, p. 698.

men whose experience and economic self-interest were usually bound up with the international economy, it was easy for them to view the Marshall Plan as a device for restoring the operation of a system with which they were familiar. All that was needed to guarantee success was the adherence to business principles, and on this score both "progressives" and "fundamentalists" were agreed that professional civil servants were incompetent and unreliable architects of such an undertaking. To free the enterprise from the shackles of politics and bureaucracy, businessmen must design and administer the plan. The ultimate purpose of Congress in establishing ECA as an independent agency under Paul Hoffman was to remove it from the unsanctified hands of the State Department. Only a special breed of business executives was deemed worthy of the task and these were to be recruited on a leave-of-absence basis from finance and industry. Thus the balance would be swung in favor of the redemptive power of "production" and against the "tragic" possibility of "an international WPA with the waste of man-hours, money and materials that we commonly associate with a program of spending for the sake of spending." [15]

POINT FOUR

In contrast to Bretton Woods, the British Loan, and the Marshall Plan, the "Point Four" program proposed by President Truman in 1949 raised the issue not of government intervention in an established market system but of America's long-term role in foreign economic development. The President had envisaged Point Four as "a bold new program for making the benefits of our scientific advances and industrial progress available for the improvement and growth of under-developed areas." The proposal underscored the opportunity for sharing our "know-how" as a means of forestalling the spread of communism. At the same time, by calling for the investment of American capital in these areas, the proposal also implied the opportunity to foster the development of private enterprise. The policy alternatives connected with the implementation of Point Four thus continue to reflect the difference of perspectives held by "fundamentalists" and "progressives" among the business elite.

The fact that Point Four was to operate in underdeveloped countries stimulated most of the witnesses for industry and business to regard the program as an instrument for the furtherance of private enterprise. Spokesmen such as Austin Foster (National Foreign Trade Council), R. W. Gifford (Detroit Board of Commerce), and Spruille Braden were agreed that "technical co-operation programs should be authorized only with foreign countries which have indicated their firm intention to co-operate in fostering private enterprise by the adoption of treaties with the United States giving our nationals assurance of equitable and nondiscriminatory treatment."[16] This same approach was embodied in a bill introduced in the House by Representative Christian Herter who argued:

---

[15] ERP, p. 674.

[16] Testimony by Austin Foster in *International Technical Cooperation Act of 1949*, Hearings before the House Foreign Affairs Committee, 81st Cong. 1st Sess., p. 113 (hereinafter cited as ITCA 1949). Similar statements may be found in *Act for International Development*, Hearings before the Senate Committee on Foreign Relations, 81st Cong., 2d Sess.

If . . . one's philosophy believes that the private enterprise system is the most effective in the long run . . . as judged by experience we have had over the last 150 years, then I think it is of the utmost importance to let foreign nations know that . . . there is a limit to which this country will go [in] supplying government funds, unless those nations are willing to be reasonable from the point of view of possible private investments.[17]

That economic assistance programs should serve to further private enterprise, that government's role should be confined to creating a climate conducive to private investment, are the familiar earmarks of the "fundamentalist" perspective. So too is the tendency to justify this position by pointing out that this is the way America became great.

The spirit if not the purpose of the "fundamentalists" in supporting Point Four was in essence contrary to that enunciated by President Truman. The Administration bill recognized that the United States had to participate actively in the economic development of backward countries: this entailed the idea of sharing, without the prospect of material return. Against this, the "fundamentalist" position implies an aloofness on the part of the United States government, a freedom from responsibility apart from maintaining the legal and commercial framework essential to the protection of private property, private investment and enterprise. In keeping with this, the "fundamentalist" was anxious to dissociate the program from any connection with the United Nations. The international agencies may be doing a splendid job, said Austin Foster, "but I do not think that that program will ever result in the emphasis on private enterprise methods which is what I think most of the people in this country believe is the right way of doing things, and your U.N. programs are just as likely to be devised on Socialistic lines." [18]

Even with respect to the transmission of technical knowledge — the key purpose of the program — the "fundamentalists" argued that the real job can only be accomplished as an integral part of the capitalistic investment process. In contrast to health, education, and agricultural development there is industrial development which, according to Mr. Herter, "is a commercial product. . . . It is not something that somebody has got to give away. It has always been a part and parcel of private investment, the know-how that goes with the . . . enterprise." [19]

Nelson Rockefeller took the lead in expounding the value of the Point Four program as it was originally intended. In a manner reminiscent of the "progressives' " approach to the Marshall Plan, Rockefeller stressed the need to improve these countries' productive capacity "in order to produce larger volumes of goods at lower cost, thus putting greater power into the hands of labor and consequently greater purchasing power in the hands of the people." [20]

---

[17] *Ibid.*, p. 185. Speaking for the Detroit Board of Commerce, Mr. R. W. Gifford declared that "our motives would be better understood" if technical assistance were put "on a clear-cut business basis." Gifts make enemies, self-interested commercial relations make friends. *Ibid.*, p. 322.

[18] *Ibid.*, p. 120.

[19] *Ibid.*, p. 185.

[20] ITCA 1949, p. 79.

To accomplish this, Rockefeller would extend the role of government beyond the mere protection of foreign investments. "Government must perform two basic functions. One is this program of direct technical aid. . . . The other is the creation of a framework which would permit business, labor and private capital to do the main job." [21] Yet this "framework" was to be broader than that envisaged by the "fundamentalists." Rockefeller did not balk at the prospect of interdependence at many levels. "The more ties we can make between established institutions in this country with institutions abroad, the better it is." [22]

This particular point was bolstered in the course of the hearings by the welling up of a deep flowing moral and religious strain in American culture. The image of backward peoples waiting for help recalled the precedent set by private philanthropy and religious missionary work. This was well exemplified by the statements of Representative Walter Judd, a former missionary to China and also by those of such surprising people as Senator Fulbright of Arkansas. Each in his own way cherished a vision of the role of Point Four: that of a few devoted technicians or county agents going into a backward country and working economic and spiritual miracles with a combination of American ingenuity and human brotherliness. In the place of programs which try to modernize primitive economies overnight, people like Judd and Fulbright preferred "to work with the people and teach them things like home canning, for example . . . or the rudiments of refrigeration." [23] They saw Point Four in effect "as an expansion and extension of the kind of work American missions and other private groups have been doing for decades." [24] And they justified this approach by pointing to the limitations on a backward country's ability to absorb technological change without suffering social disruption; indeed this faith in the virtues of gradualism and change at the "grass roots" sometimes blinded Fulbright to the value of "impact" programs designed to achieve striking gains or to give the people some hope for the future. [25]

The contrast between "fundamentalist" and "progressive" perspectives revealed by these divergent responses to Point Four can be summed up as follows: "Fundamentalists" viewed the proposal within a framework of assumptions which strictly dichotomized the sphere of government and the sphere of private enterprise. In their view, the investment and market system was the only proper medium for transmitting the technical knowledge required for economic development. The United States has no obligation to help those who are not willing to employ private enterprise to help themselves; moreover it would be dangerous and unavailing for the American government to go beyond the protection of private investment in supporting economic development.

The "progressive" perspective is characterized by a genuine reluctance to confine Point Four to such mutually exclusive policy alternatives. Raising the level of living in underdeveloped countries calls for the best use of resources,

---

[21] *Ibid.*, p. 83.
[22] *Ibid.*, p. 95.
[23] *Mutual Security Act of 1951*, Hearings before the Senate Foreign Relations Commitee, 81st Cong. 1st Sess., p. 443 (hereinafter cited as MSA 1951).
[24] Jonathan B. Bingham, *Shirt-sleeve Diplomacy* (New York: Day, 1954), p. 173.
[25] MSA 1951, pp. 442–43.

public or private. "We cannot," said Rockefeller, "have competition between the two but a working together of private and Government in the accomplishment of the objective." [26] The "progressives" accept the premise that economic development is worth the effort no matter how unprepared the backward countries are and believe that this can be accomplished through international co-operation with public and private financing, combining high-level planning with intimate contact at the "grass roots." The "progressives' " perspective is thus significant in committing them to seek new ways for solving a long-range problem.

The Mutual Security Program

By the spring of 1950 the United States possessed the rudimentary elements of an economic strategy but there still existed great uncertainty as to the precise function and long-run needs of economic and technical assistance. There was a growing concern that the amount of investment funds, both private and public, available to underdeveloped countries would continue to fall far short of their needs, which were likely to increase as development got under way. The onset of the Korean war introduced the issue of military security as a consideration in our economic strategy. These were the principal considerations around which debate turned in the preparation of the Mutual Security Acts of 1951 through 1953.

The difference in perspective of "fundamentalists" and "progressives" is apparent in their responses to the ambiguity and indefinite duration of our obligation to assist the underdeveloped countries. The "progressives' " perspective was revealed in the report prepared by Gordon Gray (submitted November 10, 1950)[27] and the report by the United States International Development Advisory Board under the chairmanship of Nelson A. Rockefeller (submitted March 7, 1951).[28] These reports had been requested by the President for guidance in the formulation of long-term United States economic assistance policy.

Both of these reports were characterized by a much franker recognition than hitherto of the magnitude and complexity of the problem posed by the underdeveloped countries and of their economic and political relation to the security and prosperity of the free world. The Rockefeller Report was somewhat more aggressive than the Gray Report in expressing its "belief in the prime importance of private capital," but both were frank to recognize that the conditions necessary to attract private investment depend to a great extent upon what governments, including our own, are prepared to contribute in the form of development assistance, investment guarantees, etc. Both groups recommended that two new international agencies be created under the general supervision of the International Bank: (1) a new International Development Authority for the purpose of making grants to underdeveloped countries for projects "that cannot be financed entirely on a loan basis"; (2) an International Finance Corporation "with author-

---

[26] ITCA 1949, p. 94.

[27] *Report to the President on Foreign Economic Policies*, Washington, November 10, 1950, pp. 1–131 (hereinafter cited as Gray Report).

[28] *Partners in Progress, A Report to the President* (The International Development Advisory Board), March, 1951, pp. 91–92.

ity to make loans to private enterprise." [29] Both of these signified the willingness of the "progressives" to enter into long-range government-sponsored development financing in order to meet the needs of the underdeveloped countries.

As usual, the "fundamentalists" were agitated by the seemingly indefinite duration of foreign dependence upon the United States and by the call for an unorthodox departure from the normal operation of the market system, a departure which threatened the image of American autonomy upon which the "fundamentalists' " whole position rests. Spokesmen for the "fundamentalists" pointed out the grave danger that "Point Four aid could . . . continue into the indefinite future" and "that the amounts might increase." [30] The rapidly growing program of aid is "a serious long-term threat to the already overburdened American taxpayer." [31] The "fundamentalists" were especially disturbed that the plight of the backward countries should in any way be a major concern of the United States. They argued that the United States ought to "conserve its strength for the long haul" and expressed the fear that foreign outlays would lead to "further loss of confidence in our national solvency." [32] Their concern for the future of the underdeveloped countries was confined to the expansion of markets for American goods. "There is a sphere for Government action as well as for private enterprise" but only if the two "go hand in hand, each to its appointed task." [33] The appointed tasks of government are to prepare the diplomatic path for private enterprise and to restrict itself to those unprofitable functions which are "beyond the scope and authority of private enterprise." [34]

In the end the Mutual Security Programs for 1951 through 1953 were passed under the aegis of military security. Here another significant difference distinguishes the "progressive" and "fundamentalist" perspectives. Both the Gray and Rockefeller Reports underscored the importance of economic development assistance to the defense policies of the United States. "The more deeply we have explored the relationship of economic development to defense the more impressed we have been with how truly inseparable they are." [35] In short, "economic development when brought within the necessary broad strategy of a total foreign policy, will play an important part in our mobilization for defense." [36] But it was clearly not the intention of the "progressives" who had always resisted contaminating foreign aid with political expedients, to exploit it now for narrowly military ends. The statement for CED by Meyer Kestnbaum emphatically argued that it would be a costly error to regàrd rearmament and security as synonymous. "The Marshall Plan . . . was successful precisely because it recognized and emphasized the economic and social aspects of European security. . . . The rearma-

---

[29] *Ibid.*, p. 84; Cf. Gray Report, pp. 13–14.

[30] *Mutual Security Act of 1952*, Hearings before the Senate Foreign Relations Committee, 82d Cong. 2d Sess., p. 531.

[31] *Ibid.*, p. 536.

[32] *Ibid.*, pp. 531–33.

[33] MSA 1951, p. 770

[34] *Ibid.*, p. 770.

[35] *Partners in Progress*, p. 50.

[36] *Ibid.*, p. 53.

ment program must be regarded as supplementing, not replacing, the co-operative effort to build a productive, stable, and united Western Europe." [37]

By contrast the "fundamentalist" seemed to find in military security the only powerful justification for foreign aid to underdeveloped countries. "We recognize that the Point Four program derives its primary importance from the national interests in the United States as, therefore, an implement of national defense." [38] Naturally Administration witnesses found it expedient to point out that economic assistance contributed to a proportionately larger military effort on the part of our allies; that it was cheaper to support a Turkish soldier for $200 a year than an American at $3,500 or $4,500; that economic assistance was being undertaken on a strictly temporary basis; that it would be used to benefit rather than hurt domestic economic interests; and that it would eventually permit the United States to pursue its economic interests free of any obligation to other countries. Blandishments such as these had a great appeal to the "fundamentalists." [39] Unfortunately it was the temporary character and the overriding importance attributed to military security that weakened the political appeal of MSA and reduced its effectiveness as a program for development assistance. [40]

The International Finance Corporation

Before the shortcomings of MSA could be fully understood and a new departure undertaken, the "fundamentalists" had to grapple for the first time with the responsibility for taking the initiative in charting the course of foreign policy. For with the Republican victory of 1952, the Executive branch came to be dominated by businessmen of a marked "fundamentalist" stripe. When the Eisenhower Administration confronted the issue of development assistance it had to reconcile the necessity for continuing what already existed with the desire to bring the program into line with the principles of free enterprise, minimal government and balanced budgets.

The difficulty in solving this problem is clearly demonstrated by the struggle within the Administration over the question of whether America should support the adoption of any new international lending agencies for development assistance.

---

[37] MSA 1951, p. 791.

[38] *Ibid.*, p. 769.

[39] Furthermore, it was argued that since the three programs — military, economic, and technical assistance — "were all trying to do essentially the same thing," greater efficiency and economy could be achieved by an administrative consolidation of the three. The Mutual Security Act of 1951 provided for a Director of Mutual Security with authority to co-ordinate all three foreign aid programs. Even though the administration of the military assistance program was left in the Department of Defense, the organizational arrangement was bound to create suspicion in the minds of those receiving economic or technical assistance that they were being tied into the American military program. To make matters clear to the neutral nations, Congress, under Section 511 (6) of the Mutual Security Act of 1951, provided that no economic or technical assistance should be supplied to any nation unless the President found that the supplying of such assistance would strengthen the security of the United States.

[40] Most of the assistance voted was of a direct military type, and of that having a high "development assisting" content most went to the seven countries with which we had large-scale military arrangements: China (Taiwan), Greece, Indo-China, Korea, Pakistan, the Philippines, and Turkey. Howard C. Petersen, *Needed: A New Foreign Aid Policy* (New York: Committee for Economic Development, April, 1957).

One of the agencies recommended in the Rockefeller Report of 1951 was an International Finance Corporation with authority to make loans in local and foreign currencies to private enterprise without the requirement of government guaranties and also to make non-voting equity investments in local currencies in participation with private investors.[41] On the surface it appeared that the new Administration was united in its resistance to IFC.[42] The Treasury Department under George Humphrey, the Board of Governors of the Federal Reserve System and the Export-Import Bank opposed the new agency because an international institution in equity ownership of private enterprises ran counter to the principles of free enterprise. The Department of State, though it saw in the proposal "a convenient and relatively inexpensive vehicle for supporting its policy in the field of international economic affairs," [43] felt constrained to support the Treasury viewpoint in keeping with the ideological premises which seemed to prevail within the Administration.

These Administration views were strongly seconded by spokesmen for business interests. The National Foreign Trade Council maintained that the United States government "must make it clear, by word and action," that American public funds would not be used for development and investment projects which, under proper conditions, could be financed by private capital.[44] To do so "might well deter, rather than promote, the creation of such mechanisms." [45] Mr. Clarence B. Randall, sometime economic advisor to the President, hopefully declared:

It would seem to follow that the foreign economic policy of the United States should be devoted to the furtherance of our three basic principles. These are: Reliance upon private effort and intelligence called forth by proper incentives; the governing control of rigorous free competition; and the registering of choice through free competition.[46]

In conformity with such attitudes, strongly held and vigorously expressed, United States economic policy marked time during the period between 1952 and 1954. But the world was not standing still. By the autumn of 1954 pressure from the underdeveloped countries through the channels of the United Nations and of the Organization of American States threatened to lead to an open breach with the United States. The Soviet Union, taking advantage of their frustration and chagrin with the United States, had begun to offer dazzling trade and loan agreements to anyone willing to negotiate.

Suddenly, on November 9, 1954, Secretary of the Treasury Humphrey announced that the United States government was prepared to support IFC. Two features are worth noting in connection with this surprising reversal of position. First, most of the pressure for it came from a stratum of businessmen and bankers

[41] *Partners in Progress*, pp. 84–85.

[42] Much of the analysis in this section rests upon the findings of B. Matecki, *Establishment of the International Finance Corporation and United States Foreign Policy* (New York: Praeger, 1957), pp. 1–194.

[43] *Ibid.*, p. 80.

[44] 1952 Declaration of the National Trade Convention as quoted in Matecki, *op. cit.*, p. 85.

[45] *Ibid.*, p. 86.

[46] *New York Times*, Novembr 2, 1954.

of a roughly "progressive" outlook, strategically situated on various United States delegations to the United Nations and within the International Bank. Secondly, its ratification by the United States government was secured by the elimination of the provision for public equity financing ("international bureaucracy"!) so as to limit the role of IFC to that of merely buying debentures in the enterprises without the right of active participation in their management. This modification was at the instance of Mr. Eugene Black, president of the International Bank, and is a good example of the influence which "progressives" manage to exert by devising workable compromises consistent with American capitalistic precepts.[47]

However, the very features that made IFC attractive to the business and banking mind were those which limited its effectiveness as an instrument of United States economic strategy. First, IFC was inadequately funded to meet the growing needs of the underdeveloped countries. Second, the American Congress was becoming restive with the Mutual Security Program which seemed to involve the continued expenditure of hundreds of millions of dollars in grants with little or no promise of their eventual recovery. Some new formula more compatible with traditional business values than MSA and more effective in meeting the needs of the underdeveloped countries still had to be found.

THE DEVELOPMENT LOAN FUND

The search for this new formula took the form of a series of studies authorized by the Congress and the Executive which led eventually to the establishment of the Development Loan Fund, a United States agency authorized to make loans on easy terms to underdeveloped countries. On July 11, 1956, the Senate passed Resolution 285, creating the Special Committee to Study the Foreign Aid Program (hereafter referred to as the Special Committee). The Senate instructed this Committee to make " exhaustive studies of the extent to which foreign assistance by the United States Government serves, can be made to serve, or does not serve, the national interest, to the end that such studies and recommendations based thereon may be available to the Senate in considering foreign-aid policies for the future." [48] On the basis of this directive the Special Committee outlined

[47] Mr. Isador Lubin, a permanent member of the United States delegation to the United Nations, paid tribute to the role of the "progressives" in this process when he remarked that what he could not accomplish under a Democratic administration, businessmen achieved under a Republican. These men seem to have been displaced to the periphery of policy-making by the "fundamentalist" oligarchy (Humphrey, Wilson, Hollister, and Herbert Hoover, Jr.) which came in with the Eisenhower Administration. United Nations delegates J. David Zellerbach (president of Crown Zellerbach Corp. and later chairman of the CED) and Preston Hotchkis, seconded by Senator H. Alexander Smith, appear to have exerted the strongest influence on behalf of IFC both at Washington and among the "top officers" of the leading New York banks. Eugene Black and Robert Garner, president and vice-president respectively of the International Bank, kept the IFC concept alive during these years in their contacts with the United States Treasury Department and with American banking associations. These businessmen and bankers were prepared to have their feelings about IFC favorably influenced not only because they were in direct contact with the world crisis through the United Nations, but because they were internationally minded; otherwise it is doubtful that they would have been at the UN to begin with. The full details of these relationships are brilliantly presented in Matecki, op. cit., pp. 129–51.

[48] Foreign Aid Program, Compilation of Studies and Surveys prepared for the Special Senate Committee to Study the Foreign Aid Program, 85th Cong. 1st Sess. (July, 1957), p. iv (hereinafter cited as FAP Studies 1957).

a series of studies to be undertaken by private institutions in the United States. Almost simultaneously President Eisenhower appointed his own committee, the President's Citizen Advisors on the Mutual Security Program under the chairmanship of Mr. Benjamin Fairless, former Board chairman of the United States Steel Corporation.[49] The Committee for Economic Development also prepared a statement on national policy entitled "Economic Development Assistance."[50] In addition, the International Development Advisory Board under the chairmanship of Mr. Eric Johnston submitted a report to the President calling for "A New Emphasis on Economic Development Abroad." [51]

In taking the initiative Congress recognized the need for determining whether economic development assistance was to be a long-run obligation of the United States government or not. Once again the recommendations of the various organizations and committees were sharply divided by "fundamentalist" and "progressive" perspectives. The elements of the "progressive" position are to be found in the Report of the Center for International Studies (M.I.T.) to the Special Committee, in that of the Committee for Economic Development, and in the IDAB report to the President submitted by Eric Johnston. The "fundamentalists," position found its most sophisticated advocacy in the report of the American Enterprise Association[52] to the Special Committee, in the report of the Fairless Committee to President Eisenhower and in Mr. Fairless' testimony before the Special Committee.

From these two sets of reports it can be seen that the perspectives of "fundamentalists" and "progressives" remain as divergent today as they were at the onset of the cold war. The M.I.T., CED, and IDAB reports virtually agreed that "in the near future, foreign private capital is not likely to play a major role in the

---

[49] The members of this group were, in addition to Mr. Fairless, Colgate Darden, Jr., president of the University of Virginia; Richard R. Deupree, board chairman of Proctor and Gamble; Whitelaw Reid, chairman of the New York Herald Tribune; Walter Bedell Smith, vice-chairman, American Machine and Foundry Corp.; Jesse W. Tapp, chairman of the Bank of America; and John L. Lewis, president of the United Mine Workers of America.

[50] This statement was prepared under the general guidance of the following members of the Committee for Economic Development: Howard C. Petersen, Fidelity-Philadelphia Trust Co.; Frank Altschul; Thomas D. Cabot, Godfrey L. Cabot, Inc.; S. Sloan Colt, Bankers Trust Company; Gardner Cowles, Des Moines Register & Tribune and Cowles Magazines, Inc.; Jay E. Crane, Standard Oil Company (New Jersey); William C. Foster, Olin Mathieson Chemical Corporation; H. J. Heinz, II; T. S. Petersen, Standard Oil of California; Philip D. Reed, General Electric Company; Beardsley Ruml; Harry Scherman, Book-of-the-Month Club, Inc.; H. Christian Sonne; Wayne C. Taylor, Heathsville, Virginia.

[51] This report was prepared by Eric Johnston; Gardner Cowles; Dr. Robert Daniel, Virginia State College; Harvey S. Firestone, Jr.; J. Peter Grace, W. R. Grace & Co.; Dr. Wilton Halverson, University of California; Mrs. J. Ramsay Harris, U.S. Committee for UNICEF; Lloyd Mashburn, AFL–CIO; Lee W. Minton, AFL–CIO; Dr. W. I. Myers, Cornell University; Herschel D. Newsom, National Grange; William M. Rand, deputy director, Mutual Security Agency; and Laurence F. Whittemore, chairman of the board, The Brown Co.

[52] The American Enterprise Association, Inc., is a research organization. Its study report on American Private Investment, Foreign Economic Development, and the Aid Programs was carried out under the joint direction of Dr. W. Glenn Campbell, director of research, and Dr. Wilson Schmidt of George Washington University, who were aided by a group of top academic economists. A detailed account of the background to the foreign aid legislation of 1957 is to be found in H. Field Haviland, Jr., "Foreign Aid and the Policy Process: 1957," American Political Science Review, LII (September, 1958), 689–724.

development of either Asia or Africa." [53] This position evoked from Mr. Fairless the flat assertion: "I can't go along with that." [54]

The "fundamentalists," sensing that a crucial point had been reached in the evolution of American economic policy, argued that the time for government-sponsored economic and technical assistance programs was past. Either the foreign countries desirous of American investment should create the conditions necessary to induce private investment and development or the United States should recognize that such countries are either unable or unwilling to help themselves.[55] Government grants or loans are no proper substitute for private investment. "Intergovermental charity . . . is ordinarily an inferior instrument of international co-operation. It has no natural limits; it is certain to be condemned at home for excess and abroad for deficiency. It is likely to make the recipient suspect ulterior motives and hidden designs. The donor is likely to make it a pretext for demands for repayment in political rather than businesslike form." [56]

The "progressives" countered this argument by denying that the purpose of government assistance should be to influence the recipients. Assistance should not be looked upon a means of securing friendship and gratitude but rather as a means of resolving a strictly economic problem without letting a doctrinaire insistence upon private enterprise defeat the purpose.

Although both groups assumed the inherent autonomy of the market system, and agreed that it should not be adulterated by spectacular or sensational projects designed to have a political or psychological impact, they disagreed on the value of planning for economic development. "Progressives" stress the importance of the recipient country's having a national development plan whereas the "fundamentalists" roundly condemn such planning as a self-defeating strategy for the free nations. Milton Friedman, economist from the University of Chicago, testifying on behalf of the American Enterprise Association, bitterly attacked the tendency of the M.I.T. Report to "take as a prime test of whether a country is making an effective effort on development whether they have a centrally designed and co-ordinated development program. . . . I do not think we can successfully compete with the Soviet ideology by accepting its basic premises." [57] To accept central planning in place of the free market "is likely to make the efforts of the Soviets more successful." [58]

The most significant feature of the proposed Development Loan Fund was that of making loans available "on more generous terms" than either the Export-Import Bank or the International Bank for Reconstruction and Development were prepared to offer. It was proposed that the Fund Administrator have considerable discretion in setting interest rates, periods of maturity, etc., and it was anticipated that many of the Fund's loans might have to provide for repayment in local cur-

---

[53] FAP Studies 1957, p. 288.

[54] *The Foreign Aid Program*, Hearings before the Senate Special Committee, 85th Cong. 1st Sess. (March and April, 1957), p. 360 (hereinafter cited as FAP Hearings 1957).

[55] FAP Hearings 1957, p. 127.

[56] FAP Studies 1957, p. 592.

[57] FAP Hearings 1957, pp. 128–29.

[58] *Ibid.*

rencies which could be utilized at the discretion of the Administrator. These "soft" loans represented the effort to reconcile the demands of an autonomous market system with the strategic imperatives of foreign policy.

Characteristically the "fundamentalists" were opposed to such a practice. The Fairless report declared flatly that "loans by the United States repayable in the inconvertible currencies of foreign nations are undesirable, and the practice of granting them should be terminated." [59] Mr. Fairless made it clear that he was adamantly opposed to soft loans "because we feel that the 'soft loan' principle undermines the real loan" and "the drift will be to all soft loans." [60] The report of the American Enterprise Association also expressed fear that "governmental loans carrying especially easy terms as a kind of gift will create misunderstanding in the borrowing country about the rate of return on private loans or investments that is appropriate and commensurate with the risk." [61]

Both "progressives" and "fundamentalists" agree that the underdeveloped countries can benefit from America's experience with private enterprise but disagree on the means by which this benefit should be exported. "Fundamentalists" assume that the essence of the American achievement lies in overcoming the hazards of entrepreneurship by self-discipline and sacrifice; and these qualities can develop only where people must face the risk of failure. If development is slow in many countries it can be assumed that those people are uninterested in raising their standards, "as is clear from their reluctance to make the resources available by voluntary savings." [62] They could improve their real income "simply by rearranging the allocation of resources." [63] Since the United States made its way by voluntary savings, why cannot the underdeveloped countries of today do likewise? But it is precisely the futility of expecting such self-reliance to emerge, under the conditions prevailing in those countries, that motivates the "progressives" to alter those conditions. The "progressive" believes that initiative and self-reliance, indispensable to private enterprise, must be induced by the employment of American economic assistance to establish a system of economic incentives. It is precisely the "progressives'" confidence and willingness to employ unorthodox devices that distinguishes them from the "fundamentalists."

CONCLUSION

We began our study with the assumption that by analyzing the foreign policy perspectives of the business elite we would gain insight into the process by which it exercises power over American foreign policy. We contended that the business elite exercises this power by confining debate within traditional conceptions of how economic resources should be employed. [64] We have seen that in considering

---

[59] *Ibid.*, pp. 370–71.
[60] *Ibid.*, p. 371.
[61] FAP Studies 1957, p. 602.
[62] *Ibid.*, p. 581.
[63] *Ibid.*, p. 585.
[64] Debate has been confined not only by the traditional conceptions of how economic resources should be used but also by the special attention which businessmen have received from Congress and the Administration. The testimony of other groups — religious, civic and labor — if solicited at all, has been accepted in a perfunctory, almost ritualistic, manner. The

new proposals for foreign economic assistance business spokesmen are constrained to reconcile the employment of an economic strategy with the traditional premises of American capitalism. We have discovered that some businessmen ("progressives") are consistently able to overcome the limitations imposed upon their judgment by these premises. With equally striking consistency we have noticed a coincidence between the "fundamentalists' " opposition to new departures in foreign economic policy and their tenacious adherence to traditional precepts.

In contrast to the "progressives," "fundamentalists" stress the impossibility of reconciling governmental controls with the freedom of enterprise, the autonomy of the market with other forms of social and political control; and they insist that the American system of enterprise cannot be exported unless the underdeveloped countries adopt it of their own free will, leaving us free of the gratuitous political commitments which would result if we went beyond orthodox business methods. By contrast the "progressives" look further afield for the contingencies on which the survival of American capitalism rests. They have consistently approved new departures in foreign economic policy; they have demonstrated a willingness to employ government as an instrument for fostering economic development in the backward countries; and they are confident that this will not impair our economic freedom or our political autonomy. This perspective has been strengthened by the "progressives' " capacity to apply ideas and advice acquired from their own experience in government.

To the extent that the United States possesses a foreign economic strategy it has been developed largely with reference to the conflicting perspectives of the business elite. When we examine the sequence of foreign aid programs since World War II it appears that United States policy has been a series of attempts to reconcile our traditional conception of how economic resources should be used, with the need to apply these resources in foreign societies and in response to the demands of political strategy. The achievements in this direction are more consistent with the perspective of the "progressives" than with the perspective of the "fundamentalists."

However, the "progressives' " initiative in sponsoring new departures in foreign economic policy should not obscure their basic commitment to the traditional precepts of American capitalism, nor the limitations involved in pursuing political goals in foreign countries by means of an economic strategy. By and large, "progressives" have tended to assume that increased production and its consequent raising of the level of material well-being will inevitably result in political stability. Their preoccupation with reconciling foreign economic assistance with the premises of American capitalism has confined them to a search for economic and financial innovations of the sort represented by the International Finance Corporation and the Development Loan Fund.

---

business community's access to the decision-making apparatus of the United States government has been analyzed statistically in David S. McLellan and Charles E. Woodhouse, "Businessmen in Foreign Policy," *Southwestern Social Science Quarterly*, XXXIX (March, 1959), 283–90. A paper, "American Foreign Assistance: the Dilemmas of a Tutelary Role," presented at the 1959 meeting of the American Sociological Society, examines the implications of the business perspective in the administration of aid programs abroad.

Assuming that our political purpose is to prevent the spread of Soviet influence, we can ask whether the "progressives" are aware of the political consequences which economic development may entail. Do they appreciate its potential for disrupting the traditional social structure of the aided country, opening the way for new bonds of social and political allegiance on the basis of new ideologies? Do they have a conception of the type of internal political order which is necessary for rapid economic development in backward countries? Do they appreciate the gulf that separates conditions in backward societies from the conditions in our country which make it possible to sustain a social order based upon traditional capitalist precepts?

BIG BUSINESS AND GOVERNMENT POLICY IN POST-NEW DEAL AMERICA: FROM DEPRESSION TO *DETENTE*

Prof. Kim McQuaid*

Our interest in the Business Roundtable stems primarily from our interest in antitrust policy and thus in the Federal Trade Commission, a 5-member agency that is supposed to be a prime maker of that policy in America. Reports have it that, during a recent campaign by several rival candidates for an FTC post, a small-business supporter of one such contender received a phone call from an official of the Roundtable branding the man in question a *"radical"* and urging the listener to switch sides, i.e., to write a letter to the White House saying he'd changed his mind and was now in favor of the Roundtable's own applicant for that seat on the FTC. *The latter in fact got the nod from Jimmy Carter and now sits on the agency, busily writing lengthy decisions and delivering laborious speeches that fully justify the Roundtable's faith in him.*

The TNEC 'Farce'

That incident raises a number of rather large questions, beginning with whether it's a one-time fluke or the way our FTC commissioners are routinely chosen by the White House. How many of the others got their jobs that way? Does the Roundtable, the principal spokesman for monopoly in America, now get to pick its own antitrust judges and, if so, how long has this been going on? We'll be exploring those issues further, needless to relate, in our future issues of this journal and, in the meantime, are pleased to present some of

*Prof. McQuaid teaches at Lake Erie College, Painesville, Ohio.

the historical background on them in the paper below. We were already clear, for example, that modern American presidents kill major antitrust cases in exchange for corporate campaign contributions and the like but we didn't know until now that they'd gone so far as to crank them up in the first place precisely for the purpose of securing—in exchange for their later abandonment—corporate "cooperation" in other areas. Professor McQuaid's account below of how FDR did just that in a confrontation with U.S. Steel once—and how his aides privately characterized the monumental TNEC probe of the late 1930s as "a farce put on for public consumption"— adds a most intriguing dimension to a variety of the deeper antitrust problems. If there's anyone in our audience who is aware of any other incidents of this kind or who can add any further historical insights here, we'd love to hear from you. And that goes double for anyone who might know of any additional instances where the Roundtable has either supported or opposed any candidate for a seat on the FTC.

Editors

■

Updating the 'Image'

This paper is concerned with the interaction between big businessmen and federal bureaucrats in the formulation and implementation of public policy, with the emphasis upon the dynamics of these relationships. For too long debates as to the nature and extent of corporate influence in the nation's political affairs have been couched in idioms bequeathed to us by the Muckraking journalists of the Progressive Era, an imagery that can—and oft-times does—portray big business-men as paunchy gentlemen in top hats and vests pulling strings with politicos dangling from them or as gray eminences who employ unsavory characters to lurk about in hotel rooms dispensing graft.[1] Such imagery is badly out-of-date, not least because it generally confines itself to the actions of *individual* capitalists or individual firms.

---

[1] Notes will be found at the end of the article. Ed.

Changing the Corporate Guard

The most important thing to understand about big-business and government relations during the past 40 years is that corporate efforts to influence American public policy have become considerably more organized than they were in the days of the "Robber Barons," with the ad hoc and individual being progressively replaced by the *institutional* and collective. This does not mean, however, that big-business' role in national policy councils can be understood merely by looking at the statements and lobbying activities of long-established organizations like the National Association of Manufacturers (NAM) and the United States Chamber of Commerce. The influence of groups such as these has decreased in recent decades, with new types of big-business organizations replacing them as focal points of corporate influence in Washington. These new business groups are exemplified by three organizations currently active on the national political scene, the Business Council (BC), the Committee for Economic Development (CED), and the Business Roundtable.[2] Though hardly household words, these three groups do not depend upon public recognition for their effectiveness. In this and other important ways they differ from the capitalist organizations that have preceded them, with five major characteristics serving to distinguish the new from the old in the realm of corporate organizational dynamics.

Rank Hath Its Privileges

First, the Business Council, Business Roundtable, and the CED draw their membership from among the leaders of the nation's largest corporations—those that occupy favored niches on the *Fortune* 100 and *Fortune* 500 lists. None of these three organizations is in any sense a mouthpiece for "small" or "medium-sized" firms (those with 5,000 employees or less). The CED, currently chaired by Fletcher L. Byrom, the chairman of the board of Koppers Company, is the most egalitarian of the three corporate think-tanks since it allows large corporations to be represented by vice presidents as well as their top-most officers. The Business Council, now headed by Reginald Jones of General Electric, and the Business Roundtable, presently chaired by Thomas A. Murphy of General Motors, are hardly so accessible: *Their* members are confined to the chief executive officers (chairmen or presidents) of the corporations and financial institutions that occupy the commanding heights of the U.S. economy. Lesser figures need not apply.[3]

Of Births and Midwives

The Business Council, the CED, and the Business Roundtable are also organizations which federal officials have had an important hand in creating. The Business Council, for example, was a quasi-public advisory agency created under the aegis of the Commerce Department in the early months of the New Deal. CED, in its turn, was established in 1943 as part of a cooperative endeavor between businessmen and bureaucrats to forward post-war reconversion planning aimed at avoiding a renewal of the Great Depression. Finally, the Business Roundtable took shape in 1972 as part of a campaign to increase big-business' political clout in Washington. Though the Roundtable was the most "privately" created of the three organizations being discussed here, it too enjoyed substantial measures of indirect support within the Executive Branch of the federal government at the time of its birth.

'Yes, But...'

The third major difference between the Council, Round-table, CED, and earlier organizations concerns the type of *stands* they take on important policy issues. While broad-gauged business groups like the U.S. Chamber and the NAM have tended until very recently to simply oppose legislation they don't like, big-business outfits like the three being discussed here have increasingly tended to substitute a strategy of "Yes, but..." for a strategy of "No."   By arriving first and proposing consistently—and by being careful to offer positive as opposed to negative positions—the Roundtable, Council, and CED attempt to set the limits of public debate and condition the impact and scope of pending legislation.

Keeping a Low Profile

The economic strength of the elite corporations making up the membership of the Council, the Roundtable, and the CED is undeniably vast but that doesn't mean they use any and all opportunities to belligerently defend free enterprise. Far from it. The managers of America's largest corporations have come a long way from the New Deal days when it was hardly unusual for the chairman of the board of General Motors or DuPont to call the President of the United States a communist and a part of this process has been a growing realization of the virtues of minimizing visibility, exposure, and opposition. Such relatively sophisticated approaches can and do allow the leadership of the larger American corporations to be as content to defend existing powers and procedures as they are to demand their extension.[4]

Not 'Whether' But 'Who'

Fifth and lastly the Business Council, the Roundtable, and the CED are organizational creations of a corporate elite increasingly conscious of the fact that neo-Classical economic precepts which see the "economic" and the "political" as entirely separate and distinct realms are less and less capable of describing the reality of a world in which big business and the state are tied together by a dense web of political, economic, and social relationships. Such corporate leaders are hardly socialists. Rather, they are capitalists who have come to understand that the fundamental public-policy questions that they and their successors will have to deal with revolve not around the question of whether additional measures of "planning" will be undertaken by public and private authority but around the question of *who* will do the "planning" and how they will go about performing it.

In the Beginning

To help insure that efforts aimed at enhanced coordination and control of the nation's economic life do not threaten the existence of the largest American corporations, the leaders of these institutions have organized themselves to forward "planning" procedures which take place *within* the market system as opposed to those which would supersede it. In this process of accommodating big businessmen to changed realities, organizations such as the Business Council, CED, and the Business Roundtable have served— and will continue to serve—important roles. These changes have not been instantaneous, however, and those groups that have led them did not spring up full-blown overnight but evolved rather over the period of the past four decades. During this time their structure, functions, strategy, and aims have undergone important transformations, thus illustrating the transition from an era of Depression to an era of Detente in corporate-governmental affairs. Some necessarily abbreviated history is therefore in order and, to begin our tale, we must go back in time to the climactic months of the early New Deal, June of 1933 to be precise.

The Government As 'Enforcer'

In 1933 the rhetoric of "partnership" and "cooperation" was in the air. Three years of economic catastrophe had educated big businessmen to their need for federal assistance. Managers of the nation's largest corporations pressured Washington to increase its role as an industrial "referee and umpire." Organized industry, argued businessmen like Gerard Swope of General Electric, must create a system of rules and administer a set of regulations to forward economic and social recovery and these regulations, in turn, should meet certain minimum standards aimed at preserving the interests of workers and consumers. As such standards were agreed upon, the *government must enforce the rules set down by big business.* The crucial decisions regarding economic recovery must remain in private hands, with Washington not "regulating" industry but using its police powers, rather, to sponsor enlightened corporate behavior.[5]

Rise of the 'Welfare State'

As historians have long recognized, such collectivist corporate logic was initially persuasive to Franklin Delano Roosevelt and other important New Deal administrators. Quick passage of the National Industrial Recovery Act and the creation of the National Recovery Administration (NRA) served to accent the extent to which national leaders called upon big business to organize itself to solve problems under the auspices of the federal government.[6] Less understood, however, is the fact that NRA was but one facet of a hoped-for collaboration between organized industry and the state. Secure in the knowledge that *economic recovery in a capitalist system could not take place without the cooperation of the managers of the nation's largest corporations*, the Roosevelt administration sponsored the creation of an organization aimed at bringing big-business leadership into an ongoing advisory relationship with the Executive branch of the federal government. The "Business Council," as this agency eventually came to be known, served as a major forum for corporate-governmental contact and cooperation during the transition from an era of welfare capitalism to the era of the welfare state.[7]

Behind Closed Doors

Organizationally speaking, the Business Council was a highly unusual advisory agency, one that was required to obey none of the regulations that were applied to every other advisory board in the federal government. The Council's membership, for example, was not determined by government officials. Instead, its 60 (later 65) active members were selected by a "membership committee" made up of the leaders of some of the largest corporations in the country and these same corporations—including General Electric, Standard Oil of New Jersey (Exxon), U.S. Steel, and General Motors—have themselves provided most of the Council's chairmen. Though charged with the responsibility of preparing confidential reports and studies on the broad range of domestic and foreign policies "affecting the business interests of the country," the Council was in no sense administered by federal bureaucrats. Said bureaucrats, indeed, did not even possess the power to determine the agendas for Council meetings nor did they bother to keep minutes of Council deliberations. Council meetings were regularly addressed by high Cabinet officials, civil servants, military men, and foreign dignitaries but reporters were never allowed direct access to such meetings nor were copies of such speeches generally made available to the public.[8]

The New Deal 'Mutiny'

Strange as its structure was—and remained—the Business Council existed to perform important functions. Its bureaucratic and corporate sponsors alike hoped that it could become a sort of General Staff to administer the recovery programs being launched by the first Roosevelt administration and this it emphatically did. They also believed that the Council could provide a necessary and securely-private forum for government and business leaders to work out compromises on matters of political and economic import and in this, too, their hopes were realized.[9] This is not to say that the Business Council had an altogether happy relationship with Franklin Delano Roosevelt or succeeding Presidents. Far from it. By the summer of 1935, indeed, the NRA was moribund and important Council members were in open revolt against New Deal labor-relations and banking policies. The heads of General Motors and DuPont, among others, absented themselves from Council functions and rumors were afoot that the organization was doomed.[10]

They *Need* Each Other

The Council, however, did not die. Even in the worst periods of friction between corporate and governmental interests, Council meetings continued to be attended by capitalists from the nation's largest firms and joining them were their opposite numbers from the commanding heights of the federal government. None of it was accidental. Businessman and bureaucrat needed each other's cooperation to deal with the continuing problems of depression and, while the *terms* of that cooperation were debatable, the *necessity* for it was not. Henry Ford might continue to act as if he were an independent sovereign negotiating with lesser potentates in Washington but in this he was increasingly eccentric. American big businessmen had to recognize—whether they wanted to or not—that the federal government was never again going to assume a well-nigh-invisible presence in the nation's economic affairs. Such corporate leaders as W. Averell Harriman (Union Pacific, Brown Brothers, Harriman), Juan Trippe (Pan American), Thomas J. Watson (IBM), and scores of others continued to make use of the opportunities for contact and compromise that the existence of the Business Council made possible.[11]

The Management 'Talent Pool'

Government leaders, too, were coming to have a vested interest in the Council's existence. As the New Deal progressed, federal officials assumed wider and wider responsibilities for preserving the public welfare and complex programs were created which demanded specialized experience and skill to administer. Lacking adequate reserves of trained manpower, federal leaders often found themselves forced to recruit personnel from outside Washington. State governments were an important source of talent but so, too, were the larger American corporations whose managerial staffs composed the largest single pool of administrative expertise the nation possessed. The Business Council provided an important center for such recruitment of corporate talent.[12]

FDR and U.S. Steel

Government leaders also recognized the usefulness of the Council as a private forum. Even during the worst periods of stress between the public and the private sectors, businessmen and bureaucrats continued to use Council meetings as a base from which to work out political compromises far from the public eye, one of the most interesting of which involved the Roosevelt administration and the U.S. Steel Corporation. Late in 1937 the Democrats had been placed in political jeopardy by the onset of a severe "Roosevelt recession" and in short order a private meeting was arranged between the President and Myron C. Taylor, chairman of U.S. Steel. At this meeting Roosevelt proposed that U.S. Steel assist in the recovery effort by cutting the prices it charged for its products without, at the same time, cutting the *wages* it paid to its workers. Taylor, not surprisingly, responded that his corporation preferred to cut *both* wages and prices and Roosevelt replied that such actions might be acceptable to him if U.S. Steel would agree to provide him with its confidential cost-of-production and profit statistics. Taylor ignored Roosevelt's suggestion.

Playing the Antitrust 'Card'

Within a few months, however, the Democrats had upped the political ante. Roosevelt allowed liberal New Dealers in Congress to create a "Temporary National Economic Committee" to investigate "monopoly power" in the United States and the Antitrust Division of the Department of Justice also announced its intention to launch an ambitious program of prosecutions. The steel industry was widely rumored to be a particular target of the New Deal's antitrust attentions. In

June of 1938 U.S. Steel started negotiating with Roosevelt in earnest. First, chairman Myron C. Taylor announced his corporation's intention to cut prices on its products without lowering wages and then informed U.S. Steel's representative on the Business Council, Edward N. Stettinius, Jr., to try and make sure that U.S. Steel did not become the target of an antitrust investigation.[13]

Steel and 'Statesmanship'

Stettinius made haste to comply. On June 13, 1938, he and 15 other Business Council members met with high administration officials in Washington. The federal representatives—including the Attorney General, the head of the Antitrust Division of the Justice Department, the assistant secretaries of Commerce and Treasury, and several high-ranking White House advisers—used the meeting to calm corporate sensibilities. U.S. Steel's "statesmanship" was specifically praised and, indeed, so laudatory did one high-ranking bureaucrat become that he suggested the federal government might divert *all* of the steel orders it was then placing for an expanded defense program to U.S. Steel in order to increase the corporation's volume of business "to a point where it would be unnecessary for it to make a wage cut." U.S. Steel's lawyers soon deemed acceptance of such federal largesse "extremely unwise" but its bargaining with the White House continued behind the scenes, climaxing in a secret meeting between Stettinius and Roosevelt on September 1st, 1938.

The 'Ripple Effect'

At this latter meeting Stettinius allowed Roosevelt to examine his corporation's confidential profit and cost-of-production data for a 10 year period. As Roosevelt pored over the materials, Stettinius argued that U.S. Steel's agreement to cut prices without cutting wages was causing it to lose $36 million a year. Roosevelt replied that he understood

Stettinius' position but that a corporation as massive as U.S. Steel could not cut wages without causing an industrial ripple effect which would "spread like wildfire throughout the country" and threaten Administration programs aimed at assisting economic recovery.   U.S. Steel, then, should plan on maintaining the status quo.

Selling Antitrust 'Protection'

After more sparring the real bargaining commenced. Roosevelt began by asking Stettinius what U.S. Steel's "time schedule on this whole [wage cutting] business" was and Stettinius replied that U.S. Steel's leadership could no longer honor its "obligation" not to cut wages.   Roosevelt than informed Stettinius that he "hoped" that U.S. Steel would not cut wages for "a certain period of time," by which he meant the forthcoming 1938 elections.   After the elections wages might be lowered and Roosevelt would attempt to "work out a face-saving plan" for John L. Lewis and the C.I.O. Stettinius, for U.S. Steel, then added that his corporation felt a "keen sense of obligation" for the messages that Roosevelt had delivered to them through his aide Harry Hopkins, these being in all probability (though they were never explicitly discussed in the available record) Presidential assurances that U.S. Steel would *not* be a target for an antitrust investigation *if* it cooperated on the wage question. After more pleasantries, the meeting closed.

The TNEC 'Farce'

That U.S. Steel had made a deal to avoid antitrust prosecution is supported by Stettinius' subsequent records of his meetings with high administration officials at Business Council functions.   By the end of September, indeed, the Attorney General, the head of the Antitrust Division of the Justice Department, and the chairman of the Temporary National Economic Committee had all assured him that U.S. Steel was in no antitrust danger. *He was also told that the antimonopoly drive being mounted by the federal government was largely a farce put on for public consumption.*[14]   U.S. Steel's experience in its bargaining with Roosevelt in that 1937-38 recession had hardly been cost-free but, by making use of the confidential forum provided by the existence of the Business Council, its management had been able to come to a workable compromise with Roosevelt. It had lost the wage-cutting battle but, in return for keeping wages up until after the 1938 elections, it had gained its freedom from the antitrust threat.   Stettinius might not have liked the price his corporation had had to pay but he could not ignore the usefulness of an organization through which such bargaining contacts had been maintained.

The War Games

A year after the events described above, the uses of the Council as a means of channeling corporate influence into Washington were decisively accented by the outbreak of World War II.   As big businessmen streamed in to administer the mobilization drives, the Council became, in the words of one of its wartime chairmen, "the nucleus for industrial cooperation" and "the principal instrumentality for drafting the services of important members of management" for use by the federal government.   As the war progressed, the Council increasingly became a recruiting station for corporate expertise for an expanding Executive branch.[15] The organizational imperatives of modern war did more, however, than to simply increase the usefulness of the Business Council.   It also helped persuade the relatively liberal members of the Council to seek to broaden the scope of corporate influence in federal councils by creating a research agency that could provide big businessmen with long-term proposals and perspectives on questions of the broadest national import.   The creation of this new avenue for collective corporate expression marked the beginnings of a second stage in the evolution of organized business influence.

Post-War Planning and the CED

By the first months of 1942 the war was fueling an economic recovery that the New Deal itself had never been able to provide. Millions of jobless men and women were finally able to find employment in an industrial sector that was finally operating at peak capacity. But could prosperity and full employment survive the cessation of that massive armaments production? Would an America victorious in war be forced to endure another wrenching depression after peace returned? Such questions were very much on the minds of influential Business Council members even before America's entry into the war and, in the wake of Pearl Harbor, efforts to establish a research and planning committee to coordinate businessmen's reconversion efforts were intensified. Federal officials, academics, and interested businessmen outside of the Business Council made haste to cooperate. By June of 1942 an organization aimed at achieving a healthy post-war economy had been created, the Committee for Economic Development (CED).[16]

Chip Off the Old Block

Business Council members were only one factor in the birth of the CED but their support was central to the success of that new organization. As a recent student of it notes, the older Business Council had "acted as a sounding board for the original proposal [to create the CED] and as a cosponsor of the organization during its gestation. Most of the leaders of the CED, moreover, were [initially] drawn from the ranks of the Council; of the 20 trustees who served on the CED board in 1942, 14 had served or were then serving on the [Council] and three of the remaining six were appointed to the Council the next year."[17]

Widening the Net

CED differed, however, from its organizational parent in two important ways. The Council's role was primarily that of a forum for contact between businessman and bureaucrat and a recruitment center for corporate expertise. The CED, on the other hand, had longer-term goals which required it, unlike the Council, to develop a large *research* component and this fact, in turn, led CED to open its membership to academics (primarily economists) as well as big businessmen. (The latter, however, reserved all posts on the CED's board of directors for themselves.) It was also a private as opposed to a quasi-governmental organization and this allowed its member corporations—most of whom were also represented on the Business Council—to reach a wider range of business associations without whose cooperation CED's reconversion planning could not succeed. Chief among these were the National Association of Manufacturers and the U.S. Chamber of Commerce, organizations whose leaders had long been disenchanted with the New Deal and its works and also with business groups that had "cooperated" with Roosevelt,[18] including the Business Council.

Coming to Terms With 'Liberalism'

CED was created to put forth a positive "businessmen's program" for post-war economic stability but this did not mean that it was part of a corporate attempt to "roll back" the New Deal. CED, like the Business Council, stood as institutional evidence of a growing urge for *detente* between big businessmen and an expanded federal government with broadened responsibilities for the orderly management of a capitalist economy. Its wartime leadership had provided, for example, important assistance to Treasury officials in the creation of the pay-as-you-earn system of "withholding taxation" that has been the centerpiece of the federal income-tax system from 1943 to the present. CED's leadership did not, moreover, expect the expenditures that increased levels of federal taxation had made possible would return to pre-New Deal levels after the war and, indeed, those leaders advocated federal annual budgets which were more than twice as high as the $8.5 billion maximum spent by New Deal administrators.[19]

The 'Keynesian' Revolution

Following the defeat of the Axis powers, politician and businessman alike braced for the depression that all feared would return. None came. Relief was soon followed by trepidation, however, among the relatively conservative business groups which had hitherto cooperated with Washington officials via umbrella organizations such as the CED and by 1946 relations between the NAM, the U.S. Chamber of Commerce, and the Truman administration had degenerated badly. Both associations had, in addition, ceased most of their organized collaboration with the CED. The latter's leaders, however, continued to announce its public support for federal activities which were anathema to right-wing businessmen who equated the welfare state with creeping socialism, including federal responsibilities for the provision of old-age pensions, unemployment insurance, and protection of the right of workers to organize and bargain collectively. CED reports also accepted the necessity of federal public-works spending during periods of economic emergency and even went so far as to cautiously support short-term deficit spending by the federal government. Though hardly "Keynesians," CED's member corporations were ever-so-slowly coming to terms with the fact that federal debt was not simply household borrowing on a continental scale.[20]

The Full Employment Bill of 1946

CED's willingness to recognize the legitimacy of key elements of the New Deal heritage paid handsome dividends. The influence of the organization rose throughout the immediate post-war period and that influence, in turn, enabled CED leaders to take an important role in determining the shape of America's post-war politics. CED and BC members had great influence, for example, in the creation and administration of the "Marshall Plan" for Western European economic recovery and, beyond the foreign-affairs field, CED leaders also played key roles in determining the fate of the

"Full Employment Bill of 1946," perhaps the single most important piece of domestic reform legislation introduced during the immediate post-war period.

NAM and the 'Reds'

As originally introduced in Congress, this latter bill had called upon the federal government to assume a number of clearly-mandated responsibilities for the relief of joblessness. Washington bureaucrats would forecast yearly economic performance and outline fiscal and monetary strategies conducive to achieving full employment. Levels of federal investment, expenditure, and taxation would then be arranged in a manner consistent with this economic goal and, if necessary, the federal government should also serve as an employer of last resort. The bill thus enlarged on New Deal welfare precedent by allowing for an expanded and continuous federal presence in the management of the industrial economy. Businessmen generally opposed this proposed extension of federal welfare responsibility but the differing ways in which they did so underlined the distance that big businessmen had come since the onset of the Depression. Traditional pan-industrial business organizations like the NAM and the U.S. Chamber reacted viscerally, speaking of communists within the federal government. But the chief executive officers of the large corporations who belonged to the Business Council and the CED were more sophisticated. They spoke of *modifying* the full-employment proposal and in fact CED leaders Beardsley Ruml and Ralph Flanders cooperated with congressional moderates to replace the bill with their own program.

Taking Out the 'Action' Words

The CED-backed proposal passed in Congress and ultimately became the Employment Act of 1946. Federal responsibilities to guarantee "full" employment were replaced with a call for "maximum" employment of those "willing and able to seek work" in "a manner calculated to foster and promote free enterprise." The legislation neglected, however, to *define* full employment. It created a Council of Economic Advisers within the executive branch to advise the President on economic policy and prepare an annual report on the state of the nation's economy but the law established no machinery for translating governmental proposals into action. Federal administrators "fostered" and "promoted" but they failed to act. Using a strategy of arriving early and proposing consistently, the big business-men of the BC and CED were thus making creative use of their 15 years of organizational experience with reform-minded Democratic administrations and, in the process, they were learning to make new sorts of bargains and to maintain a new type of presence in the nation's public-policy councils.[21]

Minding the Store for Ike

Such lessons were not forgotten in the decades following the end of World War II. Throughout the onset of the Cold War and on into the comparative "normalcy" of the 1950s, CED's stature remained high in corporate and governmental circles alike. When Republican Dwight David Eisenhower assumed the Presidency in 1953 he made haste to appoint men identified with both the Business Council and the CED to high administrative posts, including at various times the Secretaries of Army, Defense, Treasury, HEW, and Commerce. Other BC and CED members served as Under-secretaries of Commerce and Defense, as consultants to the Departments of State and Treasury, the U.S. Army, and the National Security Council, and as ambassadors to Great Britain, Canada, and Italy.[22]

Coming of the 'Protesters'

As time passed the extent of the direct interlocking between the Business Council and the CED gradually diminished and CED became a recruiting ground for corporate expertise in its own right. CED's leadership also began to conceive of its organization's role as a corporate "think-tank" in an increasingly ambitious way. From the realm of fiscal and monetary policy (where its research interests had originally been confined), CED moved out to address broader social questions, including labor relations, urban policy, and race relations.[23] In the process, however, CED began running into trouble, particularly after the Democratic Presidents arrived back in Washington in 1961. Democratic leaders John F. Kennedy and his successor Lyndon Johnson had no desire to offend big business but, as the troubled decade of the 1960s progressed, the administrations they headed found themselves forced to deal with vexing issues at home and abroad that were not easily resolvable by the use of established corporate or bureaucratic logic. The anti-war and civil-rights protest of the period underlined, for example, some of the challenges of changing political realities and the latter emphasized the ascent of new political-interest groups such as the nonwhite and the young into positions of national prominence.

The Hodges Rebellion

In their efforts to respond to these new clienteles and challenges, the Democrats often found themselves at odds with the big businessmen of the BC and CED and engaged in open war with the NAM and U.S. Chamber, particularly in the realm of social welfare and labor-relations policy. Such a growing disjunction of interests between organized business and the federal government did not, however, mean that the usefulness of CED and the Business Council was at an end. The limits of cooperation between businessmen and bureaucrats were strained but not broken, yielding a process of accommodation that was illustrated by an event that occurred in the immediate wake of John F. Kennedy's inauguration, the "disaffiliation" of the Business Council from the U.S. government. In its simplest terms, this crisis in Council-government relations was a question of privacy. Luther Hodges, Kennedy's appointee as Secretary of

Commerce, was a retired North Carolina textile manufacturer who was suspicious of the Council's big-business membership and its confidential access to high federal officials. He proposed to restructure the Council in three major ways. First, he wanted the Secretary of Commerce to have the power to select candidates for Council membership and to set the agendas for Council meetings. Second, he wanted Council meetings opened to the press when—and only when—they were being addressed by federal representatives. Third, he wanted the Council to appoint more businessmen from "small" and "medium-sized" firms.

Getting Rid of the 'Agitator'

The Council's leaders wanted little or nothing to do with Luther Hodges or his demands. They grudgingly appointed five small businessmen to membership in their organization but stonewalled Hodges' other proposals. Compromise was attempted but, after a Council meeting at a plush Virginia resort was attended by no Administration representative save Hodges, the Council's membership voted overwhelmingly to avenge this slight to their organizational status by leaving the offices in the Commerce Department they had occupied for 30 years and re-establishing themselves as a "private" association. Hodges threatened retribution but none came and, barely a month after the Council's disaffiliation, high White House aides were busily restoring the advisory interlocks the Council had long maintained with cabinet level departments, the Council of Economic Advisers, and the White House itself. Relations between the Council and the Executive branch remained strained, particularly after the steel price-hike crisis of 1962 had pitted Kennedy against U.S. Steel (and Business Council) chairman Roger Blough but, following Kennedy's death, Lyndon Johnson made haste to improve his administration's relations with organized big business in general and the Business Council in particular. Perhaps the clearest signal of this *rapprochement* was launched immediately after the 1964 elections when Johnson replaced Secretary of Commerce Luther Hodges with John T.

Connor of Allied Chemical, a long-time member of the Business Council.[24]

Recession of the '70s

As the Business Council's successful transition from a quasi-public to a private organization had demonstrated, federal bureaucrats, like their corporate opposite numbers, had a strong interest in maintaining the existence of a forum where contacts with elite elements of corporate America could be maintained. Such a recognition of mutual interest preserved Council and CED stature vis-a-vis the government but it did little or nothing to protect either big businessmen or the federal bureaucracy from political pressure emanating from *outside* the government itself. As the 1960s progressed, the pressure facing corporate America had grown markedly. New waves of political-constituency groups appeared on the Washington scene. War protesters and advocates of Negro rights were succeeded by environmental, consumer protection, womens rights, and other spokesmen whose combined demands posed new challenges to business. As the 1970s began, businessmen's difficulties were compounded by recessionary uncertainties, increasingly-polarized political reactions to the Presidency of Richard M. Nixon, and a slowly developing awareness that a post-war era of "cheap energy" was coming to an end.

Coming of the 'Roundtable'

In such unsettling political circumstances American big business searched for new organizational tools through which to exercise its influence. The CED provided one already-existent foundation upon which to build but, by the late 1960s, its cohesion as a research and policymaking body had been eroded by the failure of its membership to achieve a consensus on a series of broad social questions regarding which the organization had, all-too-optimistically, decided to formulate policies. CED's business members were also

becoming increasingly concerned that the organization was
becoming a creature of its academic staff or, as Leonard Silk
of the *New York Times* colorfully put it, that "the golf pros
were taking over the clubhouse."[25] The Business Council
had similarly unsuitable organizational attributes,
particularly the fact that its usefulness as a forum for contact,
cooperation, and recruitment depended upon the *confidentiality* of the organization's proceedings. This
confidentiality, in turn, had led the Council to insist that none
of its members seek to use it as an organizational base from
which to lobby openly for specific legislation, gain public
recognition, or do anything that might be likely to get his own
name in the papers. Members who did attempt such actions
were (in the words of one confidential Council statement)
"quietly dropped in due course."[26] A new organizational
form for big-business influence was thus required and it was
achieved in 1972 with the formation of the "Business
Roundtable," the third leg of the corporate policymaking
infrastructure that exists in the United States today and that
is, as we shall see, an organization which demonstrates
important elements of continuity with the two that preceded
it.

A Lobbying Arm for Big Business

The Business Roundtable was expressly designed as a
lobbying agency rather than a contact forum (the Business
Council) or as a research and policymaking assembly (the
CED). It is important to understand, however, that the same
large corporations represented on the Council and CED are
also intimately involved in the affairs of the Business
Roundtable. Two firms, American Telephone and
Telegraph and General Electric, were particularly important
in its creation. In March of 1972 ATT and GE leaders met
with high-level Nixon administration advisers, including
Secretary of Treasury John Connally and Arthur Burns,
chairman of the Federal Reserve Board, meetings at which
those corporate officials were warned that "business had to
shape up in sophistication and techniques in Washington or

or else go down the political tube." Those warnings spurred action. Before the end of the month, ATT and GE hosted a meeting of about a dozen chief-executive-officers of major American corporations, accompanied by their chief Washington representatives. At this conference, strategies were mapped out to increase big businessmen's returns on their political investments, including the creation of a new organization, the Business Roundtable.[27]

The 45 Who Count

The Roundtable's membership is overwhelmingly drawn from the nation's largest firms. In 1976, for example, chief-executive-officers of 9 of the top 10, 37 of the top 50, and 63 of the top 100 of the nation's industrial companies were represented at its functions. Its chairmen have in recent years included the leaders of corporations like GE, DuPont, and General Motors. These are of course busy men and the entire membership—currently numbering about 200[28]—meets together only once each year. The Roundtable, however, does not depend upon mass meetings for organizational effectiveness. Instead, a 45-man "Policy Committee" is delegated major administrative responsibilities, including oversight of the deliberations of over a dozen "task forces" which formulate position papers on specialized topics, including national planning and employment, government regulation, labor legislation, energy, taxation, consumer interests, national health insurance, and environmental legislation. Policy Committee members are, in addition, publicly affiliated with the Roundtable. *All other member-ships are kept secret to the greatest possible extent.*[29]

Strategy Versus Ideology

The Roundtable's Policy Committee meets in New York approximately six times a year to perform its major functions, the first of these being the mapping out of the organization's short-term legislative and lobbying priorities. Secondly, the

Policy Committee serves as a ratification board for all reports, recommendations, and other policy statements issued under the Roundtable's imprimatur. On the first point, its lobbying efforts are of a type not seen before in Washington. First, Roundtable lobbying is selective, with only a small number of bills or issues being chosen for attention during a given legislative session. Secondly, its members do not merely lobby *against* particular legislation but push, instead, *for* substitute bills, those with amendments aimed at preserving big-business interests. A strategy of "Yes, but..." is substituted, as noted, for the strategy of "No" associated with broader-based business pressure-groups like NAM and the U.S. Chamber.[30]

The Winning Approach

To further increase their effectiveness, Roundtable CEOs lobby Washington bureaucrats and legislators directly rather than depending primarily upon the services of their corporations' paid lobbyists. To add still more to the political returns of such face-to-face contacts, CEOs are regularly asked to lobby politicians representing *areas* in which their firms have large corporate installations. At such meetings, Roundtable members are expected to put forward views upon which the organization has been able to achieve a workable consensus and any *other* issues that they may wish to discuss *individually* are not advertised as Roundtable positions. Articles in a variety of national newspapers and magazines in recent months have acknowledged the Roundtable's stature as one of the most successful lobbies on the contemporary Washington scene.[31]

'A Rose By Any Other Name'

Given the undoubted influence of the Business Roundtable, it is important to understand that the organization is controlled by the same corporations—and the same men—who make up the membership of the Business Council and who are well-represented on the Board of Directors of the CED. The instrument of this control is the Roundtable's "Policy Committee." *The 45 corporate leaders who compose this body have the final say in Roundtable decisions*: The other 135 to 155 member-corporations of the organization must play by Policy Committee rules if they wish to take part in Roundtable affairs. That Policy Committee, however, *is very largely the membership of the Business Council under another name.* In 1977-1978, no less than 37 of the 45 CEO's on the Roundtable Policy Committee were also members of the Business Council, an interlock of 82%. During 1978-1979, 35 of the 47 members of the Policy Committee—approximately 75%—were also members of the Council. One-third of the Roundtable's Policy Committee also served on the Board of Directors of the CED during the same period, including the CED's chairman.[32]

The Interlocking 'Directorate'

Such large-scale interlocking between the Business Roundtable, the Business Council, and the CED is not an accidental phenomenon nor is it a particularly surprising one. As this paper has attempted to demonstrate, big businessmen's efforts to influence public policy have become progressively more *collective* and institutionalized since the New Deal era. Initially, the chief-executive-officers of the nation's largest corporations grouped themselves into a forum where advisory contacts with federal officials might be confidentially maintained. They did so, moreover, at the invitation of Franklin D. Roosevelt's New Deal administrations and later, during World War II, federal officials again cooperated with the Business Council to create the CED, an agency which provided a long-term research and planning component to big-businessmen's public-policy efforts. Finally, in 1972, the leaders of the same corporations whose names had long been associated with both the Business Council and the CED cooperated to produce yet a third type of big-business policy agency, the lobbying-oriented Business Roundtable. To help insure continuity of operations,

Council and CED activists moved in to staff the Roundtable's directorate, the Policy Committee.

'The More Things Change...'

The Roundtable, Council, and CED are thus three different facets of the same overarching organizational impulse, one that has been at work within this nation's big-business community throughout the last four decades. For too long the historians of American business have ignored this fact, oft-times contenting themselves with the thought that "things changed after the New Deal" and that businessmen have been increasingly required to take the federal government into account as a basic condition for their entrepreneurial existence. How businessmen have sought to bargain with the government, what types of institutions they have established to assist them in those efforts, and what collective interests American big-businessmen have sought to preserve are topics that have not yet been much discussed.[33]

A New 'Iconography'

In the future, however, interested scholars must start paying more attention to the structure and operations of organizations such as those described here. For too long the capitalist iconography of the Progressive Era has obscured the fact that big-businessmen are no longer behaving as unilateral or individualistic actors. The larger American firms have, in recent decades, come more and more to understand the virtues and the necessities of reaching accommodations with a vastly-enhanced federal government holding wide responsibilities in the area of mass welfare and economic operations. In the process of accommodating themselves to these changed realities, American big-businessmen have created a new organizational world, one in which the Business Council, Business Roundtable, and CED have played—and will continue to play—central and important roles.

It Isn't Going Away

It is too soon, of course, to know whether the Business Roundtable—only seven years old at this writing—will prove to be as stable as the two sister organizations that preceded it. Some current evidence (e.g., the Carter administration's use of Roundtable officials to draft and then help pass the "anti-boycott" legislation designed to counter Arab embargoes on trade with Israel by U.S. corporations) suggests that the Roundtable has achieved a secure stature in Washington. Whether the Roundtable survives as a specific organization, however, it appears quite likely that the *type* of structure it represents will live on under whatever name the future may have in store.[34]

■

REFERENCES

[1] The two classic statements here are Lincoln Steffens, *Shame of the Cities* (New York, 1904) and David Graham Phillips, *Treason of the Senate* (Stanford, Calif.: Academic Reprints, 1950). The current spate of books on such wealthy families as the Rockefellers, Mellons, Guggenheims, and the like fall generally within this same tradition.

[2] One of the reactions of the Chamber and NAM to their loss of influence has been to propose mergers with each other. These efforts have so far proven abortive, not least because the Roundtable was to have become the Advisory Policy Council for the resulting Chamber-NAM organization, thus increasing the influence of the largest U.S. corporations in its affairs. See, e.g., "Business Lobbyists Blend Their Voices," *Business Week* (June 21, 1976), p. 31.

[3] A membership list of the Roundtable's Policy Committee, including interlocks with the BC and CED, is presented below.

[4] See, e.g., Charles Kindleberger, *Power and Money* (New York, 1970), pp. 56-57; Lester M. Salamon and John J. Siegfried, "Economic Power or Political Influence: The Impact of Industry Structure on Public Policy," *American Political Science Review*, Vol. 71 (September 1977), pp. 1026-1043; and Irving Shapiro (president of DuPont), "Government and Business: Adversaries or Partners for the Public Good?," *Vital Speeches* (November 15, 1974), pp. 87-90.

[5] The best single source for businessmen's opinions in the 1930-1933 period is probably R. F. Himmelberg, *The Origins of the NRA* (New York, 1976). Another useful book is Herman Krooss, *Executive Opinion* (Garden City, New York, 1970).

[6]   The best sources for the gestation of the NRA are Ellis W. Hawley, *The New Deal and The Problem of Monopoly* (Princeton, N.J., 1966); Leverett S. Lyon, et al., *The National Recovery Administration* (Washington, 1935); Charles F. Roos, *NRA Economic Planning* (Bloomington, Indiana, 1937); and Hugh S. Johnson, *The Blue Eagle from Egg to Earth* (Garden City, N.Y., 1935).

[7]   The term "Business Council" is used throughout the text for simplicity. In fact the original name of the organization was the "Business Advisory and Planning Council of the Department of Commerce," subsequently changed to the "Business Advisory Council" in 1934 and to the "Business Council" in 1961. For the organization's birth, see Kim McQuaid, "The Business Advisory Council of the Department of Commerce, 1933-1961: A Study in Corporate-Governmental Relations," in Paul Uselding (Ed.), *Research in Economic History*, Volume I (Greenwich, Conn.: JAI Press, 1976), pp. 171-197.

[8]   A good source for Council structure is Hobart Rowen's *The Free Enterprisers: Kennedy, Johnson and The Business Establishment* (New York, 1964). See also Gerald R. Rosen, "The Blue Ribbon Business Council," *Dun's Review* (January 1970), pp. 37-41; "An Association That Shuns The Limelight," *Association Management* (January 1976), pp. 77-81; and Gerald R. Rosen, "Business' Most Powerful Club," *Dun's Review* (December 1976), pp. 69-71, 94.

[9]   For Business Council influence in early New Deal industrial recovery and labor relations policy, see Kim McQuaid, "The Failure of Corporate Revival During The Early New Deal," *The Historian* (August 1979).

[10]   The *New York Times* carried such rumors in 1935 and again in 1936. See McQuaid, note 7, supra.

[11]   One of the most useful surveys of big business public-policy efforts remains a decade-old doctoral thesis written from a Marxist perspective, David Eakins, "The Development of Corporate Liberal Policy Research in the United States, 1885-1965" (University of Wisconsin, 1966).

[12]   For an example of the federal government's need for corporate expertise in formulating and administering its social welfare programs, see Edward D. Berkowitz and Kim McQuaid, "Businessman and Bureaucrat: The Evolution of the American Social Welfare System, 1900-1940," *Journal of Economic History*, Vol 38 (March 1978), pp. 132-141. The influence of big businessmen in the war mobilization is covered in Bruce Catton, *The Warlords of Washington* (New York, 1948); Eliot Janeway, *The Struggle for Survival* (New Haven, 1956); Geoffrey Perrett, *Days of Sadness, Years of Triumph: The American People, 1941-1945* (Baltimore, 1972); John Morton Blum, *"V" Was For Victory* (New York, 1976); and Richard Polenburg, *War and Society: The United States, 1941-1945* (Philadelphia, 1972).

[13]   Edward Stettinius later went on to succeed Taylor as U.S. Steel's chairman and, during the later stages of World War II, to serve as the nation's Secretary of State.

[14]   Data as to the sequence of the confidential meetings between U.S. Steel and various Roosevelt administration leaders is contained in a bound notebook entitled "Washington Notes" dictated by E. N. Stettinius, Jr., at

various times during September and October of 1938. This notebook is in Box 64 of the *Stettinius Papers*, Alderman Library, University of Virginia, Charlottesville. See also Myron C. Taylor to Stettinius (June 16, 1938), Box 63, *Stettinius Papers*.

¹⁵ William Batt (BC chairman) to Stettinius (May 20, 1940), Box 627, *Stettinius Papers*. See also the agenda for the BC meetings of November 14-16, 1941, with accompanying listing of official mobilization positions occupied by BC members (Box 627, *Stettinius Papers*). Other sources on the BC during the wartime years include Box 76 of the *Lou Holland Papers*, Harry S. Truman Library, Independence, Missouri, and Box 70, *Will Clayton Papers*, Truman Library.

¹⁶ Two of the best surveys of the early history of the CED are Karl Schriftgeisser, *Business and Public Policy: The Role of the Committee for Economic Development, 1942-1967*, and Robert Brady's neglected essay, "The CED—What Is It and Why?," *Antioch Review*, Vol. 4 (Spring 1944), pp. 21-46.

¹⁷ Robert Collins, "Positive Responses to the New Deal: The Roots of the Committee for Economic Development, 1933-1942," *Business History Review* (Autumn 1978), pp. 388-389. Secretary of Commerce Jesse Jones was one who termed the Business Council a "co-sponsor" of the CED during its creation. See Jesse Jones to S. Clay Williams (June 25, 1942), File #102517/36, RG 40, National Archives, and Box 40 of the *Paul Hoffman Papers*, Truman Library.

¹⁸ For the extent of NAM and Chamber cooperation with CED during its first years, see Brady (1944), p. 22, and Schriftgeisser (1968). For internal BC awareness of the fact that the "tie-in" between BC members, NAM and the Chamber could be better carried out through a CED not identified with the New Deal, see S. Clay Williams to Jesse Jones (July 2, 1942), RG 40, File #102517/36, National Archives. It should be noted that BC leaders tried to recruit pro-New Deal staffers as well as conservatives. John Kenneth Galbraith, for example, was offered the post of Research Director for CED in 1943 by BC member Ralph Flanders (J.K. Galbraith interview, July 11, 1977).

¹⁹ The peacetime federal budget had peaked at $8.5 billion in 1939. CED advocated a federal budget of approximately $18 billion a year in the immediate post-war period and in fact federal expenditures between 1946 and 1949 never fell below $33 billion a year. Eakins thesis, note 11, supra, pp. 334-5. Beardsley Ruml was the CED leader most closely associated with changes in the federal income-tax collection mechanisms. For a discussion of some of the effects of these changes, see J.R.T. Hughes, *The Governmental Habit: Economic Controls From Colonial Times to the Present* (New York, 1977), p. 207.

²⁰ See, for example, William Benton, "The Economics of a Free Society: A Declaration of American Economic Policy," *Fortune*, Vol. 30 (October 1944), pp. 163-5. On proto-Keynesianism among BC and CED members, see Dennison, Flanders, Leeds, Filene, *Toward Full Employment* (New York, 1938).

²¹ The classic volume on the Employment Act is Stephen Bailey, *Congress Makes A Law* (New York, 1961). See also Otis L. Graham, Jr.,

Toward A Planned Society: From Roosevelt to Nixon (New York, 1976), pp. 88-90; Karl Schriftgeisser, *Business Comes of Age: The Story of the CED* (Englewood Cliffs, N.J., 1960), pp. 96-97. Daniel Patrick Monyihan has noted an important element of significance in America's failure to pass full employment legislation in the immediate wake of World War II. It thereby became—along with Canada—the only one of the world's democracies *not* to institute "a postwar economic policy that gave the first priority to continued full employment. Accordingly, it became impossible to base other social policies on the presumption that all able-bodied persons in need of income would [be able to] obtain it first of all by working." This fact, in its turn, has helped to make the structure of America's "welfare state" a considerably more *ad hoc* proposition than is the case in various Western European and Scandinavian nations. Monyihan, *The Politics of A Guaranteed Income: The Nixon Administration and the Family Assistance Plan* (New York, 1973), pp. 94-95.

²² For a listing of BC members' government service as of 1955, see U.S. Congress, House of Representatives, Committee on the Judiciary, Antitrust Subcommittee, "WOC's and Government Advisory Groups," *Hearings*, August 10, 1955, Part II, 84th Congress, 1st session (Washington, 1955), pp. 960-967. See also Hobart Rowen, "America's Most Powerful Private Club," *Harper's*, Vol. 221 (September, 1960), pp. 79-84; Schriftgeisser, *Business and Public Policy*, p. 53; Eakins thesis, note 11, supra, pp. 451-497.

²³ Frank V. Fowlkes, "Washington Pressures and CED's Impact on Federal Policies Enhanced by Close Ties to Executive Branch," *National Journal* (June 17, 1972), pp. 1015-1024.

²⁴ The best single source for Council and governmental relations during the Kennedy/Johnson period is Hobart Rowen, *The Free Enterprisers: Kennedy, Johnson, and the Business Establishment* (Philadelphia, 1964), especially pp. 61-79. See also Bernard Nossiter, *The Mythmakers: An Essay on Power and Wealth* (Boston, 1964); Jim Heath, *John F. Kennedy and the Business Community* (Chicago, 1969). Primary source materials for the period include the *Walter Heller* and *Theodore Sorensen Papers* at the JFK Library in Waltham, Massachusetts. The oral history memoirs of Luther Hodges, Thomas J. Watson, Jr., Frederick Kappel, and Myer Feldman at the Kennedy Library are also extremely useful.

²⁵ Interview with Leonard Silk (January 11, 1979) and interviews with businessmen active in CED councils, including James E. Robison, retired vice president, Textron (February 24, 1977) and Walter Blass, director of corporate planning, New York Telephone (April 5, 1978).

²⁶ "Observations of a BAC Wife" (memo dated January 16, 1961). This report, plus the accompanying "Advantages and Disadvantages of BAC" statement of the same date, provide a useful summary of internal Council dynamics. The two reports are available in Box 126 of the John W. *Snyder Papers*, Truman Library, Independence, Missouri.

²⁷ Bryce N. Harlow to author (January 18, 1979). Harlow, the chief Washington representative for Procter and Gamble since 1970 and a high White House staff assistant to Richard Nixon in 1969-1970, was a participant in the activities described here.

²⁸ Peter Slavin, "The Business Roundtable: New Lobbying Arm of

Big Business," *Business and Society Review*, Number 16 (Winter, 1975-1976), pp. 28-32, and Steven Rattner, "Big Industry Gun Aims at Hill," *New York Times* (March 7, 1976), Section 111, p. 7.

[29] The Roundtable position papers published thus far, including those on energy, inflation, taxation policy, and the makeup of corporate boards of directors, are available from the Roundtable's New York or Washington offices (405 Lexington Avenue 10017 and 1801 K St., N.W. 20006).

[30] Rattner, note 28, supra; Barry M. Hager, "Business Roundtable: New Lobbying Force," *Congressional Quarterly* (September 17, 1977), pp. 1964-1968; Walter Guzzardi, Jr., "Business is Learning How to Win in Washington," *Fortune* (March 27, 1978), pp. 53-54; and John W. Post, Executive Director of the Business Roundtable, to author (September 18, 1978).

[31] "Business' Most Powerful Lobby in Washington," *Business Week* (December 20, 1976), p. 60; Juan Cameron, "The Tax Education of Jimmy Carter," *Fortune* (January 16, 1978), p. 58; R.W. Merry and A.R. Hunt, "Business Lobby Gains More Power as it Rides Anti-Government Tide," *Wall Street Journal* (May 17, 1978), pp. 1, 17; Martin Tolchin, "Carter's Corporate Brain Trust," *New York Times* (July 24, 1978), pp. D-1, D-2; "Business Lobbying: Threat to the Consumer Interest," *Consumer Reports*, Vol. 43 (September, 1978), pp. 529-531; Thomas Ferguson and Joel Rogers, "Labor Law Reform and Its Enemies," *The Nation* (January 6-13, 1979), pp. 19-20; and Adam Clymer, "Like Carter, Potomac Power is Ambiguous," *New York Times* (January 8, 1978), Section XLL, pp. 26, 30. Ralph Nader's "Congress Watch" organization has sponsored an investigation of the Business Roundtable's influence and its report, prepared by Andrew Buchsbaum, a student at Harvard University, is due out shortly.

[32] For the extent of these interlocks, see the appendix below.

[33] An honorable exception here is Raymond A. Bauer, Ithiel DeSola Pool, and Lewis A. Dexter, *American Business and Public Policy: The Politics of Foreign Trade* (Chicago, 1972), as is J.R.T. Hughes, *The Governmental Habit*, note 19, supra. It should also be noted that various Neo-Marxist scholars have made major efforts to investigate the extent of cooperation and interlocking between big-business organizations like those described in this essay, an important recent contribution to this literature being G. William Domhoff, *The Powers That Be: Processes of Ruling Class Domination in America* (New York, 1978).

[34] For the Roundtable's efforts on the anti-boycott legislation, see the author's "Back-Door Policymaking," *Working Papers for a New Society* (July/August 1979), pp. 50-54.

Historical Antecedents
of Military-Industrial Criticism*

by Earl A. Molander
Portland State University

THE outcry that rose against the military-industrial complex and most specifically against the aerospace/defense industry in the 1960s was in some respects a distinctive phenomenon of the period. It grew out of the public concern for dramatic increase in the size of the peacetime defense budget in the late 1950s, was catalyzed by Eisenhower's warning against "the acquisition of unwarranted influence...by the military-industrial complex" in his 1961 farewell address, and came to full bloom as a part of public reaction to American involvement in the Vietnam War and the movement to make American business more "socially responsible." In reflecting on this criticism, many observers find it unique not only in its integration of the criticisms which previously had been directed at the military and industry as separate institutions, but also in its simultaneous attack on the military and industry as a unified body.[1] This paper will endeavor to show that the unified attack on the military and industry in the 1960s also has some strong antecedents in recent American history. Particularly, it will show that those aspects of military-industrial complex criticism that focus on the aerospace/defense industry are part of an historical movement which has concerned itself specifically with military-industrial integration in the arms business. Because of its deep roots in American culture, and Western culture generally, this historical criticism of the arms business was in many respects as important in bringing the military-industrial complex attack to popularity as the unique conditions which prevailed in America in the 1960s. Before beginning, it is important that the reader understand that our effort is

only to demonstrate the origins of military-industrial complex *criticism*, not the military-industrial complex itself.

One need not go back very far in American history to find a precedent for military-industrial criticism. In the 1930s there was a visceral attack both in Europe and America on armaments manufacturers. In this country, the "Merchants of Death" scandal, culminating in a Congressional investigation headed by Senator Nye of North Dakota, had a dramatic impact on American attitudes towards the arms industry.[2] Even more recently, it was a popularly held view at the end of World War II that there had been a Japanese military-industrial complex — a "Gumbatsu-Zaibatsu complex," as one contemporary Russian writer has called it — behind Japanese military expansion, and an equally sinister German military-industrial complex behind the Nazi movement.[3] Like the contemporary attack on the military-industrial complex, these movements perpetuated an historical distrust of military-industrial relationships which had existed in Amierican society since the 1890s.

To fully understand the origins of the military-industrial complex criticism, one must begin with the long-standing distrust of profits, dating at least to classical times, and the equally long-standing concern over economic motives in warfare.[4] The distrust of businessmen and the broad concern with the economic motives in warfare are established historical facts and might in themselves be enough to have laid the foundations for military-industrial criticism. But there are three other historical movements that also are important. First, from its earliest beginnings, the movement to establish a permanent peace through disarmament, in America as well as in Europe, focused on the costs of standing armies, their equipment, and warfare itself; on the threat to liberty presented by a peacetime defense establishment; and on the enmity and

danger of war growing out of armaments expansion in neighboring nations.[5] Although the Quakers argued against armaments from the early 17th century onward, and Washington warned against the threat to liberty of "overgrown military establishments," the mainstream of American public opinion to the end of the 19th century was largely unsympathetic to the disarmament movement.[6]

A second concern which helped lay the foundation for military-industrial criticism was the traffic in arms — specifically, the dispute over the rights of neutrals to sell military goods to belligerents in wartime. From Jefferson's early defense of the United States Neutrality Act of 1793 onward, Americans have found themselves scrutinizing the operation of the American arms industry in the international arms market.[7] Finally, criticism of military-industrial relations is set against a public concern with the price, quality, and delivery of military supplies sold to the government that dates at least to the French and Indian War. Profiteering during that war, the Revolution, and the Civil War sparked a number of Congressional investigations whose reports were highly critical of military suppliers; but in no instances were contractors brought to trial.[8]

These three separate concerns all touched indirectly on the relationship between the military and its industrial suppliers. Although there occasionally appeared in each a sense of an unusual symbiosis between the two, the idea of a "military-industrial complex" with far-reaching consequences for American society was never articulated.

The late 19th and early 20th century brought together these three concurrent streams of thought — the peace and disarmament movement, the desire to control the arms traffic, and the scrutiny of government contracting practices. In addition, the concept of a "military-industrial complex" was then first articulated. In the

* A condensed version of the essay which will appear in the forthcoming volume *War, Business, and American Society*, edited by B. Franklin Cooling, reprinted with the permission of the Kennikat Press.

311

early 1890s, European nations and the United States began a race to build heavy naval armor which saw such exorbitant prices being paid by the U.S. Navy for the heavy armor plate that it caused a Congressional investigation. The Senate Committee on Naval Affairs was charged:

> ...to inquire whether the prices paid or agreed to be paid for armor for vessels of the Navy have been fair and reasonable; also, whether any prices paid have been increased on account of patent processes used for the introduction of nickel, or for cementation by the Harvey process; and if so, whether the increases in price are fair and reasonable; whether the issuance of any of the patents was expedited at the request of the Navy Department; whether such patents were properly issued and were for inventions not previously known or used, and who were and are the owners of such patents; whether any officers of the Government were interested therein, or at the time when any contracts were made were, or have since been interested in the patents or employed by the owners thereof, and whether any legislation is necessary to further promote the manufacture and cheapen the price of armor for vessels of the Navy.[9]

Although never specifically articulated, implicit in this charge is unquestionably the idea of military-industrial collusion in the exploitation of the public purse. When the Committee found considerable evidence to substantiate these claims, the government responded with legislation to fix prices and prohibit the employment of retired or furloughed military officers by government contractors, but because of contractor resistance, it was never effectively enforced.[10]

BEGINNING in 1900, the problem of military-industrial integration became the concern of the international peace movement. The movement enjoyed spectacular growth in the period between the Spanish-American War and 1914, and was instrumental in giving broad publicity to the Second Hague Conference of 1907, which again considered the international traffic in arms, although its only action was to reaffirm the rights of neutrals to export arms to belligerents.[11] The movement also focused its attention for virtually the first time on the manufacturers of armaments, especially the large European firms — Schneider-Creusot in France, Krupp in Germany, Vickers and Armstrong in England, and Skoda in Czechoslovakia.

In the United States, the peace movement found itself in conflict with the newly formed (1902) Navy League whose dedication to expansion of the Navy appeared to peace advocates to be less an outgrowth of

patriotism than of the vested interests of some of its officers and supporters in the manufacture of war materials. This conflict reached its peak in 1914 when Representative Clyde H. Tavenner of Illinois denounced the League on the House floor, accused its membership of profiteering, fraud, and false patriotism, and called for the nationalization of the arms industry.[12] One particularly vexing problem for Tavenner was the frequent pigeonholing by Navy Department officials and naval officers of efforts to construct a government armor plant while the arms firms and their military representatives were able to maintain high prices for armor plate, guns, and ammunition. In 1911, another Illinois Congressman, Henry T. Rainey, had a similar concern. He pointed to the interests of Gens. A.R. Buffington and William Crozier, successive heads of the Bureau of Ordnance in the War Department, in gun carriage patents they had sold to the Bethlehem Steel Company as a factor in that department's resistance to government manufacture.[13] This led Tavenner to conclude that:

> ...(T)he ammunition ring and the armor ring...are composed of practically the same concerns which for a good many years have had a strangle hold on both Army and Navy.[14]

The attention given to armaments in the early 1900s was an outgrowth not only of the peace movement but also of a series of armament scandals which rocked the major European powers. In England, there had been a number of minor scares and "scraps" (drives to scrap existing armaments and build new and better ones) which received some publicity, but none so much as the "Naval Scare of 1909," in which it was revealed that H.H. Mulliner, managing director of the Coventry Ordnance Company, had for three years been anonymously circulating a false rumor that the Krupp Steel Works was greatly expanding its capacity to enable it to outfit an enormously increasing Germany Navy.[15] The famous "Putiloff Affair" drew equally wide publicity in France. The Putiloff factory was a Russian munitions factory in St. Petersburg, jointly financed by Schneider-Creusot of France and Skoda of Czechoslovakia, then a Krupp subsidiary, and using Schneider patents. When a rumor began circulating in France that Schneider intended to sell its interest in the Putiloff factory to Krupp, Frenchmen became enraged at the possibility of French armament secrets being funneled to Germany through Krupp's access to Schneider patents.[16]

The attack on the armaments industry during this pre-war period had all the elements of the Merchants of Death scandal 20 years later, including charges of industry

participation in war scares, international armaments cartels, and manipulation of the news media, as well as charges of conflict of interest on the part of government officials who awarded armament contracts. Some good examples of this genre include The National Labor Press' "The War Trust Exposed," the Union of Democratic Control's "The International Industry of War," the National Peace Council's "The War Traders," the World Peace Foundation's "Syndicates for War," and Philip Snowden's "Dreadnoughts and Dividends."[17] The idea of a military-industrial complex was not altogether foreign to these early critics. Perris speaks of "the association of political power and the private trade in arms," and Snowden quotes Lord Welby, former head of the Treasury in Britain, as saying, "We are in the hands of an organization of crooks. They are politicians, generals, manufacturers of armaments and journalists."[18] Particularly notable is McCullough's projection of a military-industrial complex that would encompass the entire society:

> ...it is probable that if we in England go on for the next half century as we have gone on for the past half century, so large a proportion of the moneyed classes, of the legislators, bishops, newspaper proprietors, and skilled mechanics will be interested in military aeroplane works and in armament factories of one kind or another that the militarist snowball will have become an avalanche which nothing can check.[19]

The beginning of hostilities in Europe in the summer of 1914 stemmed the growing tide of armament criticism in Europe. But in the United States, criticism of the arms business continued through 1915 and 1916, largely because of the continuing debate in Congress and the press as to the legality, morality, and good sense of preferential arms sales by American firms to the Allies but not to Germany. The principle arguments on each side of this question were summarized in *The Independent*:

> The argument that the exportation of munitions to the Allies should be stopped may be reduced to the following propositions:
>
> 1. It makes our country a workshop of death.
> 2. It is for profits, not patriotism.
> 3. It compromises us in the eyes of humanity.
> 4. It makes us an ally of the Allies.
> 5. *It fosters an industry whose interest will be to extend militarism in the United States.* (emphasis added)
> 6. It theoretically enables a small state to buy arms when attacked, but practically this right is of little value, as the small state is likely to be completely invested by its greater and more warlike antagonist.

The official justification by the Secretary of State of the exportation of arms can be epitomized as follows:
1. It is the accepted rule of international law, which no nation should break.
2. It is and has been the universal practise of nations — Germany and Austria included.
3. It is unneutral in that it would deprive England of her superiority on sea and not Germany of her superiority on land.
4. It enables the United States to keep a small military establishment in time of peace.
5. It enables all nations to go without storing up vast reservoirs of military supplies.
6. It thus tends to the peaceful method of settling international disputes.[20]

Almost unnoticed in this period was an article by Shailer Matthews in the *Journal of Political Economy* which went far deeper than other writings in exploring the possibility that expanded American arms manufacturing capability could lead to a militarized economy and society. In warning of the dangers inherent in the private manufacture of armaments, Matthews noted that "...the propaganda for preparedness become(s) a means of perpetuating the...private business in war materials..." and warned of "...the tendency of business like that of Krupp and Armstrong to fasten war upon civilization in the interests of industrialism."[21]

AMERICAN entry into the war in 1917 aborted arms criticism in this country, just as it had in Europe three years before. There were some, like Senator George W. Norris of Nebraska, who believed that munitions makers and Wall Street financiers were pushing us into the war to guarantee their profits; but they were a minority. Most Americans were supportive of the munitions makers' contribution to the war effort, even when it became apparent near the end of the war that many were profiting immensely from it.[22]

Following the war, the League of Nations made numerous attempts to secure international agreement on limiting the manufacture and trade in armaments. The Covenant of the League of Nations even included provisions which stated:

The Members of the League agree that the manufacture by private enterprise of munitions and implements of war is open to *grave objections* (emphasis added)....
...The League (is entrusted) with general supervision of the trade in arms and ammunition with the countries in which control of this traffic is necessary to the common interest.[23]

Within two months of the Treaty of Ver-

sailles, the Convention for the Control of the Trade in Arms and Ammunition was signed by 28 powers at St. Germain-en-Laye, prohibiting to certain territories the export of arms and munitions used in war, except for the use of the signatory governments. But the Convention was never ratified by the major arms producers, including the United States, and never went into effect. There followed a series of meetings in Geneva throughout the early 1920s to secure international support for the principle of arms trade control, spurred on by wars in China, Mexico, and Morocco, fought with arms manufactured in Europe, Japan, and the United States. These efforts also met with failure in the large arms exporting nations. The United States eventually sent a delegation to Geneva which signed the Arms Traffic Convention of 1925, but the Convention languished in the Senate Committee on Foreign Relations until 1934.

Criticism of the arms business among the general public was present but not widespread in the United States in the 1920s. Revelation of the extensive war profits made by many American firms brought some criticism immediately after the war, but then was largely forgotten. A number of writers picked up the theme of the League of Nation's Temporary Mixed Commission on Armaments whose 1921 report argued that armament firms had:

1. Been active in fomenting war scares and in persuading their own countries to adopt warlike policies and to increase their armaments;
2. Attempted to bribe government officials both at home and abroad;
3. Disseminated false reports concerning the military and naval expenditures of various countries in order to stimulate armament expenditures;
4. Sought to influence public opinion through the control of newspapers in their own and foreign countries;
5. Organized international armament rings through which the armaments race has been accentuated by playing off one country against the other;
6. Organized international armament trusts which have increased the price of armaments to governments.[24]

These were the "grave objections" to which the Covenant of the League had alluded.

Americans were as apathetic to setting limitations on their arms industry as they were to joining the League of Nations. In fact, in early 1928, the political climate was so favorable to American munitions firms that Secretary of War Davis proposed that these firms be given contracts for "educational munitions making" to develop the advanced technology and production

equipment that would be necessary should there be another war.[25]

In the late 1920s the rapid turnabout in American sentiment began, which saw virtually the entire country join the hysterical attack on armaments manufacturers, culminating in the Nye Committee Investigation in 1934. As Americans again began to look abroad, they saw that in the decade since the end of the World War, the League had been largely unsuccessful in its efforts to institute international organization and outlaw war and armaments traffic. In Congress, the Burton Resolution in 1928 and the Capper and Porter Resolutions in 1929 were introduced to "prohibit the exportation of arms, munitions, or implements of war to any nation which is engaged in war with another."[26] Although each failed to secure Congressional approval, their debate renewed public interest in arms control. Then, in August 1929, it was revealed that three large American shipbuilding firms had employed one William Shearer to sabotage the Geneva Naval Conference of 1927.[27] Considerable press coverage provoked a half-hearted Senate Investigation, and although it did nothing, the public's interest in the arms business was further aroused. The signing of the Kellogg-Brand pact that same month, renouncing war as an instrument of national policy, was the first official indication of the end to American isolationist thinking.

In the early 1930s, war clouds again appeared on the horizon. Japan invaded Manchuria, Italy conquered Ethiopia, and the Gran Chaco war broke out. More importantly, Hitler came to power and, in defiance of the Versailles Treaty, Germany began to rearm. The fear of war again took hold of the minds of many Americans, and they began to search for ways to avoid another world conflict. In 1931, Congress established the War Policies Commission to study proposals for removing profit from war, and the Commission's star witness, Bernard Baruch, published his own treatise, *Taking the Profits out of War*. In 1932, the United States sent a delegation to the General Disarmament Conference at Geneva, which for the first time had broad public support for American participation in international control of private (and state) arms manufacture.

At home, the popular press again turned its attention to the role of the armaments industry in warfare. In the fall of 1931, *The Living Age* and *The World Tomorrow* carried articles attacking the European armaments firms for their false patriotism and indiscriminate trafficking in arms.[28] In 1932, taking their lead from British and French press, *The Literary Digest, The Nation*, and *The New Republic* joined the fray, accusing the international armaments industry of sabotaging the latest Geneva Disarmament Conference. A series of three articles by historian Charles A. Beard in *The New Republic* attacking the Navy League was perhaps the most important work in this early period, not only because of Beard's notoriety, but because the articles focused exclusively on the abuses of American, not European, armaments firms.[19] These journals continued their attack on the munitions industry through 1933, and then in the spring of 1934, two books, Englebrecht and Hanighen's *Merchants of Death* and Seldes' *Iron, Blood and Profits*, and an article in the much-respected business magazine *Fortune* (reprinted with wide distribution in *The Reader's Digest*), brought the American munitions makers into the view of most American citizens.[20] These works so aroused the American public and Congress to the supposed evils of private arms manufacture that when Senator Nye's proposal for an investigation of the munitions industry was finally brought to a vote on 12 April 1934, two months after it had first been introduced, there was not a single dissenting voice.[21]

The day-to-day proceedings of Senator Nye's Munitions Committee hearings were given generous coverage in newspapers and magazines for the next two years. Yet when the Committee had finished its hearings and prepared its report, the members were almost unanimous in their view that the evidence did not support the "Merchants of Death" charge.[22] When the Committee finally closed its doors in 1936, the possibility of a new war in Europe was becoming clearer, and by 1939, the "Mer-

chants of Death" had once again become the "Arsenal of Democracy."

Critics of the Nye Committee have been legion, including President Truman, who called it " …pure demagoguery in the guise of a Congressional Investigating Committee." The Committee was accused of having mistreated witnesses, having excessively pursued newspaper publicity and, in their attack, having given aid and comfort to enemies of the American system. The aspect of the Committee most criticized was its alleged contribution to the passage of the neutrality laws of 1935-1937. The laws were felt by many to have delayed the buildup of American military strength for World War II by as much as two years, a charge hotly denied by former committee members.[23]

The "Merchants of Death" criticism of the 1930s did not have the broad social, eonomic, and political concern of the "military-industrial complex" criticism of the 1960s, or the earlier armaments criticism which preceded World War I. It tended to linger on the evidence of specific abuses of arms firms without putting them into a broader context, other than the inherent dangers to international war. Only rarely was the suggestion made that the arms industry and its activities were deeply rooted in our social, economic, and political structure, or that its reform would have a dramatic effect on this structure.[24] Even in recommending nationalization of the industry, as so many critics did, including the Nye committee, the focus was almost exclusively on relieving these abuses.

Although the armaments industry shared the criticism of excessive business influence on the Office of Production Management during World War II, which arose out of the Truman Committee hearings, the industry was largely free of criticism from 1936 until the military-industrial complex debate in the 1960s.[25] It is ironic that it is in this period that critics assert the armaments firms made their most significant inroads into American economic and political life.

Summation

The combined attack on the military and industry derives, as we have endeavored to show, from historical movements to control armaments, the arms trade, and arms profiteering. Although varying in origin and content, by the start of the 20th century they were all focused on the arms industry and its relation to the military establishment. The concept of a *unified* "military-industrial complex" dates to the start of the century as well, particularly in the attack on the joint military-industrial promotion of war scares in Europe and the conflict of interest and profiteering charges against military officers and their sometime industrial employers in this country. These early attacks did not charge the military-industrial *domination* of society as did the attacks of the 1960s, although a number of writers anticipated that possibility. However, it is clear they had laid a solid ideological groundwork on which such a charge eventually would be constructed.

Earl A. Molander is Assistant Professor of Business Administration at Portland State University. His primary areas of interest include the social and political environment of business and the weapons acquisition process. This article was accepted for publication in July 1975.

1. The most thoroughgoing analysis of antimilitarism in American intellectual history is contained in Arthur A. Ekrich, Jr., *The Civilian and the Military* (New York: Oxford University Press, 1956). For American attitudes toward business, see Miriam Beard, *A History of Business* (Ann Arbor: Ann Arbor Press, 1962), Part II.
2. The phrase is from H. C. Engelbrecht and F. C. Hanighen, *Merchants of Death*(New York: Dodd, Mead & Company, 1934). The committee investigation is reported in *Munitions Industry*, Hearings Before the Special Committee to Investigate the Munitions Industry, U.S. Senate, 73rd and 74th Congress, 1934-1936. For an excellent analysis of the committee proceedings and findings, see John E. Wiltz, *In Search of Peace* (Baton Rouge, Louisiana State University Press, 1963). A near-simultaneous British Parliamentary investigation is viewed in Phillip Noel-Baker, *The Private Manufacture of Armaments*

(New York, Oxford University Press, 1937), the most thoroughgoing statement of the criticism of the armaments industry in the post-World War I period.
3. I. Sergiyenko, "Gumbatsu — Zaibatsu Complex Again," *New Times* (Moscow), 17 Mar. 1970, 25-27. For an excellent review of the role of Japanese industrial giants, the Zaibatsu, in World War II and before, see Theodore A. Bisson, "Can We Trust a 'Zaibatsu' Japan," *Amerasia*, 8, Oct. 1944, 291-302. An American investigation of the Zaibatsu's wartime role was highly critical of the entire industrial structure of Japan, not just its armaments industry, charging that Japanese politics had been dominated by the military and the large industrial combines — the Zaibatsu — since the Meiji restoration in 1868. See *Report of the Mission on Japanese Combines*, U.S. Department of State Publication 2628, Pt. I, Mar. 1946, vii. For the role of German business in the Nazi era, see Alfred Schweitzer, *Big Business and the Third Reich* (Bloomington, Indiana University Press, 1964), and Josiah E. DuBois, Jr., *Generals in Grey Suits* (London, Bodley Head, 1953).
4. See Miriam Beard, *A History of Business* (Ann Arbor: Ann Arbor Press, 1962), Pt. I; and Richard Lewinsohn, *The Profits of War Through the Ages* (New

York: Garland Publishing, Inc., 1972, originally published by E. P. Dutton and Co., 1937).
5. See Merle Curti, *Peace or War: The American Struggle, 1636-1936*, (New York: W. W. Norton & Co., 1936); and Merze Tate, *The Disarmament Illusion* (New York: Macmillan, 1942), for the history of the disarmament movement in America.
6. Curti, *Peace or War*, 16-17, 21.
7. See Elisabeth M. Garber, *Control of the Sales of Munition of War* (Washington: Government Printing Office, 1941), 77th Congress, 1st Sess., Doc. 19; and Elton Atwater, *American Regulation of Arms Export* (Washington, D.C.: Carnegie Endowment for International Peace, 1941).
8. Richard Kaufman, *The War Profiteers* (Indianapolis: Bobbs-Merrill, 1970), 5-8. Although Robert Morris, chairman of the committees of Congress with authority over finances and government finances, has drawn considerable attention from historians for his exploitation of the public purse during the war, his activities, although criticized at the time, went unprosecuted. A Senate resolution to investigate his activities was never acted upon. See Senate Journal, 1st Congress, 8 Feb. 1790, 22-24. A Civil War investigation of profiteering is reported in U.S. Congress, House,

MILITARY AFFAIRS

select Committee, "Government Contracts," Report no. 2, 37th Congress, 2nd sess., 17 Dec. 1861, 34.

9. U.S. Congress, Senate Committee on Naval Affairs, "Prices of Armor for Vessels of the Navy," Report no. 1453, 54th Congr., 2nd Sess., 1895, 1.

10. Kaufman, 10.

11. Charles Noble Gregory, "Neutrality and the Sale of Arms," The American Journal of International Law, 10, 1916, 547.

12. Clyde H. Tavenner, "Why Congress should take the profit out of war and the preparation for War." Extension of remarks in the House. Congressional Record, 1, 17, app., 12 May 1914, 551-560. Of interest is the fact that the Rock Island government arsenal, where the bulk of any expansion of government arms manufacture could be expected to take place, was located in Tavenner's home district.

13. Gilson Gardner, "Feeding the War Ring," Harper's Weekly, 60, 13 Mar. 1915, 246.

14. Tavenner, 558.

15. George Herbert Perris, "The War Traders," London: National Peace Council, 1914, 27-31.

16. The full particulars of the rather complex background to this affair are described in Engelbrecht and Hanighen, 28-139. In this same period in Germany, Dr. Karl Liebknedt was denouncing the political influence of Krupp and other German armaments firms in securing government contracts.

17. J. T. Walton Newbold, "The War Trust Exposed," Manchester: The National Labour Press, 1916; Union of Democratic Control, "The International Industry of War," Pamphlet #7, London, 1915; Perris; Francis McCullough, "Syndicates for War," World Peace Foundation Pamphlet

Series, July 1911, no. 2, p. III; and Philip Snowden, "Dreadnoughts and Dividends," World Peace Foundation Pamphlets, 1914.

18. Perris, 11; and Snowden, "Dreadnoughts and Dividends," 10.

19. McCullough, 3.

20. "Selling Death," The Independent, 83, 6 Sept. 1915, 312-313.

21. Shailer Matthews, "Some Larger Aspects of the Trade in War Materials," Journal of Political Economy, 1916, 17-19.

22. Albert W. Atwood, "Americans Made Rich and Powerful by the War," The American Magazine, 81, Feb. 1916, 17-20+. A Federal Trade Commission investigation in 1918 concluded that profiteering did indeed exist and that "much of it is due to advantages taken of the necessities of the times as evidenced in the war pressure for heavy production (but) some of it is attributable to inordinate greed and barefaced fraud." Federal Trade Commission, "Profiteering," U.S. Congress, 2d Sess., Doc. no. 248, 27 June 1918, 5.

23. Article 8, sec. 5, and Article 23.

24. As quoted in John Gunther, "Slaughter for Sale," Harper's, 168, May 1934, 659.

25. See " 'Education' Munitions Making as 'Peace Insurance,' " The Literary Digest, 98, 14 Jan. 1928, for the Secretary's recommendations and the response they drew in the press.

26. In 1922, a similar resolution had been introduced in the Congress, but was never reported out of committee. For a discussion of the differences among these resolutions, see L. H. Woolsey, "The Porter and Capper Resolutions against Traffic in Arms," American Journal of International Law, 23, Apr. 1929, 379-383.

27. Engelbrecht and Hanighen, 205-217.

· 28. Francis Delaisi, "Corruption in Ar-

maments," The Living Age, 341, Sept. 1931, 50-56; and H. C. Engelbrecht, "The Bloody International," The World Tomorrow, 14, Oct. 1931, 317-320.

29. "Munition Makers Balk Disarmament," The Literary Digest, 113, 23 Apr. 1932, 14; "Villains of the Disarmament Drama," The Literary Digest, 114, 9 July 1932, 10; Robert Dell, "Sabotage at Geneva," The Nation, 135, 7 Sept. 1932, 209-210; and Charles Beard, "Big Navy Boys," The New Republic, 69, 20 Jan. 1932, 258-262, 27 Jan. 1932, 287-291, and 3 Feb. 1932, 314-318.

30. Engelbrecht and Hanighen; George Seldes, Iron, Blood, and Profits (New York Harper's, 1934); and "Arms and the Men," Fortune, 9, Mar. 1934, 52-57+.

31. Wiltz, 36.

32. Ibid., 231.

33. Ibid., 215-220, 227-231.

34. One exception to this generalization is Paul Hutchinson, who noted the testimony of Eugene R. Grace, president of Bethlehem Steel Co., before the committee. Grace said, "When you talk of profits and the necessities to prosecute a war, . . . it is the whole social structure that is involved." Paul Hutchinson, "The Arms Inquiry," The Christian Century, 52, 15 May 1935, 666.

35. U.S. Congress, Senate, Special Committee to Investigate the National Defense Program, Investigation of the National Defense Program, Additional Report, (Washington D.C.: Government Printing Office,1942), 77th Congress, 2d Sess., Report 480, especially Pt. 5, 15 Jan. 1942. Harold Lasswell's 1941 article on "The Garrison State," often cited as a forerunner of military-industrial criticism, actually focused exclusively on the growing influence of the military, a related, but differentiable concern. American Journal of Sociology, 46, Jan. 1941, 445-468.

STEEL AND THE STATE: INDUSTRY POLITICS AND BUSINESS POLICY FORMATION, 1940-1989[*]

HARLAND PRECHEL
University of Maryland Baltimore County

Whether states are autonomous and whether unity exists within the capitalist class are questions that have long been debated by political and historical sociologists. I suggest that these questions are historically contingent, and conceptualize the state as an organization that is affected by its own structure and agendas, and by the political coalitions in its environment. I evaluate competing explanations of state business policy formation by examining policies that affected the U.S. steel industry between 1940 and 1989. There are four major findings: (1) organizations that represent political coalitions of capitalist groups in the state's environment form the basis of collective action and constitute the means to exercise political and economic power; (2) differential rates of accumulation affect business unity; (3) business policy is affected by the state's structure and agendas and the way in which its agendas conflict or coincide with the interests of the steel industry; (4) as the state's authority extends over more areas of economic activity and as it establishes more complex enforcement structures, state autonomy declines because these new structures provide class segments with legitimate mechanisms within which class members can exercise their political power.

There is considerable disagreement among sociologists who investigate the political behavior of business as a determinant of state policy. Several studies that emphasized forces external to the state argued that agreement exists within the capitalist class, intraclass conflicts are resolved outside the state, and a coherent classwide rationality influences policy. Others have argued that the state is only semi-autonomous in its relationship with capitalist groups, and that the content of policy is the outcome of the state's efforts to mediate class and intraclass conflict. In rebuttal to these arguments, the state-centered perspective emphasizes the autonomous political action of the state. After many years of debate and little prog-

ress toward resolution, it cannot be demonstrated that the capitalist class is unified or fragmented (see Mizruchi 1989a, p. 402; 1989b), or that states are autonomous or the instruments of the capitalist class. There are two important interrelated obstacles to the resolution of these debates. First, the concepts within each perspective are articulated in such a way that they cannot account for historical variation. Second, the empirical studies that document the "state-centered," "class-wide," and "class-segment" perspectives lack sufficient historical depth. That is, they do not operate within a sufficiently long time frame to determine the variations in these relationships in different historical contexts. What is needed, therefore, are modifications in the *conceptualization* of these variables, and historical studies that investigate the *conditions* under which class unity and state autonomy exist.

In this article I analyze historical data on the United States steel industry. My four objectives are to: (1) develop a theoretical perspective that emphasizes the organizational state and its environment and that accounts for historical variation, (2) describe the ways in which the accumulation process affects class unity under different historical conditions, (3) examine the effects on policy formation of the capitalist class and class segments and the state's structure and

[*] Direct all correspondence to Harland Prechel, Department of Sociology, University of Maryland Baltimore County, Baltimore, MD 21228. I have benefitted substantially from comments on this paper from Pat Akard, Robert Antonio, Dan Clawson, and Mark Mizruchi, five anonymous *ASR* reviewers and Gerald Marwell. Critical comments on earlier drafts by Stephen Bunker, Derek Gill, Scott McNall, Jill Quadagno, George Ross and David Willer were also helpful. Earlier versions of this paper were presented at the 83rd annual meeting of the American Sociological Association, Atlanta, (1988), and at the Program in Comparative International Development Colloquium at the Johns Hopkins University (1988).

agendas, and (4) evaluate the competing explanations of business policy formation. I argue that the class-wide, class-segment, and state-centered perspectives are necessary to understand the policy formation *process* but, by themselves, are insufficient and that the *organizational state environment* perspective developed herein provides a more inclusive explanation of capital-state relations.

CLASS UNITY, CLASS SEGMENTS, AND STATE AUTONOMY AS INDEPENDENT PERSPECTIVES

The classwide rationality argument maintains that consensus exists within business (Miliband 1969, p. 47-8). Some adherents of this approach have argued that a dominant coalition of banks exercises hegemony over corporations and takes into account the long-run interest of the economy (Mintz and Schwartz 1985; Bearden 1987; Kotz 1978). Others have argued that class-wide rationality is articulated by an inner circle (e.g., Useem 1982, 1984) consisting of members of the capitalist class who sit on multiple corporate boards and act on the basis of what is best for business as a whole. This argument suggests that "by virtue of the intercorporate networks in which it rests, it [the inner circle] has the informal organizational ties, the formal organizational capacity, and the general vision of business needs to serve aٖ a vehicle for classwide political mobilization" (Useem 1983, p. 119-20).

In contrast, the class-segment perspective suggests that divisions emerge among major business sectors because of the differential rates of accumulation within the various segments of capital (Aglietta 1979, pp. 215-6; Offe 1975, p. 133; Poulantzas 1978). Class segments conform to the relationship each branch of capital has with the economy, and are strongest in industries where economic concentration is high (Baran and Sweezy 1966; Mizruchi and Koenig 1986). As a consequence of their distinct location in the social process of production, *class segments* have specific political economic requirements and concrete interests that may be contradictory to those of other class segments and, therefore, the potential to develop a specific variant of intraclass consciousness and common action in relation to other class segments (Zeitlin, Neuman, and Ratcliff, 1976 p. 1009; Zeitlin 1980, p. 6). As a result, whereas market constraints that are shared by economic

sectors result in similar political behavior (Mizruchi 1989a, p. 412-15; Mizruchi and Koenig 1986), conflicting economic interests generate opposing political interests (Berg and Zald 1978). Moreover, the policy formation process itself generates political divisions among class segments because business policies do not affect all capitalist groups equally. Business policy designed to overcome blockages to accumulation in the economy as a whole or in one segment of capital often impedes accumulation in other segments. In summary, the class-segment argument suggests that just as the economic realm is not dominated by a unified logic of accumulation, the political realm is not occupied by a single class or class segment, but by several dominant class segments whose composition can vary historically (Poulantzas 1978, p. 93).

In contrast to the class-unity and class-segment perspectives, state-centered arguments suggest that the political action of the state is autonomous from these external forces and the state's organizational structure and agendas are important forces in shaping policy (e.g., Amenta and Carruthers ·1988; Skocpol 1980).[1] States are conceived as organizations that formulate and pursue goals that are not simply a response to the demands or interests of social groups, classes, or society (Skocpol 1985, p. 9; Block 1980). The state is an organizational political power with a life and structure of its own that is independent of the dynamics of capital accumulation, and its responses to the economy are traceable to administrative arrangements, government institutions, and political parties (Skocpol 1980).

A REFORMULATION: HISTORY, THE ORGANIZATIONAL STATE, AND ITS ENVIRONMENT

Despite previous research, little progress has been made toward the resolution of these debates. For every empirical study that appears to demonstrate business unity, another can be offered that suggests the opposite (see Bauer, de

---

[1] Despite the emphasize state-centered arguments place on the autonomous state, they also suggests that state autonomy "can come and go" Skocpol (1985, p. 14). Block (1977) suggests that during serious depressions and postwar reconstruction periods state managers can pay less attention to business opinion and concentrate on responding to popular pressure.

Sola Pool, and Dexter 1968; Pfeffer 1987). Although the debate over state autonomy has a shorter history, empirical studies also confirm both sides of this argument (see Martin 1989).

In part, these findings arise because state autonomy and class unity are too often interpreted as empirical absolutes, rather than understood as theoretical constructs. My point is that the central concepts in this debate — class unity and state autonomy — should be conceptualized as *ideal types* that exist only rarely at the empirical level, but that serve as abstractions that provide a *means* to aid in the description of the empirical level (Weber 1949, pp. 92-3). Class unity can be seen as existing at one end of a continuum, with class divisions at the other. Likewise, in a separate continuum state autonomy can be considered at the opposite end of the continuum from the concept of the state as an instrument of the capitalist class. The key issue to understand when considering capital-state relations is not whether class segments are united or divided, but rather the *conditions* under which the capitalist class is more or less unified or divided. Similarly, the key issue is not whether states are autonomous from the capitalist class or class segments but rather the *conditions* under which the state is more or less autonomous.

I adopt a perspective common in organizational theory. I conceptualize the process of policy formation within the state as affected by: (1) internal organizational arrangements, and (2) changes in the environment, which include the degree of economic power of single capitalist groups, political unity among capitalist groups, and the historical conditions under which these outside groups attempt to influence policy. I argue here that a useful view of the relationship between the capitalist class and the state is one that begins by explaining how capitalist groups might come to have different interests, and allowing for the possibility of conceptualizing class power and state power as independent variables whose relationship must be ascertained in specific historical circumstances.

Research that has been sensitive to historical variation in the relationship between state and outside interests has demonstrated, for example, that the strength of specific class segments in Chile depended on the historical circumstances and on the nature of other relationships that differentiated or integrated the class segments (Zeitlin 1984). Historical vari-

ation in the constellation of dominant class segments also had an important effect on the final content of the Wagner Act (Domhoff 1987). Similarly, analyses of business policy formation during the late 1970s and early 1980s suggest that business unity was a response to the class-wide capitalist concern with the declining rate of accumulation in the economy as a whole. However, unity among business interests collapsed after conflict emerged over the solution to the 1981 recession and deficits that followed President Reagan's economic program (Akard 1988).

An explanation of how economic interests are expressed must also account for how economic groups mobilize politically (Dahl 1961). Organizations that represent powerful political coalitions (March and Olsen 1984; Therborn 1978, pp. 37-42) are the basis of collective action, and constitute the primary means to exercise power in modern society (Hall 1986, p 14; Offe and Wiesenthal 1980, pp. 76-80). However, organizations as political coalitions are not restricted to capitalist groups (e.g., Business Roundtable). They also represent noncapitalist (e.g., unions) and international political coalitions such as the European Economic Community (hereafter EEC). Organizations that represent political coalitions affect policy by pressuring the state to amend legislation when existing policies conflict with their economic interest, and provide the basis to forge alliances with other political coalitions when their interests coincide.

This emphasis on political actors in the state's environment is compatible with the thesis in organizational theory that structures and goals/agendas affect decisions (Simon 1957) and with the state-centered argument that state structures and goals/agendas affect policy. The state's *agendas* are defined by its claim to being the guardian of universal interests and its attempt to preserve the state's unity (Rueschemeyer and Evans 1985). Agendas that emerge from this claim include economic stability, international relations, and national defense. Although the state's agendas are often generated outside the state and are endorsed by the capitalist class as a whole, they may not be shared at all times by all capitalists groups because general policies may undermine the specific accumulation needs of class segments. For example, the state's agenda to maintain free-trade policies, which has been a key issue to ensure stable political relations with the EEC in the post World War

II era (Cline 1983), may not be shared by capitalist groups whose market shares are eroded by imports from the EEC. Similarly, the capacity of capitalist groups in the state's environment to affect policy does not preclude state structures from affecting policy. Just as changes in the environment affect organizational decisions and structures, existing structures affect future action (March and Olsen 1976; Prechel forthcoming 1991). *Structure* includes the formal procedural rules, compliance procedures, and standard operating procedures that define the relationship among organizational units, and between the organization and its environment. The state's structure is important because legislation changes laws, rules, and procedures, which simultaneously alter the organizational structure by redefining the relationship among organizational units and the parameters of the state's formal authority (also see Clegg 1981). Existing structures are important, first, because they establish the parameters for future policy. Second, existing structures affect policy through the alignment they provide for competing interests both inside and outside the state, which has consequences for implementation. State structures that do not specify adequately procedural rules that define jurisdictions within the state often result in conflict over policy implementation. Policies that can only be implemented with great difficulty have less chance of acceptance than those whose implementation is more straightforward (Beetham 1987).

In summary, this *organizational state environment* perspective conceptualizes the *state* as an organization that is affected by its own structure and agendas and by political coalitions in its environment. The state is a complex organization with agendas and with a structure that includes separate large "supra-units" (i.e., executive, judicial, legislative) and disparate subunits (e.g., treasury, commerce). Whereas the organizational arrangements within the state become the accumulated product of a history of past policies, these arrangements develop into an organizational structure and a network of interests both inside and outside the state that constrain present choices.

This analysis evaluates four propositions. First, during recessions and depressions the capitalist class unifies behind a business policy favorable to accumulation. Despite the potential loss of confidence in the capitalist class during economic downturns, the state's agenda to ensure economic stability, in conjunction with

capitalist class unity,[2] results in business policies that are favorable to conditions of accumulation in the dominant economic sectors. Second, during periods of steady economic growth, when there is less threat to economic stability, class segments pursue their independent economic agendas, which reduces political unity. Under these conditions powerful capitalist class segments influence business policy by pursuing a logic of accumulation that may conflict with the state's goals to ensure accumulation in the economy as a whole, through their ability to develop coalitions with other political actors and their capacity to manipulate the state structure in such a way that the enforcement of existing laws interferes with the state's agendas. Third, despite the lack of unity among capitalist class segments, the state is least autonomous during periods of rapid economic growth. When the rate of accumulation is at acceptable levels, the state has less power over class-segments because they are not dependent on the state to ensure accumulation. Fourth, as the state's authority is extended over more areas of economic activity and more complex enforcement structures are established (e.g., laws, rules, procedures), state autonomy may decline because these new structures provide class segments with legitimate mechanisms within which to exercise their political power.

THE CASE STUDY

This paper analyzes legislation that affected the integrated steel industry (which manufactures steel from raw materials) during the middle and late stages of the oligopolistic era (1940-1961) through the era of global competition (1962-1989).[3] The steel industry was selected for three reasons. First, it represents a large segment of capital. The steel industry generated the largest

---

[2] Class unity and class power are conceptualized as independent variables. Hence, this analysis does not suggest that when the capitalist class is unified it always has the capacity to influence business policy. Rather, capitalist class segments unify because they do not have the political clout to independently influence business policy.

[3] Whereas the integrated steel industry manufactures steel from raw materials (e.g., limestone, coal, iron ore), minimills produce steel from scrap and, therefore, have significantly lower capital investments, a different social organization of production, and a narrower product line and market niche. As a result, they have different political economic requirements and concrete interest.

proportion of the Gross National Product (GNP) in the manufacturing sector between 1929 and 1958 and only two industries had a higher share of the GNP in 1974 (U.S. Department of Commerce 1960-1979). Second, the political and economic actions of the steel industry have implications for industrial output and employment, accumulation in other sectors of the economy, and defense preparedness. Third, economic concentration is high in the steel industry. In 1947, the eight largest steel corporations shipped 66 percent of the total value of steel shipments (U.S. Census of Manufacturers 1972), and by 1950 they accounted for more than 75 percent of all domestic steel production (U.S. Federal Trade Commission 1977, p. 53). The high degree of economic concentration in the steel industry makes it an appropriate object of analysis to determine whether class segments that control large segments of capital have the capacity to organize politically and influence business policy.

If classwide rationality is correct, the business community will be in agreement on policies that affect the steel industry, and there will be few disagreements within the state over the content of legislation affecting the steel industry. In contrast, the class-segment argument will be confirmed if political conflict over business policy emerges among capitalist class segments and if the state mediates economic conflict among capitalist class segments by formulating new policies or redefining existing policies. The state-centered argument will be supported if the state's responses to the economy appear to be autonomous and traceable to the state's agendas and administrative arrangements. The organizational state-environment argument will be supported if the conditions of accumulation affect capitalist class unity, class segments manipulate the organizational structure of the state to achieve desired outcomes, and new legislation is affected by state agendas, existing legislation, and the organizational structure of the state.

THE INTEGRATED STEEL INDUSTRY AS A CLASS SEGMENT, AND ITS ACCUMULATION STRATEGY

The integrated steel industry is a class segment because it is a group within a class that shares interests with the class as a whole but, by virtue of its common and specific relations to the means of production, also has interests that often

conflict with those of other segments of the same class. The high degree of internal economic concentration and the number of interlocking networks (Fusfield 1958; Scheuerman 1986) allowed for extensive planning and coordination, which provided the steel industry with the capacity to unify its economic and political power and act as a class segment. The way in which the steel industry pursued its political and economic interests resulted in particular relations to the accumulation process as a whole and to other capitalist groups.

The capacity of the steel industry to act as a class segment was established by the early 1900s when its oligopolistic market structure made it possible to pursue a coherent accumulation [4] strategy. The capital accumulation strategy included price setting, and coordination between production capability and market demand, which ensured a high *capability utilization rate*: the ratio between actual output and production capability. Since accumulation is closely tied to utilization rates, the steel industry resisted expansion during periods of economic growth because unused capability undermined accumulation on the downside of the business cycle. That is, because of its specific location in the social process of production, the steel industry had its own political economic requirements and concrete interests. As a result, under certain historical conditions the interests of the steel industry were contradictory to those of other capitalist groups. For example, the strategy of the steel industry to control production capability had important effects on other capitalist groups because steel was necessary to build the nation's infrastructure (e.g., roads, bridges, factories) and ensure accumulation in the economy as a whole, and to manufacture many important consumer commodities and ensure accumulation within other industries, (e.g., automobile, appliance).

---

[4] Accumulation is the mobilization, transformation, and exploitation of inputs in such a way that the total capital of the corporation increases (Marx 1976, p. 711-61; also see Bowles and Edwards 1985, p. 86-9; Sweezy 1970, p. 92-4; Szymanski 1977, p. 35). Capital accumulation is used, rather than profits, because it reflects the overall financial position of the corporation. In addition to profits, accumulation includes maintaining a strong liquidity position for capital investment and reducing debt. These variables determine the financial strength of the corporation, the value of its stock, and the financial worth of the corporation. Most importantly, accumulation includes reinvestment of capital, which is necessary in the long-term to realize profits.

An analysis follows of how the steel industry's specific location in the social process of production, its accumulation strategy, its particular relations with other political economic actors (including the state), and the historical variation in these relations affected the content of business policy. The American Iron and Steel Institute (hereafter AISI) is the organization within which the steel industry developed its political and economic strategy (Congressional Quarterly 1968, p. 158).

THE POLITICAL ECONOMY OF THE WAR AND POST-WAR EXPANSION

As World War II intensified, the demand for military-industrial products from Europe increased. Although the steel industry was unable to meet the wartime demand, it did not reinvest. To meet its politico-military obligations to the Allies, the U.S. government encouraged the private sector to redirect production toward the war economy and expand production capability. However, top executives in the steel industry maintained that low profits during the depressed 1930s, and wartime price controls, left the industry without sufficient capital to finance the construction of additional capability.

In response to the steel industry's resistance, the federal government revised the depreciation allowance of the Internal Revenue Code to provided capital for reinvestment (Burn 1961, p. 64). However, this legislation did not stimulate the level of investment that the federal government considered adequate to ensure a strong national defense and to meet its politico-military obligations to the Allies. Under the direction of the War Production Board the federal government in 1943 became directly involved in productive activity and constructed 29 modern integrated steel plants wholly with government funds and engaged in 20 joint-ventures with private corporations (Hogan 1971, pp. 1459-63; Sobel 1984, p. 169). The total cost of this expansion, almost $2.7 billion, was divided between the steel corporations and the government. When the war concluded, the War Assets Administration sold these properties to private enterprise considerably below construction costs.[5]

When the domestic economy returned to peacetime activity demand increased in virtu-

ally every steel consuming industry. Although demand exceeded the production capability of the industry, there was little threat that new steel companies would be formed in this capital-intensive industry because collusion among steel producers made it possible to cut prices and force new competitors out of the market. Despite the increased demand and pressure from the federal government to increase steelmaking capability, the steel industry did not expand. Citing the rapid decline in capability utilization rates to 35 percent following WWI, AISI maintained that capability estimates should include economic downturns, and expansion would not be profitable when the post-war economic boom subsided (American Iron and Steel Institute 1947). AISI argued that expansion would undermine long-term profits because an economic downturn would occur once the immediate consumer needs were filled.

Conflict among capitalist groups emerged in Congress when representatives from small businesses and the oil and agricultural machinery industries argued that an inadequate supply of steel undermined growth in their industries (U.S. Congress 1948). In late 1949, the Executive Branch entered the debate and publicly criticized the steel industry for failing to expand. President Truman, the Department of Agriculture, and the Small Business Administration argued that a steel shortage would limit business activity throughout the economy and suggested that Congress authorize the construction of steel capability if the steel industry did not reinvest (U.S. Congress 1950, p. 788-91). In addition, several members of Congress maintained that the steel shortage was undermining economic growth and would raise prices, fuel inflation, and threaten national security (U.S. Congress 1950). The steel industry disagreed sharply with this conception and argued that adequate capacity existed (U.S. Congress 1950). The Executive Branch and Congress both viewed the steel industry's failure to comply with its agenda as the outcome of inter-dependent decision-making and oligopolistic resistance to ensure higher prices.

Conflicts among these capitalist groups and between the steel industry and the government reemerged when the U.S. entered the Korean War. To meet its national security objectives, the federal government passed the *Defense*

---

[5] For example, between 1940 and 1944 the federal government invested over $471 million into a steel plant in Geneva, Utah and sold these properties to the U.S. Steel Corporation for $40 million after the war (U.S. Congress 1946, p. 8).

Production Act of 1950 to encourage expansion of production capability. This legislation redefined the depreciation period from 20 years to depreciate 100 percent of investments to five years to depreciate 85 percent of investments, which increased cash flow and provided reinvestment capital. Despite these lucrative tax breaks, the steel industry did not reinvest. The federal government defined the steel shortage as a threat to national security, and in 1952 the President nationalized the steel industry under Executive authority of the Defense Production Act of 1950. Although the Supreme Court ruled President Truman's decision unconstitutional, these events demonstrate that the state's agendas to ensure economic growth and a strong national defense had an important effect on business policy. These business policies, in conjunction with political pressure from the federal government, generated a rapid rate of investment in the steel industry. Between 1952 and 1960 the industry's production capability increased from 109 to 149 million tons (American Iron and Steel Institute 1960). In 1957 and 1960, respectively, the federal government financed 45 and 60 percent of these investments (*Fortune* 1966, p. 228).

In summary, two types of conflict contributed to the redefinition of business policy and state intervention in the accumulation process. First, economic conflict emerged between the steel industry and the steel consuming industries because their logics of accumulation did not coincide at this historical juncture. This conflict reemerged at the political level when political coalitions representing capitalist groups in the steel consuming industries convinced members of Congress and the Executive Branch that the steel shortage undermined growth within their respective industries (U.S. Congress 1948). Second, conflict emerged between the state and the steel industry because the accumulation strategy of the steel industry impeded the state's agendas to ensure economic stability and national security. The state mediated these conflicts by implementing new legislation that provided financial incentives for the steel industry to reinvest. The state redefined business policy because the steel industry had the capacity to pursue a unified accumulation strategy, despite the resistance of other capitalist groups and the state itself.

Although this business policy ensured the state's national security and economic agendas, it had detrimental consequences for the

steel industry because the market did not justify the expansion. While the growth in steel capability averaged 3.9 percent between 1950 and 1960, growth in steel consumption was 0.4 percent (Barnett and Schorsch 1983, p. 23). Moreover, capital investments at this historical juncture, in conjunction with three critical events in the next decade, undermined the long-term profitability of the U.S. steel industry. First, by the end of the 1950s the much more efficient basic oxygen furnace (BOF) was available for commercial use, which made the open hearth steelmaking facilities outdated by the time construction was completed. Second, the domestic steel industry invested in Canadian ore deposits. In the 1960s, however, higher quality iron ore was discovered in Brazil, Venezuela, and Australia. Japanese and European steelmakers purchased these raw materials, which reduced their production costs and increased the quality of their steel. Third, the construction of large ocean vessels lowered the cost of transporting raw materials. These events significantly lowered production costs for foreign steelmakers, which eliminated the cost advantages U.S. steel producers enjoyed in the immediate post-WWII era.[6] In short, state intervention in the accumulation process resulted in *premature capitalization*: investment prior to technological advances and adequate market demand.

THE EMERGENCE OF GLOBAL COMPETITION

The high manufacturing cost and oligopolistic pricing structure in the steel industry made domestic markets lucrative to foreign steel producers and industries that were able to replace steel products (i.e., aluminum, plastic). By 1959, steel imports exceeded exports for the first time. Most importantly, whereas consumption increased by 1.8 percent per year in the 1960s and 1970s, domestic steel shipments grew at an annual rate of one percent (Barnett and Schorsch 1983, p. 50). That is, foreign steel-

---

[6] The cost of shipping ore from Brazil to Japan dropped by 60 percent from 1957 to 1968 (Crandall 1981, p. 23; Walter 1983, p. 490). The effects of changes in raw material prices, shipping costs, and technology lowered the cost of producing steel in Japan by approximately $25 a net finished ton from 1957 to 1967 (Crandall 1981, p. 23). Moreover, wages in the United States were higher than in Japan (Goldberg 1986, p. 48).

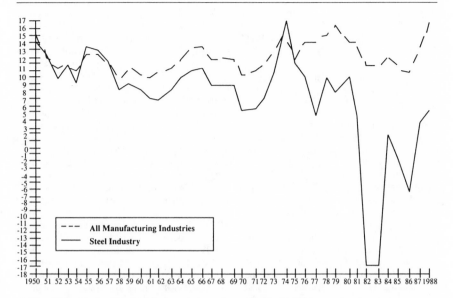

Figure 1. Rate of Return on Equity in the Steel Industry and All Manufacturing Industries

Sources: U.S. Federal Trade Commission. 1950-1982. *Quarterly Financial Reports for Manufacturing Corporations*, Washington, DC: Government Printing Office.
Department of Commerce. 1983-1988. *Quarterly Financial Reports for Manufacturing, Mining & Trade Corporations*, Washington, DC: Government Printing Office. (The 1988 data includes only the first and second quarters.)

makers captured almost one-half of the expansion in steel demand, and the domestic steel industry found itself in a *scissors crisis*: expanded capability and insufficient demand (Barnett and Schorsch 1983, p. 33). As global competition intensified, profits in the steel industry dropped from 11.4 percent (1957) to 6.2 percent (1961) (see Figure 1).

The declining rate of return in the steel industry during the second half of the 1950s coincided with the eroding balance of trade and profits in the manufacturing sector as a whole. By early 1961, as profits steadily declined, the Executive Branch became increasingly convinced that state intervention was necessary to end the 1960-61 recession and proposed a tax credit to stimulate reinvestment and modernization of industry to ensure U.S. competitiveness in global markets (U.S. Congress 1961, p. 5; 1962, p. 84). The business community opposed this policy and lobbied for accelerated depreciation allowances (Congressional Quarterly Almanac 1961). Business interests prevailed and the subsequent *Revenue Act of 1962* included both the accelerated depreciation allowances and a seven percent tax credit (U.S.

Federal Trade Commission 1977). As with the Defense Production Act of 1950, the dominate manufacturing capitalist groups supported this policy because it facilitated accumulation in this segment of the economy.

The Revenue Act increased cash flow in the steel industry from $900 million (1961) to $1.7 billion (1965) (*Fortune* 1966, p. 135). By the mid-1960s, the steel industry had replaced many of its open hearth furnaces with the BOF and was producing lighter, stronger, higher quality steel. However, there was a contradictory dimension to this strategy. Although the BOF was more efficient, the additional steelmaking capability lowered utilization rates, which increased per-unit costs. Moreover, the competitive market conditions, in conjunction with pressure from the Executive Branch, restricted price increases.[7] As the marketplace established

---

[7] The federal government viewed higher steel prices as inflationary, and monitored steel wage and price increases throughout the 1960s. In 1962, for example, a major confrontation occurred between President Kennedy and the steel industry over price increases (Congressional Quarterly Almanac 1962, p. 1017). Similarly, during the 1968 labor negotia-

quality standards and prices, steel profits declined to 7.7 percent in the 1960s compared to 11.2 percent for all manufacturing industries (see Figure 1).

CLASS UNITY, STATE AGENDAS, AND THE POLITICS OF THE DECLINING OLIGOPOLY

As competition intensified, accumulation in the steel industry became increasingly associated with its capacity to organize as a political coalition. In contrast to its antagonistic relations with both the state and other capitalist groups in the oligopolistic era, the steel industry's strategy in the era of global competition was to align its interests with other capitalist groups and the agendas of the state. On the one hand, the steel industry's political strategy incorporated the state's argument that a strong steel industry was necessary to ensure national security and long-term economic growth. On the other hand, it attempted to establish a political coalition with other capitalist groups and the United Steel Workers of America (USW). The primary objective of the steel industry was to establish import quotas.

AISI maintained that import quotas were necessary because low wages abroad and government subsidies represented unfair competition, which eroded the balance of payments, created unemployment, and increased dependence on foreign steel (U.S. Congress 1968, p. xxv-xxix). By 1967, a political coalition including USW[8] and the textile, oil, and steel industries obtained enough support in Congress to introduce import quota legislation. President Johnson, however, threatened to veto this protectionist legislation because it would jeopardize the credibility of the U.S. commitment to international trade agreements and could result in trade retaliation by foreign nation-states (Congressional Quarterly 1968, p. 157).

tions President Johnson pressured the steel industry and the USW to keep wage and price increases at a minimum (Council on Wage and Price Stability 1977; U.S. Federal Trade Commission 1977, p. 267-305).

[8] In the late 1950s, the USW rejected the steel industry's argument that imports were responsible for declining profits and employment opportunities. However, by 1963, when foreign competition began to pose a serious threat to wages and job opportunities, the USW leadership supported the industry's argument that protectionist legislation was the best means to ensure employment (Bernstein 1975; Scheuerman 1986, p. 133-4).

Despite this opposition from the Executive Branch, Senator Hartke of Indiana and 36 cosponsors introduced a steel import quota bill. To forestall the imposition of mandatory import quotas, the Japanese and German steelmakers approached the House Ways and Means and Senate Finance Committees to establish guidelines to restrict voluntarily exports. In 1968, the State Department negotiated a three-year (1969-1971) *Voluntary Restraint Agreement* (VRA) with European and Japanese corporations to provide the steel industry with the opportunity to modernize and reestablish its competitive position in the global economy.

Although imports dropped in the short-term, many foreign producers shifted to different and often higher value products not covered by VRAs, which maintained or increased the value of their imports (U.S. Federal Trade Commission 1977, p. 74). VRAs did not solve either the balance of trade or steel import problem, and in 1971 steel imports increased to 17.9 percent of the market share and profits in the steel industry dropped to less than one-half of the average for all manufacturers (see Figure 1). AISI renewed its lobbying efforts and sought more stringent enforcement measures and more specific product coverage. In May 1972, the Nixon administration established a second set of VRAs (1972-1974) that included more stringent and comprehensive controls. The 1972-74 VRAs, however, were not tested in the marketplace because demand for steel in the global economy temporary increased from 640 (1971) to 783 (1974) million tons. As result, prices significantly increased, imports declined to 12.4 percent (1973) of the market share, and profits in the U.S. steel industry reached record levels (see Figure 1). Although VRAs did not establish import quotas, they signified the transition from corporate revenue generating legislation to an indirect form of protectionism by regulating imported steel (see Table 1).

Despite record profits in the steel industry and the accelerated depreciation allowances under the *Revenue Act of 1971*,[9] AISI continued to lobby for import quotas because VRAs did not establish a solid legal basis to block imports. However, a political solution to the accumulation constraints in the steel industry became more complicated as the steel industry

[9] Legislation that accelerates depreciation allowances is temporary. Hence, by 1971, the accelerated depreciation allowances defined by the Revenue Tax Act of 1962 were eliminated.

Table 1. State Business Policy that Affected the Steel Industry, WWII-1989

Legislation	Corporate Revenue Generating	Voluntary Agreements	Protectionist Legislation	Designed to Benefit All Manufacturing	Steel Industry
Revision of the Internal Revenue Code (WWII)	×			×	
Defense Production Act of 1950	×			×	
Revenue Act of 1962	×			×	
1969-71 VRAs (1968)		×			×
Revenue Act of 1971	×			×	
1972-4 VRAs (1971)		×			×
Trade Act of 1974			×		×[a]
Soloman Plan Trigger Price Mechanism (1978)		×[b]			×
Trade Agreements Act of 1979			×		×[a]
Trigger Price Mechansim (1980)			×		×
ERTA (1981)	×			×	
Steel Industry Compliance Act (1981)	×				×
Fair Trade in Steel Act of 1983			×		×
Steel Import Quotas (1984)			×		×
Steel Import Quotas (1989)			×		×

[a] These laws are placed in this category because key components of them were written for the steel industry.

[b] Although there were some revenue generating dimensions to the Soloman Plan, the most important aspect of this legislation was its protectionist dimensions.

became less central to economic growth and other capitalist groups (e.g., computer, electronics) began to benefit from free-trade. In addition, the Executive Branch continued to be concerned that protectionist policies would initiate a trade war with the EEC, where the United States had a substantial trade surplus.

THE POLITICS OF REDEFINING THE STATE-STRUCTURE

The conflicting interest of capitalist groups, especially those in the heavily energy dependent manufacturing sector, were redirected toward a concern with accumulation in the economy as a whole when the Organization of Petroleum Exporting Countries (OPEC) quadrupled its oil prices in 1973. The interest of these capitalist groups coincided with the concern in Congress and the Executive Branch that shifts in the global economy would undermine domestic economic stability. To take advantage of this new political climate, as in the late 1960s, the steel industry articulated its interest in such a way that it was consistent with the interests of other political actors and the state's agendas. With the support of USW and other industries with protectionist interests (i.e., tex-

tile, footwear, glass), AISI argued that assistance was necessary to finance the expansion programs necessary to meet future demand, that without a viable steel industry the economy would become dependent on imports and vacillations in the global economy, and that a weak manufacturing sector would threaten national security and economic stability (U.S. Congress 1973, p. 3962). The political clout of this coalition led to the formation of the *Congressional Steel Caucus*, which defended the interest of the domestic steel industry in Congress.

To avoid mandatory import quotas, the Nixon administration introduced legislation (1973) that provided the steel industry with protectionist possibilities while minimizing the threat of foreign retaliation that quotas would have created. A crucial component of the subsequent business policy was the *Trade Act of 1974*, which redefined dumping. Whereas the 1921 anti-dumping (AD) law defined *dumping* as the sale of foreign products below prices in their domestic market (Scheuerman 1986, p. 123-4), the Trade Act of 1974 required foreign firms to demonstrate that their prices included the full cost of production, a 10 percent mark-up for fixed costs, and an eight percent rate of return (U.S. Congress 1978, p. 11). Most importantly, the trade act redefined two dimensions of the state structure that established the legal basis to enforce protectionism. First, it increased the authority of the Executive Branch by formalizing presidential power to impose import quotas. Second, although the Trade Act gave the Executive Branch a significant degree of autonomy over enforcement of the dumping laws, it established the organizational structure and legal mechanism to file complaints against foreign steel corporations that did not comply with AD laws (Congressional Quarterly 1974). This legislation designated the shift from voluntary trade agreements to establishing the legal mechanism within the state to restrict imports (see Table 1). This dimension of the state structure became the cornerstone of AISI's political strategy throughout the 1970s.

In 1976, AISI pressured the Executive Branch to enforce the Trade Act when the demand for steel on the global market declined and imports increased from 12.4 (1973) to 14.1 (1976) percent. The Ford administration, however, was concerned over trade retaliation and favored reestablishing VRAs. Although Japanese producers agreed to reduce imports, EEC refused. To avoid plant closing and retaliation from EEC, President Ford imposed a three-year import quota on European specialty steel (*Iron Age* 1976, p. 22). The failure to protect the large carbon steel markets meant that the quotas had little effect on imports.

As imports escalated, beginning in March 1977 the steel industry filed dozens of AD suits against European and Japanese steel producers under the Trade Act of 1974. This political action is important because it denotes a strategic shift within the steel industry from exerting political or economic pressure on the state to using the state's legal structure to achieve its economic goals. However, President Ford did not litigate the AD suits because he was concerned that such action would initiate a trade war with foreign nation-states. Moreover, the banking industry pressured the Executive Branch to avoid protectionist policies because trade restrictions would undermine the ability of less developed countries to repay their loans (*Forbes* 1984).

After the steel industry failed to obtain protectionism from the Executive Branch, it refocused its political strategy on the public and Congress. The steel industry organized a media campaign to solicit support from industrial communities affected by imports. As unemploy-

ment increased, political coalitions within these communities (i.e., local governments, USW locals) exerted pressure on their representatives in Congress to obtain a political solution (Bensman and Lynch 1988; Hoerr 1988; Reutter 1988). Meanwhile, AISI intensified its lobby efforts in Congress and argued that "unfair foreign competition" was responsible for declining profits (see Figure 1). These lobbying efforts resulted in an expansion of the Congressional Steel Caucus to 180 members by 1977, which made it one of the largest political coalitions on Capitol Hill. The accumulation constraints of the steel industry reemerged as political conflict within the state when the Chairman of the House Ways and Means Committee criticized the Executive Branch for failing to resolve the steel crisis (U.S. Congress 1977, p. 42). This conflict reached a high point when members of the Congressional Steel Caucus introduced five protectionist bills in October 1977 (Congressional Quarterly 1977, p. 2467-69).

As was the case with previous administrations, President Carter did not enforce AD laws because they conflicted with the state's agendas. Specifically, he was concerned that protectionism would initiate a trade war with foreign nation-states, interfere with the Tokyo Multilateral Trade Negotiations, and reduce the supply of steel, increase prices and stimulate the already rapid rate of inflation (Levine 1985, p. 12; Jones 1986, p. 119). Despite the perceived effects of AD laws on these agendas, the Executive Branch could not ignore the domestic political implications of plant closing, the unemployment of thousands of steel workers, and the erosion of the economic base of entire communities.

To mediate this political economic crisis in such a way that the outcome did not undermine the state's agendas, President Carter established the White House Conference on Steel to complete a detailed analysis of the industry. The subsequent *Solomon Plan* liberalized depreciation schedules and issued $365 million in loans to steel companies and depressed steel communities (U.S. Congress 1978). The most important dimension of this legislation was the *Trigger Price Mechanism* (TPM) under which the Treasury Department monitored 84 categories of steel products, representing 90 percent of all steel imports (U.S. Office of Technological Assessment 1981). Based on the cost of producing and transporting Japanese steel to the

U.S., beginning in May 1978 the TPM established a minimum pricing formula for imported steel. While this legislation induced U.S. steel companies to withdraw their AD complaints, it also increased protectionism beyond the 1974 antidumping legislation. Although TPM did not substantially alter the flow of imports until 1979, it provided a pricing system that allowed producers to raise prices, which increased their profits.

However, TPMs only protected U.S. markets from Japanese imports, and the steel industry argued that subsidized steel from Europe continued to penetrate domestic markets. When the Tokyo Multilateral Trade Negotiations were completed, the AISI intensified its efforts to restrict imports of European steel and with the support of the Steel Caucus Congress passed the *Trade Agreements Act of 1979*. This legislation required the federal government to prosecute AD and *countervailing duty* (CVD) (i.e., laws regarding subsidies foreign steel makers received from their governments) allegations within 150 days (Congressional Quarterly Almanac 1979, p. 294; U.S. General Accounting Office 1989).[10] Most importantly, it subjected the actions of the International Trade Commission (ITC) to judicial review, which provided the steel industry with a more effective legal basis to force the Executive Branch to act on AD and CVD litigation and thereby reduced its autonomy over enforcement of protectionist legislation.

In March 1980, when EEC imports began to surge, the politically unified steel industry filed AD petitions against 75 percent of all imported steel, which included steel from seven European countries (Walter 1983, p. 492). To avoid taking legal action which would threaten international relations, the Executive Branch suspended the TPM. To resolve this international political crisis President Carter established the Steel Tripartite Advisory Committee (STAC). With the support of the EEC which recognized the added strength of the new AD and CVD laws, the Executive Branch negotiated a new set of TPMs that were 12 percent higher than the 1978 TPMs. The STAC also recommended liberalization of depreciation rules, tax investment credits, and relaxation of pollution con-

trols to improve capital flows. In return for these concessions by the state, the steel industry dropped its AD suits.

In summary, the lack of an enforcement mechanism in the Trade Act of 1974 ensured state autonomy over implementation of protectionism. However, the redefinition of the state structure and dumping provided the steel industry with the legal mechanism to file AD complaints and established a legal basis to argue that foreign steelmakers violated U.S. trade laws. The Trade Act became a critical dimension of the steel industry's political strategy; it *legitimated* protectionist arguments in Congress and to the public, from whom the steel industry solicited support to establish stronger forms of protectionism. This political strategy resulted in The Trade Agreements Act of 1979, which required the state to act on AD and CVD complaints. The Trade Agreements Act was the outcome of the capacity of the steel industry to legitimate its protectionist arguments and establish political alliances with other capitalist groups. Whereas the Trade Act of 1974 was important because it created an organizational structure to file AD complaints and legitimated the protectionist arguments, the Trade Agreements Act of 1979 was important because it designated a shift from political struggles over the principle of protectionism to redefining the state structure in such a way that the steel industry could force the state to administer existing forms of protectionism. These Acts were important because they provided mechanisms to initiate litigation against steel producers in foreign nation-states. In short, this class segment redefined business policy in such a way that it increased protectionism and reduced state autonomy over enforcement of protectionism.[11]

GLOBAL POLITICAL CONFLICT AND THE REDEFINITION OF STATE STRUCTURES, EARLY 1980S

By 1981, TPMs no longer provided an effective means to ensure accumulation within the steel industry. Foreign steel producers avoided TPM regulations by including hidden rebates, falsifying price statements on customs declarations, and establishing importing firms to resell steel below the trigger prices (*The Economist*

---

[10] The Trade Agreements Act of 1979 also transferred the authority over protectionism from the Treasury to the Commerce Department because of the perception in Congress that it was a more effective enforcement unit.

[11] It is important to emphasize that the VRAs and the TPMs were proposed by the Executive Branch, and were regarded by the steel industry as temporary solutions.

1981, p. 75; *Business Week* 1981, p. 44). As profits declined and imports increased, the steel industry intensified its efforts to establish import quotas. However, import quotas were not compatible with the increased emphasis on free-trade in the Reagan administration, and the Executive Branch continued to be concerned that protectionism would undermine international political relations and initiate a trade war with EEC. The political position of the steel industry was strengthened when the back-to-back recessions in the early 1980s increased business unity and dominant segments of the capitalist class established a unified political coalition that pressured the federal government to stimulate accumulation in the economy as a whole (Akard 1990; Clawson and Neustadtl 1989).

In response to the first recession, the Reagan administration proposed the *Economic Recovery Tax Act of 1981* (ERTA). Though skeptical of the policy, a coalition of business organizations agreed to support it in return for the inclusion of accelerated depreciation schedules, which business groups had been lobbying for since 1978 (Congressional Quarterly, 1981a, p. 1133; 1981b, 1431). The most active business coalition was organized by the American Business Conference and *The Carlton Group*, which was formed in 1975 and included representatives from the Business Roundtable, the National Association of Manufacturers, the American Council for Capital Formation, the Committee for Effective Capital Recovery, and the Retail Tax Committee. The business segment of the ERTA, the *Accelerated Cost Recovery System*, (ACRS) liberalized depreciation schedules and tax credits. This legislation provided the steel industry with an estimated $400 million between 1982 and 1983 (Scheuerman 1986, p. 163). It has been estimated that ACRS write-offs were so generous that profits from new investments were higher after, rather than before taxes (McIntyre and Tipps 1982, pp. 32-7). To enable low-profit industries such as steel to take full advantage of these tax breaks, a special tax-leasing provision was implemented that allowed low-profit corporations to sell their unused tax credits to more profitable corporations. The government also passed the *Steel Industry Compliance Act* in 1981, which amended the *Clean Air Act* and allowed steel corporations to postpone compliance with air pollution standards if they reinvested. The Steel Industry Compliance Act is important because

it was the first corporate revenue generating legislation that affected only the steel industry. It demonstrates the capacity of a class segment to redefine business policy to facilitate accumulation in a single industry.

Although this business policy facilitated accumulation and temporarily halted the steel industry's efforts to enforce protectionism under AD and CVD laws, it did not resolve permanently the political crisis. The tax breaks did not restore profits and several European producers continued to sell steel in U.S. markets considerably below their production costs. During the 1981-82 recession imports increased to 18.9 (1981) and 21.8 (1982) percent, utilization rates dropped to 48.4 percent (1982), and the steel industry did not realize a profit for the first time since the 1930s. In January 1982, as in the past, the steel industry used the organizational structure of the state to achieve its economic objectives. The seven largest U.S. steel corporations filed 110 AD charges against 41 foreign producers, which included every major foreign steel producing country except Japan (Walter 1983, p. 493). As the investigation proceeded through the ITC and the Commerce Department, EEC attempted to obtain a political solution and in May 1982 the Commerce Secretary and the Under Secretary for International Trade opened negotiations with EEC.

International political conflict escalated again in June when the Commerce Department issued a preliminary ruling on $1.4 billion of imported steel against corporations in West Germany, Italy, Britain, Belgium, the Netherlands, Luxembourg, France, Brazil, and South Africa (Walter 1983, p. 496). These trade violations were subject to an immediate bond of 20 to 25 percent of the import values to be forfeited if the final decision supported the preliminary ruling. In response, EEC developed a list of products exported by the United States that benefitted from U.S. government subsidies. EEC maintained that the action of the U.S. government violated the Versailles Summit commitment to continued trade liberalization, which challenged the legality of U.S. trade policy under the General Agreement on Tariffs and Trade (GATT).

In addition, domestic political conflict emerged between the steel industry and USW. Although USW and the steel industry fought bitterly over labor issues, they had agreed on tax policy since the 1940s, and beginning in 1974 USW supported the steel industry's protectionist strategy. The political alliance between the USW and the steel industry dissolved when employment in the steel industry dropped from 449,000 (1978) to 289,000 (1982) (American Iron and Steel Institute 1983, p. 15), and many steel corporations disinvested from steel. USW argued that the steel industry used revenue from the existing business policy for diversification and refused to support legislation that did not mandate modernization.

To resolve the domestic and international political crises, the Executive Branch intensified negotiations with EEC and reached an agreement to limit exports of 10 categories of steel if AD complaints were withdrawn. The steel industry would not agree to this proposal because it did not include the legal means to block imports. In response, Congress passed a narrowly defined trade law that amended the *Tariff Act of 1930* by requiring a valid export license for steel products (Congressional Record 1982). This agreement went into effect in November 1982 with an official ending date of December 1985 when EEC agreed to stop subsidizing its steel industries. The amendment, however, proved inadequately protectionist to ensure the accumulation goals of the steel industry because, as in the past, the EEC diverted exports toward other product lines. In addition, EEC limited steel imports from Newly Industrializing Countries (NICs) such as Brazil and Korea, which diverted their exports to U.S. markets. By 1983, foreign steelmakers captured over 20 percent of the U.S. market share.

To increase protectionism, the steel industry pursued three interrelated political strategies. First, it continued to use the organizational structure of the state to achieve its accumulation goals, and in January 1984 the steel industry filed dozens of AD complaints against EEC producers under the Trade Act of 1979. Second, Bethlehem Steel Corporation with the support of USW petitioned for import restrictions under section 201 of Article XIX of GATT, which allows a government to impose temporary trade protection for an industry that has suffered serious injury due to a surge in imports (Congressional Quarterly 1989, p. 631). Third, the steel industry broadened its political base. By 1983, it had obtained the support of the Congressional *Trade Reform Action Coalition*, which represented other industries threatened by imports including the textile, chemical, footwear, steel, nonferrous metal, metalworking, and television industries. In response

to the unified lobby efforts of these capitalist groups the House passed the *Fair Trade in Steel Act of 1983*. This legislation limited imports in 47 product lines to 15 percent of the domestic market, and "mandated" modernization.[12] The Steel Act simultaneously increased protectionism and resolved the conflict between the USW and the steel industry. However, this legislation allowed the Secretary of Commerce to "amend or lift the quota in cases of short supply" (U.S. Congress 1984), and the steel lobbyist continued to argue that the Executive Branch had too much discretion over enforcement of trade laws.

The steel industry's efforts to use the state structure to realize its accumulation goals succeeded when, in June 1984, the ITC voted to place import quotas on most steel products (International Trade Commission 1984, p. 11). The decision by the ITC forced President Reagan, who was campaigning for reelection, to revise his free-trade agenda. On the one hand, enforcement of the ITC recommendations could have initiated a trade war and/or international legal battles. On the other, failure to support the steel industry and the USW ran the risk of losing electoral votes to Senator Mondale in key steel manufacturing states including Illinois, Indiana, Maryland, Ohio, Pennsylvania, and Texas. To avoid implementing the protectionist recommendations of the ITC, while maintaining political support during an election year, President Reagan replaced the ITC recommendation with a new set of VRAs (1984-1989) that set imports at 18.5 percent of the market share. However, these agreements were no longer "voluntary." This legislation included a licensing system that prevented foreign steelmakers from switching their product mix (Reagan 1984; U.S. Trade Representative 1984), which made it possible to enforce the quotas on a product-by-product basis. This more precise legislation significantly reduced the autonomy of the Executive Branch over enforcement of the quotas.

The import quotas were the outcome of the steel industry's long-term political strategy (1967-1984) and its capacity: (1) to articulate its interests in such a way that it was able to establish alliances with other capitalist groups

---

[12] Although this legislation required steel corporations to reinvest into steel operations (U.S. Congress 1984), the amount was not defined and a mechanism to monitor the rate of reinvestment was not established.

and USW during crucial historical junctures, (2) to pressure Congress to implement a protectionist judicial system of trade dispute settlement, and (3) to use the subsequent state structure in such a way that enforcement of existing legislation would have conflicted with the state's agenda to maintain stable relations with foreign nation-states.[13]

ACCUMULATION AND THE REEMERGENCE OF INTRACLASS CONFLICT, 1985-1989

Economic growth in the late 1980s, the accelerated depreciation allowances, tax investment credits, and import quotas have contributed to a significant turnaround in the U.S. steel industry. These business policies increased the rate of reinvestment, and the concomitant modernization reduced U.S. steel manufacturing cost below Japanese production costs. Imports dropped to the lowest levels since 1981, capability utilization rates were the highest in the last two decades (i.e., 89.2 percent), steel prices increased, the steel industry reported profits of 2.3 billion dollars, and several of the large integrated producers reported profit levels that were among their highest in the last three decades (American Iron and Steel Institute, 1968-1988). Despite this significant increase in the rate of accumulation, the steel industry continued to lobby the Executive Branch and Congress, where by early 1989 it obtained 240 co-sponsors to extend the import quotas. In addition, the steel industry began to prepare several hundred anti-dumping cases to litigate under the AD laws if the quotas were not renewed (Congressional Quarterly 1989, p. 631). The steel industry maintained that a five-year continuation of the import quota system was necessary to protect domestic markets from subsidized foreign steel.

Although George Bush promised to renew the import quotas during his presidential campaign and both the House and Senate introduced legislation to extend the quotas for an additional five years (Congressional Quarterly 1989, p. 630), the 1990 quotas were revised. There are two important historical conditions that contributed to the revision of this business policy. First, protectionism had re-emerged as

---

[13] Economic analysis of international steel trade suggests that between 1976 and 1983 import relief for steel was not warranted (Grossman 1986).

a threat to stable international relations. The 1989 European Economic Summit defined protectionism as the most significant trade issue, and GATT officials became increasingly critical of import quotas and proposed to strengthen trade rules against protectionist legislation (New York Times, 1989b). Second, a political coalition representing a wide range of steel consuming industries lobbied Congress and the Executive Branch to eliminate the quotas. These political actors included the Coalition of American Steel Using Manufacturers, which alone represented 370 companies. In addition, the Precision Metal Forming Association, the American Institute for Imported Steel, the Texas Association of Steel Importers, the West Coast Metal Importers, the Steel Service Center Institute, and the National Grange were also members of this political coalition (Congressional Quarterly 1989, pp. 629-32; New York Times 1989a, 1989c; Baltimore Sun 1989). This political coalition represented firms that could not negotiate the low prices enjoyed by the large steel consumers. They argued that import quotas created steel shortages, generated higher steel prices, and eroded the profits of steel consuming industries (Congressional Quarterly 1989, p. 629).

As in the past, the threat to stable international relations and conflict among capitalist groups was resolved by redefining business policy. The new business policy reduced the steel quotas to two and one-half years and increased the foreign market share to 20.2 percent. To retain the support of the steel industry, the Bush Administration established the Steel Trade Liberalization Program to eliminate foreign steel subsidies by mid-1992 when the new quotas expire.

In summary, two types of conflict contributed to the reformulation of this business policy. First, conflict emerged between the state and the steel industry because enforcement of the import quotas, which ensured accumulation in the steel industry, undermined the state's agenda to maintain political stability with foreign nation-states. Second, conflict emerged among domestic capitalist groups because protectionist legislation that ensured accumulation in the steel industry constrained accumulation within other capitalist segments. Conflict at the economic level emerged as political conflict because the logics of accumulation among the various capitalist segments did not coincide at this historical juncture, and existing business policy did not affect all segments equally. These conflicts were mediated within the state by formulating new business policy that reduced state autonomy over enforcement of protectionism.

FINDINGS

There are several important findings from this case study. First, organizations that represent political coalitions of capitalist groups in the state's environment were a basis of collective action and constituted a means to exercise political and economic power. AISI was the organizational vehicle that forged alliances with other capitalist groups and articulated a strategy to realize the steel industry's political economic interests within a wide range of historical conditions. This organization established an economic strategy to limit expansion of production capability in the oligopolistic era and a political strategy to obtain protectionism in the era of global competition when the economic strength of the steel industry declined. The political and economic power of this class segment resulted in business policies that have financed a significant proportion of each major expansion and modernization project within the steel industry since the 1940s.

Second, differential rates of accumulation affected business unity. Business unity among domestic capitalist groups was highest when OPEC oil prices (i.e., 1973) and foreign competition (i.e., 1979-82) undermined accumulation in the economy as a whole. These threats to accumulation from the global economy resulted in political alliances among several capitalist groups which lobbied Congress and the Executive Branch to implement policies to overcome constraints to accumulation. In contrast, business was less unified during periods of rapid economic growth. This finding suggests that when the conditions of accumulation declined, the capitalist class mobilized and moved toward the unified end of the class unity/division continuum to exercise control over business policy.

Third, when the accumulation strategy of the steel industry undermined accumulation significantly in other capitalist groups (i.e., post WWII, late-1980s), these accumulation constraints emerged as political conflicts that were mediated within the state by revising business policy. Moreover, the state's structure and agendas and the way in which the agendas conflicted or coincided with the interests of the steel industry affected the content of the subsequent business policy. State intervention in the oligopolistic era occurred in the form of corporate revenue generating business policy because the steel industry's strategy to limit production capability undermined the state's agendas to ensure steady economic growth, a strong national defense, and to meet its military-politico obligation to foreign nation-states. Similarly, corporate revenue generating business policies were implemented in the era of global competition to ensure the state's agenda to maintain steady economic growth (e.g., 1962, 1981). After 1974, when protectionist policies were incorporated into the state structure, the steel industry used the state's organizational structure of trade dispute settlement to force the state to enforce litigation against foreign steel producers. A key component of the steel industry's political strategy was the coordinated filing of AD complaints (i.e., 1977, 1980, 1982, 1984), which if enforced would have conflicted with the state's foreign policy agenda. The Executive Branch, therefore, resisted enforcement of the AD laws. However, the enforcement mechanism within the state structure established under the Trade Agreements Act of 1979 provided the steel industry with the organizational mechanism to force the state into conflicts that required solutions. The resolution of each conflict resulted in a new business policy that redefined the state structure and the parameters of its formal authority. The capacity of this class segment to establish a long-term unified political strategy and to manipulate the state structure explains how the steel industry obtained the highest form of protectionism in the history of the United States during the Reagan administration, one of the most adamant free-trade administrations in the post-World War II era.

Fourth, the state was least autonomous in relation to the steel industry during periods of rapid economic growth when the state's national defense and economic stability agendas were dependent on a steady supply of steel. Under each of these *conditions* the state implemented business policies favorable to accumulation before the steel industry expanded production capability. When economic stability became less dependent on domestic steel and the rate of accumulation in the steel industry declined, the steel industry was able to exercise less control over the state. This suggests that the state moves toward the less autonomous end of the continuum during periods of rapid economic growth, and toward the autonomous end of the continuum when the rate of accumulation declines (also see Block 1977). However, despite the steel industry's weakened economic position in the 1970s and 1980s, the cumulative affects of its political strategy steadily reduced the autonomy of the state. Once a system of trade dispute settlement was established within the organizational structure of the state, rather than attempting to influenced legislation through its lobbying efforts where success was dependent on support in Congress, the steel industry manipulated the organizational structure of the state to achieve its economic agendas. Despite consistent opposition, especially from the Executive Branch, its strategy to use the laws governing trade dispute settlement significantly increased the capacity of the steel industry to exercise power over the state. For example, in 1982 the steel industry rejected the state's proposed business policy, and refused to withdraw AD complaints until the state implemented a licensing agreement to govern steel trade.

In short, state structures and agendas were important *not* because they ensured state autonomy as state-centered arguments suggest (Skocpol 1980, 1985), but rather because they provided the means for this class segment to exercise control over the state. Although organizational structures may be a key to the state's capacity to engage in economic transformation (Rueschemeyer and Evans 1985, p. 51, 59), these structures also provided class segments with the mechanisms to exercise control over the state.[14] Organizational structures simultaneously extended the state's authority over more spheres of economic activity and established the legal mechanisms, which provided class segments with the capacity to define the content of state authority. In the long-term, by manipulating the existing state structure, this class segment redefined protectionism and reduced state autonomy over enforcement of protectionism. These findings suggest that state agendas and structures constitute critical dimensions of capital-state relations. This class segment, the steel industry, was able to exercise control over the state when: (1) the state's national defense and economic stability

agendas depended on accumulation within the industry, and (2) existing state structures provided the mechanism to pursue political economic strategies that conflicted with the state's agendas.

In addition, this case study provides some insights into variations in the capitalist state. In Western Europe where the textile, auto, and steel industries have historically controlled the economy (Kurth 1979, p. 33), a long-term business policy to subsidize the steel industry exists. In contrast, no one sector has been dominant in the postwar United States (Kurth 1979), and despite the importance the state has placed on a viable steel industry to ensure its national defense and economic agendas, there has been no mandate for a coherent business policy concerning steel production. Instead, there have been a series of short-term policies that have frequently contradicted one another and placed significant financial burdens on society.[15] These business policies, for example, provided reinvestment capital for the steel industry, which encouraged over-expansion and investment into technology that was outdated by the time its was constructed. In addition, estimates suggest that the higher steel prices that followed the 1984 import quotas alone cost consumers seven billion dollars annually (*New York Times* 1989b).

DISCUSSION

This case study has addressed one of the central theoretical problems of historical sociology: the conditions under which groups that share an interest act, or fail to act, on that interest (Tilly 1981). Such studies require historical grounding to identify the means of action that are available to groups. By developing a theoretically explicit conception of the relationship between the organizational state and political coalitions in its environment, I have sought to illustrate the historical conditions that shaped and transformed business policy that affected the steel industry. I identified two themes that affected the content of business policy: conflict between the accumulation goals of a powerful class segment and the agendas of the state, and conflict among capitalist groups. Both conflicts occurred at the economic level and were medi-

---

[14] Rueschemeyer and Evans' argument is based on an analysis of semiperipheral states, where the capitalist class maybe more homogeneous and/or more or less organized than the capitalist class in the United States.

[15] For other examples of the short-term dimensions of U.S. economic policy see Bluestone and Harrison (1982), and Shonfield (1965).

ated at the political level (also see Quadagno 1984). The historically specific conditions of accumulation that defined class alliances, the state's agendas, and the particular laws and structure of the state that governed trade dispute settlement affected business policy. Once the protectionist mechanisms were incorporated into the state structure, each change in business policy redefined the state structure and the parameters of its formal authority.

This case study demonstrates that constraints to accumulation compel action. That is, significant changes in the accumulation process require a response. Although *a* response is *necessary* to ensure or recreate the conditions of accumulation, the *character* of the specific action taken is shaped by the political and economic context. The historical variation in the conditions of accumulation structured the motives and actions of the steel industry as well as its interests and the opportunities for satisfying them. The specific form of the steel industry's actions were affected by the legal relationship between the steel industry and the state; the laws governing trade dispute settlement and the organizational structure of the state determined the range of possible alternatives available to the steel industry in the pursuit of its political economic interests. The process that recreates the conditions of accumulation is both dynamic and reflexive; business policy changes the state structure, which in turn shapes future action (also see Beetham 1987; Burawoy 1983, 1984; Staples 1987). State structures become the product of past policies, which become congealed and develop a network of interests around them, both inside and outside the state. These structures affect policy outcomes through the alignment they give to competing interests, and through their consequences for policy implementation. Those policies that are difficult to enforce (e.g., VRAs, TPMs, ADs) are replaced with more effective policies (e.g., quotas).

Moreover, unity within the capitalist class varies historically, and is affected by the accumulation opportunities and constraints of the specific capitalist groups. Although class segments pursue their own political and economic interests, they establish political alliances with other capitalist groups when their own political and economic power is inadequate to implement business policies to overcome obstacles to accumulation. Capitalist class unity depends on how the historically specific accumulation opportunities and constraints and the respec-

tive relationship of class segments to the state differentiates or integrates class segments.

Finally, although other capitalist groups frequently supported the political agendas of the steel industry, this case study demonstrates that class unity is not necessary to exercise control over the state. Class segments that have the financial resources and legal expertise can exercise a significant degree of control over the state, despite resistance from other capitalist groups and from the state itself. The capacity of a class segment to exercise control over the state and affect business policy increases significantly once the state is structured in such a way that it has the organizational capacity to reproduce the conditions of accumulation for that class segment. The outcome of the concerted political action of this class segment has been, beginning in 1978, a rapid proliferation of legislation to facilitate accumulation solely within the steel industry (see Table 1).

This analysis leaves us with an important question: Is the steel industry an exception to the way in which relations between class segments and the state are articulated? I would argue that the steel industry is not an exception. In addition to the steel industry, this study has also demonstrated that steel consuming capitalist groups successfully pursued their economic interests politically. To demonstrate that some class segments do not successfully pursue their economic interests politically would require studies of different capitalist groups during different historical periods. Through such studies, we could further develop an analytic framework for understanding the how historical conditions affect the relationships between the capitalist class and class segments and the state.

HARLAND PRECHEL is an Assistant Professor of Sociology and an Affiliate Assistant Professor of Policy Sciences at the University of Maryland Baltimore County. His current research examines the effects of the political and economic environment on corporate change (1940 - 1990), and the effects of recent applications of rational calculation and cybernetic technologies on the organizational structure and the distribution of authority in a U.S. steel corporation.

REFERENCES

Aglietta, Michel. 1979. *A Theory of Capitalist Regulation*. London: New Left Books.
Akard, Patrick. 1988. "Economic Policy in a Capi-

talist State: The Humphrey-Hawkins Bill and the Revenue Act of 1978." Paper presented at the Annual Meeting of the American Sociological Association (Atlanta).

_____. 1990. "Corporate Mobilization and the Transformation of U.S. Economic Policy, Recent History Versus Recent Theories of the State." Paper presented at the Annual Meeting of the Midwest Sociological Society, Chicago.

Amenta, Edwin and Bruce Carruthers. 1988. "The Formative Years of U.S. Social Spending Policies." *American Sociological Review* 53:661-78.

American Iron and Steel Institute. 1947. "Address of the President." *Yearbook.* New York: AISI.

_____. 1957-1988. *Annual Statistical Report.* New York: AISI.

Baltimore Sun. 1989. June 18, pp. 1D, 6D.

Baran, Paul and Paul Sweezy. 1966. *Monopoly Capital.* New York: Monthly Review Press.

Barnett, Donald and Louis Schorsch. 1983. *Steel Upheaval in a Basic Industry.* Cambridge: Ballinger Publishing Company.

Bauer, Raymond, Ithiel de Sola Pool, and Lewis Dexter. 1968. *American Business and Public Policy: The Politics of Foreign Trade.* New York: Atherton Press.

Bearden, James. 1987. "Financial Hegemony, Social Capital and Bank Boards of Directors." Pp. 48-59 in *The Structure of Power in America: The Corporate Elite as a Ruling Class,* edited by Michael Schwartz. New York: Holmes & Meier.

Beetham, David. 1987. *Bureaucracy.* Minneapolis: University of Minnesota Press.

Bensman, David and Roberta Lynch. 1988. *Rusted Dreams: Hard Times in a Steel Community.* Berkeley: University of California Press.

Berg, Ivar and Mayer Zald. 1978. "Business and Society." *Annual Review of Sociology* 4:115-43.

Bernstein, Meyer. 1975. "The Trade Policy of the United Steelworkers of America." Pp. 229-84 in *Toward a New World Trade Policy* edited by C. Fred Bergsten. Lexington: Lexington Books.

Block, Fred. 1977. "The Ruling Class Does Not Rule." *Socialists Review,* 7:6-28.

_____. 1980. "Beyond Relative Autonomy: State Managers as Historical Subjects." *The Sociologist Register,* ed. Ralph Miliband and John Saville. London: Merlin Press.

Bluestone, Barry and Bennett Harrison. 1982. *The Deindustrialization of America: Plant Closings, Community Abandonment, and the Dismantling of Basic Industry.* New York: Basic Books, Inc.

Bowles, Samuel and Richard Edwards. 1985. *Understanding Capitalism.* New York: Harper & Row Publishers.

Burawoy, Michael. 1983. "Between the Labor Process and the State: The Changing Face of Factory Regimes under Advanced Capitalism." *American Sociological Review* 48:587-82.

_____. 1984. "Karl Marx and the Satanic Mills: Factory Politics under Early Capitalism in England, the United States, and Russia." *American Journal of Sociology,* 90:247-82.

Burn, Duncan. 1961. *The Steel Industry, 1939-1959: A Study in Competition and Planning.* Cambridge: Cambridge University Press.

Business Week. 1981. April 13.

Clawson, Dan and Alan Neustadtl. 1989. "Interlocks, PACs, and Corporate Conservatism." *American Journal of Sociology* 94:749-73.

Clegg, Stewart. 1981. "Organization and Control." *Administrative Science Quarterly* 26:545-62.

Cline, William. 1983. *Trade Policy in the 1980s.* Washington, DC: Institute for International Economics.

Congressional Quarterly Almanac. 1961. Washington, DC, Congressional Quarterly, Inc.

_____. 1962. Washington, DC, Congressional Quarterly, Inc.

_____. 1979. Washington, DC, Congressional Quarterly, Inc.

Congressional Quarterly Weekly Report. 1962. Washington, DC, Congressional Quarterly, Inc., October 27.

_____. 1968. Washington, DC, Congressional Quarterly, Inc., February 2.

_____. 1974. Washington, DC, Congressional Quarterly, Inc., December 28.

_____. 1977. Washington, DC, Congressional Quarterly, Inc., November 19.

_____. 1981a. Washington, DC, Congressional Quarterly, Inc., March 7.

_____. 1981b. Washington, DC, Congressional Quarterly, Inc., August 8.

_____. 1989. Washington, DC, Congressional Quarterly, Inc., March 25.

Congressional Record. 1982. H 8388, October 1.

Council on Wage and Price Stability. 1977. *Prices and Costs in the U.S. Steel Industry.* Washington, DC: U.S. Government Printing Office, October.

Crandall, Robert. 1981. *The U.S. Steel Industry in Recurrent Crisis: Policy Options in a Competitive World.* Washington, DC: The Brookings Institute.

Dahl, Robert A. 1961. *Who Governs?* New Haven: Yale University Press.

Domhoff, William. 1987. "The Wagner Act and Theories of the State: A New Analysis Based on Class-Segment Theory." *Political Power and Social Theory* 6. Greenwich: JAI Press Inc.

The Economist. 1981. March 28.

Forbes. 1984. "Taking It To The Courts." January 2.

Fortune. 1966. "Steel is Rebuilding for a New Era." October.

Fusfield, Daniel. 1958. "Joint Subsidiaries in the Iron and Steel Industry." *American Economic Review,* 48:578-87.

Goldberg, Walter. 1986. *Ailing Steel: The Transoceanic Quarrel.* New York: St. Martin's Press.

Grossman, Gene. 1986. "Imports as a Cause of Injury: The Case of the U.S. Steel Industry." *Journal of International Economics* 20:201-23.

Hall, Peter. 1986. *Governing the Economy: The Politics of State Intervention in Britain and France.* New York: Oxford University Press.

Hoerr, John. 1988. *And the Wolf Finally Came: The Decline of the American Steel Industry.* Pittsburgh: University of Pittsburgh Press.

Hogan, William, 1971. *Economic History of the Iron and Steel Industry in the United States,* Lexington: Lexington Books.

International Trade Commission. 1984. "Carbon and Certain Alloy Steel Products." Publication 1553. Washington, DC: U.S. International Trade Commission.

Iron Age. 1976. "Why Specialty Steel Won its Case for Quotas." 218:3 (July 19).

Jones, Kent. 1986. *Politics vs Economics in World Steel Trade.* London: Allen & Unwin.

Kotz, David. 1978. *Bank Control of Large Corporations in the United States.* Berkeley: University of California Press.

Kurth, James. 1979. "The Political Consequences of the Production Cycle: Industrial History and Political Outcomes." *International Organization,* 33:1-34.

Levine, Michael. 1985. *Inside International Trade Policy Formulation.* New York:Praeger.

March, James and Johan Olsen. 1976. *Organizational Choice under Ambiguity.* Olso: Universitetsforlaget.

_____. 1984. "The New Institutionalism: Organizational Factors in Political Life." *American Political Science Review* 78:734-49.

Martin, Cathie Jo. 1989. "Business Influence and State Power: The Case of U.S. Corporate Tax Policy." *Politics and Society,* 17:189-223.

Marx, Karl. (1887) 1976. *Capital.* Volume 1. New York: Vintage Books.

Miliband, Ralph. 1969. *The State in Capitalist Society.* New York: Basic Books, Inc., Publishers.

Mintz, Beth and Michael Schwartz. 1985. *The Structure of Power in American Business.* Chicago: University of Chicago Press.

Mizruchi, Mark. 1989a. "Similarity of Political Behavior among Large American Corporations." *American Journal of Sociology,* 95:401-24.

_____. 1989b. "Cohesion, Structural Equivalence, and Similarity of Behavior: An Approach to the Study of Corporate Political Power." Preprint series in the Center for the Social Sciences at Columbia University.

Mizruchi, Mark and Thomas Koenig. 1986. "Corporate Political Consensus." *American Sociological Review* 51:482-91.

McIntyre, Robert and Dean Tipps. 1983. *Inequality and Decline.* Washington, DC: Center on Budget and Policy Priorities.

New York Times. 1989a. February 13, p. D2.

_____. 1989b. June 28, p. D5.

_____. 1989c. July 24, p. D1.

Offe, Claus. 1975. "The Theory of the Capitalist State and the Problem of Policy Formation." Pp. 125-44 in *Stress and Contradiction in Modern Capitalism,* edited by Leon Lindberg, Robert Alford, Colin Crouch, and Claus Offe. Lexington: D.C. Heath and Company.

Offe, Claus and Helmut Wiesenthal. 1980. "Two Logics of Collective Action." *Political Power and Social Theory* 1:67-115.

Pfeffer, Jeffrey. 1987. "A Resource Dependence Perspective on Intercorporate Relations." Pp. 25-55 in *Intercorporate Relations: The Structural Analysis of Business,* edited by Mark Mizruchi and Michael Schwartz. New York: Cambridge University Press.

Poulantzas, Nicos. [1978] 1974. *Classes in Contemporary Capitalism.* London: Verso.

Prechel, Harland. forthcoming 1991. "Irrationality and Contradiction in Organizational Change: Transformations in the Corporate Form of a U.S. Steel Corporation." *The Sociological Quarterly,* 32 (August).

Quadagno, Jill. 1984. "Welfare Capitalism and the Social Security Act of 1935." *American Sociological Review* 49:632-47.

Reagan, Ronald. 1984. "Steel Import Relief Determination" (Memorandum for the U.S. Trade Representative), 18 September.

Reutter, Mark. 1988. *Sparrows Point: Making Steel — The Rise and Ruin of American Industrial Might.* New York: Summit Books.

Rueschemeyer, Dietrich and Peter B. Evans. 1985. "The State and Economic Transformation: Toward an Analysis of the Conditions Underlying Effective Intervention." Pp. 44-77 in *Bringing the State Back In,* edited by Peter Evans, Dietrich Rueschemeyer, and Theda Skocpol. Cambridge: Cambridge University Press.

Scheuerman, William. 1986. *The Steel Crisis: The Economics of Politics of a Declining Industry.* New York: Praeger.

Simon, Herbert. 1957. *Administrative Behavior.* New York: Macmillian.

Shonfield, Andrew. 1965. *Modern Capitalism: the Changing Balance of Public and Private Power.* New York: Oxford University Press.

Skocpol, Theda. 1980. "Political Response to Capitalist Crisis: Neo- Marxist Theories of the State and the Case of the New Deal." *Politics and Society* 10:155-201.

_____. 1985. "Bringing the State Back In: Strategies of Analysis in Current Research." Pp. 3-43 in *Bringing the State Back In,* edited by Peter Evans, Diertrich Rueschemeyer, and Theda Skocpol. Cambridge: Cambridge University Press.

Sobel, Robert. 1984. *The Age of Giant Corporations: A Microeconomic History of American Business 1914-1984.* Westport: Greenwood Press, Inc.

Staples, William. 1987. "Technology, Control, and the Social Organization of Work at a British Hardware Firm, 1791-1891." *American Journal of Sociology* 93:62-88.

Sweezy, Paul (1942) 1970. *The Theory of Capitalist Development.* New York: Monthly Review.

Szymanski, Al. 1977. "Capital Accumulation on a World Scale and the Necessity of Imperialism." *The Insurgent Sociologist*, 2:35-53.

Therborn, Goran. 1978. *What Does the Ruling Class do When it Rules?* London: New Left Books.

Tilly, Charles. 1981. *As Sociology Meets History.* New York: Academic.

Useem, Michael. 1982. "Classwide Rationality in the Politics of Managers and Directors of Large Corporations in the United States and Great Britain." *Administrative Science Quarterly* 27:199-226.

_____. 1983. "The Corporate Community: Its Social Organization and the Rise of Business Political Activity in the United States and United Kingdom. *Organizational Theory and Public Policy* edited by Richard Hall and Robert Quinn. Beverly Hills: Sage Publications.

_____. 1984. *The Inner Circle: Large Corporations and the Rise of Political Activities in the U.S. and U.K.* New York: Oxford University Press.

U.S. Census of Manufacturers. 1972. Volume I.

U.S. Congress. 1946. Senate, Surplus Property Subcommittee of the Committee on Military Affairs, "War-Plant Disposal: Acceptance of Bid of United States Steel Corporation for Geneva Steel Plant: Report Pursuant to S. Res. 129."

_____. 1948. Senate, Hearings before the Special Committee to Study Problems of American Small Business. "Problems of American Small Business." 80th Congress, 2nd Session.

_____. 1950. House of Representatives, Subcommittee on Study of Monopoly Power of the Committee on the Judiciary. "Study of Monopoly Power: Hearing." 81st Congress, 2nd Session.

_____. 1961. House of Representatives, 87th Congress. 1st session: "Message from the President of the United States Relative of Our Federal Tax System," April 20. House Document No. 140.

_____. 1962. Senate, Committee on Finance, Hearing, Revenue Act of 1962, 87th Congress, 2nd Session, April.

_____. 1968. Steel Imports, Staff Study of Senate Committee on Finance, Senate Document no. 107, 90th Congress.

_____. 1973. House of Representatives, Committee on Ways and Means. Trade Reform Act of 1973. Hearing of HR 6767, 93rd Congress, 1st session, pp. 3957-4031.

_____. 1977. House Ways and Means Committee on Trade, Hearing on World Steel Trade: Current Trends and Structural Problems, 95th Congress, September 30.

_____. 1978. House of Representatives. Hearing Before the Subcommittee on Trade of the Committee on Ways and Means. Reprint in Administration's Comprehensive Program for the Steel Industry. Originally titled "A Comprehensive Program for the Steel Industry, Report to the President Submitted by Anthony M. Soloman, Chairman Task Force, December 6, 1977.

_____. 1984. "The Effects of Import Quotas on the Steel Industry," Congressional Budget Office.

U.S. Department of Commerce. 1960-1979. *Statistical Abstract of the United States.* Washington, DC: Government Printing Office.

_____. 1983-1988. *Quarterly Financial Reports for Manufacturing, Mining, & Trade Corporations,* Washington, DC, Government Printing Office.

U.S. Federal Trade Commission — Securities and Exchange Commission. (1974) 1950-1982. Quarterly Financial Reports for Manufacturing Corporations.

_____. 1977. Staff Report on the United States Steel Industry and its International Rivals: Trends and Factors Determining International Competitiveness.

U.S. General Accounting Office. 1989. "Import Duties: Assessment of Duties on Unfairly Priced Imports Not Reviewed" (September).

U.S. Office of Technological Assessment. 1981. Technology and Steel Industry Competitiveness. (June).

U.S. Trade Representative. 1984. "Brock Announces President's Steel Decision," (Press Release), 18 September.

Walter, Ingo. 1983. "Structural Adjustment and Trade Policy in the International Steel Industry." Pp. 483-525 in *Trade Policy in the 1980s,* edited by William C. Cline. Washington, DC: Institute for International Economics.

Weber, Max. 1949. *The Methodology of the Social Sciences.* Translated and edited by Edward Shils and Henry Finch. New York: The Free Press.

Zeitlin, Maurice. 1980. *Classes, Class Conflict, and the State.* Cambridge: Winthrop.

_____. 1984. *The Civil Wars in Chile (or the Bourgeois Revolutions That Never Were).* Princeton: Princeton University Press.

Zeitlin, Maurice, W. Lawrence Neuman, and Richard Ratcliff. 1976. "Class Segments: Agrarian Property and Political Leadership in the Capitalist Class of Chile." *American Sociological Review,* 41:1006-29.

THE

YALE REVIEW

VOL. LXV · PUBLISHED IN OCTOBER 1975 · No. 1

THE "MILITARY-INDUSTRIAL COMPLEX" MUDDLE

By JEROME SLATER AND TERRY NARDIN

THE phrase "military-industrial complex" is now common in political debate, journalism and, increasingly, academic scholarship in the United States. It appears both in substantive controversy concerning questions of public policy and in scholarly controversy concerning the explanation of the phenomena that the phrase is thought to describe. But despite its popularity the concept of a military-industrial complex embodies a highly misleading analysis of contemporary American politics and policy. In particular, we will argue, it presupposes an implicit theory of politics that is notably deficient in its analysis of the policy process as well as in its implications for the substance of public policy.

The popularity of the concept of a military-industrial complex has arisen in the context of the following features of recent American history: a large military establishment supported by vast military budgets; the consequent creation of substantial economic, political, bureaucratic, and psychological interests in the continuation of high levels of military expenditures; and the rise of participation by the military in making American foreign policy, largely free from public examination. There is a concomitant decline in the influence of the Department of State, the Congress, and of public opinion. In addition to these incontrovertible facts, the military-industrial-complex literature stresses the existence of other, more problematic, trends, notably the coordination and integration of groups interested in continuing high military expenditures, through extensive formal and informal relationships, particularly between the military and the government bureaucracy, Congress, corporations, industrial associations, veterans groups, and military-oriented scientists and academicians; and massive and largely successful efforts by these groups and organizations to militarize attitudes throughout American society—through propaganda, deceit, and manipulation of public opinion—in order to forestall opposition and preserve their privileged positions. The overall result of these developments is seen to be pathological, in both policy substance and process: militarist foreign policies in both cold and hot war, and the erosion of democracy and political accountability, as crucial decisions have come to be increasingly dominated by military and industrial elites able to evade public scrutiny and capable of working their will free from effective political opposition or the normal regulation of the constitutional order. (The works upon which our analysis of the literature of the military-industrial complex is based are identified in the earlier, fully documented version of this paper that was published in *Testing the Theory of the Military-Industrial Complex*, edited by Steven Rosen [Lexington Books, 1973].)

In most of the literature, the concept of a military-industrial complex functions as both a description and an explanatory theory of what is being described. Sometimes, though, the military-industrial complex notion is intended as an atheoretical description: simply as a name or label for an area of concern focusing on some or all of the actual or presumed phenomena listed above. In a few instances, especially in the more recent literature, the phrase is used in a low-key, relatively neutral way merely as a fashionable synonym for what formerly would have been called "the military establishment." On rare occasions the term is accepted, even embraced, by those who wish to thank God for the military-industrial complex and defend it against its detractors. Overwhelmingly, though, those who make use of the notion of a military-industrial complex use it as a political symbol for institutions and policies that they wish to condemn.

Some are primarily concerned with waste, inefficiency, or corruption in the weapons-procurement process, alleged to arise out of excessively close ties between the defense industry and the Pentagon. Others have more fundamental concerns, which are the larger purpose and direction of American policy and the processes by which it is made.

Thus, while the phrase appears in a number of contexts and types of discourse, its most comfortable home remains political debate, where it functions as a metaphor closely associated with the criticism of American institutions. It is scarcely coincidental that the term became popular at the very time when disenchantment with American foreign and military policies was spreading. Indeed, it is reasonable to guess that this disenchantment usually precedes the postulation of a military-industrial complex as a causal agent. Something is wrong here, the argument runs, and an explanation that goes behind the official mythology is required. By contrast, those who approve of American policies seldom worry about the existence of a military-industrial complex, or make use of that conception in their explanation of those policies; instead, they typically emphasize the pluralistic (open, competitive, diversified, nonhierarchical; that is, *legitimate*) nature of the policy process. While it is not logically necessary or inevitable that there be such a nearly perfect correlation between views on policy process and policy substance, it is easy to understand the powerful psychological connection: if one accepts the basic premises of American foreign and military policies in recent decades then no further explanation for the large military budgets or the increased role of the military in government, economy, and society is required—they are seen as rational responses to the international situation.

It is likely that some of the deficiencies even in the more academic analyses of a military-industrial complex arise from the inherent difficulties of adapting a concept derived from partisan controversy to the descriptive and explanatory purposes of political science. One such difficulty is that controversy about public affairs tends to be characterized by the search for pragmatic explanations aimed at identifying factors which can and should be manipulated to bring about change, rather than by a search for complete explanations that take account of factors which, while important; are beyond the reach of practical influence. Furthermore, such controversy often focuses on the identification of individuals or groups that seem to be politically and morally responsible for the occurrence or persistence of disapproved events, policies, or situations, and against whom pressure can be mobilized to effect reform. The phrase "military-industrial complex" strongly suggests—and the concept to which it refers typically embodies—an implicit causal theory, or selective set of assumptions, of this kind. In particular, it suggests that the cause of militarism in the United States today lies in the existence and actions of some entity (an agent or group of agents) with an interest in militarism as well as the power to bring it about. To speak, as participants in this particular controversy so frequently do, of "*the* military-industrial complex" as if it were an entity, motivated by interest, and possessing power by reference to which a causal explanation of certain features of American society and politics can be framed, is thus to make certain questionable assumptions about power, motivation, causation, and explanation. These assumptions, far from being defended in the literature, are seldom explicitly stated, and are in all probability largely unrecognized. Thus, even those writers who are apparently engaged only in what they intend as atheoretical description are in fact likely to be operating within a framework of assumptions that is subject to considerable dispute. It is this framework of assumptions, which in fact constitutes a theory of the military-industrial complex, that we wish to examine.

There seem to be four main variants within the literature on the military-industrial complex: the complex as a ruling class, as a power elite, as a governing bureaucracy, and as a loose coalition of powerful groups. Many of the central themes in the current literature—the importance of economic interests, the dependence of political upon economic power, the concept of false consciousness—are rooted in Marxian class analyses of the nineteenth and early twentieth centuries. Contemporary writers working within this tradition (e.g., G. William Domhoff and

Gabriel Kolko) focus on the wealthy as a self-conscious class dominating American policies and institutions. The military as such plays only a subordinate role, but because the interests of the corporate rich are dependent upon imperialist foreign policies, the military definition of reality prevails throughout society. In the power elite conception, the military-industrial complex is portrayed as a small, relatively unified, and frequently conspiratorial group whose members, linked by ties of class, vocation, economic interest, education, and personal friendship, are drawn primarily from the military leadership, industrial firms engaged in military production, bureaucrats in key positions in the executive branch, and a few key members of Congress. The power elite conception differs from the ruling class conception of the military-industrial complex chiefly in giving government and military institutions equal or greater importance than the corporate rich. Thus, it is not wealth that is the dominant tie binding the elite, but power—particularly the power to make the crucial decisions concerning war and peace. C. Wright Mills is of course the intellectual father of current writers in this vein (e.g., Richard J. Barnet, Fred J. Cook, Sidney Lens, and John M. Swomley).

In a third variant, the core of the military-industrial complex is said to be the nonelected bureaucrats or managers in the executive branch, with the military and its industrial allies playing a supporting but distinctly secondary role. The unprecedented power of these new "state-managers" or "national security managers" derives from the importance of their positions in the organization of both government and the economy, each of which has itself become highly centralized because of the dynamics of modern industrial society and the permanent international crisis of our times. The main interest or motivation of the bureaucratic managers is to maintain or expand their power; thus their entrenchment in power and sheer bureaucratic momentum ensure the continuation of the cold war and the militarization of American society. Authors of works emphasizing the bureaucracy are again Richard J. Barnet, and Bert Cochran, John Kenneth Galbraith, and Seymour Melman.

The final model of the military-industrial complex is one comprising a loose coalition of powerful groups linked by common interests in militarized policies: the industrial sector is interested mainly in profits, the political, military, and bureaucratic sectors mainly in power. There is no one ruling class or power elite, no internal organization or integrated structure, no conscious coordination or planned action within the complex. The shared perceptions of reality and the common actions and policies that emerge from these perceptions—the pursuit of high military budgets and bellicose cold-war policies—are simply a function of the "coincidences of interest" or "symbiotic ties" that link otherwise noncentrally coordinated organizations and groups (e.g., this was President Eisenhower's view). Recent writers who have this view in common are Galbraith, Adam Yarmolinsky, and, to a considerable extent, Marc Pilisuk and Thomas Hayden.

Despite their considerable differences, these four main variants of the military-industrial-complex theory have a number of significant substantive commonalities: (1) the military-industrial complex is an entity, a specifiable group of human actors; (2) this group is relatively small and unrepresentative of American society as a whole; (3) yet it has great political power and is opposed by little or no countervailing power, especially in the area of foreign and military policy; (4) this power is exercised mostly covertly, in activities and organizations other than (or at least in substantial addition to) the formal and constitutional institutions of government—the military-industrial complex, that is, constitutes a "state within a state"; (5) the exercise of power by the military-industrial complex is motivated by and exerted on behalf of its private interests, defined in economic or power terms; (6) this leads to militarist policies which serve these interests rather than the public interest; (7) the result is a political *process* that is to a great extent undemocratic and which produces *policies* that are irrational, pathological, and dangerous. In short, the military-industrial complex, consisting of groups with economic and institutional interests in cold-war policies and high military expenditures and linked by shared values and beliefs as well as by overlapping or symbiotic positions in the economic, social, and political structure of American society, is America's dominant institution, exercising power over a broad range of military, foreign, and domestic policies in ways which have consequences for even seemingly remote aspects of American life.

This conception presupposes certain problematic ideas about power, motivation, causation, and explanation. One of the more notable of these ideas is the assumption that the proper way to explain the occurrence or persistence of events, policies, or situations is by reference to the actions and power of individuals or groups with an interest in those outcomes. Such a view—which in effect is a conspiracy theory—radically oversimplifies the explanation of social and political events. For one thing, it underestimates the level of mere accident and drift in human life, particularly the unintended and unforeseen consequence of actions taken with quite different ends in mind. As conspiracy theories are invented to explain disapproved events, their main concern is to attach some rational purpose to an historical progression of events which would otherwise be meaningless to condemn as *policy*, and for which identifiable men or groups could be blamed. Conspiracy theories also restrict the range of potentially valid types of explanation to those which refer to agents, motives, actions, and powers. They particularly miss the possibilities for explanation which refer to social wholes of various kinds (such as beliefs, rules, practices, and institutions) and, in general, overlook a wide range of factors which must be considered in any reasonably complete explanation of social and political events. The point is not that such explanatory factors or perspectives never enter into theories of the military-industrial complex—they sometimes do—but rather that the framework of assumptions embodied in such theories hinders them from moving very far or very consistently away from the style of analysis characteristic of conspiracy theories.

It is beyond the scope of this paper to analyze militarism (or, to say it more neutrally, the increased role of military factors in American domestic and foreign policy) on different substantive and methodological premises from those presupposed by the theory of the military-industrial complex. But it might help to clarify our criticism of that theory to suggest briefly some elements, other than the interests and actions of powerful groups, which would enter into a more complete theory of the military dimensions of American politics, elements which are ignored or slighted by the military-industrial-complex theory. We have already mentioned the argument of some that there is a real Communist challenge *requiring* a military response. Alternatively, to the extent it can be shown that political officials and elites genuinely *believe* in the existence of such a threat for reasons not plausibly attributable simply to their "interests," regardless of the extent to which that belief is founded on reality, then to that extent a long step has been taken in accounting for the phenomena attributed to the power of a military-industrial complex. At a different level of abstraction, one might point simply to the nature of the international political system, the near anarchic structure of which creates genuine, deep-rooted anxieties about security, action-reaction patterns of conflict, and competitive arms races. Recent literature on the Soviet "military-industrial complex" suggests that this structural factor has similar effects on nations with very different institutions, ideologies, and political practices. Transnational historical developments, too, such as the growth of modern industrialism, with its uncontrolled, exploding technological "advances," especially when linked to the "worst possible contingency" styles of military planning that have their roots in global insecurities, seriously exacerbate arms races and political tensions.

Besides these factors, there are certain characteristics of American political beliefs or mythologies and political institutions that play a role in explaining American foreign and military policies. For example, what has been called "liberal messianism" in foreign policy, although not associated with or plausibly attributable to any specific group, does, because of its expansive conception of America's mission in the world, imply an assertive foreign policy and a military establishment going beyond that required for "security." And at the institutional level there is the well-known conservative structural bias of the political system, which not only overweights in Congress the more militaristic forces within American society but, more broadly, fragments power and thus makes change from established policies particularly difficult. The conservative impact of these forces on policy may be strengthened by a more general human reluctance to reexamine fundamental premises or to alter established practices and institutions even long after their validity or sense has come to be regarded as more and more dubious.

To take account of these kinds of factors is not only to go beyond an explanation of the military dimensions of American society in terms of the interests and actions of powerful groups, but to reveal those interests and actions as themselves products of an historically changing context of technologies, beliefs, institutions, and situations. From this perspective, the so-called military-industrial complex begins to look like a consequence of recent changes in American society rather than like a cause. Possibly the reason that the concept of a military-industrial complex as a causal entity is so popular is that in America institutions appear more accessible to criticism and reform than other more intangible or complex factors contributing to militarism. And, as we have already noted, the emphasis in debates about American militarism has been on the identification of factors which might be manipulated in order to effect social and political change, and particularly on the identification of men who seem to be responsible and whose power must be curtailed. To the extent that pragmatic, action-oriented theories are subject to this kind of selectivity, their usefulness is limited.

Another kind of selectivity in the formulation of theory occurs when assumptions about political motivation are oversimplified. The first assumption is that men are invariably motivated by "interests" defined in terms of their immediate economic or political gain. A second assumption is that in politics men act to maximize those interests. A final assumption is that these interests can be easily and directly inferred from class, social, or institutional position. These assumptions are not equal to the complexity of actual political behavior. The point is not that "interests" never determine political action, only that they do not invariably do so. To imagine the military-industrial complex as sufficiently united, organized, and self-conscious to act as an entity in politics is questionable, but even if it did so act we would still be obliged to discover, rather than presume, in whose interests and to what ends it acts.

There are several ways of interpreting such actions. One is that the complex genuinely seeks to exercise its power in the public interest, and because it correctly understands reality (it is rational to pursue active anti-Communist policies and maintain high military budgets), it in fact does so. Insofar as these policies also further its own economic and political interests, this is a coincidental and unavoidable by-product. This view was implicit in the broad anti-Communist consensus in the United States of the late 1940's and 1950's, but it rarely makes an appearance in the literature on the military-industrial complex. More common is the view that the complex genuinely seeks to act in the public interest, but it misperceives reality—in good part, no doubt, because its own interests unconsciously distort its perceptions—and ends by acting in its own interests but against the public interest. A final possibility, and the one that is prevalent in the military-industrial-complex literature, is that the complex deliberately misrepresents reality in order to legitimate its own power and further its own particular interests; there is no genuine need for large military budgets and anti-Communist policies, and those who comprise the military-industrial complex know it. It is not our purpose to make judgments about the relative validity of these possibilities, but only to make clear the extent to which theories of the military-industrial complex rest upon unacceptably narrow and simplistic assumptions about individual and group motivation and thus result in a sadly partial and misleading analysis of American politics.

Another question is whether it makes sense to conceive the military-industrial complex as an entity with sufficient internal coherence and group-consciousness to have and act upon "interests." We have already noted how common it is for the phrase "military-industrial complex" to be used as if it referred to such an entity. An initial problem here is that most of the literature is vague or inconsistent concerning the kinds of individuals or subgroups that "belong" to the military-industrial complex; the criteria for belonging are seldom made the subject of explicit discussion. Nearly all accounts agree in including as central to the complex the higher officials of the executive branch, particularly those in the Department of Defense; high-ranking military leaders; the top managers and principal owners of industrial corporations judged significantly dependent on military contracts; and Congressional leaders, especially the ranking members of committees consistently supporting high military expenditures. Beyond this inner core, however, there begins to be disagreement; it is often unclear whether other groups are properly regarded as members of the complex, "associate members," or merely as a sympathetic environment for the complex. Among these other groups are the leaders of labor unions whose members are dependent upon military related and generated employment, and at times even the membership of those unions in their entirety; industrial and military associations of various kinds; veterans groups; many of the nation's scientists and engineers; universities in which military research is being undertaken or which are otherwise dependent upon financial support from the Department of Defense; Congressmen belonging to military reserve units, holding stock in defense corporations, or simply supporting high military budgets and sharing the cold-war consensus; the foreign service, intelligence agencies, and the Atomic Energy Commission; parts of the mass media; local business associations and civic groups in communities which benefit from heavy defense spending; and various religious bodies and spokesmen.

It is apparent that the criteria for membership in the complex are unclear and shifting, and to a considerable extent they undermine other premises of the military-industrial-complex theory as an account of who makes high policy and for what ends. At least six criteria for membership can be discerned: participation in high-level policy-making (the inner core); participation, at any level, in any government agency involved in foreign or military policy (the foreign service, intelligence agencies, AEC); economic, bureaucratic, or career interests (corporations, unions, scientists, academicians, etc.); ideological support for cold-war politics (conservative Congressmen, church groups, editors, etc.); and emotional attachments to the military (veterans groups, Congressmen in reserve units). Yet once membership in the complex is conceived to include groups beyond those identified as the inner core, the military-industrial-complex theory loses most of its force, which rests on the premise that high policy in the United States is the work of a small, largely nonofficial, and unrepresentative elite group or coalition. In some versions, indeed, the complex seems to include most of both national and local governments, as well as a substantial proportion of the population at large. While these versions might conceivably reflect an insight into the pervasiveness of militarism in American society, they are certainly inconsistent with the notion of a military-industrial complex as a coherent entity possessing interests and powers. For one thing, insofar as the existence of the complex itself is thought to be explained by the power of vested economic or institutional interests, then the inclusion of groups which have no such interests denies the premise. Moreover, the more inclusive one conceives the military-industrial complex to be, the less sense it makes to speak of it as an entity, until (in the more extreme versions) it is a mere list of all groups or individuals within American society, with or without "power," that support high military expenditures and the main lines of American foreign policy since 1945, for whatever reasons.

While a less inclusive conception of the complex is thus required if the theory of the military-industrial complex is to make sense, such a conception would not necessarily be correct. That is, there would still be room for debate concerning the internal coherence and agreement of even the least inclusive collections of men and groups that have been proposed as constituting the military-industrial complex. Any such debate would have to take into account the fact that the history of American foreign and defense policy is replete with examples of disagreement among the presumptive members of the complex. The response of defenders of the military-industrial-complex theory to this argument is usually that the *range* of disagreement, however significant it might appear to some participants and outside observers, is "really" quite narrow. All policy members are said to share the same cold-war perspective, the same "military definition of reality," as Mills put it, the same devotion to capitalist expansion, as many Marxists and current revisionist historians would have it.

A particularly interesting case study on the problem of whether it is more persuasive to emphasize agreement or disagreement within the military-industrial complex would be an examination of Robert McNamara's tenure as Secretary of Defense. From one perspective, certainly that of the majority of writers on the complex, McNamara stood at its very center, indeed was perhaps the prime example of the intertwining of business, bureaucratic, political, and military power at the highest levels of policy-making. Yet, from another perspective—that held by a wide variety of former policy-makers and outside observers—McNamara was the center of raging conflict that rent the complex, if he was not in fact "the 'complex's' greatest foe." How are such differences of interpretation to be resolved? Clearly it is the case that in any group there will always be *some* areas of agreement as well as *some* diversity and disagreement. Whether it is what unites or what divides that is more significant is a question to which there can be no general answer; one must ask "significant for what?" If we take as the criterion of significance in the present dispute the ability to explain particular policy outcomes (such as high military expenditures), as writers on the military-industrial complex largely do, then the kinds of agreement among those said to comprise the complex seem to be of such generality as to permit marked disagreement at the level of operational policy.

The concept of a military-industrial complex as an entity coherent enough to have and pursue interests of a certain kind is incomplete, within the framework of assumptions we are discussing, without the attribution of *power* to the complex. For it is power which completes the picture of an American society whose purposes and policies are distorted by the complex, and provides the explanatory link between the existence of a complex and these distortions. Our discussion of the concepts of power presupposed by the theory of the military-industrial complex will focus on the *criteria* according to which power is attributed to the complex, and the *scope* and *kind* of power attributed to it.

How can we determine whether or to what extent the military-industrial complex has power? One approach is to infer power by examining who benefits from particular policies: those who gain are presumed to be powerful. This method is implicit in much of the military-industrial-complex literature. The crucial point to be made about it is that it assumes rather than demonstrates that there is a causal relationship between the desires and demands of some group, and outcomes which satisfy those desires. But this assumption rests on a *post hoc, ergo propter hoc* fallacy. Not only is it the case that in the absence of evidence supporting a causal relationship we cannot assume that outcomes are explained by the desires or demands of particular groups rather than by other factors, but strictly speaking we cannot even exclude the possibility that the outcomes occurred *despite* those demands.

Another common assumption of the military-industrial-complex literature is that power can be inferred from institutional position: the elites of the major economic, military, and political institutions are presumed to be powerful. Yet to have power in general is not necessarily to have the power to achieve some specific end. Neither can we assume that because someone *might* have brought about a certain state of affairs, he *did* bring it about. With respect to particular outcomes, then, institutional elites may or may not have had power, for institutional position provides us mainly with information about potential power, which in fact for a variety of reasons is frequently not translated into actual power when relevant policy issues are decided.

A third method of ascertaining power would be to examine specific cases of decision-making to see who participates, and with what results. We have already observed that case studies are rare in the military-industrial-complex literature; when they occur, they quite frequently fail to support the attribution of power to business firms or military agencies. What we know in general about the foreign policy decision-making process in the United States suggests strongly that the main participants are official elites, especially in the executive branch, rather than any behind-the-scenes unofficial elites. In particular, businessmen appear to play only the most minimal role, and the military participate mainly as distinct subordinates to the President and his advisors, and even then usually make their weight felt only on matters directly within their realm of presumed expertise. This is not to say that various business or military groups are without indirect influence on policy (for example, through legislative lobbying or campaign financing), only that there is very little evidence of direct or unusual participation by them in the decision-making process. Finally, the case studies do not support attributions of power to a coherent military-industrial entity for, as we have said, there exist conflicts of interest, as well as common interests, among military and industrial groups. Therefore, proven instances of military or industrial influence on decision-making still fail to support attributions of power to a military-industrial *complex.*

Implicit in the decision-making case study approach is the assumption that power consists in being able to "prevail" over opposition. Those whose views or ends most often prevail in policy conflicts have the most power. This criterion for inferring power, though common, is a bad one. The notion of "prevailing," widely shared among both "power elite" theorists and their "pluralist" critics, obscures just those distinctions (for example, among coercion, persuasion, exchange, and authority) that are crucial for the resolution of debates about the nature of power, power elites, power structures, and the like. But even if we adopt it, the results are inconclusive. From one perspective it would appear that, if there is a military-industrial complex, it has suffered a whole series of setbacks in recent years, beginning with public and Congressional opposition to the war in Vietnam, to general military spending, and to a considerable extent even to the military establishment itself. Military spending (projected for fiscal 1972) declined in terms both of its percentage share of the federal budget and of overall Gross National Product. Indeed, if one discounts for inflation, non-Vietnam defense spending has declined in absolute as well as relative terms. According to Assistant Secretary of Defense Moot (*New York Times*, July 30, 1972) "the cost of all research and development, construction, and all major procurement from industry together has grown just $300 million in the past nine years"; it is military pay raises (a total of $21 billion since 1964), voted for by a diverse Congressional majority including doves seeking the establishment of an all-volunteer military, that have accounted for most of the recent increases in the absolute size of the military budget.

One should also note the present ailing state of the aerospace industries, the heart of the industrial sector of the military-industrial complex, in part resulting from the elimination or substantial cutback of many weapons systems strongly urged on the executive branch by the defense establishment and its industrial allies, e.g., nuclear-powered airplanes; the Skybolt, Navaho, Snark, and Nike-Zeus missiles; the B-70 bomber; and the ABM (anti-ballistic missile). It is quite characteristic of the literature to point with great alarm to the "pressures" of the complex on behalf of these and other weapons systems but somehow to fail to notice how often those pressures *fail*.

Certainly, however, from another perspective what is more impressive is what the military and its suppliers continue to get even in the face of these apparent adversities: the defense budget is still over $80 billion, most of the recent Congressional attacks on specific weapons-projects have been weathered, the SALT (strategic arms limitation talks) agreements seem to have had little immediate impact on the arms race, and so on. What this juxtaposition of two reasonable perspectives suggests, of course, is the frequent extreme difficulty of ascertaining who "prevails" in conflicts. Take, for example, the ABM conflict prior to the SALT agreements—did the pro- or anti-ABM forces prevail when Congress decided to build two missile sites rather than the twelve initially requested by the Nixon Administration and its corporate and military allies? Or, take the Congressional decision in which by a margin of one vote a large loan to the Lockheed Corporation was authorized. Should we be more impressed with the power of Lockheed to get the Nixon Administration and Congress to subsidize its operations, or with the fact that a major corporation presumably standing at the very heart of the complex barely was able to avoid bankruptcy? Congressman William Moorhead likened Lockheed's tactics to that of "an 80-ton dinosaur who comes to your door and says, 'If you don't feed me, I will die.' And what are you going to do with 80 tons of dead, stinking dinosaur in your yard?" Attributions of power to a military-industrial complex, at least insofar as power is associated with the notion of prevailing, thus vary according to whether it is the successes of the complex or its reverses, what it gets or what it fails to get, that strike the observer as most significant. But the criterion of prevailing is too crude a notion, and one too closely tied to one's judgments about how much military spending is justified or rational, to bear the theoretical weight it has been asked to carry.

Thus, the criteria according to which power is attributed to a military-industrial complex are indecisive, and involve logical fallacies or conceptual confusion. What about the *scope* of power attributed to the military-industrial complex? Over what range of public policy is the complex said to have power? There seem to be five main possibilities envisaged in the literature, listed here in order of increasing scope: the distribution of the military budget, the overall size of the military budget, foreign and military policy in general, the entire range of public policy, and the structure, ethos, and direction of American society. The scope of power enjoyed by the complex is commonly taken to be very great, including at least the determination of American foreign and defense policies and the general setting of priorities within American public policy. Most of the *specific arguments* made by theorists of the military-industrial complex, however, are relevant only to the complex's alleged power over the distribution of the military budget or, at most, to its overall size.

In essence, the argument concerning the distribution and size of the military budget is that a close, nonadversary, symbiotic "team" relationship has developed between the military and its industrial suppliers because of the interchange of personnel between the two institutions (over 2000 former high-ranking officers are employed by the hundred largest military contractors; top industrialists move from their corporations to stints in the Defense Department and back again); because of the practice of letting arms contracts and deciding their terms through industry-Pentagon negotiations rather than through competitive bidding; and because of the mutually dependent relationship between the Pentagon and its top suppliers. In contrast with the past, the argument runs, most of the largest defense industries (aircraft, electronics) are not diversified but do most of their business with the government; conversely, the Pentagon is dependent on the experience, technological expertise, and massive production capabilities of the largest of its suppliers. This close relationship, in turn, is thought to lead to favoritism, waste, inefficiency, and even corruption. The evidence most commonly adduced in support of this argument is that over two-thirds of military prime contracts go to the hundred largest companies, that enormous cost overruns are typically tolerated by the Pentagon, and that billions of dollars' worth of new military-weapons systems have had to be canceled because of their poor operational performance or instant obsolescence.

However, the facts do not necessarily support these conclusions drawn from them. While there is admittedly at least some waste, corruption, and inefficiency attributable to an excessively close industry-Pentagon relationship, other factors are clearly also important. The uneven distribution of military largesse can be explained by factors other than political influence or favoritism. The largest corporations can afford huge outlays for research and development and presumably have the experience and technological skills necessary to produce advanced weapons-systems. Climate and geography play important roles (aircraft and missile work takes place where the climate permits all-year testing and launching, large military bases are thought to be most appropriately located in outpost areas like Alaska or Hawaii or in less densely populated areas like the South and Southwest, naval installations and shipbuilding facilities obviously have to be in ports, etc.). Also, lack of competition in the awarding of major contracts is often unavoidable for technical, not political, reasons. Similarly, cost overruns, late deliveries, and poor performance are not due simply to inefficiency or corruption but also to the inherent problems and uncertainties involved in advanced technology. Finally, the disposition of the Pentagon to overlook poor performance and to rescue floundering corporations by means of government loans or subsidies can be explained in great part by the belief that, come what may, the national interest requires the continued existence of the military's major industrial suppliers.

As for the effects of industry-Pentagon relationships on the overall size of the budget, what counts as "waste" or evidence of corruption, and what is thought to be the inevitable by-product of technological change, healthy interservice and industrial competition, or a sound policy of covering all bets (even when it is known that some will not work out), depends upon interpretations, evaluations, and judgments concerning a wide range of matters, including the nature of the international environment and the appropriate American response to it. Put differently, the implicit argument that the relationship between the military and the defense industry biases the weapons procurement process to such a degree that the United States spends far more on defense than is "necessary" or than it otherwise would, cannot be proven by simply pointing to the amount of money spent on weapons systems that cost more than original estimates or proved to be less effective or reliable than expected.

More important, even if the facts cited by the relevant theorists supported all the implications drawn from them, these facts would be germane primarily to that part of the argument concerned with the distribution of the military budget, only partially to its overall size (since no one would claim that without the structural biases attributed to the military-industrial complex the United States would spend little or nothing on defense), and not at all to the alleged power of the complex over matters of broader scope. Thus the centrally important theme, implicit or explicit, that there is a military-industrial complex which exercises a broad range of power within American society, is not supported by evidence or logic, but rests instead upon assertion or indirection.

Finally, what about the *kind* of power attributed to the military-industrial complex? Implicit in most of the literature is the argument that the source of the complex's power lies in the availability to it of both positive and negative sanctions: the complex has power because it is able to use its extensive economic and political resources to reward its friends and punish its enemies. Such a conception of power overlooks a number of possibilities, however, one of which is that a complex might achieve its ends (assuming, again, for purposes of discussion, that it existed as an entity, had ends, and succeeded in furthering them) not because it had power in the sense of control over sanctions, but *influence*, defined as the capacity to persuade both public officials and public opinion of the validity of its preferred policies without recourse to sanctions. Thus, to the extent that various supposed members of a military-industrial complex have "prevailed" in decisions concerning military policy, it may be because Presidents and Congressional committees have been convinced by their arguments or deferred to their presumed expertise, rather than that they have brought irresistible economic and political power to bear. Perceptions of whether it is power or influence that is at work vary in quite predictable ways. Those who disagree with the rationale of particular policy decisions usually explain them as the result of the exercise of power, whereas those who agree with them rarely see "power" or "pressures" at work, let alone illegitimate power, but only persuasion, or perhaps simply a necessary response to an obvious reality.

Yet another possibility is that an agent's power is not based on his capacity to overcome resistance, whether by sanctions *or* by persuasion, but on the absence of any opposition at all, or the availability of positive support. For most of the postwar period there existed a cold-war consensus in America (shared by groups with no "interests" in the cold war as well as by those who might be said to have such interests) so deep that there were few significant conflicts over military expenditures, and hence little opposition over which a military-industrial complex would be forced to prevail. Indeed, if we were to accept the usual conception of power as the capacity to achieve ends over opposition, we would be forced to conclude that for most of the postwar period in the United States there was little basis at all for attributing power to a military-industrial complex. On the other hand, if power is conceived simply as the capacity to achieve ends, then it would make sense to attribute power of a kind to the executive bureaucracy, the military, and perhaps other institutions alleged to form part of a military-industrial complex, but it would be power which derived primarily from the fact that such institutions gave expression to and were supported by a public consensus.

A few writers on the military-industrial complex are aware that the existence of a general cold-war consensus in American society throughout most of the postwar period poses serious problems for the view of the complex as an unrepresentative elite imposing its will on society. They meet this problem by claiming that the consensus was not spontaneous or not in some sense "genuine," but was created, imposed, or manipulated by the complex itself, through its control over the instruments of mass communication, education, and socialization. In this way the power of the complex manifests itself not, or rather not only, in concrete policy decisions but in its ability to determine what issues become matters of public decision at all and to shape the terms in which such issues are framed. If there is no overt conflict of interests between the majority and the elite, it is because the majority are victims of a "false consciousness" of their true interests, deliberately fostered by a controlling military-industrial complex. Thus, it is not so much that the complex prevails over opposition as that it prevails by ensuring that no opposition arises in the first place. The main works emphasizing the deliberate and successful efforts of the military-industrial complex to inculcate in mass public opinion a false view of the world are those of Cook, Pilisuk and Hayden, Barnet, and Melman.

The argument does not seem very persuasive. The notion that

a single coherent elite, with a vested interest in the cold war or militarism, controls the major instruments of information and education is not demonstrated but simply asserted, and moreover is implausible on its face. The media, the schools, the churches, etc. are neither controlled by such an entity nor are they monolithic in their content. Indeed, most careful studies of the influences of the mass media conclude that their capacity to mold attitudes is highly exaggerated. Finally, the notion of an elite-controlled consensus is embarrassed by the recent explosion of very real popular *dissent* over American foreign and military policies.

The major fallacy in the kinds of analyses we have been discussing is that they rest on a false underlying premise, namely that the existence of a "wrong" or "false" consensus (i.e., one based on erroneous or oversimplified conceptions of reality) can only be explained by the actions of an identifiable group with both the power and motivation to create it. Because this premise is wrong, our rejection of the notion that the cold-war consensus in the United States has been deliberately created from above by no means commits us to the view that this consensus was (or is) either substantively correct or rationally arrived at. The irrationalities of American foreign and military policies are better explained by a pattern of fears, misconceptions, myths, and desires, shared by elites and masses alike, and historically rooted in the structure of American norms, practices, and institutions. Thus, the current state of American society is not explained primarily by the "power" of *any* particular individual, group, or institution, let alone by the power of a military-industrial complex. If this general analysis is correct, clearly the central claims of the theorists attributing power to the military-industrial complex collapse.

To reject the framework of assumptions within which discussion of American militarism and the military-industrial complex has been largely carried out is obviously not to deny everything that has been said in the course of that discussion. Clearly, one may reject the explanatory theory developed within this framework while accepting contentions that some serious wrongs in

American politics and society constitute or are traceable to militarism, that some individuals and groups have a stake in high military expenditures and militarist policies, and that these individuals or groups may have some effect on the process and substance of policy-making. Nor is to reject the theory necessarily to deny the value of the military-industrial-complex literature as exposé or as sources of information on military procurement practices and the like. What is objectionable in this body of literature is the inflation of observations about American politics into an overblown theory which exaggerates the unity and coherence that exists among groups, exaggerates their efficacy in controlling policy, and exaggerates the scope of policy affected by their actions; which neglects other crucially important factors that must be taken into account in understanding the military aspects of American society; and which is tied to a restrictive and misleading model of explanation in terms of the deliberate actions and powers of agents. It is our conclusion that the main consequence of the concept of a military-industrial complex has been to oversimplify and misdirect the analysis of power and militarism in American politics.

The Interplay of Ideology and Advice in Economic Policy-Making: The Case of Political Business Cycles

M. Stephen Weatherford
University of California

Political business cycle models propose an attractive rationale for presidents to manipulate the economy: it is a way to win votes. But there is little empirical support for the hypothesis. The problem with positing that vote maximization leads to political business cycles is clear: the incentive is universal; the facilitating economic and political conditions occur frequently; but the outcome occurs seldom. Why is it that only some presidents respond to the incentive only some of the time? What features of an administration might help us explain or predict the occurrence of such cycles? The issues here are not limited to economic policy-making: they raise questions about goal-setting and policy coordination. Focusing on economic policy helps to structure observations within an important but bounded context.

This paper focuses on two critical aspects of economic policy-making: the president's economic ideology summarizes the administration's goals; the organization of economic advice provides a means through which they might be sought. The empirical section concentrates on economic policy-making in the two post-war administrations most in need of explanation: the Eisenhower years, when there were opportunities but no electoral cycles; and the Nixon administration, the most egregious instance of the political business cycle *genre*. The concluding section elaborates the classification and tentatively maps other administrations into the model.

The political science and economics literature on political business cycles has flourished recently (Keech, 1980; and Monroe, 1984, review this literature), motivated by the straightforward assumption that presidents respond to the electoral incentive by manipulating the economy in order to win votes. However plausible this proposition in the abstract, it has received little unambiguous empirical support. Its earliest version— hypothesizing a pre-election boom in every even-numbered year, or only in presidential election years (e.g., Tufte, 1978)—is clearly overstated (Stigler, 1973; MacRae, 1977; Barry, 1985). More complex formulations have followed (Frey, 1978; Hibbs, 1977), proposing that Democrats opt to raise employment and Republicans concentrate on lowering inflation, thus pursuing votes by appealing to their core class constituencies. But

*For their valuable comments on earlier drafts of this paper, I want to thank John H. Kessel, Lorraine M. McDonnell, and several anonymous reviewers.

the evidence is no kinder to this model. Tests of hypotheses about variation in fiscal policy, monetary policy, public sector growth, or spending patterns corrected for bipartisan counter-cyclical policies (Golden and Poterba, 1980; Beck, 1982b; Lowery and Berry, 1983; Lowery, 1985; Lewis-Beck and Rice, 1985) show some evidence of fluctuation, but the model's image of neat partisan patterning is nowhere apparent. Moreover, much evidence suggests that the most important differences in the use of stabilization policy occur between administrations rather than between parties (cf. Beck, 1982a; Lowery, 1985; Woolley, 1985). Given the available data, it is impossible to resolve this dispute on statistical grounds, and recent exchanges have taken the form of debates about parsimony and the preferability of each researcher's a priori beliefs about how the American political system works (cf. Hibbs, 1983; Beck, 1982a; 1983).

Although insufficient support exists in these data for advancing some simple, general model, two inferences can be drawn from the cumulation of research to date:

—Political business cycles—the manipulation of the economy for electoral ends—probably do occur, but they are unusual, and they appear most plausibly traceable to particular administrations rather than to party differences.

—Given that most of the variation in this phenomenon is at the level of administrations and presidents, it is logical to turn our attention away from quantitative indicators of aggregate economic activity and toward the properties that may foster political business cycles in particular presidential administrations.

The problem with positing that vote maximization motivates political business cycles is clear: the incentive is universal; the facilitating economic and political conditions occur frequently; but the outcome occurs seldom. Why is it that only some presidents respond to the incentive only some of the time? What features of the adminstration might help us to explain or predict the occurrence of such cycles?

This paper focuses on two aspects of an administration's economic policy-making apparatus—the president's economic ideology, and the organization of advice—arguing that these are critical indicators of the potential that a president will resort to economic manipulation, if other economic and political circumstances allow. The paper's empirical section compares two cases, the Eisenhower and Nixon administrations, and the concluding section elaborates the classification and proposes a tentative mapping to fit other administrations into the model.

THE INTERPLAY OF IDEOLOGY AND ECONOMIC ADVICE

The potential benefits of a political business cycle are obvious, but pursuing the policy entails probable costs. Some of these attach to the likelihood of the president's (or his party's) being credibly accused of political manipulation. Macroeconomic policy-making is high politics: it is of unusual public visibility, and national elites perceive it to be of great importance and seriousness. This entails that the risks to a president are high: successfully disguising such a policy will be more difficult than in a less visible issue area, and the political costs if discovered will be great. Other costs attach in a more conventional way to implementing the policy. Even if the risk appears worth taking, the political resources required to persuade and coordinate the formally independent efforts of several governmental institutions will be substantial. Even at this stage, the policy's success is not assured: the president's control over relevant policy instruments, while considerable, is hardly sufficient to assure that the outcome matches his intentions. Attempting to use stabilization policy to win votes would require not only that a president be unusually risk-accepting, but also that his sense of the legitimate ends of political power be unusually broad. We expect governments to employ macroeconomic policy instruments for stabilization or even long-run alterations in the balance of politico-economic advantage, but not to use national economic policy to serve short-term political ends (cf. Barry, 1985). Finally, pursuing a political business cycle strategy entails opportunity costs: pressing the policy will absorb political resources and send the economy along a path that will inhibit the administration's ability to seek its longer-run political economic goals, such as diminishing the size of the public sector or redistributing income. If we are interested in explaining or predicting the occurrence of political business cycles, then the question is: Which administrations have such weak economic policy ambitions that they might pursue a risky electoral tactic?

The importance to the president of a clear, firmly held, salient vision of the long-term goals toward which his economic policy is directed—a well-formed economic ideology—is as a counterpoise to more myopic demands. With a relatively weak commitment to long-range goals, the president is open to all manner of diffuse, short-run economic and noneconomic incentives; the electoral demands of his party colleagues and his own ambition are only two of the more pressing among these. But holding to a steady policy course in the face of inevitable economic shocks and political pressures also requires effective organization of information and instruments. Thus, the presient's ability to assemble and use effectively his potential resources of economic advice provides the means to map these goals onto policy options and to prioritize programs so as to hold the administration's policy on course (Light, 1982). Investigating advisory arrangements will show the extent to which he involves himself in economic policy in a consistent and thematic way;

and it will indicate the contribution of his advisory system, both as a source of information and as a political broker in promoting the administration's program.

The President's Economic Ideology

An administration's economic ideology proposes answers to questions about the interaction between private and public economic power and the ends to which governmental economic activity is directed (Weatherford and McDonnell, 1984). These ideas will influence the president's interpretation of ambiguous economic indicators, his selection of particular policies from the menu of options in a given situation, and his preference for specific policy instruments to achieve a given macroeconomic goal. His economic ideology is related to elections and campaigns, but that relation is by no means simple or direct. His image of the most desirable economic outcome for the nation is a part of the policy agenda for which the voters chose him (and hence of the standards by which his performance will be judged [cf. Brody, 1983]), and it shapes his interactions with groups and interest organizations. No president will be insensitive to the preferences of these multiple overlapping audiences, but his ideology is not a proxy for those influences. It is, rather, a tool that allows him to select from their demands, to meld them, or to adopt a novel option. And in crisis or uncertainty, the president's own economic lodestone will be the surest guide among a set of alternatives whose future effects can be only dimly gauged.

It is not, however, the content of the president's economic ideology that is most important for this analysis; rather it is the salience of economic issues, especially allocative or distributive (Musgrave, 1959) concerns, among the president's policy priorities, and the clarity and firmness with which he holds his economic goals. Presidents vary in their interest in and commitment to mastering the economy as a locus of policy challenges, and in the care and attention they allocate to managing economic policy. A president with a well-formed economic ideology has an image of the state of the economy toward which he would like his administration to guide the country. This image entails more than an interest in keeping the economy moving smoothly along the established growth path—it also involves a concern with setting the direction of national economic development. The image may be liberal or conservative, but it goes beyond stabilization to include prominent concerns with achieving allocative or distributive goals. A president for whom economic goals are clear and salient need not regard economic policy as his major area of concern (Cronin, 1980 p. 146; but contrast Light, 1982, p.7), but he will bring a clearer conception of long-run policy goals and greater continuity to his pursuit of them. For such a president, the opportunity costs argue against using his economic policy instruments to pursue a political business cycle.

But a president's priorities may be more exclusively centered on foreign policy or domestic social policy: for such a president, economic policies will be directed largely toward coping with the most recent economic emergency, and they will be vetted less closely for their consistency with his broader purposes and commitments. Such a president's economic beliefs and intentions will be limited essentially to stabilization goals, and are better described as "strategy" (cf. Neustadt, 1980, for such a definition of presidential ideology): they may bear only a weak resemblance to "ideology" as a relatively clear set of prior beliefs. This president will have less compunction about using economic policy resources to assure his re-election.

The Organization of Economic Advice

Holding a clear and salient image of his administration's intended achievements for the economy will strengthen the president's resolve agains pressures for short-term policy digressions, but maintaining consistency also requires careful policy selection and coordination.[1] As governmental responsibilities for managing the economy have grown, their exercise has frequently been channeled not toward universalistic economic policy agencies but into existing departments that claim the new authority on grounds of subject-area specialization. The result is to carry the tendency toward fragmented authority even further than in other realms of government policy (Heclo, 1983; Heclo and Salamon, 1981). The problem of integrating diffused power is exacerbated by the weak institutional position of the Council of Economic Advisors, formally the most likely agency to perform as policy coordinator (Pierce, 1971). Although its mandate is broader than those of the Treasury or OMB, it has no operational authority and only weak links to other agencies (cf. Heller, 1966; Saulnier, 1969). Its coordinative capacity is latent, dependent on the president rather than initiatives by Council members. If the president does not view economic policy as sufficiently interesting

---

[1] Much of the best research on advisory resources has centered on foreign policy (Allison, 1971; George, 1972, 1980; Allison and Szanton, 1976; Cottam and Rockman, 1984) or concentrated on the White House staff and the interplay between staff and Cabinet (R.T. Johnson, 1974; Hess, 1976; Price and Siciliano, 1980; Campbell, 1983; Helco, 1976, 1983; Randall, 1979; Nathan, 1983). More recent work on advisory arrangements in the domestic policy area are more immediately applicable (Kessel, 1983, 1984; Light, 1982), for these studies bring us closer to the special character of the economic policy-making process. As in many areas of presidency research, however, the most useful sources are often historical studies of particular institutions or administrations (Flash, 1965; Stein, 1969, 1984b; Norton, 1977, 1985; Porter, 1980, 1981, 1983; Pierce, 1971; Berman, 1979; Reichley, 1981).

and important to justify his active participation (cf. Nourse, 1953; Nourse and Gross, 1948); if the members of the Council are not compatible in ideology and, to some extent, political style with the president (cf. Burns, 1975b; Ackley, 1966; Kilborn, 1983; Smith, 1984); and if they fail to work at the task of continuously creating a presidential demand for their supply of advice and expertise (Okun, 1976; Heller, 1966; cf. Flash, 1965), then the CEA's potential capacity to plan policy and coordiante specific initiatives will be lost.

Every president perceives that he is constrained by the antinomy between control and openness. His ability to advance consistent and coherent policy requires that he establish his priorities and that his advisors select only the most critical issues for his personal involvement, and it demands that specific decisions be integrated into a pattern whose programmatic unity is readily visible (Light, 1982): these requisites press the advisory system toward centralization and hierarchy. At the same time, the diffuse nature of the economic policy system and the multiplicity of channels through which relevant problems enter put a high premium on openness (George, 1972; R.T. Johnson, 1974). Besides the CEA, the Treasury, Federal Reserve, OMB, Cabinet departments, White House staff and Congress are potential sources of economic policy inputs (cf. Pierce, 1971; Cronin, 1980). An inclusive advisory process broadens the information base and enhances the legitimacy of decisions, helping to rally agency heads whose positions have lost and thus contributing to the forcefulness of the administration team (Porter, 1980). But these requisites lead to a flatter institutional structure and more equal, collegial interactions.

A president constructs his advisory system by melding elements from these paradigms, and in a policy realm where institutional traditions for aggregating advice are weakly defined, it is natural to expect considerable variation from one president to the next. Although there is no neat, abstract standard against which to judge the organization of economic advice, recent commentators on executive organization concur in arguing:
—against a narrow and exclusive advisory process;
—for a more collegial system relying on the CEA and the Cabinet, rather than on staff or shifting ad hoc arrangements; and
—for an organization that elevates economic policy to a primary position in its own right, rather than viewing economic decisions as adjuncts of domestic social policy, budget policy, or foreign policy (Porter, 1980, 1983; Destler, 1980; Bryant, 1983).

RESEARCH DESIGN AND CASE SELECTION

The political business cycle approach seems to have reached the stage of diminishing returns, because the within-administration variables on which explanations now center concern issues of process, whose components are not readily quantifiable. At the same time, these studies bring the advantages of abstractness and generalizability, in a method that fosters systematic comparison across administrations. The comparative case study approach allows a design in which some of the methodological strengths of the more "scientific" approach can be melded with the sensitivity to process typical of institutional studies of the presidency and policy (cf. Eckstein, 1975; Yin, 1984).[2]

Case selection aims to provide empirical instances rich in theoretically indicated contrasts, but in which differences in crucial variables appear against a background of similarity broad enough to justify comparison (Przeworski and Teune, 1970, chs. 2, 5). Moreover, administrations should be classifiable from observations that could have been made prior to the opportunity for producing a PBC. This research concentrates on the first terms of presidents Eisenhower and Nixon, summarizing their economic goals and the early organizational phase of each administration, outlining the way in which the advisory system worked and the extent of contact with the president, and then surveying the role of the advisory network in each president's first great economic challenge—for Eisenhower, the 1954 recession; for Nixon, the decision to impose wage and price controls.

These two presidencies differ on the dependent variable, the occurrence of a political business cycle, more clearly than any other pair of post-war administrations. Indeed, in some respects, the two are

---

[2] The advantages of the comparative case study approach on grounds of internal validity spring from its suitability for tracing operational links and interpersonal transactions over time, and for observing phenomena in context (cf. Thomas, 1983). Challenges to external validity note that the population of presidents is small and each somehow unique, thus inhibiting generalization from one or a few cases to the universe of presidents. An appreciation for the complexity of the economic policy process strengthens this argument: the problem is not simply that the number of cases is small, but that the number of potentially relevant variables will virtually always be larger (Campbell, 1975; Yin, 1981). This challenge implicitly adopts the perspective of sampling theory as its criterion for validity. The comparative case study method, however, is more appropriately evaluated in terms of its ability to produce theoretically critical replication. Like experimental science, the case study method is typically implemented where it is only possible to observe a small number of instances of the phenomenon. In this situation, research follows a cross-experiment rather than a within-experiment design, and cases are chosen not because they are "representative" of some enumerated population, but because of their potential productivity in theory-testing (Yin, 1984). Any particular case will produce results similar to expectations on the basis of current knowledge ("literal replication"), or else yield dissimilar findings whose differences can be anticipated ("theoretical replication"). As with series of replicative experimental tests, the robustness of the theory is a function of the number and variety of successfully explained outcomes, and contradictory results provide guidance for revising and retesting the theory's propositions (cf. Hersen and Barlow, 1976; e.g., Szanton, 1981).

deviant cases: Nixon because the pre-election boom of 1972 is the most egregious instance of the genre (and consequently stands as the centerpiece of Tufte's 1978 popularization); Eisenhower because conditions were ripe for a political business cycle in 1954, 1958, and 1960, yet he explicitly abjured the temptation (a perversity which prompts Tufte [1978, cf. pp. 18, 51] to wish this presidency out of the analysis). Because these two administrations stand at extreme points on the continuum of dependent variable outcomes, their careful observation is especially appropriate: it should allow us to view sources of variation in clear relief.

Moreover, the two administrations differ on each of the critical independent variables: the clarity, firmness, and salience of the president's economic goals; and the continuity and skill with which he utilized his advisory resources. Eisenhower's unambiguously primary economic goal was to ensure the value of the currency by combating the economy's natural tendency toward inflation. Nixon's conservative economic ideology, on the other hand, was anchored neither in a philosophical subscription to the principles of free enterprise nor even in the tenets of small business Republicanism, and his interpretation of GOP losses in 1958 and 1960 made him willing to abandon his economic principles if other goals were at stake. The contrast between their uses of economic advice is similar: Eisenhower repeatedly demonstrated great interest in economic issues and policy selection, and he provided an environment in which his advisors' tenure was stable, their prestige within the administration high, and their criticism encouraged and carefully considered. Nixon's economic advisory arrangements, while depicted as identically "centralized" and "formalistic" with Eisenhower's (R.T. Johnson, 1974, 1979), operated in fact in an environment of shifting personnel, generally low prestige, and suspicion of critical arguments.

Systematic comparison requires a foundation of similarity, however, and on other dimensions the two administrations show as much likeness as might be expected in realistic historical situations. Neither is an "economic" presidency: both chief executives were more interested in foreign policy and saw that as the source of potentially greater achievements. Moreover, both presidencies shaped and established an economic policy direction before the supply shocks of late 1973 brought such a fundamental change in the character of policy challenges (cf. Gordon, 1980; Blinder, 1979; Eckstein, 1978). This research avoids the potential pitfalls to comparison entailed by this step-change in the complexity of economic management, by focusing on policy-making in two pre-OPEC administrations.

The economic situations facing the two presidents also bear strong resemblance to each other. Early in both administrations, unemployment rose steeply, and recession thinned legislative totals in the first midterm election. The public and political elites had become acclimated to higher average levels of unemployment and inflation in the 1970s, but the short-run economic dynamics and political pressures were quite similar. Indeed, looking at declining business conditions suggests that it should have been Eisenhower rather than Nixon who lost patience with Republican orthodoxy. For instance, unemployment worsened from a low of 1.8% to a high of 5.8% in the first Eisenhower administration, while its deterioration under Nixon was only about two-thirds of that (from 3.3% to 6.1%); on average, each month brought .16% more unemployment during Eisenhower's first two years, but .11% for the same period of the Nixon administration.[3] Both in the mid-1950s and the early 1970s, the president was surrounded by politicians from both parties and by public clamor to ameliorate the pain of recession and stimulate economic growth (cf. Sundquist, 1968; Nixon, 1978; Burns, 1957a; Humphrey, 1965), and both administrations' policies were opposed by a majority of professional economists (Eisenhower's classical orthodoxy by a growing Keynesian majority [Stein, 1969]; Nixon's use of controls by a similar majority convinced of their distorting effects on the market [Blinder, 1979]). Both presidents were sensitive to public demands and to the economic and potential electoral costs of sustained recession (cf. Eisenhower, 1960; Nixon, 1962, 1978; cf. Burns, 1975a, 1984; Stein, 1984a, 1984b; McCracken, 1984). Viewed in its historical context, the economic situation confronting Eisenhower in 1953-54, and the elite political pressure to which it gave rise, is closely comparable to the nexus of economic conditions and political pressures facing Nixon in 1970-71.

The more narrowly political aspects of the context also contribute to overall comparability. Both presidents took office after a long period of Democratic party dominance that had built widespread public support for liberal innovations in economic management, and both owed their electoral victories in large measure to foreign policy promises, not to challenging Democratic economic policies (cf. Leuchtenberg, 1983; Stein, 1984a). The content of the economic ideology of the two presidents bore strong resemblance: both intended to pursue traditional Republican goals of diminishing governmental interference in the market; both were concerned about the corrosive effects of inflation on economic activity and on social and personal rectitude; and both felt that excessive federal taxes were stifling the productive potential of corporations and investors. Finally, the two administrations shared personnel: Nixon's conception

[3] These coefficients are from the regression of the monthly unemployment rate against time, coded 1,2,..., 24, for the administration's first two years. Data are from *Business Conditions Digest* (Bureau of Economic Analysis, Social and Economic Statistics Administration, U.S. Department of Commerce, various years). Similar differences are apparent in deflated GNP and in the index of leading indicators.

of governmental organization had been strongly influenced by his vice-presidential experience under Eisenhower; and two of his major economic advisors, Arthur Burns and Paul McCracken (along with other members of the economic advisory staff), had served prominently in the Eisenhower administration.

ECONOMIC IDEOLOGY, ADVICE, AND POLICY

Ideology

As the first Republican president since Hoover, Eisenhower shaped a notion of modern Republicanism that was consistent with the level of government social spending bequeathed him by the New Deal "fiscal revolution" (Stein, 1969), just as it could accommodate balancing the federal budget over the business cycle rather than annually. But his clear first priority was to guard against what he viewed as the economy's natural tendency toward overexpansion and inflation (Eisenhower, Cabinet Meeting, January 12-13, 1953 [WF-C]; to Brundage, April 21, 1956 [WF-DDE]; 1960; Ferrell, 1981). By any reckoning, he accomplished virtually complete success with this goal, but at the economic cost of lost output (Gordon, 1980) and, it is generally agreed, at the political cost to his party of congressional election losses in 1954 and 1958, and perhaps even the loss of the presidency in 1960 (cf. Friedman, 1980). For our purposes, however, the most notable characteristic of Eisenhower's economic management is not its accomplishments but the way in which the policy process worked. It was infused throughout by the president's unwavering world view—an image that sought to minimize the role of government in the private economy, and that believed an economy operating below capacity would right itself but that an inflationary outbreak demanded prompt corrective action by government. This economic ideology gave impetus and direction to Eisenhower's selection of advisors and to his management of the economy (cf. Burns, 1984; Saulnier, 1984).

Nixon entered office in 1969 with a narrow electoral margin, after a campaign that had focused on Vietnam and social issues. To the extent that there was an economic issue in 1968, it was inflation, but even the Republican party's approach was largely ritualistic. As president, Nixon spoke out as vehemently against government's role in the marketplace as Eisenhower had, and the fundamental elements of his broad economic ideology are essentially identical. But Nixon was little inclined to concentrate on mastering economic policy: it was not an area of competence for him and learning it would have required a disproportionate investment; it had never been the party's winning issue and he would not be able to alter public attitudes toward economic conservatism;

and, unlike foreign policy, there was little promise that a president could make his mark on history simply by managing the economy (Nixon, 1978; cf. Safire, 1975, p. 246-62; Wills, 1970). Stein remarks that "one extremely important aspect of Mr. Nixon's initial attitude toward economic policy was that he did not want to have much to do with it" (1984b, p. 138); and McCracken emphasizes "Nixon's lack of interest in economics," suggesting that "Mr. Nixon may even have had an almost psychological block about economics" (1984b, p. 327; cf. Evans and Novak, 1971, p. 180).

Nixon opposed inflation on partisan grounds, but he was convinced that a decade of prosperity and price stability had fostered a public opinion that regarded unemployment and lagging growth rather than inflation as the more severe threat. Stein suggests that this attitude— whatever was done on the inflation front could not be allowed to raise unemployment—was "part of a more general schizophrenia" in Nixon's approach to economic policy-making: "Nixon felt that he ought to be for the traditional virtues. . . . But he also wanted to be a 'modern' man and recognized as such by intellectuals and liberals. He was impatient with the dull, pedestrian and painful economics of conventional conservatism. . . . In an early meeting in 1969, he said that we should have some 'fine tuning.' He associated that term with sophistication and expertise, even though in the conventional conservative view he was praising the devil's prescription" (Stein, 1984b, p. 135; cf. Evans and Novak, 1971, p. 177-80).

Although Eisenhower and Nixon held economic ideologies that were quite similar in content, they differed widely in the clarity and consistency of their economic beliefs, in the economy's salience among their policy concerns, and in the degree of their personal involvement in economic policy-making (cf. Burns, 1984; McCracken, 1984). Their construction and use of economic advisory systems show corresponding differences.

The Organization of Economic Advice

Three characteristics distinguish Eisenhower's organization and use of economic advice: his concerted effort, early in the administration, to institutionalize a formal advisory system with clear lines of authority; the unambiguous attribution to the CEA of the primary role for coordinating multiple information sources and implementing agencies; and his continuing willingness to foster the work of advisors representing quite distant positions within the broad ambit of conservative views, and to use their advice to meld a philosophically coherent policy.

At Eisenhower's accession, there was widespread doubt about whether a formal advisory apparatus should continue to exist. The combined effect of Keyserling's often obtrusive advocacy and President Truman's unpopular programs had so annoyed influential members of Congress that funds for the Council had been cut by 25% for fiscal 1953. By spending this allocation in the first three quarters of the year, the CEA avoided curtailing activities or staff, but such measures meant that the Council would officially cease to exist just as the new president took office. In response to Eisenhower's request ("I have found since assuming office that the Council of Economic Advisors did not have the status it should have. . . . My intention is to reinvigorate that body . . ." [Eisenhower, 1953]), Congress voted partial funding for the final quarter, on the proviso that the appropriation was to be used for only a single advisor and small staff.

Arthur Burns's nomination to chair the Council was announced during the hearings and helped to ease the appropriation's passage. His anti-Keynesian writings (cf. Burns, 1954, pp. 3-25) had recommended him to Gabriel Hauge, Eisenhower's Administrative Assistant for Economic Affairs, and his work as Director of Research at NBER impressed Democratic Congressmen with his scholarly credentials. Burns's proposals for reconstituting the Council were strongly centralizing: Where the Employment Act had spoken of three essentially equal economic advisors, Reorganization Plan No. 9 vested responsibility for staffing and communicating with the president solely in the Chairman. At Burns's request, the president formed an Advisory Group on Economic Growth and Stability, comprising the Treasury, Agriculture, Commerce and Labor departments, along with the Federal Reserve and Bureau of the Budget, and headed by Burns (Eisenhower, 1953, pp. 355-59). The "Tuesday Group," a parallel committee at the senior staff level, was formed under David Lusher of the CEA. These groups monitored the economy, focused policy discussions, and channeled dissemination of the president's policies: they ensured the Council's central place in economic policy formation. Eisenhower's military background and the resulting high value he placed on reliable staff work, along with the close personal relationship he and Burns developed, enhanced the Council's position and Burns's autonomy. Regular appropriations for the CEA were restored in the FY 1954 budget, and Burns's personnel choices, while made in consultation with Hauge, reflected a mandate to assemble his own CEA. Flash's summary statement—that the Council had been "revitalized along Burns-Eisenhower lines" (1965, p. 110)—must be interpreted to imply Eisenhower's version of modern Republicanism rather than the traditional views associated with the Taft wing of the Party and with Humphrey or Anderson at the Treasury.

The CEA and Treasury were the primary sources of economic advice, and George Humphrey at Treasury was the administration's most influential economic spokesman.[4] Burns's contacts with Cabinet departments and executive agencies made his active participation indispensable, and on specific policy decisions his expertise and personal persuasiveness with the president evened the balance between the two advisors (cf. Burns, 1984; Stein, 1969). By the middle of 1953, Burns had become part of the administration's top echelon of policy advisors, along with Hauge, Sherman Adams, John Foster Dulles, and Humphrey.[5] A philosophical but distinctly empirical conservative, Burns often disagreed with the ritualistic big-business conservatism of Humphrey, but Eisenhower elicited from these potential adversaries the same sort of constructive give-and-take he sought within other advisory networks (Greenstein, 1982, ch. 4). Below the level of formal consultation, the informal interplay of personal styles and philosophical approaches was tempered by loyalty to Eisenhower, and it produced a level of discussion and debate on economic policy that was more penetrating and better balanced than the president would have received from either alone (cf. Eisenhower to Burns, February 19, 1955 [WF-DDE]; Burns, 1957a, 1984; Humphrey, 1965; Ambrose, 1984; Eisenhower, 1978).

In contrast to the organization of economic advice under Eisenhower, the status and influence of economic specialists in the Nixon adminstration were never clearly established; no agency held stable, predictable authority for policy coordination; and rather than drawing policy out of the interplay of different economic arguments from multiple advisors, the president tended to shift from one to another depending on what policy he favored on other grounds.

Previous administrations had shaped a distinct role for economic advisors: the Heller Council's successful activism and the visibility of Ackley and Okun implied that economists were to be regular contributors to national policy leadership. But Nixon's economic oganization took shape slowly, and the growing centralization of domestic policy under Erlichmann weakened the voice of economic advisors and inhibited their access to the president (cf. Cronin, 1980). For the first year, Burns served as a Special Counselor in the White House, while McCracken and the Council, assisted by a staff largely carried over from the previous administration, attempted cautiously to lower inflation. Although Burns was quite close to the president, he was outmaneuvered by Moynihan in the White House, and he was reticent to intrude on McCracken's prerogatives as Council chair (cf. Safire, 1975; Silk, 1972). Moreover,

[4] Eisenhower said of Humphrey: "George is synonymous with money. If it is a question of money, then you must clear it with George" (Finer, 1960, p. 50; cf. Childs, 1958; Anderson, 1969).

[5] Eisenhower's 1954 State of the Union address, outlining his administration's policy goals, was authored by the group, and Burns was a "prime participant" in developing this agenda (Neustadt, 1955).

neither McCracken nor Kennedy at Treasury or Mayo at the Budget Bureau was personally close to Nixon, nor had they the forceful personalities needed to secure regular access by penetrating the gatekeepers around the president (Stein, 1984b).[6] Lines of consultation were never clearly defined: Cabinet secretaries frequently end-ran the Council to secure exceptions for favored programs, and the president and others, responding to group demands, occasionally even committed the administration to inconsistent policies (Stein, 1984a; McCracken, 1984, p. 328; 337ff). Where no formal channels existed, informal ad hoc groups— breakfast meetings, personal contacts, etc.—promoted some coordination, but they carried no analytical or operational mandate.

The style or tone of the president's interaction with his economic advisors also conditions their influence and indicates his involvement with the policy area. In this respect, too, the contrast between administrations is clear. Eisenhower remarked to Burns at their first meeting that "I don't want a long report, because I don't know how to read." Burns responded by preparing careful oral expositions of the economic outlook and policy options for each of their weekly meetings (Burns, 1984, p. 95). Most of Eisenhower's advice came to him by way of personal conferences, and when advisors disagreed or several perspectives needed to be heard simultaneously, the president scheduled sessions in which he listened carefully to personal presentations of each alternative (cf. Greenstein, 1982). Burns and Saulnier both emphasize that the president's interest was high, his comprehension of the issues thorough, and his questions acute during these sessions (Burns, 1984, p. 98ff; Saulnier, 1984, p. 127ff). The pattern and style of interactions among the president and members of the Troika resembled multiple advocacy, with Hauge the central broker among interests (George, 1972, 1980).

President Nixon "was much more inclined to want a paper that he could look at" (McCracken, 1984, p. 327). But unlike foreign policy, where the president's interest and eagerness for further information were great, he found meetings with his economic advisors tedious and their detailed written arguments too academic (Stein, 1984a). The meager salience of economic policy meant that it received his primary attention only at moments of crisis, and that even at those times his lack of familiarity with issues and infrequent communication with his advisors occasionally

[6] McCracken, who served on the CEA in both administrations, draws a sharp contrast between the organization and processing of economic advice under Eisenhower and Nixon. In the Eisenhower White House, the structure was clearly articulated, lines of authority unambiguous, and communication with the president regular. "In the Nixon administration, you had to find your way around. . . . By a process of trial and error, the structure began to form" (McCracken, 1984, p. 329).

resulted in policy choices whose economic implications were not adequately researched or fully considered.

At the operational level, economic policy-making under Nixon was characterized by ambiguous attributions of authority, both inside the government and as the administration's public spokesman, by dramatic shifts in leadership, and by a decisional procedure that was inevitably political rather than professional. In this sense, the relatively neglected status of the CEA among economic policy influences, or the policy shifts accompanying the admission of Connally and Shultz to the administration's inner circle, typify a system in which the advisory network was never stably integrated into the decision process (cf. Kessel, 1983, 1984). Professionals as diverse as Greenspan and Okun reacted to the neglected status of economic advice in the administration, concerned that short-term economic and political demands would readily deflect policy from its course.[7]

Eisenhower: Policy for the 1954 Recession

The primary cause of the 1954 recession was the dramatic cut made by the incoming president in Truman's FY 1954 budget proposals (cf. Gordon, 1980). Made possible by the cessation of hostilities in Korea, and carried out as part of a foreign policy campaign pledge, it was unusual not only in its size but also in that it was undertaken with virtually no systematic consideration of probable economic impact. Although the Federal Reserve had earlier embarked on a monetary policy designed to tighten credit conditions, the new administration cut federal expenditures by about 20% (3% of GNP) over a period of less than a year (*Economic Report*, 1956, tables D-1, D-11, D-12), and no compensating measures offset the impact on aggregate demand. The decision was taken before Burns arrived in Washington to begin setting up the new Council, and its shortsightedness from a macroeconomic perspective underlines how his sensitivity to stabilization issues

[7] Arthur Okun's (1976) response to Nixon's decision in April 1969 to request suspension of the 7% investment tax credit, for instance, focused on advisory arrangements rather than on the outcome of the decision: "I must say that the nature of that decision, and the kind of rhetoric used to justify it, concerns me a lot more that the substance of the decision. It was not the kind of decision-making to instill confidence in the Administration's procedures. Nearly all, if not all, of the President's principal economic and financial advisors were on record as saying that they wanted to stick with the credit. Maybe they had a change of heart, but at least it does raise the question of who is giving the advice to the President and on what basis he is making his decisions if he does not come out on the side of his principal advisors" (*New York Times*, May 25, 1969, sec. 3, p. 1.). Alan Greenspan's reluctance to serve on the Council in the Nixon administration (after having been a valued advisor during the campaign and transition) was based on similar qualms about the salience of economic policy and the weak integration and influence of economic advisors (cf. Reichley, 1981, p. 64; Greenspan, 1984).

contributed to the administration's later economic deliberations (cf. Burns, 1954, pp. 107-84).

Once the policy was in place, Burns's options were limited. His own and the Council's tenuous status with Congress put fiscal initiatives out of the question. But during the second and third quarters of 1953, Burns was in frequent contact with Chairman Martin of the Federal Reserve, urging various measures to ease monetary conditions.[8] Although it is impossible to assess the precise extent of Burns's influence on Fed policy, in the period from May to July 1953, the Board did increase the money supply by open market operations, lower the discount rate, and decrease reserve requirements, and these monetary policy actions were the most important measures taken to end the recession (Samuelson, 1956; Gordon, 1980).

Public and press attention, however, centered on large-scale public works as anti-recession policy, and the CEA was the focus of political pressure. The Council and Bureau of the Budget did draw up a list of projects that could be initiated if justified, but even this extent of planning was undertaken only reluctantly (cf. U.S. Congress, 1954). Eisenhower, Burns and Humphrey agreed that public works programs should be used "only as a last resort" and that the long lag before such spending would have in effect made it inappropriate for combating the brief cyclical downturn the administration perceived (Burns, 1957a; cf. Stein, 1969).

Humphrey and Burns were in less agreement on other countercyclical measures, and here the president's ability to meld opposing positions into a consensual advisory network can be credited with improving the resultant policy (cf. Lilienthal, 1964, p. 7). At several decision points, the CEA chairman and the Treasury secretary were in concert on the administration's conservative principles, but Burns pressed the president to allow the budget to move into deficit so as not to defeat the automatic stabilizers (Stein, 1969), and he argued the case for varying mortgage terms and other flexible credit policies as countercyclical instruments (*Economic Report*, 1954; Flash, 1965, p. 129). Burns eventually brought both Humphrey and the president into agreement with his proposal to accelerate federal spending (U.S. Congress, 1954, p. 33)—the president concurred on countercyclical grounds, and Humphrey acquiesced once convinced that the program was broadly consistent with balancing the budget and reducing the federal debt (Flash, 1965, p. 153-57; Stein, 1969). The policy was a well-articulated compromise: by combining a visible sign of the administration's acceptance of responsibility for stabilization with its ideological concern for fiscal probity, it stands as a good example

---

[8] Since Martin was not a member of the Cabinet, his informal ties to administration policy-makers were centered on Burns (cf. Anderson, 1969; Burns, 1957b; Flash, 1965).

of the way Eisenhower's economic advisory network functioned to innovate programmatic content for his modern Republicanism.

Over the balance of the first term, Burns frequently played the role of confident, modern conservative, working to adapt the president's long-term program to immediate conditions, and thus to reconcile Republican principles with countercyclical responsibilities. Indeed, Humphrey and Burns fit neatly into the roles of ideologue and empiricist in the contrast Burns described in an essay written just before joining the administration: "The business cycle of a speculative thinker may be one phenomenon; the business cycles of experience are many" (1954, p. 181). The president, whose military background had honed his managerial skills and whose interest quickly built his self-confidence as a consumer of economic intelligence, purposely brought these distinct strains of Republican conservatism together in the service of his economic goals.

Nixon: The 1970-71 Recession and the Turn to Controls

In spite of his attacks on the liberal economics of his predecessors, and his apparent commitment to conservative orthodoxy, the aspiration of Nixon's policy of "gradualism" owed more to the Heller Council than to any past Republican programs. Inflation was seen as a problem of fine tuning: policy aimed to bring economic growth slowly down to a rate consistent with price stability, and to hold it there long enough to assure a "soft landing" with the minimum possible rise in unemployment (McCracken, 1984, p. 341; U.S. Congress, Joint Economic Committee, 1969). The administration continued the income tax surcharge, postponed excise tax reductions, initiated user charges in several minor programs, and impounded expenditures approved by Congress. The package produced a dramatic shift in the trajectory of fiscal policy, from a $25 billion deficit in FY 1968 to a $1.4 billion surplus in FY 1969, and was abetted by a drop in money supply growth from 1968's 6.5% to 2.8% in the first half of 1969. The Council's initial timetable called for unemployment to rise to 4-4.5% during 1969, with the effect on prices coming shortly after, so that policy could return to a neutral or slightly stimulative posture by mid-1970. The effect on aggregate economic activity was substantial and quick: GNP in constant dollars declined from 729.2 billion in 1969-II to 719.3 billion in 1970-IV, and unemployment rose from 3.6% to 5.8% by the midterm congressional elections. But inflation persisted, with the CPI moving from 110.6 to 118.6 over the period. The CEA attempted to educate the president in the tenets of monetarism and the inertial role of engrained inflationary expectations, but Nixon was not interested in the details of policy or in his advisors' explanations for its failure to produce the desired results (Stein, 1984b; McCracken, 1984).

Until mid-1971, the CEA directed administration policy and served as its chief expositer to the public, while the president took very little interest and no active part in policy design. At a Camp David meeting in June, McCracken proposed to continue the program of gradualism but with a shift to mildly expansionary policy, a plan the president and his new Treasury secretary, John Connally, strongly opposed for its inflationary potential. During the following week, Nixon called the members of the Council into the Oval Office and informed them that, although he "would welcome any memoranda" from them, "John Connally was going to be his official spokesman . . . and [they] were not to promote contrary ideas in public" (Stein, 1984a, p. 369).

Connally's elevation is only the most obvious manifestation of a fundamental shift in the process of economic policy-making midway through the administration's term. The initial arrangement, although never formalized, was a collegial process in which McCracken, Kennedy and Mayo met regularly, and the other CEA members participated actively in analyses and recommendations—with only the most superficial presidential consultation (cf. Stein, 1984b). When the predicted results of gradualism failed to appear, however, the response was typically Nixonian: the Council was left in place, while policy determination was removed to the more politically forceful Connally. The president "wanted a more aggressive, dramatic, leading role. But he didn't think he could produce that himself, and he didn't find that he got much help in that direction from his scholarly and low-key team of economic advisors and officials" (Stein, 1984b, p.152).

Neither McCracken and the Council nor Shultz at OMB took an active part in setting the administration's course toward the New Economic Policy's combination of controls with demand stimulus (Cameron, 1972). Indeed, during the period from June to December 1971, economic policy-making was "personalized" in much the same way that foreign policy was centered on the Nixon-Kissinger relationship. Stein suggests that Connally "was operating pretty much as the chief decision maker in the economic field—not in the role of an advisor to the President, but in the role of somebody who has the President's authority in making decisions' (1984a, p. 370; cf. Safire, 1975, pp. 497-508). The commitment to implement wage and price controls was made by Connally and the president in early summer, with promulgation of the price freeze tentatively scheduled for September.[9] It was implemented in mid-August when Connally and the president perceived the gold crisis as an opportunity to "seize the initiative" by means of a dramatic policy shift

---

[9] Shultz and McCracken were informed of the decision soon after it was taken, but the other members of the CEA and the Federal Reserve Board did not learn of it until some time later (Cameron, 1972; Stein, 1984a).

on both domestic and international fronts. There was, of course, no necessary connection between policies adopted to meet domestic stagflation and international monetary disequilibrium, and McCracken had argued at the Camp David meeting in mid-August for a much narrower response addressed solely to the international imbalance (cf. McCracken, 1984; Cameron, 1972; DeMarchi, 1975; Stein, 1984b). Overall, policy coordination during this period was haphazard: not only were domestic and international segments of the New Economic Policy adopted largely independently of each other (cf. Odell, 1982; Gowa, 1984), but once the president and Treasury secretary had concluded that controls were needed, coordination with existing policies was also neglected. Stein, for instance, remarks that "monetary policy was one subject not considered at Camp David" (1984b, p. 179), and Blinder (1979) suggests that this neglect may explain the inconsistent components of a program that combined controls with a strongly stimulative tax cut.

Just as Eisenhower had been pressured in 1954—by Republican as well as Democratic members of Congress and by a vocal, respected portion of the business community—to adopt more activist fiscal policy, so Nixon was beset during the 1970-71 recession with claims that gradualism had resulted in "overkill." In 1954, the president persevered out of a firm belief that aggressive governmental involvement was inconsistent with maintaining a vital market economy. His policy was vindicated, but he had persisted with it in the face of mixed and generally unencouraging economic data. In 1971, Nixon faced the same sort of mixed economic signals and the same vehement pressures from political and business elites, but in the economy his policies were guided by no firmly held conception of long-term goals: he responded by undertaking one of the most radical reversals of policy in the modern period. Most observers, both liberal and conservative, agree that, had the administration persisted with is gradualist policies, their efficacy would have been visible within a quarter or so and the economy would have been healthier in the medium and longer run (cf. Blinder, 1979; Eckstein, 1978; Kosters, 1975; Fellner, 1976; Stein, 1984b). In a policy area to which he devoted only intermittent attention and on which his own beliefs were an unsettled mix of conservative nostrums conflated with the strong desire to be perceived as an activist president, Nixon lacked the ideological focus to take a stand against political pressures. Controlling prices while cutting taxes responded to political demands with a policy so dramatic as to silence his critics.

How much independent influence could Nixon's advisors have exercised at this critical juncture? If Nixon's move to controls was inevitable, the advisory system would deserve attention as a separate indicator of the low salience and inconsistent ideas animating the administration's economic policy, but would not stand as a potential causal explanation. Advisory arrangements, however, are not purely endogenous: advisors frequently do exercise significant influence over presidential decisions, and their effect is greatest in areas at the periphery of the chief executive's concerns. Could his advisors have steered Nixon away from controls, convinced him to stay the course of gradualist, market-oriented Republican orthodoxy? While it is by no means assured that access to the appropriate presidential documents could settle this question, those papers are not available. It is notable, however, that each of the advisors most strategically placed and most strongly opposed to controls—McCracken, Shultz, and Stein—reports having felt torn between his own conviction of the best policy and the president's urging that he go along with the team, even when the coach could not decide which goal was theirs. Each felt that resignation would influence the president's course, and each seriously considered resigning in defense of his convictions, but none could bring himself to leave. McCracken's reflections a decade later evoke the situation: "But if you decide you don't like the whole damn game plan, then you get off the team. . . . After all, there is a place for resignation in a democracy. In my own case, the point at which, in retrospect, perhaps I should have resigned was in the latter part of 1971 when the President went to wage and price controls. I had opposed that sort of thing, not only within the administration, but for a long period of time. . . . I would have to say in all candor that perhaps the game plan had changed enough at that point that I should have said 'I've got to step off the team'" (1984, p. 326; cf. p. 350; Stein, 1984a; Shultz and Dam, 1977).

CONCLUSION

Eisenhower epitomized the chief executive who sets an economic policy course early in the administration and holds tightly enough to its central tenets to resist the naturally occurring shocks and pressures that threaten to elevate short-term stabilization problems above long-term allocative and distributive goals. Rather than being stifled or ignored, conflict is channeled toward contributing to the unity and feasibility of the administration's position. Such a president is not inflexible, but his compromises are few and carefully considered. Their consideration is the business of his economic advisory network. If the members of that network are well chosen, and if the president fosters their work and integrates them with other issue and influence networks, then his ideological goals will be translated into policy as effectively as other circumstances permit.

Economic policy-making under Nixon marked the opposite pole of this continuum. Here the chief executive is relatively indifferent to economic issues unless a crisis looms; his advisory network is accumulated and arranged in an almost haphazard fashion; and it is typified by excessive duplication and informal arrangements that undermine rather than complement the formal organization. Nixon's ambivalence about the appropriate foundations, goals, and styles of economic policy-making is apparent in a series of shifting advisory arrangements marking major changes in his administration's approach to managing the national economy. The agencies involved in economic policy-making were not so much encouraged to confront and negotiate their differences as they were simply ignored; decision making on economic issues was less a matter of compromising interests than of selective attention.

The president's economic ideology helps to explain this difference. By posing long-range goals as primary, it entails a set of priorities that will condition his response to virtually every economic emergency: it shapes short-run stabilization policy to serve allocative and distributive goals. Presidents with clear, salient goals for economic policy will resist the attraction of using stabilization instruments for short-run electoral gains: they are unlikely to produce political business cycles.

But there is another dimension to this distinction. Among those presidents less consistently motivated by long-run political economic goals, it is useful to distinguish those who conscientiously and attentively build an advisory apparatus, and who regard its research and advice as critical to economic decision making. Although such a president is guided by no strong allocative or distributive goals, he ranks economic stabilization as one of the administration's primary tasks. For presidents in this category, the requisites of good economic policy will take precedence over electoral concerns when conflicts arise, and they will accept the advice of their economic experts that short-term manipulation of the economy is unsound policy. Contrast this pattern with that of a president concerned with economic policy only if a crisis threatens, whose advisory agencies are ignored, overruled, or frequently supplanted. For such a chief executive, economic policy—even the quarter-to-quarter conduct of stabilization policy—is of distinctly inferior priority. When resource conflicts or goal incompatabilities arise, economic plans can be and often are compromised. The formal advisory network whose task it is to maintain the administration's macroeconomic morality may be either ignored or forced to compromise its own virtue. The table below tentatively maps the post-war presidencies into this typology.[10]

[10] It is worth emphasizing that the placements of other administrations in this table are tentative. This is especially the case with the current administration, where placement in cell III, rather than cell II, appears justified by the shifting status of the CEA, OMB

TABLE 1

THE INTERPLAY OF ECONOMIC IDEOLOGY AND ADVISORY ARRANGEMENTS:
A TENTATIVE MAPPING OF POST-WAR PRESIDENTS

President's Economic Ideology

Economic Advisory Arrangements	Clear preferences; economic issues have high salience	Vague long-run goals; economic issues generally have low priority
Advisory organization and lines of communication clearly established; economic advisors have high prestige and influence within the White House and Administration	II Eisenhower Kennedy	I Ford Carter
Advisory organization relatively unstable, not well integrated into structures of White House or administration influence; formal advisors may be ignored or bypassed by the president	III Reagan	IV Johnson Nixon

The table helps to place particular administrations in terms of these two critical components of economic policy-making, and it helps to depict the relationship between ideology and the organization and use of economic advice. While space limitations prohibit fully elaborating the justification for each placement, among post-war presidents with relatively strong economic ideologies, Eisenhower is notable, but the Kennedy and Reagan administrations should be grouped in the same column. Each had a clear impression of the primary economic mission of his presidency—for Kennedy, the attempt to move the national economy permanently onto a steeper growth path; for Reagan, the attempt to reduce the size of government and thus to alter the balance in the economy between public and market decision making—and each

and even Treasury as particular advisors have come and gone. The table itself is offered as illustrative and intended to stimulate the further research that would ultimately underlie the employment of this typology to classify the post-war administrations.

regarded economic policy as the most important domestic issue. In contrast, the Nixon administration was characterized by ambivalent economic ideas and wide swings of policy. Presidential economic ideology was a similarly ambivalent policy guide in the Johnson, Ford and Carter administrations. For Johnson and Nixon, the concern with foreign affairs and noneconomic domestic issues held higher priority than economics, and those issues were given correspondingly more careful, continuous presidential attention. The commitment of Ford and Carter to particular economic goals went little beyond conventional partisan rhetoric. Both were strongly concerned with economic stabilization, but without a firm drive toward achieving some larger economic goal, their stabilization policies were ad hoc rather than thematic, reacting to each cyclical disturbance as a separate event. Economic policies in these administrations served neither the accomplishment of long-run political economic goals nor the enhancement of the president's electoral chances.

But the economic policies of Ford and Carter were quite different from those of Johnson and Nixon, who occupy the same column, and the difference can be traced to distinctions in the way they organized and integrated their advisory networks. Both Greenspan in the Ford administration and Schultze in the Carter years occupied critical positions in the networks of communication and influence in the White House: their access to the president was regular and unproblematic, and their advice was taken seriously and occasionally resulted in postponing an initiative because of its macroeconomic effects. In both these administrations, economic and political advisors debated whether to stimulate the economy before the election, and in both cases the president sided firmly with his economic advisors (Greenspan, 1984; Schultze, 1984; Carter, 1982). In the Johnson administration, in spite of the impressive credentials and strong national policy ambitions Ackley and Okun brought to the Council, their advice was occasionally ignored at critical points, they were sometimes omitted from decision circles on issues where economic considerations were important, and, when trade-offs were unavoidable—as on the question of a tax increase in 1966—stabilization goals were sacrificed to foreign or domestic ones (King, 1985; Anderson and Hazelton, 1986, ch. 3; Johnson, 1971, p. 444 ff).

Finally, note that arraying administrations across the categories of this typology shows how these two components of the economic policy process work as partially independent themes in explaining political business cycles. A president who is committed to long-run allocative or distributive aspirations is unlikely to neglect his circle of economic advisors, so that both the counterpoise of clear economic goals and the consciously instrumental organization of advice toward their achievement will militate against political manipulation of the economy. But most presidents do not enter office with clear intentions in the economic realm, and among this group some may be willing to manipulate short-term policy instruments for electoral ends. Carefully examining how the president organizes and uses his economic advisory resources gives us a purchase on this distinction. It would be mistaken to imply that administrations in cell IV will inevitably respond to the electoral incentive by attempting short-term manipulation of the economy. But if political business cycles occur, it is reasonable to expect them to take place under administrations of this type.

REFERENCES

(Primary source material is cited under the name of the person quoted [e.g., material from the Vanderbilt Oral History Project on the CEA: v. Hargrove and Morley, eds., below] or, for materials from the Eisenhower Library, according to the Library's catalogue conventions [e.g., WF-C indicates Ann Whitman file—Cabinet Series; WF-DDE, the President's diary series].)

Ackley, Gardner. 1966. The Contribution of Economists to Policy Formation. *Journal of Finance*, 21: 176ff.
Allison, Graham. 1971. *Essence of Decision*. Boston: Little-Brown.
Allison, Graham, and Peter Szanton. 1976. Organizing for the Decade Ahead. In Henry Aaron and Charles L. Schultze, eds., *Setting National Priorities: The Next Ten Years*. Washington, DC: Brookings.
Ambrose, Stephen E. 1984. *Eisenhower, v. 2: The President*. New York: Simon and Schuster.
Anderson, James E., and Jared E. Hazleton. 1986. *Managing Macroeconomic Policy: The Johnson Presidency*. Austin, TX: University of Texas Press.
Anderson, Patrick. 1969. *The President's Men: White House Assistants of Franklin D. Roosevelt, Harry S. Truman, Dwight D. Eisenhower, John F. Kennedy, Lyndon B. Johnson*. Garden City, NY: Doubleday.
Barry, Brian, 1985. Does Democracy Cause Inflation? Political Ideas of Some Economists. In *The Politics of Inflation and Economic Stagnation*. Leon N. Lindberg and Charles S. Maier, ed., Washington, DC: Brookings.
Beck, Nathaniel. 1982a. Parties, Administrations and American Macroeconomic Outcomes. *American Political Science Review*, 76: 83-94.
————. 1982b. Presidential Influence on the Federal Reserve in the 1970s. *American Journal of Political Science*, 26: 415-45.
————. 1983. Beck, contra Hibbs, contra Beck:... a Rejoinder to Professor Hibbs. Mimeo, Department of Political Science, University of California, San Diego.
Berman, Larry. 1979. *The Office of Management and Budget. 1921-1979*. Princeton, NJ: Princeton University Press.
Blinder, Alan S. 1979. *Economic Policy and the Great Stagflation*. New York: Academic Press.
Brody, Richard A. 1983. Public Evaluations and Expectations, and the Future of the Presidency. In James S. Young, ed., *Problems and Prospects of Leadership in the 1980s*. Lanham, MD: University Press of America.
Bryant, Ralph C. 1983. *Controlling Money*. Washington, DC: Brookings.
Burns, Arthur F. 1954. *The Frontiers of Economic Knowledge*. Princeton, NJ: Princeton University Press (for the National Bureau of Economic Research).

———. 1957a. *Prosperity without Inflation*. New York: Fordham University Press.

———. 1957b. An Economist in Government. *Forum*, 1: 4-6.

———. 1984. Oral History Interview: The Council of Economic Advisors Under Chairman Arthur F. Burns. In *The President and the Council of Economic Advisors*. See Hargrove and Morley, 1984.

Cameron, Juan. 1972. How the U.S. Got on the Road to a Controlled Economy. *Fortune*, 85: 74ff.

Campbell, Colin. 1983. *Governments Under Stress: Political Executives and Key Bureaucrats in Washington, London, and Ottawa*. Toronto: University of Toronto Press.

Campbell, Donald, T. 1975. Degrees of Freedom and the Case Study. *Comparative Political Studies*, 8: 178-93.

Carter, Jimmy. 1982. *Keeping Faith*. New York: Bantam.

Childs, Marquis. 1958. *Eisenhower: Captive Hero*. New York: Harcourt.

Cottam, Richard W., and Bert A. Rockman. 1984. In the Shadow of Substance: Presidents as Foreign Policy Makers, In David P. Forsythe, ed., *American Foreign Policy in an Uncertain World*. Lincoln, NE: University of Nebraska Press.

Cronin, Thomas E. 1980. *The State of the Presidency*, 2d ed. Boston: Little-Brown.

DeMarchi, Neil. 1975. The First Nixon Administration: Prelude to Controls. In Craufurd D. Goodwin, ed., *Exhortation and Controls: The Search for a Wage-Price Policy, 1945-71*. Washington, DC: Brookings.

Destler, I.M. 1980. *Making Foreign Economic Policy*. Washington, DC: Brookings.

Eckstein, Harry. 1975. Case Studies and Theory in Political Science, In Fred I. Greenstein and Nelson W. Polsby, ed., *The Handbook of Political Science: Strategies of Inquiry*, Reading, MA: Addison-Wesley.

Eckstein, Otto. 1978. *The Great Recession*. Amsterdam: North-Holland.

Economic Report of the President as Transmitted to the Congress. 1954-1956; 1970-72. Washington, DC: U.S. Government Printing Office.

Eisenhower, Dwight D. 1953-1956. *Public Papers of the Presidents of the United States*. Washington, DC: U.S. Government Printing Office.

———. 1960. *Waging Peace*. Garden City, NY: Doubleday.

———. 1978. *The Papers of Dwight David Eisenhower: The Chief of Staff*, v. VI-IX, ed. Louis Galambos. Baltimore: The Johns Hopkins University Press.

Evans, Roland E., Jr., and Robert D. Novak. 1971. *Nixon in the White House*. New York: Random House.

Fellner, William. 1976. *Toward a Reconstruction of Macroeconomics: Problems of Theory and Policy*. Washington, DC: American Enterprise Institute.

Ferrell, Robert H. 1981. *The Eisenhower Diaries*. New York: Norton.

Finer, Herman. 1960. *The Presidency: Crisis and Regeneration*. Chicago: University of Chicago Press.

Flash, Edward S., Jr. 1965. *Economic Advice and Presidential Leadership*. New York: Columbia University Press.

Frey, Bruno. 1978. *Modern Political Economy*. Oxford: Martin Robertson.

Friedman, Milton. 1980. Financial Markets in the Post-war Period. In Martin Feldstein, ed, *The American Economy in Transition*. Chicago: University of Chicago Press.

George, Alexander L. 1972. The Case for Multiple Advocacy in Making Foreign Policy, *American Political Science Review*, 76: 751-85.

———. 1980. *Presidential Decision-making in Foreign Policy*. Boulder, CO: Westview Press.

Golden, D., and J. Poterba. 1980. The Price of Popularity: The Political Business Cycle Reexamined. *American Journal of Political Science*, 24: 696-714.

Gordon, Robert J. 1980. Postwar Macroeconomics. In *The American Economy in Transition*. See Milton Friedman, 1980.

Gowa, Joanne. 1984. State Power, State Policy: Explaining the Decision to Close the Gold Window. *Politics and Society*, 13: 91-117.

Greenspan, Alan. 1984. Oral History Interview: The Council of Economic Advisors Under Chairman Alan Greenspan. In *The President and the Council of Economic Advisors*. See Hargrove and Morlay, 1984.

Greenstein, Fred I. 1982. *The Hidden Hand Presidency*. New York: Basic.

Hargrove, Erwin C., and Samuel A. Morley, eds. 1984. *The President and the Council of Economic Advisors*. Boulder, CO: Westview.

Heclo, Hugh. 1976. *A Government of Strangers*. Washington, DC: Brookings.

———. 1983. One Executive Branch or Many? In Anthony King, ed., *Both Ends of the Avenue*. Washington, DC: American Enterprise Institute.

Heclo, Hugh, and Lester M. Salamon. 1981. *The Illusion of Presidential Government*. Boulder, CO: Westview Press.

Heller, Walter. 1966. *New Dimensions of Political Economy*. Cambridge, MA: Harvard University Press.

Hersen, M., and D.H. Barlow. 1976. *Single-case Experimental Designs: Strategies for Studying Behavior*. New York: Pergamon.

Hess, Stephen. 1976. *Organizing the Presidency*. Washington, DC: Brookings.

Hibbs, Douglas A., Jr. 1977. Political Parties and Macroeconomic Policy. *American Political Science Review*, 71: 1467-87.

———. 1983. Comment on Beck. *American Political Science Review*, 77: 447-51.

Humphrey, George M. 1965. *The Basic Papers of George M. Humphrey as Secretary of the Treasury*, ed. Nathan R. Howard. Cleveland: Western Reserve Historical Society.

Johnson, Lyndon Baines. 1971. *The Vantage Point*. New York: Holt Rinehardt and Winston.

Johnson, Richard Tanner. 1974. *Managing the White House*. New York: Harper.

———. 1979. Presidential Style. In Aaron Wildavsky, ed., *Perspectives on the Presidency*. Boston: Little-Brown.

Keech, William R. 1980. Elections and Macroeconomic Policy Optimization. *American Journal of Political Science*, 24: 345-67.

Kessel, John H. 1983. The Structures of the Carter White House. *American Journal of Political Science*, 27: 431-63.

———. 1984. The Structures of the Reagan White House. *American Journal of Political Science*, 28: 231-59.

Kilborn, Peter. September 18, 1983. The Testing of Martin Feldstein. *New York Times*.

King, Ronald F. 1985. The President and Fiscal Policy in 1966: The Year that Taxes Weren't Raised. *Polity*, 17: 685-714.

Kosters, Marvin H. 1975. *Controls and Inflation: The Economic Stabilization Program in Retrospect*. Washington, DC: Brookings.

Leuchtenberg, William. 1983. *In the Shadow of FDR*. Ithaca, NY: Cornell University Press.

Lewis-Beck, Michael S., and Tom W. Rice. 1985. Governmental Growth in the United States. *Journal of Politics*, 47:2-30.

Light, Paul C. 1982. *The President's Agenda*. Baltimore, MD: The Johns Hopkins University Press.

Lilienthal, David E. 1964. *The Atomic Energy Years, 1945-50*. New York: Harper.

Lowery, David. 1985. The Keynesian and Political Determinants of Unbalanced Budgets: U.S. Fiscal Policy from Eisenhower to Reagan. *American Journal of Political Science*, 29: 428-60.

Lowery, David, and William D. Berry. 1983. Growth of Government in the United States: An Empirical Assessment of Competing Explanations. *American Journal of Political Science*, 27: 665-94.

McCracken, Paul W. 1984. Oral History Interview: The Council of Economic Advisors Under Chairman Paul W. McCracken. In *The President and the Council of Economic Advisors*. See Hargrove and Morley, 1984.

MacRae, C. Duncan. 1977. A Political Model of the Business Cycle. *Journal of Political Economy*, 85: 239-63.

Monroe, Kristen Renwick. 1984. *Presidential Popularity and the Economy*. New York: Praeger.

Musgrave, Richard A. 1959. *The Theory of Public Finance*. New York: McGraw-Hill.

Nathan, Richard. 1983. *The Administrative Presidency*. New York: Wiley.

Neustadt, Richard. 1955. Presidency and Legislation: Planning the President's Program. *American Political Science Review*, 49: 980-1018.

_____. 1980 [1960]. *Presidential Power*. New York: Wiley.

Nixon, Richard M. 1962. *Six Crises*. New York: Doubleday.

_____. 1978. *The Memoirs of Richard Nixon*. New York: Grosset and Dunlap.

Norton, Hugh. 1977. *The Employment Act and the Council of Economic Advisors, 1946-76*. Columbia, SC: University of South Carolina Press.

Norton, Hugh S. 1985. *The Quest for Economic Stability: Roosevelt to Reagan*. Columbia, SC: University of South Carolina Press.

Nourse, Edwin G. 1953. *Economics in the Public Service: Administrative Aspects of the Employment Act*. New York: Harcourt, Brace.

Nourse, Edwin G., and Bertram M. Gross. 1948. The Role of the Council of Economic Advisors. *American Political Science Review*, 42: 283-95.

Odell, John S. 1982. *International Monetary Policy: Markets, Power and Ideas as Sources of Change*. Princeton, NJ: Princeton University Press.

Okun, Arthur. 1976. The Economist and Presidential Leadership. In Ryan C. Amacher, Robert D. Tollison, and Thomas D. Willett, eds., *The Economic Approach to Public Policy: Selected Readings*. Ithaca, NY: Cornell University Press.

Pierce, Lawrence C. 1971. *The Politics of Fiscal Policy Formation*. Pacific Palisades, CA: Goodyear.

Porter, Roger B. 1980. *Presidential Decision Making*. Cambridge, MA: Harvard University Press.

_____. 1981. The President and Economic Policy: Problems, Patterns, and Alternatives. In *The Illusion of Presidential Government*. See Heclo and Salamon, 1981.

_____. 1983. Economic Advice to the President: From Eisenhower to Reagan. *Political Science Quarterly*, 98: 403-26.

Price, Don K., and Rocco C. Siciliano. 1980. *A Presidency for the 1980s*. Washington, DC: National Academy of Public Administration.

Przeworski, Adam, and Henry Teune. 1970. *The Logic of Comparative Social Inquiry*. New York: Wiley.

Randall, Ronald. 1979. Presidential Power versus Bureaucratic Intransigence: The Influence of the Nixon Administration on Welfare Policy. *American Political Science Review*, 73: 795-810.

Reichley, A. James. 1981. *Conservatives in an Age of Change*. Washington, DC: Brookings.

Safire, William. 1975. *Before the Fall*. New York: Doubleday.

Samuelson, Paul A. 1956. The Economics of Eisenhower: A Symposium. *Review of Economics and Statistics*, 38: 371-73.

Saulnier, Raymond J. 1969. *The Strategy of Economic Policy*. New York: Fordham University Press.

_____. 1984. Oral History Interview: The Council of Economic Advisors under Chairman Raymond J. Saulnier. In *The President and the Council of Economic Advisors*. See Hargrove and Morley, 1984.

Schultze, Charles. 1984. Oral History Interview: The Council of Economic Advisors under Chairman Charles Schultze. In *The President and the Council of Economic Advisors*. *See* Hargrove and Morley, 1984.

Shultz, George P., and Kenneth W. Dam. 1977. *Economic Policy Beyond the Headlines*. Stanford, CA: Stanford University Alumni Association.

Silk, Leonard. 1972. *Nixonomics*. New York: Praeger.

Smith, Adam. March 18, 1984. Why Feldstein Hangs Tough. *New York Times Magazine*, p. 34ff.

Stein, Herbert, 1969. *The Fiscal Revolution in America*. Chicago: University of Chicago Press.

———. 1984a. Oral History Interview: The Council of Economic Advisors under Herbert Stein. In *The President and the Council of Economic Advisors*. *See* Hargrove and Morley, 1984.

———. 1984b. *Presidential Economics*. New York: Simon and Schuster.

Stigler, George. 1973. Aggregate Economic Conditions and National Elections. *American Economic Review*, 64: 160-67.

Sundquist, James. 1968. *Politics and Policy*. Washington, DC: Brookings.

Szanton, Peter, 1981. *Not Well Advised*. New York: Russell Sage Foundation.

Thomas, Norman C. 1983. Case Studies. In George C. Edwards III and Stephen J. Wayne, eds., *Studying the Presidency*. Knoxville, TN: University of Tennessee Press.

Tufte, Edward R. 1978. *Political Control of the Economy*. Princeton: Princeton University Press.

U.S. Congress, Joint Committee on the Economic Report. 1954-1956; 1969-72. *Hearings on the Economic Report of the President*. Washington, DC: U.S. Government Printing Office.

Weatherford, M. Stephen, and Lorraine M. McDonnell. 1984. Presidential Ideology in Economic Policymaking. *Policy Studies*, 12: 691-704.

Wills, Gary. 1970. *Nixon Agonistes*. Boston: Houghton-Mifflin.

Woolley, John T. 1985. Elections, Administration, Parties and Monetary Policy in the United States: Another Look at the Use of Reaction Functions in the Study of Monetary Policy. Paper for the annual meeting of the Midwest Political Science Association, Chicago.

Yin, Robert K. 1981. The Case Study Crisis: Some Answers. *Administrative Science Quarterly*, 26: 58-65.

———. 1984. *Case Study Research: Design and Methods*. Beverly Hills, CA: Sage.

Thomas W. Zeiler

Kennedy, Oil Imports, and the
Fair Trade Doctrine

In his efforts to secure passage of the Trade Expansion Act of 1962, John F. Kennedy had to placate not only oil and coal interests at home, but also traditional trade partners like Venezuela abroad, and he also had to foster the broad national security aim of retaining domestic oil reserves. This article argues that Kennedy was able to utilize a fair trade doctrine to gain enactment of legislation that would both lower trade barriers and assist domestic producers hurt by increased imports.

President John F. Kennedy believed in the principle of free trade, but he sympathized with producers hurt by imports and recognized the political necessity of placating protectionists in Congress. His position on oil imports exemplified this tension between free trade and protectionism. A powerful bloc of oil- and coal-state legislators could scuttle his top legislative priority for 1962, the Trade Expansion Act (TEA); without this bill, the president could not lower tariffs on a reciprocal basis with other nations, maintain a liberal world trade regime, and meet the challenge of the rising European Economic Community to America's leadership in the global economy. In pursuit of votes, he forged a policy that limited oil imports but assured passage of the TEA.

This accomplishment was impressive because oil import policy was of concern to numerous influential interests. Divided into producers, refiners, and sellers and between vertically integrated, multinational large-scale producers and independent domestic producers and refiners, the industry represented a complex trade problem for Kennedy. On the protectionist side were independent oil producers

THOMAS W. ZEILER is a lecturer in history at the University of Colorado, Boulder. This project was funded in part by a John F. Kennedy Library Foundation grant and the Visiting Scholars Program at the Carl Albert Congressional Research and Studies Center, University of Oklahoma. I would particularly like to thank archivist John Caldwell.

Business History Review 64 (Summer 1990): 286–310. © 1990 by The President and Fellows of Harvard College.

from states that relied on strong domestic production for their economic health, and coal producers who hoped to limit imports of residual fuel oil, used for heating along the Atlantic seaboard, in order to expand the market for coal. On the liberal trade side, residual fuel users demanded freer trade in petroleum as a way of lowering fuel prices, and exporting nations sought increased access into the United States for their oil. Kennedy backed liberal trade in oil not only on principle and economic grounds, but also because America's security depended on safely transported, reliable supplies of petroleum imports, which would help conserve U.S. deposits. Clearly, he faced a politically complicated task in trying to satisfy all of these interests and passing his trade bill.

He did so by adhering to the "fair trade" doctrine. Similar to the "managed trade" terminology of the 1970s, the fair trade approach aimed to protect national economies by permitting government intervention in the free-market system through the regulation of imports and exports.[1] The doctrine enabled Kennedy to reduce trade barriers while aiding domestic sectors hurt by imports. It consisted of two parts.

One part focused on trade liberalization. Boosting American exports and those of other Western nations would spur economic growth, fund military and aid commitments that were causing a U.S. balance-of-payments deficit, and thereby bolster national security. In practice, Kennedy used the doctrine to seek advantages for all traders, often sacrificing protection of U.S. producers for the good of the global capitalist trade order. Yet liberal trade confronted domestic economic and political realities. Conditions in Massachusetts while he was a senator had made Kennedy aware of the harmful effects of imports on declining industries. Thus, the other half of the fair trade doctrine hinged on aiding import competitors by a novel assistance program included in the TEA. Since the measure would not be put into effect until the bill passed, however, Kennedy selectively restricted imports to help injured interests and to appease the congressional blocs most capable of derailing his trade bill. In short, fair trade in oil helped America and its partners enjoy the mutual benefits of expanded commerce without undue injury to vulnerable interests.

---

[1] Joan E. Spero, *The Politics of International Economic Relations*, 3d ed. (New York, 1985), 122. For the free trade/protectionist dualism, see Stefanie A. Lenway, *The Politics of U.S. International Trade: Protection, Expansion, and Escape* (Marshfield, Mass., 1984); Vinod K. Aggarwal, *Liberal Protectionism: The International Politics of Organized Textile Trade* (Berkeley, Calif., 1985); Jock A. Finlayson and Mark W. Zacher, "The GATT and the Regulation of Trade Barriers: Regime Dynamics and Functions" in *International Regimes*, ed. Stephen D. Krasner (Ithaca, N.Y., 1983).

Fair trade addresses a debate over postwar U.S. trade policy. A "hegemony" school argues that oil companies penetrated foreign markets solely for the benefit of American exporters but closed the door of the U.S. market to competitive imports. Such a policy extended U.S. hegemony over the global oil regime. These scholars also contend that decisions taken by domestic and international petroleum interests, with the tacit approval of the executive branch, determined policy.[2]

A "comparative advantage" school, meanwhile, maintains that the United States sought profits for the most efficient producers, often sacrificed its markets to imports in doing so, and in many cases could not prevent the erosion of its trade edge in oil in the face of rising foreign competition. These historians point out that national security requirements—the need to procure and store petroleum in case of a war or emergency—overrode the pursuit of profits. They add that decision-making was based on political pluralism, necessitated by the tangle of competing interests and the dominant role of Congress in bargaining with the president before passing trade legislation.[3]

The formulation and results of Kennedy's oil import policy bear out the comparative advantage school's position. Decision making revolved around interbranch politics between Congress, which represented interest groups, and the president, who pushed free trade

[2] Stephen E. Ambrose, *Rise to Globalism: American Foreign Policy Since 1938*, 5th ed. (Baltimore, Md., 1988); William A. Williams, *The Tragedy of American Diplomacy* (New York, 1972). For decision making, see John M. Blair, *The Control of Oil* (New York, 1976); Robert Engler, *The Politics of Oil: A Study of Private Power and Democratic Direction* (New York, 1961); Michael J. Hogan, "Corporatism: A Positive Appraisal," *Diplomatic History* 10 (Fall 1986): 363–72; Thomas J. McCormick, "Drift or Mastery? A Corporatist Synthesis for American Diplomatic History," *Reviews in American History* 10 (Dec. 1982): 321–28; David S. Painter, *Oil and the American Century: The Political Economy of U.S. Foreign Oil Policy, 1941–1954* (Baltimore, Md., 1986), 206–7.

[3] William H. Becker and Samuel F. Wells, eds., *Economics and World Power: An Assessment of American Diplomacy since 1789* (New York, 1982); Thomas W. Zeiler, "Free-Trade Politics and Diplomacy: John F. Kennedy and Textiles," *Diplomatic History* 11 (Spring 1987): 127–42. For decision making and the security argument, see Irvine Anderson, *The Standard-Vacuum Oil Company and the United States East Asian Policy, 1933–1941* (Princeton, N.J., 1975); Burton I. Kaufman, *The Oil Cartel Case: A Documentary Study of Antitrust Activity in the Cold War Era* (Westport, Conn., 1978); Stephen D. Krasner, *Defending the National Interest: Raw Materials and U.S. Foreign Policy* (Princeton, N.J., 1978); Lenway, *The Politics of U.S. International Trade*, chaps. 1–4; Gerald D. Nash, *United States Oil Policy, 1890–1964* (Pittsburgh, Pa., 1968); Robert A. Pastor, *Congress and the Politics of Foreign Economic Policy, 1929–1976* (Berkeley, Calif., 1980), chaps. 1–4; Stephen J. Randall, *United States Foreign Oil Policy, 1919–1948: For Profits and Security* (Kingston, Ont., 1985); Michael B. Stoff, *Oil, War, and American Security: The Search for a National Policy on Foreign Oil, 1941–1947* (New Haven, Conn., 1980).

and security aims. This process permitted Kennedy to pursue liberal trade, offering efficient foreign producers a growing share of the U.S. oil market if Congress passed the TEA.

Origins of the Kennedy Policy

Kennedy's oil import problem stemmed from the immediate post-war era. With its booming industry in need of oil, America in 1948 became a net importer of petroleum for the first time since the First World War. The Cold War was another catalyst for oil imports. For defense purposes, the United States hoped to keep this vital commodity available to its allies, conserve its own deposits by importing from foreign sources with secure access routes to America, and buoy the economies of oil-dependent Middle Eastern and South American nations. Yet rising imports had a downside; they displaced U.S. independent oil and domestic coal producers in the American market and caused production to stagnate.

As a result, well-organized forces put pressure on Congress to limit imports. Oil-state legislators attached a "national security" amendment to the trade bill of 1955, providing for restrictions when imports impaired domestic production of goods required in an emergency. Two years later, rising oil imports compelled "voluntary" controls by U.S. importers. Dwight Eisenhower's administration soon replaced these ineffective restraints with the Mandatory Quota Program of 1959. The program limited imports to 9 percent of estimated domestic demand but exempted Canada and Mexico from quotas in order to maintain their safely imported, overland supplies. The plan also placed a ceiling on fuel oil imports at their 1957 level. Inimical to free trade, the quota program was well ensconced by the time Kennedy arrived in Washington.[4]

His prior stand on oil burdened Kennedy, however. Of all the presidential aspirants, he had been singled out as the most "openly hostile" to the petroleum industry. Opposed to quotas and the deple-

---

[4] Douglas R. Bohi and Milton Russell, *Limiting Oil Imports: An Economic History and Analysis* (Baltimore, Md., 1978), chaps. 1–3; Nash, *United States Oil Policy*, 202–6; Edward W. Chester, *United States Oil Policy and Diplomacy: A Twentieth Century Overview* (Westport, Conn., 1983), chaps. 1, 3, pp. 140–57; Burton I. Kaufman, *Trade and Aid: Eisenhower's Foreign Economic Policy, 1953–1961* (Baltimore, Md., 1982), 89–90. For a history of oil policy, see U.S., Senate Subcommittee on Multinational Corporations of the Committee on Foreign Relations, *Report on Multinational Oil Corporations and U.S. Foreign Policy*, 93d Cong., 2d sess., 1975 [hereafter cited as *Multinational Oil Hearings*].

tion allowance tax break to producers, he was one of twelve members of the New England Senate delegation who opposed restrictions on fuel oil. Failing to persuade Eisenhower to exempt residual fuel oil from limits, Kennedy censored the quota program as a "completely unjustified, uneconomic and shortsighted action," which not only raised prices but "cuts athwart our trade position, unnecessarily damages our relations in this hemisphere, and does not contribute to our national defense and security."[5] Such a view did not sit well with U.S. producers, so he moderated his rhetoric during the campaign of 1960, though in early 1961 secretary of the interior Stewart L. Udall revised quotas and increased fuel oil imports. Asked about the future of controls on residual oil, Kennedy the fair trader responded that "we have to consider the needs of the coal industry and domestic producers, the needs of New England, and we are trying to reach a balance which will protect the public interest."[6]

Nevertheless, oil producers wondered if Kennedy would swing the concept of import controls away from national security, and thus protection of domestic production, and toward reducing quotas to help the economies of foreign producers. Assistant secretary of the interior and oilman John M. Kelly argued that defense requirements should take precedence. Total petroleum imports had risen over 63 percent since 1954, and U.S. crude production had not kept pace with foreign output. But Kennedy rejected Interior's suggestion to cut import quotas by 50,000 barrels a day because he opposed protectionism, high fuel prices, and potential injury to less-developed countries (LDCs). As oil leaders had feared, the president shifted the focus of import policy from the national to the international level in order

---

[5] Kennedy to George W. Mills, 19 March 1959, box 724, Pre-Presidential Papers [hereafter cited as PPP], John F. Kennedy Library, Boston, Mass. [hereafter cited as JFK Library). See also *Petroleum Week* 11 (8 Jan. 1960): 13; *Oil and Gas Journal* 58 (18 July 1960): 62; Speech, "The Economic Problems of New England: A Program for Congressional Action," no. 3, 25 May 1953, box 774; New England Senate Delegation to the President, 5 March 1959, box 724.

[6] *Public Papers of the President of the United States, John F. Kennedy, 1961*, 138 [hereafter cited as *Public Papers, 1961*]. See also Briefing Paper, Oil Import Situation, 1960, box 993, PPP; Justinus Gould to Cong. Wright Patman, 16 May 1961, box 288, Papers of Tom Steed [hereafter cited as Steed Papers], Carl Albert Congressional Research and Studies Center, Congressional Archives, University of Oklahoma, Norman, Okla. [hereafter cited as Albert Center]; *New York Times*, 18 Feb. 1961, 25; Senator Robert C. Byrd to the White House, 17 Feb. 1961, box 23, White House Staff Files—Myer Feldman, JFK Library [hereafter cited as Feldman files]; *Oil and Gas Journal* 59 (27 Feb. 1961): 56; Bohi, *Limiting Oil Imports*, 149–50.

to ensure friendly trade relations with other nations and to preserve American supplies.[7]

National security considerations undergirded Kennedy's trade program as well as his resistance to oil import restrictions. Both Moscow and Washington viewed petroleum as a critical commodity in their economic competition, and the Soviet Union had emerged as the second-ranking producer behind the United States by the time Kennedy took office. Italy had already responded to Soviet overtures by selling or bartering construction material for Eastern-bloc oil. The State Department now worried about Soviet penetration in the politically unstable LDCs, many of whom turned to Russian financing for exploration and drilling when international oil companies refused such help.[8]

Venezuela

Kennedy feared that Venezuela, the largest source of American petroleum imports, would fall prey to communism. With the highest per capita income in Latin America, Venezuela was a test case for his Alliance for Progress. The world's top oil exporter, the nation had become the sixth largest customer for U.S. goods, spending over $1 billion on imports from the United States on the strength of its petroleum revenue and bilateral trade agreements. The bellwether of the Latin American oil industry, Venezuela nevertheless had economic problems. The country had endured a severe recession in 1959–60, an unemployment rate of 12 percent, a decline in oil drilling of 42 percent since 1959, and a deficit of over $800 million. As a result

---

[7] *Oil and Gas Journal* 60 (8 Jan. 1962): 29; John M. Kelly, In Support of Proposals to Amend the Oil Import Program, Charts 6 and 7, 21 Nov. 1961, box 23, Feldman files; Summary Minutes of the Interdepartmental Committee of Undersecretaries on Foreign Economic Policy, 13 Dec. 1961, box 32, Papers of Kermit Gordon, JFK Library [hereafter cited as Gordon Papers]; Myer Feldman to the President, 14 Dec. 1961, box 63, President's Office File, JFK Library [hereafter cited as POF]; U.S., House Hearings before Subcommittee No. 4 of the Select Committee on Small Business, *Small Business Problems Created by Petroleum Imports*, pt. 1, 87th Cong., 1st sess., 1961 [hereafter cited as *Petroleum Hearings—I* or *II*], Clarence W. Nichols, State Department, 198.

[8] Summary Record of Meeting on World Oil Problems, 15 Jan. 1962, box 33, Gordon Papers; George Feldman, "The OECD, the Common Market, and American Foreign Policy," attached to Lawrence O'Brien to Cong. John McCormack, 10 Jan. 1962, box 237, White House Central Files, JFK Library [hereafter cited as WHCF]; Remarks of Stewart L. Udall to the American Petroleum Institute Meeting, 27 July 1961, box 93, Papers of Stewart L. Udall, Special Collections, University of Arizona; *Petroleum Management* 34 (April 1962): 1.

of the world oil surplus and consequent weakening of prices, oil investment and exports, composing one-fourth of Venezuela's gross national
product (GNP) and over 90 percent of its total overseas sales, were
sluggish.[9]

Economic difficulties jeopardized political stability. Venezuelans
remembered Eisenhower's tolerance of the brutal dictatorship of Perez
Jimenez, and they had shown their disfavor to vice-president Richard
Nixon in 1958 by attacking his car in Caracas. Now, Kennedy courted
the government of moderate president Rómulo Betancourt in order
to protect Venezuela's new democratic institutions. Betancourt had
recently survived a bombing attempt on his life from left-wing insur-
gents. From the right, he faced an entrenched ruling class that chafed
at reforms of all kinds. As White House aide Arthur Schlesinger
warned, Betancourt's downfall could guarantee another Fidel Castro
or Juan Peron. To keep him in power required a strong economy,
particularly in the petroleum sector. But since its inception, the quota
program had threatened Venezuelan petroleum production and
enraged minister of mines and hydrocarbons Juan Pablo Perez
Alfonzo.[10]

Perez Alfonzo was a follower of Brazilian economist Raúl Prebisch,
who claimed that the "terms of trade" gave the manufactured goods
of advanced industrial nations a price edge over the raw materials of
the LDCs, thereby perpetuating a cycle of one-sided benefits for the
advanced countries. The minister addressed this problem by trying
to raise plummeting world oil prices, reduce output, and control
exports. To these ends, Perez Alfonzo helped form the Organization
of Petroleum Exporting Countries (OPEC) in 1960 and criticized the
U.S. quota program. Caracas understood the political pressures on
Eisenhower and Kennedy and recognized that the program had stabilized prices and allowed a sustained growth of exports. Yet Venezuela

[9] *Oil and Gas Journal* 59 (25 Dec. 1961): 81; *New York Times*, 31 Aug. 1961, 39; *Petroleum Management* 34 (May 1962): 12; Stephen G. Rabe, *The Road to OPEC: United States Relations with Venezuela, 1919–1976* (Austin, Texas, 1982), viii, 109–10, 123–29; Arthur M. Schlesinger, Jr., *A Thousand Days: John F. Kennedy in the White House* (Boston, Mass., 1965), 766; *Wall Street Journal*, 3 July 1961, 1, 10; *Petroleum Week* 12 (6 Jan. 1961): 40; William G. Harris, "The Impact of the Petroleum Export Industry on the Pattern of Venezuelan Economic Development" (Ph.D. diss., University of Oregon, 1967), 1; General Economic Situation [Venezuela], 5 Dec. 1961, box 235–238, National Security File, JFK Library [hereafter cited as NSF].

[10] Rabe, *The Road to OPEC*, 97–140; Rómulo Betancourt, *Venezuela: Oil and Politics* (Boston, Mass., 1979), 387–88; Current Political Situation in Venezuela, boxes 235–38, NSF; Arthur Schlesinger, The Current Crisis in Latin America, Part 1, 1961, box 121A, POF.

feared losing its historically favorable position in the U.S. market to Mideast and Canadian oil, and Perez Alfonzo complained that his country did not receive an exemption from the program as Canada and Mexico did. In 1961 Betancourt sent a letter to the departments of State and Interior noting the harmful effects of quotas, and asked United Nations ambassador Adlai Stevenson to end the "abuses and injustices" of oil restrictions.[11]

Oil was a main topic of conversation during Kennedy's visit to Venezuela in December, 1961, the first ever by a U.S. president. Drawing on Interior's arguments, the president said that the oil program actually helped Venezuela. Because of the overland exemption from U.S. controls, Canada's western provinces sold oil profitably in the American upper Midwest. Canada therefore saw no need to build a pipeline to its eastern provinces, where a large market remained dependent on oil from Venezuela. Also, decontrolling residual products would lower prices and impair Caracas's exchange rate. Moreover, fuel oil, of which Venezuela provided almost all of America's imports, was not severely limited, and Kennedy had abandoned plans to reduce crude quotas. In sum, Venezuelan oil would not be put at a disadvantage in the U.S. market.[12]

Nevertheless, Kennedy recognized the dangers inherent in Venezuela's economic and political situation. In response, he doubled loans to Caracas to $100 million in 1961 and encouraged Venezuela to take an active role in the Latin American Free Trade Association in order to promote its exports through a common market. As a fair trader, Kennedy permitted some Latin American discrimination against U.S. goods as a way of stabilizing the region's economies. He also promised to hold consultations with Betancourt before changing the oil quota program, installing a hotline between the Oval Office and Betancourt's chambers to facilitate such communications.[13]

---

[11] Rabe, *The Road to OPEC*, 117–20, 158–60; R. K. Pachauri, *The Political Economy of Global Energy* (Baltimore, Md., 1985), 56–58; Franklin Tugwell, *The Politics of Oil in Venezuela* (Stanford, Calif., 1975), chap. 3; American Embassy, Caracas to Secretary of State, 5 May 1961, box 192, NSF; *Multinational Oil Report*, 88; Foreign Service Dispatch, Caracas to the Department of State, 5 Dec. 1961, box 24, Feldman files; Position Paper, The President's Visit to Venezuela and Colombia, Oil Import Program, 6 Dec. 1961, box 235, NSF; *Petroleum Week* 12 (10 March 1961): 24; A Request for Elimination of Restrictions on the Import of Residual Oil Filed with the Office of Civil and Defense Mobilization, *Petroleum Hearings—I*, 309.

[12] Betancourt, *Venezuela*, 389; John Kelly to Myer Feldman, 22 Oct. 1961; Feldman to the President, 14 December 1961, box 24; Feldman to the President, 15 Dec. 1961, box 23, Feldman files.

[13] *Public Papers, 1961*, 808. See also *Foreign Commerce Weekly* 66 (11 Sept. 1961): 39; *Department of State Bulletin* 45 (11 Sept. 1961): 463–64, 467–69; Briefing, The President's Trip

Interest-Group and Congressional Pressures

Back home, Kennedy prepared to net votes for the TEA. In early December 1961, he had announced that the Office of Emergency Planning (OEP) would review the quota program. The undertaking of this study, due out in mid-1962, worried oil producers about the future of controls but won praise from the coal industry, which thought the quota program was inadequate. In general, the energy sector believed that 1962 would be a "showdown year" for trade issues.[14]

Well before the TEA campaign, the coal and oil factions spelled out their plights. Indeed, the coal industry was in dire straits. Although world coal production had risen by 35 percent from 1950 to 1962, U.S. output had dropped 13 percent. Of the ten principal coal-producing states, only Virginia, Tennessee, and Missouri mined more coal in 1962 than in 1950. Meanwhile, nearly one-fifth of American mines had closed, and employment had dropped by 65 percent, or 272,000 workers. Indeed, these conditions existed mainly because coal exports to Canada and Europe had been halved, while railroads had shifted to diesel and consumers to natural gas. To be sure, residual fuel imports had captured the eastern seaboard, but the market provided only a minor part of coal's traditional purchasers.[15]

The industry hoped to stake out a certain portion of the eastern market to help coal compete with residual products. Kennedy supported modernization plans to achieve these ends, which led a West Virginia legislator to point out that "the President is killing us with kindness," but "we're not going to get what we really want."[16] The industry wanted Kennedy to increase exports; Germany and Canada discriminated against U.S. coal, yet both received special treatment for some of their key exports to America (including Canadian oil). But most observers erroneously perceived imports as a bigger problem. The major coal associations, companies, and the United Mine Work-

---

to Venezuela and Colombia, Dec. 1961, box 235, NSF; *Public Papers, 1961*, 804; John M. Kelly Oral History, JFK Library [hereafter cited as Kelly Oral History], 21.

[14] *Oil and Gas Journal* 59 (11 Dec. 1961): 50–51; Stewart Udall to the President, 2 Feb. 1962, box 23, Feldman files; "Steed Fears U.S. Oil Policy Not Adequate," *Oklahoma City Times*, 24 Nov. 1961, box 1, Steed Papers; *Oil and Gas Journal* 59 (11 Dec. 1961): 51; ibid. 60 (8 Jan. 1962): 3.

[15] Commodity Research Bureau, *Commodity Yearbook, 1963* (New York, 1963), 82–83; *Petroleum Hearings—I*, 185.

[16] *Business Week* 1699 (24 March 1962): 32. See also Thomas Kennedy, UMW, to President Kennedy, 28 June 1961, box 489, WHCF; *Oil and Gas Journal* 60 (24 Sept. 1962): 85–86; *Public Papers of the Presidents of the United States, John F. Kennedy, 1962* (Washington, D.C., 1963), 709 [hereafter cited as *Public Papers, 1962*]; ibid., 249–50.

ers (UMW) cited residual fuel oil imports as injurious to Appalachia, a testing ground for the New Frontier domestic agenda. Informally supported by management, the UMW, demanding a "permanent rigid quota on residual oil imports," opposed the TEA.[17]

Oil producers linked up with coal interests. Since they supplied only 10 percent of the residual products consumed in America, independents cared more about crude than about fuel oil imports. They allied with the coal industry primarily out of a fear that decontrol of any petroleum product implied an easing of crude quotas. The Independent Petroleum Association of America (IPAA) and state organizations expressed disappointment that Kennedy refused to cut quotas by 250,000 barrels a day, or even by 50,000 following Udall's recommendation.[18]

The independents cited imports, which they claimed had absorbed market growth, and loopholes in the quota program as the causes of stagnation in the industry. They complained that the "overland exemption" enabled Canada to dominate the markets of the Upper Midwest. Also bothersome was the "Brownsville Shuffle," a crafty transshipment maneuver that permitted Mexico to squeeze an additional amount of its oil across the border. In the interest of "national security," the IPAA offered a plan to limit imports to 14 percent of

[17] Coal and the Trade Expansion ACt, 30 March 1962; Energy Policy: Coal, Hydroelectric Power, Natural Gas, and Oil, 2 Feb. 1962, box 31, White House Staff Files—Howard C. Petersen, JFKL [hereafter cited as Petersen files]; U.S., House Subcommittee on the Impact of Imports and Exports on American Employment of the Committee on Education and Labor, *Impact of Imports and Exports on Employment (Coal and Residual Fuel Oil)*, pt. 1, 87th Cong., 1st sess., 19–20 June 1961 [hereafter cited as *Coal and Residual Import Hearings*], Harry Gilroy, "U.S. Coal Men Face New Woes in Declining European Market," 199; U.S., House Ways and Means Committee, *Trade and Expansion Act of 1962*, 87th Cong., 2d sess., 1962, pt. 3, Thomas Kennedy, 1714 [hereafter cited as *TEA—House*]; Senators Robert C. Byrd and Jennings Randolph to Lawrence O'Brien, 28 June 1961, box 5, Feldman files; U.S., Senate Committee, *Trade Expansion Act of 1962*, 87th Cong., 2d sess., 1962, pt. 2, Senator Paul Douglas (D–Ill.), 568 [hereafter cited as *TEA—Senate*]; *Coal and Residual Imports Hearing*, G. Don Sullivan, National Coal Association, 38; *Petroleum Hearings—II*, C. J. Potter, Rochester and Pittsburgh Coal Company, 465; *TEA—House*, pt. 3, Thomas Kennedy, 1714; Henry Wilson to Lawrence O'Brien, 20 Dec. 1961, box 3, White House Staff Files—Henry H. Wilson, JFK Library; Mike Manatos to Lawrence O'Brien, 14 March 1962, box 1, White House Staff Files—Mike Manatos, JFK Library [hereafter cited as Manatos files]; Joseph Moody, National Coal Policy Conference, to Secretary Udall, 3 May 1962, box 5, Feldman files.

[18] *New York Times*, 17 Dec. 1961, 3: 1, 7; *Oil and Gas Journal* 59 (18 Dec. 1961): 40; press release, Texas Independent Producers and Royalty Owners Association (TIPRO) Information Service, 11 March 1962, box 23, Feldman files; TIPRO Information Service to President James F. West, 2 April 1962, box 14, Petersen files; E. A. Smith, Oklahoma Independent Petroleum Association to Robert Bleiberg, 8 Dec. 1961; Joseph Moody to Cong. Tom Steed, 1 Dec. 1961, box 288, Steed Papers.

domestic production, instead of estimated demand. Oil interests girded for a "tough fight" with Kennedy, willing to trade support for the TEA for this new restriction.[19]

Oil imports were partially to blame for industry hardships. Indeed, crude output in the country still more than doubled that of the closest competitors, Russia and Venezuela. Since 1950, production had risen 25 percent, and output in 1961 had topped the previous boom year of 1957. Residual oil production had fallen, but this drop was by choice, since the independents concentrated on refining the more profitable crude. Nonetheless, surplus world production and eroding prices had increased imports, which took an increasing share of U.S. demand. Excess capacity, coupled with rising imports, idled drilling and prompted worker layoffs. In Texas, exploration fell 44 percent from 1958 to 1961, as the glutted market limited production from an average of twenty-one days a month in 1952 to just over eight days a month in 1961. Louisiana, Kansas, Oklahoma, and New Mexico suffered similar fates.[20]

Calls for import restrictions found sympathetic ears in Congress. Many legislators faced reelection; many in the Southwest relied on oil industry leaders to bankroll their campaigns. Though gratified by Kennedy's attention to Appalachia, the House coal bloc had soured on oil import policy. Arch Moore (D–W.Va.) and John Dent (D–Pa.), who initiated hearings on imports by focusing on coal and residual fuel oil problems, mobilized the coal bloc with the support of powerful leaders such as Thomas Morgan (D–Pa.), chairman of the House Foreign Relations Committee.[21]

The House oil bloc marched with its coal cohorts. Representative Tom Steed (D–Okla.) led oil protectionists. Steed's hearings on oil imports in late 1961 had been a platform for independents to criticize the quota program. He and Arch Moore proposed an amendment to the TEA that endorsed the IPAA plan of limiting imports to 14 percent of domestic production. He described the Steed-Moore

---

[19] *TEA—House*, pt. 3, Harold Decker, IPAA, 1724; Memorandum for Meeting with Prime Minister Diefenbaker [1961], box 113, POF; Chester, *United States Oil Policy and Diplomacy*, 138–39.

[20] *Commodity Yearbook, 1963*, 245, 247; *Petroleum Hearings—I*, 66, 496; *Petroleum Hearings—II*, 540; Bohi, *Limiting Oil Imports*, 22–23, 25.

[21] For campaign bankrolling from oil producers, see Robert A. Caro, *The Path to Power: The Years of Lyndon Johnson* (New York, 1983), 663. *Congressional Record—Appendix*, vol. 108, reel 11, 10 Jan. 1962, Cleveland M. Bailey, A12, A14, and 7 Feb. 1962, Arch A. Moore, A943; *Coal and Residual Imports Hearing*, Dent, 139; Legislative Highlights, 26 Feb. 1962, box 50, POF.

JFK, Congressman Steed, and LBJ · Tom Steed of Oklahoma received close attention from the Kennedy administration. He led the oil-state protectionists in the House against the TEA and increased petroleum imports. (Photograph reproduced courtesy of the Carl Albert Center Congressional Archives, University of Oklahoma, Norman, Okla.)

amendment as a weapon with which the oil-coal alliance would make a "final" stand against oil imports.[22]

Protectionists united in April 1962. Thirty-three members of Congress introduced bills identical to the Steed-Moore amendment. A bipartisan group of 110 House and Senate members endorsed a pamphlet published by the National Coal Policy Conference calling for import restrictions. In general, the seventy-nine House members attacked imports, and an additional eighty-four members of Congress

[22] *Oil and Gas Journal* 60 (7 May 1962): 63; ibid. 59 (4 Dec. 1961): 102; ibid. 59 (27 Nov. 1961): 64–65; *Petroleum Hearings—I*, Steed, 2, 413; Minutes of Meeting, Subcommittee No. 4, House Small Business Committee, 18 July 1961, and Record of Meeting between Steed and leaders of the Oklahoma Independent Petroleum Association, 21 Dec. 1961, box 288, Steed Papers, *Congressional Record—House*, vol. 108, pt. 5, 18 April 1962, Steed, 6958, and pt. 11, 20 July 1962, 14385; Steed and Moore to Colleagues, 12 April 1962 and attached bill, box 307, Steed Papers.

from twenty-three states expressed similar disgruntlement in the *New York Times*. Kennedy could not ignore the outcry, especially since it involved several members of the Ways and Means Committee, which controlled trade legislation in the House.[23]

If not for a powerful "consumer" bloc, Kennedy might have responded with some restrictions. The New England Council and the Independent Fuel Oil Marketers of America spearheaded efforts toward relaxing quotas. They argued, as Senator Kennedy had, that imports of residual fuel were not responsible for coal problems. Instead, consumers used fuel oil on the Atlantic seaboard because coal was no longer a significant source of energy there and because residual fuel oil was too heavy to transport inland economically. Besides, U.S. producers did not turn out enough residual fuel for consumers' needs. Meanwhile, consumer interests complained that import controls raised fuel prices and had bankrupted three large New England marketers.[24]

Consumers had a plausible cause. Since 1950, stocks and production of residual fuel oil in the United States had fallen by 17 and 30 percent, respectively. Oil for industrial and heating purposes had not filled the gaps in the market created by the change to other energy sources by railroads, utilities, and ocean-going vessels. Also, since producers earned about a dollar less per barrel for residual oil than for crude, independents concentrated on the more lucrative crude. Before the war, residual fuel oil accounted for over half the output of U.S. refineries; in 1962, production was a paltry 9.6 percent (see Table 1). Editors of the *Oil and Gas Journal* conceded that removing fuel oil controls would have little effect on producers and would hurt coal interests only if prices dropped appreciably, and that Venezuela should supply America's fuel oil demand.[25]

The lack of logical underpinning for import controls on residual fuel prompted pressure for their removal by the House consumer bloc, led by Silvio Conte (R), Hastings Keith (R), and Thomas Lane (D)

[23] "Congress Speaks on Domestic Fuels, Oil Imports, and National Security," National Coal Policy Conference, Inc., March 1962, box 30, Petersen files; *Congressional Record—House*, vol. 108, pt. 8, 13 June 1962, Exhibit 1, Advertisement from the *New York Times*, 1 April 1962, 10429.

[24] John Evans, Independent Fuel Oil Marketers to the President, 28 Aug. 1962, box 23, Feldman files; *Coal and Residual Import Hearings*, Humble Oil and Refining Co., 128–30; *TEA—Senate*, pt. 2, John H. Lichtblau, Petroleum Institute Foundation, 566; John Evans to Myer Feldman, 30 April 1962, box 23, Feldman files; *Petroleum Hearings—I*, Charles W. Colsen and James S. Couzens, New England Council, 291, 294–95; *TEA—House*, pt. 3, Edward M. Carey, Independent Fuel Oil Marketers, 1830.

[25] *Commodity Yearbook*, 1963, 1, 245–48; *Petroleum Hearings—I*, 445–46; *Oil and Gas Journal* 59 (27 Feb. 1961): 57–58.

Table 1
U.S. Oil Production, Yields, and Imports, 1952–1970
(millions of barrels)

	Production		Yield Resid. from	Imports		
Year	*Crude*	*Total*	*Petroleum*	*Crude*	*Resid.*	*Total*
1952	2,289.8	453.9	18.5%	209.6	128.4	348.5
1954	2,315.0	416.8	16.4	239.5	129.1	384.0
1956	2,617.3	426.7	14.7	341.8	162.8	525.6
1958	2,449.0	363.4	12.9	348.0	182.3	620.6
1960	2,574.9	332.1	11.2	371.6	233.2	664.1
1962	2,676.2	295.7	9.6	411.0	264.3	759.8
1965	2,848.5	268.6	8.6	452.0	345.1	900.8
1968	3,160.9	275.8	8.0	472.3	409.9	1,039.0
1970	3,350.7	257.5	6.6	483.3	557.8	1,248.0

Sources: Douglas R. Bohi and Milton Russell, *Limiting Oil Imports: An Economic History and Analysis* (Baltimore, Md., 1978), 22–23; Commodity Research Bureau, *Commodity Yearbook, 1963* (New York, 1963), 245, 248; ibid., *1971*, 253–54.

of Massachusetts. In all, the bloc numbered roughly seventy-five House members from Atlantic coast states. They urged the president to "show his genuine belief in freer trade by removing barriers to residual oil imports" and ending "protection gone wild."[26]

The TEA in the House

This line-up of conflicting interests placed Kennedy in a difficult position. Udall raised the ceiling on residual imports by 10 percent in April 1962, which enraged the coal bloc but pleased the consumer faction. A refusal to amend the TEA with the Steed-Moore limit brought "rumblings" from Steed, who visited the president in March 1962. Kennedy opposed the Steed-Moore amendment because it might invite a flood of clauses for other commodities and because oil imports could be slowed "administratively" through the quota program. Though aware of oil-state conditions, he believed security interests would be badly served by cutting off LDCs from the Ameri-

[26] *Congressional Record—Appendix*, vol. 108, reel 11, 7 March 1962, Hastings Keith, A1980, and "Protectionism in Oil," *Boston Herald*, 30 Dec. 1961, A1718. See also *Congressional Record—Appendix*, vol. 107, reel 11, 12 Sept. 1961, Dante B. Fascell (D–Fla.), A7167 and Silvio Conte, A7542; Mike Manatos to Lawrence O'Brien, 8 Nov. 1961, box 1, Manatos files.

can market and throwing them into the laps of the Soviet bloc.[27] As general policy, fighting the Cold War outweighed protectionism.

For the political short term, however, Kennedy decided that passage of the TEA took precedence. To pacify oil interests, Kennedy retained the national security provision. Though Steed adamantly refused to back off his 14 percent amendment, Kennedy assured him privately that his quota revision plan was under consideration. Recovery programs for Appalachia and a tariff increase on glass imports also helped to convince coal-state legislators of Kennedy's concern for their region. Kennedy's key ally was Ways and Means Chairman Wilbur Mills, who engineered a defeat of the Steed-Moore amendment in committee by a vote of 15–10 on 23 May 1962. Arguing that the measure would tie the president's hands in trade policy, Mills enabled the TEA to remain unfettered by protectionist amendments.[28]

On 28 June 1962, the trade bill sailed through the House, in large part because of the application of the fair trade doctrine. Of the one hundred and eight representatives who petitioned for oil import limits, seventy-one voted for the TEA. Among those opposing the bill were twenty-four anti-New Frontier Republicans and intractable protectionists such as Steed, Moore, and Dent. Coal-state representatives backed the TEA, including two-thirds of the West Virginia delegation and over half of Pennsylvania's members. Two-thirds of the oil-state legislators from Louisiana, Oklahoma, Texas, Kansas, and New Mexico sided with Kennedy, as did twenty of the thirty-three cosponsors of the Steed-Moore amendment. Not surprisingly, four-fifths of the consumer bloc favored the bill.[29]

[27] Henry Wilson to Lawrence O'Brien, 23 Feb. 1962, box 14, White House Staff Files—Lawrence O'Brien, JFK Library [hereafter cited as O'Brien files]; Lawrence O'Brien to the President, 6 March 1962 and attached memorandum from Cong. Tom Steed, My Proposed Conference with the President, box 50, POF; Address by Udall to the IPAA, 30 April 1962, Udall Papers; "Petty's Oil Letter," in *The Oil Daily*, 28 March 1962, attached to James West to Lindley Beckworth, 6 June 1962, box 14; Question to Harold Decker, IPAA, on his testimony before the House Ways and Means Committee [1962], box 10, Petersen files.

[28] *TEA—House*, pt. 2, Udall, 804; Howard Petersen to Johnny Mitchell, 25 April 1962, box 599, WHCF; Proposed Exchange of Letters between the President and Congressman Clark Thompson, 11 May 1962, box 23, Feldman files; Truman Richardson to Ross U. Porter, 14 March 1962, box 307, Steed Papers; *Congressional Record—Senate*, vol. 108, pt. 9, 5 July 1962, Cleveland M. Bailey, 12798; Ways and Means in *World Oil* 154 (1 Aug. 1962): 23; Myer Feldman to the President, 25 June 1962, attached to Memorandum for Congressman Clark C. Thompson, box 23, Feldman files; W. E. Turner to Cong. Tom Steed, 28 March 1962, box 307, Steed Papers.

[29] *Congressional Quarterly—Almanac* 18 (1962): 618–19.

The Kennedy-Kerr Deal

Kennedy's tightrope act faced a similar challenge in the Senate, which oil producers viewed as their last "thin thread of hope" for protection. The battle lines were drawn for the TEA fight. The twelve-member New England delegation represented the consumer bloc. The voice of the coal forces was newcomer Robert C. Byrd (D-W.Va.), and Robert S. Kerr (D-Okla.) led the oil bloc. Earlier, twenty-seven oil- and coal-state senators had complained to Secretary Udall about the adverse effects of oil imports. Eighteen had warned the president that imports jeopardized national security, and thirty had endorsed the pamphlets signed by their counterparts in the House. Altogether, the oil-coal bloc comprised thirty-nine senators from half the states in the union.[30]

Kerr commanded the Senate oil-coal forces. The second-ranking Democrat on the Finance Committee (which directed trade bills) and part owner of Kerr-McGee Oil Company, he had reached the apex of his power by 1962. Kerr had handed the White House one of its worst defeats over the Medicare bill in 1961, so the president was well aware of the "King of the Senate" 's influence. As the story goes, Kennedy, looking ahead to his legislative agenda for 1962, announced that he would visit Kerr's ranch in late October 1961. Before the trip, a jealous Oklahoma governor J. Howard Edmondson, a possible replacement for Lyndon Johnson as vice-presidential running-mate in 1964 and a Kennedy intimate, flew to Hyannisport, found the president on a golf course, and demanded to know the purpose of Kennedy's trip. The president responded, "Why Howard, I'm going to Oklahoma to kiss Bob Kerr's ass."[31] Kennedy knew he was Kerr's "legislative captive."[32]

---

[30] *World Oil* 154 (1 Aug. 1962): 14, 18. See also "Platt's Oilgram," 4 May 1962, attached to Henry Wilson to Myer Rashish, 10 May 1962, box 14, Petersen files; *Oil and Gas Journal* 60 (27 Aug. 1962): 43–44; *Congressional Record—Senate*, vol. 107, pt. 2, 20 Feb. 1961, New England Delegation to the President, 7 Feb. 1961, 2363; Mike Manatos to Lawrence O'Brien, 7 April 1962, box 327, O'Brien files; Sen. Harry Byrd to the President, 12 April 1962, box 599, WHCF; *Coal and Residual Hearings*, G. Don Sullivan, National Coal Association to Secretary Udall, 9; *Congressional Record—House*, vol. 107, pt. 3, 2 March 1961, Robert C. Byrd, 20801 and 18 Senators to President Kennedy, 3137–38.

[31] Anne H. Morgan, *Robert S. Kerr: The Senate Years* (Norman, Okla., 1977), 221, also 209–10, 242.

[32] Morgan, *Kerr*, 232–33. See also Myer Rashish Oral History, JFK Library, 28–30; Luther Hodges to the President, Memorandum Reporting the Status of the Trade Expansion Act, 20 Aug. 1962, box 51, POF. The "whales" included Richard B. Russell (D–Ga.), Carl Hayden (D–Ariz.), Allen Ellender (D–La.), and James Eastland (D–Miss.).

Senator Kerr Shows Off His Prize Bull · Kennedy visited the Oklahoma ranch of Senator Robert Kerr in October 1961 in order to win the support of the so-called King of the Senate for New Frontier legislation in 1962. The Trade Expansion Act was the top item on the agenda. (Photograph reproduced courtesy of the Carl Albert Center Congressional Archives.)

This relationship gave Kerr leverage. His congressional allies, senior senators called "whales" by Johnson, dominated the president's "minnow" friends. Kerr's power of persuasion with these veterans was a card he could play ruthlessly. For instance, he explained that he could not break the logjam in Congress over the tax bill of 1962 unless Kennedy backed the senator's pet public works scheme, the Arkansas River Navigation Project. A smiling Kennedy replied, "You know, Bob, I never really understood the Arkansas River bill before today," and accepted it. Kerr also chaired the Aeronautical and Space Sciences Committee, which funded the National Aeronautical and Space Administration (NASA) and could determine whether Kennedy would send an American to the moon.[33] He could also make or break the Trade Expansion Act.

In order to win favors for Oklahoma, promote himself in the Senate, and undercut the power of his rival on the Finance Committee, chairman Harry F. Byrd (D-Va.), Kerr championed the cause of the oil interests. He had opposed the last two trade bills, helped write

[33] Morgan, *Kerr*, 210, 233.

the protective national security amendment, and pushed for the Mandatory Quota Program. Now, willing to abandon the protectionist camp in return for political favors, Kerr advocated liberal trade as beneficial to Oklahoma and responded tepidly to the Steed-Moore amendment. The national security clause would be sufficient, he argued, if the president tightened the quota program. Throughout the spring and summer of 1962, Kerr visited the White House to work out an "understanding" with Kennedy that would restrict oil imports.[34]

The eventual deal lived up to this goal. Taking 1961 as a base period, Kennedy agreed to limit crude imports to 12.2 percent of domestic production in order to prevent imports from growing faster than U.S. output. The revised program adopted the Steed method of allocating quotas, aimed to reduce imports by an estimated 70,000 barrels a day, limit imports from Canada, and expand consumption of domestic crude on the West Coast. In return, Kerr corraled votes for the TEA. Reversing his erstwhile protectionism, Kerr persuaded thirty-four of the thirty-nine senators who had endorsed restrictions and all of the southwestern oil-state delegation to accept the trade bill. Every senator but two from the coal states followed suit, and nine of the twelve New England delegation members sided with Kennedy. Dissent came either from staunch protectionists or from the president's Republican foes.[35] The fair trade strategy of conceding moderate protectionism in oil for general trade liberalization under the TEA was a success.

[34] Robert Kerr to John Cosey, 4 May 1955, box 34; Kerr to Cleo Ingle, 13 April 1955, box 34; Kerr, "The Reader Writes: Senator Kerr's Amendment," *Christian Science Monitor,* 26 July 1958, box 1; Address to the Midyear 1958 Meeting of the IPAA, 29 April 1958, box 8; press release, Kerr and Senator A. S. Monroney (D–Okla.), 28 Feb. 1959, box 18; Transcript of Television Show on the Trade Expansion Act of 1962, Washington, D.C., 14 June 1962, box 25, Papers of Senator Robert S. Kerr, Albert Center [hereafter cited as Kerr Papers]; press release, 28 March 1962, box 56, Petersen files; *Oil and Gas Journal* 60 (23 April 1962): 65; ibid. 60 (30 July 1962): 90; press release, Kerr and A. S. "Mike" Monroney (D–Okla.), 20 June 1962, box 56, Petersen files; "Kerr, Steed on Different Sides on Oil Amendment," *Oklahoman,* 1 April 1962, box 307; Kerr to Thomas Williams, 16 April 1962, box 4; Kerr to J. Howard Edmondson, 21 May 1962, box 4, Kerr Papers; Morgan, *Kerr,* 233.

[35] Kelly Oral History, 43–46; Luther Hodges to Myer Feldman, 2 August 1962, box 23, Feldman files; Kerr to E. A. Smith, 8 Oct. 1962, Kerr Papers; *Congressional Quarterly—Almanac* 18 (1962): 289; Transcript of Television Show on the Trade Expansion Act of 1962, 14 June 1962, box 25; Statement by Senator Robert S. Kerr, Trade Bill-Compensation for Import Damage, 9 Oct. 1962, box 25; Statement by Senator Robert S. Kerr on Trade, 9 Oct. 1962, box 11, Kerr Papers; Harold Decker to the IPAA, 12 Oct. 1962 and attached copy of *Congressional Record,* statement of Russell Long, box 11, Kerr Papers; *Congressional Quarterly—Almanac* 18 (1962): 688.

Signing the Trade Expansion Act • President Kennedy signed the act on 11 October 1962 after granting concessions to a few major industries, including oil. To the far right is Senator Kerr. Behind Kennedy's head is Senator Wilbur Mills of Arkansas, who defeated the protectionist Steed-Moore oil amendment to the TEA in the Ways and Means Committee (Photograph reproduced courtesy of the John F. Kennedy Library, Boston, Mass.)

Two loose ends remained before Kennedy could feel satisfied. The first concerned the OEP report, deliberately released in September after the Senate vote. When the OEP recommended more liberal quotas, the watchdog Kerr readied a bill to tighten them in case Kennedy did not. At once, the president declared that the OEP plan was "not acceptable," and on 30 November 1962 he had Udall announce a revised Mandatory Quota Program identical to that agreed on with Kerr. Earlier, the IPAA had given Kerr a standing ovation for his efforts and thanked Kennedy for the special treatment.[36]

The other loose end was the foreign response to the revised program. Canada had sought to boost its oil exports in the American market and succeeded, despite the new 12.2 percent restriction. The

[36] A Report to the President by the Petroleum Study Committee, OEP, 4 Sept. 1962, box 23, Feldman files; *Public Papers, 1962*, 715; press release, Proclamation 3509, 30 Nov. 1962, box 23, Feldman files; Bohi, *Limiting Oil Imports*, 107; *New York Times*, 1, 29; Kelly Oral History, 42; Myer Feldman to Harold Decker, 19 Dec. 1962, box 13, Petersen files; Robert Kerr to E. A. Smith, 8 Oct. 1962, box 4; Remarks of Kerr to the IPAA Annual Meeting, Dallas, Texas, 29 Oct. 1962; "Kerr's Magic Sways Oilmen," *Oklahoman*, 4 Nov. 1962, box 11; Statement by Harold Decker 30 Nov. 1962, box 25, Kerr Papers.

United States did not squeeze off Canada's imports or revoke Ottawa's overland oil exemption. As a result, Canadian sales to America surpassed those of the Middle East by 1966 and of top exporter Venezuela by 1972, resulting in an overall rise of 21 percent from 1962 to 1973. The United States also worked out an agreement to sustain Mexico's negligible exports, permit the "Brownsville Shuffle" to continue, and retain the overland exemption until 1971.[37] Oil trade was fair; a steady expansion of oil imports into the United States persisted.

U.S.–Venezuelan Dialogue

For Venezuela, the situation was more complicated. During 1962, Betancourt had quelled leftist rebellions and stabilized his democracy. With recovery from the recent depression under way, oil production increased. Also, relations between Washington and Caracas grew more cordial after the Kennedy visit. Even Perez Alfonzo, though demanding preferential treatment for Venezuelan oil in the American market, had moderated his recriminations against the import quota program during a trip to the United States in April 1962. Indeed, he realized Venezuela would be the chief beneficiary from the raised fuel oil ceiling that occurred that month. The revised program, however, threatened to derail these improved relations. The American embassy in Caracas reported Venezuelan indignation over the new restrictions. Betancourt "had worked up quite a head of steam" after a briefing by Perez Alfonzo on the new quota program and was allegedly reconsidering his proposed visit to Washington in early 1963 unless concessions were forthcoming.[38] Kennedy immediately dispatched White House aide Myer Feldman to Venezuela for consultations.

Betancourt and Perez Alfonzo issued a list of grievances. The revised program, they asserted, contradicted Kennedy's pledge never to change the system unilaterally. Moreover, although Venezuela was one of America's oldest and most important suppliers of petroleum

[37] Report by the United States Delegation to the United States–Canadian Discussions of Petroleum Policies and Programs, 13–14 Dec. 1962, box 104, POF; Bohi, *Limiting Oil Imports*, 107, 132–34; Rabe, *The Road to OPEC*, 198.

[38] AUSAID-Caracas to the Department of State, 21 Sept. 1962, box WH–23, Papers of Arthur M. Schlesinger, Jr., JFK Library; *International Commerce* 68 (2 July 1962): 33; ibid. 68 (27 Aug. 1962): 47; ibid. 68 (29 Oct. 1962): 68; Robert J. Alexander, *Romulo Betancourt and the Transformation of Venezuela* (New Brunswick, N.J., 1982), 554–57; U.S. Ambassador C. Allan Stewart to the Secretary of State, 2 July 1962, box 92; CIA Reference Biographic Register of Juan Pablo Perez Alfonzo; Visit to the United States of Venezuelan Minister of Mines and Hydrocarbons Dr. Juan Pablo Perez Alfonzo, April 1962, box 192, NSF.

Betancourt Visits Washington · In February 1963, President Rómulo Betancourt of Venezuela visited Kennedy in Washington, D.C. The two talked about the revised U.S. oil import program and the future of Venezuelan petroleum exports. (Photograph reproduced courtesy of the John F. Kennedy Library.)

in the hemisphere, it did not enjoy an exemption from the quota program as Canada and Mexico did. This lack of preference not only "disregarded" that Venezuela was an "integrated Sister-Republic" with the United States, but it also restricted profitable crude exports, leaving Venezuela with the mere "bones" of the American residual products market. Another complaint was a new method of "quota trading." The revised system reduced the percentage of imports allocated to "historical" importers, those U.S. companies who bought foreign (mostly Venezuelan) oil before 1957. The rules now allowed "inland" refiners, which did not directly use imported oil, to swap their quota allotments for domestic petroleum. Quota trading cut imports; Venezuela estimated a loss of revenue of $35 million. Betancourt wished to eliminate this process, charging that the allocation of permits for imports encouraged speculation by greedy refiners. He desired that they use Venezuelan oil.[39]

---

[39] Report of Myer Feldman on Discussions with President Betancourt on the United States Oil Import Program, Attachment 1, New Regulations on the Oil Import Restrictions—

Feldman responded with a firm defense of the Kennedy program. On the lack of preferences for Venezuela, he repeated that without the overland exemption, Canada would have cut off Venezuelan exports to the Montreal area by building a pipeline from its oil-producing provinces. In addition, Canada's position in the U.S. market was fixed under the quota program, whereas Caracas had an increased sales potential once American consumption expanded. Venezuela's rising exports during 1962 confirmed the nation's competitiveness in the United States.

Admittedly, the revised quota program would slow Venezuelan crude sales, continued Feldman, but Caracas could look forward to increased demand in Europe and in the markets it dominated, such as the Caribbean and Canada. Though residual oil did not reap such high profits as crude, it still offered "attractive opportunities." Venezuela virtually owned the American fuel oil market, supplying about 86 percent of the residual fuel oil consumed there either directly or through the Netherlands Antilles. These exports had climbed 30 percent over the past three years and could rise further.

Kennedy also disliked the speculation involved in quota trading. But Feldman explained that quota trading aided domestic producers, who were required to expand their sales to inland refiners who had been penalized by the allocation advantage of historical importers under the previous system. Phasing out this competitive edge for importers was only fair. Besides, an elimination of quota trading would hurt Caracas by forcing inland refiners to transport oil from the coast at an uneconomical cost, thereby depressing prices and resulting in less revenue for Venezuela.[40]

In the end, Betancourt and Perez Alfonzo accepted the U.S. position. The administration's claim that Venezuela would encounter steady growth in exports was borne out over time. Since Venezuela also produced nearly all of the oil exported from the Netherlands Antilles, its exports to America increased by 18 million barrels a year from 1962 to the first oil crisis in 1973. Thus Venezuela remained America's top oil supplier until 1976 if Caribbean sources are added to its export total. Also, though Kennedy rejected an OEP recommendation in February 1963 to eliminate controls on residual products,

---

First Personal Impressions of Dr. Juan P. Perez Alfonzo, box 104, POF; Betancourt, *Venezuela*, 390–91.

[40] Betancourt, *Venezuela*, 391; Report by Myer Feldman on Discussions with President Betancourt on the United States Oil Import Program, box 104, POF; White House Situation Room to General McHugh for the President, 23 Dec. 1962, box 192, NSF.

limits on fuel oil ended in 1966. American imports of crude rose by 15 percent, to 483,293 thousand barrels a day, but fuel oil imports more than doubled to 557,845 thousand barrels a day by the end of the decade. The ratio of residual fuel oil imports to U.S. domestic consumption leapt from 48.2 percent in 1962 to 69.4 percent in 1970. Since it sent nearly nine-tenths of this fuel oil, Venezuela profited considerably.[41]

The hegemony school blames restrictive U.S. oil policy for Venezuela's meager gains in petroleum sales, which prevented the nation from diversifying its oil-based economy. But blame must also be placed on Venezuela. The country's high cost structure, brought about by its tariffs and overvalued exchange rate relative to other LDCs, restrained growth in export sectors other than petroleum. Venezuela was largely responsible for not using its considerable earnings from oil exports to build a solid industrial base necessary for economic diversity and growth.[42]

The critics also overlook the rise in U.S. imports at America's expense. Fuel oil imports climbed while coal exports to Europe and Canada plunged until 1970. Oil imports grew by 65 percent from 1962 to 1973, the U.S. share of world production dropped, and purchases from overseas filled a growing percentage of demand and consumption, taking more of the market away from domestic producers (see Table 2).[43] U.S. energy producers were hurt in trade.

At the same time, the effects of the Trade Expansion Act sent American trade into deficit with Venezuela and other producers. Hegemony scholars contend that this imbalance was warranted by America's overall world trade surplus and its domination of the Venezuelan economy. Yet as secretary of state Dean Rusk informed Betancourt in late 1962, the oil import program would in no way affect the rising tide of all Venezuelan exports to the United States. He was right. The U.S. trade deficit with Venezuela more than doubled between 1960 and 1976, when it totaled $896 million. By 1976, moreover, the United States suffered a global trade deficit of almost $6 billion, when fifteen years before it had enjoyed a $5 billion sur-

---

[41] Ambassador C. Allan Stewart to the Secretary of State, 30 Dec. 1962, box 192, NSF; Rabe, *The Road to OPEC*, 198; Magin A. Valdez, "The Petroleum Policies of the Venezuelan Government" (Ph.D. diss., New York University, 1971), 6–7; Shaffer, *The Oil Import Program*, 95; Bohi, *Limiting Oil Imports*, 146; Commodity Research Bureau, *Commodity Yearbook, 1971* (New York, 1972), 254.

[42] Rabe, *The Road to OPEC*, 116; Harris, "The Impact of the Petroleum Export Industry," 12, 77, 93, 102.

[43] *Commodity Yearbook, 1971*, 93, 253; Bohi, *Limiting Oil Imports*, 23.

Table 2
U.S. Petroleum Imports from Venezuela, Canada,
and Mexico, 1950–1976
(millions of barrels)

Year	Venezuela[a]	Canada	Mexico	Total U.S. Oil Imports
1950	229	—	18	309
1955	307	—	23	470
1960	451	44	6	687
1962	440	91	18	760
1963	442	97	17	775
1964	464	109	17	827
1967	473	164	18	926
1970	536	280	15	1,248
1973	627	484	6	2,283
1976	357	219	32	2,670

[a]Including petroleum imported from the Netherlands Antilles.

Source: Stephen G. Rabe, *The Road to OPEC: United States Relations with Venezuela, 1919–1976* (Austin, Texas, 1892), 198.

plus.[44] The commercial benefits brought to other countries by the TEA, coupled with domestic injury, proved that America was a magnanimous fair trader and validated the comparative advantage school's position.

Conclusion

Kennedy's fair trade approach to oil imports revealed the political nature of oil trade policy. Indeed, decision making on the TEA, as Theodore Lowi claimed, represented a most "vulgar pluralist view of American politics."[45] The oil concession indicated that Kennedy was neither a free trade ideologue nor a selfish protectionist. He perceived that he had little choice but to protect oil interests. By resisting them, the TEA might fail in Congress. By meekly submitting to them, the TEA might be altered and its effectiveness for trade liberalization undermined. Interbranch horsetrading was a middle course that pacified producers and Congress and preserved the TEA intact.

[44] Secretary of State Rusk to the American Embassy, Caracas, 20 Dec. 1962, box 192, NSF; Rabe, *The Road to OPEC*, 194.
[45] Theodore Lowi, "American Business and Public Policy: Case Studies and Political Theory," *World Politics* 16 (July 1964): 685.

The oil quotas did not grant American energy producers immunity from import injury. The door remained ajar to U.S. markets. The tradeoff regarding oil was that America maintained its deposits of petroleum to be used in the event of wartime shortages. In a broader sense, the TEA ensured that America would reciprocally boost exports in which it enjoyed a comparative advantage and maintain leadership over the global trade order. Increases in oil imports, decreases in coal exports, and the halving of the American trade surplus by the end of the 1960s showed that other nations did not suffer unduly from U.S. trade policies, and that America, to an extent, did. Considering the political constraints on Kennedy, trade was as fair as possible.

In the end, Kennedy's oil import policy, based on the delicate balance of the fair trade doctrine, satisfied all parties. Oil and coal producers were protected, and consumers enjoyed the general trend toward trade liberalization. Canada and Venezuela publicly criticized but privately accepted the revised program. In fact, Betancourt expressed satisfaction with U.S. oil import policy during his visit to Washington in February 1963.[46] The U.S. military and other policymakers welcomed the continued conservation of American petroleum reserves, in part the result of increased imports. And Kennedy won a strategic victory that helped pass the Trade Expansion Act and allowed him to pursue his goal of liberal trade.

[46] Betancourt, *Venezuela*, 390; Ambassador C. Allan Stewart, to the Secretary of State, 2 Jan. 1963, box 24, Feldman files; *Public Papers of the Presidents: John F. Kennedy, 1963* (Washington, D.C., 1964), 188.

ACKNOWLEDGMENTS

Collins, Robert M. "American Corporatism: The Committee for Economic Development, 1942–1964." *Historian* 44 (1982): 151–73. Reprinted with the permission of the International Honor Society in History. Courtesy of Yale University Sterling Memorial Library.

Critchlow, Donald T. "The Political Control of the Economy: Deficit Spending as a Political Belief, 1932–1952." *Public Historian* 3 (1981): 5–22. Reprinted with the permission of the University of California Press. Courtesy of Yale University Sterling Memorial Library.

Cuff, Robert D. "Ferdinand Eberstadt, the National Security Resources Board, and the Search for Integrated Mobilization Planning, 1947–1948." *Public Historian* 7 (1985): 37–52. Reprinted with the permission of the University of California Press. Courtesy of Yale University Sterling Memorial Library.

Cuff, Robert D. "An Organizational Perspective on the Military-Industrial Complex." *Business History Review* 52 (1978): 250–67. Reprinted with the permission of the Harvard Business School. Courtesy of Yale University Sterling Memorial Library.

Draper, Hal. "Neo-Corporatists and Neo-Reformers." *New Politics* 1 (1961): 87–106. Courtesy of Yale University Seeley G. Mudd Library.

Griffith, Robert. "Dwight D. Eisenhower and the Corporate Commonwealth." *American Historical Review* 87 (1982): 87–122. Reprinted with the permission of the author. Courtesy of Yale University Sterling Memorial Library.

Hogan, Michael J. "American Marshall Planners and the Search for a European Neocapitalism." *American Historical Review* 90 (1985): 44–72. Reprinted with the permission of the author. Courtesy of Yale University Sterling Memorial Library.

Hogan, Michael J. "In the Shadow of the Left: The Postrevisionist History of American Economic Diplomacy." *Reviews in American History* 13 (1985): 276–81. Reprinted with the permission of Johns Hopkins University Press. Courtesy of Yale University Sterling Memorial Library.

Hogan, Michael J. "Revival and Reform: America's Twentieth-Century Search for a New Economic Order Abroad." *Diplomatic History* 8 (1984): 287–310. Reprinted with the permission of *Diplomatic History*. Courtesy of Yale University Sterling Memorial Library.

Libecap, Gary D. "The Political Economy of Crude Oil Cartelization in the United States, 1933–1972." *Journal of Economic History* 49 (1989): 833–55. Reprinted with the permission of Cambridge University Press. Courtesy of Yale University Sterling Memorial Library.

Long, Norton. "American Business and American Liberals: Slogans or Responsibility?" *Political Quarterly* 29 (1958): 166–77. Courtesy of Yale University Sterling Memorial Library.

Martin, Albro. "Uneasy Partners: Government-Business Relations in Twentieth-Century American History." *Prologue* 11 (1979): 91–105. Reprinted with the permission of the author and *Prologue*. Courtesy of Yale University Seeley G. Mudd Library.

May, Ann Mari. "President Eisenhower, Economic Policy, and the 1960 Presidential Election." *Journal of Economic History* 50 (1990): 417–27. Reprinted with the permission of Cambridge University Press. Courtesy of Yale University Sterling Memorial Library.

McLellan, David S. and Charles E. Woodhouse. "The Business Elite and Foreign Policy." *Western Political Quarterly* 13 (1960): 172–90. Courtesy of Yale University Sterling Memorial Library.

McQuaid, Kim. "Big Business and Government Policy in Post-New Deal America: From Depression to *Detente*." *Antitrust Law & Economics Review* 11 (1979): 41–71. Reprinted with the permission of Antitrust Law and Economics, Inc. Courtesy of Yale University Law Library.

Molander, Earl A. "Historical Antecedents of Military-Industrial Criticism." *Military Affairs* 40 (1976): 59–63. Reprinted with the permission of *Military Affairs*. Courtesy of Yale University Sterling Memorial Library.

Prechel, Harland. "Steel and the State: Industry Politics and Business Policy Formation, 1940–1989." *American Sociological Review* 55 (1990): 648–68. Courtesy of Yale University Law Library.

Slater, Jerome and Terry Nardin. "The 'Military-Industrial Complex' Muddle." *Yale Review* 65 (1975): 1–23. First published in the *Yale Review*, copyright Yale University. Courtesy of Yale University Law Library.

Weatherford, M. Stephen. "The Interplay of Ideology and Advice in Economic Policy-Making: The Case of Political Business Cycles." *Journal of Politics* 49 (1987): 925–52. Reprinted from the *Journal of Politics*, by permission of the author and the University of Texas Press. Courtesy of Yale University Sterling Memorial Library.

Zeiler, Thomas W. "Kennedy, Oil Imports, and the Fair Trade Doctrine." *Business History Review* 64 (1990): 286–310. Reprinted with the permission of the Harvard Business School. Courtesy of Yale University Sterling Memorial Library.